GED® TEST REASONING THROUGH LANGUAGE ARTS (RLA) REVIEW

Other titles of interest from LearningExpress

GED® Test Preparation
GED® Test Mathematical Reasoning Review
GED® Test Flash Review: Mathematical Reasoning
GED® Test Flash Review: Reasoning through Language Arts
GED® Test Flash Review: Science
GED® Test Flash Review: Social Studies

GED® TEST REASONING THROUGH LANGUAGE ARTS (RLA) REVIEW

LEARNING EXPRESS®

NEW YORK

ISBN-13: 978-1-61103-048-8

Printed in the United States of America

9 8 7 6 5 4 3 2 1

For more information on LearningExpress, other LearningExpress products, or bulk sales,
please write to us at:
  224 W. 29th Street
  3rd Floor
  New York, NY 10001

CONTENTS

CHAPTER 1   **Introduction to the GED® RLA Test**   1

About the GED® RLA Test   2

Question Types   2

How to Use This Book   7

Test Taking Tips   7

Eliminating Answer Choices   9

Keeping Track of Time   10

Preparing for the Test   11

The Big Day   12

Good Luck!   12

CHAPTER 2   **Diagnostic Test**   13

Part I   17

Part II   29

Answers and Explanations   30

CHAPTER 3   **Reading Comprehension: Big Picture Tools**   37

Reading the Passages   38

Tips for Fiction Passages   40

Tips for Nonfiction Passages   41

Author's Purpose   42

Point of View   45

Theme   47

Synthesis   51

Reading More Closely   55

CONTENTS

Interpreting What You Read		57
Quiz		59
Answers and Explanations		62
Review		65
CHAPTER 4	**Reading Comprehension: Close-Reading Skills**	67
	Make Connections	67
	Main Idea and Supporting Details	68
	Reading Comprehension Review	73
	Summarizing	77
	Fact and Opinion	79
	Organizational Structure	81
	Inferences	87
	Making Comparisons between Passages	89
	Quiz	90
	Answers and Explanations	97
	Review	101
CHAPTER 5	**Language and Grammar: Reading Skills**	103
	Word Parts	103
	Parts of Speech	106
	Context Clues	118
	Multiple Meaning Words	119
	Frequently Confused Words and Homonyms	120
	Literary Devices	121
	Language and Grammar Review	123
	Answers and Explanations	125
	Review	128
CHAPTER 6	**Language and Grammar: Grammar Skills**	129
	GED® Test Strategies	129
	Sentence Construction	130
	Capitalization	136
	Using Apostrophes to Create Possessive Nouns and Contractions	140
	Sentence Punctuation	142
	Sentence Structure	145
	Usage	145
	Mechanics	146
	Organization	146
	Quiz	148
	Answers and Explanations	149
	Review	151

CONTENTS

CHAPTER 7   **The Extended Response Essay: Tips and Scoring**   153

About the GED® Test Extended Response Question   153

Before You Write Your Essay   154

What's in an Essay   155

How Your Essay Will Be Scored   160

Extended Response Practice   163

Extended Response Practice Sample Essays   169

CHAPTER 8   **The Extended Response Essay: Planning and Revising**   173

How to Write a Powerful Essay   173

Thinking Styles   174

Organization of Your Essay   179

Example of an Extended Response Essay   181

Revising an Essay   189

Sample Extended Response Question   189

Practice Essay   191

The Final Steps   195

Quiz   195

Answers and Explanations   198

A Final Word   206

Review   208

CHAPTER 9   **GED® RLA Practice Test 1**   209

Part I   210

Part II   226

Answers and Explanations   232

CHAPTER 10   **GED® RLA Practice Test 2**   249

Part I   250

Part II   267

Answers and Explanations   275

ADDITIONAL ONLINE PRACTICE   291

GED® TEST REASONING THROUGH LANGUAGE ARTS (RLA) REVIEW

1 ▶ INTRODUCTION TO THE GED® RLA TEST

This book is designed to help people master the basic reading skills and concepts required to do well on the GED® Reasoning through Language Arts (RLA) test. Many people who are preparing for this particular GED® test have not been in a school setting for some time. This means reading skills have gotten rusty or have been forgotten altogether. Others may have been in a school setting, but have not mastered various essential reading skills. By focusing on basic reading skills, this book will give its readers a better grasp of key reading concepts.

This book is not designed to prepare people to take the GED® test immediately afterward. Instead, its goal is to provide the necessary foundation of reading skills required for the GED® Reasoning through Language Arts test. Without these fundamental skills, it would be difficult for a person to prepare for the test effectively, much less earn a passable score. However, once these basic reading skills are understood, a person is then on the right path toward learning the concepts needed to succeed on this particular GED® test.

About the GED® RLA Test

In previous versions of the GED® test, the Language Arts section was divided into two separate tests: Reading and Writing. The new GED® test combines these into a single test. Questions in this section will ask you to do things like identify the main idea or theme in a reading passage or determine the meanings of words within a passage. The RLA section also tests your knowledge of grammar, sentence structure, and the mechanics of language. Sharpening your reading and writing skills is important for the GED® test, and not only for the Reasoning through Language Arts section: The GED® Social Studies test and the GED® Science test also measure your ability to understand and communicate ideas through writing.

The Reasoning through Language Arts test will contain a number of reading passages, each 400 to 900 words in length. Approximately 75% of these passages will be nonfiction, and the other 25% will be fiction.

Because the new GED® test is all given on the computer, you will see a number of different question types that are more interactive than the usual multiple-choice questions.

How Is the Test Delivered?

You will take your GED® test on a computer. Although you absolutely do not need to be a computer expert to take the GED® test, you should be comfortable using a mouse and typing on a keyboard.

How Long Is the Test?

You can choose to take all four GED® tests at once, or you can take each test separately. The entire exam will take about seven hours to complete. The timing for each subject area alone is as follows:

- Mathematical Reasoning—115 minutes
- Reasoning through Language Arts—150 minutes (including a 10-minute break)
- Science—90 minutes
- Social Studies—90 minutes

Question Types

The traditional **multiple-choice** questions will still be the main type you will see on the RLA test, and each item will have four possible answer choices to select from. This is a change from previous GED® tests, which had five choices for each multiple-choice item. There is still only one correct answer choice for each item. This eliminates the possibility of answer choices such as "All of the above" or "Both A and B," and allows you to focus on selecting the one correct answer.

On the RLA test, all multiple-choice items will refer to a reading passage; each passage will be followed by six to eight items. The layout for multiple-choice items related to a passage will be split-screen—the passage will appear on the left, and the multiple-choice items will appear on the right.

Drag and Drop

For these questions, you will need to click on the correct object, hold down the mouse, and drag the object to the appropriate place in the problem, diagram, chart, or graph that you're given.

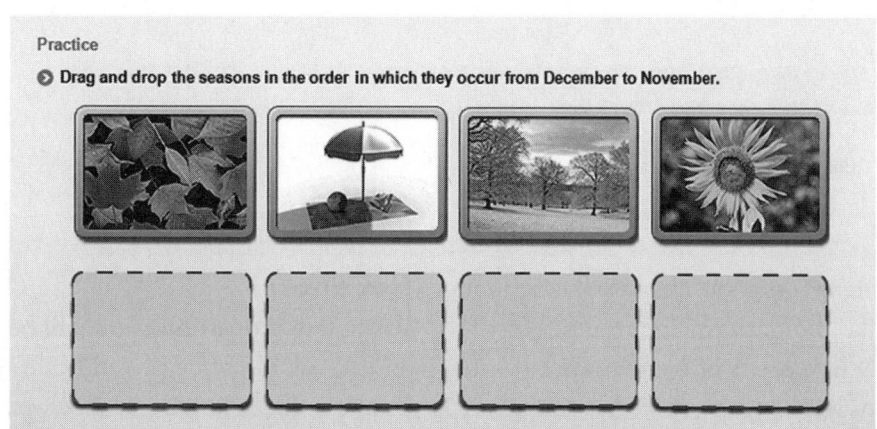

Drag-and-Drop

Drag-and-drop questions have two areas—one area shows all of the answer choices, and the other area is where you will move the correct answers. You will need to drag one or more answer(s) from the first area to the second area.

To answer a drag-and-drop question, click and hold the mouse on an answer and move it (drag it) to the correct area of the screen. Then let go of the mouse (drop it). You can remove an answer and switch it with another answer at any time.

Try the practice question below.

Practice

⊙ **Drag and drop the seasons in the order in which they occur from December to November.**

Of course, within this book you can't drag and drop items. For the purposes of *GED® Test Reasoning through Language Arts (RLA) Review*, you will choose from a list of items, as you would on a typical drag-and-drop question, and write the correct answer(s) in the appropriate spot.

Drop Down

In drop-down questions, you will need to select the answer or phrase to complete a sentence or problem from a menu that drops down with the click of a button.

Practice

⊙ **Select the appropriate word from each drop-down menu to complete the sentence correctly.**

[▾] am trying to become more skilled at weaving before winter [▾]

She
I
They
He

Check Answer

Drop-down questions are very similar to multiple-choice questions, so you will not see them in the two tests within this book.

Fill-in-the-Blank

A fill-in-the-blank question asks you to type information into one or more blank space(s). There are no answer choices given to you—you must come up with what you think is the correct answer and type it in the blank.

To answer the question, type in what you think is the correct word or phrase for each blank.

Try this practice question.

 Henry has $5 more than Oliver, and the same amount of money as Murray. Together, they have $85. How much money does Oliver have?

_____ dollars.

The fill-in-the-blank questions in this book look almost exactly like the ones you'll encounter in the online test, but here you will of course have to write in your answer instead of typing it.

Fill-in-the-Blank

These questions ask you to manually type in answer(s) to a problem rather than choose from several choices.

Hot Spot

For hot-spot questions, you will be asked to click on an area of the screen to indicate where the correct answer is located. For instance, you may be asked to plot a point by clicking on the corresponding online graph or to click on a certain area of a map.

Hot Spot

Hot spot questions ask you to choose a certain place on an image.

To answer the question, click on the correct spot of the image provided. You can change your answer by simply clicking on another area.

Now, you try.

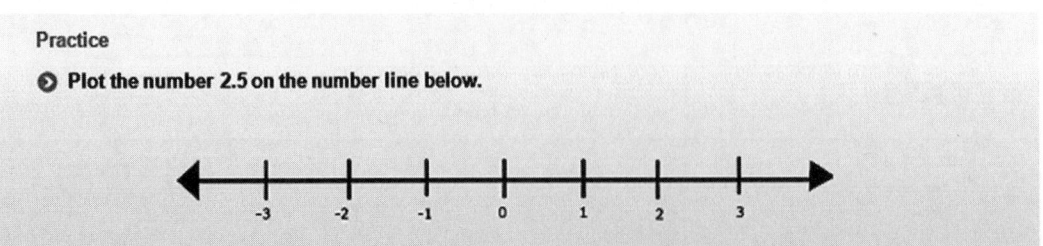

Practice

Plot the number 2.5 on the number line below.

In this book, you will be asked to draw a dot on a specific point or to circle a certain part of a diagram.

Short Answer

Short-answer questions are similar to fill-in-the-blank questions—you must type your response on the provided lines. However, these questions require you to write a paragraph instead of a word or two, usually in response to a passage or an image. Each should take about 10 minutes to answer.

Short Answer and Extended Response

These question types ask you to respond to a question by typing your answer into a box. With short answer and extended response questions, your answer will range from a few sentences to an essay. Like with fill-in-the-blank, there are no answer choices given to you.

You should feel comfortable typing on a keyboard in order to answer these questions, since there is a time limit for each test.

- Short answer questions can be answered with just a few words or sentences—they will probably take about 10 minutes to complete.

- Your extended response question is an essay, and is much longer—it will take 45 minutes to complete.

To answer these question types, enter your response into the text box provided. Here is an example of a response box:

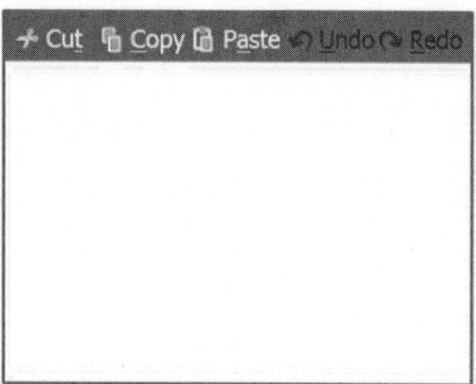

Notice that at the top of the box you will find tools to help you edit your answer if necessary.

Like fill-in-the-blank questions, short-answer questions in this book look as they will online—you will just write in your answer instead of typing it.

Extended Response

For extended response questions on the RLA exam you will be given 45 minutes to read one or two informational articles (a total of 550 to 650 words) and type a response on a computer using a simple word-processing program. This question requires you to read the prompt (the passage provided), create an argument based on it, and write a strong essay with evidence and examples.

When using this book, you can choose to either hand-write your essay or type it on a computer.

When and Where Can I Take the Test?

There are three testing opportunities per year in each subject area. To find a GED® test center, visit the link below, choose your location, and enter your zip code: www.gedtestingservice.com/testers/locate-a-testing-center.

You can sign up for any or all of the GED® tests online at this link, depending on the availability of spots in your area.

How Much Will the Test Cost?

Each of the four GED® tests costs $30, for a total of $120 for all four tests. You can pay for any or all parts of the test you are ready to take. There may be additional fees, depending on the state in which you take the test. Check the official GED® test website for complete test information.

How Are the Tests Scored?

A minimum score of 145 is required to pass each test. Each question on the GED® test is assigned a different point value depending on its difficulty. You will find out your score or scores on the same day you take the exam.

Reasoning through Language Arts

There are 48 questions and one Extended Response question on the RLA test. You will have 150 minutes to complete the entire exam, with one 10-minute scheduled break.

For most of the questions on the RLA test, you will be given a reading passage, followed by 6 to 8 questions that test your ability to understand and analyze what you have read.

Drop-down items are mostly used on the GED® RLA exam to test grammar and English-language mechanics. Drop-down questions are inserted in the middle of paragraphs. You will be asked to "drop down" a menu with several sentence choices, and choose the one that fits best grammatically in the sentence.

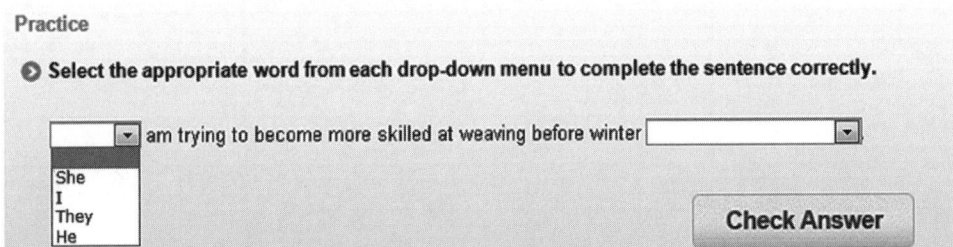

Passage Types for Reading Questions

Twenty-five percent of the reading passages on the RLA test will be literature. This includes historical and modern fiction, as well as nonfiction like biographies or essays. You might generally think of literature as fiction (invented stories), but literary texts can also be nonfiction (true stories).

Seventy-five percent of the reading passages will be from informational texts, including workplace documents (like memos or letters). These passages will often cover topics in social studies and science. The RLA test also will feature historical passages that are considered part of the "Great American Conversation." These include documents, essays, and speeches that have helped shaped American history.

There are no poetry or drama passages on the RLA test.

Extended Response Question

As you learned earlier in the chapter, the extended response item requires you to find and use information from the reading passage (or passages) to answer the question in a well-thought-out essay. You will be asked to analyze an issue and likely also asked to provide an opinion on what you have read. You will have 45 minutes of your total RLA time to complete this essay—that includes brainstorming, writing a draft, writing a final version, and proofreading your work.

How to Use This Book

In addition to this introduction, *GED® Test Reasoning through Language Arts (RLA) Review* also contains the following:

- **The LearningExpress Test Preparation System.** Being a good test taker can boost anyone's GED® test score. Many of the skills and strategies covered in this book will be familiar to anyone who has taken many multiple-choice tests, but there is a large difference between being "familiar with the strategy" and being "excellent at using the strategy." Our goal is to get you into that second category, and this chapter offers you the means to do so.
- **A Diagnostic Exam.** It's always helpful to see where your reading skills stand. Therefore, we recommend taking the diagnostic test before starting on the content chapters. By taking the diagnostic test, you should be able to determine the content areas in which you are strongest and the areas in which you might need more help. For example, if you miss most of your questions on the nonfiction passages, then you know that you should pay extra attention when the book discusses the best ways to approach nonfiction passages.

  The diagnostic test does not count for any score, so don't get caught up on how many you got right or wrong. Instead, use the results of the diagnostic test to help guide your study of the content chapters.
- **Content Chapters.** These chapters form the heart of the book. Here we cover the basic reading concepts discussed earlier. To help you understand all these ideas, every chapter has sample questions, helpful tips, and summaries, as well as explanations of the concepts being discussed. We recommend reading these chapters in order and not skipping around, as many of the concepts in the earlier chapters are built on in the later chapters.

- **Two Practice Tests.** Once you have a better grasp of the basic reading skills, the best thing to do is to practice those skills. Both our practice tests are designed to be similar to the real GED® Reasoning through Language Arts test in terms of question types and passage content.

  Taking these tests under timed conditions will help you gain familiarity with taking a timed reading test, which can help you in your GED® test preparations. However, if you would prefer to work on the questions untimed in order to focus on mastering the basic concepts of the content chapters, that's not a bad idea, either. Either way is helpful preparation.

Test Taking Tips

Selecting the Best Answer

You know all the reasons why test takers should read the passages and questions carefully. Now comes the part that makes all the difference: selecting the best answer. When all is said and done, this is the part of the test that matters most. To do well on the GED® test, it is essential that you select the best possible answer to each question.

Try to Answer the Question before Reading the Choices

As soon as you finish reading the question, think about what the best answer would be. Then, see if your answer is among the choices listed. If so, there's a good chance that it is correct, but don't mark the answer right away. Read all the choices first to be sure your answer is really the most complete option.

Read Every Choice

As you read the answer choices, you may determine that the first choice looks really great. But don't stop there! Read every single choice, no matter how wonderful any one of them appears to be. You may find that one of the first answers looks good but that the last one is even better.

Read Each Choice Carefully

Remember how important it is to be sure you read every single word in a question? The same holds true for reading each answer choice. Read each choice slowly and carefully, paying attention to every word. Take the time to read each answer choice twice before making your selection. Slight differences in wording can make one answer choice better than the others.

Use the Information in the Passage

Make sure that you choose an answer based solely on the information in the passage. You may already know a lot about the topic, which is great; however, the correct answers are in the passage. This test is not asking about what you knew before you read the material; it only wants to find out whether you are able to identify the correct information in this text.

Avoid Careless Mistakes

There will probably be answers you know right off the bat. Don't rush on these. Even if a question appears to be easy, read the question and answer choices carefully before making your selection. Careless mistakes can lower your score.

Watch Out for Absolutes

If certain words are found in answer choices, they should catch your attention. Look for words such as these:

- always
- never
- forever
- every

It is unlikely that the correct answer choice includes these inflexible words. Very few things are *always* true or *never* occur. Be suspicious if an answer choice suggests otherwise.

Pay Attention to Except and Not

Be sure you read every word in a question and pay close attention to the words *except* and *not*. It is easy to overlook these words by reading too quickly, and they completely change the question.

One trick for correctly answering these questions is to cover *except* or *not*, read the question, then look for the answer choice that does *not* belong.

Read Each Question for What It Is

Have you ever read a test question and wondered, *"What is this* really *asking?"* It can be easy to read too much into a question. Try not to do that on this test. The good news is, there are no trick questions on the GED® test. Just pay attention to what is being asked and select the best answer.

Choose the Best Answer

As you look through all the answer choices, you may find that more than one could be correct. Make sure that the answer you choose *most completely* answers the question. Just because a statement is true or looks like an acceptable choice does not mean it is the *best* answer. Carefully evaluate each choice before making a selection. Also, make sure your choice is the best answer *based on the passage*, not based on your own assumptions or beliefs.

> **TIP**
>
> Tempting answer choices are often listed before the best answer choice. Read all the answers carefully and make sure you completely understand each option before selecting the best response.

Read the Question Again

After you have selected your answer, read the question one more time. Make sure that your choice actually answers the question that was asked. Read the question, the appropriate section of the passage, and any visual aids, then read your answer choice. Does your answer make sense? If so, great! If not, now is your chance to try again.

Trust Your Instincts

Did you know that your first answer is usually correct? If you know that you have carefully read the passage and each answer choice, you have probably selected your best choice.

You may have time at the end of the test to look back over some of your answers. Unless you find an obvious mistake that you are certain about, don't change your answers. Research has shown that your first answer is usually right.

Answer Every Question

Make sure you do not leave any answers blank. Any question that is not answered is considered wrong, so take your best guess. There is no guessing penalty, so it is better to guess than to not answer a question.

BOOST

If you have been diagnosed as having a learning disability or physical handicap, you may be entitled to special accommodations for taking the GED® test. Be sure to check with the testing center you will be attending ahead of time to find out what, if any, documentation you might need to provide.

Eliminating Answer Choices

There may be times when you have no idea which answer choice is correct, and your only option is to take your best guess. In this situation, it is important to eliminate as many incorrect answer choices as possible, then select among those that remain.

Think of it this way: If you randomly choose one of the four answer choices, you have a 1 in 4 chance of getting it right. That's a 25% chance. Not bad, but definitely not in your best interest.

Suppose you are able to eliminate one of the answer choices. Now, you have a 1 in 3 chance of guessing correctly. Your odds just increased to 33%. Eliminate two choices and you have a 1 in 2 chance of answering correctly. This 50% chance of getting the answer right is much better than what you started with. Now, your random guess is much more likely to be the correct answer.

A few hints follow on how to make your best guess. These are only hints and will not work every single time. It is always better to use what you know and select the best answer based on the passage. Use these hints if your only option is making a random guess.

Look for Similar Answers

If you find that two of the answer choices are almost exactly the same, with the exception of a few words, eliminate the other answers and select between these two.

Also Look for Opposite Answers

You may notice that two of the answer choices are opposites.

> Which is true about the duck-billed platypus?
> **a.** It lays eggs.
> **b.** It is a bird.
> **c.** It does not lay eggs.
> **d.** It is a vegetarian.

Notice that choices **a** and **c** are opposites, and obviously, both cannot be correct. So, you can automatically eliminate at least one of these answers. In this case, choice **a** happens to be correct. However, keep in mind that in another question, it is possible that both of the opposite answers could be wrong.

Get Rid of Extremes

Sometimes one answer may seem very different from the rest. In this case, eliminate the extreme answer.

Where did the story take place?

a. Alabama
b. Florida
c. Georgia
d. Paraguay

The answer choices here include three southern states and a foreign country. Paraguay seems a little extreme among the other choices in the list. If you are going to try to eliminate an answer so that you can make your best guess, Paraguay might be the most logical choice to eliminate.

Look for Grammatical Hints

Some questions may require you to choose the answer choice that correctly completes a sentence. Look for any choices that do not fit grammatically and eliminate these. For example, if the beginning of the sentence is written in past tense and an answer choice is in present tense, there's a good chance that the answer is incorrect.

If you are asked to choose a missing word or to identify a word with the same meaning, eliminate any choices that are a different part of speech.

The attorney was late for the meeting and asked us to brief her quickly on what had taken place so far.

What best tells the meaning of *brief* in the sentence?

a. concise without detail
b. to summarize in writing
c. a synopsis of a document
d. to give necessary information

In the sentence, *brief* is a verb, so the correct answer will also be a verb. Choice **a** is an adjective, and choice **c** is a noun. These can be eliminated, leaving only answers **b** and **d**, which are both verbs. In this case, **d** is the best choice.

Keeping Track of Time

Remember that this is a timed test. Being aware of how much time has passed and how much time remains can make a tremendous difference in your overall performance.

Wear a Watch

Be sure to wear a watch on the day of the test. Check the time as the test begins and figure out the time at which the test will end. The test administrator will probably update you on how much time remains throughout the test. However, it's a good idea to be able to check for yourself.

Don't Rush

Remember the old saying "Slow and steady wins the race"? Yes, there is a time limit. Yes, you need to pace yourself. However, if you rush, you'll be more likely to make mistakes. Work quickly, but most important, work carefully.

It's better to answer some of the questions and get them right than to answer most of the questions and get them wrong.

Keep an eye on your watch, but keep your focus on doing your best.

> **TIP**
>
> Most people who have not passed the GED® test actually had the knowledge needed to pass. So what was the problem? They ran out of time. Don't let this happen to you! Pace yourself, monitor the time, and keep moving.

Use Your Time Wisely

Don't spend too much time trying to select a single answer. If a question has you stumped, take your best guess and move on. You can always come back later if you have extra time at the end. Wasting time on one tricky question can prevent you from having time to answer another that you might think is a breeze.

> **TIP**
>
> Sometimes, if you skip a tough question and come back to it later, you will find it easier to answer the second time around. Information and clues in other questions may help you figure out the best answer.

Wrap Things Up at the End

You already know the importance of keeping an eye on the time. If you find that there are only a couple of minutes left and you have not yet finished the test, start guessing. Any answer that is left blank will automatically be marked wrong. Go ahead and take a stab at any remaining questions; quickly get an answer marked for every test item. At this point, what have you got to lose? You may or may not get them right, but at least you tried, and as previously noted, there is no guessing penalty.

Preparing for the Test

Like so many things, the key to doing well on the GED® test is preparation. You're already on the right track by reading these chapters. A few other tips to help you prepare are discussed in this section.

Practice, Practice, Practice

Taking a practice test, such as the ones in this book, is a terrific way to be sure you are ready. These practice tests help you in several ways:

- You will know what types of questions to expect.
- You will become comfortable with the format of the test.

- You will learn about your own strengths and weaknesses.
- You will be aware of what you need to study.

As you take the practice tests, pay attention to the types of questions you get right and those that are more challenging. For example, you may find that the questions about main ideas are really easy. That's great! You might also find that you miss a lot of the questions that deal with themes. No problem. Now you know what skills to study.

Create Opportunities for Even More Practice

You probably read different types of passages all the time, either in magazines or newspapers, in novels, or on the Internet. As you read, think about the types of questions you will find on the GED® test. Then, ask yourself questions about your reading material. For example, you might ask yourself:

- What is the main idea of the passage I just read?
- What details support the main idea?
- What were the conflict and resolution in this story?
- What context clues helped me determine the meanings of unfamiliar words?
- What is the theme (or tone or mood) of the passage?

Another idea is to work with a friend and write questions for each other based on passages you select. You could also summarize passages, underline key words, circle the main idea of each paragraph, and highlight supporting details.

Know Yourself

Figure out what works best for you. For example, not everyone benefits from reading the questions before reading the passage. Some people may find it helpful to scan a passage for the main idea before reading; others may not. Try different strategies as you work through the practice questions and pay attention to which strategies you find most comfortable and most beneficial.

Be Ready the Day Before the Test

Being ready mentally and physically can help you do your best on the test. Here are some suggestions:

- Start studying and preparing in advance; don't plan on cramming for the test in the few days before you are scheduled to take it.
- The day before the test, take a break and relax. Go for a walk, call a friend, or see a movie. Don't stay up late to study.
- Have anything you want to take with you ready ahead of time. Set out your pencils, sweater, watch, or anything else that you need to take to the test location in the morning.
- Make sure you get plenty of sleep the night before the test. If you're concerned that you won't be able to fall asleep, get up extra early the morning before the test. That way, you'll be ready for bed early that evening.

The Big Day

You've studied, you're well rested, and now you're ready to take the GED® Reasoning through Language Arts exam! Now that test day is here, make the most of it.

Get Off to a Good Start

First, set your alarm early enough so that you won't have to rush. Not only will you feel more relaxed and have time to get settled before the test starts, but you also might not be allowed to enter the testing center if you are late. Make sure that being on time is one thing you won't have to worry about.

Then, be sure to eat a well-balanced breakfast. You need to keep your energy up, and you certainly don't want to be distracted by the sound of your stom-

ach growling. If today is going to be a long day of testing, bring a bottle of water, a piece of fruit, or some trail mix to snack on between sessions.

Also, dress in comfortable, layered clothes and bring a sweater. Feeling like your shoes are too tight or being too hot or too cold can be distractions. Do everything you can to be sure you feel great and are on top of your game today!

Keep Your Cool

You've studied, you've practiced, and now you're ready. Don't let your nerves get the best of you. Getting worked up will not help you get your highest possible score. In the overall scheme of things, the GED® test is just a test. If things don't go as well as you'd hoped today, consider this a practice run. You have three chances in a calendar year to pass the test. Try to stay calm and focus on doing your best.

Carefully Read the Directions

If you are unsure about the directions or what exactly you are supposed to do, be sure to ask the test administrator before you begin the test. He or she cannot help you with specific test questions or vocabulary, but you may be able to get the information you need to clarify the test's instructions.

Good Luck!

Now that you are familiar with the GED® test, you can begin your powerful practice. The exams in this book are designed to be as close as possible to the actual tests you will see on test day. Each question in the exams that come with this book is accompanied by a very detailed answer explanation—you will be able to see not only why the correct answer is right but also why each of the other choices is incorrect. You will also see sample essays at all levels for the Extended Response items.

Best of luck on your GED® test study journey and on your test-taking experience!

2 ▶ DIAGNOSTIC TEST

CHAPTER SUMMARY
This is the first of the three practice tests in this book based on the GED® Reasoning through Language Arts test. Use this test to see how you would do if you were to take the exam today.

This diagnostic practice exam is of the same type as the real GED® Reasoning through Language Arts test. It consists of 50 multiple-choice questions and one essay question. These questions test your skills in comprehension (extracting meaning), application (using information), analysis (breaking down information), and synthesis (putting elements together).

The answer sheet you should use for the multiple-choice questions is on the following page. Then comes the exam itself, and after that, the answer key. Each answer on the test is explained in the answer key to help you find out why the correct answers are right and why the incorrect answers are wrong.

Diagnostic Test

1.	ⓐ ⓑ ⓒ ⓓ	18.	ⓐ ⓑ ⓒ ⓓ	35.	ⓐ ⓑ ⓒ ⓓ
2.	ⓐ ⓑ ⓒ ⓓ	19.	ⓐ ⓑ ⓒ ⓓ	36.	ⓐ ⓑ ⓒ ⓓ
3.	ⓐ ⓑ ⓒ ⓓ	20.	ⓐ ⓑ ⓒ ⓓ	37.	ⓐ ⓑ ⓒ ⓓ
4.	ⓐ ⓑ ⓒ ⓓ	21.	ⓐ ⓑ ⓒ ⓓ	38.	ⓐ ⓑ ⓒ ⓓ
5.	ⓐ ⓑ ⓒ ⓓ	22.	ⓐ ⓑ ⓒ ⓓ	39.	ⓐ ⓑ ⓒ ⓓ
6.	ⓐ ⓑ ⓒ ⓓ	23.	ⓐ ⓑ ⓒ ⓓ	40.	ⓐ ⓑ ⓒ ⓓ
7.	ⓐ ⓑ ⓒ ⓓ	24.	ⓐ ⓑ ⓒ ⓓ	41.	ⓐ ⓑ ⓒ ⓓ
8.	ⓐ ⓑ ⓒ ⓓ	25.	ⓐ ⓑ ⓒ ⓓ	42.	ⓐ ⓑ ⓒ ⓓ
9.	ⓐ ⓑ ⓒ ⓓ	26.	ⓐ ⓑ ⓒ ⓓ	43.	ⓐ ⓑ ⓒ ⓓ
10.	ⓐ ⓑ ⓒ ⓓ	27.	ⓐ ⓑ ⓒ ⓓ	44.	ⓐ ⓑ ⓒ ⓓ
11.	ⓐ ⓑ ⓒ ⓓ	28.	ⓐ ⓑ ⓒ ⓓ	45.	ⓐ ⓑ ⓒ ⓓ
12.	ⓐ ⓑ ⓒ ⓓ	29.	ⓐ ⓑ ⓒ ⓓ	46.	ⓐ ⓑ ⓒ ⓓ
13.	ⓐ ⓑ ⓒ ⓓ	30.	ⓐ ⓑ ⓒ ⓓ	47.	ⓐ ⓑ ⓒ ⓓ
14.	ⓐ ⓑ ⓒ ⓓ	31.	ⓐ ⓑ ⓒ ⓓ	48.	ⓐ ⓑ ⓒ ⓓ
15.	ⓐ ⓑ ⓒ ⓓ	32.	ⓐ ⓑ ⓒ ⓓ	49.	ⓐ ⓑ ⓒ ⓓ
16.	ⓐ ⓑ ⓒ ⓓ	33.	ⓐ ⓑ ⓒ ⓓ	50.	ⓐ ⓑ ⓒ ⓓ
17.	ⓐ ⓑ ⓒ ⓓ	34.	ⓐ ⓑ ⓒ ⓓ		

Part I

Directions: Choose the *one best answer* to each question.

Questions 1 through 7 refer to the following excerpt from a novel.

Will Anne Miss Green Gables?

It was a happy and beautiful bride who came down the old carpeted stairs that September noon. She was the first bride of Green Gables, slender and shining-eyed, with her
(5) arms full of roses. Gilbert, waiting for her in the hall below, looked up at her with adoring eyes. She was his at last, this long-sought Anne, whom he won after years of patient waiting. It was to him she was coming. Was
(10) he worthy of her? Could he make her as happy as he hoped? If he failed her—if he could not measure up to her standards. . . .

But then, their eyes met and all doubt was swept away in a certainty that everything
(15) would be wonderful. They belonged to each other; no matter what life might hold for them, it could never alter that. Their happiness was in each other's keeping and both were unafraid.
(20)   They were married in the sunshine of the old orchard, circled by the loving and kindly faces of long-familiar friends. Mr. Allan married them and the Reverend Jo made what Mrs. Rachel Lynde afterwards
(25) pronounced to be the "most beautiful wedding prayer" she had ever heard. Birds do not often sing in September, but one sang sweetly from some hidden tree while Gilbert and Anne repeated their vows. Anne heard it
(30) and thrilled to it. Gilbert heard it and wondered only that all the birds in the world had not burst into jubilant song. The bird

sang until the ceremony was ended. Then it wound up with one more little, glad trill.
(35)   Never had the old gray-green house among its enfolding orchards known a merrier afternoon. Laughter and joy had their way; and when Anne and Gilbert left to catch their train, Marilla stood at the gate
(40) and watched them drive out of sight down the long lane with its banks of goldenrod. Anne turned at its end to wave her last goodbye. She looked once more at her home and felt a tinge of sadness. Then she was
(45) gone—Green Gables was her home no more. It would never be again. Marilla's face looked very gray and old as she turned to the house which Anne had filled for years with light and life.

Adapted from L.M. Montgomery,
Anne's House of Dreams

1. Which of the following words best describes what Gilbert feels toward Anne?
  a. love
  b. respect
  c. gratitude
  d. nervousness

2. What happened when Gilbert's and Anne's eyes met?
  a. He wondered whether he was worthy of her.
  b. He wondered what their life would be like.
  c. He realized they were meant for each other.
  d. He thought Anne would miss Green Gables very much.

3. Based on the excerpt, what was probably the hardest change for Anne?
  a. becoming a wife
  b. saying goodbye to Marilla
  c. not being free to do what she wanted
  d. Green Gables not being her home any longer

4. Based on the excerpt, which description best characterizes the relationship between Marilla and Anne?

   a. Marilla felt tired from having taken care of Anne.

   b. Marilla raised Anne from childhood and cared about her.

   c. Marilla was sad that Anne left because she would have to leave, too.

   d. Marilla and Anne disagreed about Gilbert being a good husband.

5. Which of the following best describes what the author means when she says "this long-sought Anne" (lines 7 and 8)?

   a. Anne was no longer a young woman.

   b. Anne did not fall in love with Gilbert right away.

   c. Anne was patient with Gilbert.

   d. Anne had nearly married someone else.

6. Of the characters in this excerpt, whose inner thoughts are hidden from the reader?

   a. Anne

   b. Gilbert

   c. Marilla

   d. Mr. Allan

7. How does the bird's singing relate to Gilbert's and Anne's marriage?

   a. The bird's singing was distracting to those watching the service.

   b. The bird's singing mirrored the joy of the wedding service.

   c. The bird's singing seemed to suggest sad events in the future.

   d. The bird's singing was worrisome to the bridal couple.

Directions: Choose the *one best answer* to each question.

Questions 8 through 14 are based on the following passage.

Raymond Dean
Green Valley Farm
3421 Rte 32
Stone Ridge, NY 12430

Dear Mr. Dean:

(A)

(1) I am presently a student at ulster county community college and my field of study is agriculture. (2) I am studying all types of farming techniques, and only prefers organic methods for growing vegetables. (3) I have learned much about the latest techniques for growing food organically and I know that since you are one of the largest organic growers in the area, I will learn a great deal more from you and your employees.

(B)

(4) This is why I would like to apply for a summer position with your farm. (5) I hope to get a permanent job with you after I graduate. (6) I believe the experience of working with the Green Valley Farm professionals would, enhance my education greatly. (7) I want to let you know that I would consider an unpaid internship at your farm. (8) That is how anxious I am to work with you. (9) Maybe I could borrow some money from my parents or get a second job to support myself. (10) I am enclosing my resume as well as my references from teachers and a former employer.

(C)

(11) I first learned about your farm from a teacher. (12) He has high regard for your work. (13) He was suggesting that I write you and make this request. (14) I hope I will hear from you. (15) In the near future.

Sincerely yours,

Mark Tanzania

8. Sentence (1): I am presently a student at <u>ulster county community college</u> and my field of study is agriculture.

Which is the best way to write the underlined portion of the sentence?
- **a.** ulster county Community College
- **b.** Ulster county community college
- **c.** Ulster County Community college
- **d.** Ulster County Community College

9. Sentence (2): I am studying all types of farming <u>techniques, and only prefers</u> organic methods for growing vegetables.

Which is the best way to write the underlined portion of this sentence?
- **a.** techniques, so I prefer
- **b.** techniques which are
- **c.** techniques, but prefer
- **d.** techniques that don't prefer

10. Sentences (4) and (5): This is why I would like to apply for a summer position with your farm. I hope to get a permanent job with you after I graduate.

Which is the most effective combination of sentences (4) and (5)?
- **a.** I am applying for a summer job, but I hope to get a permanent position.
- **b.** Applying for a job now in the hopes that you will hire me after I graduate.
- **c.** I would like to apply for a position with your farm, today, and then later after I graduate.
- **d.** I would like to apply for a summer position with your farm in the hopes of having a permanent job with you after I graduate.

11. Which revision would improve the effectiveness of paragraph (B)?
- **a.** move sentence (5) after sentence (10)
- **b.** move sentence (9) to the end of the paragraph
- **c.** remove sentence (6)
- **d.** remove sentence (9)

12. Sentence (6): I believe the experience of working with the Green Valley Farm professionals would, enhance my education greatly.

Which correction should be made to sentence (6)?
- **a.** insert a comma after <u>professionals</u>
- **b.** replace <u>working</u> with <u>to work</u>
- **c.** change <u>believe</u> to <u>believed</u>
- **d.** remove the comma after <u>would</u>

13. Sentences (11) and (12): I first learned about your farm from a teacher. He has high regard for your work.

Which is the most effective combination of sentences (11) and (12)?

a. First I learned about your farm from a teacher he has high regard for your work.

b. I learned about your farm from a teacher who has high regard for your work.

c. My teacher has high regard for your work, I learned about your farm.

d. A teacher who has high regard for your work and I first learned about your farm.

14. Sentence (13): He was suggesting that I write you and make this request.

Which correction should be made to sentence (13)?

a. change <u>make</u> to <u>made</u>

b. change <u>you</u> and <u>make</u> to <u>you. Make</u>

c. change <u>was suggesting</u> to <u>suggested</u>

d. change <u>was suggesting</u> to <u>have suggested</u>

Questions 15 through 18 refer to the following excerpt from a short story.

Will He Appear on National Television?

"I think half the world has shown up for this audition." Gene was talking on his cell phone to his girlfriend. "I can't wait to perform. I know I'm in fine voice, and they are going to

(5) love the song I chose."

"Well, good luck. I will be thinking of you."

Although he sounded upbeat with his girlfriend, in truth Gene was anything but

(10) confident. He had staked so much on the audition, and he had no idea what the judges would really think of him. He realized for the first time that he was scared. Even so, he wanted to succeed so much he could almost

(15) taste it. Just imagine competing on national television. He took a long breath in. It was hard to believe he was actually going to perform for the judges.

He had arrived exactly at nine and had

(20) been in line for over three hours. He could hear his heart beating loudly. Right then, Gene heard his name being called. He went into the building and was ushered into the audition room.

(25) "Yes, I'm here," he answered.

Gene looked at the judges sitting at the table. They seemed bored and unimpressed.

"Well, what are you going to sing for us today?" one of the judges asked him. "Time

(30) After Time," Gene told him, his voice quavering a bit.

"Okay, let's see what you've got," said another judge who was tapping the table with a pencil.

(35) Gene felt a knot in his throat and didn't know if he could go on. He remembered what his voice coach told him: "Just take a moment before you start. Close your eyes. Take a deep breath, and then let go." Gene

(40) closed his eyes and took a breath and then a sweet voice began emanating from his mouth. The judges seemed to disappear. He could have been anywhere. He was in his own world.

(45) Suddenly it was over, and he stood in front of the judges feeling very alone and vulnerable. He could feel the sweat on his brow.

"Well, that was a surprise," said the first
(50) judge. "I never would have predicted that."

"What do you think? Does he go through?" All four of the judges gave him a thumbs up. "You're in, kid," the first judge said. "Don't make us regret our decision."

(55) "Oh, no, sir. You won't regret it," Gene said as he nearly skipped out of the room.

15. Based on the excerpt, what does Gene most likely think about the audition?
   a. It will give him a chance to make a good living.
   b. It is something he had wanted to avoid.
   c. It is a chance for him to be discovered.
   d. It will make him famous in a short time.

16. When does the scene in this excerpt take place?
   a. early morning
   b. late afternoon
   c. early afternoon
   d. early evening

17. Which is the best description of Gene's performance?
   a. a good try but not good enough
   b. a fine voice but without true conviction
   c. a bit slow to start but ultimately wonderful
   d. a showy voice but not much rhythm

18. What is the main effect of the author's use of phrases such as "could almost taste it," "took a long breath in," and "beating loudly"?
   a. to show how long Gene had been waiting
   b. to show that Gene was talented
   c. to show that Gene had been exercising
   d. to show how important the audition was to Gene

Questions 19 through 25 are based on the following passage.

Gorée Island

(A)

(1) Europeans played a large part in bringing slaves to America from west africa.
(2) European countries sent out explorers who sailed down the west coast of Africa.
(3) They came in contact with the people there. (4) They traded with them, but they also captures many of the people. (5) These people were sent to the New World where they became slaves. (6) Most of them ended up working on farms and plantations.

(B)

(7) Some Africans were sent from Gorée, a small island off the coast of what is now Senegal. (8) There are about nine and a half million people in Senegal today. (9) They stayed in dungeons until the ships from the New World came to take them to America and the Caribbean. (10) Some Africans also profited from the slave trade. (11) A group of free African women, called *signares*, sold food to the European traders for the enslaved people and also owned many slaves herself.

(C)

(12) Today the dungeons where they stayed are a museum. (13) Hundreds of people visit this museum each year to see where the slaves were held. (14) They view the dungeons and the House of the Slaves, which is where the masters lived. (15) Their is a memorial statue right outside the house showing African slaves in chains. (16) A visit there would be very educational. (17) You will learn a great deal from the guides about what happened there.

19. Sentence (1): Europeans played a large part in bringing slaves to America from west africa.

Which correction should be made to sentence 1?

a. replace <u>played</u> with <u>were playing</u>

b. insert a comma after <u>America</u>

c. insert a period after <u>large part</u>

d. change <u>west africa</u> to <u>West Africa</u>

20. Sentences (2) and (3): European countries sent out explorers who sailed down the west coast of Africa. They came in contact with the people there.

The most effective combination of sentences (2) and (3) would include which group of words?

a. coast of Africa while they

b. coast of Africa where they

c. coast of Africa instead of

d. coast of Africa but they

21. Sentence (4): They traded with them, but they also <u>captures</u> many of the people.

Which is the best way to write the underlined portion of this sentence?

a. had been captured

b. was capturing

c. will capture

d. captured

22. Which revision would improve the effectiveness of paragraph (B)?

a. move sentence (7) to the end of the paragraph

b. remove sentence (8)

c. remove sentence (9)

d. move sentence (11) to the beginning of the paragraph

23. Sentence (11): A group of free African women, called *signares*, sold food to the European traders for the enslaved people and also owned many slaves herself.

Which correction should be made to sentence (11)?

a. change <u>owned</u> to <u>owns</u>

b. change <u>A group</u> to <u>A groups</u>

c. insert a comma after <u>people</u>

d. replace <u>herself</u> with <u>themselves</u>

24. Sentence (15): Their is a memorial statue right outside the house showing African slaves in chains.

Which correction should be made to sentence 15?

a. move <u>right</u> to the end of the sentence

b. replace <u>Their</u> with <u>There</u>

c. change <u>is</u> to <u>are</u>

d. change <u>slaves</u> to <u>Slaves</u>

25. Sentence (17): You will learn a great deal from the guides about what happened there.

The most effective revision of sentence (17) would begin with which group of words?

a. If you go, you

b. Even if you go, you

c. However, you

d. Learning a lot

Questions 26 through 31 refer to the following employee memo.

What Will the New Procedures Do?

Memo
To: Employees of IMPEL
From: Management
Re: New Security Procedures
(5)   Date: June 15
As a result of some incidents that have occurred with unauthorized persons in secure parts of Building A, as of June 30, new procedures will go into effect for security in
(10)   that building. From now on, all employees reporting to work should enter through the employee entrance at the side of the building on Murray Street. No employee is to enter through the main entrance. In order to be
(15)   admitted, each employee must have a valid photo ID. The ID needs to be swiped to unlock the door. Make sure not to allow another person to enter with you even if you know the person. Each employee needs to
(20)   swipe his or her own ID in order to be registered as being on the job.

The main entrance will be for visitors only. The receptionist there will call the party that the visitor is coming to meet so that he
(25)   or she can come to the main desk to escort the guest to his or her office. Visitors will be given temporary passes, but they cannot have full run of the office.

In addition, all employees will also be
(30)   required to log in on their computer when they begin work and log out when they take a break. Make sure to log out and in when taking lunch breaks.

If an employee sees someone whom he
(35)   or she believes is unauthorized to be in Building A, that employee should take immediate action and report the event to Mr. Shields, our head of security. Do not

(40)   approach the person, but simply call Mr. Shields's office. His extension is 890. If there is no answer, make a written report and e-mail it to cshields@impel.com.

If employees have any questions regarding these regulations, please contact
(45)   the Human Resources department at extension 550. Ms. Hardy will be able to respond to your queries. Thank you for your cooperation in this matter. We feel that with these additional procedures, our workplace
(50)   will be made more secure for everyone concerned. Ideally, this will result in improved work output, since any possibility of a security breach will be prevented.

26. Which of the following best restates the phrase "security breach" (line 53)?
   a. a compromise in the safety of the office
   b. a blow to the confidence of employees
   c. a distraction because of an employee's personal problems
   d. a defense against employees not doing their jobs

27. Based on the excerpt, which of the following can be inferred about management?
   a. They are concerned about the safety of employees.
   b. They believe that the office is completely secure.
   c. They want employees to fill out time sheets.
   d. They want to track employee work habits.

28. Which of the following could be prevented by the new security procedures?
   a. visitors entering through the main entrance
   b. employees swiping IDs to open doors
   c. employees entering through the side entrance
   d. unauthorized persons wandering around Building A

29. Imagine an employee sees a person in Building A without an ID badge. According to the memo, which of these actions should the employee take?
a. call Mr. Shields's office to make a report
b. tell the person to leave the building
c. call the receptionist in the main entrance
d. report the event to Ms. Hardy

30. Which of the following best describes the style in which this memo is written?
a. complicated and unclear
b. academic and dry
c. straightforward and direct
d. detailed and technical

31. Which of the following best describes the way in which the memo is organized?
a. by listing information in the order of importance
b. by sequence of events
c. by presenting a problem and then a solution
d. by comparing and contrasting issues

Questions 32 through 37 refer to the following excerpt from a novel.

Will His Mother Let Him Leave?

"Beatrice," he said suddenly, "I want to go away to school. Everybody in Minneapolis is going to go away to school."

Beatrice showed some alarm.

(5)   "But you're only fifteen."

"Yes, but everybody goes away to school at fifteen, and I *want* to, Beatrice."

On Beatrice's suggestion, the subject was dropped for the rest of the walk, but a
(10)   week later she delighted him by saying, "Amory, I have decided to let you have your way. If you still want to, you can go away to school."

"Yes?"

(15)   "To St. Regis's in Connecticut."

Amory said nothing, but he felt a bolt of excitement along his spine.

"It's being arranged," continued Beatrice. "It's better that you should go away.
(20)   I'd have preferred you to have gone to Eton and then to Christ Church, Oxford. But it seems impracticable now—and for the present, we'll let the university question take care of itself."

(25)   "What are you going to do, Beatrice?"

"Heaven knows. It seems my fate to spend my years in this country. Not for a second do I regret being American—indeed, I think that regret is very typical of ignorant
(30)   people. I feel sure we are the great coming nation, yet"—and she sighed, "I feel my life should have slipped away close to an older, mellower civilization, a land of greens and autumnal browns. . . ."

(35)   Amory did not answer, so his mother continued, "My regret is that you haven't been abroad. But still, as you are a man, it's better that you should grow up here under the snarling eagle—is that the right term?"

(40)   Amory agreed that it was.

"When do I go to school?"

"Next month. You'll have to start East a little early to take your examinations. After that you'll have a free week, so I want you to
(45)   go up the Hudson and pay a visit."

"To who?"

"To Monsignor Darcy, Amory. He wants to see you. He went to Harrow and then to Yale—became a Catholic. I want him
(50)   to talk to you. I feel he can be such a help." She stroked his auburn hair gently. "Dear Amory, dear Amory. . . ."

Adapted from F. Scott Fitzgerald, *This Side of Paradise*

32. Which of the following best expresses the main idea of the excerpt?
   a. A boy's mother agrees to let her son go to a boarding school.
   b. A boy's mother would like her son to visit schools in other countries.
   c. A boy wants to make his mother happy.
   d. A boy wants to get away from his hometown.

33. Based on the information in this excerpt, which of the following would Beatrice most likely prefer to do?
   a. learn about American history
   b. have a potluck dinner with friends
   c. spend time in England
   d. teach English to schoolchildren

34. Why does Beatrice most likely think it is better for Amory to grow up in America?
   a. He would not like Europe.
   b. He is good at sports.
   c. Schools are easier in America.
   d. He was born in America.

35. Based on Beatrice saying, "I feel my life should have slipped away close to an older, mellower civilization, a land of greens and autumnal browns" (lines 31 to 34), what does she suggest about America?
   a. She thinks it is similar to England.
   b. She believes it is a land of great energy.
   c. She assumes it is a weak country with little future.
   d. She decides then to adopt it as her home.

36. How does Amory calling his mother by her first name influence the excerpt?
   a. It shows that Amory and his mother are not close.
   b. It shows that Beatrice wants to appear to be Amory's sister.
   c. It shows that Beatrice resents being a mother.
   d. It shows that Amory and his mother's relationship is not typical.

37. Why does Beatrice want Amory to visit Monsignor Darcy?
   a. She thinks that Monsignor Darcy can convince Amory to go to school closer to home.
   b. Monsignor Darcy is Amory's uncle.
   c. She wants Amory to become Catholic.
   d. She feels that Monsignor Darcy can help Amory because he went to Harrow and Yale.

Questions 38 through 42 refer to the following excerpt from a review.

What Does the Reviewer Think of *Last Fight*?

Last Fight may be one of the biggest blockbusters of the summer, but it doesn't live up to the buzz around it. In this science fiction tale of epic proportions, viewers are

(5)   propelled forward to a future when Earth is populated by androids and humans. These survivors of an ancient civilization live in a sterile world covered by a plastic dome. The dome is for protection from aliens who

(10)   attack Earth on a regular basis. It also cuts down on such environmental problems as air pollution and global warming.

      The plot centers around a young man named Raal and his quest to forge a peace

(15)   between the humans and the aliens. His is a

difficult task, considering the aliens have no desire to stop trying to overcome Earth and its inhabitants. While Raal (George Armstrong) is a likeable character, he lacks the ability to
(20) change expression to any extent. As a result, his acting range is quite limited. He is something of a dreamer, and perhaps the message here is that there is no place for dreamers in the future, but I will not detail
(25) the plot or the ending. I don't want to spoil it for those people who may actually want to view the film. Still, let it be said that events do not go well for young Raal.

The high point of the movie for me
(30) was the performance by veteran actor Bruce Cameron as the sage Kel. He has shown over and over his ability to transform even the most mundane character into someone fascinating to watch. It may be worth seeing
(35) the film just for his performance.

Besides being far-fetched, the movie concentrates too much on special effects, including 3-D, but that of course may be a draw for many viewers. Its cost was also
(40) enormous. Not much that is green is in this film.

38. Which of the following is the main idea of the excerpt?
- **a.** The author is giving the reasons movies should not use special effects.
- **b.** The author is detailing the kind of acting that he prefers.
- **c.** The author is providing his impressions of a science fiction movie.
- **d.** The author is explaining why he enjoys science fiction movies.

39. Which of the following best expresses the reviewer's opinion of *Last Fight*?
- **a.** It was too expensive to make and is too long.
- **b.** It was enjoyable because there was some great acting in it.
- **c.** The reviewer hopes that most people will turn out for the movie.
- **d.** It has little depth and relies too much on special effects.

40. If it is known that the author of this review had written numerous science fiction scripts, none of which were ever made into a movie, how would this most likely affect the reading of this review?
- **a.** The experiences of the author give his or her opinion greater value.
- **b.** The author's knowledge of the genre may be questioned.
- **c.** Much of the negativity might be construed as sour grapes.
- **d.** The author's personal experiences have no influence on the review whatsoever.

41. Which of the following best describes the style in which this review is written?
- **a.** technical
- **b.** humorous
- **c.** academic
- **d.** ornate

42. According to the author, which word best describes *Last Fight*?
- **a.** provocative
- **b.** lighthearted
- **c.** solemn
- **d.** overblown

Questions 43 through 50 are based on the following passage.

How to Write a Cover Letter

(A)

(1) A cover letter that accompanies your résumé is of great importance, the cover letter gives the employer a general impression of you. (2) In fact, if the cover letter don't interest the potential employer, the employer may opt not to read through the résumé at all. (3) So make your cover letter effective by keeping it short and bring up points that will interest the reader.

(B)

(4) Before you start to write, make sure you have an updated résumé. (5) Then research the company so you can include information about itself that might relate to the position you are hoping to fill. (6) Research will also help you prepare for an interview. (7) When you are ready to write your letter make sure to include the name of the person the title, the correct company name, and address. (8) If you don't know the name of the person to who you are writing, use "Dear Sir/Madam."

(C)

(9) When you get to the body of the letter, use the first paragraph to say why you think you would be good for the position.
(10) Also include, why you would want to work for the company. (11) Use the next paragraph to tell about your experience and matching it to the job. (12) Let the employer know that you are enthusiastic about the prospect of working for the company.
(13) The last paragraph should be brief.

(14) Should include a strong statement that will make the employer want to interview you. (15) At the end of the letter, give your contact, information and conclude with either "sincerely yours" or "yours truly."

43. Sentence (1): A cover letter that accompanies your résumé is of great importance, the cover letter gives the employer a general impression of you.

Which correction should be made to sentence (1)?
   a. insert a comma after <u>résumé</u>
   b. remove the comma
   c. replace <u>gives</u> with <u>give</u>
   d. replace the comma with <u>because</u>

44. Sentence (2): In fact, if the cover <u>letter don't interest</u> the potential employer, the employer may opt not to read through the résumé at all.

Which is the best way to write the underlined portion of sentence (2)?
   a. letter did not interest
   b. letters don't interest
   c. letter haven't interest
   d. letter doesn't interest

45. Sentence (3): So make your cover letter effective by keeping it short and bring up points that will interest the reader.

Which correction should be made to sentence (3)?
   a. change <u>keeping</u> to <u>will keep</u>
   b. change <u>interest</u> to <u>interesting</u>
   c. change <u>it</u> to <u>its</u>
   d. change <u>bring</u> to <u>bringing</u>

46. Sentence (5): Then research the company so you can include information <u>about itself</u> that might relate to the position you are hoping to fill.

Which is the best way to write the underlined portion of sentence (5)?

a. about yourselves
b. about herself
c. about himself
d. about yourself

47. Sentence (7): When you are ready to write your letter make sure to include the name of the <u>person the title</u>, the correct company name, and address.

Which is the best way to write the underlined portion of sentence (7)?

a. person; the title
b. person, the title,
c. person. The title
d. person and the title

48. Sentence (8): If you don't know the name of the person <u>to who</u> you are writing, use "Dear Sir/Madam."

Which is the best way to write the underlined portion of sentence (8)?

a. to which
b. that
c. which
d. to whom

49. Sentence (11): Use the next paragraph to tell about your experience <u>and matching</u> it to the job.

Which is the best way to write the underlined portion of sentence (11)?

a. getting to have matched
b. and to have matched
c. and to match
d. yet to match

50. Sentence (14): Should include a strong statement that will make the employer want to interview you.

What correction should be made to sentence (14)?

a. insert <u>It</u> before <u>Should</u> and use lowercase <u>should</u>
b. change <u>will make</u> to <u>is making</u>
c. replaced <u>interview</u> with <u>interviewing</u>
d. change <u>employer want</u> to <u>employer. Want</u>

Part II

1 Question

Read the following passages. Then, read the prompt and write an essay taking a stance. Use information from the passages to support your essay.

President Franklin Roosevelt's Message to Congress on Establishing Minimum Wages and Maximum Hours, May 24, 1937

"Today, you and I are pledged to take further steps to reduce the lag in the purchasing power of industrial workers and to strengthen and stabilize the markets for the farmers' products. The two go hand in hand. Each depends for its effectiveness upon the other. Both working simultaneously will open new outlets for productive capital. Our Nation so richly endowed with natural resources and with a capable and industrious population should be able to devise ways and means of insuring to all our able-bodied working men and women a fair day's pay for a fair day's work. A self-supporting and self-respecting democracy can plead no justification for the existence of child labor, no economic reason for chiseling workers' wages or stretching workers' hours.

Enlightened business is learning that competition ought not to cause bad social consequences which inevitably react upon the profits of business itself. All but the hopelessly reactionary will agree that to conserve our primary resources of man power, government must have some control over maximum hours, minimum wages, the evil of child labor and the exploitation of unorganized labor."

Letter to the Editor Regarding Minimum Wage Increase, January 3, 2014

Dear Editor:

I have seen many people speak out in support of raising the minimum wage in recent weeks, but I have yet to see anyone offer an informed alternative view. The truth is, if we increase the minimum wage for all American workers, we will undoubtedly do irreparable harm to our economy. The more we keep government from intruding into the workplace, the better.

Raising the minimum wage means that employers have to come up with the extra money to pay their workers more. How will they do this? By firing workers to reduce costs, or by charging more for their goods and services. If they fire workers, then those workers will now be earning less than they did before . . . not exactly a great solution to raise the standard of living. If they raise the price of goods and services, then people will have to spend more on life essentials such as food and transportation. So the benefit of higher wages will be eaten up by the increased expenses faced by the average worker.

When I was growing up, I made twenty-five cents an hour washing cars. I used that money to put myself through college to get my engineering degree. I used that degree to get a job designing bridges for the state of Texas. I didn't sit there at the car wash complaining about how little I earned; I used that opportunity to better myself. I just wish more people these days were willing to do the same.

Sincerely,

Ralph Phillips

Prompt

These two passages present different arguments regarding the issue of minimum wage. In your response, analyze both positions to determine which one is best supported. Use relevant and specific evidence from the passages to support your response.

Answers and Explanations

Part I

1. a. Although Gilbert may feel *respect* and *gratitude*, the word that best describes his feelings is *love*. It is clearly indicated in his actions. *Nervousness* is not supported by the excerpt.

2. c. This choice is clearly supported by what the excerpt says happened when their eyes met—"and all doubt was swept away in a certainty that everything would be wonderful." The other choices may enter into the scene between them, but they do not occur when their eyes met.

3. d. It is clear from the ending of the excerpt that this was the biggest and hardest change for Anne. That is why she felt a "tinge of sadness." The other choices are not supported.

4. b. There are hints in the excerpt that support this answer, such as Marilla looking "gray" when Anne was leaving and how Anne had filled the house with "light and life." The other choices are not supported by the text.

5. b. Based on the information in the excerpt, this is the correct answer. The text says that Gilbert had won her "after years of patient waiting." This supports choice **b**, not the other choices.

6. d. The author gives the readers clues about what all the other characters are thinking, but the reader does not learn anything about Mr. Allan.

7. b. The text says that not many birds sang in September but that one sang sweetly while Gilbert and Anne repeated their vows. It even "wound up with one more little, glad trill" after the ceremony was over, seeming to mirror the joy of the wedding service.

8. d. Choice **d** is correct because it capitalizes all the words that make up the proper name of the college. Choices **a**, **b**, and **c** are incorrect because they capitalize some, but not all, of the words in the proper name.

9. c. The best revision of this sentence reads, "I am studying all types of farming techniques, but prefer organic methods for growing vegetables." Therefore, choice **c** is the best response. Choices **a**, **b**, and **d** change the meaning of the sentence.

10. d. Choice **d** is the best answer. This contains all the relevant information that is needed. Choice **a** is very general, and it is unclear what permanent position is wanted by the letter writer. Choice **b** is grammatically incorrect because it lacks a subject for the verb *applying*. Choice **c** is awkward and unclear.

11. d. Choice **d** is the best response, since this information is not central to the main point of the letter, which is asking for an internship. Choice **a** doesn't make sense when it is moved. Choice **b** doesn't work since the information is not material to the topic. Choice **c** would mean removing an important sentence from the paragraph.

12. d. Choice **d** is correct because it removes an unnecessary comma from the sentence. Choice **a** is not correct because it would insert an unnecessary comma. Choices **b** and **c** are not correct because these contain the wrong forms of the verbs.

13. b. Choice **b** is the best response. This sentence replaces the repetitive *he has* with the pronoun *who*. Choice **a** is a run-on sentence so it is incorrect. Choice **c** does not combine the sentences, but simply puts an inappropriate comma between them. Choice **d** improperly joins the sentences with *and*.

14. c. Choice **c** is correct because this action happened once in the past and is not ongoing. Choice **a** is not correct because the verb *made* is in the past tense, not the present tense, the way it should be. Choice **b** is the wrong answer because it creates a phrase and doesn't address the verb problem. Choice **d** uses an incorrect form of past tense.

15. c. This is the best answer. The audition will give him a chance to be discovered. The audition will not make him become famous or give him a chance to make a good living.

16. c. The excerpt says Gene got to the audition site at 9:00 A.M. and had been waiting more than three hours (line 20). That would make the time after noon.

17. c. This answer reflects what happens in the story. At first he was slow to start, but then he sang very well and passed the round of auditions.

18. d. This answer reflects the feelings that Gene was having about the audition. For instance, a person's heart often beats loudly—or seems to beat louder than usual—when a person is experiencing an important moment in life.

19. d. Choice **d** correctly capitalizes a proper noun. Choice **a** changes the verb into an incorrect tense. Choice **b** inserts a comma that is not needed, and choice **c** makes the second sentence a fragment.

20. b. Choice **b** is correct because it combines the ideas in both sentences with the relative pronoun *where*. Choice **a** uses a transition word that changes the meaning of the sentences. Choice **c** creates a confusing sentence, and choice **d** changes the meaning of the sentences.

21. d. Choice **d** is correct because the verb form fits the subject, and the tense is correct as well. Choice **a** is not correct because the tense and the verb in the first part of the sentence do not match the subject. Choices **b** and **c** are both incorrect because they pick incorrect tenses—one in the past continuous tense and the other in the future tense.

22. b. Choice **b** is correct. This sentence has nothing to do with the main topic of the paragraph, which concerns the slaves being held in Gorée Island. Choice **a** is not correct because this is a topic sentence and clearly the opening of the paragraph. Choice **c** has important information about the slaves in it. Choice **d** wouldn't make logical sense.

23. d. Choice **d** is correct since the subject (*women*) is plural, not singular. Choice **a** is incorrect because this is the wrong verb tense for the sentence. Choice **b** is grammatically incorrect since *a* is singular and *groups* is plural. No comma is needed after *people*, so choice **c** is incorrect.

24. b. Choice **b** is correct because it replaces the homonym *their*, a possessive pronoun, with *there*, meaning *that place*. Choice **a** does not make sense. Choice **c** would result in a verb that does not agree with the subject. Choice **d** is incorrect because there is no reason to capitalize *slaves*.

25. a. Choice **a** is correct because this phrase links a visit to Gorée Island with learning from the guides. Choice **b** is incorrect because it changes the meaning of the sentence. Choice **c** uses an inappropriate transition. Choice **d** is wrong because it turns the sentence into a dependent clause.

26. a. This phrase means that the security was somehow broken, so choice **a** is correct. This can be seen in the very first section of the memo: "As a result of some incidents that have occurred with unauthorized persons in secure parts. . . ." The other choices are not suggested by these words. They have nothing to do with security being compromised.

27. a. The point of the memo is that there were some security incidents that needed to be addressed. Based on the memo, choice **b** is clearly not correct, and the others are not suggested by the memo, either.

28. d. If you read the memo carefully, you will see that this is the one option that the new regulations will help prevent. It is mentioned in the first paragraph.

29. a. Again, a close reading of the text will reveal that this is what an employee is to do first if a stranger is seen in Building A. This can be found in the fourth paragraph.

30. c. The memo is direct and to the point. It is not technical. It's quite clear and not at all academic.

31. c. The memo states a problem at the beginning and then describes the new regulations that will solve it—a way to keep unauthorized people out of secure parts of Building A.

32. a. This choice is clearly correct. It contains the main idea of the excerpt. The dialogue is about a boy wanting to go away to school and his mother finally agreeing to it.

33. c. It seems clear from the dialogue in the excerpt that Beatrice would prefer to be in England rather than do any of the other activities. She seems not to mind America, but she does long for England.

34. d. This is the most logical choice, although it is never actually stated in the excerpt. There is no mention of the father, although he may or may not live in America. The other choices are not supported by the passage, either.

35. b. This is the only choice suggested by the lines spoken by Beatrice. She is comparing England's mellow nature to America's energetic spirit.

36. d. This is the best and most all-encompassing answer. This mother and son do not seem like most mothers and sons. The way they relate and talk suggests an atypical relationship.

37. d. This is the most obvious reason that Beatrice wants Amory to meet Monsignor Darcy. She says he went to Harrow and Yale, and she wants Amory to talk to him.

38. c. This is what the review is mostly about. The reviewer does address the other answer choices, but they do not represent the main intent of the review.

39. d. Based on what the reviewer says about the movie, this is the best answer. He says the main character's acting is bad. He does not mention the length of the film, either.

40. c. This is the most logical choice. People reading the review would take into consideration that the reviewer has never had any of his or her science fiction scripts made into a movie. This would definitely taint the review, as he or she might be overly critical.

41. b. The review is somewhat *humorous*, or at least that is its intention. Although the 3-D aspect of the film is mentioned, that's not really enough to call the review *technical*. A technical review would probably have discussed the 3-D aspect at more length. None of the other choices properly describes the writing style of the review.

42. d. This word best describes what the reviewer feels about the movie. Overall, the reviewer is not very impressed with the film, so a positive choice like **b** could be eliminated. None of the other choices accurately describes the author's opinion.

43. d. Choice **d** is correct because it adds an appropriate conjunction to join the two sentences. Choice **a** inserts an unnecessary comma, and by removing the existing comma you create a run-on sentence, so both choices **a** and **b** are incorrect. Choice **c** replaces the correct form of the verb with an incorrect form.

44. d. Choice **d** is correct because the singular verb *doesn't* agrees with the singular noun *letter*. Choice **a** is incorrect because this is the wrong verb tense for this sentence. Choice **b** is incorrect, not because of the verb, but because of the plural form of *letter*. The sentence is referring to one letter, not multiple ones. Choice **c** is incorrect because this is a plural form of the verb.

45. d. Choice **d** is correct because it uses a verb that is parallel to *keeping*. Choices **a** and **b** are incorrect because they use an incorrect form of the verb. Choice **c** is not correct because it changes the pronoun object into a possessive.

46. d. Choice **d** is correct because this pronoun refers back to the antecedent *you*. Choice **a** is incorrect because it refers to more than one *you*. Choices **b** and **c** are incorrect because they refer to either *she* or *he* as antecedents.

47. b. Choice **b** is correct because commas are used between lists of items. Choices **a** and **c** are incorrect because they create sentence fragments. Choice **d** is not correct because *title* is not the last item in the list of items.

48. d. Choice **d** is correct because the preposition *to* takes the objective form of the pronoun *who*. Choice **b** is incorrect because *that* refers to an animal or thing, but not a person. Also, *which* does not refer to a person, so choices **a** and **c** are incorrect.

49. c. Choice **c** is correct because it matches the preceding verb *to tell*. Choices **a** and **b** are incorrect because they do not match *to tell*. Choice **d** is incorrect because it creates a confusing sentence.

50. a. Choice **a** is correct because it adds a subject to properly complete the sentence. Choice **b** changes a correct verb form into an incorrect one, as does choice **c**. Choice **d** is incorrect because it turns the sentence into two fragments.

Part II

Sample 6 Scoring Essay

President Roosevelt and letter-writing citizen Ralph Phillips represent perspectives on the minimum wage from very different time periods. During Roosevelt's administration, the country was facing its worst Depression in history; in 2014, the country had rebounded from a dramatic Recession but was deeply divided on both who was responsible for the crisis, and how it should be addressed.

Among FDR's New Deal initiatives was a proposal to establish a minimum wage and maximum hours for American workers. In this message to Congress, he suggests that protecting and investing in the American workforce would improve conditions for industrial workers and for farmers who are dependent on market demand, drawing on Americans' sense of ability and resourcefulness, ideals of democracy, and national ego. He cites child labor and exploitation of unorganized labor as the primary justifications for these measures.

However, Ralph Phillips' letter focuses on the downsides of such an initiative—employers required to adhere to an increased minimum wage would be forced into "firing workers to reduce costs" or "charging more for their goods," which would increase the burden on the workers it was meant to help. He justifiably points out that workers will need to be fired in order for employers to pay the remaining workers more. While these logistical concerns might initially appear to be more persuasive than FDR's appeal to the enlightened American spirit of enterprise, Phillips concludes with a petulant "I made twenty-five cents an hour washing cars" anecdote that willfully ignores class and economic realities of the modern era. He even appears hypocritical—he thinks the government should stay out of the private employment arena, but took a job for a government office! Besides, nobody could put themselves through college making a quarter an hour today—Phillips thus proves himself to be one of the "hopelessly reactionary" individuals FDR despaired of reaching in his message. FDR's address is best supported because he addressed it to a legislative body that could make a difference and sought to inspire Congressional leadership to intervene on behalf of the American worker.

This essay introduces compelling evidence from each source, organizes its points logically by moving from beginning to end in each essay, then comparing the two, and concludes by making an argument about which essay is better supported, and why. It demonstrates fluency in Standard American English conventions, including spelling and grammar.

Sample 3 Scoring Essay

In his message to congress, President Franklin Roosevelt says that the government should assist people to prevent exploration and child labor, even if it damages the economy. America is rich enough to paying workers fairly for their work. Ralph Phillips wrote a letter to the editor saying about how it would be to hard to have a minimum wage because of it having increase costs for employers and actually basically reduce employment.

He worked hard to put himself through school and says everyone should—but what if you can't even find a car wash job? What if you have other obstacles? Roosevelt may have less of plans but he is at least talking to the right people instead of just giving up.

This essay uses less specific, more simplistic evidence from each source, and features no direct quotes or broader context. Its organization is basically logical but lacks a coherent beginning-middle-end structure or specific analysis of each argument. The grasp of Standard American English is weaker—the pronoun "He" in the second paragraph is clear and there are other syntax issues.

Sample 0 Scoring Essay

They both make differnt points about minimum wagers in America. Phillips says the min. wage would only do bad things to the economy and supports his argument with personal stories about working hard. So he is more persuasive. roosevelt says America is rich and so should pay its workers more no matter what.

This essay fails to introduce its sources, what types of documents they are, or when they were written. There are no specific quotes, the essay is much too brief, and its structure is disorganized—it draws a conclusion before analyzing FDR's argument. The grammar, spelling, and syntax are all substandard.

Extended Response

For this prompt, an extended response should include some discussion of how the two passages differ in viewpoint regarding the issue of minimum wage. Specifically, Roosevelt's message to Congress emphasizes the need for government to establish livable requirements for wages and working conditions, while the letter to the editor asserts that government should keep out of private enterprise as much as possible. A successful extended response should also analyze the arguments presented in each passage. For the Roosevelt passage, the arguments focus on an appeal to emotion and charitable cooperation among all Americans. For example, Roosevelt refers to the way a "self-respecting democracy" should run. The letter to the editor, on the other hand, relies largely on personal experience to support its argument. Mr. Phillips also offers a logical argument regarding the effects of a minimum wage increase that some could consider one-sided; following the logic of this argument, workers should be paid as little as possible to keep everyone employed and to keep the price of goods low. A keen reader might even note the potential conflict between Mr. Phillips's assertion that government should stay out of the affairs of business, and the fact that he got a job working for the government.

3 ▶ READING COMPREHENSION: BIG PICTURE TOOLS

CHAPTER SUMMARY

Many of the questions on the GED® RLA test are designed to uncover how well you understand and think about what you read. You'll need to read the passage carefully in order to answer the question correctly. In some cases, the answer will be obvious to you; in other cases, you'll have to do a little detective work to figure out the correct choice.

Answers and explanations for all practice questions are at the end of the chapter.

This chapter covers tips and strategies for answering questions about big picture concerns like Author's Purpose, Point of View, and Theme, as well as how to read effectively and efficiently, how to select and eliminate answers, and how to manage your time.

Reading the Passages

Pay Attention to the Purpose Question

As you may already know, each passage is preceded by a purpose question. This question is printed in bold and is there to give you a purpose and focus as you read. Use this question to your benefit. Read it carefully, and think about what you might read about in the passage.

Suppose the following is one of the purpose questions on your test:

Who Is Knocking?

How can this help you? Well, before you even begin reading, you know that in the passage, you will read about someone knocking. Because the purpose question doesn't tell you who that is, you know you need to look for that information as you read. For some reason, this is going to be important for you to know.

> The purpose question is just there to provide a focus for your reading; you will not have to answer this question.

Read the Questions First

Another way to help you focus on important information as you read a passage is to take a quick look at the questions *before* you begin reading. This will help you know what information to look for in the passage.

1. How does the author feel about the topic?

By reading the questions ahead of time, you know you need to look for words and details that offer clues about the author's attitude toward the subject matter. This could help focus your attention as you read and possibly save time in the long run.

First Scan, Then Read

You may find it helpful to quickly scan the passage to identify the main idea, then go back and read the passage carefully. Knowing the main idea first can help you identify supporting details as you read. This also lets you know what information you should be looking for when you read the passage slowly and critically the second time.

Use Context Clues

Don't get upset if you come across an unfamiliar word in a passage. Use what you have learned about context clues to figure out the meaning. Try doing the following:

- Notice how the word is used in the sentence.
- Read the surrounding sentences.
- Look for hints such as synonyms, antonyms, examples, and definitions.
- Think about what would make sense in the context of the passage.

To correctly answer the questions, it is imperative that you completely understand each passage.

Notice Important Details

As you read, pay attention to words, phrases, and details that seem to be important to the meaning of the passage. Be on the lookout for the information listed here:

- key words
- names of real people
- names of characters
- names of locations
- dates
- headings
- specific details
- clues about mood or tone
- hints about the theme
- point of view

> **TIP**
>
> If a word is in *italics* or CAPS or is <u>underlined</u> or **bold**, it is probably important. Pay close attention to this information.

Read Everything

As you read, you may come across information that is set off in brackets. These are explanatory notes that can provide valuable information.

> *Information in brackets [such as these] can be helpful in selecting the best answer.*

It may be tempting to skip over the information in the brackets, especially if you're beginning to feel the time crunch. Don't skip anything. Be sure to read all the information you've been given. It may be there for a good reason.

Classify Information

As you read, be sure to recognize the difference between the main idea and supporting details. Also, be sure to recognize whether a statement is a fact or an opinion. Classifying statements correctly can help you completely understand the passage and mentally organize the ideas you have read.

Don't Forget the Visuals

Any time a passage includes visual displays, pay close attention to them! They are probably there for a reason and often include extremely valuable information that will deepen your understanding of the passage. Visual aids that you might find include the following:

- maps
- charts
- graphs
- diagrams
- illustrations
- photographs

Read the titles, labels, and captions as well as the information contained within the visuals themselves.

Read the Passage Completely

Some people find it helpful to read the questions before reading the passage. That's great; however, you need to read the passage completely before trying to actually *answer* the questions, even if the questions appear to be simple. Most of the questions will require you to understand the entire passage completely in order to correctly answer them. Remember, this is not the time to assume that you know what the passage is about. Read the entire text carefully, then answer the questions.

Carefully Read the Questions

This may seem obvious, but it is vital that you read each question carefully and make sure you completely understand exactly what is being asked. In fact, read each question twice. How can you select the correct answer if you misread or do not understand the question?

> *Which of the following is least likely to occur next?*

Suppose you read this question too quickly. You might miss the word *least*. This one simple word completely changes the question. Overlooking one word in a question could cause you to select the wrong answer choice.

Also, it may be tempting to assume that you know what the question is asking, especially if several similar questions are grouped together and you're feeling rushed for time. But remember—just because it would be logical for a certain question to come next, there's no guarantee that it will.

Pay Attention to Line Numbers

Some questions may refer to line numbers in the passage. Be sure to refer back to the passage and read the information in that line again. It is important to understand the words and information in the correct context.

> *What is the meaning of the word* buffet *in line 17?*

You're probably familiar with the word *buffet* and could easily give a definition. But, this word does have several meanings. Without reading line 17, how will you know which meaning is correct?

> *(17) Heavy raindrops and hail continued to buffet the tiny cabin throughout the night.*

Now that you've read the word in the correct context, you will be able to select the appropriate meaning.

TIP

Any information that is offered within a question is important! It would not be there if you didn't need it.

Tips for Fiction Passages

Prose fiction passages involve imaginary people and events. While you may see prose fiction passages that contain arguments and evidence to support a viewpoint or conclusion, the author's main intent for prose fiction is generally to entertain. These passages are more likely to focus on tone, style, setting, point of view, and making inferences about the characters and the world.

Make Inferences

Often in prose fiction passages, the author intentionally leaves out some information. This requires readers to make inferences about the plot, characters, or setting. Use the information that is implied to "fill in the blanks" and create your own complete mental picture. For example, you can infer what type of person a character is by paying attention to what other characters say or think about him. You can put together information about the sights, sounds, and smells described in a story to infer the setting.

> *As Maxwell stepped outside, he noticed the sounds of the cows mooing in the distance and could make out the silhouette of the barn on the opposite side of the field. This was nothing like the city he was used to.*

> What is the setting of the story?
> **a.** a barn
> **b.** a big city
> **c.** a farm
> **d.** a zoo

The writer mentions a city, but this is not the setting. Because we know that Maxwell hears cows and can see a barn on the other side of the field, we can infer that he is on a farm (choice **c**). If the barn were the setting, he would be in it or near it; it would not be in the distance.

Notice Names

Pay close attention to the names of people and places, as well as to dates and key words. These are often important to remember if you are going to accurately understand the story.

Pay Attention to Details

Details can help you determine many things about a story. This information is invaluable when answering questions about plot, conflicts, mood, point of view, and theme. If you get to a question about one of these and are unsure of the answer, look back in the passage and see what insight the details can offer.

Tips for Nonfiction Passages

The GED® RLA test focuses on three types of nonfiction reading passages. These have been chosen to ensure that you have an understanding of practical reading and writing situations that you might encounter in the professional world.

Informational Science Passages

These passages will focus on one of two areas within the scientific realm. The first is human health and other biology; this may include topics such as respiration and the interdependence of animal species. The second is energy-related systems; this may include topics such as photosynthesis, climate, and gas combustion.

The emphasis of these passages is not to test you on unfamiliar scientific principles; you will not be expected to provide additional scientific knowledge on the topics presented. These passages will likely focus on your ability to correctly understand the steps in a process, and your ability to explain how the steps relate to each other.

Informational Social Studies Passages

These passages will focus on the theme of the Great American Conversation, which includes discussion of elements of American government and how it relates to society. The passages featured here will likely include excerpts from well-known historical documents, such as the Preamble to the U.S. Constitution, as well as other writings of significant figures in American history. These passages may also include texts from modern-day political figures, and can appear in forms as various as speeches, letters, laws, or diaries.

Informational Workplace Passages

These passages are meant to resemble the kinds of documents you are likely to encounter in a modern workplace setting. These documents may include letters, e-mails, instruction manuals, memos, or lists of policies, among others.

The purpose of the nonfiction passages on the test may be to entertain, inform, or persuade readers. The testing standards of the GED® Reasoning through Language Arts test place a particular emphasis on the understanding and analysis of arguments and evidence, so expect passages that focus on presenting a viewpoint or position on an issue. Regardless of their purpose, these passages are based on actual people, topics, or events and will offer information, facts, and details about the topic.

Notice Details

Watch for details such as statistics, dates, names, events, section headings, and key words that are included in the passage. You may see these again when you get to the questions. However, do not select an answer choice simply because it matches something from the passage; many incorrect answer choices are also taken from the text. This is to ensure that you are understanding the passage and not just skimming for a correct answer.

Pay Attention to Descriptive Language

Descriptive language can offer clues about an author's views on a topic. For example, if an author describes a car as a "beast," that author probably feels that the vehicle is very big or powerful. After you find the main idea, begin looking for language, facts, and details that reveal or support the author's point of view.

Look for Evidence

Keep in mind that each paragraph of a nonfiction passage will have a main idea. The rest of the paragraph will include details to support the main idea. As you read, search for this evidence. Facts, examples, descriptions, and other information that helps explain the main idea are essential to understanding the text and will probably be the subject of at least some of the questions.

Draw Your Own Conclusions

Some types of nonfiction passages will include opinions on a particular topic. In some cases, you will be given two passages that offer different views on the same topic. Pay special attention to the evidence and reasons presented to support the view presented in each passage. Then, draw your own conclusions regarding the author's ability to present and support that opinion. For the extended response item on the test, reaching your own conclusions and expanding on the evidence and views presented in the passages is critical if you want to score well.

Author's Purpose

To fully understand what we read, we need to be able to figure out why the passage was written. An author always has a reason, or purpose, for writing. The **author's purpose** for writing a passage is usually one of the following:

- to entertain
- to inform
- to persuade

Understanding the author's reason for writing can help you better understand what you read. Different types of texts usually have different purposes. Many stories, plays, magazine articles, poems, novels, and comic strips are written to **entertain**. They may be fiction or nonfiction and may include facts, opinions, or both, but the purpose for writing them is to tell a story. These are intended to entertain readers and are meant for pleasure reading.

This summer while vacationing in Florida, I went parasailing with my mom. It was the most thrilling adventure I'd ever had! We floated from a giant parachute, hundreds of feet above the water, and soared over the beaches.

This passage was written to entertain. It was intended to tell a story about the author's adventure. It does not try to teach any information, nor does it try to convince you to share an opinion about the topic.

Textbooks, encyclopedias, and many newspaper articles are written to **inform**. Their purpose is to give the reader information or to teach about a subject. Such passages will usually contain mostly facts and may include charts, diagrams, or drawings to help explain the information.

Parasailing is a sport in which a rider is attached to a large parachute, or parasail. The parasail is attached to a vehicle, usually a boat, by a long tow rope. As the boat moves, the parasail and rider rise up into the air.

This paragraph teaches readers about the sport of parasailing. It contains facts and information about the topic. Readers may enjoy reading about the subject, but the author's reason for writing the passage was to inform.

Other material, such as commercials, advertisements, letters to the editor, and political speeches, are written to **persuade** readers to share a belief, agree with an opinion, or support an idea. Such writing may include some facts or statements from experts, but it will most likely include the author's opinions about the topic.

One of the most dangerous sports today is parasailing. Each year, many people are seriously injured, or even killed, while participating in this activity. Laws should be passed that prohibit such reckless entertainment. If people want to fly, they should get on an airplane.

The author of this paragraph wants to convince readers that parasailing is a dangerous sport. The text includes not only opinions, but also facts that support the author's stand on the subject. Notice that strong words and phrases, such as *seriously injured, should,* and *reckless,* are included to stir up emotions in the readers. The author's purpose for writing this passage was to persuade readers to agree with his or her beliefs about parasailing.

BOOST

Did you know that the GED® test was originally created for military personnel and veterans who did not finish high school? That was in 1942. Five years later, New York became the first state to make the test available to civilians. By 1974, the GED® test was available in all 50 U.S. states.

Let's practice what you've learned about recognizing the author's purpose. Read the paragraph and determine whether it was written to entertain, inform, or persuade.

It was a quiet summer evening. The moon was full, and the sky seemed to hold a million stars. Outside, only the sounds of the crickets could be heard.

What was the author's purpose for writing this passage?

_____

Did you recognize that the author's purpose was to entertain? The text did not try to teach anything or convince you to hold a certain opinion. It was simply written for the reader to enjoy.

Read the passage for key information and answer the following five questions.

Instructions for License Renewal

A driver's license must be renewed every four years. A renewal application is sent approximately five to seven weeks before the expiration date listed on the license. Individuals who fail to renew within three years of the license expiration date are not eligible for a renewal and must repeat the initial licensing process. To renew a license, you must visit a Motor Vehicles Agency. You must present a completed renewal application; your current driver's license; acceptable proof of age, identification, and address; and proof of social security in the form of a Social Security card, a state or federal income tax return, a current pay stub, or a W-2 form. You must also pay the required fee. If all the documents and payment are in order, your photo will be taken and a new license will be issued.

1. What documents does one need to renew a driver's license?

2. What documents represent proof of social security?

3. How often must one renew a driver's license?

4. How does one obtain the renewal form?

5. True or False: You can renew your driver's license by mail.

Read the following passage and determine the meaning of the italicized word from its context.

6. By the time our staff meeting ended at 8:00, I was *ravenous*. I had skipped lunch and hadn't eaten since breakfast.

Ravenous means
a. like a raven, birdlike.
b. extremely hungry, greedy for food.
c. exhausted, ready for bed.
d. angry, quite upset.

Read the passage and answer the six questions that follow.

Robert Johnson is the best blues guitarist of all time. Johnson had a tremendous impact on the world of rock and roll. Some consider Johnson the father of modern rock: His influence extends to artists from Muddy Waters to Led Zeppelin and the Rolling Stones. Eric Clapton has called Johnson the most important blues musician who ever lived. It is hard to believe that Johnson recorded only 29 songs before his death in 1938, yet he left an indelible mark on the music world. Again and again, contemporary rock artists return to Johnson, whose songs capture the very essence of the blues, transforming our pain and suffering with the healing magic of his guitar. Rock music wouldn't be what it is today without Robert Johnson.

7. According to the passage, from what musical tradition did Robert Johnson emerge?
a. rock and roll
b. jazz
c. blues
d. classical

8. Johnson died in
a. 1927.
b. 1938.
c. 1929.
d. 1940.

9. True or False: Johnson influenced many rock artists, including Led Zeppelin and the Rolling Stones.

10. Contemporary rock artists turn to Robert Johnson for
a. musical influence.
b. life lessons.
c. recovery from painful injuries.
d. advice.

11. The most appropriate title for this article would be
a. "A Fleeting Life"
b. "The World's Greatest Musician"
c. "Blues Guitar Legend Robert Johnson"
d. "Learning the Guitar"

12. Indicate whether the following sentences are *fact* or *opinion*:
a. Robert Johnson is the best blues guitarist of all time.
b. Eric Clapton has called Johnson the most important blues musician who ever lived.
c. Rock music wouldn't be what it is today without Robert Johnson.
d. Robert Johnson died in 1938.

Read the passage and answer the eight questions that follow.

There will be dire consequences for residents if a shopping mall is built on the east side of town. First, the shopping mall will interfere with the tranquil and quiet atmosphere that we now enjoy. Second, the mall will attract a huge number of shoppers from a variety of surrounding areas, which will result in major traffic congestion for those of us who live here. But most importantly, to build the shopping mall, many of us will be asked to sell our homes and relocate, and this kind of displacement should be avoided at all costs.

13. The main idea of this passage is that the shopping mall would
   a. be great for the community.
   b. not change things much.
   c. be bad for the community.
   d. be a good place to shop.

14. *Displacement* is a good word choice because
   a. it is compatible with general reading level and the formal writing style of the article.
   b. the writer likes to impress readers by using big words.
   c. it is the only word that is suitable or appropriate.
   d. it is easy to understand.

15. This passage is organized
   a. in chronological order.
   b. by cause and effect.
   c. by order of importance.
   d. both **b** and **c**

16. This passage uses which point of view?
   a. first person
   b. second person
   c. third person
   d. no point of view

17. This passage is written from whose perspective?
   a. that of the residents
   b. that of an outside consultant
   c. that of the shopping mall developer
   d. the reader's perspective

18. The choice of the word *dire* suggests that the consequences of the merger would be
   a. minimal.
   b. expected.
   c. disastrous.
   d. welcome.

19. Which words best describe the style of this passage?
   a. informal, conversational
   b. descriptive, storylike
   c. formal, businesslike
   d. scattered, confusing

20. The tone of this passage is
   a. sad.
   b. foreboding.
   c. threatening.
   d. joyous.

Point of View

It is important to think about who is telling the story. This narrator may be someone who is a part of the story, or it may be someone outside of the events. The **point of view** refers to who is telling the story, which makes a difference in how much information the reader is given.

Some stories use a **first-person** point of view. In this case, one of the characters is telling the story, and readers see the events through this person's eyes.

After the game, Henry and I grabbed a pizza with the rest of the team. We hung out for a couple of hours, then headed home. By then, I was totally exhausted.

Notice that when an author uses a first-person point of view, the narrator uses the pronouns *I, me, us,* and *we,* and it seems as if the character is speaking directly to the reader. The narrator knows only his or her own thoughts and feelings, not those of the other characters, and often shares his or her attitudes and opinions with the readers.

Other stories use a **third-person** point of view, in which the narrator is not a character in the story and does not participate in the events.

> *After the game, Deon said he would join Henry and the rest of the team for pizza. They stayed for a couple of hours before heading home, exhausted.*

When a story is told from the third-person point of view, the narrator will use pronouns such as *he, she,* and *they* when discussing the characters. Also, the narrator often knows the thoughts and feelings of every character.

Let's practice what you've just reviewed. Read the next three paragraphs, think about who is telling the story, and determine the point of view of the passage.

> *As soon as the bell rang, a tall, thin woman with dark hair rose from behind the desk. The class quieted as she began to speak.*
>
> *"Good morning, class," she stated. "I am Ms. Wolfe, and I will be your English teacher this semester. Go ahead and open your books to the table of contents, and let's get started."*
>
> *Ms. Wolfe picked up the text from her desk, and opened it to the first page.*

What is the point of view of this passage?

_____

This passage is written in the third-person point of view. The narrator is not a character in the story. Notice that the pronoun *I* is included in the passage. However, it is spoken by one of the characters, not the narrator.

Read the passage and answer the question that follows.

> Ms. Crawford has been a model citizen since she moved to Springfield in 1985. She started out as a small business owner and quickly grew her business until it was one of the major employers in the region. In 1991, her company was profiled in *BusinessWeek* magazine. Her innovative business model includes a great deal of community work and fundraising, the rewards of which have brought deep and lasting benefits to Springfield and its citizens. Today, she is being honored with Springfield's Citizen of the Century Award to recognize all her cutting-edge efforts on behalf of our community.

21. This paragraph uses what point of view?
   a. first-person point of view
   b. second-person point of view
   c. third-person point of view
   d. It can't be determined from the information provided.

Read the passage and answer the question that follows.

> There will be dire consequences for residents if a shopping mall is built on the east side of town. First, the shopping mall will interfere with the tranquil and quiet atmosphere that we now enjoy. Second, the mall will attract a huge number of shoppers from a variety of surrounding areas, which will result in major traffic congestion for those of us who live here. But most importantly, to build the shopping mall, many of us will be asked to sell our homes and

relocate, and this kind of displacement should be avoided at all costs.

22. This passage uses which point of view?
   a. first person
   b. second person
   c. third person
   d. no point of view

Theme

As we read, we look for and try to understand the messages and information that the author wants to share. Sometimes, the author's message is very obvious. Other times, we have to look a little harder to find it. The **theme** of a story is its underlying message. In a fable, the moral of the story is the theme. In fiction, this overall message is usually implied, rather than being directly stated, and may involve the following:

- attitudes
- beliefs
- opinions
- perceptions

The theme often leaves you with ideas, a conclusion, or a lesson that the writer wants you to take away from the story. Often, this lesson relates to life, society, or human nature. As you read, think about what the author's message might be. Consider the characters' words and actions, the tone, the plot, and any repeated patterns to see what views of the writer these portray.

Think about the story of the three little pigs. One could say that the theme of this story is that it is best to do a job the right way the first time. The author does not directly state this message, but this is a lesson or opinion that readers might take away from the story.

As an example, say you're reading a novel about a poor woman's journey from Korea to the United States in the 1940s. It may describe the details of the character's childhood on a farm in Korea, the boat trip that she took as a young adult to San Francisco, the elderly man who swindled her out of her life savings because she didn't speak English, the difficulties she had finding a job, and the satisfaction she ultimately felt as she worked hard to make a living. These are the facts of the plot, but the theme of the novel is something very different. Here are some possible themes:

- The theme could be *a message or lesson*. For instance: *You can reach your goals more easily if you block out your problems and focus only on your goal.*
- The theme could be *a question*. For instance: *Do you lose part of yourself when you leave your culture? Is it better to stay where you are and face the difficulties there, or do you become more of your real self when you leave your culture and make your own way in the world?*
- The theme could be *a specific idea about life or people*. For instance: *Desperation brings out the very worst in people and the very best.*
- The theme could also be *a simpler, more general concept*. For instance, perhaps the novel is an exploration of the theme of youth and aging.

Note that more than one theme may be valid for a work of fiction, and other readers may come to a different conclusion than you do. This is part of the reward of reading fiction—seeing the ideas behind what you read and discussing those ideas with other people. (Often these are ideas about life, which will be interesting to you as you make your own way in the world.)

NOTE

Although a work of fiction may have more than one possible theme, don't worry that this will cause confusion on the GED® RLA test. Every question about theme on the GED® RLA test will have only one, clearly correct answer. There are no "trick" questions on the exam.

Finding the Theme

As you read a work of fiction closely, pay attention to the following elements in order to find the theme:

- **Repetition:** Note whether the author repeats certain words, phrases, symbols, actions, or ideas, or whether certain characters reappear throughout a story. This is often a clue that those words, phrases, characters, and so on have a special importance in the story—and to the theme.

- **Connections:** In many stories, one specific thing may not be repeated, but if you look closely, you'll find that the writer uses repetition in a more complicated way. For example, let's say the first chapter of a book takes place in a house by a river,

which is flooding after a bad storm. The climax of the book takes place on a train that's traveling through the dusty plains of Texas. The end of the book takes place on a street in New York City, where children have uncapped a fire hydrant and are playing in the water. While a river, a plain, and a fire hydrant are very different things, there is a pattern running through the book: water—either too much or too little. Ask yourself if this pattern helps to reveal the theme.

- **Timing:** Consider when events occur in a story and whether there is a pattern. For example, let's say in one short story, whenever the main character, a firefighter, puts on his firefighting uniform in the morning, a mouse—a common symbol for cowardice and weakness—peeks its head out of a hole in the wall. Is this pattern a reminder that we all have to battle our weaknesses? Or that even when someone acts bravely, he or she is still vulnerable? Patterns are usually connected to the theme and can help us understand it.

- **Omission:** Often it's what a writer *doesn't* write about that's most important. Is there a detail or event that's glaringly left out of the story? This may be directly tied to the theme.

Practice

Read the passage and answer the questions that follow.

Four Simple Tips to Help You Land a Great Job

Whether you're just graduating and entering the job market for the first time or you're changing careers, searching for a job is never easy. In today's high-tech society, many potential employers are turning to social media to learn more about you.

"Before you even walk through the door for your first interview, it is highly likely the person waiting on the other side has seen more than just your resume," says Lauren Berger, CEO of Intern-Queen.com. "The way you present yourself online speaks volumes to hiring managers about your tech savvy and comfort level with social media—both critical skills demanded by virtually every employer."

With technology playing an established role in our lives and social networks easily accessible to potential employers, establishing a strong digital footprint and personal brand is crucial to success. So how can you use technology to land that first job and make the best first impression?

Here are four top tech tools and social media tips for landing your dream job:

1. Get organized. While it may seem like a minor detail, one of the first things you should do is get a professional e-mail address. The college e-mail or cutesy address you created back in high school won't impress a job recruiter.

2. Leverage your networks and set informational interviews. Make a target list of employers you'd like to work for and do some research about them, identifying one person from each company whom you'd like to meet. Reach out to that person and explain that you're really interested in the company and what his or her department does. Then ask if he or she will take five minutes to sit down and tell you how he or she got started and give you some advice.

3. Put your best "digital foot" forward. You have one chance to make a first impression, so make sure it's a good one. This means not only dressing professionally but also using your style (both online and off) to demonstrate your personal interests. Building your personal brand and establishing relationships within the industry will help open doors to opportunities you may not have discovered otherwise. Make sure that your online presence is up to date and also reflects your best attributes. This includes maintaining a consistent resume and work experience information across your networks to build familiarity among possible recruiters.

4. Lead with your strengths. Ask your friends and previous employers what your strengths are, and use specific examples during your interview to highlight them. You can also use this opportunity to demonstrate your experience with technology. If you are consistently told how well organized you are, share a previous work experience that demonstrates how you used technology and what value this brings to the employer. If you have a laptop or a tablet computer, consider bringing it to the interview to show off your portfolio of work. This instantly demonstrates you're on the cutting edge of new technology—a value for any employer.

These seemingly simple tips can help you stand out from the crowd and boost your chances of finding that great job.

23. Of the following choices, which skills does the author emphasize as being important to potential employers?
- **a.** leadership and the ability to resolve conflict
- **b.** digital literacy and expertise with Internet communications
- **c.** loyalty and a strong work ethic
- **d.** creativity and knowledge of computer hardware

24. Based on the passage, which of the following statements would the author most likely make when advising someone who was recently laid off and is in the process of applying for jobs?
- **a.** Update your career wardrobe and hire a professional to revise your resume.
- **b.** Consider getting retrained in a field that is growing in career opportunities.
- **c.** Evaluate how your job qualifications can be demonstrated through the use of technology.
- **d.** Schedule as many informational interviews as you can at each company you are interested in, and attend a weekly job-support group.

Common themes you may have found in reading might include:

- Crime does not pay.
- It is important to be honest.
- Be happy with what you have.
- Money cannot buy happiness.
- Keep going when things get tough.
- Do not be afraid to try something new.

Give it a try. Look for the theme as you read the following passage.

> Camilla usually looked forward to Friday nights, but this week was the definite exception. Instead of going to the movies with her friends, she would be stuck at home, helping Mom get ready for tomorrow's garage sale. As she walked into the house, Camilla could see that Mom was already prepared for the long night ahead of them.
>
> "Hey, get that scowl off your face and throw on your overalls," Mom called out cheerfully. "It won't be that bad."
>
> Camilla changed clothes and headed to the garage, dragging her feet the whole way. Mom was elbow deep in an old cardboard box. She pulled out a raggedy, old stuffed dog.
>
> "Mr. Floppy!" Camilla cried, excited to see her old friend. "I haven't seen him in years!"
>
> "Your very first soft friend," Mom reminisced. "I'm assuming you'll be keeping him? Or would you like a 25-cent price tag to stick on his ear?"
>
> Camilla set the old dog aside. She would definitely keep him. She helped Mom empty the rest of the box, sticking price tags on other old toys and books. They continued through the boxes, stopping to look through old photo albums together, telling funny stories about some of the useless gifts they'd collected, laughing at the hand-me-down clothes that had arrived at their house over the years, and modeling the silliest of them.
>
> After a few hours, Mom looked at her watch. "Wow! It's nearly 8:00 already. Should we order a pizza?"
>
> Camilla couldn't believe how late it was. She looked at her mom—who was wearing dusty overalls, five strands of Aunt Edna's old beads, and Granny's wide-brimmed Sunday bonnet—and couldn't help but laugh out loud. This was the best Friday night she could remember.

What is the theme of the story?

a. Memories are a special part of life.

b. It is important to get rid of old items.

c. Families should spend weekends together.

d. Sometimes things turn out to be better than expected.

At the beginning of the story, Camilla did not want to spend the evening helping her mom. By the end, she was having a great time. Choice **d** is the theme of this story. Some of the other answer choices represent ideas that were presented in the story, but the underlying message that the author wanted to portray is that things can turn out to be more fun than we think they will be.

Synthesis

Suppose you were doing a research paper. You would select a topic, then to be sure you learned as much as possible, you would search a variety of texts to find information about that topic. After reading each of your sources, you would put together all the information you learned. This combination of information would provide a clear understanding of the subject.

As readers, there are times when we have to combine information to gain a complete understanding of the text. **Synthesis** means putting ideas from multiple sources together. Sometimes, readers synthesize information from different parts of a single text. Other times, they must put together information from more than one text.

Read the passage below.

Roger quietly walked to the shelf. He pulled his ball cap down on his head as he quickly looked at the items neatly lined up in front of him. Then, he grabbed a package of crackers, shoving it into his backpack as he hurried to the door, trying not to make any sound.

Think about what you know so far. Roger is being quiet; he grabs something off of a shelf and tries to quickly sneak out the door. What do you think is happening? Now, continue reading.

Roger's mom heard him opening the front door. She put the sleeping baby in her cradle, then hurried to see her son. "Honey, did you find something in the pantry to take for a snack?"

"Yeah, Mom," Roger replied. "I found the peanut butter crackers and grabbed a package. Those are my favorites. Thanks for getting them."

"Do you want me to drive you to baseball practice so you're not late?" Mom asked.

"No, I don't want you to wake Amy. I know she hasn't been sleeping much lately."

"You're a good big brother and a great son. Be careful."

Did this new information change your mind about what was happening? You may have thought Roger was being sneaky or doing something he should not have been doing. When you synthesize the new information, you gain a deeper understanding of the situation. Roger is being quiet so he doesn't wake up his sister, he's taking crackers that his mom bought for him off of a shelf in the pantry, and he's in a hurry to get to practice.

When you synthesize information, ask yourself:

- Why is this new information relevant?
- Why was the new information given?
- How does it relate to the first part of the passage?
- How does this help me gain a deeper understanding of what I've read?
- In what ways does the new information change my ideas about the passage?

Another common type of question found on the GED® Reasoning through Language Arts exam is an **extended synthesis** question. First, you will read a passage. Then, you will be given a question. An additional piece of information about the passage or the author will be given within the question itself. You will have to combine the new information with what you read in the text to gain a deeper understanding of the passage.

First, figure out how the new information relates to what you previously read. Then, try to determine how this information helps you understand the reading passage in a deeper or different way.

Let's try an example. Be sure to read the passage carefully so that you will be able to understand the question that follows.

The winter had been especially cold. A thick, snowy blanket had covered the landscape for what seemed like months. Each day, the stack of firewood beside the house grew visibly smaller and smaller. This concerned Ella terribly. She continued to hope that the snow would be gone before the firewood.

Ella turned away from the window and returned to her writing. Somehow, writing about summer made the house feel warmer. Feeling the sun's bright rays on her face, walking barefoot in the green grass, fishing with her family, swimming in the refreshing water—these were things Ella dreamed and wrote of during the long winter months.

Here's an extended synthesis question:

The author of the passage lived during the nineteenth century in the midwestern United States. Based on the information in the story, as well as knowing the information about the author, which of the following best explains Ella's concern over the firewood?
  a. Most nineteenth-century homes had large fireplaces.
  b. There was not much firewood available during the 1800s.
  c. Winters in the midwestern United States are extremely cold.
  d. Before electricity, people depended on firewood for heat and cooking.

Keep in mind that to correctly answer this question, you need to combine the information in the passage with the new information given in the question. Several answer choices could make sense. For example, it is true that many nineteenth-century homes had fireplaces and that winters in parts of the United States can be very cold. However, these facts do not consider the pieces of information that you need to synthesize.

From reading the passage, you know that Ella needs firewood. After learning the time period during which she lived, you are able to see how important firewood was for her survival. During the nineteenth century, homes did not have electricity. People had to have firewood to warm their homes and cook their meals. Choice **d** best synthesizes the information from both sources.

Let's try another example. Read the passage carefully, then read the question. Determine how the information in the question is related to the passage.

As the real estate agent walked up to the home, she admired her own photo on the "For Sale" sign in the front yard. She was anxious to get this home sold. Once inside with the homeowners, she explained the next step in selling their house.

"Your beautiful home has been on the market for several weeks now without any offers. We need to consider our options. The carpet is definitely a little bit worn in one bedroom, the bathroom wallpaper is a bit out of date, and the front yard could use some new flowers. These issues could be deterring potential buyers. I think it is time we lower the price of your home by at least 15%, if you want to get it sold."

The real estate agent will qualify for a large bonus if she sells one more house within the next month. Which of the following best describes the agent's motives in the passage?
   a. Her first concern is selling the house quickly so she can get the bonus.
   b. Her profit depends on the house selling for the highest possible price.
   c. She knows it is best for the owners to get the best price for their home.
   d. Her clients' home is currently overpriced for the neighborhood.

Based on the information in the passage, we do not know whether the home is overpriced, so choice **d** is incorrect. Choices **b** and **c** may be true. However, these do not take into consideration the additional information provided within the question. This information lets us know that if the house sells quickly, the agent will receive a large bonus. When added to the information in the passage that states that she wants to lower the price of the house, we can figure out that her moti-

vation for dropping the price is to sell the house quickly so that she can get the bonus. So, the correct answer is choice **a**.

> ## TIP
>
> Remember to carefully read the extended synthesis questions. Look for the additional information within the question and think about how this information relates to the passage. The information is there for a reason. You will be expected to use it as you consider your answer.

Compare and Contrast

We spend a good deal of our lives comparing and contrasting things. When we want to explain something, for example, we often **compare** it to something else (showing how two or more things are similar). We might say, for example, that mint chocolate chip ice cream tastes just like a peppermint-filled chocolate, or that our new boss looks a lot like Will Smith. When we want to show how things are different or not alike, we **contrast** them. We might say that our friend Sam looks nothing like his brother Pat, or that Italian is a much harder language to learn than Spanish.

Comparing and contrasting are common techniques in writing, too. They can be used for many reasons—for example, to describe a character more colorfully or to provide support for an argument that the writer is making.

Transitions Used to Compare and Contrast

As you read the next passage, about gardeners and parents, notice the transitional words and phrases that indicate when the writer is comparing (showing similarity) and when the writer is contrasting (showing difference). There are several transitional words and phrases writers use to show comparison and contrast.

Here are some words and phrases that can be used to show *similarity*:

- similarly
- likewise
- like
- just as
- in the same way
- and
- also

These words and phrases can be used to show *difference*:

- on the other hand
- on the contrary
- however
- nevertheless
- conversely
- yet
- but

Practice

Read the passage and answer the questions that follow.

Gardeners and Parents

Planting a garden is a lot like having a family. Both require a great deal of work, especially as they grow and as the seasons change. As summer days lengthen, your plants become dependent on you for sustenance, much like your children depend on you for food and drink. Like a thirsty child asking for a drink of water, your plants do the same. Their bent, wilted "body" language, translated, issues a demand much the way your child requests milk or juice. When their collective thirsts are quenched, you see the way they both thrive in your care. The fussy child becomes satisfied, and the plant reaches toward the sun in a showy display. You might also find that you have to clean the space around your plants much like you would pick up toys and clothes that have been left helter-skelter in your toddler's room. Similarly, plants shed spent petals, roses need to be pruned, and weeds need to be pulled. To keep children healthy, parents protect their children against disease with medicine, and gardeners do the same with insect repellent. To nourish them, parents give children vitamins, and gardeners use fertilizer, as both promote healthy growth. As children grow and become adults, they need less and less care. However, here's where the similarity ends. While plants die or become dormant during winter, children still maintain a vital role in the family unit.

---

25. In this passage, the writer compares being a parent to being a _____.

26. Which of the following pairs shows a **contrast**, not a comparison, between being a parent and being a gardener?
  a. Parents give vitamins to children to keep them healthy; gardeners give fertilizer to their plants to keep them healthy.
  b. Parents pick up toys and clothes in their children's room; gardeners pull up weeds around their plants.
  c. Children remain an important part of the family after they grow up; plants die or become dormant after the growing season ends.
  d. Children ask parents for milk or juice when they are thirsty; plants bend or wilt when they need water, showing gardeners that they are thirsty.

Reading More Closely

As you practice more and more with reading passages, you will begin to notice how specific sentences or paragraphs relate to each other and to the passage as a whole. When you are aware of how an author has structured his or her writing, it will help you understand the writer's meaning even better. Structure, word choice, description, and detail all give shape to a text and affect its meaning.

The following excerpt is from the speech that John F. Kennedy gave when he was sworn in as president in 1961.

> ### EXCERPT
>
> The world is very different now. For man holds in his mortal hands the power to abolish all forms of human poverty and all forms of human life. And yet the same revolutionary beliefs for which our forebears fought are still at issue around the globe—the belief that the rights of man come not from the generosity of the state, but from the hand of God.

As you read this passage closely, you should pay attention to certain words or phrases and how they build on each other.

The phrase *mortal hands* has a more powerful meaning than if the word *mortal* was not included. Words such as *revolutionary beliefs* and *forebears* reinforce Kennedy's appeal to the audience to make a connection with the birth of the nation.

The structure and word choice of the passage affect its tone and meaning and support Kennedy's purpose to inspire his audience. Later on in the speech are six paragraphs that all begin with the same pattern:

> *To those old allies whose cultural and spiritual origins we share. . . .*
> *To those new States whom we welcome to the ranks of the free. . . .*
> *To those peoples in the huts and villages across the globe struggling to break the bonds of mass misery. . . .*
> *To our sister republics south of our border. . . .*
> *To that world assembly of sovereign states. . . .*
> *Finally, to those nations who would make themselves our adversary. . . .*

This is a great example of the use of **repetition** and **parallel structure** to strengthen meaning and focus the listener's attention.

Practice

Read the passage and answer the questions that follow.

"The Magnolia Tree," from the Memoir *Cross Creek* (1942), by Marjorie Kinnan Rawlings

I do not know the irreducible minimum of happiness for any other spirit than my own. It is impossible to be certain even of mine. Yet I believe that I know my tangible desideratum. It is a tree-top against a patch of sky. If I should lie crippled or long ill, or should have the quite conceivable misfortune to be clapped in jail, I could survive, I think, given this one token of the physical world. I know that I lived on one such in my first days at the Creek.

The tree was a magnolia, taller than the tallest orange trees around it. There is no such thing in the world as an ugly tree, but the magnolia grandiflora has a unique perfection. No matter how crowded it may be, no matter how thickly holly and live oak and sweet gum may grow up around it, it develops with complete symmetry, so that one wonders whether character in all things, human as well as vegetable, may not be implicit. Neither is its development ruthless, achieved at the expense of its neighbors, for it is one of the few trees that may be allowed to stand in an orange grove, seeming to steal nothing from the expensively nourished citrus. The young of the tree is courteous, waiting for the parent to be done with life before presuming to take it over. There are never seedling magnolias under or near an old magnolia. When the tree at last dies, the young glossy sprouts appear from nowhere, exulting in the sun and air for which they may have waited a long hundred years.

The tree is beautiful the year around. It need not wait for a brief burst of blooming to justify itself, like the wild plum and the hawthorn. It is handsomer than most dressed only in its broad leaves, shining like dark polished jade, so that when I am desperate for decoration, I break a few sprays for the house and find them an ornament of which a Japanese artist would approve. The tree sheds some of its leaves just before it blooms, as though it shook off old garments to be cleansed and ready for the new. There is a dry pattering to earth of the hard leaves and for a brief time the tree is parched and drawn, the rosy-lichened trunk gray and anxious. Then pale green spires cover the boughs, unfolding into freshly lacquered leaves, and at their tips the blooms appear. When, in late April or early May, the pale buds unfold into great white waxy blossoms, sometimes eight or ten inches across, and the perfume is a delirious thing on the spring air, I would not trade one tree for a conservatory filled with orchids. The blooms, for all their size and thickness, are as delicate as orchids in that they reject the touch of human hands. They must be cut or broken carefully and placed in a jar of water without brushing the edges, or the creamy petals will turn in an hour to brown velvet. Properly handled, they open in the house as on the tree, the cupped buds bursting open suddenly, the full-blown flowers shedding the red-tipped stamens in a shower, so that in a quiet room you hear them sifting onto the table top. The red seed cones are as fine as candles. They mature slowly from the top of the tree down, as a Christmas tree is lighted.

27. To what does the author compare magnolia blooms?

   a. orchids

   b. candles

   c. Christmas trees

   d. jade

28. The passage describes the yearly cycle of a magnolia tree. Select the answer that puts the following statements in chronological order:

   1. The tree is covered in flower buds.

   2. The tree grows fresh green leaves.

   3. The air around the tree is perfumed.

   4. Leaves fall off the tree.

   a. 3, 2, 4, 1

   b. 2, 3, 4, 1

   c. 1, 2, 4, 3

   d. 4, 2, 1, 3

Interpreting What You Read

As we touched on, your job as a reader is not only to understand the literal meaning of a word, paragraph, article, or book, but to read between the lines in order to discover the full meaning of the text. Just as in spoken conversation, where you have many ways to communicate what you are thinking—through a joke, a story, even a facial expression—writers have many techniques to communicate with their readers.

Text with layers of meaning is often more colorful, more convincing, more emotional, or more meaningful than text that simply spells out what the author is trying to say in a clear, factual way.

It's important to try to pick up on a writer's clues, just as, for example, you would pick up on a look of disappointment when a friend says, "That's fine." You immediately recognize that your friend does not really think that whatever happened is fine. This section describes the techniques that writers use—many of which you probably have already picked up on—and how to identify them.

Interpreting Specific Words

On the GED® RLA test, you may be asked to figure out the definition of vocabulary words by looking at their **context**—the words and meanings that surround the vocabulary words.

For an example of how to do this, read the following paragraph about one of the nation's favorite pastimes.

Reality TV

Most reality TV shows center on two common motivators: fame and money. The shows transform waitresses, hairdressers, investment bankers, counselors, and teachers, to name a few, from obscure figures to household names. A lucky few successfully parlay their 15 minutes of fame into celebrity. Even if you are not interested in fame, you can probably understand the desire for lots of money. Watching people eat large insects, reveal their innermost thoughts to millions of people, and allow themselves to be filmed 24 hours a day for a huge financial reward seems to have mass appeal for viewers. Whatever their attraction, these shows are among the most popular on television, and every season, they proliferate like weeds in an untended garden. The networks are quickly replacing more traditional dramas and comedies with reality TV programs, which earn millions of dollars in advertising revenue. Whether you love it or hate it, one thing is for sure—reality TV is here to stay!

One of the more difficult words in the paragraph is *obscure*. With a little detective work, we can determine the definition of that word by looking at how it is used in the paragraph. Let's look at the context in which it appears:

> *The shows transform waitresses, hairdressers, investment bankers, counselors, and teachers, to name a few, from obscure figures to household names.*

Given the sentence, what can we tell about *obscure*? Well, since the shows transform waitresses, hairdressers, investment bankers, counselors, and teachers from one position—*obscure* figures—to another position—household names—that immediately tells us that an obscure figure and a household name are two different things.

Furthermore, we know from the sentence that the people in question are involved in typical, everyday jobs (waitresses, hairdressers, bankers, etc.) and that from this position, they are transformed into household names, which means they achieve some level of fame and notoriety. Now you can take a pretty good guess at the meaning of *obscure*.

Before they become household names, the waitresses, hairdressers, investment bankers, counselors, and teachers are

A. famous and notorious.
B. unknown and undistinguished.
C. unique and distinctive.

The correct answer, of course, is **B**. It certainly can't be **A**, because we know that these people are not yet famous. The reality shows will make them famous, but until that happens, they remain *obscure*. Answer **C** doesn't really make sense because we know from the passage that these people are waitresses, hairdressers, investment bankers, counselors, and teachers. Now, these are all very respectable jobs, but they are fairly common, so they wouldn't be described as unique or distinctive. Furthermore, we can tell that **B** is the correct answer because we can substitute the word *obscure* with the word *unknown* or *undistinguished* in the sentence and both would make sense.

How Much Context Do You Need?

In the previous example, you would still be able to understand the main message of the passage even if you didn't know—or couldn't figure out—the meaning of *obscure*. In some cases, however, your understanding of a passage depends on your understanding of a particular word or phrase. Can you understand the following sentence, for example, without knowing what *adversely* means?

> *Reality TV shows will adversely affect traditional dramas and comedies.*

What does *adversely* mean in this sentence? Is it something good or bad? As good a detective as you may be, there simply aren't enough clues in this sentence to tell you what this word means. But a passage with more information will give you what you need to determine meaning from context.

> *Reality TV shows will adversely affect traditional dramas and comedies. As reality TV increases in popularity, network executives will begin canceling more traditional dramas and comedies and replacing them with the latest in reality TV.*

In the passage, *adversely* most nearly means

A. mildly, slightly.
B. kindly, gently.
C. negatively, unfavorably.
D. immediately, swiftly.

The correct answer is **C**, negatively, unfavorably. The passage provides clues that allow you to determine the meaning of *adversely*.

Quiz

Now you've had a chance to review some of the skills needed to comprehend reading passages.

Directions: Read the following passages and choose the *one best answer* to each question.

Questions 29 through 33 refer to the following passage.

What Will Happen with the Painting?

After hours of rummaging through the various items that had been donated to the charity over the weekend, Natasha was ready to head home for the day. She had sorted the
(5)   clothing, books, toys, housewares, and sporting goods into the appropriate bins and would tackle the task of pricing the items in the morning. With any luck, the items would find their place on the store shelves by
(10)   tomorrow afternoon and be sold quickly.

As she turned to lock the door to the storeroom, Natasha noticed a framed canvas leaning against the wall. She wondered where it had come from and why she hadn't
(15)   noticed it before now. She bent over to examine the artwork and was amazed at the bold colors and brushstrokes of the oil painting and the detail in the carved wooden frame. At the bottom corner of the
(20)   piece, she noticed the signature of a world-famous artist. Amazed, she stared at the painting wondering whether it was authentic or a fake. Natasha carefully traced the frame with her finger, looking for any imperfections.
(25)   She couldn't help but wonder why someone would part with such a beautiful, and possibly valuable, piece of art. She carefully covered the painting with a sheet and placed it in a closet where it would be safe.

(30)   Natasha could not stop thinking about the painting. Her mind was filled with questions that kept her awake most of the night. Where had it come from? Was it really the work of a famous artist? Why would
(35)   someone give away a piece of art that could potentially be worth thousands of dollars? Finally, she got out of bed and went to the computer. She found the name of an art history professor at the nearby university.
(40)   Maybe some of Natasha's questions would finally be answered.

29. Which is most likely the author's purpose for writing this passage?
a. to tell readers a true story
b. to inform readers about art history
c. to entertain readers with a fiction tale
d. to teach readers about a famous artist

30. Which is the meaning of the word *authentic* in line 22?
a. old
b. genuine
c. famous
d. beautiful

31. Read the following sentence from the second paragraph:
Natasha carefully traced the frame with her finger, looking for any *imperfections*.

What is the meaning of *imperfection*?
a. perfect
b. improvement
c. type of disease
d. a flaw or defect

32. Which statement is an example of a text-to-world connection readers might make with the passage?

    a. I remember when I found a high-fashion coat at a garage sale for only $5.

    b. Art appreciation has been on the rise in major cities.

    c. I need to clean out my attic and donate what I find to charity.

    d. An art history book I read mentioned that people sometimes don't realize they own valuable pieces of art.

33. Natasha spent many years working in an art museum and has a keen eye for valuable oil paintings. The charity she now volunteers with donates money to the local children's hospital, which is known for its impressive research program. Which sentence most accurately describes Natasha?

    a. She has a large art collection that she hopes to expand.

    b. She plans to return to the university and teach about art.

    c. She is generous and genuinely cares about helping others.

    d. She hopes to work in the field of medicine or research someday.

Questions 34 through 38 refer to the following passage.

Will Others Change Their Minds?

Since I was a boy, it has been difficult to make friends. Many assumed that all aristocrats thought themselves better than others, but that was not the case. I never
(5) believed that being a member of the highest social class made me more important than anyone.

In the streets, people stepped far out of my way, as if trying to avoid me. I smiled and
(10) tried to make eye contact, but no one would meet my gaze. Groups of friends gathered on street corners and in cafes, laughing together. Loneliness filled my heart, and I longed to be a part of one of their groups. Yet somehow, I
(15) would be excluded by circumstances that many would call fortunate.

One day, I stopped at the farmers' market in town to buy a piece of fruit. As I paid the gentleman, a woman sneered and
(20) said, "Don't you have servants to do your shopping for you?" Several other customers giggled and turned their backs. Smiling politely, I thanked the man for the fruit and walked away, listening to the whispers
(25) behind me.

As I walked away, I noticed a young boy sitting alone beside the bakery. He was crying, and many people walked past him without stopping. I sat down beside him on
(30) the ground and asked why he was upset.

"I can't find my mother. I stopped to look in the window of the bakery. When I turned back around, she was gone," the boy explained.
(35) I put my arm around him, explaining that he was wise to stay in one place so that his mother could find him. "You must feel lonely," I said. "I feel lonely, too, sometimes.

(40) We'll stay here together until your mother returns."

Very soon, a frantic young woman came running down the street, calling out, "William! William, where are you?"

(45) The boy jumped up, and his mother ran to us and scooped up her son in her arms, asking if he had been afraid.

"No, Mama," William explained. "This man kept me company."

(50) The woman looked at me and seemed surprised, then smiled warmly and thanked me. William gave me a hug, then walked away, hand in hand with his mother. As they walked away, I realized a crowd had gathered to watch the commotion. One person in the

(55) crowd smiled at me, then another, then another. For the first time, I no longer felt like a lonely outsider.

34. Which sentence from the passage reveals its point of view?
   a. I smiled and tried to make eye contact, but no one would meet my gaze.
   b. Groups of friends gathered on street corners and in cafes, laughing together.
   c. "Don't you have servants to do your shopping for you?"
   d. He was crying, and many people walked past him without stopping.

35. Considering the point of view from which the story is told, which of the following is true?
   a. The narrator is not one of the characters in the story.
   b. The narrator knows the motivations of all the characters in the story.
   c. Readers will know the thoughts and feelings of only one character.
   d. Readers will know the thoughts and feelings of all the characters.

36. Reread the first paragraph. Which would best describe someone who is an *aristocrat*?
   a. friendly
   b. gloomy
   c. helpful
   d. wealthy

37. Which statement is an example of a text-to-self connection that readers might make with the passage?
   a. It was hard for me to make friends after I moved to a new town, and for a while, I felt like an outsider.
   b. Farmers' markets are growing in popularity.
   c. There was a missing child on the news last night, but he was found this morning, safe and sound.
   d. Our social studies book talks about class conflict throughout history.

38. What is the theme of the story?
   a. Friendship is a necessary part of life.
   b. It is difficult to find happiness without having great wealth.
   c. Even young children are able to make a difference in the world.
   d. It is important not to judge people before getting to know them.

Answers and Explanations

1. Completed renewal application; current driver's license; acceptable proof of age, identification, and address; proof of social security; money to pay required fee

2. Social Security card, state or federal income tax return, current pay stub, W-2 form

3. Every four years.

4. It is sent five to seven weeks before the current license expires.

5. False: You can renew only by visiting a Motor Vehicles Agency.

6. **b.** Because the writer hadn't eaten since breakfast, she is *extremely hungry, greedy for food.*

7. **c.** According to the passage, Robert Johnson emerged from the *blues*.

8. **b.** According to the passage, Robert Johnson died in 1938.

9. **True.** Johnson did influence many rock artists, including Led Zeppelin and the Rolling Stones.

10. **a.** The author mentions that contemporary rock bands such as Led Zeppelin and the Rolling Stones were influenced by Johnson's music. Johnson's legendary musical influence is communicated when the author writes, "Again and again, contemporary rock artists return to Johnson." Based on the text, the logical conclusion is that the contemporary artists are turning to Johnson for musical inspiration.

11. **c.** Although "A Fleeting Life" might be an appropriate description for Johnson's brief life span, it describes only one aspect of his life. On the other hand, specifying that Robert Johnson is a blues guitar legend is more specific and descriptive.

12. **a.** Is an **opinion**. It is debatable whether Johnson is the best blues guitarist of all time. Choice **b** is **fact**. This is verifiable information. Choice **c** is **opinion** because this is a debatable proposition. Choice **d** is **fact**. According to the passage, Robert Johnson died in 1938.

13. **c.** The first sentence is the topic sentence, which establishes that the shopping mall will be bad for residents of the town. The remaining sentences support that idea.

14. **a.** The style of the article is businesslike and formal, and is targeted to a sophisticated reader who would be capable of understanding a word such as *displacement*. Therefore, *displacement* is compatible with the style of the article.

15. **d.** The writer warns the readers of the effects that a shopping mall will have on residents of the town and arranges those effects in order of importance, saving the most important effect for last.

16. **a.** The first-person point of view is reflected in the use of the pronouns *us* and *we*.

17. **a.** The writer says that the shopping mall will have "dire consequences" for the residents and then uses the pronouns *us* and *we*, which identify the writer with the residents.

18. **c.** The effects the writer includes here are all very serious, especially the third effect—displacement. The writer has chosen the word *dire* to emphasize that seriousness.

19. **c.** The passage avoids any unnecessary description or details and uses formal rather than casual language.

20. **b.** Each sentence explains a negative effect that the shopping mall will have on the residents, and the negativity of this passage is heightened by the word *dire* and the phrase "avoided at all costs."

21. Answer: Choice **c** is correct. This paragraph uses the objective third-person point of view. There is no *I* or *we* (first person) or *you* (second person), and the only pronouns the paragraph uses are the third-person pronouns *she* and *her*.

22. Answer: Choice **a** is correct. The first-person point of view is reflected in the use of the pronouns *us* and *we*.

23. b. The main idea of the article is that employers are increasingly using social media, so using social media and other tech tools can improve your chances of finding a job. In the third paragraph, the author states, *With technology playing an established role in our lives and social networks easily accessible to potential employers, establishing a strong digital footprint and personal brand is crucial to success.* The writer then goes on to suggest tips for improving the way readers use e-mail and other Internet communications.

24. c. The underlying premise of the article is that having strong computer-literacy skills is important during job searches. More specifically, the author advises readers, *Make sure that your online presence is up to date and also reflects your best attributes.*

25. In this passage, the writer compares being a parent to being a **gardener**. Throughout the passage, the writer lists the many ways that he or she thinks being a parent is similar to being a gardener.

26. c. The last sentence of the passage points out one difference between being a parent and being a gardener: after parents raise their children, the children still maintain an important role in the family, but after gardeners raise plants, the plants die or go dormant in the garden.

27. a. The author states, *The blooms, for all their size and thickness, are as delicate as orchids in that they reject the touch of human hands.*

28. d. According to the author, on magnolia trees, *there is a dry pattering to earth of the hard leaves and for a brief time the tree is parched and drawn, the rosy-lichened trunk gray and anxious. Then pale green spires cover the boughs, unfolding into freshly lacquered leaves, and at their tips the blooms appear. When, in late April or early May, the pale buds unfold into great white waxy blossoms, . . . the perfume is a delirious thing on the spring air.*

29. c. This passage was written to entertain. It is not a true story, and although art history and a famous artist are mentioned, the author did not intend to teach readers about these topics.

30. b. The passage tells us that Natasha wondered whether the painting was "authentic or a fake." *Fake* is given as an antonym of *authentic*. So, *authentic* means *real*, or *genuine*.

31. d. The root of *imperfection* is *perfect*. The prefix *im-* means "not," so *imperfections* cause something to be not perfect. An *imperfection* is a flaw or defect that makes something not perfect. If you thought the answer was *perfect*, you selected the root of the word. If you chose "type of disease," you may have confused the word with *infection*.

32. b. Choices **a** and **c** are examples of text-to-self connections because they relate ideas from the passage to something personal. Choice **d** makes connections between the passage and other texts that have been read previously, so it is an example of a text-to-text connections. Choice **b**, making a connection between the passage and something happening in the world, is a text-to-world connection.

33. c. This is an example of an expanded synthesis question. To answer it correctly, you must combine the information given in the question with what you read in the passage. Because Natasha used to work in a museum and recognizes valuable oil paintings, she probably had a pretty good idea that the artwork was worth a lot of money. The charity that now has the painting donates its money to the children's hospital, which uses some of the money for research. Natasha was obviously excited about the painting being given to the charity, which is probably because the money it raises will be given to the hospital. If she is so excited, she must really care about the people who will benefit from the donation.

34. a. This passage was written from the first-person point of view. The narrator is one of the characters in the story, and he uses pronouns such as *I* and *me*. Notice that it sounds as if the narrator is talking directly to the reader.

35. c. Because the story tells a first-person account of the events, only the narrator's thoughts and feelings will be revealed to the readers. The narrator is a character in the story, and he knows only his own ideas and motivations, unless the other characters reveal their thoughts and feelings to him.

36. d. Context clues in the first paragraph explain that an *aristocrat* is "a member of the highest social class." Generally, people in this class have a lot of money. In this story, the aristocrat was also friendly, helpful, and possibly even gloomy. However, by definition, aristocrats are usually wealthy. As you read, remember to look for context clues in the sentences surrounding the word they help to define. In this case, the word *aristocrats* is used in one sentence, and the definition or explanation is in the sentence that follows.

37. a. Choices **b** and **c** are examples of text-to-world connections because they relate ideas from the passage to real-world events. Choice **d** makes connections between the passage and other texts that have been read previously, so they are examples of text-to-text connections. Choice **a**, making a connection between the passage and something personal, is a text-to-self connection.

38. d. In this passage, people made assumptions about the narrator without getting to know him. As it turned out, these assumptions were incorrect. After others saw his helpfulness and the way he cared for the little boy, they became aware of his true personality. The narrator longed for friendships and showed that he felt helping the little boy was important, but these ideas were not the overall message the author wanted to portray. Choice **b** is the opposite of what the narrator believed, as he did have great wealth but was not happy.

REVIEW

In this chapter, you have learned several strategies to help you better comprehend reading materials:

1. Point of view refers to who is telling the story. First-person point of view is when one of the characters tells the story and readers see the events through his or her eyes. Third-person point of view is when the story is told by a narrator who is outside of the story and does not participate in the events. However, he or she is often aware of the thoughts and feelings of all the characters.

2. Authors usually write for one of the following purposes: to entertain, to inform, or to persuade.

3. The theme of a story is the author's underlying message. Usually, these beliefs, attitudes, or perceptions are not directly stated; instead, the theme is a lesson that readers take away from the story. The words and actions of the characters, the tone, the plot, and repeated patterns in the story help to reveal the theme.

4. Synthesizing information means putting together information from multiple sources or from more than one location within a source. Combining information can help readers gain a deeper understanding of the text.

5. Making connections between the text and what they already know helps readers better understand the material. The types of connections readers make include text-to-self, text-to-text, and text-to-world.

6. Before you begin reading a passage, be sure to pay attention to the purpose question that precedes the passage as well as the comprehension questions that follow it.

7. Scan the passage first, then read it carefully, noticing important details and mentally organizing the information. Remember to read the information in brackets, the visual aids, and the captions as well.

8. After you read the passage completely, thoroughly read each question, paying close attention to any information stated within the question itself.

9. Try to answer each question before you actually read the answer choices. Then, read each choice carefully, paying close attention to every word, before selecting the best answer based on the passage.

10. When reading fiction passages, be sure to pay attention to details, such as the names of characters or places, and use the ideas that are included in the passage to infer information that the author has not included.

11. As you read nonfiction passages, look for evidence that supports the main idea of the passage. Be sure to pay close attention to details, names, dates, statistics, and descriptive language that can enhance your comprehension of the material and help you draw your own conclusions about the topic.

C H A P T E R

4 ▶ READING COMPREHENSION: CLOSE-READING SKILLS

CHAPTER SUMMARY
This chapter teaches you to identify main ideas and supporting details, summarize passages, distinguish fact from opinion, recognize organizational structure, and make inferences—key close-reading skills you'll need to succeed on the GED® Reasoning through Language Arts test.

While the previous chapter focused on higher-order concerns like the Author's Purpose and Point of View, this chapter provides more nuts-and-bolts tools that you'll use to answer questions about fiction and nonfiction texts. Now that you've mastered the bigger picture, it's time to zoom in and learn to break excerpts down and identify their component parts. When close-reading, or examining excerpts for elements that help you gain insight into the meaning of the text as a whole, you'll need to be able to focus on individual elements and understand what they contribute to the larger work.

Make Connections

To better comprehend text, it is important for readers to **make connections** between what they are reading and what they already know. Not only does this help readers gain insight, but it also helps to make the material more personal and relevant. This gives readers a deeper understanding of what they read.

There are three main types of connections that great readers make:

1. text-to-self
2. text-to-text
3. text-to-world

The connections readers make are neither correct nor incorrect. The same text may remind different readers of very different things. Connections with texts are personal, and they will mean different things to different readers. The important thing is that readers connect with the text in a way that makes it meaningful and understandable to them.

Text-to-Self

Connections that readers make between the reading material and their own personal experiences are **text-to-self** connections. These make the reading more personal. Statements that could help you make such connections include the following:

- This reminds me of when I . . .
- If I were this character, I would . . .
- If this ever happened to me, I might . . .

Think about the story we read about Camilla on page 50 and the garage sale. Perhaps it reminded you of a garage sale you had, of a time you came across sentimental items, or of a situation in which time flew by with your family. These would be text-to-self connections.

Text-to-Text

Text-to-text connections occur when readers are able to make connections between the reading material and a text that they have previously read. To make such connections, think about whether the text reminds you of any of the following:

- a different book by the same author
- a book with similar characters, settings, or plots
- a book that includes similar situations or events

- a book about a similar topic
- information you read in a textbook, newspaper, or magazine

Did Camilla's story remind you of another character who reconnected with his or her mom? Have you ever read an article about having a garage sale? Can you think of a book about discovering your family history? If so, these would be examples of text-to-text connections.

Text-to-World

Connections that readers make between the reading material and something that happens in the real world are **text-to-world** connections. To make this type of connection, think about whether the text reminds you of:

- information you read on the Internet
- something you saw on TV or heard on the radio
- events that are happening in the real world

If you connected Camilla's story to a television documentary on relationships between parents and teenagers or if it reminded you that there is a garage sale happening in your neighborhood this weekend, you made a text-to-world connection.

Main Idea and Supporting Details

Every passage you read, regardless of the type of material, has a main idea. The **main idea**, sometimes called the *big idea*, is the central message of the text. To determine the main idea, first identify the topic of the text. Then, think about the major point that the writer is trying to tell readers about the topic. For example, if the topic of a passage is loggerhead sea turtles, the main idea could be as follows:

Loggerhead sea turtles return to the beach where they were born to lay eggs.

This would be the most important idea that the writer wants you to take away from the passage. The rest of the passage would contain information to help explain the main idea. Examples, information, facts, and details that help to explain and describe the main idea are the **supporting details**. These help to strengthen readers' understanding of the main idea.

In the passage about sea turtles, supporting details could include the following sentences:

The turtles crawl onto the beach at night.

They dig a hole in the sand and lay their eggs in the hole.

After covering the nest with sand, the turtles return to the ocean.

Each of these supporting details gives information about the main idea.

There are four basic types of supporting details that writers include to give readers a deeper understanding of the central message of the text. Here are the types of supporting details:

- examples
- reasons
- facts
- descriptions

Being able to identify the main idea and supporting details is helpful in organizing the information in a passage. Readers are able to recognize the central message of the text and identify examples, reasons, facts, and descriptions to clarify and explain the message.

TIP
While the topic of a passage may be as short as a single word, the main idea of a passage is always a complete sentence.

Read the following paragraph. Look for the main idea and supporting details as you read.

Before becoming the sixteenth president of the United States, Abraham Lincoln showed a pattern of behavior that caused him to earn the nickname "Honest Abe." Early in his career, he worked in the grocery business. When his partner passed away, leaving behind a mountain of debt, Lincoln not only paid off his own part of the money, but also his late partner's share because this was the honest thing to do. Later, he worked as a lawyer. During that time in history, members of the legal profession were often recognized as being dishonest. However, Lincoln earned the reputation among his colleagues as being a man who never told a lie. He even gave a lecture during which he encouraged the audience to make honesty a priority in their occupations.

What is the main idea of the passage?

_____

_____

You probably recognized that the first sentence tells the main idea of the passage. You may have stated that the main idea is:

Abraham Lincoln earned the nickname "Honest Abe."

Abraham Lincoln showed a pattern of honesty throughout his life.

People called Lincoln "Honest Abe" because of the priority he placed on honesty.

Any of these would be correct. The main idea is the most important piece of information, about which the rest of the paragraph is written. Each of these choices captures that information.

> Which of the following is a supporting detail from the passage?
> a. Abraham Lincoln was the sixteenth president of the United States.
> b. Lincoln's behavior caused him to be known as "Honest Abe."
> c. Early in his career, Lincoln worked in the grocery business.
> d. Lincoln's colleagues recognized him as a man who never told a lie.

Did you recognize that answer choice **d** supports the main idea of the passage? This statement is an example of the honesty that caused people to call Lincoln "Honest Abe." Choice **b** restates the main idea. Choices **a** and **c** both contain relevant or interesting information, but they do not directly support the main idea, so they are considered minor details rather than supporting details.

What other supporting details are contained in the passage?

_____

_____

Supporting details from the passage include *Lincoln paid off his late partner's debt as well as his own* and *he gave a lecture encouraging the audience to be honest*. These statements support the main idea by giving some reasons why he became known for his honesty.

Some reading passages include more than a single paragraph. Every paragraph will have its own main idea. The main idea is stated in the topic sentence. The **topic sentence** basically sums up what the entire paragraph tries to explain.

Look back at the paragraph about Lincoln. Can you identify the topic sentence? It is the sentence that tells the basic message of the paragraph.

> *Before becoming the sixteenth president of the United States, Abraham Lincoln showed a pattern of behavior that caused him to earn the nickname "Honest Abe."*

This is the first sentence of the paragraph, and it is the topic sentence. Notice that it also contains the main idea. The topic sentence can be anywhere in the paragraph; however, it is generally either the first or last sentence. Being able to locate the topic sentence can be helpful in determining the main idea.

Excerpted from Marjorie Kinnan Rawlings's *Cross Creek*, a Memoir about Life on a Florida Orange Grove (1942)

I see no reason for denying so fundamental an urge, ruin or no. It is more important to live the life one wishes to live, and to go down with it if necessary, quite contentedly, than to live more profitably but less happily. Yet to achieve content under sometimes adverse circumstances requires first an adjustment within oneself, and this I had already made, and after that, a recognition that one is not unique in being obliged to toil and struggle and suffer. This is the simplest of all facts and the most difficult for the individual ego to accept.

A close reading of this passage requires that you first pay attention to the year in which it was published—1942. What significant events happened in the United States around this time? The nation was recovering from the Great Depression and had just entered World War II. Rawlings is writing about the years before this, but it is important to know that these events were happening because they may shape the viewpoint of the author.

In this excerpt, Rawlings talks about living the life one wants to live, even if it means suffering difficulties, instead of having more money but being less happy. She acknowledges that the struggle she faced was not really unique—everyone experiences difficulties. Rawlings implies that complaining about one's lot in life is a waste of time. This summarizes her point of view, which may have been shaped not only by her personal experiences but by what was happening in society at this time.

What might be Rawlings's purpose for writing *Cross Creek*? Based on her style and viewpoint, the reader can conclude that she wanted to provide readers with a glimpse of life in a Southern community, including its challenges and imperfections. In reading this memoir, a person might connect on some level with the struggles that Rawlings faced.

Practice

Read the passage and answer the questions that follow.

Excerpted from the Memoir *Cross Creek* (1942), by Marjorie Kinnan Rawlings

It is always bewildering to change one's complete way of life. I was fitted by temperament and by inheritance for farm and country living, yet to take it up after some thirty years of urban life was not too easy. I had known my maternal grandfather's Michigan farm, but there I was both guest and child, and the only duties were to gather the eggs from the sweet-smelling hayloft. I had known my father's Maryland farm, but that farm was his love, his escape from Washington governmental routine, and we lived there only in the too few summers. I had no duties there at all. There was only delight; the flowering locust grove; the gentle cows in pasture; Rock Creek, which ran, ten miles away from its Washington park, at the foot of the hill of the locusts, where my brother and I learned to swim and to fish for tiny and almost untakable fishes; long walks with my father through the woods where he hoped someday to build a home; jaunts with him behind Old Dan in the carriage, to the county seat of Rockville, or to buy mules at Frederick. These things got in the blood but were no preparation for running a farm oneself.

When I bought the Florida orange grove with my inheritance that represented my share of the Maryland farm, my father's sister Madeline wrote me in lament. "You have in you," she said, "that fatal drop of Pearce blood, clamoring for change and adventure, and above all, for a farm. I never knew a Pearce who didn't secretly long for a farm. Mother had one, Uncle Pierman was ruined by one, there was your father's tragic experience. I had one, once." I see no reason for denying so fundamental an urge, ruin or no. It is more important to live the life one wishes to live, and to go down with it if necessary, quite contentedly, than to live more profitably but less happily. Yet to achieve content under sometimes adverse circumstances requires first an adjustment within oneself, and this I had already made, and after that, a recognition that one is not unique in being obliged to toil and struggle and suffer. This is the simplest of all facts and the most difficult for the individual ego to accept. As I look back on those first difficult times at the Creek, when it seemed as though the actual labor was more than I could bear, and the making of a living on the grove impossible, it was Martha who drew aside a curtain and led me in to the company of all those who had loved the Creek and been tormented by it.

1. Madeline's attitude toward the writer's decision to purchase the farm could best be described as
   a. nostalgic for days gone by.
   b. enthusiastic but concerned.
   c. understanding but foreboding.
   d. indifferent.

2. The passage suggests which of the following about the writer's decision to purchase the farm in Cross Creek?
   a. She deeply regretted her decision because of the amount of work required to run the farm.
   b. She was ready to separate from her domineering family and live on her own on the farm.
   c. She was enthusiastic about owning the farm and appreciated the experiences that prepared her for this endeavor.
   d. She had a deep desire for rural life and knew she must fulfill this longing to be truly happy.

3. In the last sentence, *the Creek* refers to
   a. a farm in Michigan.
   b. an orange grove in Florida.
   c. Rock Creek, ten miles from Washington, DC.
   d. a farm in Maryland.

4. The phrase *it was Martha who drew aside a curtain* is a metaphor that could be best interpreted as
   a. Martha opened the curtains of the author's house, filling it with sunlight.
   b. Martha gave the author clarity by offering an inside perspective.
   c. Martha alleviated some of the author's burden at the Creek by opening the curtains and doing other household tasks.
   d. none of the above.

Reading Comprehension Review

Use the following passage to answer questions 5 and 6.

FDA Widens Look at Arsenic in Apple Juice

Some consumers are understandably surprised to learn that arsenic is present in water, air, and soil, and as a result, it can be found in certain foods and beverages, including apple juice and juice concentrates. Arsenic is present in the environment as a naturally occurring substance and also as a result of contamination from human activity, such as past use of fertilizers and arsenic-based pesticides, which may still be in the soil, explains Donald Zink, PhD, senior science adviser at the U.S. Food and Drug Administration's (FDA's) Center for Food Safety and Applied Nutrition. "While environmental contaminants like arsenic are unavoidable in food," says Zink, "the goal is to keep the levels of arsenic that people consume over the course of their lives as low as possible."

That's where the FDA and the U.S. Environmental Protection Agency (EPA) come in. Their job is to monitor food and the environment and take action when needed to protect the American public. The FDA has been testing and monitoring fruit juices, including apple juice, for arsenic content for more than 20 years, says Michael R. Taylor, the FDA's deputy commissioner for foods. "We are confident in the overall safety of apple juice consumed in this country because we continue to find that apple juice, on average, contains low amounts of arsenic."

In fact, the FDA's most recent tests done in 2010 and 2011 show on average about three parts of arsenic in every one billion parts of apple juice. That is lower than the 10 parts per billion (ppb) set by the EPA as the maximum level allowed in public drinking water.

"Our test results over many years support the overall safety of apple juice," says Taylor, "but we see a small percentage of individual samples tested that contain higher levels of arsenic. We want to minimize the public's exposure to arsenic in foods as much as we can." For that reason, the FDA plans to consider all the relevant evidence, and based on this work, it may set a guidance or other maximum level to further reduce arsenic in apple juice and juice products.

To further protect the public's health, the FDA is also taking the following actions:

- Enhancing its surveillance of arsenic in apple juice and juice concentrate. The agency will shortly have results for an additional 90 samples of apple juice and juice concentrate and soon after will sample additional types of juice and juice concentrates.

- Continuing to test samples of apple juice imported into the United States from China. The most recent results included more than 70 samples from China, and 95% of these contained less than the 10 ppb level used for drinking water.

- Working with the EPA to coordinate the review of the risk assessment being prepared and discussing other steps the two agencies can take to reduce the overall levels of arsenic in the environment and in foods.

The bottom line is that the FDA is working hard to ensure the safety of the foods people consume and to do so based on the best science. And the best thing families can do is to consume a variety of foods and beverages and follow a well-balanced diet consistent with the Dietary Guidelines for Americans.

5. What is *arsenic*?
- **a.** It is a preservative added to apple juice and other fruit juices to increase their shelf life.
- **b.** It is a naturally occurring element that can be hazardous to your health if you consume too much of it.
- **c.** It is a vitamin found in apple juice and other fruit juices that can be hazardous to your health if you consume too much of it.
- **d.** It is an artificial sweetener used in beverages to reduce calorie levels.

6. In the following sentence, what does *10 ppb* mean? *The most recent results included more than 70 samples from China, and 95% of these contained less than the 10 ppb level used for drinking water.*
- **a.** 10 percent per beverage
- **b.** 10 parts of pesticides in beverages
- **c.** 10 parts per billion
- **d.** none of the above

Use the following passage to answer questions 7 and 8.

Excerpted from *Army Letters from an Officer's Wife, 1871–1888*, by Frances M.A. Roe

Fort Lyon, Colorado Territory, October 1871.

After months of anticipation and days of weary travel we have at last got to our army home! As you know, Fort Lyon is fifty miles from Kit Carson, and we came all that distance in a funny looking stage coach called a "jerkey," and a good name for it, too, for at times it seesawed back and forth and then sideways, in an awful breakneck way. The day was glorious, and the atmosphere so clear, we could see miles and miles in every direction. But there was not one object to be seen on the vast rolling plains—not a tree or a house, except the wretched ranch and stockade where we got fresh horses and a perfectly uneatable dinner.

It was dark when we reached the post, so of course we could see nothing that night. General and Mrs. Phillips gave us a most cordial welcome—just as though they had known us always. Dinner was served soon after we arrived, and the cheerful dining room, and the table with its dainty china and bright silver, was such a surprise—so much nicer than anything we had expected to find here, and all so different from the terrible places we had seen since reaching the plains. General Phillips is not a real general—only so by brevet, for gallant service during the war. I was so disappointed when I was told this, but Faye says that he is very much afraid that I will have cause, sooner or later, to think that the grade of captain is quite high enough. He thinks this way because, having graduated at West Point this year, he is only a second lieutenant just now, and General Phillips is his captain and company commander.

It seems that in the Army, lieutenants are called "Mister" always, but all other officers must be addressed by their rank. At least that is what they tell me. But in Faye's company, the captain is called general, and the first lieutenant is called major, and as this is most confusing, I get things mixed sometimes. Most girls would. A soldier in uniform waited upon us at dinner, and that seemed so funny. I wanted to watch him all the time, which distracted me, I suppose, for once I called General Phillips "Mister"! It so happened, too, that just that instant there was not a sound in the room, so everyone heard the blunder. General Phillips straightened back in his chair, and his little son gave a smothered giggle—for which he should have been sent to bed at once. But that was not all! That soldier, who had been so dignified and stiff, put his hand over his mouth and fairly rushed from the room so he could laugh outright. And how I longed to run some place, too—but not to laugh, oh, no!

These soldiers are not nearly as nice as one would suppose them to be, when one sees them dressed up in their blue uniforms with bright brass buttons. And they can make mistakes, too, for yesterday, when I asked that same man a question, he answered, "Yes, Sorr!" Then I smiled, of course, but he did not seem to have enough sense to see why. When I told Faye about it, he looked vexed and said I must never laugh at an enlisted man—that it was not dignified in the wife of an officer to do so. And then I told him that an officer should teach an enlisted man not to snicker at his wife, and not to call her "Sorr," which was disrespectful. I wanted to say more, but Faye suddenly left the room.

(continues)

> Yesterday morning, directly after guard-mounting, Faye put on his full-dress uniform—epaulets, beautiful scarlet sash, and sword—and went over to the office of the commanding officer to report officially. The officer in command of the post is lieutenant colonel of the regiment, but he, also, is a general by brevet, and one can see by his very walk that he expects this to be remembered always. So it is apparent to me that the safest thing to do is to call everyone general—there seem to be so many here. If I make a mistake, it will be on the right side, at least.

7. Who is Faye?
  a. the person to whom Frances Roe is writing
  b. the general's wife
  c. Frances Roe's husband
  d. a soldier whom Frances Roe gets to know at Fort Lyon

8. In general, what seems to be Frances's attitude toward army protocol?
  a. disinterested and bored
  b. interested but furious
  c. devoted and serious
  d. curious but questioning

Use the following passage to answer questions 9 and 10.

Excerpted from the Short Story "To Build a Fire" (1908), by Jack London

Day had broken cold and grey, exceedingly cold and grey, when the man turned aside from the main Yukon trail and climbed the high earth bank, where a dim and little traveled trail led eastward through the fat spruce timberland. It was a steep bank, and he paused for breath at the top, excusing the act to himself by looking at his watch. It was nine o'clock. There was no sun nor hint of sun, though there was not a cloud in the sky. It was a clear day, and yet there seemed an intangible pall over the face of things, a subtle gloom that made the day dark, and that was due to the absence of sun. This fact did not worry the man. He was used to the lack of sun. It had been days since he had seen the sun, and he knew that a few more days must pass before that cheerful orb, due south, would just peep above the sky line and dip immediately from view.

The man flung a look back along the way he had come. The Yukon lay a mile wide and hidden under three feet of ice. On top of this ice were as many feet of snow. It was all pure white, rolling in gentle undulations where the ice jams of the freeze-up had formed. North and south, as far as his eye could see, it was unbroken white, save for a dark hair-line that curved and twisted from around the spruce-covered island to the south, and that curved and twisted away into the north, where it disappeared behind another spruce-covered island. This dark hair-line was the trail—the main trail—that led south five hundred miles to the Chilcoot Pass, Dyea, and salt water; and that led north seventy miles to Dawson, and still on to the north a thousand miles to Nulato, and finally to St. Michael on Bering Sea, a thousand miles and half a thousand more.

(continues)

But all this—the mysterious, far-reaching hair-line trail, the absence of sun from the sky, the tremendous cold, and the strangeness and weirdness of it all—made no impression on the man. It was not because he was long used to it. He was a newcomer in the land, a *chechaquo*, and this was his first winter.

The trouble with him was that he was without imagination. He was quick and alert in the things of life, but only in the things, and not in the significances. Fifty degrees below zero meant eighty-odd degrees of frost. Such fact impressed him as being cold and uncomfortable, and that was all. It did not lead him to meditate upon his frailty as a creature of temperature, and upon man's frailty in general, able only to live within certain narrow limits of heat and cold; and from there on it did not lead him to the conjectural field of immortality and man's place in the universe. Fifty degrees below zero stood for a bite of frost that hurt and that must be guarded against by the use of mittens, ear flaps, warm moccasins, and thick socks. Fifty degrees below zero was to him just precisely fifty degrees below zero. That there should be anything more to it than that was a thought that never entered his head.

9. Which of the following best expresses the theme of the passage?
   a. A person must have rigorous training to face the harsh elements of nature.
   b. It is extremely foolish to travel alone in unknown terrain.
   c. A person must learn to see beyond the facts to understand the meaning of life.
   d. With hard work and perseverance, a person can triumph over any adversity.

10. Which words describe the man as he appears in the passage?
   a. innocent, heroic
   b. knowledgeable, matter-of-fact
   c. rebellious, observant
   d. religious, young

TIP

Sometimes, the main idea is suggested but not directly stated. Remember to ask yourself what the topic is and what the most important thought is about the topic. This will help you determine the main idea of the text.

Summarizing

Have you ever given a book report or written a research paper? In either case, you read information from a text, then restated the most important ideas in your own words. This is called **summarizing**.

Being able to summarize information is one way to show how well you understood what you read because it requires you to focus on the main points and explain them. Think back to a research paper you have written. Chances are, you read a number of articles or books about your topic; however, your paper was probably only a few pages long. That's because you only included key pieces of information in your summary. You chose the main idea and the most important supporting details and restated these in the report.

Think back about the paragraph we read about "Honest Abe." What information in the text was the most important? How could you restate that in your own words?

> *Abraham Lincoln was known as "Honest Abe" for many reasons. He showed honesty in his early work life, set an example of honesty as a lawyer working among many dishonest colleagues, and encouraged others to practice honesty as well.*

This summary has two sentences in it. The original paragraph about Lincoln was considerably longer. Because a summary focuses on only the most important information, it is generally much shorter than the original text. In fact, you might summarize an entire book in only a few sentences or paragraphs.

Read the following paragraph.

> *In the midst of New York Harbor stands a 305-foot tall, 225-ton symbol of freedom and democracy: the Statue of Liberty. "Lady Liberty," as she is affectionately known, was a gift of friendship from France and was dedicated on October 28, 1886. Officially named "The Statue of Liberty Enlightening the World," this highly recognizable structure contains much symbolism. For example, the torch itself is a symbol of enlightenment. The tablet of law held in her left hand contains Roman numerals representing the date of our country's independence, July 4, 1776.*

> *Finally, the crown on the head of the statue has seven rays, one for each of the seven continents.*

> *The statue is covered in copper, about the thickness of two pennies. Natural weathering has caused the copper to turn a light green color. When the statue was restored for its 100th birthday, the torch was replaced, and the new torch was covered with a thin layer of 24 karat gold. During the day, the sun's reflection lights the torch; at night, it is lighted by 16 floodlights.*

To summarize the passage,

- determine the most important idea.
- decide what information can be left out.
- restate the information using your own words.

Now, let's summarize the passage.

What is the main idea of the entire passage?

_____

What are two important supporting details?

_____

_____

Write a summary of the passage in your own words.

_____

_____

_____

You probably recognized that the main idea is one of the following:

> *The Statue of Liberty is an important symbol.*

> *The Statue of Liberty is a huge monument that represents many things.*

Remember, there is not a single correct way to state the main idea. The important thing is that you recognize which information is the most important.

Next, figure out which supporting details are key. The size of the Statue of Liberty is definitely interesting. It could even be the central idea of another passage. However, in this example, these facts are not some of the supporting details that must find their way into a summary. The same is true about the date the statue was dedicated and the fact that the copper has turned green over the past century and a half. These are ideas that could be left out when you summarize the passage.

The most important supporting details would be those that address the symbolism associated with the statue. Information about the significance of the torch, the tablet, and the crown should be included in a thorough summary.

> **TIP**
>
> Don't forget! A summary must use your own words, not the words of the author. Restate the ideas that you read and make sure you are not copying what is written in the text.

Just like the main idea, there is more than one correct way to summarize a passage. Yours may be similar to the following summary:

> *The Statue of Liberty was a gift from France that symbolizes a number of ideas that are important to our country. The torch represents enlightenment, the tablet recognizes the date of our country's freedom, and the crown acknowledges the seven continents in the world.*

> Remember learning that each paragraph has its own main idea? See if you can find the main idea in the second paragraph about "Lady Liberty." If you recognized the main idea as the fact that the Statue of Liberty is coated with a thin layer of copper, you're exactly right! Supporting details include information about the thickness of the copper and the fact that it has changed colors due to weathering.

Remember that understanding the author's purpose is critical to understanding the text itself. If the author's purpose in the previous passage was to persuade readers that the Statue of Liberty was long overdue for restoration, then the supporting details the author chose would probably have focused on the statue's recent state in a negative way. The author might have presented evidence that the structure represented a safety hazard due to its age, or that its weathered copper covering was an eyesore for those who visited it. As written, however, the passage is clearly written to inform the reader.

Fact and Opinion

You probably learned the difference between fact and opinion when you were younger. A **fact** is a true statement that can be proven.

> *California is located on the west coast of the United States.*

This is a fact. Look at any atlas, encyclopedia, or geography book, and you can verify, or prove, that this statement is true.

An **opinion** is a statement that reflects someone's personal views. Not everyone will agree with an opinion.

> *California's beaches are the most beautiful in the whole country.*

Many people would probably agree with this statement. However, this is the writer's personal view. If you were to talk with people sitting on the beaches in Hawaii, North Carolina, or Florida, you'd most likely find at least a few who disagree.

TIP

Words such as *beautiful, best, worst, should, terrible*, and *wonderful* often indicate an opinion. Look for clues that help you determine that a statement shares the feelings or beliefs of the author.

Writers often use a combination of facts and opinions to share their ideas. Being able to distinguish between these statements can help you gain a complete understanding of the passage. Strong readers are able to interpret the information in a passage and form their own opinions.

Four inches of snow fell overnight.

Can this be proven? Absolutely. A ruler or a weather report can be used to check how much snow fell. Because this statement can be proven, it is a fact.

We have had too much snow this winter.

Can this be proven? We could prove that snow has fallen, but how much is too much? Not everyone would agree that there has been too much snow. In fact, some people might think there has not been enough. This statement tells how someone feels about the snow, so it is an opinion.

Facts and opinions are both useful. They not only help writers get their point across; they can be useful to readers as well.

Suppose you want to buy tickets to a play and are trying to decide which play to attend. You would need to know facts such as where each play is being per-

formed, the times and dates of the shows, and the cost of the tickets. These facts are helpful in making up your mind. But, you'll probably want to find some opinions, too. You could read reviews or talk to friends to find out which theaters offer the best seats, which actors and actresses are the most entertaining, and whether a particular play is completely boring.

The author's purpose for writing a piece can impact whether the text includes mostly facts, mostly opinions, or a combination of both:

- If the author's purpose is *to inform*, the text is likely to contain mostly facts.
- If the author's purpose is *to entertain*, a combination of facts and opinions will be included.
- If the author's purpose is *to persuade*, you can definitely expect to find opinions. However, facts that support or promote the author's opinion may also be included.

TIP

As you read nonfiction passages, look for facts that give information about the topic. If opinions are included, be sure to recognize them for what they are—the personal feelings of the writer, not verifiable information.

As you read the following paragraph, determine which statements are facts and which are opinions. Ask yourself:

1. Can this statement be proven or verified?
2. Would everyone agree with this statement?

The drama club of Meadowbrook Middle School put on a stage presentation of The Elves and the Shoemaker *earlier this month. The students performed before a sold-out crowd for all three performances. The highlight of the evening was a dance by the elves during the second act. Even the principal was seen laughing until tears filled her eyes. It was the first live performance the students put on this year, although plans for a spring musical were announced at the end of the evening. It is sure to be a huge success!*

A woodwind ensemble from the school band provided music before the show as well as during the intermission. This impressive group of young musicians was enjoyed by all. The amazing talent present in the school was obvious in everyone involved, from the actors and actresses to the stagehands and technical crew. Ticket sales for the performances earned nearly $900 for the school's fine arts department.

Did you determine which statements from the review of the play were facts and which were opinions?

Facts from the passage:

- The drama club of Meadowbrook Middle School put on a stage presentation of *The Elves and the Shoemaker* earlier this month.
- The students performed before a sold-out crowd for all three performances.
- Even the principal was seen laughing until tears filled her eyes.
- It was the first live performance the students put on this year, although plans for a spring musical were announced at the end of the evening.
- A woodwind ensemble from the school band provided music before the show as well as during the intermission.
- Ticket sales for the performances earned nearly $900 for the school's fine arts department.

Each of these statements could be proven by checking the school calendar, looking at the program for the performances, or checking with the accountant for the fine arts department. Even the statement about the principal could be verified through a photograph or video. She might even admit it.

Opinions from the passage:

- The highlight of the evening was a dance by the elves during the second act.
- It is sure to be a huge success!
- This impressive group of young musicians was enjoyed by all.
- The amazing talent present in the school was obvious in everyone involved, from the actors and actresses to the stagehands and technical crew.

All these are opinions because there could be people who would not agree with the author. For example, some audience members might have thought the highlight of the evening was when the musicians played, not when the elves danced. Also, *amazing* and *impressive* are words that often indicate an opinion.

Organizational Structure

When you write, whether the text is a story, a letter, or a research paper, you probably spend time planning the order in which you will present your ideas. It would not make sense to randomly write down your thoughts without any pattern or logical order. Before writing, you probably organize similar ideas together or tell actions and events in the order in which they happened. Without using some sort of organization, not only would you have trouble getting your thoughts across accurately, but your readers would also become terribly confused.

Writers want their texts to make sense. The whole point of writing is to share information and ideas with an audience, and writers carefully consider how to best arrange this information so that readers are able to follow their thoughts and fully understand the passage. The **organizational structure** of a passage is the way a writer arranges his or her ideas.

Common types of organizational structures that writers may choose include *sequence, cause and effect, compare and contrast, problem and solution, classification*, and *description*.

Understanding how information is presented can help readers

- organize and understand the passage.
- anticipate what ideas might be presented next.
- think about what information to look for.
- make predictions.
- connect ideas from different parts of the text.

To recognize which organizational structure an author has used, think about what he or she wants readers to know. If an author wants to be sure readers understand the order in which events occurred, sequence is probably used. If he or she wants readers to know what led up to a particular event, a cause and effect structure is likely to be found. Recognizing and understanding each type of organizational structure can make a big difference in how well you comprehend the material.

Now, let's talk about each type of organizational structure in a little more detail.

Sequence

The **sequence** of events is the order in which the events are discussed in a passage. When readers are able to recognize that a text uses a sequential organizational structure, they know that details, ideas, and events will be presented in a specific order. Often, the sequence used is either time order or order of importance.

Time order means that ideas and events are presented chronologically, or in the order in which they actually happened. Often, words and phrases such as the following indicate time order:

- first
- second
- next
- then
- last
- before
- after that
- following
- by the time
- as soon as

Writers often use time order when the correct order is important. For example, history books are often written in time order by beginning with the earliest events and leading up to the most recent. Correct order would also be important when readers are expected to follow steps in a particular sequence, such as directions, how-to articles, and recipes.

Of all days for it to happen, my alarm clock didn't go off this morning. As soon as I opened my eyes and saw sunlight, I knew it would be a race to make it to the bus on time. The first thing I did was jump in the shower, wash my hair quickly, then jump right back out. Next was the dash to the closet. Shirt on, jeans zipped, shoes tied, and down the stairs. By the time I reached the kitchen, Mom had my peanut butter toast wrapped in a napkin and ready to go. I ran out the door, and before it even slammed behind me, the bus pulled up to the curb. Yes! I made it!

The transition words in the paragraph help readers know exactly when each action happened. On the lines below, list the events of the paragraph in the correct order.

_____

_____

_____

_____

You probably figured out that the events occurred in this order:

1. The alarm clock did not go off.
2. The speaker opened his or her eyes.
3. The speaker showered.
4. The speaker got dressed.
5. Mom wrapped up the toast in a napkin.
6. The speaker ran out the door.
7. The bus reached the curb.
8. The door slammed.

Another sequence writers may use to organize their writing is by **order of importance**. They might choose to tell the most important idea first, followed by ideas that decrease in importance. This is a good way to catch the readers' attention by beginning with the strongest point.

> Did you know that newspaper articles are often organized in order of importance? The most important information is usually listed at the beginning of the article, followed by less important information. The reason for this is that some readers do not take the time to finish the entire article. This organizational structure ensures that those readers do not miss the most important ideas.

Conversely, writers may begin by telling the least important idea, then list ideas or events in increasing order of importance, telling the most important idea last. This leaves readers with the strongest point freshest in their minds.

The Tri-City Tigers won the district soccer championship on Friday night! The final score was 5–2 in what was a very exciting game. Jackson Greenwood scored three goals for the

Tigers. Coach Abbott placed each team member in the game at some point. It was truly a victory for all!

The fact that the Tigers won the championship is the most important idea in the paragraph, so it is stated at the beginning. The final score is the second most important piece of information, so it is stated next. Jackson scoring two goals is next in importance, followed by the fact that all the players were involved in the win.

If the writer had chosen to tell the events in order of least to most importance, the paragraph could have been organized as shown here:

All members of the Tigers soccer team got a chance to play in Friday night's game, thanks to Coach Abbott. Jackson Greenwood scored three goals for his team. The final score of the exciting game was 5–2, giving the Tri-City Tigers the title of district champs!

Cause and Effect

As you know, a *cause* is something that makes something else happen. An *effect* is what happens as a result of the cause. For example, if you go to bed late, you'll be tired in the morning. Going to bed late is the cause; being tired in the morning is the effect.

At times, there is a cause and effect relationship between events in a passage. Authors may choose to use a **cause and effect** organizational structure, which focuses on such relationships, in the text. Recognizing a cause and effect structure lets readers know that they should be on the lookout for things that are the result of a given event. It also helps readers understand how events in the passage are related to one another.

Darnell studied every night for a week, so he got an A on his science exam.

How are these events related? Did one thing happen as a result of the other? Yes. Studying every night *caused* Darnell to do well on the test. He got an A *because* he studied so much. So, studying every night is the cause; getting an A on the exam is the effect.

Often, writers will include clues—words that signal a cause and effect relationship. Examples of such words are listed here:

- because
- then
- as a result
- so
- due to
- therefore
- since
- when
- if

Ella fixed French toast for breakfast since it was her parents' anniversary.

In this sentence, the clue word *since* indicates a cause and effect relationship. In the sentence about Darnell, the clue word *so* signaled the relationship.

Notice that either the cause or the effect can come first. In Darnell's example, the cause is first; in Ella's example, the effect is first. To determine which event is the cause and which is the effect, ask yourself which event is the result of the other.

Now it's your turn. Read the following paragraph. As you read, look for cause and effect relationships.

During the past quarter, our company had a record number of sales. As a result, we also saw a significant increase in profits. So, over the next few weeks, we will be able to hire additional employees in several departments to take on some of the workload. Current employees will also receive a bonus in their next paycheck as recognition for their contribution to our company's continued success.

What signal words were included to offer clues about the cause and effect relationships?

_____

As a result and *so* were used to highlight two of the relationships. However, you probably noticed that more than two relationships existed. Signal words are not always included. Be sure to read carefully and think about how the events in a passage are related, whether signal words are included or not.

Did you recognize all the cause and effect relationships in this paragraph?

The *cause*:

- a record number of sales for the company

The *effects*:

- a significant increase in profits
- the hiring of additional employees
- a bonus for current employees

Notice that a single cause had more than one effect. The opposite may also be true; a single effect can be the result of several causes.

Compare and Contrast

When we *compare*, we tell how two or more things are alike. When we *contrast*, we tell how two or more things are different. Writers often use a **compare and contrast** organizational structure to explain ideas, events, people, or objects by describing the ways in which they are alike or different. When readers recognize a compare and contrast structure in a passage, they look for similarities and differences between the topics.

Signal words often alert readers that things are alike or different in some way.

Similarities	Differences
■ also	■ but
■ like	■ yet
■ both	■ only
■ alike	■ differ
■ similar	■ unlike
■ likewise	■ rather
■ the same as	■ although
■ at the same time	■ however
■ in the same ways	■ different
■ in the same manner	■ less than
	■ better than
	■ nevertheless
	■ on the contrary

By comparing and contrasting, writers are able to help readers gain a clear understanding of their ideas.

Chinchillas are small animals that are slightly larger and rounder than squirrels. Both animals are generally gray or brown in color. The chinchilla often has a bushy tail similar to that of a squirrel, although its ears are more round, like those of a mouse.

The comparisons and contrasts in this paragraph help describe chinchillas in a way that gives readers a clear picture of these animals.

What signal words did you notice in the paragraph?

_____

You probably recognized that *slightly larger and rounder than*, *both*, *similar to*, *although*, and *like* pointed out similarities and differences between the various animals.

There are two types of compare and contrast organizational structures that writers often use. **Whole-to-whole comparisons** completely discuss the first idea, event, or item and then completely discuss the second. For example, if a writer were comparing and contrasting sports, he might completely explain baseball, then completely describe soccer.

Part-to-part comparisons discuss one particular aspect of each topic, then discuss another aspect, and so on. For example, a writer might discuss the number of players on baseball and soccer teams, then discuss how points are scored in each game, and then discuss the rules for each game.

Problem and Solution

If an author elects to use a **problem and solution** organizational structure, a problem is discussed and is then followed by one or more solutions to the problem. When readers recognize this structure, they know that as they read, they should look for possible ways to solve the problem.

Construction of the new auditorium at Forest Lakes Middle School is scheduled to begin in early April, which will interfere with the school's planned Spring Fling Carnival because construction equipment will occupy a large portion of the area normally used for the event. The carnival committee believes it may be possible to reschedule the carnival for the middle of March, prior to groundbreaking on the construction project. If that is not possible, the committee may consider moving some of the activities indoors, reducing the need for some of the outside space. It has also been suggested that an alternative location, such as the nearby Little League fields, be used for the event.

What problem is the topic of the paragraph?

_____

The problem is that there may not be enough space for the school carnival after construction has begun on the new auditorium.

What solutions are suggested?

_____

_____

_____

Three possible solutions are suggested: change the date of the carnival, move some of the activities indoors, and change the location of the event. In a longer passage, the problem might be introduced in one paragraph, with each solution being discussed in separate paragraphs.

Classification

Sometimes, writers divide information about a topic into smaller sections that each focus on a group of related ideas or objects. This organizational structure is called **classification**, and writers use it to arrange ideas and information into categories. Each category contains ideas that are similar in some way.

Readers can recognize that classification has been used if the passage talks about different kinds of things, such as different kinds of animals, different types of transportation, or different kinds of sports. This structure lets readers know that ideas in each section will be somehow related.

TIP

Sometimes, section headers will be a clue that the organizational structure is classification. For example, a passage about animals might include section headers such as *mammals*, *reptiles*, *birds*, *amphibians*, and *fish*.

Dear Friends,

We are pleased that you are planning a trip to our resort! We are sure that you will find the vacation package that best suits your needs. Vacation packages are grouped into three categories. You may make your selection at any time prior to your arrival.

Room-only packages include your hotel room and access to the resort's three swimming pools. You may also enjoy the exercise equipment in the gym at no additional charge.

Bed-and-breakfast packages include your hotel room as well as access to the pools and gym. Breakfast in any of the resort restaurants is also included, or you may choose to order your morning meal from our room service menu.

All-inclusive packages include not only the offerings of the previous packages, but also lunch and dinner from any of the resort restaurants or room service. Each guest may enjoy three meals and two snacks each day, all included in the price of the package.

We look forward to your stay and would be happy to answer any questions. Feel free to contact us at any time for further assistance.

Sincerely,

Resort Manager

This passage uses a classification organizational structure. What is the topic of the letter?

_____

What were the categories that the information was divided into?

_____

You probably recognized that the topic is the resort's vacation packages, and the categories the packages are divided into include *room-only*, *bed-and-breakfast*, and *all-inclusive* options.

Description

When an author chooses a **description** as the organizational pattern for a passage, he or she will introduce the topic, then discuss attributes and characteristics that describe it. When readers recognize this organizational pattern, they know to anticipate finding details, attributes, examples, and characteristics that will help explain the topic.

> *For more than 200 years, the White House has been home to the presidents of the United States and is undoubtedly the most recognizable residence in the country. A view of the front reveals a two-story structure with rows of rectangular windows, columns in the center of the building, and our nation's flag flying over the roof. Indoors, the home boasts six levels, including 132 rooms, 35 restrooms, and 28 fireplaces. For recreation, the First Family can enjoy a tennis court, jogging track, swimming pool, movie theater, and bowling alley, all without leaving the comfort of their very famous home.*

In this paragraph, the topic was introduced in the first sentence. The following sentences describe what the White House looks like from the outside, the structure of the inside, and the recreational features of the building. Each of these details helps give the reader a clear picture of the topic.

Inferences

Sometimes, writers come right out and directly state everything they want readers to know. Other times, a writer will make suggestions about a person, place, event, or object without directly stating the information. To gain a complete understanding of the passage, readers have to read between the lines and construct meaning about the information in the text. An educated guess based on clues in the passage is an **inference**.

To make an inference, consider

- clues and hints in the passage.
- your own prior knowledge.
- observations.
- details in the text.

Making inferences is similar to drawing conclusions.

When readers make inferences, they recognize ideas that are implied.

> *Elliot showed his little brother around the school, making sure he would be able to find his locker, classrooms, and most importantly, the cafeteria.*

What information is implied in this sentence? Based on what we read, what we already know, and what makes logical sense, we can infer several things:

> *Elliot's brother is unfamiliar with the school.*
>
> *Elliot's brother is a new student.*
>
> *Elliot already attends the school.*

These ideas were not directly stated. However, if we read between the lines, we can infer that they are most likely true.

TIP

Keep in mind that inferences are not random, wild guesses. They are based on information that you have been given as well as what you already know. Inferences are *logical* conclusions.

BOOST

Did you know that about 71% of people who take the GED® test have already reached at least grade 10? In fact, one in ten college freshmen earn their GED® test credential before arriving on campus!

At times, you will have to make inferences to determine different things about a passage, such as the main idea, purpose, tone, or point of view. You will have to pay attention to the details in the text to infer this information.

To gain a complete understanding of the text, readers may have to make **multiple inferences** by considering information from various parts of the text. This requires readers to think about their purpose for reading, evaluate the importance of ideas and details, then decide what information is key to understanding what the writer wants them to know about the passage.

For example, suppose you are reading a passage describing how to make a birdhouse. Based on the purpose of the text, you know that it is essential to find the steps necessary to complete the project. If you came across information describing why birds migrate in the winter, you could categorize these facts as being unimportant to the purpose of this particular passage. If you came across information telling you to first measure a piece of wood, you would know that this detail is essential in understanding the text.

Readers also might need to consider information from various parts of the text to make strong predictions. Think of each piece of information as a piece to a jigsaw puzzle. The more pieces you have, the better equipped you will be to predict what the finished puzzle will look like. Consider each piece of information as it relates to what you have already read. Then, use this combination of ideas to infer what is likely to happen next in the text.

Considering all the pieces of information in a passage can also be helpful in making inferences about the author. What authors say, as well as what they do not say, can help readers recognize their attitudes, beliefs, biases, prejudgments, and opinions about the topic.

Four bands performed at the school's Winter Wonderland Formal. The ultimate hip-hop band Sticks and Stones rocked the crowd first. Nearly every student was on the dance floor the entire time they played. The drumbeat of their signature hit "Keep Movin'" undoubtedly stuck in everyone's heads for days. After their set, the bands Golden Child, Harvey's Dudes, and Stumped also played.

Which inference could be made about the passage?

a. The author is the drummer in a hip-hop band.

b. Sticks and Stones was the audience's favorite musical group.

c. Nearly all the students attended the Winter Wonderland Formal.

d. The author believes Sticks and Stones was the best band at the dance.

The author's opinion about the bands is obvious. You could probably read between the lines and infer that the author really enjoyed the performance by Sticks and Stones. Think about all the words and details he or she included when talking about the band. Then, think about what he or she *didn't* say; the author only quickly mentioned the other bands, without giving any information about the bands or their performances. Choice **d** is the best answer.

Connotative Meaning

Authors use words in certain ways to help them describe characters or events and create a particular mood or tone.

The **connotative** meaning of a word is its suggested meaning, as opposed to the literal or exact definition. For instance, if you are angry with someone and refer to him or her as a "rat," you are suggesting that the person is mean or disgraceful, not an actual rodent.

Writers use **figurative** language to create images with words and express ideas in creative ways. Figurative devices include metaphors and similes.

Making Comparisons between Passages

A number of questions on the GED® Reasoning through Language Arts test will involve comparing two passages that contain related ideas. For example, the text of Lincoln's Emancipation Proclamation might be followed by an excerpt from a speech by Confederate President Jefferson Davis regarding slavery. In this case, the two passages provide opposing viewpoints of a single issue. In other cases, the passages might deal with the same idea or theme but offer differences in style, tone, or even purpose. In any case, the most important questions to ask when comparing two passages are:

In what ways are the two passages similar?

In what ways are the two passages different?

When two passages are paired together, you will often encounter a question about the main idea or theme that is common to both passages. If you can identify the ways in which the two passages are similar, this will help you determine whether they share a single idea or theme. When two passages are placed together on the GED® test, you can be sure that they are related in some way—it's up to you to figure out exactly how they are related.

When comparing passages, remember to look at both the content and the form of the passages. Two passages with dramatically different forms, such as an e-mail and a news article, might actually contain the same main idea but differ in structure, style, tone, or intended audience. By contrast, two passages that are both excerpted from persuasive essays might share the same form, style, and intended audience, but offer opposing arguments and evidence on a topic.

For the extended response item on the GED® Reasoning through Language Arts test, you may be required to write a short essay comparing two passages that contain related ideas. When writing, it is especially important to mention the specific details in each passage that support the main idea. You may even want to quote small amounts of text from each passage to support your analysis. Be careful to avoid drawing comparisons between elements that are not important to the main idea or theme. For example, two passages may both be written in an informal style, but unless that style is important to understanding the author's purpose, it should not be brought up as a key point in your response.

Quiz

Now that you've had a chance to review some of the skills needed to comprehend nonfiction, read each of the following passages, then choose the one best answer to each question.

Directions: Choose the *one best answer* to each question.

Questions 11 through 15 refer to the following passage.

What Is Included in a Healthy Diet?

Most people recognize the importance of a healthy lifestyle. Part of this includes enjoying a balanced diet. Each day, people need to eat foods from each food group to
(5) be sure they are getting the benefits offered by each type of food.

It is recommended that people enjoy between 6 and 11 servings of food from the grain food group. These foods include
(10) bread, rice, pasta, and cereal. Those made from whole grains offer the most health benefits. Enjoying whole grain toast for breakfast, a sandwich on a wheat pita for lunch, and whole wheat pasta for dinner are
(15) ways to ensure that plenty of servings of these foods have found their way onto our plates.

We all know the benefits of eating plenty of fruits and vegetables, but do we
(20) really get enough every day? It is recommended that people enjoy three to five servings of vegetables and three to four servings of fruit every day. That may sound like a lot, but whipping up a fruit smoothie
(25) at the beginning of the day, having veggies and dip as a snack, and adding fresh berries to a yogurt parfait for dessert are ways to think outside of the box—a box of fruit snacks, that is.

(30) Getting enough protein doesn't have to mean eating two to three burgers each day. Did you know that beans, eggs, and nuts are considered protein as well? Sure, a burger, fish, chicken, or steak would be great at
(35) lunch or dinner, but including eggs at breakfast or a handful of almonds in the afternoon can cut down on the amount of meat in your diet, while still guaranteeing the protein your body needs.

(40) We all know the importance of dairy for strong teeth and bones. But don't feel that you have to drown yourself in skim milk to get your two to three servings a day. Remember that fruit and yogurt parfait?
(45) That's a yummy way to get a full serving of dairy. And how about the grilled cheese sandwich on wheat for lunch? Cheese is another way to get some dairy into your diet.

Eating a balance of food from each
(50) group is essential to staying healthy and feeling your best. Remember to mix it up. Try new things and be sure to get the servings you need each day.

11. Which statement from the passage is an opinion?
   a. Most people recognize the importance of a healthy lifestyle.
   b. Those made from whole grains offer the most health benefits.
   c. That's a yummy way to get a full serving of dairy.
   d. Cheese is another way to get some dairy into your diet.

12. Which organizational structure is used in the passage?
   a. sequence
   b. classification
   c. cause and effect
   d. problem and solution

13. What is the main idea of the passage?

   a. We need to include plenty of dairy in our diets.

   b. Most foods can be grouped into five basic types.

   c. A balanced diet is an important part of a healthy lifestyle.

   d. There are creative ways to be sure we eat the right nutrients.

14. Which detail supports the main idea of the third paragraph?

   a. A fruit smoothie can help us get enough servings of fruit.

   b. A box of fruit snacks offers an entire serving of fresh fruit.

   c. We all know the benefits of eating plenty of fruits and vegetables.

   d. We need between six and nine servings of vegetables and fruits daily.

15. Which choice best summarizes the passage?

   a. A balanced diet includes plenty of grains, fruits and vegetables, dairy, and protein to help us stay healthy. These foods can be incorporated into our diets in creative ways throughout the day.

   b. Protein and dairy are important foods that come from many sources. Meats, nuts, and eggs offer our bodies the protein we need, while milk, yogurt, and cheese give us dairy for strong bones and teeth.

   c. Eating the right kinds of foods is important to staying healthy. Exercise, plenty of sleep, and eating a balanced diet ensure that we have enough energy every day as well as the nutrients we need to build muscles.

   d. Each day, we need 6 to 11 servings of grains, especially whole grains. We can get these nutrients from breads, cereals, rice, and pasta. Including these foods at every meal will ensure that we get enough of them.

Questions 16 through 20 refer to the following passage.

What Types of Jobs Are Available?

Currently, Fairhaven Fine Furnishings has a job opening available in the warehouse. Daily job requirements include unloading trucks of furniture and accessories delivered
(5) by the manufacturers, organizing these items in the warehouse, locating and preparing items to fill customer orders, and loading these items onto our company's trucks for delivery. This job requires
(10) employees to be able to lift at least 100 pounds, operate a forklift, and demonstrate exceptional record-keeping abilities, as maintaining accurate inventory is of utmost importance. This job offers many
(15) opportunities for future advancement within the company. Many of Fairhaven's current management team members began their careers working in the warehouse. This is a full-time position, paying $17.75 per hour.
(20) Health insurance, including vision and dental benefits, will be available after 90 days, assuming the employee receives an acceptable performance evaluation at that point.

(25)   Fairhaven Fine Furnishings also has openings available for a data entry clerk and a receptionist. Both positions require exceptional computer skills, and applicants will need to demonstrate adequate abilities
(30) prior to being hired. The receptionist must also have excellent communication and customer service skills, as he or she will be responsible for answering phone calls and greeting customers as they enter our
(35) showroom. Likewise, the data entry clerk must demonstrate strong communication skills, as this position requires interacting with company representatives from our various departments as well as

(40) representatives from each of the companies that provide our products. However, the data entry clerk will not be communicating directly with Fairhaven's customers. The receptionist position is full-time and pays

(45) $10.50 per hour. The data entry position is 20 hours per week and pays $12.35 per hour. Both positions include health insurance benefits following an acceptable 90-day performance evaluation. The company will

(50) also contribute toward vision and dental benefits, making a greater contribution toward these benefits for full-time employees than those working part-time.

Applicants for any of these positions

(55) must first submit a completed resume, including work and salary history, and a list of three professional references. After these documents have been reviewed by a department manager, qualified applicants

(60) will be contacted for a telephone interview. The final step in the hiring process will be a personal interview with our hiring team.

16. Based on the passage, which of these statements is a fact?
   a. Fairhaven Fine Furnishings would be a great place to work.
   b. The receptionist position is better suited for a woman than a man.
   c. All the available positions offer some health insurance benefits.
   d. The phone interview is the most important step in the hiring process.

17. What is the organizational structure of the first paragraph?
   a. sequential
   b. description
   c. cause and effect
   d. problem and solution

18. Which is true about the second and third paragraphs?
   a. The second paragraph uses classification to group similar ideas.
   b. The steps in the application process are listed in a random order.
   c. Signal words indicate a cause and effect structure in the paragraphs.
   d. Two job positions are compared and contrasted in the second paragraph.

19. Which inference can best be made, based on the information in the passage?
   a. The data entry clerk is the most important position.
   b. Warehouse employees are valued very highly within the company.
   c. The company is likely to hire the first applicant for each of the jobs.
   d. The receptionist position will be the most difficult for the company to fill.

20. What is the main idea of the third paragraph?
   a. Some applicants will be invited to interview in person.
   b. There are several steps involved in the hiring process.
   c. Department managers will contact qualified applicants by phone.
   d. Only the most qualified applicants will meet with the hiring team.

Use the following passage to answer questions 21–23.

Imani P. Jones
421 Carroll Street
Franklin, NY 10821
(512) 555-4390

May 22, 2014

Shanice Childress-Harris
Owner
Luxalot Florists, Inc.
80 River Street
Franklin, NY 10821

Dear Ms. Childress-Harris:

I am writing to register a complaint about the floral displays that were prepared and delivered by Luxalot Florists for my son DeAndre Jones's wedding on May 18. After consulting with your assistant, Maurice Thomas, on February 13 and again on March 1, we thought that our desires were understood and that Maurice and the rest of the team had a clear plan for the wedding's floral designs.

We asked for Luxalot to deliver two standing bouquets for the entrance to the chapel, one larger standing bouquet for the altar, and 18 centerpieces for the tables at the reception. Maurice asked us what colors we preferred, and we told him that the wedding's color scheme was white, yellow, and fuchsia. He suggested that a beautiful combination in these colors would be First Snow tulips, Sunray roses, and Hot Pink ranunculus. He also wanted to add a few stems of filler flowers, such as baby's breath and Queen Anne's lace, which I thought was a good idea to reduce the overall cost.

I was shocked to see a completely different combination of flowers than the one we had discussed on the day of the wedding. The bouquets consisted primarily of baby's breath and Queen Anne's lace, and the other flowers were carnations, lilies, and irises. At the reception, we saw that the centerpieces had the same combination and also learned that only 14 centerpieces had been sent, so four tables were not adorned with flowers.

I am writing to you to request a refund of half ($2,700) of the amount I paid for the flower displays ($5,400). I would ask for a full refund, but the flowers that did arrive were very fresh and in the correct color scheme.

I await your prompt response to this matter.
Sincerely,

Imani P. Jones

21. In the first sentence of the letter, the word *register* means
   a. a machine that calculates and holds money at a store.
   b. registrar.
   c. formally submit.
   d. withdraw.

22. Based on the information in the second paragraph of the letter, we can infer that the definition of *fuchsia* is
   a. the color white.
   b. bright pink.
   c. a type of flower.
   d. none of the above.

23. Based on the letter, which is NOT a reason why the writer wants a refund?
   a. The flower displays contained too many inexpensive flowers.
   b. The flower displays contained the incorrect types of flowers.
   c. Luxalot did not send the correct number of flower displays.
   d. The flower displays were in the wrong colors.

Use the following passage to answer questions 24–27.

Is Your Drowsiness Dangerous?

Despite common misconceptions, anyone—regardless of gender, weight, or fitness level—can develop obstructive sleep apnea, a life-threatening condition characterized by episodes of complete or partial airway obstruction during sleep. As many as 12 million to 18 million American adults have untreated sleep apnea, and the experts at the American Academy of Sleep Medicine are recommending the following steps for diagnosis and treatment to significantly improve overall health, mood, and productivity.

First, be aware of the risk factors. Your risk of sleep apnea increases between middle and older age and with the amount of excess body weight you carry. In general, men have a greater likelihood of developing the disease. However, menopause is a risk factor for sleep apnea in women. Your risk is also higher if family members have been diagnosed with sleep apnea. Smoking is another significant risk factor, as well as being a detriment to your overall health.

In addition to these more commonly known risk factors, many people don't realize that they're in greater danger of developing sleep apnea if they already suffer from other common diseases. "Seven in ten type 2 diabetics and 30% to 40% of adults with hypertension also have obstructive sleep apnea," says Dr. M. Safwan Badr, president of the American Academy of Sleep Medicine. "As a result, patients with these conditions should pay close attention for potential symptoms and then seek necessary treatment."

(continues)

It's important to watch for symptoms. While the symptom most commonly associated with sleep apnea is snoring, not everyone who snores has the disease. However, when snoring is paired with choking, gasping, or pauses in breathing during sleep, it's a more likely indicator of sleep apnea. Sleep apnea symptoms also may appear during the daytime and include morning headaches, excessive sleepiness, trouble concentrating, memory or learning problems, and general moodiness, irritability, or depression.

"Sleep apnea can make you wake up in the morning feeling tired, even though you believe you've had a full night of sleep," says Badr. "During the day, you may feel incredibly fatigued because you're actually waking up numerous times throughout the night and your body isn't getting the rest it needs."

If you suspect that you have the risk factors and symptoms of sleep apnea, it's important that you are evaluated by a board-certified sleep-medicine physician right away. Left untreated, sleep apnea may have a serious impact on your overall health, even increasing your risk of death. The sleep-medicine physician will have the training and expertise to diagnose your condition. He or she will conduct a thorough physical examination and sleep evaluation, asking questions like whether symptoms began when you gained weight or stopped exercising, and whether your partner or roommate has complained that you snore or make choking noises in your sleep. If the sleep physician determines that you are at risk for obstructive sleep apnea, then you will be scheduled for a sleep study.

Once diagnosed, the recommended treatment for sleep apnea is continuous positive airway pressure (CPAP) therapy, which provides a steady stream of air through a mask to gently keep the patient's airway open throughout the night, making it easier to breathe. In patients with moderate or severe sleep apnea, it's estimated that CPAP therapy reduces the ten-year risk of heart attack by 49% and stroke by 31%.

"Treating sleep apnea provides all the benefits of improved sleep, including increased alertness during the day and improved memory and cognitive function," says Badr. "Clinical evidence also shows that sleep apnea treatment lowers blood pressure, thus decreasing your risk of cardiovascular disease, and improves nighttime glucose levels and insulin sensitivity among type 2 diabetics."

—*Adapted from an article published on Brandpoint.com.*

24. According to the passage, what are some of the symptoms of sleep apnea?
   a. heartburn, nausea, and upper abdominal pain when awake
   b. migraines, excessive eating, and chest pain at night
   c. choking, gasping, and pauses while breathing during sleep
   d. type 2 diabetes, menopause, and hypertension

25. Which statement best expresses the main idea of the passage?
   a. Sleep apnea primarily affects people with hypertension and diabetes.
   b. Everyone should be aware of the risk factors and signs of sleep apnea and get tested if there is reason for concern.
   c. As many as 12 million to 18 million American adults are living with sleep apnea but have not been treated.
   d. Sleep apnea is a condition that can be successfully treated with continuous positive airway pressure (CPAP) therapy.

26. How does the author present and develop the key ideas of this passage?
   a. by listing facts and advice related to sleep apnea
   b. by presenting a chronological order of the development of sleep apnea as a person ages
   c. by describing the differences between people who have sleep apnea and those who don't
   d. by giving examples of patients who have been treated successfully for sleep apnea

27. Based on the passage, we can infer that the author has which of the following viewpoints?
   a. To accurately identify and treat sleep apnea, it's better to see a board-certified sleep-medicine doctor than to see another type of doctor.
   b. The medical profession overdiagnoses sleep apnea, causing increased anxiety and irritability in patients.
   c. It's a shame that sleep apnea is so difficult to diagnose, leaving many Americans untreated.
   d. Screening for sleep apnea must be part of a person's annual checkup with one's primary-care physician.

Answers and Explanations

Chapter Practice

1. c. Madeline recognizes the family instinct to own a farm, but she calls it "fatal" and mentions other family members' bad experiences.

2. d. There are several lines in the passage that support this choice. The narrator says that she was *fitted by temperament . . . for farm and country living* and that her experiences on farms as a child *got in the blood.* Her father's sister made a similar observation: *You have in you that fatal drop of Pearce blood, clamoring for change and adventure, and above all, for a farm.* The narrator adds that *I see no reason for denying so fundamental an urge, ruin or no. It is more important to live the life one wishes to live, and to go down with it if necessary, quite contentedly, than to live more profitably but less happily.*

3. b. The second paragraph starts off with a reference to the Florida orange grove that the narrator purchases. She doesn't mention it by name at first, but she does in the last sentence. You can also assume that *the Creek* is short for *Cross Creek*, which is the name of the book.

4. b. In the sentence before this line, the author says that she was troubled by the hard work at the Creek and the difficulty of making a living on the grove. Relief came when someone named Martha *drew aside a curtain* and welcomed her into the group of people who had a history with the farm. This implies that by pulling back the curtain, Martha was clearing up some of the writer's confusion or angst by sharing information about the grove in the past.

Reading Comprehension Review

5. b. The first paragraph states that *arsenic is present in the environment as a naturally occurring substance.* We can infer that it is hazardous—or hurtful—to people's health because it is referred to as a *contaminant.* Another important reason is because officials are trying to keep apple juice safe by making sure that arsenic levels are very low; that implies that arsenic at higher levels makes food unsafe.

6. c. The term *parts per billion (ppb)* is mentioned in the third paragraph in the same context—discussing the amount of arsenic found in drinks.

7. c. There are several clues throughout the letter that Faye is Frances's husband, but the biggest one appears in the fourth paragraph: *When I told Faye about it, he looked vexed and said I must never laugh at an enlisted man—that it was not dignified in the wife of an officer to do so. And then I told him that an officer should teach an enlisted man not to snicker at his wife, and not to call her "Sorr," which was disrespectful. I wanted to say more, but Faye suddenly left the room.* We can infer that this was a private disagreement between a husband and a wife. Faye thought that Frances had not acted like a dignified wife, but Frances said that Faye should have stood up for her: *I told him that an officer should teach an enlisted man not to snicker at his wife, and not to call her "Sorr," which was disrespectful.* Faye may have taken this comment personally, because he suddenly left the room.

8. d. She seems interested in the ins and outs of army protocol—she describes details and tries to figure out the rules of rank—but she also questions why things are as they are.

9. c. The writer hints at this point when he notes that *all this—the mysterious, far-reaching hair-line trail, the absence of sun from the sky, the tremendous cold, and the strangeness and weirdness of it all—made no impression on the man.* The ideas presented in the last paragraph also support this theme.

10. b. Although the writer criticizes the man for not thinking deeply about his circumstances and about life in general, the man does seem knowledgeable. He knows about the path of the sun, he knows the exact temperature, and it's suggested that he knows the exact path of the trail he is on. *Matter-of-fact* is also a good description for the man. There are many reasons to think that the man focuses on the world around him in a straightforward way. For example, the writer notes that *He was quick and alert in the things of life, but only in the things, and not in the significances.* The last three sentences of the passage offer further evidence that he is matter-of-fact.

11. c. Not everyone would agree that a certain food is *yummy*, which makes this statement an opinion. The other answer choices all include statements that could be proven. Most people do know that a healthy lifestyle is important, and the information about whole grains and cheese could be verified in a health or science textbook.

12. b. The types of foods needed to stay healthy are classified by similarities. Each of the food groups discussed is a category. Information about the types of food in each category, as well as the number of servings needed daily, is included in that section of the text.

13. c. The importance of a balanced diet is the main point that the author wants readers to understand. Including plenty of dairy is a detail that supports the main idea. While it is true that most foods can be grouped into five basic types, this is not the main point of the passage.

14. a. Choice **d** states the main idea of the third paragraph, and choice **a**, the statement that fruit smoothies are one way to get enough servings of fruit, supports this idea. Fruit snacks are mentioned in the passage, but nothing is said about them actually offering a serving of fruit. Choice **c** is also a statement from the passage; however, it does not support the main idea.

15. a. Choice **a** restates the main idea and the most important details from the passage. Choice **b** summarizes the third and fourth paragraphs, while choice **d** summarizes the second paragraph. The information in choice **c** is true; however, it includes information that was not mentioned in the paragraph.

16. c. By reading the job descriptions, we can prove that each position offers insurance benefits. Because the statement can be verified, it is a fact. Not everyone would agree with the other three answer choices, so they are opinions.

17. b. The topic of this paragraph is the warehouse employee position. This topic is introduced in the beginning of the paragraph, then the remainder of the sentences describe the position. The requirements, hours, salary, and benefits are all explained. The order of the information is not important, there is not a problem to discuss, and no events result in the occurrence of other events.

18. d. The words *both* and *likewise* indicate ways in which the two jobs are similar. *However, on the other hand,* and *greater* point out differences between the two positions. The third paragraph uses a sequential organizational structure, listing the steps in the order in which they will occur. *First, after,* and *final* are clues to the structure used in this paragraph.

19. b. Several clues help you read between the lines in this passage. Notice that the warehouse employee receives a much higher salary and more benefits than the others. Also, the passage states that the warehouse job "offers many opportunities for future advancement" and that "many of Fairhaven's current management team members began their careers working in the warehouse." Such advancement is not mentioned for either of the other available positions. These hints indicate that warehouse employees are valued highly within the company.

20. b. The main idea of this paragraph is implied rather than directly stated. Readers are able to infer this information by reading the entire paragraph. Although it is not the main idea, readers can also infer the idea that only the most qualified applicants will meet with the hiring team in person because the other steps seem to narrow down the field to only those best suited for the job. Choices **a**, **c**, and **d** are supporting details.

21. c. The letter writer is indeed submitting her complaint to the owner of Luxalot and writing it in a formal way. The word *register* has many meanings. One of them is a machine that calculates and holds money at a store (*cash register*), but that doesn't make sense in this sentence. We are looking for a different meaning of the word *register*. Also note that in the sentence, *register* is used as a verb, whereas a machine that calculates and holds money at a store is a noun.
Registrar means an official record keeper (for instance, the person at a school or college who keeps records and helps to sign up students for classes). Finally, the letter writer is presenting her complaint to the owner of Luxalot and wants the owner to take action. She is not withdrawing, or removing, her complaint.

22. b. The word is used in the statement that *the wedding's color scheme was white, yellow, and fuchsia.* Then, in the next sentence, the writer mentions the types of flowers that would fit that combination of colors: *First Snow tulips, Sunray roses, and Hot Pink ranunculus.* We can deduce that First Snow tulips are white flowers (because snow is white), that Sunray roses are yellow flowers (because the sun is yellow), and that Hot Pink ranunculus are fuchsia-colored flowers. *Fuchsia* probably means hot—or bright—pink.

23. d. This is not a reason why the writer is dissatisfied. At the end of the letter, she explains, *I would ask for a full refund, but the flowers that did arrive were . . . in the correct color scheme.* Choice **a** is a reason why the writer is dissatisfied. She mentions that the original plan was to use *a few stems of filler flowers, such as baby's breath and Queen Anne's lace, which I thought was a good idea to reduce the overall cost.* We can assume that baby's breath and Queen Anne's lace are inexpensive flowers because Mrs. Jones calls them *filler flowers* and because if they are used, the cost goes down. Then, on the day of the wedding, *The bouquets consisted primarily of baby's breath and Queen Anne's lace*—not *a few stems,* as had been discussed. This all adds up to mean that the displays contained too many inexpensive flowers. Choice **b** is an incorrect choice because the writer says that the plan was to use mainly tulips, roses, and ranunculus. Instead, the company delivered mainly *baby's breath and Queen Anne's lace, and the other flowers were carnations, lilies, and irises.* Choice **c** is an incorrect choice because she says that she ordered 18 center-pieces, but only 14 were delivered.

24. c. All three of these symptoms are listed in the article as possible signs that a person suffers from sleep apnea. Migraines are a type of headache, and the article does mention that headaches could be a symptom, but it specifies *morning* headaches. Also, the article does not mention excessive eating or chest pains as signs of sleep apnea. (Sleep apnea may cause heart attacks—which can cause a person to feel chest pain—but that does not mean that chest pain is a sign of sleep apnea.) Choice **d** is incorrect because each of these is mentioned as a *risk factor* for developing sleep apnea—people who have type 2 diabetes or hypertension or who are going through menopause may be more likely to develop sleep apnea, but this doesn't mean that these conditions are *symptoms* of having sleep apnea. (If you don't quite understand this point, consider this everyday example: Standing outside in the freezing rain would be a *risk factor* for getting a cold. The *symptoms* of having indeed come down with a cold would be coughing, sneezing, and a runny nose.)

25. b. The writer starts off by saying that *anyone—regardless of gender, weight, or fitness level—can develop obstructive sleep apnea*, which suggests that everyone should be knowledgeable about the condition. At different points in the article, the author also states: *First, be aware of the risk factors*; *It's important to watch for symptoms*; and *If you suspect that you have the risk factors and symptoms of sleep apnea, it's important that you are evaluated by a board-certified sleep-medicine physician right away*. Choice **a** is incorrect because although, according to the article, a large portion of people who have hypertension and type 2 diabetes also have sleep apnea, that does not mean that sleep apnea primarily affects people with those conditions. In fact, the first paragraph of the article stresses that *anyone* can develop sleep apnea. Choices **c** and **d** are not main ideas of the passage.

26. a. The author presents facts about the symptoms, diagnosis, and treatment of sleep apnea, and advises readers to pay attention to risk factors and symptoms and to get tested if they think they may have sleep apnea. *Chronological* means ordered by time from start to finish, as in a time line. The author does not discuss the development of sleep apnea over time. The author also does not discuss specific people who have sleep apnea.

27. a. This choice is supported by these sentences in the article: *If you suspect that you have the risk factors and symptoms of sleep apnea, it's important that you are evaluated by a board-certified sleep-medicine physician right away. . . . The sleep-medicine physician will have the training and expertise to diagnose your condition. He or she will conduct a thorough physical examination. . . .* The author emphasizes the skill of board-certified sleep-medicine doctors when it comes to sleep apnea, never mentions other types of doctors (here or elsewhere in the article), and encourages readers to visit a board-certified sleep-medicine doctor if they think they may have sleep apnea. All of this suggests that when it comes to sleep apnea, the author probably thinks that it is better to see a board-certified sleep-medicine doctor than to see another type of doctor. Choice **b** is incorrect because overdiagnosis is not mentioned or implied in the article. Instead, the author discusses sleep-medicine doctors' ability to diagnose sleep apnea accurately. Choice **c** is incorrect because the author does not say or imply that sleep apnea is difficult to diagnose. Instead, one of the big messages of the article is that many people with sleep apnea are going untreated simply because they've never asked to be screened in the first place. The author does not imply choice **d** in the article.

REVIEW

In this chapter, you learned several strategies to help you better comprehend nonfiction reading materials:

1. The main idea is the central message of a passage. Supporting details help to strengthen readers' understanding of the main idea.

2. To summarize is to restate the most important information in your own words. Be sure to think about the main idea and the most important details when creating a summary.

3. Writers include both facts and opinions to express their ideas. Facts are provable and can be verified; opinions tell someone's personal thoughts or ideas, may vary from one person to another, and cannot be verified.

4. Organizational structure refers to the way ideas are arranged in a passage. Common structures include sequence, cause and effect, compare and contrast, problem and solution, classification, and description.

5. When sequence is used to organize a passage, ideas may be listed in time order or in order of importance. Writers may choose to begin with either the most important or least important idea.

6. A cause and effect structure points out how ideas or events are related. A cause is the reason another event occurs; an effect is the result of one or more causes.

7. To compare is to show how ideas, events, or objects are similar; to contrast is to point out ways in which the topics are different. A compare and contrast structure focuses on these similarities and differences.

8. A problem and solution structure introduces a problem, then discusses one or more possible ways to solve the problem.

9. When a writer uses classification as the organizational structure, he or she groups similar ideas together in categories.

10. A description introduces a topic, then provides information and details to explain the topic to readers.

11. To make an inference means to read between the lines and determine what the writer is telling readers without directly stating that information.

12. At times, readers will need to make multiple inferences to fully understand a passage. This may require putting together bits of information located throughout the text to figure out what the writer wants readers to understand.

5 ▶ LANGUAGE AND GRAMMAR: READING SKILLS

CHAPTER SUMMARY
This chapter will help you build the foundation you need to understand the fiction and nonfiction passages found on the GED® Reasoning through Language Arts test. You will learn to identify word parts, prefixes, suffixes, context clues, multiple word meanings, the author's point of view and purpose, and theme. It will also teach you to make predictions and synthesize what you read.

Many of the questions on the GED® RLA exam are designed to test your knowledge of grammar, word usage, and language mechanics. Make sure you are prepared by carefully reviewing this chapter and answering the practice questions. Answers and explanations for all practice questions are at the end of the chapter.

Word Parts

To understand what a passage is about, you have to be able to determine the meanings of its words. Words are formed from a combination of root words, prefixes, and suffixes. **Root words** are the foundation of words.

Prefixes are added to the beginning of words to change their meanings. **Suffixes** are added to the ends of words to change their meanings.

Look at the following example:

unexpected = un + expect + ed

In the word *unexpected*, *un-* is the prefix, *expect* is the root word, and *-ed* is the suffix. These parts work together to give the word meaning. Think about the differences in the meanings of the following sentences:

We expect her to call by 1:00 today.
We expected her to call by noon yesterday.
The fact that she did not call was unexpected.

Adding the suffix *-ed* to the end of the word changes it to past tense. Adding the prefix *un-* to the beginning tells that the event was *not* expected.

Mario is an honest man.

Let's look at the underlined word, *honest*. We know that honest means "truthful" or "trustworthy." So, the sentence lets us know that Mario can be trusted.

Mario is a dishonest man.

In this sentence, the prefix *dis-* has been added to the root word *honest*. This prefix means "not," so we know that *dishonest* means "not honest." Adding the prefix has changed the meaning of the sentence. Now we know that Mario cannot be trusted.

Emily handled the package with care.
Emily was careless with the package.

The first sentence tells that Emily was gentle with the package. However, when the suffix *-less* is added to the root word *care*, the meaning changes. This suffix means "without," so *careless* means "without care."

Emily was careful with the package.

This sentence uses the same root, *care*, but adds the suffix *-ful*. This suffix means "full of," so Emily was full of care when she handled the package.

Following are lists of some common prefixes and suffixes and their meanings. Knowing the meanings of these word parts can help you figure out meanings of words and help you better understand what you read.

Prefixes

- *co-*: with
- *de-*: to take away
- *dis-*: lack of, opposite of
- *ex-*: out of, previous
- *extra-*: outside, beyond
- *il-, in-, im-, ir-*: not
- *inter-*: between, among
- *mis-*: wrongly, badly
- *non-*: without, not
- *pre-*: before
- *post-*: after
- *re-*: again
- *sub-*: lower, nearly, under
- *super-*: above, over
- *trans-*: across
- *un-*: not

Suffixes

- *-able, -ible*: able to, can be done
- *-ant*: one who
- *-en*: made of
- *-er*: comparative, one who
- *-ful*: full of
- *-ive*: likely to
- *-ize*: to make
- *-less*: without
- *-ly*: in a certain way
- *-ment*: action, process
- *-ness, -ity*: state of
- *-or*: one who
- *-ous*: full of
- *-tion*: act, process

Now, use what you know about word parts to determine the meaning of the underlined word in the following sentence. Write the meaning of the word on the line underneath.

It seemed illogical for her to drop out of the campaign.

_____

Breaking the underlined word into word parts can help determine its meaning. The word *illogical* is made up of the prefix *il-*, meaning "not," and the word *logical*. If something is logical, it makes sense. So, if it is illogical, it does not make sense.

> **TIP**
>
> Keep in mind that groups of letters are considered a prefix or suffix only if they are added to a root word. For example, *mis-* is a prefix when added to the root word *spell* to create the word *misspell*. However, these letters are not a prefix in the words *mistletoe* or *misty*.

Sometimes, thinking of a word with a similar root can help you figure out the meaning of an unfamiliar word.

The captain watched the sails underline{deflate} as he attempted to guide the boat to the dock.

Suppose you do not know the meaning of *deflate*. Ask yourself, "Do I know a word that has a similar root?" You probably already know that *inflate* means to fill something with air or to make something larger.

Dad will underline{inflate} the balloons before the party.

Using what you know about the meanings of word parts, you can figure out that *deflate* means that the air has gone out of something, or it has gotten smaller.

Let's try another example:

Brian carries his underline{portable} CD player everywhere he goes.

Portable contains the root *port* and the suffix *-able*. *Port* means "to move," so *portable* means that the CD player is "able to be moved."

The company plans to underline{export} 75% of its products overseas.

Suppose you are unsure of the meaning of *export*. Do you know a word that has a similar root? *Portable* and *export* have the same root. You know that the prefix in *export*, *ex-*, means "out of" and *port* means "to move," so *export* means "to move out." So, the company plans to move its products out and send them overseas.

The island underline{imports} most of its fruit from other countries.

If *export* means "to move out," what do you think *import* means? It means "to move in" or "to bring in."

Now you try. What words could help you determine the meaning of the underlined word in the following sentence? Write the words on the line underneath.

She tried to underline{visualize} the author's description of the animal.

_____

Vision and *visible* both have roots that are similar to that of *visualize*. *Vision* is the sense of sight. If something is *visible*, it is able to be seen. So, to *visualize* means "to see something."

Here are a few sets of words with similar roots. Knowing sets of words with similar roots can help you determine word meanings. What other words could you add to each set in the list below? What other groups of words can you think of that have similar roots?

- adjoin, conjunction, juncture
- anniversary, annual, biannual

- audible, audience, audio
- benevolent, benefit, beneficial
- chronic, chronological, synchronize
- civic, civilian, civilization
- contradict, dictate, dictionary
- describe, prescribe, transcribe
- design, signal, signature
- empathy, pathetic, sympathy
- evacuate, vacancy, vacuum
- exclaim, exclamation, proclaim
- mystify, mystery, mysterious
- pollutant, pollute, pollution
- telescope, telephone, television
- terrain, terrestrial, territory

Parts of Speech

Verbs

Verbs are the heart of a sentence. They express the action or state of being of the subject, telling us what the subject is doing, thinking, or feeling. They also tell us when that action or state of being occurs—in the past, present, or future—and they can communicate more complicated ideas, for instance whether something happens often or whether there is a possibility that something will happen in the future.

Infinitive and Simple Present Tense

An **infinitive** is the base form of the verb plus the word *to*, such as *to go*, *to dream*, and *to eat*. The infinitive form can be used in many ways in a sentence.

Here are some examples:

> *Tong promises* to return *by noon.*
> To walk *was the most logical decision.*

One of the most common mistakes in English involves the infinitive. People often say *try and* do something rather than the correct *try to* do something. For example:

Incorrect: Try and *come to work on time tomorrow.*
Correct: Try *to come to work on time tomorrow.*

Incorrect: *I'll* try and *buy the tickets at the box office rather than online.*
Correct: *I'll* try *to buy the tickets at the box office rather than online.*

This may be tested on the GED® test, so make sure you know the difference.

Simple present tense is the verb form that communicates facts or indicates that something occurs on a regular basis. For example:

> *The assistants* commute to work on the subway, *but their boss takes a limo.*
> *I* commute to work every morning on the subway.
> *She* speaks English.
> *I am* from Philadelphia.
> *Dogs* bark, and cats meow.
> *In the Caribbean, the water* is aqua blue.
> *Marissa* runs five miles every weekend.

The simple present tense of regular verbs is formed as follows, using the verb *to drive* as an example:

	SINGULAR	PLURAL
First person (I/we)	Base form (drive)	Base form (drive)
Second person (you)	Base form (drive)	Base form (drive)
Third person (he/she/they)	Base form plus -s or -es (drives)	Base form (drive)

Present Continuous Tense

Present continuous tense is the verb form that describes what is happening now, at this exact moment. It ends in *-ing* and is accompanied by one of the following helping verbs: *am*, *is*, or *are* (the present tense of the verb *to be*). For instance:

> *Adam* is driving to the fair.
> *They* are driving to the picnic.

Gerunds

Words that end in -ing don't always function as verbs. Sometimes they act as nouns and are called **gerunds**. They can also function as adjectives.

Examples:

Tracy enjoys running *on the beach.*
> Here, *running* serves as a noun—it is the thing that Tracy enjoys.

The loading *dock is outside the back door.*
> Here, *loading* serves as an adjective—it describes the dock.

Here is an example of how the same word can have three different functions:

verb:	*He is* screaming *loudly.*
gerund (noun):	*That* screaming *is driving me crazy.*
adjective:	*The* screaming *boy finally stopped.*

When correcting sentences on the GED® RLA test, do not assume that a word that ends in -ing is a verb. You will need to read closely to determine how the word functions in the sentence. Here are a few guidelines for identifying and using gerunds:

1. Gerunds are often used after a preposition.
   Keza thought that by taking *the train she would* save money and time.
   Noriel was afraid of offending *her host, but she couldn't eat dinner.*
2. Gerunds frequently follow these verbs:

admit	dislike	practice
appreciate	enjoy	put off
avoid	escape	quit
can't help	finish	recall
consider	imagine	resist
delay	keep	risk
deny	miss	suggest
discuss	postpone	tolerate

We should discuss buying *a new computer.*
I quit smoking.

Past Tense

Simple past tense is the verb form that expresses what happened at a specific moment in the past.

It rained *for three hours yesterday.*
She opened *the door and* welcomed *the guests.*

Past Participle

The **past participle** of a verb consists of its past form, accompanied by the helping verb *have, has,* or *had* (e.g., have cared, has forgiven, had thought, etc.). This is true of both regular and irregular verbs.

Past Continuous Tense

The **past continuous tense** indicates that an action happened in the past and continued for some time. It's used with the helping verb *was* or *were*.

She was walking *when the rain started.*
While they were singing, *the phone rang.*

Past Perfect Tense

Used with the helping verb *had*, the **past perfect tense** indicates that an action happened in the past before another action happened in the past. This may sound confusing, but it's a tense that you probably often use in everyday speech. Look at these examples:

Yesterday, Theresa told me that she thought Harry had played *too much golf during their honeymoon.*

Notice that the sentence places us at one point in time—when Theresa was talking and thinking—and it uses the past perfect to look back at an earlier point in time, when something may have happened during her honeymoon.

> *Jack's vacation was cut short when he broke his ankle in London, but he* had had *the time of his life in Paris.*

In this sentence, we're placed at the time when Jack's vacation was cut short, and we're looking back at the time when he enjoyed himself in Paris.

> *Aisling's parents* had *always* wanted *her to become a doctor, but in college she decided to become an English major.*

The time that Aisling's parents wanted her to become a doctor happened before the time that she decided to become an English major.

Past Perfect and the Conditional

On the GED® test, you may be asked to use the past perfect in another situation: **conditional sentences** set in the past.

You probably use the conditional all the time in everyday life without knowing it. It follows this general pattern: *If this happens, then that happens.* Look at these examples:

> *I will go inside* if *you tell me to.*
> If *you don't know where those cookies came from, you shouldn't eat them.*

Now look at these examples of conditional sentences set in the past. They all include the past perfect:

> *I would have brought sunscreen if I had known it was going to be so hot and sunny.*

> *If you had really wanted to keep that job, you would have gotten to work on time.*
> *If someone had called to tell me that the doctor's office was closed, I would have stayed in bed.*

> ## NOTE
> Conditional sentences in the past often include the words *would have.*

Regular versus Irregular Verbs

Most English verbs are regular—they follow a standard set of rules for forming the simple past tense. Usually, add *-ed.*

> *He interrupted me when I was typing.*

If the verb ends with the letter *e*, just add *-d.*

> *The prisoners* escaped.

If the verb ends with the letter *y*, change the *y* to an *i* and add *-ed.*

> *I carried the water pitcher to the table.*

Irregular Verbs

About 150 English verbs are irregular—they don't follow the standard rules for changing tense.

Many irregular verbs form the past tense by changing the vowel to *a*. For example:

Present	Simple Past
begin	began
sing	sang
spring	sprang
come	came
overcome	overcame
run	ran

Other irregular verbs are more "irregular," such as these:

Present	Simple Past
bite	bit
bring	brought
dig	dug
hear	heard
leave	left
plead	pled
send	sent

In English, as in many other languages, the essential verb, *to be*, is highly irregular:

Subject	Present	Simple Past
I	am	was
you	are	were
he, she, it	is	was
we	are	were
they	are	were

Using a Consistent Tense

A common writing mistake is to jump between verb tenses when it is not necessary or correct to do so. You may be asked to spot this mistake on the GED® RLA test.

If a writer indicates that a certain action takes place at a certain time, he or she should be consistent in the use of verb tense when writing about that action elsewhere in the sentence (or paragraph or story). Review the following examples:

Incorrect: *She* left *the house and* forgets *her keys in the kitchen.*
Correct: *She* left *the house and* forgot *her keys in the kitchen.*

Incorrect: *Jon signed up* to run the marathon, but after talking to his doctor, he *decides* it would be too strenuous.

Correct: *Jon signed up* to run the marathon, but after talking to his doctor, he *decided* it would be too strenuous.

Subject–Verb Agreement

In grammar, agreement means that verbs should agree with their subjects. If the subject is singular, the verb should be singular. If the subject is plural, the verb should be plural. Because we often use incorrect grammar when we speak, identifying correct subject–verb agreement can be challenging.

Read the following examples, which highlight common agreement errors:

Incorrect: The president, *along with his wife and two daughters*, are *going to Hawaii on vacation.*
Correct: The president, *along with his wife and two daughters*, is *going to Hawaii on vacation.*

Although we know that four people are going on vacation—the president, his wife, and their two daughters—the sentence really has only one subject: *the president.* The phrase *along with his wife and two daughters* is just a side point; it is set off with commas and is not essential to the grammar of the sentence. Since the real subject, *the president*, is singular, the verb should be singular too: *is.*

> ### NOTE
>
> It's easy to read sentences such as the first example and think that they are correct. That is because a plural word—in this case, *daughters*—is the word that comes right before the verb. The phrase *two daughters are* sounds natural, even though in this sentence it is not correct. Make sure to keep in mind what the real subject of a sentence is, so you know what verb form is necessary.

Incorrect: *The jury* have *left the courtroom to make* their *decision.*

Correct: *The* jury has *left the courtroom to make* its *decision.*

Although *jury* refers to a group of people, the actual word *jury* is a singular noun—it means all of the jury members taken as a whole.

Here are examples of other nouns that may seem plural at first but are usually treated as singular and take a singular verb: *team, family, group, band, committee, tribe, audience,* and *flock.*

Incorrect: *That* boxer don't *have a chance against Carl.*

Correct: *That* boxer doesn't *have a chance against Carl.*

Although the first sentence may sound correct in casual speech, the word *boxer* is singular, so it should be followed by a singular verb form. *Don't* is a plural form.

How to Get Subject–Verb Agreement Right

Your main challenge when deciding if a sentence has correct subject–verb agreement will probably be determining who or what serves as the subject of the sentence.

In most cases, this should be simple and will come naturally to you. But as you saw in the previous examples, sometimes the real subject is not immediately obvious.

Here is another example. Can you identify the subject of the sentence?

Only one of the students was officially registered for class.

In this sentence, the subject is *one*, not *students.* Although it may seem as if the students are perform-

ing the action, the true subject of the sentence is the *one* student—whoever that person may be—meaning that the sentence requires the singular verb *was.*

Here's another example:

Vanessa and Erin are going to join the committee.

It's easy to see that there are two subjects in this sentence: *Vanessa* and *Erin.* The verb is correctly plural: *are.*

Now review these similar sentences:

Either Vanessa or Erin is going to join the committee.

Neither Vanessa nor Erin is going to join the committee.

In both cases, even though there are still two names—*Vanessa* and *Erin*—the subject is singular. In the first case, only one of them is going to join the committee (we don't know who, but it will be only one of them). In the second case, neither one will; *neither* also requires a singular verb.

NOTE

If one plural and one singular subject are connected by *or* or *nor*, the verb form must agree with the closer subject. For instance:

Neither Vanessa nor the teachers want to join the committee.

Neither the teachers nor Vanessa wants to join the committee.

Let's go back to our original example:

Vanessa and Erin are going to join the committee.

There are two nouns at the start of the sentence, and it is clear that there are two subjects: *Vanessa* and *Erin.*

Now take a look at this example:

Peanut butter and jelly is my favorite type of sandwich.

Although the phrase *peanut butter and jelly* is made up of two nouns, we know that the term *peanut butter and jelly* refers to one thing: a particular type of sandwich filling. In this case, you'd treat the whole phrase as one subject, so you would use a singular verb form (*is*).

Here are other examples of subjects that may look plural at first glance but are really singular:

Spaghetti and meatballs *was my grandmother's favorite dish.*
The New York Times *is delivered to my door every morning.*
The United States *has never won the Olympic gold in that sport.*

Here is one last type of sentence that often causes subject–verb agreement problems: sentences that start with words such as *There's*, *Here's*, and *What's*. Note that in these sentences, the subject comes *after* the verb. For example:

There's my dog, playing by the park bench.

The subject of the sentence is *my dog*.

Incorrect: There's *still three empty seats.*
Correct: There are *still three empty seats.*

Don't forget that *There's* is really a shorthand (or contraction) of the phrase *There is*. Since the subject of this sentence—*seats*—is plural, the sentence requires a plural introduction: *There are*.

Incorrect: What's *the side effects of this medication?*
Correct: What are *the side effects of this medication?*

Similarly, *What's* is a contraction of *What is*, which is incorrect here because the subject of this sentence is plural: *side effects*.

Practice

For each sentence, fill in the blank with either *is* or *are*.

1. Red Rocks _____ their favorite concert venue in Colorado.

2. Julio, as well as the rest of the band, _____ excited about performing at Red Rocks.

3. Two members of the band _____ still back at the hotel.

4. Everyone _____ supposed to be onstage right now!

5. Where _____ Julio and the guitar player?

For the following three questions, select the best revision of the underlined part of the sentence.

6. Catherine <u>is gone</u> to the store later today.
  a. go
  b. will go
  c. went
  d. has gone

7. Gerald and Yolanda <u>have visited</u> me yesterday.
  a. visited
  b. are visiting
  c. visits
  d. had visited

8. Neither you nor your cousins <u>appearing</u> in the photograph.
  a. appears
  b. is appearing
  c. appear
  d. to appear

Pronouns

In order to understand the correct use of pronouns, you must first have a clear understanding of what a noun is. **Nouns** are words that identify objects.

> **People:** students, brother, David, neighbor
> **Places:** New York City, ocean, university, Jupiter
> **Things:** books, Saturday, bathing suit, the U.S. Navy
> **Ideas and qualities:** beauty, faith, anger, justice

A **pronoun** is a word that replaces or refers to a noun. Consider the following examples:

> Sheldon *prefers cereal to toast and jam.*

This can be rewritten with a pronoun as:

> He *prefers cereal to toast and jam.*

> *Last Friday,* Josh *drove to* Kathy *and* Tina's *cabin.*

This can be rewritten with pronouns as:

> *Last Friday,* he *drove to their cabin.*

> Jackson *doesn't care about anyone except* Jackson.

This can be rewritten with pronouns as:

> He *doesn't care about anyone except* himself.

There are many pronouns in the English language, depending on what type of noun the pronoun is replacing and how the pronoun functions in a sentence. Here are some examples of pronouns: *I, you, she, he, we, they, it, this, that, myself, ourselves, whoever, whomever, mine, yours.*

Pronouns and Antecedents

When a pronoun is used in a sentence, it should be clear what noun(s) it is substituting for or referring to. That noun is called an **antecedent**. For example:

> Adam *had fun while* he *was on vacation in Puerto Rico.*

The pronoun *he* is another way of saying the word *Adam. Adam* is the antecedent of *he.*

Here is another:

> My grandparents *first met when* they *were in college.*

The plural pronoun *they* stands in for the plural noun *grandparents,* which is the antecedent.

This may seem simple enough, but confusion over pronouns and antecedents can arise in more complicated sentences. You may be asked to spot or correct this type of problem on the GED® RLA test.

Consider this incorrect sentence:

> *Despite what the president told the reporters,* they *are not going to authorize military action.*

The sentence may sound correct to the ear, but if we give it some thought, do we really know what is meant by the pronoun *they*? (To put it another way: Do we know what the antecedent is of *they*?)

They is a plural pronoun, so it can't refer to *the president,* which is a singular noun. It could refer to *the reporters,* which is a plural noun, but that doesn't make sense logically—reporters are not in charge of the military.

Does *they* mean some other group of people (members of a committee or army generals)? Or should it be changed to *he,* to mean *the president*?

As you can see, when there is no obvious antecedent to a pronoun, the meaning of an entire sentence can be unclear.

Beware of *They*

Another common pronoun problem arises when the writer is discussing a person (singular) but isn't sure what gender to use—*she/her/her* or *he/him/his*—so tries to keep things vague by using a plural pronoun (*they/them/their*) instead. Consider this example:

> If a student *is late to class three times,* they *will be reported to the principal.*

The pronoun *they* doesn't work here because it's plural but its antecedent is the singular noun *student.* Here is a correct way to rewrite the sentence:

> If a student *is late to class three times,* he or she *will be reported to the principal.*

Or you could rephrase the sentence this way:

> If students *are late to class three times,* they *will be reported to the principal.*

Subject Pronouns and Object Pronouns

When editing sentences for correct pronoun use, you will need to determine whether the pronoun is the subject or the object of the sentence. Consider the following sentence:

> Jane brought Jack to the dentist.

Jane is the subject of the sentence—the person who is acting out the verb *brought.* *Jack* is the object—the person who is receiving the action of the verb.

If we wanted to swap out the words *Jane* and *Jack* with pronouns, we would need to use a subjective pronoun for *Jane* and an objective pronoun for *Jack.* Note the correct sentence, after a couple of incorrect tries:

Incorrect: She *brought* he *to the dentist.*
Incorrect: Her *brought* him *to the dentist.*
Correct: She *brought* him *to the dentist.*

Here is a list of subject and object pronouns. Make sure you know the difference:

Subject	Object
I	me
you	you
he	him
she	her
it	it
we	us
who	whom
they	them

Who versus Whom

This brings us to one of the most common grammar problems in the English language: using the word *who* (a subjective pronoun) when the word *whom* (an objective pronoun) is called for. This error could appear on the GED® RLA test, so make sure you know how to spot it.

Consider the following examples:

> Who *made dinner last night?*

Who is the subject of this sentence. Whoever that mysterious meal-preparing person is, he or she performed the action of the sentence (making dinner).

> Whom *should John invite to your party?*

Here, *John* is the subject of the sentence. John is going to perform the action of the sentence (inviting one or more guests). *Whom* is the object of the sentence: it refers to one or more persons who will receive the action of the sentence (John's invitation).

An easy way to test whether you should use *who* or *whom* in a sentence is to swap it for another pronoun that you're more familiar with and check to see if that makes sense.

Let's try out this trick on the following sentence:

[Who/Whom] *is Jake going to marry?*

First, let's try to answer the question with the word *she*. It is a subjective pronoun, so it will test whether the subjective pronoun *who* would work in the sentence.

[Who/Whom] *is Jake going to marry? Jake is going to marry* she.

That is clearly not grammatical. Now let's try an objective pronoun, *her*:

[Who/Whom] *is Jake going to marry? Jake is going to marry* her.

That makes sense, so we know that we need another objective pronoun—*whom*—for the question:

Whom *is Jake going to marry?*

Here is another example:

Incorrect: *Ms. Dee is the teacher* who *I always ask for advice.*
Correct: *Ms. Dee is the teacher* whom *I always ask for advice.*

When deciding whether to use *who* or *whom*, look at the core phrase: *I ask _____.*

I ask her would be grammatical, not *I ask she*. Therefore, in our sentence, we need to use the same type of pronoun as *her* (objective). That means we need to use *whom*.

Incorrect: *Gordon is the man* whom *lives down the street.*
Correct: *Gordon is the man* who *lives down the street.*

To determine *who* versus *whom*, the core phrase is: _____ *lives down the street.*

Let's test it:

Him *lives down the street.*
He *lives down the street.*

The second sentence, with the subjective pronoun *he*, is correct, so we should use *who* in our sentence.

Now take a look at these more advanced examples to prepare for the GED® RLA test.

The same rules for *who* and *whom* apply to *whoever* and *whomever*.

Incorrect: *I'll play chess with* whoever.
Correct: *I'll play chess with* whomever.

The core phrase here is: *I'll play with _____.* The missing word is an object of the preposition *with*, so we need to use the objective pronoun *whomever*.

Let's do that test again, just to be sure. Let's try the sentence with a subjective pronoun, *she*:

I'll play chess with she.

That is clearly not correct. The subjective pronoun *whoever* is therefore not correct. Now let's try the objective pronoun *her*:

I'll play chess with her.

That's a perfect fit, so the objective pronoun *whomever* must be right.

Practice

For each of the following questions, fill in the blank with *who*, *whom*, *whoever*, or *whomever*.

9. _____ are you taking to the dance?

10. _____ is making that noise had better quiet down!

11. That man over there is the customer _____ complained about me to my boss.

12. _____ is taking you to the dance?

Possessive Pronouns

Like possessive nouns (such as *Carla's, the house's, the three players'*), possessive pronouns show ownership. However, possessive pronouns do *not* use apostrophes.

> **Incorrect:** *The purple and green balloons were* their's.
> **Correct:** *The purple and green balloons were* theirs.
> **Incorrect:** It's *tail was long and furry.*
> **Correct:** Its *tail was long and furry.*

Note that some possessive pronouns function as adjectives and are used to describe a noun. For instance: *my* car (*my* describes the noun *car*), *her* tennis shoes (*her* describes the noun *tennis shoes*), and *your* strawberries (*your* describes the noun *strawberries*).

Other possessive pronouns function as nouns themselves, for instance:

> *The blue car is* mine.
> *Those tennis shoes are* hers.
> Yours *are sweeter than* ours.

Make sure you are familiar with the spelling of both types of possessive pronouns:

Possessive (adjective)	Possessive (noun)
my	mine
your	yours
his	his
her	hers
its	its
our	ours
whose	whose
their	theirs

Read the following sentence. Then replace the underlined words with the correct pronouns:

> When Lisa and Jim's friend Tony arrived home from Iraq, <u>Lisa and Jim</u> took <u>Tony</u> to <u>Tony's</u> favorite restaurant and told <u>Tony</u> to order whatever <u>Tony</u> liked.
> When Lisa and Jim's friend Tony arrived home from Iraq, *they* took *him* to *his* favorite restaurant and told *him* to order whatever *he* liked.

Lisa and Jim translates to *they* because *Lisa and Jim* serves as a subject of the sentence (Lisa and Jim are the people who are performing the main action—taking Tony to dinner).

Tony's is a possessive noun, which translates to the possessive pronoun *his*.

To figure out the rest of the answers—pronouns that replace the word *Tony*—ask yourself whether *Tony* is a subject (performing an action) or an object (receiving an action). If he's the subject, make it *he*. If he's the object, make it *him*.

Pronouns Combined with Other Nouns

Often pronouns are combined with other subjects or objects in a sentence. For instance, in the following sentence, there is one subject (*Ruth*) and two objects (*Peter* and _____):

> *Ruth drove Peter and* _____ *to the football game.*

Do you know which pronoun should fill in the blank?

> Ruth drove Peter and *me* to the football game.
> Ruth drove Peter and *I* to the football game.

Although the second sentence may sound correct, it is not. (It may sound correct to you because we hear this type of phrasing all the time. Many people use it because they think it sounds more proper or formal, but in reality it is poor grammar.)

The first sentence is right. The word *me* is an objective pronoun, which is what is needed in the grammar of this sentence. *I* is a subjective pronoun, which is incorrect here.

There's an easy trick for finding the correct pronoun in situations such as this (when a pronoun is combined with another noun and you want to know what type of pronoun to use): **Cross out the other phrase**—here, *Peter and*—**and then see what pronoun you need**. Here it would be:

Ruth drove me *to the football game.*

You would never say:

Ruth drove I *to the football game.*

Practice

For each of the following questions, choose the pronoun that fits best.

13. Joe had _____ temperature taken at the doctor's office on Tuesday.
   a. its
   b. his
   c. him
   d. none of the above

14. Someone forgot to lock up _____ shoes and gym bag.
   a. his or her
   b. his or hers
   c. their
   d. there

15. The closet is so dark! I can't tell which coat is _____ and which is _____.
   a. your, my
   b. yours, mine
   c. our, their
   d. our, they're

Dangling and Misplaced Modifiers

A **dangling modifier** is a misplaced word or phrase. If a word or a phrase is placed incorrectly in a sentence, the meaning of the sentence can be misinterpreted.

How to Spot Dangling Modifiers

Incorrect: *Running for the bus, my backpack fell in the street.*

This suggests that the subject of the sentence—*my backpack*—was running for the bus, which we know is not correct!

The phrase *Running for the bus* is a **dangling modifier** because it describes the action of the person speaking, but that person is not mentioned in the sentence.

Here is the sentence written correctly:

Correct: *As I was running for the bus, my backpack fell in the street.*

When editing sentences for dangling modifiers, pay attention to words that end in *-ing* and appear at the beginning of the sentence. This can signal a sentence that has a dangling modifier. For example:

Incorrect: *Searching the entire house, the key was under the table.*

This sentence says that the key searched the entire house, which doesn't make sense.

Correct: *After searching the entire house, he found the key under the table.*

NOTE
Most dangling modifiers occur at the beginnings of sentences, but they can appear at the ends of sentences, too.

How to Spot Misplaced Modifiers

Now let's look at a similar type of error: **misplaced modifiers**. These are phrases or clauses that appear in the wrong spot in a sentence, so it seems as if they describe one thing when they really are intended to describe something else.

For example:

Incorrect: *Ten minutes later, a sad-looking man in a dirty suit with yellow teeth entered the room.*

Correct: *Ten minutes later, a sad-looking man who wore a dirty suit and had yellow teeth entered the room.*

The suit didn't have yellow teeth—the man did.

Incorrect: *She gave homemade treats to the kids wrapped in tinfoil.*

Correct: *She gave the kids homemade treats wrapped in tinfoil.*

The kids weren't wrapped in tinfoil—the treats were.

Only, Just, Barely, and Nearly

The words *only, just, barely, nearly,* and *almost* should appear right before the noun or verb being modified. Their placement determines the message of the sentence.

Only Peter ran to the store. (No one else but Peter went.)

Peter only ran to the store. (He didn't walk.)

Peter ran only to the store. (He didn't go anywhere else.)

Peter ran to the only store. (There was no other store around but that one.)

Peter ran to the store only. (He ran to the store and did nothing else.)

Practice

For each of the following sentences, select the best revision.

16. Moving to Nevada, Shira's truck broke down.
    a. While Shira was moving to Nevada, her truck broke down.
    b. Shira's truck, moving to Nevada, broke down.
    c. Shira's truck broke down while moving to Nevada.
    d. The sentence is correct as is.

17. Exhausted after a long day at the office, Tom only used the treadmill for ten minutes before heading home from the gym.
    a. After Tom's exhausting day at the office, he only used the treadmill for ten minutes before heading home from the gym.
    b. Exhausted after a long day at the office, Tom headed home from the gym after only using the treadmill for ten minutes.
    c. Exhausted after a long day at the office, Tom used the treadmill for only ten minutes before heading home from the gym.
    d. The sentence is correct as is.

18. Historians have wondered whether General Thomas Herald was really a woman in disguise for more than 200 years.
    a. For more than 200 years, historians have wondered whether General Thomas Herald was really a woman in disguise.
    b. Historians have wondered, Was General Thomas Herald really a woman in disguise for more than 200 years?
    c. Historians have wondered whether General Thomas Herald, in disguise, was really a woman for more than 200 years.
    d. The sentence is correct as is.

Context Clues

Even great readers will come across unfamiliar words in a text at times. One way to figure out the meanings of these words is to use **context clues**. These are hints that are included in the sentence or passage that help readers understand the meanings of words.

Authors often use **synonyms**, or words with similar meanings, to help readers understand unfamiliar terms.

> *Beginning this semester, students will have an <u>abbreviated</u>, or shortened, day every Wednesday.*

In this sentence, the author included the synonym *shortened* to explain what he or she means by *abbreviated*. This context clue helps readers determine the meaning of a word that might be unfamiliar.

An author might also include **antonyms**, or words with opposite meanings, to clarify the definition of a word.

> *Please be advised that both <u>residents</u> and visitors are expected to park their cars on the west side of the apartment building.*

This sentence talks about *residents* and *visitors*. So, we can conclude that residents are different than visitors. Because you probably know that visitors are people who do not live in the building, we can figure out that *residents* are people who do live there.

Definitions or **explanations** are often used as context clues.

> *The <u>reluctant</u> child was not eager to share his project with the class.*

In this sentence, the author explained the meaning of *reluctant* by saying that the child was *not eager*.

Examples are another type of context clue that can be used to determine the meaning of unknown words.

> *Ms. Greene pointed out pictures of several <u>monuments</u> in the students' history books, including the Statue of Liberty, the Lincoln Memorial, and the Liberty Bell.*

This sentence includes three examples of monuments: the Statue of Liberty, the Lincoln Memorial, and the Liberty Bell. From these examples, we can figure out that a *monument* must be a famous place or structure that has a special importance.

TIP

When looking for context clues, be sure to check sentences surrounding the unfamiliar word. These clues might be contained in the sentences before or after the sentence that includes the word in question, or they may even be in another part of the paragraph.

As you read the following sentences, look for context clues that could help you determine the meanings of the underlined words. Then, answer the questions that follow.

> *We climbed all day before reaching the <u>apex</u>, or top, of the mountain. We hadn't eaten anything in several hours and were all <u>famished</u>. I was so extremely hungry that I couldn't wait for lunch. As we ate our picnic, we talked about many topics, some <u>frivolous</u>, others serious. After an hour of eating, relaxing, and enjoying the gorgeous view, we began our hike back down the trail.*

1. What is the meaning of *apex*?

_____

2. What clues helped you determine the meaning?

_____

The synonym *top* probably helped you figure out that *apex* means the top, or the highest point, of the mountain.

3. What is the meaning of *famished*?

_____

4. What clues helped you determine the meaning?

_____

The sentence explains that the hikers hadn't eaten anything in several hours. The following sentence includes the definition "extremely hungry." These context clues probably helped you figure out that *famished* means "extremely hungry" or "starving." Notice that some of the clues were in the sentence following the underlined word. Also, notice that clues were found in more than one place. Be sure to look throughout the entire paragraph for clues that can help you determine meaning.

5. What is the meaning of *frivolous*?

_____

6. What clues helped you determine the meaning?

_____

The paragraph states that some of the topics the hikers discussed were *frivolous* and others were *serious*.

This use of an antonym tells us that something that is *frivolous* is not serious.

Multiple Meaning Words

Many words have more than one meaning. As we read, it is important to know which meaning the author intends to use. Consider the use of the word *stoop* in the following sentences:

> *Li sat on the front <u>stoop</u>, waiting for her neighbor to come home.*

> *David had to <u>stoop</u> to fit into the tiny door of his little brother's clubhouse.*

> *The other candidate is constantly telling lies, but I would never <u>stoop</u> so low.*

In the first sentence, *stoop* means "a small porch." In the second sentence, *stoop* means "to bend forward." In the third sentence, *stoop* means "to do something unethical."

So, if words have more than one meaning, how are you supposed to figure out which is correct? You'll have to use context clues. Think about which definition makes sense in that particular sentence.

Read the following sentence.

> *The detective said the intruders left without a <u>trace</u>.*

Which is the meaning of *trace* in this sentence?
  a. a tiny amount
  b. a remaining sign
  c. a type of drawing
  d. to find something

In the sentence, the detective could not find any remaining sign that the intruders had been there.

Although each of the answer choices is a definition of *trace*, only choice **b** makes sense in the context of the sentence.

Frequently Confused Words and Homonyms

Quick—what's the difference between *it's* and *its*? *Know* and *no*? *To* and *too*?

Like many words in the English language, these words often confuse people because they sound the same but have very different meanings. Other frequently confused words have the same *spelling* but different meanings. All of these are called **homonyms**.

To help avoid confusion on the GED® test—and in everyday life—familiarize yourself with the following homonyms and other words (such as *affect* and *effect*) that people often mix up.

Words to Remember
affect/effect

Here are the two definitions of *affect* and *effect* that people often confuse:

> to *affect* (verb): to influence
>> Eric's childhood in rural Arkansas *affected* how he viewed the world.
>
> *effect* (noun): the result of influence
>> Eric's childhood in rural Arkansas had an *effect* on how he viewed the world.

Both words also have other meanings, which you should try not to confuse:

> to *effect* (verb): to cause something to happen, accomplish
>> Over time, the union's efforts *effected* change at the factory.

> to *affect* (verb): to pretend or make a display of
>> The designer sometimes *affected* a British accent when he went to parties, which was ridiculous because he had been born and raised in New Jersey.
>
> *affect* (noun): a feeling or emotion, or the way that a feeling or emotion is expressed physically
>> He had a calm, cool *affect*, which was disturbing because his son had just gone missing.

its/it's

> *its*: belonging to a certain animal or thing
>> The dog wants *its* bone.
>
> *it's*: the contraction of *it is*
>> *It's* too hot to go outside.

lie/lay

> *lie*: to make an untrue statement (verb); an untrue statement (noun)
>> Never *lie* on a job application, because if *the lie* is detected, you probably won't get hired.
>
> *lie, lay*: the present and past tenses of the verb *to lie*, meaning to recline or rest in a horizontal position
>> Every Sunday afternoon, I *lie* on the couch and watch movies.
>> Last Sunday afternoon, I *lay* on the couch and watched movies.
>
> *lay, laid*: the present and past tenses of the verb *to lay*, meaning to put something down
>> You can *lay* the baby down in Sarah's old crib.
>> He *laid* the baby down in Sarah's old crib.

know/no; knew/new

> *know*: to be well informed, to recognize
>> I *know* a lot about growing tomatoes.
>
> *no*: zero, none
>> I have *no* idea how to grow tomatoes.

knew: past tense of the verb *to know*

    I *knew* how to grow tomatoes when I was younger.

new: appearing or made for the first time

    I will need to buy *new* tomatoes.

through/threw

through: a preposition meaning into one side and out the other

    Don't worry—I know you will make it *through* this difficult period.

threw: past tense of the verb *to throw*

    He *threw* out his house keys by mistake!

> ## NOTE
>
> You may see the word *thru* in everyday life (for instance, at a fast-food restaurant's "drive-thru"), but it's an informal spelling that is usually not appropriate in school or work settings. You should also avoid using it on the GED® test!

then/than

then: after something has happened, next

    First I will do my laundry, and *then* I will wash the kitchen floor.

than: a word used when comparing two things

    I would rather go to Florida this winter *than* stay in Wisconsin.

Practice

Select the word that best fits each sentence.

19. Jill, go rest while I _____ out the silver and get the table ready for the party.
  a. lie
  b. lay

20. Mira _____ the congregation in song at the memorial service yesterday.
  a. lead
  b. led

21. I plan to pick up my paycheck this afternoon and _____ cash it at the bank on the corner.
  a. than
  b. then

22. It's a shame that Tim and Jean and _____ children won't be at the reunion on Saturday.
  a. their
  b. there

Literary Devices

Metaphors

Before we explain what it is, look at this example of a metaphor:

> *Janie was <u>the heart</u> of the organization: all ideas came from her and circulated back to her for her feedback.*

Here *the heart* is a metaphor—Janie was not literally a human heart, but she acted as a heart at the organization. All ideas flowed through her, just as blood is pumped out from and flows back to the heart in the human body.

A **metaphor** is a word or phrase for one thing that the writer uses to refer to another thing, showing that they are similar.

Here is another example:

> *His smile is <u>a ray of sunshine</u> that makes people feel happy, no matter how down they are.*

Of course, the smile is not literally made of sunshine. The writer is using the metaphor *a ray of sunshine* to express the positive effect of the person's smile on the people around him.

Similes

Similes are similar to metaphors, but they use the word *like* or *as*. For example:

> His smile is <u>like a ray of sunshine</u>.
> My puppy Waldo is <u>as sweet as a teddy bear</u>.
> Running errands for my boss is <u>as much fun as going to the dentist</u>.

Here's a fourth example, which comes from a very descriptive paragraph in the short story "A Rose for Emily," by William Faulkner:

> Her eyes, lost in the fatty ridges of her face, <u>looked like two small pieces of coal pressed into a lump of dough</u> as they moved from one face to another while the visitors stated their errand.

A Closer Look at Figurative Language

In some passages, the use of figurative language can be much more complicated than in the sentences in the preceding section, but if you break it down, you'll see the hidden meaning.

John F. Kennedy's 1961 inaugural address used figurative language to discuss sophisticated ideas with the audience. In the second paragraph, reprinted here, you can see several examples.

EXCERPT

We dare not forget today that we are the heirs of that first revolution. Let the word go forth from this time and place, to friend and foe alike, that the torch has been passed to a new generation of Americans—born in this century, tempered by war, disciplined by a hard and bitter peace, proud of our ancient heritage—and unwilling to witness or permit the slow undoing of those human rights to which this nation has always been committed, and to which we are committed today at home and around the world.

Let's look at the first sentence:

> We dare not forget today that we are the heirs of that first revolution.

By using the word *heirs*, President Kennedy communicates a deep sense of obligation to the American public listening to him. Hearing that word makes an audience think of family history and connection.

Now, let's look at the second sentence:

> Let the word go forth from this time and place, to friend and foe alike, that the torch has been passed to a new generation of Americans—born in this century, tempered by war, disciplined by a hard and bitter peace, proud of our ancient heritage—and unwilling to witness or permit the slow undoing of those human rights to which this nation has always been committed, and to which we are committed today at home and around the world.

In this (very long) sentence, the image of a flame in the torch suggests the power and intensity of Kennedy's call to action. The metaphor gains even more intensity and atmosphere from the image of an Olympic marathon—the torch has been passed—in which a runner literally passes a lighted torch to the next runner in the relay team.

Before you take the GED® test, practice your grammar skills by building sentences and reviewing how the parts fit together. Engage in active reading, ask yourself questions, and review the language mechanics present in the passages you read. The more you review the information presented in this section, the more successful you will be on the GED® RLA test.

Language and Grammar Review

For questions 23–27, select the correct version of the underlined sentence or portion of a sentence in the passage.

Millennials Take New Approach to Work-Life Balance
—*Adapted from an article published on Brandpoint.com*

23. More and more, Millennials are on the road for work. In an average month, one in four business-traveling Millennials travels overnight for work at least once per week. As the line between "personal" and "business" grows thinner and thinner for this generation, <u>Millennials are increasingly finding adventure thru business.</u>
   a. Millennials are increasingly finding adventure threw business.
   b. Millennials are increasingly finding adventure through business.
   c. Millennials are increasingly found to have adventure through business.
   d. This is correct as is.

24. More than any other group, Millennial business travelers are likely to add on extra days to their work-related trips for leisure travel (84%), according to the Hilton Garden Inn Discovery and Connection Survey.

   <u>As the economy improves business travel across the nation is on the rise.</u> According to the Global Business Travel Association, U.S. business travel is expected to grow 5.1% in 2013.
   a. As the economy improves, business travel across the nation is on the rise.
   b. As the economy improves business travel, the nation is on the rise.
   c. As the economy improves, business travel across the nation rose.
   d. The sentence is correct as is.

25. As more Millennials hit the road for work, they are keeping top of mind a few simple business travel perks to fulfill their appetite for personal adventure and discovery:

   Fly for free. <u>Those flying for business can earn airline miles in they're name.</u> These business miles quickly add up, allowing travelers to upgrade seats or add another destination without accruing additional cost. Business travelers can then use these miles to bring a friend or loved one on the trip with them—quickly transitioning from business to family vacation or romantic getaway once the weekend hits.
   a. Those flying for business can earn airline miles in there name.
   b. Those flying for business can earn airline miles in your name.
   c. Those flying for business can earn airline miles in their name.
   d. The sentence is correct as is.

26. Earn hotel perks. Frequent stays in hotels offering rewards programs can grant business travelers <u>benefits such as free overnight stays late checkout and complimentary breakfast</u>. These extras turn a business trip into much more, especially when additional nights are used to extend a business trip into a vacation.

  a. benefits such as free overnight stays, late checkout and complimentary breakfast.

  b. benefits such as free overnight stays, late checkout, and complimentary breakfast.

  c. benefits such as free, overnight stays, late checkout, and complimentary, breakfast.

  d. This is correct as is.

27. Millennials continue to be at the forefront of achieving work-life balance <u>by using business travel to discover new cities, taste authentic cuisines, explore different cultures, and connecting with new people across the globe</u>.

  a. by using business travel to discover new cities, taste authentic cuisines, explore different cultures, and connect with new people across the globe.

  b. by using business travel to discover new cities, taste authentic cuisines, explore different cultures, while connecting with new people across the globe.

  c. by using business travel to discovering new cities, tasting authentic cuisines, exploring different cultures, and connecting with new people across the globe.

  d. This is correct as is.

28. Choose the sentence that contains correct capitalization.

  a. She and i are really hoping the Brooklyn Nets do well this year.

  b. She and I are really hoping the Brooklyn Nets do well this Year.

  c. She and I are really hoping the Brooklyn nets do well this year.

  d. She and I are really hoping the Brooklyn Nets do well this year.

29. Select the answer choice that contains correct punctuation.

  a. "I married him because I thought he was a gentleman. I thought he knew something about breeding, but he wasn't fit to lick my shoe." Says Catherine, a character in *The Great Gatsby*.

  b. "I married him because I thought he was a gentleman," Catherine, a character in *The Great Gatsby*, says, "I thought he knew something about breeding, but he wasn't fit to lick my shoe."

  c. "I married him because I thought he was a gentleman," Catherine, a character in *The Great Gatsby*, says. "I thought he knew something about breeding, but he wasn't fit to lick my shoe."

  d. None of the above is correct.

For questions 30 and 31, select the word that best completes the sentence.

30. Melissa's friend asked _____ for a ride home.
    a. they
    b. hers
    c. she
    d. none of the above

31. To _____ are you speaking?
    a. who
    b. whom
    c. when
    d. none of the above

Answers and Explanations

Chapter Practice

1. b. Jill, go lie down while I *lay* out the silver and get the table ready for the party.

2. b. Mira *led* the congregation in song at the memorial service yesterday.

3. b. I plan to pick up my paycheck this afternoon and *then* cash it at the bank on the corner.

4. a. It's a shame that Tim and Jean and *their* children won't be at the reunion on Saturday.

5. Red Rocks *is* their favorite concert venue in Colorado. By itself, the word *rocks* is plural, of course, but *Red Rocks* is a proper noun—it's the name of one specific place in Colorado. Since *Red Rocks* is a singular noun, we need to use *is*.

6. Julio, as well as the rest of the band, **is** excited about performing at Red Rocks. The subject of this sentence is *Julio*, not *Julio, as well as the rest of the band*. Why? The phrase *the rest of the band* is set off with commas as a side point. Since the subject of the sentence, *Julio*, is a singular noun—one person—we need to use *is* (the singular form of the verb *to be*).

7. a. *Visited* is the simple past tense form of the verb *to visit*, which makes sense in this sentence because we know this happened yesterday, not last week or right now.

8. c. When a singular subject and a plural subject are connected by *nor*, the verb must agree with the closer subject—in this case, the plural *cousins*. This choice, *appear*, is the correct verb form for a plural subject.

9. *Whom* are you taking to the dance? Here, the mystery person will be taken to a dance—an action will be performed on him or her. Therefore the mystery person is an object, and we need to use a pronoun that works with objects: *whom*.

10. *Whoever* is making that noise had better quiet down! When deciding whether to use *who/whoever* or *whom/whomever*, you need to ask if the person in question is the subject of the sentence (performing the action) or the object (receiving the action). Here, the mystery person being yelled at is the subject of the sentence—he or she is making the noise—so we need to use *whoever*, a pronoun for subjects. If the person were the object, we'd need to use *whomever*, a pronoun for objects.

11. That man over there is the customer *who* complained about me to my boss. In the second part of the sentence, the customer performed the action—*complained*—so he or she is the subject. We need to use *who*, a pronoun for subjects.

12. **Who** is taking you to the dance? The mystery person here is performing the action—taking you to the dance. Therefore, he or she is the subject. We need to use a pronoun that works with subjects: *who*.

13. b. We need a possessive pronoun that fits with *Joe*—a singular male noun. That is *his*.

14. a. We don't know the gender of the person who forgot to lock up the shoes and gym bag, but we know it is one person (*someone* is singular). As a result, we need to use *his or her* (singular possessive pronouns).

15. b. These possessive pronouns are used correctly and make sense in this sentence.

16. a. *Moving to Nevada* is a dangling modifier. We all know that it was *Shira* who moved to Nevada—the truck didn't move to Nevada. But based on the structure of this sentence, *moving to Nevada* modifies *Shira's truck*. The revision in this choice corrects that problem.

17. c. In the original sentence, the word *only* is in the wrong spot, and this choice moves it to where it belongs, right before *ten minutes*. What's wrong with the original sentence? The word *only* modifies the wrong thing; the sentence says that Tom *only used the treadmill* at the gym. We know that this is not correct, of course. Tom surely did many things at the gym: he must have opened the front door, walked over to the machines, and selected a treadmill; maybe he changed into his gym clothes, drank some water, and said hello to a friend, too.

18. a. The problem with the original sentence is that the phrase *for more than 200 years* modifies the wrong thing—it suggests that the general may have been in disguise for 200 years. This doesn't make any sense—people don't live for 200 years! This choice correctly places *for more than 200 years* right before *historians have wondered*—it's the wondering that's been happening for 200 years.

19. Two members of the band *are* still back at the hotel. What is the subject of this sentence—*Two members* or *the band*? It is *two members*. As a result, we need to use the verb *are*.

20. Everyone *is* supposed to be onstage right now! The word *everyone* may refer to a lot of people, but the word itself is singular. Therefore we need to use *is*.

21. Where *are* Julio and the guitar player? There are two subjects in this sentence: *Julio* and *the guitar player*. Therefore we need to use *are* (the plural form of the verb *to be*).

22. b. Because the sentence includes the phrase *later today*, we know that we need a future verb form. The sentence should read: *Catherine will go to the store later today*.

Language and Grammar Review

23. b. This sentence correctly changes *thru* to *through*, which is the proper spelling.

24. a. It is hard to tell because the underlined sentence is not punctuated properly, but there are really two clauses here. The first clause (*As the economy improves*) is a dependent clause, so it should be joined with a comma to the independent clause that follows (*business travel across the nation is on the rise*).

25. c. The word *they're* should be changed to the possessive pronoun *their*. *They're* is a contraction meaning *they are*.

26. b. This sentence includes a list of three things: (1) *free overnight stays*, (2) *late checkout*, and (3) *complimentary breakfast*. In a series, there should be commas (or semicolons, in special situations) after every item except for the last one. This revision follows that rule.

27. a. The problem with the sentence in the passage is that it contains a series that is not parallel. There is a list of four items, and the first three items are worded in a similar way (*discover . . . , taste . . . , explore . . .*), but the fourth item is different (*connecting . . .*). This revision corrects the problem. It changes the fourth item, *connecting with new people*, to *connect with new people*, which matches the verb form in the other items. The phrase *connect with new people* also fits grammatically with the first part of the sentence. The phrase *connecting with new people* didn't work. Why? Remove the first three items of the series to see what we were really saying with *connecting*. The sentence would read: *Millennials continue to be at the forefront of achieving work-life balance by using business travel to . . . connecting with new people across the globe*, but this doesn't make any sense.

28. d. The pronoun *I* and the proper noun *Brooklyn Nets* are both correctly capitalized.

29. c. This is correct punctuation and organization of a quote.

30. d. This sentence calls for an object pronoun, explaining whom Melissa's friend asked for a ride. None of the choices are appropriate pronouns.

31. b. Let's rewrite this sentence: *You are speaking to _____*. The speaker (*you*) is the subject—he or she is performing the action of the sentence (talking to someone). What we need here is an object pronoun, for the person being spoken to. *Whom* is an object pronoun and makes sense in this sentence.

REVIEW

In this chapter, you have learned two strategies to help you better comprehend reading materials:

1. Breaking unfamiliar words into word parts, such as prefixes, suffixes, and root words, can be helpful in determining a word's meaning. Thinking of words with similar roots can also help readers figure out the meaning of unknown words.

2. Context clues such as synonyms, antonyms, definitions, and examples can be helpful in figuring out the meanings of unknown words. These clues may be in the same sentence as the unfamiliar word or in the surrounding sentences and paragraph.

LANGUAGE AND GRAMMAR: GRAMMAR SKILLS

CHAPTER SUMMARY

This chapter covers GED® test writing tips and strategies that will help you be successful on exam day. You'll learn to recognize and correct errors in sentence structure, usage, mechanics, and organization, as well as identify the purpose of various parts of an essay.

As you've seen in previous chapters, the GED® Reasoning through Language Arts exam tests both reading and writing skills. Don't let that get you worried—the good news is that preparing for one part helps you to prepare for the other. And of course, the more you practice, the better your score will likely be.

GED® Test Strategies

In this chapter, we focus on basic grammar and writing skills. The topics covered include:

- sentence structure
- usage
- mechanics
- organization

In addition, we also go over some GED® test tips and strategies. Together with the information provided in previous chapters, these proven tools for exam success will help you prepare for and excel on test day.

Sentence Construction

Sentence construction refers to the way sentences are created: how we join together subjects, verbs, objects, and other elements to express a complete thought.

Complete Sentences

You can't just string words together to create a sentence. To form a complete sentence, you need to have three basic elements:

1. A **subject**: This is who or what the sentence is about.
2. A **predicate**: This states what the subject is or does.
3. The sentence must express a **complete thought**.

Look at this example:

The phone is ringing.

This is a short but complete sentence. Why? It satisfies the three requirements:

1. It has a subject: *the phone.*
2. It has a predicate: *is ringing.* It explains what the subject is doing.
3. It expresses a complete thought. We know what happened and what was involved.

Now look at these examples:

Sit down.
Don't run.
Give me a break.

Are they complete sentences? Yes. These are very short, complete sentences that command, or tell, someone to do something. You can see that each has a predicate, but where is the subject? When it comes to commands, grammar experts think of the subject as being built into the command—the subject is the person being spoken to. What's important to remember is that commands can stand on their own as real sentences.

If a string of words doesn't have a subject or a predicate, it is a **sentence fragment**. Sentence fragments cannot stand on their own.

Practice

Identify the subject and the predicate of the following sentences.

1. The woman in the lobby is waiting for Mr. Williams.
   Subject: _____
   Predicate: _____

2. Mr. Williams went downstairs.
   Subject: _____
   Predicate: _____

Independent and Dependent Clauses

One of the building blocks of writing is the **clause**: a string of words that includes a subject and a predicate. Some clauses express a complete thought and can stand on their own as sentences. These are called **independent clauses**.

Other clauses, however, express an incomplete thought and cannot stand on their own. These are called **dependent clauses**. They need to be attached to an independent clause in order to fully make sense.

Here are some examples of both types:

Independent clause: *It started snowing.*
Dependent clause: *After Emily won the contest.*

Notice that the first clause expresses a complete idea (it began to snow) and that it is a grammatically correct sentence on its own.

But the dependent clause is incomplete—it's begging for a resolution. (After Emily won the contest, *what happened?*) As is, this clause is not a sentence; it's a sentence fragment. To create a grammatically correct sentence in this case, you can do two things:

- Simply remove the word *after*:
  Emily won the contest.
- Attach the dependent clause to an independent clause using a comma:

After Emily won the contest,	*she jumped up and down in excitement.*
dependent clause	independent clause

Here's another example:

> **Dependent clause:** *That you should avoid eating in order to lose weight.*

As is, it's not a real sentence. To create a real sentence in this case, you can:

- Remove the word *that*:
  You should avoid eating in order to lose weight.
- Attach the dependent clause to an independent clause; for instance:

Potato chips and cookies are two foods	*that you should avoid eating in order to lose weight.*
independent clause	dependent clause

Coordinating Conjunctions

You probably use **coordinating conjunctions** all the time without realizing that they have a name; they are words that are used to connect independent clauses together to create one longer sentence. There are seven coordinating conjunctions: *for, and, nor, but, or, yet,* and *so.* You can use the acronym FANBOYS to remember them.

Here's an example of how they're used:

> **Independent clause:** *It's going to rain this afternoon.*
> **Independent clause:** *I still want to go to the game.*

We can use the coordinating conjunction *but* (plus a comma) to join them together:

> *It's going to rain this afternoon,* but *I still want to go to the game.*

Subordinating Conjunctions

Another way to connect clauses is to use a **subordinating conjunction**—words such as *after, because,* and *unless.*

As an example, let's join together these two independent clauses:

> **Independent clause:** *No one takes out the garbage.*
> **Independent clause:** *It smells horrible in the garage.*

Depending on which conjunction we choose, we'll communicate additional information about the situation in the garage. For example:

> *It smells horrible in the garage* because *no one takes out the garbage.*

By using *because,* we're making the point that the odor is caused by the fact that no one takes out the garbage. If we choose a different conjunction, we'll describe a different scenario and make a different point. For instance:

> Even though *it smells horrible in the garage, no one takes out the garbage.*

Here's another example of two independent clauses and ways to connect them:

> **Independent clause:** *Jonathan quit.*
> **Independent clause:** *I had to work overtime.*
> *I had to work overtime* after *Jonathan quit.*
> Because *Jonathan quit, I had to work overtime.*

You may have noticed that when you add a subordinating conjunction to an independent clause, you create a **dependent clause**. For example, in the example just given, *Jonathan quit* is an independent clause. Even though it's just two words, it can function as a real sentence all by itself. But if you add a subordinating conjunction, it no longer can stand on its own as a real sentence. For example, *Because Jonathan quit* is not a complete thought. It prompts the reader to ask, *Because what?*

Here's a list of common subordinating conjunctions:

SUBORDINATING CONJUNCTION	USE	EXAMPLE
because since so that in order that	to show cause and effect or purpose	• We are attending class *because* we want to pass our GED® test. • *Since* I no longer work at Cost Club, I can't receive an employee discount. • I lived next to Beekman Junior College *so that* I could walk to school every day.
before after while when whenever until once as soon as as long as	to show time or time sequence	• *Before* I lived in Mason City, I lived in Des Moines. • I break out in hives *whenever* I eat strawberries. • I can handle the stress at work *as long as* I exercise daily.
though although even though whereas	to show contrast	• Peter passed the test *even though* he was very nervous. • Wendy loves to read books for school, *although* she gets distracted easily. • Jake was horrible at keeping a budget, *whereas* Bob always had his money in order.
if unless whether	to show a condition	• *If* you study hard and come to class, you will succeed. • You cannot take the exam *unless* you have proper identification.
as though as if as much as	to show similarity	• She looked *as though* she had seen a ghost. • *As much as* I want to visit my daughter, I don't think I'll be able to until next year.
where wherever	to show place	• The children want to know *where* their parents used to live.

Practice

Read the two clauses, and then choose which sentence does NOT combine them correctly.

3. **Independent clause:** *I moved to Paris.*
   Independent clause: *I learned how to speak French.*
   a. I moved to Paris, so I learned how to speak French.
   b. After I moved to Paris, I learned how to speak French.
   c. I learned how to speak French after I moved to Paris.
   d. I moved to Paris, wherever I learned how to speak French.

Run-On Sentences

A **run-on sentence** occurs when one independent clause runs right into another independent clause without proper punctuation. Sometimes no punctuation is used at all, while other times there is just a comma between the two thoughts.

Here are some examples of run-on sentences:

Terri wants to leave now, she's tired.
Whether or not you believe me it's true I did not lie to you.

There are several ways to correct this type of error. You can:

- Add a *period*, a *question mark*, or an *exclamation point* to create separate sentences.
- Add a *conjunction* (and a comma, if needed) to join the clauses together.
- Add a *semicolon*, *colon*, or *dash* to join the clauses together.
- *Rewrite* one or more of the clauses.

Here are a few ways to correct the earlier examples:

Terri wants to leave now—she's tired.
Terri wants to leave now because she's tired.
Whether or not you believe me, it's true. I did not lie to you!
Whether or not you believe me, it's true; I did not lie to you.
Whether or not you believe me, it's true—I did not lie to you.

Practice

Select the revision that is NOT a good way to correct the run-on sentence.

4. Greenville is in the middle of nowhere, it's a really boring place to grow up.
   a. Greenville is in the middle of nowhere. It's a really boring place to grow up.
   b. Greenville is a really boring place to grow up; in the middle of nowhere.
   c. Greenville is a really boring place to grow up because it's in the middle of nowhere.
   d. Greenville is a really boring place to grow up—it's in the middle of nowhere.

Complex Sentences

As you learned before, many sentences contain both a dependent clause and an independent clause (they're joined together by the subordinating conjunction that's built into the dependent clause). This type of sentence is called a **complex sentence**. A complex sentence can begin with either the independent clause or the dependent clause. Comma placement depends on how the sentence is constructed.

While you were sleeping / , / the thunderstorm came through the city.
Dependent clause / comma / independent clause

The thunderstorm came through the city / while you were sleeping.

Independent clause / no comma / dependent clause

Because the city received so much snow / , / school will be canceled today.

Dependent clause / comma / independent clause

School will be canceled today / because the city received so much snow.

Independent clause / no comma / dependent clause

Did you notice a pattern with the commas? When the dependent clause is tacked onto the beginning of the independent clause, a comma is needed between the two clauses. When the dependent clause is tacked onto the end of the independent clause, no comma is needed.

You can use this rule when correcting sentences on the GED® test. Be careful to understand what is being said in the sentence you are correcting, however; sometimes the meaning of the sentence or other grammar rules will affect whether you should use a comma.

Which of the following sentences is NOT correctly punctuated?

    a. Even though I ate a huge dinner, I still want to try your macaroni and cheese.

    b. I know it will be really delicious because the chef used so much cheese and cream.

    c. Please don't finish it, before I get to try a spoonful.

    d. If you don't want me to have any, just tell me.

Choice **c** is not correctly punctuated. Here, the sentence starts off with an *independent* clause. There should not be a comma.

Parallel Construction

Before we explain this idea, look at the following example:

> *When Jim was dieting, he would usually eat just brown rice, grilled chicken, salad, and treat himself to nonfat ice cream for dessert.*

Did you notice a problem with this sentence? The problem is that the elements are not all parallel. **Parallelism** is a grammar rule that says that similar elements in a sentence should be written in a similar way.

Here, the similar elements are the four things that Jim WOULD eat when he was dieting. Let's look at them:

    1. brown rice
    2. grilled chicken
    3. salad
    4. treat himself to nonfat ice cream for dessert

You may have noticed that the first three items are parallel—they're all nouns—but the fourth item is different—it's a long phrase that starts off with a verb (*treat*).

There's another problem, too. Look at the words that introduce those four items:

> *When Jim was dieting, he would usually eat just . . .*

Each of the items needs to make sense after that introduction. To test this, just plug in each of the items after the introduction.

For example, the first item makes sense:

> *When Jim was dieting, he would usually eat just brown rice.*

The second item is grammatical, too:

When Jim was dieting, he would usually eat just grilled chicken.

The third item is also grammatical:

When Jim was dieting, he would usually eat just salad.

But the fourth item doesn't make sense after the introduction:

When Jim was dieting, he would usually eat just treat himself to nonfat ice cream for dessert.

There are many ways to fix the original sentence, but here is the most obvious way:

When Jim was dieting, he would usually eat just brown rice, grilled chicken, salad, and nonfat ice cream for dessert.

We deleted *treat himself to.* Now all four items are parallel—they're all nouns.

Practice

5. Select the best revision of this sentence:
   After Tina got her GED, she had to decide whether she was going to apply to colleges, look for a better job, or staying in her current job.
   a. After Tina got her GED, she had to decide whether she was going to apply to colleges, looking for a better job, or staying in her current job.
   b. After Tina got her GED, she had to decide whether she was going to apply to colleges, look for a better job, or in her current job.
   c. After Tina got her GED, she had to decide whether she was going to apply to colleges, look for a better job, or stay in her current job.
   d. The sentence is correct as is.

6. Identify the subject of the following sentence:
   They intend to buy the company this year.
   a. company
   b. this year
   c. They
   d. intend

7. Identify the dependent clause in the following sentence:
   If you think it is a good team, go see the Heat.
   a. If you think it is a good team
   b. go see the Heat
   c. a good team
   d. This sentence has no dependent clause.

8. Identify which of the following is a sentence fragment:
   a. I went.
   b. Who wrote this?
   c. Not going to happen today.
   d. Go away.

9. Select the best revision of the following run-on sentence:
   I'm going away on business, could you please watch the house, I'll be gone this weekend and I'd be most grateful.
   a. I'm going away on business this weekend. Could you please watch the house? I'd be most grateful.
   b. I'm going away on business, could you please watch the house? I'll be gone this weekend, and I'd be most grateful.
   c. I'm going away on business. Could you please watch the house. I'll be gone this weekend. I'd be most grateful.
   d. Could you please watch the house this weekend? I'm going away on business, I'd be most grateful.

10. Select the sentence that is NOT correctly punctuated.

   a. Since I started my new job last year, my life has changed dramatically.

   b. As long as I've been working, I've never really enjoyed what I was doing until now.

   c. It's less about the pay than it is about the people—I get along great with my coworkers.

   d. I'm going to try to keep this job, until I'm old and gray.

Capitalization

After you read certain passages on the GED® test, you'll be asked to fix grammar errors contained in some of the sentences. One of the things you may need to correct is capitalization, so it's important that you learn the rules of when to use capital letters and when to use lowercase letters.

You probably already know that the first letter of the first word of every sentence must be capitalized and that the pronoun *I* should always be a capital letter, but there are many other times when you should use uppercase letters, too.

Titles and Names

Titles such as *Ms.*, *Mrs.*, *Miss*, *Mr.*, and *Dr.* are always capitalized.

Many other words in the English language—nouns such as *mayor*, *judge*, *princess*, and *chairperson*—can serve as a title when placed in front of a person's name. When they are used this way, these words should be capitalized. For example:

> *Secretary of State* John Kerry
> *President* Barack Obama
> *Aunt* Jane

Uncle Tim
Queen Elizabeth
Prince Harry
Pope Francis
Judge Judy
Ambassador Jackson
General Jack Kurutz
Private Benjamin

These words do double duty in the English language. As you can see in the list, they can serve as titles when placed in front of a person's name. But they also often serve as plain old nouns. On the GED® test, don't automatically capitalize words like *president*, *general*, or *king* when you see them. In many cases, they are simply being used as common nouns and should be lowercase. Look at these examples:

> **Used as a title:** *President* Barack Obama
> **Used as a noun:** The *president* of the United States is Barack Obama.
> **Used as a title:** *General* Jack Kurutz
> **Used as a noun:** Jack Kurutz was a heroic *general* in World War II.
> **Used as a noun and as a title:** My favorite *aunt* is *Aunt* Jane.

Proper Nouns

A **proper noun** is a specific person, place, or thing. The names of these people, places, and things should always be capitalized.

Here are some examples of proper nouns and how they should be capitalized:

People	Places	Things/Events/Etc.
Eleanor Roosevelt	United States of America	Philadelphia Eagles
Lady Gaga	China	United Airlines
John F. Kennedy	Los Angeles	Crest
George Bush Sr.	North Fourth Street	Oscar Mayer
Uncle Tim	Central Park	ESPN
Mayor Ed Koch	Union Station	NASA
Queen Elizabeth	Eiffel Tower	Saturn
	Woodside Hospital	Battle of Bunker Hill
		St. Patrick's Day
		Fourth of July
		Car and Driver (the magazine)
		Modern Family (the TV show)
		In the Name of the Father (the movie)
		"Livin' on a Prayer" (the song)

You may have noticed that some of the words in these names—such as *the* and *of*—are *not* capitalized, although we stated earlier that proper nouns should always be capitalized. Why is this?

The rules of capitalization are very detailed—and sometimes the experts differ on what they should be—but in general, in proper names the following words should be lowercase unless they are the first word of the name.

- *the, a, an* (articles)
- *to, from, on, in, of, with*, and other prepositions (some experts capitalize prepositions that have four or more letters)
- *and, but, or, yet* (conjunctions)

Remember that when these words start off the proper noun, they are capitalized, not lowercase. For example: *In Touch* (the magazine), *A Beautiful Mind* (the movie), *For Whom the Bell Tolls* (the book).

Geographical Words

As with other proper names, the names of countries, states, cities, regions, and the like—and the words that are based on them—should be capitalized. For example:

Asia, Asian
Portugal, Portuguese
France, French, Frenchwoman, Frenchman
Great Britain, British
Middle East, Middle Eastern
the South, Southern (referring to those states in the United States)
Antarctica
Rome, Roman
New York City, New Yorker
Morris County

Movies, Books, Songs, and So On

The names of books, movies, plays, TV shows, songs, albums, and the like are another type of proper noun and should be capitalized. The same goes for newspaper headlines, the titles of magazine articles, the titles of essays you write, and more. For example:

> *Romeo and Juliet* (play)
> *Back to the Future* (movie)
> *The Big Bang Theory* (TV show)
> *The Wind in the Willows* (book)
> "Mayor Vows: City Will Bounce Back from Hurricane Sandy" (newspaper headline)
> "Why Violence Is Never the Answer" (magazine article)

Events and Time Periods

As with other proper nouns, specific historical periods and events should be capitalized. Centuries should not be capitalized when used as a regular noun in a sentence, though. Look at these examples:

> the Revolutionary War
> the Great Depression
> the Middle Ages
> The twentieth century marked a turning point in technology.

Directions

Directions on the compass (*west*, *south*, *northeast*, etc.) are considered to be common nouns and are not capitalized.

Directions also sometimes serve as proper names of specific places, however. When used in this way, they should be capitalized, as all proper nouns should be.

For example:

> *The Grand Canyon is one of the biggest tourist attractions in the* Southwest.

Here, *Southwest* means a specific region of the United States—the southwest corner of the country that includes Arizona and New Mexico.

> *The school is five miles* southwest *of Santa Fe.*

Here, *southwest* means the compass direction, so it should be lowercase.

Calendar Items

The days of the week, the months of the year, and holidays all need to be capitalized. (Do not capitalize the seasons unless they are used in a proper name, in a title, or in another way that would require a noun to have an uppercase letter.) Examples:

> *Monday*
> *January*
> *Easter*
> *Fourth of July*
> *summer, fall, winter, spring*

Note this example:

> *The club's Tenth Annual* Winter *Showcase will be held in January.*

In this case, *Winter* is capitalized because it is part of a proper name—the name of a specific event—not because it's a season. The name of the event could just as easily be *Tenth Annual* Talent *Showcase.*

Proper Nouns versus Common Nouns

Here is one more important thing to think about with proper nouns: You'll often find them blended with common nouns—for example, *Crest toothpaste* or *Oscar Mayer hot dogs.*

Notice that *toothpaste* and *hot dogs* are lowercase. Why?

The word *Crest* is a proper noun—it's a brand name—but *toothpaste* is a regular old noun. It should stay lowercase. Similarly, *Oscar Mayer* is a brand name, but *hot dogs* is a common noun, so it should be lowercase.

What if you encounter an example like *United Airlines*? Should *Airlines* be capitalized? Well, this depends on whether or not it is part of the official name of the company. In this case, it is—*United Airlines* is the full, proper name of the business, so *Airlines* should be capitalized.

Just remember: if you know (or can figure out from the passage you're reading) that a word is part of a proper name, it should be capitalized. If it is just a common noun, it should be lowercase.

Now look at these examples of proper nouns blended with common nouns. Note which words are capitalized (the proper noun) and which are lowercase (the common noun):

> *The* Supreme Court justice *gave a speech at the school.*
> *I have a coupon for a free* McDonald's hamburger.
> *The* NASA *space shuttle will blast off on Sunday.*

Capitalization in Quotations

When a direct quote is included in a sentence and it's paired with a phrase like *she said*, *they shouted*, *he replied*, or *I wrote* to explain who is doing the talking (or the shouting, replying, or writing), the first word of the quotation should be capitalized.

Here are some examples:

Incorrect: *After dessert, he said quietly, "this was the worst meal of my life."*
Correct: *After dessert, he said quietly, "This was the worst meal of my life."*

Incorrect: *The chef told his assistant, "when you learn how to bake wedding cakes, you will get a raise."*

Correct: *The chef told his assistant, "When you learn how to bake wedding cakes, you will get a raise."*

Incorrect: *When I asked what her costume was, Erica replied, "a scary clown."*
Correct: *When I asked what her costume was, Erica replied, "A scary clown."*

While *A scary clown* is not a complete sentence, it is a complete quote, and it is introduced by the phrase *Erica replied*. Therefore, the first word of the quote should be capitalized.

> ## NOTE
>
> When a quoted sentence is split in two in a sentence, do not capitalize the first word of the second part, unless there is another reason to do so.

To explain this point, let's go back to one of the previous examples:

> *The chef told his assistant, "When you learn how to bake wedding cakes, you will get a raise."*

The sentence can be reworked by splitting the quote in two:

> *"When you learn how to bake wedding cakes," the chef told his assistant, "you will get a raise."*

Note that *you* should still be lowercase. This is because it is a word that is a continuation of a quoted sentence ("*When you learn how to bake wedding cakes, you will get a raise*"); it is not the first word of the quoted sentence.

Here are two more correct examples that make the same point:

> *"When you go on the boat," Carlos told us, "do not feed the sharks."*
> *Carlos told us, "Do not feed the sharks."*

Now look at this final example, to avoid confusion on the GED® test:

> *"Mia is on her way," Mike said. "She just arrived at the bus station."*

Why should *She* be capitalized? Because this is not a case of a quoted sentence being split up. Instead, there are two complete, separate sentences.

Note that the first sentence ends in a period.

> *"Mia is on her way," Mike said.*

and

> *"She just arrived at the bus station."*

She should be capitalized because it's the first word of a sentence, even though that sentence happens to be a quote.

Using Apostrophes to Create Possessive Nouns and Contractions

In English, apostrophes are an important tool that can help you create possessive words (*the dog's house, Aunt Jane's car*) as well as contractions (*they're, it's*). This lesson explains how and when to use apostrophes.

Possessive Nouns

A **possessive noun** shows the ownership that the noun has over something else. To make a noun possessive, add the following to the end of the word:

- **For most singular nouns:** Add an apostrophe and the letter *s*.
- **For most plural nouns:** Add just an apostrophe.

Look at these examples:

> Anthony's office
> the child's blanket
> the two brothers' toys
> the ladies' room
> the dog's bones [one dog has bones]
> the dogs' bones [two or more dogs have bones]

NOTE

Some plural nouns do not end in *s*, such as *children, women, mice,* and *deer*. In these cases, add an apostrophe and an *s*:
> the children's books
> the mice's cheese

When you are editing a sentence that contains a possessive noun, you will need to decide if it is singular or plural. The best way to do this is to read the entire sentence for clues.

A Mistake to Avoid

Here are some examples of a basic grammar mistake that many people make and that may be tested on the GED® test:

> **Incorrect:** *The* boy's *are building a treehouse.*
> **Incorrect:** *I just adopted two* puppy's.

What's the problem with these sentences? In each, the writer tried to make a plural word by using an apostrophe and the letter *s*. Look at the correct versions:

> **Correct:** *The* boys *are building a treehouse.*
> **Correct:** *I just adopted two* puppies.

There is no need for an apostrophe when a noun is plural. Use apostrophes when you make nouns possessive (for instance, *the* boys' *treehouse, the* puppies' *adoption*), not when you simply make nouns plural (*the* boys *have a treehouse, the* puppies *were adopted*).

Contractions

A **contraction** refers to the process of joining together two words to create one shorter word. An apostrophe replaces the letter(s) removed in the process.

The following is a list of common contractions:

aren't = are not	let's = let us	weren't = were not
can't = cannot	mightn't = might not	what'll = what will; what shall
couldn't = could not	mustn't = must not	what're = what are
didn't = did not	shan't = shall not	what's = what is; what has
doesn't = does not	she'd = she had; she would	what've = what have
don't = do not	she'll = she will; she shall	where's = where is; where has
hadn't = had not	she's = she is; she has	who'd = who had; who would
hasn't = has not	shouldn't = should not	who'll = who will; who shall
haven't = have not	that's = that is; that has	who's = who is; who has
he'd = he had; he would	there's = there is; there has	who've = who have
he'll = he will; he shall	they'd = they had; they would	won't = will not
he's = he is; he has	they'll = they will; they shall	wouldn't = would not
I'd = I had; I would	they're = they are	you'd = you had; you would
I'll = I will; I shall	they've = they have	you'll = you will; you shall
I'm = I am	we'd = we had; we would	you're = you are
I've = I have	we're = we are	you've = you have
isn't = is not	we've = we have	

For practice, replace the underlined words with the correct contractions.

> <u>Do not</u> forget that <u>we are</u> right around the corner if you <u>cannot</u> find the keys.

> **Answer:** *Don't* forget that *we're* right around the corner if you *can't* find the keys.

The contraction of *do not* is *don't*, the contraction of *we are* is *we're* (NOT *were*!), and the contraction of *cannot* is *can't*.

Contractions versus Possessive Pronouns

In English, there are a few contractions that are pronounced the same as a few possessive pronouns, and many people mistake these words. You may see questions on the GED® test that assess whether you know the difference.

Here's an example:

Correct: *The dog hurt its paw.*
Incorrect: *The dog hurt it's paw.*

The second sentence is incorrect because *it's* is a contraction of *it is*. That means that the sentence really says *The dog hurts it is paw*, which does not make any sense.

Here are some words that people commonly confuse:

Contraction	Possessive Pronoun
it's (it is)	its
you're (you are)	your
they're (they are)	their
who's (who is)	whose

REMEMBER

Contractions *always* use apostrophes. Possessive pronouns *never* use apostrophes.

An easy way to remember this is to think about what a contraction really is: in casual speech, we sometimes slide two words together, making one word. (*You are* becomes *you're*; *would not* becomes *wouldn't*; and so on.) In the process of sliding the words together, we drop out one or two of the letters. The apostrophe replaces the letter(s) that dropped out. (When we contract *you are* to make *you're*, we drop the *a*. The apostrophe replaces that *a*.)

Practice
11. Select the grammatically correct sentence.
  a. We're going to stay at my familys house.
  b. We're going to stay at my family's house.
  c. We're going to stay at my families house.
  d. Were going to stay at my family's house.

12. Select the grammatically correct sentence.
  a. Toms sister wasn't planning to come to his childrens' graduation.
  b. Tom's sister wasnt planning to come to his childrens' graduation.
  c. Tom's sister wasn't planning to come to his children's graduation.
  d. none of the above

13. Select the grammatically correct sentence.
  a. You're not going to fix that cars problems without the proper tools.
  b. Your not going to fix that cars problem's without the proper tools.
  c. You're not going to fix that cars' problems without the proper tools.
  d. none of the above

Sentence Punctuation

Proper punctuation marks are necessary when writing complete and correct sentences.

End Marks
A complete sentence must end with correct punctuation. The punctuation at the end of the sentence depends on what type of sentence it is.

  1. A statement ends with a period.
     Minnesota is known for its cold winters.
  2. A question ends with a question mark.
     Do you think it will snow tonight?
  3. An exclamation—that is, a sentence with strong emotion—ends with an exclamation point.
     Call the police!

Commas

Commas are used to indicate breaks in different parts of a sentence. People are often confused about when to use a comma—it is common to place too many commas in a sentence. The following list outlines comma rules for standard English:

1. Use commas to separate three or more items in a **series** that includes the word *and* or *or*.

   > *I lost my wallet, my gloves, and my car keys all on one day.*
   > *Add ketchup, mayonnaise, or mustard to the sandwich.*
   > *Bring the paperwork, three forms of ID, and a photo to the office.*

   Note that the comma is placed **before** *and* or *or*, not after it.

   Do not use a comma when only two items are joined by *and* or *or*. That is not a series, so it doesn't need a comma.

   Incorrect: *Bring the paperwork, and three forms of ID to the office.*
   Correct: *Bring the paperwork and three forms of ID to the office.*

2. Use a comma after an introductory phrase. An **introductory phrase** can be a prepositional phrase that begins a sentence.

   > *In the end, Jamie was glad she had worked all weekend painting her room.*
   > *After hearing the weather report, the boss moved the company picnic indoors.*

3. Use a comma before a coordinating conjunction that joins two independent clauses. An **independent clause** contains a subject and a verb and would function as a grammatically correct sentence if it stood alone. Examples of coordinating conjunctions that join independent clauses are *and, but, or, nor, for, so,* and *yet*.

   > *I wanted to go to the movies,* but *I didn't have enough money to pay for the ticket.*

   > *William completed the computer training, so* he decided to apply for a new job.*

4. Use commas to separate an appositive from the rest of the sentence if it is a **nonrestrictive appositive** that gives information about something mentioned in the sentence but it is not essential to the core meaning or grammar of the sentence. Do not use commas with restrictive appositives (e.g., *the poet Robert Burns*).

   > *Renita, the tall girl down the hall, will pick up my mail while I am on vacation.*
   > *The office will be closed on Friday, the last day of the month.*

5. Use a comma when a dependent clause comes before the independent clause.

   > *After I complete my degree, I plan to move to Los Angeles.*
   > *If you are sick, you must contact your supervisor.*

6. Use a comma to separate the year in a date.
   > *March 14, 2008, is my daughter's birthday.*

7. Use commas to separate a state name from a city name (or a country name from a city name, etc.).

   > *Kansas City, Kansas, is my birthplace.*
   > *I'd love to visit my friends in Alberta, Canada, next year.*
   > *The flight began in Beijing, China, stopped in Osaka, Japan, and arrived 12 hours later in San Francisco, California.*

Practice

14. Select the best revision of the sentence below:
    Larry my friend from high school lives next door.
    a. Larry, my friend from high school lives next door.
    b. Larry, my friend from high school lives, next door.
    c. Larry, my friend from high school, lives next door.
    d. The sentence is correct as is.

Semicolons and Colons

A **semicolon** (;) can be used to join two independent clauses. Joining two independent clauses this way suggests that the two clauses are related in meaning and of equal importance.

> *Every Friday we go out for dinner and see a movie; it is our reward for a long week at work.*

There are several instances when a **colon** (:) can be used in a sentence.

1. Use a colon after an independent clause to introduce a list.
   > *Travis requested his favorite meal for his birthday: pizza, cheese bread, and ice cream.*
2. Use a colon after an independent clause to introduce a quotation.
   > *Emily explained her reason for leaving the magazine: "It's a dead-end job, no matter how hard I work."*
3. Use a colon between two independent clauses when you want to emphasize the second clause.
   > *The result of the poll was clear: Obama would probably win the election.*

Quotation Marks

Quotation marks are used around direct quotes— that is, the words a person or character says. For example:

> *Uncle John said, "It has been years since I have seen my sister's children."*
> *"I refuse to pay for this meal," Laura shouted, "because there is a bug in my salad!"*

Put punctuation marks before the first quotation mark and inside of the final quotation mark.

Quotation marks are also used around the names of poems, song titles, short stories, magazine or newspaper articles, essays, speeches, chapter titles, and other short works. (Titles of movies, books, TV series, etc. are usually set in italics.)

> *Her daughter would not stop singing "Row, Row, Row Your Boat" as they drove to the lake.*
> *My favorite poem is "Wild Geese," by Mary Oliver.*

Practice

Select the best revision of the following sentences.

15. Do you think Ted remembered his book, pen, and paper?
    a. Do you think Ted remembered his: book, pen, and paper?
    b. Do you think Ted remembered his book, pen and paper?
    c. Do you think Ted remembered his book; pen; and paper?
    d. The sentence is correct as is.

16. He was born in February 1994 at the main hospital in Duluth Minnesota.
    a. He was born in February 1994 at the main hospital in Duluth, Minnesota.
    b. He was born in February, 1994, at the main hospital in Duluth Minnesota.
    c. He was born in February, 1994 at the main hospital in Duluth, Minnesota.
    d. The sentence is correct as is.

17. My mother said, "I like vacationing in three states: Texas New Mexico and Arizona."
    a. My mother said, "I like vacationing in three states, Texas, New Mexico, and Arizona.
    b. My mother said, I like vacationing in three states: Texas, New Mexico, and Arizona.
    c. My mother said, "I like vacationing in three states: Texas, New Mexico, and Arizona."
    d. The sentence is correct as is.

Sentence Structure

Active and Passive Voice

Active and passive voice refers to the way you write about the subject and verb. If the subject is known and is doing the action, it's an active voice. If the subject is unknown or is not doing the action, it's a passive voice.

This concept is much easier to understand with an example. Look at the following sentence:

Barry hit the ball.

Barry is the subject and he's the one doing the action. That means the sentence is written in an active voice. What if we write the following:

The ball was hit by Barry.

Now *the ball* is the subject, but it's not doing anything; something is being done to it. The subject is no longer active, so the sentence is written in a passive voice.

Generally speaking, you should use the active voice, rather than the passive voice, when you write. The GED® test will likely include some questions that test your ability to identify the passive voice and to change it to an active voice.

Usage

Throughout the history of the English language, people have developed conventional ways of speaking that enable them to understand each other. These conventions are referred to as usage. On the GED® test, usage questions commonly test the following concepts:

- verb conjugation
- verb tense
- subject–verb agreement

Subject–Verb Agreement

As previously mentioned, a subject and verb are said to *agree* when they are either both plural or both singular. Usually, to make a noun plural you add an *-s*, and to make a verb plural you take an *-s* away. For example:

The dog growls.

or

The dogs growl.

On the GED® test, you're likely to see questions that will test common errors in subject–verb agreement. Here are a few common mistakes to watch out for:

- **doesn't/don't.** Incorrect: *He don't want to go.* Correct: *He doesn't want to go.*
- **wasn't/weren't.** Incorrect: *The pens wasn't in the drawer when I looked.* Correct: *The pens weren't in the drawer when I looked.*
- **there's/there are.** Incorrect: *There's a lot of people here.* Correct: *There are a lot of people here.*
- **here's/here are.** Incorrect: *Here's the instructions.* Correct: *Here are the instructions.*

Mechanics

In reference to writing, the term *mechanics* refers to the little things that make your writing look like it should: capitalization, spelling, and punctuation. Using correct mechanics may not change the substance of your writing; that is, a word may mean the same thing whether it's capitalized or not. Correct mechanics will change how your writing is perceived.

Organization

Organization refers to placing sentences and paragraphs in order so that the reader can best understand what you're trying to say in your writing. An organized paragraph typically includes one topic sentence, placed either at the beginning or at the end of the paragraph, and a few supporting sentences. An organized essay includes an introduction with a strong thesis statement, two or more body paragraphs, and a conclusion.

There are several common ways of organizing supporting sentences and paragraphs in an essay. Three of the most common are:

1. chronological order
2. order of importance
3. cause and effect

Chronological Order

Chronological order is the order in which things happen in time; in other words, what happens first, next, and last. If you were telling a story, giving instructions, or relating an event in your essay, you would probably do well to write in chronological order.

A common mistake made by beginning writers is to skip around in time. For example, when telling about a football game, one might write:

> *Our team got a touchdown! The running back got the ball at the 48 yard line and ran it all the way to the end zone. The coach told the quarterback to go long, but instead he handed it off to the running back.*

As you can see, this is not the order in which things actually happened; that is, it's not written in chronological order and may be confusing to some. A more organized way to write the paragraph would be as follows:

> *The coach told the quarterback to go long, but instead he handed the ball off to the running back at the 48 yard line. Then the running back ran the ball all the way to the end zone. At last our team got a touchdown!*

Telling what happens first, next, and last—in that order—helps the reader keep track of what you're writing about.

TRANSITION WORDS

Transition words help readers know the direction you're going in your writing. Common transition words for chronological order include: *first, to begin, next, then, afterward, last,* and *finally.*

Order of Importance

To organize your writing based on order of importance means to put sentences or paragraphs in order from most to least important, or from least to most important. For example, let's say you're telling a coworker about your rotten weekend. Three terrible things happened to you: you lost your hat, you stubbed your toe, and you were very ill. Assuming that your illness is the most important event and losing your hat is the second most important event, you might tell the story like this:

> *This was a terrible weekend. I stubbed my toe so badly that now I can hardly walk. Even worse, on Saturday night I lost my hat. Worst of all, when I came home Saturday night I got violently ill!*

On the GED® test, you'll be expected to know when sentences or paragraphs are in the wrong order. Look for key words like *more/most*, *worse/worst*, and *better/best* to determine what order things should be in.

Cause and Effect

Cause and effect is an organizational style that either puts the entire cause of an event first, and then the effect, or vice versa. The key to this method is to be sure that the two are entirely separated and clear. For example, let's say you got in a car wreck because a deer ran out in front of you. You might write something like this:

> *(1) Last week, I had to get my front bumper replaced. (2) I also had to get my windshield replaced and the front tires realigned. (3) All this trouble came into my life because I ran into a deer last Monday.*

As you can see, the two sentences describing the effect are together at the beginning of the paragraph, while the sentence describing the cause is at the end. The paragraph would not be as well organized if you moved sentence (3) in front of sentence (2), thereby interrupting the organizational flow.

Quiz

Now that you've had a chance to review the writing skills needed to do well on the GED® test, give the following questions a try. Read each question, and then choose the one best answer for each.

18. Sentence (1): Every time my brother takes a shower, he leave a huge mess.
    Which revision should be made to sentence (1)?
    a. replace *Every* with *All*
    b. change *takes* to *take*
    c. change *leave* to *leaves*
    d. replace *mess* with *messy*

19. Sentence (1) I used to enjoy going out to dance. (2) When I was younger.
    Which revision should be made to sentence (2)?
    a. delete sentence (2) and add a sentence about dancing
    b. move sentence (2) in front of sentence (1) and add the word *However*
    c. add *for example* to the beginning of sentence (2) and *instead of* at the end of sentence (1)
    d. connect the sentences by removing the period at the end of sentence (1) and set *When* in lowercase

20. Sentence (1) She ate the cake. (2) Which the king had poisoned.
    Which revision should be made to sentence (2)?
    a. delete the word *which*
    b. change the word *Which* to *That*
    c. connect sentences with a comma instead of a period and set *Which* in lowercase
    d. add the word *And* to the beginning of the sentence

21. Sentence (1): Three of us began the race, however, only two of us finished it.

    Which revision should be made to sentence (1)?

a. move *Three of us began the race* to the end of the sentence

b. change the first comma to a period and capitalize *however*

c. delete *however* and replace with *because*

d. change *however* to *nevertheless*

22. Sentence (1): The car was smashed by a cement mixer.

    Which revision should be made to sentence (1)?

a. delete *was*

b. place a period after *smashed*

c. move *cement mixer* in front of *car*

d. change the order to *A cement mixer smashed the car*

23. Sentence (1): The last time I went to see my friend in Dallas, he's living on the south side.

    Which of the following revisions should be made to sentence (1)?

a. delete *The*

b. change the comma to a period and capitalize *he's*

c. change *he's* to *he was*

d. move *he's living on the south side* to the beginning of the sentence

For questions 24 through 26, read the sentences and then choose the best answer.

    (1) Last week I had too get my front bumper replaced. (2) I also has to get my windshield replaced and the front tires realigned. (3) All this trouble came into my life, because I ran into a deer last Monday.

24. Which of the following revisions should be made to sentence (1)?

a. move *Last week* to the end of the sentence

b. change *too* to *to*

c. delete the word *front*

d. change *has* to *had*

25. Sentence (2): I also has to get my windshield replaced and the front tires realigned.

    Which of the following revisions should be made to sentence (2)?

a. delete *also*

b. change *has* to *had*

c. add a comma after *replaced*

d. add a semicolon after *and*

26. Sentence (3): All this trouble came into my life, because I ran into a deer last Monday.

    Which of the following revisions should be made to sentence (3)?

a. delete the comma after *life*

b. move *because I ran into a deer last Monday* to the beginning of the sentence

c. add a comma after *deer*

d. change *Monday* to *monday*

27. Which of the following should a good introduction do?

a. summarize the essay

b. develop the argument

c. get the reader's attention

d. leave the reader with a sense of closure

Answers and Explanations

Chapter Practice

1. **Subject:** *the woman*; **Predicate:** *is waiting for Mr. Williams.* This is a complete sentence: it expresses a complete idea and includes a subject and a predicate. Note that the subject is *the woman*, not *the lobby*—the lobby isn't waiting for Mr. Williams.

2. **Subject:** *Mr. Williams*; **Predicate:** *went downstairs.* This is a complete sentence: It expresses a complete idea and includes a subject and a predicate.

3. **d.** This sentence uses a subordinating conjunction—*wherever*—but *wherever* doesn't make sense here. Here is a better use of *wherever* to combine two clauses: *Wherever I go with Andy, he always seems to know someone.*

4. **b.** This revision tries to blend the clauses together with a semicolon, but in the process it chops out some key words. By itself, *in the middle of nowhere* is not a clause and it doesn't make sense tacked on at the end with a semicolon.

5. **c.** The problem with the original sentence is that it contains a series (*apply to colleges, look for a better job, or staying in her current job*), but the series is not parallel. The third item (*staying in her current job*) doesn't fit with the first two, and it also doesn't make sense with the phrase that introduces the series (*she had to decide whether she was going to . . .*). This revision is correct because the third item has been fixed—it is now similar to the other two items (it starts off with the correct verb form, *stay*), and it makes sense logically in the sentence.

6. **c.** In this sentence, *They* identifies who or what is performing the action. It is therefore the subject of the sentence.

7. **a.** The first part of this sentence, *If you think it is a good team*, would be a fragment if it stood alone. It makes us wonder, okay, if we think the Heat is a good team, *then what?* It needs an additional thought to form a complete sentence.

8. **c.** *Not going to happen today* is a sentence fragment because it's missing a subject and a proper verb. If we add these elements, we can turn it into a complete sentence. For example: *The meeting is not going to happen today.*

9. **a.** This revision combines the first clause (*I'm going away on business*) and the third clause (*I'll be gone this weekend*) into one complete sentence. This is a good idea, because these clauses communicate related ideas—they provide the background information that the speaker wants the listener to know before he or she asks for a favor. This choice also turns *could you please watch the house* into its own sentence by capitalizing *could* and adding a question mark (all questions should end with a question mark). The last sentence is now its own sentence, too.

10. **d.** This sentence starts off with an independent clause and ends with a dependent clause. There is no reason for the comma.

11. **b.** Both *We're* (meaning *We are*) and the possessive *family's* are spelled correctly.

12. **c.** The possessives *Tom's* and the possessive *children's* are spelled correctly, as is *wasn't* (a contraction meaning *was not*).

13. **d.** The sentence should read: *You're not going to fix that car's problems without the proper tools.*

14. **c.** In this sentence, the phrase *my friend from high school* is a nonrestrictive appositive: it gives additional information about the subject, Larry, but is not essential to the meaning of the sentence (that he lives next door). Commas are always used to set off nonrestrictive appositives from the rest of the sentence.

15. **d.** The sentence is correctly punctuated as is.

16. a. There is no reason for commas in the date *February 1994* (a month and year), but there should be a comma between the city and state (*Duluth, Minnesota*).

17. c. This sentence requires a comma to set off the quote, quotation marks to surround the quote, a colon to introduce the list of three states (because it comes after an independent clause, *I like vacationing in three states*), and commas after the words *Texas* and *New Mexico*.

Quiz

18. c. The subject and verb must agree. The singular subject, *he*, requires a singular verb.

19. d. By itself, sentence (2) is a fragment. Connecting it to sentence (1) makes it a dependent clause of a complete sentence.

20. c. By itself, sentence (2) is a fragment. Connecting it to sentence (1) makes it part of a complete sentence.

21. b. When the word *however* is used between two clauses, you can place either a period or a semicolon at the end of the first clause.

22. d. It is preferable that sentences use an active voice rather than a passive voice. By changing the order of the words, you can have the subject be the thing doing the action.

23. c. The beginning of the sentence is written in the past tense, so the end of the sentence must also be in past tense. *He's*, which is a contraction for *he is*, is present tense.

24. b. *Too* and *to* are homonyms. *Too* means also, and is not the correct word in this sentence.

25. b. The verb *has* does not agree with the subject *I*, and also shifts the passage from past to present tense. Replacing *has* with *had* corrects these issues.

26. a. A comma is not needed in this sentence.

27. c. The purpose of an introduction is to introduce the topic and catch the reader's attention. This is your chance to make the reader want to continue reading your essay.

REVIEW

Sentence structure refers to the way words are put together to create sentences. It includes the following concepts:

- **Subjects and predicates.** A subject is who or what the sentence is about; a predicate is the verb and everything that comes after it. Every complete sentence has a subject and a predicate.
- **Independent and dependent clauses.** A clause is a group of words that includes a subject and a predicate. An independent clause is a complete sentence; a dependent clause is not complete on its own.
- **Fragments and run-ons.** A fragment is an incomplete sentence; a run-on is two complete sentences joined together with a comma or no punctuation at all.
- **Active and passive voice.** In an active voice, the subject of a sentence is doing the action. In a passive voice, the action is being done to the subject.

Usage refers to the rules that determine how words should be used in sentences. It includes the following concept:

- **Subject–verb agreement.** A verb should be made singular or plural to match its subject.

Mechanics are the nuts and bolts of writing, including punctuation, capitalization, and spelling. In regard to punctuation, one of the most important things to study is comma rules. In regard to spelling, you'll need to learn how to use homonyms correctly.

Organization refers to the way sentences and paragraphs are placed in order. There are three major types of organization:

- **Chronological order.** Events are written in the order in which they occurred in time.
- **Order of importance.** Sentences and paragraphs are written in order from least to most important, or vice versa.
- **Cause and effect.** Everything having to do with the cause is written separately from everything having to do with the effect.

On the GED® Test Reasoning through Language Arts (RLA) Review, you'll be expected to know when sentences or paragraphs are in the wrong order.

CHAPTER

7 ▶ THE EXTENDED RESPONSE ESSAY: TIPS AND SCORING

CHAPTER SUMMARY

In this chapter, you'll learn how to recognize the parts of an effective essay. You'll also learn how to use the basic steps of the writing process to plan and draft an effective essay in response to a given prompt.

About the GED® Test Extended Response Question

The GED® Reasoning through Language Arts test features one extended response item that requires you to write a short essay in response to a reading passage or pair of passages. These reading passages are between 550 and 650 words, and will focus on presenting arguments or viewpoints along with supporting evidence. Your job will be to analyze these arguments and evidence, incorporating your own knowledge and views while still focusing mainly on the author and his or her intent. Your extended response should always include evidence presented within the passage itself as the main basis for your arguments. You should also analyze or evaluate the validity of the evidence presented in the passage. Note that this test item is not about choosing the "right" or "wrong" side of an issue. It is intended to test your ability to understand, analyze, and evaluate arguments.

Before you take the GED® RLA test, practice your typing skills. On exam day, you will have a lot to say, and you don't want to waste part of your 45 minutes hunting for letters on the keyboard. A good goal for taking the GED® RLA test is to be comfortable typing sentences on a computer. When you practice essay writing, set a timer for yourself so you can see what it feels like to type with the clock ticking.

Before You Write Your Essay

Producing a great essay for the GED® test requires a step-by-step process, and many of those steps take place *before* you write it. Take the time to work through this lesson, and you'll have a good foundation for writing your best essay on test day.

ERASABLE WHITEBOARDS

When you take the GED® test, you will be provided with an erasable whiteboard to jot down notes. These are especially useful during the extended response question, as you prepare to write your essay. If you need additional whiteboards during testing, you can request a fresh one and turn in the one that you've already used. You are allowed to have only one whiteboard at a time.

Understanding the Prompt

Writing an extended response essay requires you not only to analyze the passage(s) but also to respond to a specific prompt. Take a look at this sample prompt:

PROMPT

In the following article, the pros and cons of wearing school uniforms are discussed. In your response, analyze both positions to determine which view is better supported. Use relevant and specific evidence from the passage to support your response.

Type your response in the box; you will have approximately 45 minutes to complete it.

To understand exactly what you're being asked to write about, carefully read the prompt and identify:

- **The issue** (*pros and cons of wearing school uniforms*)
- **The description of what you are asked to do** (*analyze both positions; determine which view is better supported; use relevant and specific evidence from the passage to support your response*)
- **Instructions for completing the task** (*type your response in the box; you will have approximately 45 minutes to complete it*)

Reading the Passage(s)

There's a natural tendency to want to rush into writing the essay—that's what you are being tested on, after all—and to skimp on reading the passage(s). Avoid doing this. The only way to produce a good essay is to read the passage(s) carefully, understand it/them, and pull out what you will need when you write.

Follow these **five steps** as you read the passage(s). At the end of the process, you will have good information and ideas to use as you write your essay.

1. Before you start to read, **scan the passage(s)** to get a sense of what the passage(s) is/are about and note how the information is organized.
2. **Read the passage(s).** Because you know you will definitely have to respond, as you read try to relate the information in the passage(s) to your own life experiences.
3. As you read, use your whiteboard to **write down questions** that you have about the content.
4. **Determine the author's main argument**, and write that down. Then quickly outline the main points that the author makes to support that argument and restate them in your own words.
5. **Evaluate the author's argument.** Did he or she provide good support or enough evidence for it? Why or why not? Does the way the author writes affect you emotionally? Why or why not?

What's in an Essay

An **essay** is a short piece of nonfiction writing that presents the writer's point of view on a particular subject. Remember, *short* is a relative term; in this case, it basically means *shorter than a book*. An essay can actually be as short as a paragraph or two, or as long as 50 pages. On the GED® test, you'll want to shoot for a four or five paragraph essay.

Every essay has three main parts: an **introduction**, a **body**, and a **conclusion**, also known as a **beginning**, **middle**, and **end**. In a five-paragraph essay, the first paragraph is the introduction, the last paragraph is the conclusion, and the three paragraphs in the middle are the body.

The Introduction

The *introduction* is the first paragraph in an essay. In a five-paragraph essay such as the one you'll be writing for the GED® test, the introduction is usually about three or four sentences long. It has three main purposes:

- state the main idea of the essay
- catch the reader's attention
- set the tone for the rest of the essay

Stating the Main Idea

A **main idea** is the main thing the writer wants the reader to know. The main idea of a paragraph is stated in the **topic sentence**, and the topic sentence is often the first sentence of the paragraph. Like a paragraph, an essay has a main idea. It is stated in a single sentence called the **thesis statement**, which is generally the last sentence of the introduction.

On the GED® test, your thesis statement should be a clear, concise answer to the prompt. For example, a possible thesis sentence for a sample prompt asking what you would choose if you could relive one day of your life might be as follows:

> *If I could do one thing in my life again, I would relive my wedding day.*

This is a good thesis statement because it clearly answers the question in the prompt. It also presents the main idea of the essay without trying to tell the reader too much at once.

Catching the Reader's Attention

In addition to containing the thesis statement, a good introduction starts off with a couple of sentences that catch the reader's attention. Obviously, the content of these sentences will vary widely depending on your thesis statement. A possible introduction based on the sample thesis statement provided might look something like this:

> *What if you could live one day of your life over again? Some people might choose to relive a day in order to change something about their lives. Others might simply want a second chance to enjoy a great experience. If I could do one thing in my life again, I would relive my wedding day.*

As you can see, the three sentences at the beginning of the paragraph lead into the thesis statement in a relatively engaging way. It might not be *Harry Potter*, but it's definitely better than the following approach:

> *This is my paper about the thing I would like to do over again in my life. I would like to live my wedding day over again.*

The people who grade GED® test extended responses read dozens, perhaps even hundreds of essays written from the same prompt. An essay with a clear, creative introduction will almost certainly earn a higher score than an introduction that merely states what the essay is supposed to be about.

Setting the Tone for the Essay

Finally, a good introduction sets the tone for the rest of the essay. **Tone** refers to the attitude the writer takes toward the subject and the reader. For example, your tone might be formal, informal, humorous, ironic, aggressive, or apologetic. The tone you choose depends to some extent on your purpose for writing. For example, if your purpose is to amuse the reader, your tone will be humorous.

On the GED® test, it is a good idea to use a formal tone. That means using standard English vocabulary and grammar, rather than casual slang such as you might use with a friend. You should strive to use complete sentences with correct grammar and punctuation, and to keep contractions (words like *can't*, *don't*, and *won't*) to a minimum. Using a formal tone in your writing shows respect for your readers while proving that you are able to write correctly.

To better understand the difference between formal and informal tone, take a look at the following examples. The first example is written using an informal tone. The second uses a formal tone. In both examples the thesis statement is bold so that you can easily locate it.

Example 1: *You know, living your life over again would be like a dream. I guess some people would want to go back and try to change something they messed up the first time, and some people would probably just want to relive a day when they did something really cool.* **I would totally do my wedding day again.**

Example 2: *What if you could live one day of your life over again? Some people might choose to relive a day in order to change something about their lives. Others might simply want a second chance to enjoy a great experience.* **If I could do one thing in my life again, I would relive my wedding day.**

While the first example may be a more accurate representation of how people speak, it is not an acceptable way to write an academic essay. The second example uses a tone that is appropriate to academic writing. You will be expected to write using a similar tone on the GED® test.

Notice that in both introductions the thesis statement is the last sentence of the paragraph. You should strive to structure your introductions in the same way. Just as businesspeople generally chat for a few minutes before getting down to business, a good writer strives to get the reader's attention before stating the essay's main idea.

Now you try it. Using the space below, draft and write *an introduction only* in response to the following prompt:

What is your favorite thing? Whether it is a gift you were given during your childhood or something you saved up for years for and bought, you probably have something that is special to you. Write about this special object and why it is important to you.

Introduction:

_____

_____

_____

_____

_____

The Body

The *body* is the part of the essay where you develop and defend your argument. Like the essay itself, the body can range from a single paragraph to many pages in length. For the purposes of the GED® test, however, the body of your essay should be two or three paragraphs long.

You have learned that each paragraph must have a topic sentence stating the main idea of the paragraph. As previously mentioned, it's a good idea to make the topic sentence the first sentence of the paragraph so that your reader knows right away what the paragraph is going to be about.

The following paragraph is an example of a body paragraph that might follow the sample introduction on reliving one's wedding day:

> *Reliving my wedding day would give me the opportunity to see my family together again. It was the only day of my life when my mom's and my dad's families came together to celebrate in one place. Furthermore, my*

wedding day was the last time I saw my grandfather because he passed away a few weeks later.

The first sentence is the topic sentence and states the main idea of the paragraph—that reliving the wedding day would allow the writer to see his or her family together again. The other sentences support the main idea by providing examples of how the family was united that day. As a whole, the paragraph develops the main idea of the essay, which is that the writer would like to experience his or her wedding day again.

It's your turn. Using the space provided, write a thesis and body paragraph that explores the following prompt.

> *What is your favorite thing? Whether it is a gift you were given during your childhood or something you saved up for years for and bought, you probably have something that is special to you. Write about this special object and why it is important to you.*

Your thesis:

_____

_____

Body paragraph:

_____

_____

_____

_____

_____

The Conclusion

The *conclusion* is the final paragraph of the essay. A good conclusion should accomplish the following things:

1. restate the main idea
2. give the reader a sense of closure

Restating the Main Idea

The purpose of restating the main idea in the conclusion is twofold; first, it reminds the reader of the most important thing you want him or her to remember. Second, it gives the essay a more unified feeling.

Restating the main idea, however, doesn't necessarily mean writing the exact same thing or simply switching the words around. You can be more creative this time around, including adding some extra information or restating your ideas in a new and interesting way. Here's one way to restate the thesis statement we've been working with throughout this chapter:

Original thesis:

If I could do one thing in my life again, I would relive my wedding day.

Restated:

Though I will never have the chance, I would love to be able to experience my wedding day again.

In this example, the main idea is given in both sentences, but in the second one it includes something more: the idea that reliving any moment of one's life is impossible. It adds a sense of regret to the essay that can leave the reader feeling pleasantly wistful.

Now it's your turn to write. Using the following lines, rewrite the thesis statement you wrote in the previous example as it would appear in the conclusion of your essay.

Original thesis:

_____

_____

Restated thesis:

_____

_____

Giving the Reader a Sense of Closure

To give readers a sense of closure means to make them feel satisfied with how the essay ends. It's difficult to say specifically what to do so that people come away with this feeling. It's fairly easy, however, to say what *not* to do. To ensure that readers feel a sense of closure at the end of your essay,

- don't introduce completely new ideas.
- don't only refer to narrow, specific examples.
- don't end your essay with a question.

An example of an effective conclusion for the topic of reliving some moment of your life would be:

Beautiful weather, a fairytale setting, my happy family; for one day of my life, everything was perfect. Although I know I will never have the chance, I would love to experience my wedding day again.

As you can see, the conclusion doesn't have to be long and involved. It just needs to be a long enough to tie the essay together and leave the reader feeling satisfied. Although conclusions can be difficult to write well, it becomes easier with practice.

Using the following space, write a conclusion for the essay you've been working on in the previous examples. Include the restated thesis you wrote in the last exercise.

Original thesis:

_____

_____

Restated thesis:

_____

_____

Conclusion:

_____

_____

_____

_____

How Your Essay Will Be Scored

Your extended response essay will be scored based on three traits, or elements:

- **Trait 1:** Creation of arguments and use of evidence
- **Trait 2:** Development of ideas and organizational structure
- **Trait 3:** Clarity and command of standard English conventions

Your essay will be scored on a scale where each trait is worth up to 2 points, for a possible total of 6 points. The total is then doubled, so the maximum number of possible points you can earn is 12.

Creation of Arguments and Use of Evidence

Trait 1 tests your ability to write an essay that takes a stance based on the information in the reading passage(s). To earn the highest score possible, you must carefully read the information and express a clear opinion about what you've read. You will be scored on how well you use the information from the passage(s) to support your argument.

NOTE

To earn the highest score possible, you must reference and restate information from the passage(s), not just mention information from your own personal experiences.

Your score will also be based on how well you analyze the author's argument in the passage(s), if he or she makes one. To earn the highest score possible, discuss whether you think the author is making a good argument, and why or why not.

For your reference, here is a table that the GED® test scorers will use when determining if your essay should get a score of 2, 1, or 0 for Trait 1.

TO ATTAIN A SCORE OF:	DESCRIPTION
2	■ Generates text-based argument(s) and establishes a purpose that is connected to the prompt ■ Cites relevant and specific evidence from the source text(s) to support argument(s) ■ Analyzes the issue and/or evaluates the validity of the argumentation within the source texts (e.g., distinguishes between supported and unsupported claims, makes reasonable inferences about underlying premises or assumptions, identifies fallacious reasoning, evaluates the credibility of sources, etc.)
1	■ Generates an argument and demonstrates some connection to the prompt ■ Cites some evidence from the source text(s) to support argument(s) (may include a mix of relevant and irrelevant citations or a mix of textual and non-textual references) ■ Partially analyzes the issue and/or evaluates the validity of the argumentation within the source texts; may be simplistic, limited, or inaccurate
0	■ May attempt to create an argument OR lacks purpose or connection to the prompt OR does neither ■ Cites minimal or no evidence from source text(s) (sections of text may be copied from source) ■ Minimally analyzes the issue and/or evaluates the validity of the argumentation within the source texts; may completely lack analysis or demonstrate minimal or no understanding of the given argument(s)

Development of Ideas and Organization Structure

Trait 2 tests whether you respond to the writing prompt with a well-structured essay. Support of your thesis must come from evidence in the passage(s), as well as personal opinions and experiences that build on your central idea. Your ideas must be fully explained and include specific details.

Your essay should use words and phrases that allow your details and ideas to flow naturally.

Here is a table that the GED® test scorers will use when determining if your essay should get a score of 2, 1, or 0 for Trait 2.

TO ATTAIN A SCORE OF:	DESCRIPTION
2	■ Contains ideas that are well developed and generally logical; most ideas are elaborated upon ■ Contains a sensible progression of ideas with clear connections between details and main points ■ Establishes an organizational structure that conveys the message and purpose of the response; applies transitional devices appropriately ■ Establishes and maintains a formal style and appropriate tone that demonstrate awareness of the audience and purpose of the task ■ Chooses specific words to express ideas clearly
1	■ Contains ideas that are inconsistently developed and/or may reflect simplistic or vague reasoning; some ideas are elaborated ■ Demonstrates some evidence of a progression of ideas but details may be disjointed or lacking connection to main idea ■ Establishes an organization structure that may inconsistently group ideas or is partially effective at conveying the message of the task; uses transitional devices inconsistently ■ May inconsistently maintain a formal style and appropriate tone to demonstrate an awareness of the audience and purpose of the task ■ May occasionally misuse words and/or choose words that express ideas in vague terms
0	■ Contains ideas that are insufficiently or illogically developed with minimal or no elaboration of main ideas ■ Contains an unclear or no progression of ideas; details may be absent or irrelevant to the main idea ■ Establishes an ineffective or no discernible organizational structure; does not apply transitional devices or does so inappropriately ■ Uses an informal style and/or inappropriate tone that demonstrates limited or no awareness of audience and purpose ■ May frequently misuse words, overuse slang, or express ideas in a vague or rapturous manner

Clarity and Command of Standard English Conventions

Trait 3 tests how well you create the sentences that make up your essay. To earn a high score, you will need to write sentences with variety—some short, some long, some simple, some complex. You will also need to prove that you have a good handle on standard English, including correct word choice, grammar, and sentence structure.

If you need to review any topics in grammar, usage, or mechanics, revisit Chapters 5 and 6 of this book.

Here is a table that the GED® test scorers will use when determining if your essay should get a score of 2, 1, or 0 for Trait 3.

TO ATTAIN A SCORE OF:	DESCRIPTION

2	■ Demonstrates largely correct sentence structure and a general fluency that enhances clarity with specific regard to the following skills:
	  ■ varied sentence structure within a paragraph or paragraphs
	  ■ correct subordination, coordination, and parallelism
	  ■ avoidance of wordiness and awkward sentence structures
	  ■ usage of transitional words, conjunctive adverbs, and other words that support logic and clarity
	  ■ avoidance of run-on sentences, fused sentences, or sentence fragments
	■ Demonstrates competent application of the conventions of English usage with specific regard to the following skills:
	  ■ frequently confused words and homonyms, including contractions
	  ■ subject–verb agreement
	  ■ pronoun usage, including pronoun antecedent agreement, unclear pronoun references, and pronoun case
	  ■ placement of modifiers and correct word order
	  ■ capitalization (e.g., proper nouns, titles, and beginnings of sentences)
	  ■ use of apostrophes, with possessive nouns
	  ■ use of punctuation (e.g., commas in a series or in appositives and other nonessential elements, end marks, and appropriate punctuation for clause separation)
	■ Response may contain some errors in mechanics and conventions but they do not interfere with comprehension; overall, standard usage is at a level appropriate for on-demand draft writing

1	■ Demonstrates inconsistent sentence structure; may contain some repetitive, choppy, rambling, or awkward sentences that may detract from clarity; demonstrates inconsistent control over skills listed in the first bullet under Trait 3, score of 2 ■ Demonstrates inconsistent control of basic conventions with specific regard to skills listed in the second bullet under Trait 3, score of 2 ■ May contain frequent errors in mechanics and conventions that occasionally interfere with comprehension; standard usage is at a minimally acceptable level of appropriateness for on-demand draft writing
0	■ Demonstrates consistently flawed sentence structure so that meaning may be obscured; demonstrates minimal control over skills listed in the first bullet of Trait 3, score of 2 ■ Demonstrates minimal control of basic conventions with specific regard to skills listed in the second bullet under Trait 3, score of 2 ■ Contains severe and frequent errors in mechanics and conventions that interfere with comprehension; overall standard usage is at an unacceptable level for appropriateness for on-demand draft writing OR ■ Response is insufficient to demonstrate level of mastery over conventions and usage

Avoid an Automatic Zero Score

If your essay has any of the following problems, it will *automatically* receive a score of 0:

- The entire essay is made up of text copied from the passage(s) or the prompt.
- The essay shows no evidence that the test taker has read the prompt.
- The essay is on the wrong topic.
- The essay is incomprehensible (cannot be understood).
- The essay is not in English.
- The essay section is blank.

Extended Response Practice

Use the following prompt to answer this sample extended response question. As you write your essay, be sure to:

- Decide which position presented in the passage(s) is better supported by evidence.
- Explain why your chosen position has better support.

- Recognize that the position with better support may not be the position you agree with.
- Present multiple pieces of evidence from the passage(s) to defend your assertions.
- Thoroughly construct your main points, organizing them logically, with strong supporting details.
- Connect your sentences, paragraphs, and ideas with transitional words and phrases.
- Express your ideas clearly and choose your words carefully.
- Use varied sentence structures to increase the clarity of your response.
- Reread and revise your response.

PROMPT

The following passage discusses the debate over violent video games and their effect on young people. Take no more than 45 minutes to read the passage, write your essay, and then revise it.

Violent Video Games—Are They Harmful to Young People?

The debate over the effects of video games on the behavior of youths continues today with reports of school shootings and violent acts in urban neighborhoods. Violent video games are often cited as the culprit for increased violent behavior in youths. Some people contend that these games desensitize players to violence and teach children that violence is an acceptable way to resolve conflicts. Video game supporters state that research on the topic is unsound and that no direct relationship has been found between video games and violent behavior. In fact, some argue that violent video games may reduce violence by providing a safe outlet for aggressive and angry feelings.

In testimony presented at a 2012 federal hearing addressing the regulation of the video game rating system, Cindy Marrix, a psychologist and researcher at the Media and Mind Institute at Wollash University, in Wollash, Idaho, stated there is overwhelming evidence that supports the link between violent video games and aggressive behavior in young people. Dr. Marrix stated that research shows that violent video games are more likely than other media to lead to aggressive behavior because of the repetitive nature of game activities and players' identification with violent characters.

Dr. Marrix also noted that the practice of being rewarded for many acts of violence may intensify a game player's learning of violent acts. She believes that electronic media play a significant role in the emotional and social development of youth. While there are many video games that promote learning and cooperative behavior, studies suggest that the video games that include aggression, violence, and sexualized violence may have a negative impact on children.

Research results reveal that violent video games do increase feelings of hostility and thoughts about aggression. Dr. Marrix contends that the entertainment industry must recognize the link between violent behaviors and violent video games, and that these games should depict the realistic consequences of violence to show children that violence is not an effective means of resolving conflict.

While the concerns about the effects of violent video games are understandable, there are also a number of experts who claim there is no link between video games and violence. After examination of the research evidence, several authorities have concluded that these studies do not scientifically validate the hypothesis that the games increase violence. In fact, millions of children and adults play these games without any ill effects.

Researchers Dr. Erica Trounce and Dr. Jacob Smith state that concerns about current video games are really no different than those of previous generations regarding the new media of earlier times. Drs. Trounce and Smith state that research findings that claim violent video games create violent behaviors come from poorly conducted studies and sensational news reports.

The findings of two recent studies were reported in 2014 in the scientific journal *Behind the Brain*. Participants of the first study were assigned to play either a violent or a nonviolent video game for two hours per day for 20 days. Although male participants were observed to have greater aggression during the time they played the violent game than female participants, the

(continues)

results of this study revealed no increase of real-life aggression in players of the violent games. Results of the second study indicated that a predisposition to respond to certain situations with acts of aggression, family violence, and male gender were predictive of violent crime, but exposure to violent video games was not. These results suggest that playing violent video games does not demonstrate a significant risk for future violent acts.

Worldwide video game sales are predicted to reach over $110 billion in 2016. As games get more complex and lifelike, the discussion over whether children should be allowed to be exposed to violent video games will continue.

Read the passage and construct an essay that addresses the following question: *Do violent video games promote violent behavior in youths?* In your response, analyze both positions to determine which is better supported. Use relevant and specific evidence to support your response.

_____

_____

_____

_____

_____

_____

_____

_____

_____

_____

Extended Response Practice Sample Essays

Sample Score 2 Response

There is strong reason to believe that violent video games help create a culture of violence among America's youths. The playing of violent video games can cause players to blur the line between fantasy and reality and make them believe there are no consequences for violent actions. Evidence from a variety of sources such as psychologists and scientific researchers shows that we must take steps to curb children's exposure to violent video games.

As the testimony of Dr. Cindy Marrix makes clear, violent video games have a much greater impact on the behavior of players than other forms of media. Beyond the "repetitive nature of game activities and players' identification with violent characters" that she mentions, I would also argue that the interactive component of video games makes them more dangerous than violent movies or television. This is because players actively contribute to the games' violent story lines, whereas movies and television are passive viewing experiences. Additionally, as Dr. Marrix contends, the system of rewarding game players for violent actions both desensitizes players to violence and lends positive associations to violent acts.

While the passage contains evidence against the link between violent video games and violent behavior, I do not believe it is as strong as the argument represented by Dr. Marrix. Most significantly, the study published in *Behind the Brain* does not seem to take into consideration the long-term effects of playing violent video games over a sustained amount of time. Perhaps players' levels of aggression do not rise after a few days' or weeks' worth of play, but what about over the course of 10 or 15 years? Most game players I know, whether they play violent or nonviolent games, have been doing so since early childhood. Even if many years spent playing such games does not result in violent behavior, at the very least these games

remove the danger from violent behavior and make it appear almost normal. This can't be good for players' abilities to empathize with victims of violence or fully grasp the problem of violence in the world today.

Dr. Marrix is right to call for increased vigilance on the part of both the game makers and the general public when it comes to violence in video games. As the passage predicts, these games will only get more lifelike with time, raising further questions about the relationship between simulated and real violence. Factors such as a player's psychological health and family background definitely play a part in his or her tendencies toward violence, but the influence of interactive media on a child's emotional development cannot be ignored.

About This Essay

This extended response is a Score 2 because it contains an argument that is clearly connected to the prompt. The author does this by using evidence from the passage and attributing it correctly (this means that the writer explained who or what is the source of the evidence). The writer makes reasonable inferences, makes reasonable claims, and organizes his or her points in a logical way. He or she looks at both sides of the debate with fairness and objectivity, adding personal observations only when they are relevant to the response. The language, style, and tone of the essay remain formal throughout. Sentence structure is clear and precise, and the writer has a varied vocabulary. He or she follows basic grammar rules, including proper capitalization and punctuation.

Sample Score 1 Response

This essay discusses violence and video games. In my opinion violence is a problem today but video games don't make it any worse. Video games can even help with hand eye coordination and reflexes.

The first source, Dr. Marrix, discusses why she thinks that video games lead to violence. She says that people who play video games are more aggressive than people who don't and that they have a hard time telling the difference between what's real and what isn't. Maybe there is some truth to this but I know people who have played video games for years and they are not violent. I think it depends on people's families, if their families are good and teach them not to be aggressive and violent then they should be able to play video games without resulting in social violence. Dr. Marrix believes that players "identify" with violent characters and that this makes them want to act like the characters in real life, but I think it's more like the second source, Doctor Trounce, says: "violent behaviors come from poorly conducted studies and sensational news reports." What she means is that the news media is responsible for blowing up the problem of violent video games to sensationalize a story. It really has no grounding in reality. I also agree with the study in Behind the Brain magazine, that states that there is no increase in real-life aggression when people play video games. This refutes Dr. Marrix's point that there is a link between the two. The study also backs up what I said about the importance of family in raising nonviolent children.

The article states that people are going to spend "73.5 billion" dollars on games by the end of 2013. This alone is enough to show that games are not going away and that they are very difficult to regulate because they take up such a large part of the economy. Dr. Marrix suggests they change the content of the games, but that will be difficult because so many people buy them. Instead they should let the consumers decide if they can handle the content of the games. Games like Grand theft Auto can even help people's driving abilities and even pilots sometimes train on simulators so it is proven that simulated electronic media can have positive value in society. Plus the magazine study shows that it is usually only males that have the problem with violence and video games, not the entire population. In conclusion I do not see an established link between violence and video games, at least not enough so that we have to change

our national policy toward games, like Dr. Marrix suggests.

About This Essay

This extended response is a Score 1 because the argument has some connection to the prompt, but the author wanders in making his or her point. He or she does not follow a logical progression to explain his or her argument. The writer does not analyze the evidence from the text in depth, and little is done to show how it connects to the author's thesis. The essay writer makes similar points repeatedly, using a tone that wavers between formal and casual. There are run-on sentences, some errors in punctuation and capitalization, inaccurate quotes, and awkward transitions between parts of the essay.

Sample Score 0 Response

The article says video games lead to violence I agree cuz video games r violent & lotsa people play em that r violent. i'd say ban all the video games cuz they lead to violence! The game Call of Duty's very violent, I know ppl who play it n the graffix r super real looking. Not good for society to have ppl playin these games. in the article it sez ppl get aggressive when they play too many games. I would agree wit this, they have trouble telling whats real and whats fake. The dr. in the article sez these games have "negative impact" which is true if you've ever seen how violent the games can b. other parts in the article talk bout how the games arent that violent that ppl can play them w/o being violent but I dont know, I think they raise aggression in players. games once were simpler, not so violent, but now theyre super violent, the doctors in the article even think so. ppl are gonna spend "7.53 billion" on games the article states, so its a bigger problem then really anyone can handle at this point . . . its one of the biggest parts of the media and ppl will find ways to get their games. its to bad b/c I think its bad for society to have all these people playing so many games not thinking about real problems in society like war etc. but I dunno I dont think theres a solution rite now . . . sad that ppl become so violent with games.

About This Essay

This extended response is a Score 0 because it has little or no connection to the prompt, follows no logical progression, and includes little evidence from the passage. There is very little analysis of the issue or of the studies mentioned in the passage; while there is a very general thesis, it is not fully explained. The author uses slang and shorthand spellings (for instance, "sez" and "dunno") and writes in a tone that is too casual. There are many errors in spelling, capitalization, punctuation, and basic grammar rules, and the dollar amount is quoted inaccurately. These prevent the reader from fully understanding what the writer is trying to say.

THE EXTENDED RESPONSE ESSAY: PLANNING AND REVISING

CHAPTER SUMMARY

This chapter helps you prepare to manage your writing time on exam day, practice pre-writing skills, and revise your initial draft on the spot. These skills can also transfer to writing tasks above and beyond the GED® Reasoning through Language Arts test.

How to Write a Powerful Essay

An *effective* essay is one that clearly and completely accomplishes its purpose. There are many possible purposes for an essay: to inform, to persuade, to entertain, to compare, to prove, or to disprove. The purpose of your essay on the GED® test will most likely be either to inform the reader regarding your opinion of an issue or to persuade the reader to agree with your point of view on an issue.

Planning

Writing an effective essay requires planning, something that new writers are often reluctant to do. Why? Many students are impatient and just want to get the job over with. Others worry that taking the time to plan out their essay will cause them to run out of time to write.

However, planning what you are going to write beforehand should make the writing process much smoother and easier. It will also help you come up with ideas for what to write, organize your ideas effectively, and express your ideas clearly once you start writing. Most of the writing you did in the preceding chapter was much like planning; in this chapter, you will learn how to plan more.

Prewriting Strategies

We have all been there: at that first moment before you begin to write. You open your exam book, double check your scratch paper and pencil, sigh a huge sigh, whisper to yourself, "Okay, here goes," and then . . . nothing. Blank. Nada. It happens to the best of us. And it is the hardest part about writing. But, here's the good news: Once you have gotten past those first few agonizing moments, and you begin to put your thoughts in motion, the hardest part is over! You remember that you are a person with a purpose, and you are ready to embark on your GED® extended response essay.

Organizing your thoughts before writing is absolutely critical. It is probably the most important step in the entire writing process. Before you even put fingers on keys, you have to start thinking. So, do whatever you can to put yourself in a mental state of free-flowing thought. You need to allow yourself the ability to really focus.

This chapter will include the following aspects of organizing your writing:

- Thinking styles
- Outlining
- Order of importance

Thinking Styles

This might sound more like a lesson in Zen Buddhism, but clear thinking makes all the difference in your writing performance. You can start by first figuring out what type of thinker you are. This seems funny, but isn't it obvious in everyday life how differently people think? Just try getting three small children and their grandmother to agree on what to have for dinner, and you will see what I mean. You could conceivably have ten people in a room with each person looking at the same issue in a diametrically different way. So, you have to understand what kind of

thinker you are. There are two basic thinking styles that can be associated with writing: *linear thinking* and *free association*.

Linear Thinker

You are a **linear thinker** if you organize your ideas in chronological or sequential order. If you are working with a time line, you simply list events chronologically, starting with the first event:

Example
The school library needs to be reorganized. Given its enormous size, several student volunteers will be involved in the reorganization. As a result, you need to make a chronological list—bulleted or numerical, from beginning to present—of the steps that must be taken in order to get the job done.

Sample notes: **Linear thinker** (using chronology):

- Reorganization agreed upon March 23, 2014; project to be completed May 23, 2014.
- Step 1 (March 26–April 9): Remove all books from shelves.
- Step 2 (April 16–22): Clean shelves, removing all shelf labels and notations from the old organization system.
- Step 3 (April 23, 11 A.M.): Meeting to approve new reorganization system.
- Step 4 (April 25–May 9): Donate unneeded books, order new books, and label book spines with new organization system notation.
- Step 5 (May 10–May 17): Place all books on shelves, leaving ample room for future book acquisitions.
- Step 6 (May 18–May 22): Test out new organization system, receive feedback from employees, and make necessary changes.
- Step 7 (May 23): Project completion.

If you are thinking *sequentially*, you make an outline or a list that begins with your most important ideas.

You then move down your list of thoughts in descending order of importance:

Example
You need to write an essay comparing the effectiveness of two different pieces of writing. So, you sketch a quick outline that covers what you need to say in order of importance.

Sample notes: **Linear thinker** (using sequence):

1. Introduce topic and first essay author (remembering our minimum wage essay, that would be President Roosevelt).
2. List points of support:
   a. We must "reduce the lag in the purchasing power of industrial workers and . . . strengthen and stabilize the markets for the farmers' products."
   b. Our nation has resources and a hardworking population, and we should treat people fairly, if we consider ourselves a "self-supporting and self-respecting democracy."
   c. Child labor and worker exploitation are unforgivable.
   d. "Enlightened business" means knowing that competition is not more important than the humans doing the work to earn the profits.
3. Introduce second author:
   a. Ralph Phillips, asking for "informed alternative views."
   b. Increasing minimum wage will harm the economy—government doesn't belong in the workplace.
   c. Employers will have to pay workers more, which means firing workers, raising prices, and making less profit.
   d. Phillips worked in a very low-paying job and still achieved professional stability. Why can't everyone do that?
4. Analyze the support each author provides for his argument, using specific evidence.

Free Association Thinker
You are a **free association thinker** if you use no particular sequence in your initial thinking.

You have a thought, jot it down as it comes to you, and then provide supporting details last. You might write down key words that you know will trigger your memory later. You will eventually do an outline, but you need to see all your ideas laid out on paper first.

You can refer to this type of thinking as bubble thinking. Thoughts may come to you at lightning speed, so you should write down notes as quickly as you think of them. You can then circle each separate idea in its own bubble so you can categorize them logically later. When you're done taking notes, rearrange each bubble until the essay flows sensibly.

The thinking style notes in this section are obviously very brief, but they address the important points. Of course, the length of your outline will vary depending on the level of detail you have time for, and how much you know about the essays you're responding to. The important thing to determine is what kind of thinker you are. Once you have done that, you can apply yourself to your next step: organizing your notes logically.

There are three main steps to successfully planning an essay:

1. come up with a thesis statement
2. brainstorm ideas related to your thesis statement
3. organize your ideas into an outline

The following subsections describe each step in detail.

Coming Up with a Thesis Statement
Many students find it difficult to come up with an effective thesis statement. Often, writing a thesis statement for the GED® test is as simple as answering a question about yourself, a question that may appear in

the prompt. Then all you have to do is answer it. For example:

> *What is your favorite thing? Whether it is a gift you were given during your childhood or something you saved up for years to buy, you probably have something that is special to you. Write about this special object and why it is important to you.*

The question here is *What is your favorite thing?* Your thesis statement should answer that question in a complete sentence.

Sometimes, the prompt provided is in the form of a statement. In this case, there will be a sentence that gives you instructions to *tell*, *describe*, or *explain* some-thing. Simply take the sentence that instructs you to do something and turn it into a question. For example:

> *Many people believe that humans' spirits remain on earth after they die, in the form of ghosts. Explain why you do or do not believe that ghosts exist.*

Notice that the second sentence of the prompt gives you instructions: *Explain why*. Drop the word *explain* and turn the statement into a question: *Do you or do you not believe that ghosts exist?* Again, your the-sis statement should answer that question.

Let's practice what you've learned so far. Write a thesis statement in response to the following prompt:

> *Embarrassing moments often remain clear in our memories, despite the fact that we would like to forget them. Tell about one of your most embarrassing experiences.*

Thesis statement:

_____

_____

Brainstorming Your Ideas

Brainstorm is simply another way of saying *write down anything you can think of as fast as you possibly can*. The purpose of brainstorming is to help you get all your ideas down on paper so that you can figure out how to organize them later.

So let's say you've come up with the following thesis statement: *If I could do one thing in my life again, I would relive my wedding day*. To brainstorm ideas related to this thesis, you would take out a blank sheet of paper, write your thesis at the top, and then spend about three or four minutes writing down whatever related thoughts come to you, in no particular order. Here is a sample brainstorm on this thesis statement:

- *flowers*
- *beautiful day*
- *perfect temperature*
- *no rain*
- *family together*
- *husband handsome*
- *felt like a princess*
- *beautiful hair*
- *grandmother's dress*
- *mom and dad happy*
- *mom's family and dad's family*
- *no fighting*
- *laughter*
- *great music*

At this point, the brainstorm doesn't look anything like an essay; it just looks like a bunch of ideas. The next thing to do is to sort through the mess by going over each thing you wrote down, circling related ideas, and connecting them by drawing a line between them. This leaves you with a brainstorm that looks like this:

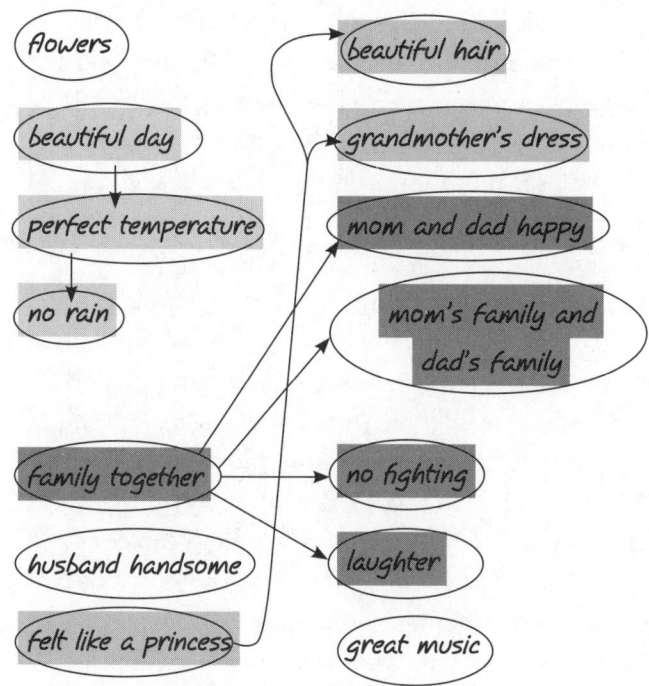

The largest groups in the brainstorm should tell you what the main ideas will be for the body of your essay. In this brainstorm, there are three ideas related to the weather (beautiful day, perfect temperature, no rain), three related to the bride's appearance (felt like a princess, beautiful hair, grandmother's dress), and five ideas related to the family (family together, mom and dad happy, mom's family and dad's family, no fighting, and laughter). That means the three body paragraphs in the essay should have to do with weather, the bride's appearance, and the family.

Collecting Details from Passages

To support your thesis, gather information from the passage(s) that will allow you to express a strong opinion. A good essay will include specific details that will help the reader understand your position.

TAKE NOTE

On the GED® test, you must include evidence from the passage(s) that supports your thesis statement and must also analyze evidence in the passage(s) that *does not* support your position.

As you jot down details from the passage(s) to use in your essay, ask the following questions:

1. Does this information support my thesis statement?
2. Does this evidence persuade the reader to believe or agree with my position?

The following is an example of a passage that presents an issue (the pros and cons of school uniforms). We will analyze this passage in the next section. Write down notes, important details, and a thesis statement as you read.

The Pros and Cons of School Uniforms for Your Child

Although uniforms have been a mainstay of private schools, public schools jumped on the bandwagon in 1994, when the California school district of Long Beach implemented school uniforms. According to the Long Beach school district, within one year after the implementation of uniforms, the fights and muggings at school decreased by 50%, while committed sexual offenses were reduced by 74%. Across the country, similar statistics abound; for example, at Ruffner Middle School in Norfolk, Virginia, the number of discipline referrals decreased by 42% once uniforms were enforced. Subsequently, fueled by these statistics, more schools across the country are implementing uniforms in public schools. Nonetheless, there are other statistics that argue that uniforms are not as beneficial as school administrators believe. Thus, the question still remains: Are public school uniforms good for your child?

There are fundamentally two benefits associated with school uniforms: a focus on learning, as well as a reduction of violence on campus. Many school administrators and parents believe that uniforms create a better learning environment at school. First and foremost, students are not distracted by how they look and therefore pay more attention to learning at school. The peer pressures of stylish dressing with the best brands are alleviated, and students can focus more on their schoolwork, rather than on social appearances. In fact, the socioeconomic differences present among students are equalized with school uniforms, minimizing the pressure to fit in with the right clothing choices.

According to the publication *School Administrator*, the mandate of uniforms on campuses has reduced tardiness, skipped classes, suspensions, and discipline referrals. In addition, with the visual uniformity present across all students, school pride has increased. Similar to athletic team uniforms, dressing cohesively increases pride, unity, and a renewed commitment to the school. With uniforms, a more professional tone is set in school, encouraging students to take their studies more seriously. Uniforms are more expensive up front, as the parent must invest in all of the staples; however, as the school year progresses, there are fewer purchases that need to be made. Last, uniforms at school reduce the prevalence of violence, which is a major concern for many public schools. Outsiders who do not belong on campus are easily identified and thus do not pose a great threat to the students. Uniforms also reduce the cliques and gangs on school campuses. When it is not easy to identify members of gangs, the fights and violence decrease. Students can no longer be distracted by who is wearing which gang color, and therefore, the campus is kept safer with less incidence of fighting.

The opponents of public school uniforms, as outlined by the ACLU's argument for the First Amendment, argue that uniforms stifle a student's need for self-expression. Students need to be encouraged to embrace their individualism, and uniforms deny that self-expression. According to opponents of uniforms, even preschoolers should have input into their wardrobes, and the need to encourage personality, confidence, and independence grows more important as the student becomes older. Without the outlet of expression in their clothing choices, students may turn to inappropriate hairstyles, jewelry, or makeup. Denying students their ability to express individualism and belief in a subculture, whether preppy, hip-hop, punk, or jock, could stymie their transition from childhood into adulthood. Controlling the socialization process could harm them as

(continues)

adults; they may not be prepared for the real world, where people are indeed judged by their appearances. In addition, others argue that uniforms may not be comfortable for all students. As it is important to ensure that the student is comfortable in order to maximize learning outcomes, uniforms may stymie academic focus. Students cannot wear their uniforms outside of school, and thus, there is the double cost of both uniforms and a casual wardrobe.

—Adapted from "Public School Uniforms: The Pros and Cons for Your Child," by Grace Chen, April 23, 2008, publicschoolreview.com.

Organization of Your Essay

A good GED® test essay starts with an introductory paragraph that presents the main idea, follows with body paragraphs that contain support for the main idea, and closes with a concluding paragraph.

Writing Your Introduction

Keep in mind these two goals as you write your introduction:

1. **Clearly state your main point or thesis statement.**

   As you write the body paragraphs, you can refer to your introduction to make sure your evidence supports the thesis.

2. **Present your plan to support your main point.**

   For example, if you are going to refer to three points of evidence from the passage(s), briefly mention them in the introduction. This will give your essay some structure—helpful for your readers, because they will know what to expect, and helpful for you, because you will have a built-in guide as you write the rest of the piece.

   It's also a good way to make sure up front that you will be able to defend your argument with evidence. If you can't find evidence to support your claim, then you need to rethink your thesis statement.

Problems to Avoid in Introductions

1. **Don't mention how you plan to write your essay.** Your position and supporting evidence should speak for themselves.

   Incorrect: *I am going to tell you why students in public schools should wear uniforms. I will present the best argument for this position that shows why this is a good thing to do. I will also explain why the information against school uniforms does not present a good argument.*

   Correct: *There are many benefits that result from mandating student uniforms in public schools. These benefits include an overall lower cost, the sense of school harmony they promote, and the respect that is associated with them. Evidence from school administrators, students, and parents supports these advantages, which outweigh the negatives of mandating school uniforms.*

2. **Don't use meaningless or empty words to sound clever or repeat the same point using synonyms.** Consider the following example:

   School uniforms are critical to student success. They are essential for helping students accomplish their best in school. Uniforms play a significant role in helping students have a positive experience in school.

   These three sentences all say the same thing!

3. **Don't make excuses for your writing.** You want to convey a clear, confident position to the reader. Don't start your essay with something like the following:

Although I'm not familiar with the debate over school uniforms, I think I would probably say that it's a good idea for students to wear them.

Building Your Argument

To write the body of your essay, you will need to provide support for your claim or thesis statement. Return to your notes to see what evidence you highlighted as you read the passage(s). On the extended response, it is okay to use evidence from your personal experiences, but much of the essay should be based on evidence found in the reading passage(s) and on your analysis of this evidence.

If the writer of the passage makes his or her own argument, you should also include an analysis of the author's argument, or arguments, in your essay. To earn the highest score possible, you should discuss whether you think the writer is making a good case, and why or why not.

NOTE

Don't try to argue a claim if you can't fully support it. If you cannot find enough evidence from the passage(s) to back up your thesis, then you will have to develop a new one.

A good way to arrange your evidence is in the order of strength: start with the weakest evidence and end with the strongest. In addition to listing details that support your thesis, you should also list details that go *against* your thesis and then talk about why you disagree with them. Arguments like this help strengthen your point.

After you have grouped your supporting evidence using the erasable whiteboard, you will be ready to construct a simple outline to draft your essay.

Constructing a Draft

One method of constructing a draft, or the first version of your essay, is to create a simple outline. You can do this on the computer in the space provided for the essay and then erase it after you finish writing the essay. You might also want to create the outline on your personal whiteboard, which has the advantage of saving space on the computer screen.

Begin by thinking about your thesis. Decide the stance you want to take, and write your thoughts into one complete sentence. For example, what thesis statement would you make for an essay about the school uniform passage?

Every extended response essay should follow this basic structure:

1. **Introduction** (states thesis)
2. **Body** (explains and supports thesis with evidence from the passage and your insights)
3. **Conclusion** (brings closure and restates thesis)

Here is an example, using the passage about school uniforms:

Thesis statement: *There are many benefits that result from mandating student uniforms in public schools.*

Body paragraph(s): Make sure these include evidence from the text, not only your opinion:

1. *Decrease in negative behavior*

   Evidence from the passage: *School administrators report a reduction in fighting, tardiness, and other discipline problems.*

2. *Increase in learning*

    Evidence from the passage: *School administrators and parents report a better focus on learning because students are not distracted by the pressure to fit in.*

3. *Professional, respectful atmosphere at school*

    Evidence from the passage: *Schools report an increase in school pride and commitment to school.*

Conclusion: *Evidence from school administrators and other experts supports these advantages, which outweigh the negatives of mandating school uniforms.*

Sometimes three paragraphs—an introductory paragraph, a body paragraph, and a concluding paragraph—are enough to make your point, but you may need more (usually extra body paragraphs).

NOTE

For an essay to be effective, each paragraph must be effective, too. This means that each paragraph must be well developed. Each paragraph should have a minimum of three sentences, but it's usually necessary to write five to eight sentences to explain your thoughts adequately.

Once you have a clear, detailed outline, you can begin to write your essay. As noted earlier, your introduction should include your claim or thesis statement. Here is an example of an introductory paragraph:

There are many benefits that result from mandating student uniforms in public schools. These benefits include an overall lower cost, the sense of school harmony they promote, and the respect that is associated with them. Evidence from school administrators, students, and parents

supports these advantages, which outweigh the negatives of mandating school uniforms.

After you have composed your introduction, write the body of the essay to support your claim, and then add a conclusion paragraph that makes a final comment and restates your thesis.

WARNING!

You *cannot* copy and paste exact text from the passage(s) into the body of your essay without using quotation marks. If you do make this mistake, your essay will receive a score of 0! You are required either to include quotation marks or to paraphrase the points (put what the author says into your own words).

Example of an Extended Response Essay

Now take a look at this great example of a high-scoring essay, which follows the structure we've discussed. The writer is responding to the prompt for the school uniform passage.

PROMPT

In the following article, the pros and cons of wearing school uniforms are discussed. In your response, analyze both positions to determine which view is better supported. Use relevant and specific evidence from the passage to support your response.

    Type your response in the box; you will have approimately 45 minutes to complete it.

Pros and Cons of School Uniforms

There are many benefits that result from mandating student uniforms in public schools. These benefits include an overall lower cost, the sense of harmony they promote, and the respect that is associated with them. Evidence from school administrators, students, and parents supports these advantages, which outweigh the negatives of mandating school uniforms.

As noted in the article by Grace Chen, evidence from schools in California and elsewhere revealed that when students were required to wear uniforms, there was a significant drop in negative behaviors on campus. For example, one school district reported that after one year of students wearing uniforms, the number of fights and muggings went down by 50%. The publication *School Administrator* had similar findings: when students wore uniforms, there was a decrease in tardiness, skipping school, and even suspensions.

School administrators and parents also report that when students are not focused on how they look or succumbing to pressure from their classmates to dress in a certain way, more attention can be paid to the task of learning in the school environment. While Chen cites the opinion that uniforms repress individual style, students have opportunities to express their style outside the school setting. Opponents also claim that there could be a greater financial cost to families if uniforms are required; however, in my experience, this is a weak argument. For example, in my school district, there is financial aid available to every family in need to help with the cost of uniforms, and in some schools, uniforms are free to qualifying families.

In addition, Chen notes that uniforms create "a more professional tone . . . in school," saying that this practice encourages students to take pride in their school and creates a sense of community. These are skills that young people need in adulthood whether they go on to college or enter the workforce. If wearing school uniforms helps students at a young age to increase their awareness of some of the things that are important for college and career readiness, then this is something school districts need to consider. A young person's ability to transition successfully to adulthood requires far more than attentiveness to his or her individual style. Many workplaces have employee dress codes, and those who do not follow the company policy for appropriate dress may face termination. Therefore, school uniforms may actually help young people develop the mind-set they need to be effective team players in the workplace.

Although some students may complain about the requirement of school uniforms, the evidence presented in this article strongly suggests that the benefits outweigh the disadvantages. Chen notes that school officials have data that prove the positive effects of uniforms: fewer behavior problems, an increase in school pride, and greater attention to learning. Based on this evidence, more districts should consider implementing uniforms in their schools.

Notice that the fourth paragraph includes a phrase from the passage, and it's correctly enclosed by quotation marks. What are the three dots in the quote? They are an ellipsis, which indicates that the essay writer removed one or more words from the original phrase. The original line in the passage is *a more professional tone is set in school*. This doesn't work grammatically in the sentence in the essay, so the essay writer removed *is set* and replaced those two words with an ellipsis.

Essay Outline

A complete essay outline will look something like this:

Introduction:
What if you could live one day of your life over again? Some people might choose to relive a day to change something about their lives. Others might simply want a second chance to enjoy a great experience.

Thesis statement:
As for me, if I could do one thing in my life again, I would relive my wedding day.

Body Paragraph #1 (Topic Sentence):
The weather was perfect on my wedding day.

Support #1:
perfect temperature

Support #2:
no rain

Body Paragraph #2 (Topic Sentence):
I felt like a princess that day.

Support #1:
beautiful hair

Support #2:
holding flowers

Support #3:
wearing my grandmother's dress

Body Paragraph #3 (Topic Sentence):
The best thing about my wedding day was seeing my family happy together.

Support #1:
mom's and dad's family there

Support #2:
no fighting

Support #3:
everyone laughing

Conclusion:
Beautiful weather, a fairytale setting, my happy family; for one day of my life, everything was perfect. Though I know I will never have the chance, I would love to experience my wedding day again.

That's it for planning. Now you know what your essay is going to be about, what the topic sentences of your body paragraphs are going to be, and what support you're going to use to back them up. You're now ready to move on to the next step: writing the essay.

Using the following outline form as a guide, create an outline for the essay topic you've been working on about your favorite object.

Introduction:

_____

_____

_____

_____

Thesis Statement:

_____

_____

Body Paragraph #1—Topic Sentence:

_____

_____

_____

_____

Support #1:

_____

_____

Support #2:

_____

_____

Support #3:

_____

_____

Body Paragraph #2—Topic Sentence:

_____

_____

_____

_____

Support #1:

_____

_____

Support #2:

_____

_____

Support #3:

_____

_____

Body Paragraph #3—Topic Sentence:

_____

_____

_____

_____

Support #1:

_____

_____

Support #2:

_____

_____

Support #3:

_____

_____

Conclusion:

_____

_____

_____

_____

Writing

Once you've thoroughly planned your essay, writing it should be a relatively simple process of expanding on what you've already written in your outline. As mentioned in previous sections, you'll want to begin your introduction with a few sentences to catch the reader's attention and lead into the thesis statement. Each body paragraph will start with the topic sentence you've already written and continue with the support you've noted to explain and develop the main idea. Finally, the conclusion will bring the essay to an end, restating the thesis and giving the reader a sense of closure.

A sample essay based on the outline in the previous section might look like this:

What if you could live one day of your life over again? Some people might choose to relive a day to change something about their lives. Others might simply want a second chance to enjoy a great experience. As for me, if I could do one thing in my life again, I would relive my wedding day.

The weather was perfect on my wedding day. Although it was supposed to rain that day, it didn't. The sun was shining, and the temperature was perfect. I could tell from the start that it was going to be a great day.

I felt like a princess that day. My hair was styled beautifully. As I walked down the aisle, I carried a bouquet of daisies, just as I had always imagined princesses doing as a little girl. I was even wearing my grandmother's wedding dress, which had a long, old-fashioned train, just as I imagine royalty must wear.

The best thing about my wedding day was seeing my family happy together. My parents are divorced, but both my mom's and my dad's families came to the wedding. For the first time in my life, they didn't fight. They were all laughing together and having a good time.

Beautiful weather, a fairytale setting, my happy family; for one day of my life, everything was perfect. Though I know I will never have the chance, I would love to experience my wedding day again.

Now it's your turn. Write an essay on your favorite object, using all the tools and strategies covered thus far. The prompt is reprinted below for your convenience.

What is your favorite thing? Whether it is a gift you were given during your childhood or something you saved up for years to buy, you probably have something that is special to you. Write about this special object and why it is important to you.

Revising an Essay

Good planning can save you a lot of time, both in writing and in revising your essay. Ideally, you should not have to make any major revisions like adding sentences or moving paragraphs around. However, it is a good idea to take the last few minutes before your time is up to read over your essay and check for proper grammar, punctuation, and word choice. Here are a few things to look out for:

- **Capitalization.** Make sure the first word of every sentence and all proper nouns are capitalized.
- **Punctuation.** Make sure you've ended each sentence with a period or a question mark, as appropriate. Also check to see that you haven't thrown in any unnecessary punctuation, like commas or apostrophes.
- **Spelling.** Double-check homonyms like *to/too*, *its/it's*, *your/you're*, and *there/their/they're*. It's easy to make mistakes with them when you're in a hurry.
- **Repetition.** If you see a word, a phrase, or an idea that has been repeated, draw a single line through the second usage.
- **Unrelated information.** If you come across a sentence that has nothing to do with the rest of your essay, draw a line through it.
- **Clarity.** If something in your essay doesn't make sense to you, it probably won't make sense to anyone else, either. Take a moment to figure out what you were trying to say and rewrite it.

If you've spent enough time in the planning phase and followed your outline well, you should need no more than five minutes to complete your revisions. When time is up, you should feel confident that you are handing in a complete and well-written essay.

Sample Extended Response Question

Read the following pair of speech excerpts, consider the prompt, and take a look at the sample essay provided.

Excerpt from President George W. Bush's Speech on Global Climate Change, June 11, 2001

Our country, the United States, is the world's largest emitter of man-made greenhouse gases. We account for almost 20 percent of the world's man-made greenhouse emissions. We also account for about one-quarter of the world's economic output. We recognize the responsibility to reduce our emissions. We also recognize the other part of the story—that the rest of the world emits 80 percent of all greenhouse gases. And many of those emissions come from developing countries.

This is a challenge that requires a 100 percent effort; ours, and the rest of the world's. The world's second-largest emitter of greenhouse gases is China. Yet, China was entirely exempted from the requirements of the Kyoto Protocol.

India and Germany are among the top emitters. Yet, India was also exempt from Kyoto. These and other developing countries that are experiencing rapid growth face challenges in reducing their emissions without harming their economies. We want to work cooperatively with these countries in their efforts to reduce greenhouse emissions and maintain economic growth.

Kyoto also failed to address two major pollutants that have an impact on warming: black soot and tropospheric ozone. Both are proven health hazards. Reducing both would not only address climate change, but also dramatically improve people's health.

Kyoto is, in many ways, unrealistic. Many countries cannot meet their Kyoto targets. The targets themselves were arbitrary and not based upon science. For America, complying with those mandates would have a negative economic impact, with layoffs of workers and price increases for consumers. And when you evaluate all these flaws, most reasonable people will understand that it's not sound public policy.

Excerpt from President Barack Obama's speech on climate change at Georgetown University, June 25, 2013

In my State of the Union address, I urged Congress to come up with a bipartisan, market-based solution to climate change, like the one that Republican and Democratic senators worked on together a few years ago. And I still want to see that happen. I'm willing to work with anyone to make that happen.

But this is a challenge that does not pause for partisan gridlock. It demands our attention now. And this is my plan to meet it—a plan to cut carbon pollution; a plan to protect our country from the impacts of climate change; and a plan to lead the world in a coordinated assault on a changing climate. . . .

Now, what you'll hear from the special interests and their allies in Congress is that this will kill jobs and crush the economy, and basically end American free enterprise as we know it. And the reason I know you'll hear those things is because that's what they said every time America sets clear rules and better standards for our air and our water and our children's health. And every time, they've been wrong.

For example, in 1970, when we decided through the Clean Air Act to do something about the smog that was choking our cities— and, by the way, most young people here aren't old enough to remember what it was like, but when I was going to school in 1979–1980 in Los Angeles, there were days where folks couldn't go outside. And the sunsets were spectacular because of all the pollution in the air.

But at the time when we passed the Clean Air Act to try to get rid of some of this smog, some of the same doomsayers were saying new pollution standards will decimate the auto industry. Guess what—it didn't happen. Our air got cleaner.

In 1990, when we decided to do something about acid rain, they said our electricity bills would go up, the lights would go off, businesses around the country would suffer—I quote—"a quiet death." None of it happened, except we cut acid rain dramatically.

See, the problem with all these tired excuses for inaction is that it suggests a fundamental lack of faith in American business and American ingenuity. These critics seem to think that when we ask our businesses to innovate and reduce pollution and lead, they can't or they won't do it. They'll just kind of give up and quit. But in America, we know that's not true. Look at our history.

Prompt

These two passages present different arguments regarding the issue of reducing greenhouse gas emissions. In your response, analyze both positions to determine which one is better supported. Use relevant and specific evidence from the passages to support your response.

Sample Response

These passages offer two significantly different views on how the United States should address its problem of greenhouse gas emissions. Both speakers concede that the United States is responsible for significant greenhouse gas emissions, and both speakers acknowledge the need for reducing these emissions. However, each speaker adopts a different attitude regarding implementation of such policies.

In this excerpt from President Bush's speech, he emphasizes the importance of an international, cooperative effort to deal with the problem. He does state that the United States generates one-fifth of the world's greenhouse gases. However, he quickly follows this information by stating that the United States is responsible for one-quarter of all economic activity, and then points out that four-fifths of the world's greenhouse gases are generated by other nations. By doing so, he attempts to explain the reason for high U.S. greenhouse emissions while also shifting the focus to other nations. Indeed, he goes on to point out how China and India are exempt from restricting greenhouse gas emissions, even though they are among the top greenhouse gas emitters.

Another key argument in Bush's speech emphasizes the economic perils of forcing drastic reductions in greenhouse gas emissions. Bush argues that to do so would devastate the U.S. economy, causing massive job layoffs and raising the cost of consumer goods. This argument also serves as the focal point in the excerpt from President Obama's speech. However, Obama refutes the claim that greenhouse gas restrictions will harm the economy. To support his position, Obama offers several historical examples where similar claims were made when businesses faced government-imposed restrictions. In each of those cases, the dire predictions of economic harm proved to be unfounded.

In essence, Bush's speech emphasizes fair play among all nations to ensure that the United States is not being held responsible for more than its share of the problem. Obama's speech emphasizes leadership by example, noting that the United States has successfully dealt with similar issues in the past. Of the two, I find Obama's position to be better supported through his use of historical examples. I also find his statement of leadership through action more compelling than Bush's call for fairness and cooperation.

Also note that the writing style is formal and that the word choice is precise in order to convey specific ideas.

Practice Essay

This practice allows you to compose your response to the given task and then compare it with examples of responses at the different score levels. You will also get a scoring guide that includes a detailed explanation of how official GED® test graders will score your response. You may use this scoring guide to score your own response.

Before you begin, it is important to note that on the official test this task must be completed in no more than 45 minutes. But don't rush to complete your response; take time to carefully read the passage(s) and the question prompt. Then think about how you would like to respond.

As you write your essay, be sure to:

- Decide which position presented in the passages is better supported by evidence.
- Explain why your chosen position has better support.
- Recognize that the position with better support may not be the position you agree with.
- Present multiple pieces of evidence from the passage to defend your assertions.

- Thoroughly construct your main points, organizing them logically, with strong supporting details.
- Connect your sentences, paragraphs, and ideas with transitional words and phrases.
- Express your ideas clearly and choose your words carefully.

- Use varied sentence structures to increase the clarity of your response.
- Reread and revise your response.

Good luck!

Please use the following to answer the essay question.

An Analysis of Nuclear Energy

1   America runs on energy. As a matter of fact, the United States is the second largest energy consumer in the world, behind China. In recent years, it can be argued that we need to ease our dependence on foreign countries that supply us with oil and develop energy at home. But where can we get the energy we need?

Benefits of Nuclear Energy

2   The U.S. Department of Energy (DOE) promotes the development of safe, domestic nuclear power, and there are many who support the idea that nuclear power is the answer. Compared to fossil fuels such as gas, coal, and oil, nuclear energy is the most efficient way to make electricity. For example, the Idaho National Laboratory reports that "one uranium fuel pellet—roughly the size of the tip of an adult's little finger—contains the same amount of energy as 17,000 cubic feet of natural gas, 1,780 pounds of coal, or 149 gallons of oil."

3   Supporters of nuclear energy cite that nuclear generators don't create great amounts of poisonous carbon dioxide, nitrogen oxides, and sulfur dioxide like the burning of fossil fuels does. The DOE reports that a nuclear generator produces 30 tons of spent fuel a year compared to the 300,000 tons of coal ash produced by a coal-powered electrical plant.

4   In terms of safety, the Nuclear Regulatory Commission ensures that each and every nuclear reactor maintains strict safety standards. Radioactive waste is contained deep underground behind steel-reinforced, 1.2-meter-thick concrete walls. The DOE also points out that "ash from burning coal at a power plant emits 100 times more radiation into the surrounding environment than a nuclear power plant."

(continues)

Arguments against Nuclear Energy

5   Opponents of nuclear energy argue that nuclear reactors endanger all life on Earth for three basic reasons. First, nuclear radioactivity is deadly and must be contained for thousands of years. Second, no matter how many safety measures are in place, accidents happen, and nuclear meltdowns are global environmental catastrophes. Finally, nuclear fuel used to generate electricity can also be used to build atomic bombs.

6   Nuclear generators use radioactive plutonium and uranium for fuel. Scientists say that exposure to a millionth of an ounce of plutonium causes cancer. Even nuclear energy proponents agree that life-threatening nuclear waste must be contained for half a million years before it becomes safe to be around. Radioactive dumps last generations.

7   Opponents of nuclear energy also cite the ever-present threat of meltdowns. Widespread radioactive contamination and death caused by the nuclear accidents at Three Mile Island, Chernobyl, and Fukushima are cautionary lessons. Researchers disagree on how possible it is to safely contain radioactivity, but it's undeniable that nuclear meltdown causes widespread contamination of the air, water, and land with deadly radioactivity. It is also verifiable that nuclear accidents have caused environmental catastrophes that continue to this day.

8   Perhaps even more disturbing than the threat of toxic waste and meltdown is the use of uranium for sinister purposes. On December 7, 2013, Reuters reported that ". . . in news that may concern world powers . . . Iran is moving ahead with testing more efficient uranium enrichment technology. . . ." Indeed, the United Nations and the entire world are worried about Iran's enhancement of uranium for use in nuclear power plants because the same enhanced uranium can be used to build atomic weaponry.

9   Opponents argue that in the same way we learned that fossil fuels are limited and destroy the environment, so must we learn from nuclear disasters. Opponents say the answer is to develop safe, clean, and renewable sources of alternative energy, such as solar, wind, tidal, and geothermal power. Why gamble? The future of the world is at stake.

PROMPT:

Nuclear energy proponents argue that it is safe and efficient, while opponents make the case for alternative energy sources, citing the deadly consequences of nuclear disaster.

In your response, analyze both positions presented in the article to determine which one is better supported. Use relevant and specific evidence from both articles to support your response.

You should expect to spend up to 45 minutes planning, drafting, and editing your response.

The Final Steps

The sample essay you just read is the final, submitted version of the essay. When you write *your* essay, you will probably need to revise your first draft before you get to this stage. You'll want to read it over carefully and make changes to improve it. Focus on improving the text (what you say) and style (how you say it), as well as fixing grammar and language errors that you may not have noticed when you were writing.

Evaluating Your Work

Use this checklist to help you evaluate your first draft to make revisions. Your response should:

- Introduce a clear point of view, distinguishing it from an opposing point of view as necessary.
- Develop the point of view and an opposing point of view fairly, give evidence for each, and point out the strengths and weaknesses of both.
- Provide a conclusion that supports the argument presented.
- Follow the rules of standard written English.

Managing Your Time

You will have 45 minutes to complete your extended response for the GED® RLA test. This requires careful planning and time management to read the passage(s) and then write your essay.

In general, you should organize your time by spending:

10–12 minutes reading the passage(s) and establishing your thesis

20–25 minutes creating a quick outline and writing your response

10–15 minutes reviewing and revising your response

When you respond to a practice essay prompt, set a timer to make sure that you are on track.

Quiz

Now that you know what's involved in writing an effective essay, use what you've learned to answer the following questions.

1. What is the purpose of a prompt?
   a. to help the student start writing about the topic
   b. to state the main idea of the essay
   c. to provide support for the main idea
   d. to suggest a possible conclusion

2. Which of the following states the main idea of an essay?
   a. thesis statement
   b. transition
   c. topic sentence
   d. introduction

3. Which of the following sentences would be a good thesis statement?
   a. My favorite object is my grandfather's old leather bag.
   b. This is an essay about my favorite object.
   c. The bag is made of leather.
   d. My grandfather's leather bag

4. Why is it helpful to brainstorm when writing?
   a. It helps give you ideas of what to write about.
   b. It takes up time.
   c. It helps you write the thesis statement.
   d. It puts your ideas in order.

5. What is the purpose of creating an outline?
   a. to organize your ideas
   b. to take up time
   c. to practice your spelling
   d. to make revision unnecessary

6. Which of the following should always state the main idea of a paragraph?
   a. topic sentence
   b. transition
   c. thesis statement
   d. introduction

7. How many main ideas should a paragraph have?
   a. one
   b. two
   c. three
   d. no fewer than two

8. Which of the following is a purpose of supporting sentences?
   a. to provide examples
   b. to state the main idea
   c. to restate the thesis
   d. to give the reader a sense of closure

9. Which of the following should a good conclusion do?
   a. state a new idea
   b. end with a question
   c. use specific examples
   d. leave the reader with a sense of closure

10. What is the purpose of revising when writing?
   a. to move paragraphs
   b. to rewrite the essay
   c. to restate the thesis
   d. to correct minor errors

11. *Practice proofreading this paragraph:*
My best friend Janet and me decide that we would bake brownis to take to the picnic that our Algebra Club was planning for Friday afternoon. We look up a recipe online, and we checked to see if either of us had all the ingredients we needed. Sure enough, everything was their and ready at Janet's house. Then we stopped by the store at lunch to get extra cute paper napkins and plates, and then we got distract looking at magazines and nail polish in the drug store next door. Suddenly the time was late, the cookies never got made we were in a hurry to get back to work. I guess cookies were just not meant to be.

Practice Essay Prompts

12. *Read the following writing prompt and write an essay that appropriately addresses it. Be sure to review and edit your work.*
Many parents give children a weekly or monthly allowance regardless of their behavior because they believe an allowance teaches children to be financially responsible. Other parents only give children an allowance as a reward for completing chores or when they have behaved properly. Explain what you think parents should do and why.

13. *Read the following writing prompt and write an essay that appropriately addresses it. Be sure to review and edit your work.*
More and more farmers and food manufacturers are genetically modifying their crops to reduce susceptibility to disease, improve flavor, and reduce costs. Do you think genetically modifying foods is a good idea? Why or why not? Use specific reasons and examples to support your position.

14. *Read the following writing prompt and write an essay that appropriately addresses it. Be sure to review and edit your work.*
Good habits improve our physical, emotional, and/or financial health. Select one of your good habits and write an essay persuading readers to make that habit a part of their lives.

15. *Read the following writing prompt and write an essay that appropriately addresses it. Be sure to review and edit your work.*
Some people think of the United States as a nation of "couch potatoes." Write an essay persuading readers to be more physically active.

16. *Read the following writing prompt and write an essay that appropriately addresses it. Be sure to review and edit your work.*
Today's top professional athletes often have salaries and bonuses in the tens of millions of dollars. Do you think these athletes deserve such high compensation? Why or why not? Explain your position and use specific reasons and examples.

17. *Read the following writing prompt and write an essay that appropriately addresses it. Be sure to review and edit your work.*
Is reading fiction a waste of time? Why or why not? Explain your answer using specific reasons and examples to support your position.

18. *Read the following writing prompt and write an essay that appropriately addresses it. Be sure to review and edit your work.*
Many people feel that the use of surveillance cameras in public places, such as parking lots, is a good idea that can help ensure our safety. Others worry that too many cameras violate our right to privacy and give law enforcement officials too much power. In your opinion, should we install more surveillance cameras in public places? Why or why not? Support your position with specific reasons and examples.

19. *Read the following writing prompt and write an essay that appropriately addresses it. Be sure to review and edit your work.*
Alexander Smith said, "The great man is the man who does a thing for the first time." Do you agree with this definition of greatness? Why or why not? Support your position with specific reasons and examples.

20. *Read the following writing prompt and write an essay that appropriately addresses it. Be sure to review and edit your work.*
Should people lease or buy new cars? Make a case for the option that you think is better. Use specific reasons and examples to support your position.

21. *Read the following writing prompt and write an essay that appropriately addresses it. Be sure to review and edit your work.*
The inventor and statesman Benjamin Franklin said, "Money never made a man happy yet, nor will it. There is nothing in its nature to produce happiness." Do you agree with this statement? Why or why not? Use specific reasons and examples to support your position.

Answers and Explanations

1. a. The prompt is meant to get you started thinking about the topic of your writing. As you write, your essay will address the prompt using details and support.

2. a. The thesis statement tells the main idea of the entire essay. Each paragraph contains a topic sentence that states the main idea of that paragraph.

3. a. The thesis statement should be a complete sentence that answers the question stated in the prompt.

4. a. Brainstorming helps you get all your ideas down on paper. After you brainstorm, you can choose which ideas to include and put these ideas in proper order.

5. a. An outline helps you organize your ideas and decide which will be the main ideas and which will be supporting details.

6. a. The topic sentence tells what the paragraph will be about. The rest of the sentences support the topic sentence.

7. a. Each paragraph should have one main idea. All of the sentences in the paragraph should explain or support that idea.

8. a. Supporting sentences help explain the main idea by providing examples and additional information.

9. d. The conclusion restates the main idea, wraps up the essay, and provides a sense of closure for the reader.

10. d. Revising is the step in which you correct errors in spelling, capitalization, and grammar. This is also the time to remove unrelated or unnecessary information, and clarify ideas as needed.

11. *Corrected version:*
Some errors were technical, like replacing "me" with "I" and making sure the tense of each verb matched ("decided," "stopped," "looked,"). Others were errors of consistency or clarity.
My best friend Janet and ~~me~~ **I** decid**ed** that we would bake ~~brownis~~ **brownies** to take to the picnic that our Algebra Club was planning for Friday afternoon. We look**ed** up a recipe online, and we checked to see if either of us had all the ingredients we needed. Sure enough, everything was ~~their~~ **there** and ready at Janet's house. ~~Then~~ **We** stopped by the store at lunch to get extra cute paper napkins and plates, ~~and~~ **but** then we got distract**ed** looking at magazines and nail polish in the drug store next door. Suddenly the time was late, the ~~cookies~~ **brownies** never got mad**e, and** we were in a hurry to get back to ~~work~~ **school**. I guess ~~cookies~~ **brownies** were just not meant to be.

12. Sample Response
Starting when I was about eight years old, my parents gave me a list of chores that had to be completed each week. If I did my chores, I got an allowance, a bit of change that I could use as I pleased. If I didn't do my chores, I didn't get my allowance. There was no other punishment, but no other punishment was necessary. That dollar or two a week was all the incentive I needed to help out around the house. Whether it was the latest Barbie or a six-pack of Hubba Bubba chewing gum, there was always something I wanted to buy. My parents could always count on me doing my chores.

I think that giving children an allowance for doing chores is a smart parenting move, for it accomplishes four important goals: It helps ensure that important work gets done around the house; it teaches children that they need to do their part to make things run smoothly for the whole family; it rewards children in a realistic, practical way for good behavior; and it helps teach children how to handle money.

I know that some people consider money for chores a form of bribery, and others feel that children should just do their chores anyway, without the incentive of an allowance. They argue that giving kids money for doing chores undermines the lesson that they need to help the family and do their part. I can understand that point of view, and when parents give their children too much money, it does undermine those lessons. But when the allowance is small, it is simply a modern version of the age-old practice of rewarding good behavior. Once children reach a certain age, money is an appropriate and effective reward that helps them learn how to be responsible and how to manage money. They get a sense of what things are worth and how much they have to save and spend to get what they want. And learning to save in order to purchase a desired item teaches them patience and helps children better understand the value of hard work.

Giving children money for doing chores is also a good introduction to the reality of the workplace. If they do the work, they get paid; if they don't do the work, they don't. Extra work can be rewarded with bonuses and extra praise; poor work may result in a pay cut or demotion.

It's important for parents to find the right amount to give. Too much money may make a child feel like hired help and will undermine the goal of teaching children to help simply because they are part of a family that must work together. On the other hand, too little money may make a child feel resentful, as if his or her work isn't worth anything to the household. What's an appropriate amount? It depends upon the amount of chores the child is expected to do and the child's age. If your nine-year-old is only expected to clean his or her room, a dollar a week is probably plenty. If your

14-year-old is expected to keep his room clean, take out the trash, water the plants, and vacuum the house, then ten dollars a week is more appropriate. Being paid for my chores helped me have a good attitude about housework, taught me how to save money and spend it wisely, and enabled me to appreciate the hard work my parents did around the house. I'm really grateful that this was the way my parents chose to handle chores in our household.

13. Sample Response

A few decades ago, manipulating genes in people, plants, and animals was just science fiction. Today, it's a reality, and genetic modification may have many positive applications in the future, including the eradication of many hereditary diseases. But like most scientific and technological advances, the genetic modification of organisms for our food supply can be as dangerous as it is beneficial. Because of the potential dangers of this technology, I think genetically altering plants and animals in the food supply is a practice that should be very tightly controlled and carefully studied before it is an accepted and common practice. Unfortunately, it may already be too late for that.

Many people don't even realize that many of their foods are genetically modified organisms (GMOs). GMOs are already prevalent in supermarkets and grocery stores across the country, but manufacturers are not required to label foods as having been made from GMOs. As a result, millions of Americans purchase and eat GMOs every day without even knowing it. Yet we don't even know if GMOs are harmful to our health. We don't really know how GMOs may affect our bodies or our ecosystem. When we mess with DNA, we may be making changes that have all sorts of dangerous repercussions, including some that we may not even realize for several generations.

One of the main concerns about GMOs is the unpredictability of the behavior of altered genes and of the bacteria, plants, and animals that interact with the altered organism. For example, a crop of corn genetically modified to be less susceptible to a particular insect may take on other unwanted characteristics due to the change. It may, for example, become *more* susceptible to another disease, or it could develop a tougher skin on its kernels, or it could decrease the crop's ability to produce vitamin E.

More frightening is the domino effect of genetically modifying foods. Any change in an organism's DNA has the potential to affect not only the organism but also anything that feeds off of it, *including us.* How do we know how GMOs might affect us on a microscopic, genetic level? We don't know, and can't know, without years of studies that track all sorts of potential outcomes over several generations.

Another fear is that transferred genes may escape from one organism into another. For example, imagine that Strain A of sweet peas was altered by adding a gene that would increase its sugar production. Through cross-pollination, this altered genetic code could enter other strains and slowly (or quickly) infect the entire subspecies. If the alteration was beneficial, this could be a good thing. But the altered gene might not act the same way in all varieties, and the change may not be a good thing in the first place, and/or it may have unintended consequences.

Genetically modifying foods is a practice that has been driven by the desire to make more food available more quickly and more cheaply than ever before. This attitude puts profit first and consumers and the environment last, and that is simply dangerous. The agribusiness needs to slow down and stop selling us GMOs until their safety is certain.

14. Sample Response

When I was 15, I wanted to get a job so I could buy a car when I turned 16. My father sat me down at the kitchen table and said, "Excellent. But only on one condition: 10% of every paycheck must go into a savings account. And you cannot touch that money except in an emergency."

"But Dad," I argued, "if I have to put 10% away, how will I ever save enough money to buy a car?"

"You'll have enough," he replied. "And you'll soon see how important it is to set money aside for savings."

I didn't believe him at the time, and in fact I often resented having to put that 10% into a separate account. But two years later when the transmission on my car blew, I didn't have to fret about coming up with the money for repairs. I was able to cover the cost easily and was back on the road in no time. It was then that I began to see the wisdom of my father's rule, which I adopted as my own. This habit has helped to give me a secure financial life, and I urge you to make this practice part of your life.

Ten percent of each paycheck may sound like a lot, and if you're on a tight budget to begin with, you might be thinking, "I just can't afford to do it." In truth, you can't afford not to do it. You never know when you are going to need an extra $100 or $1,000; life is full of surprises, and lots of them are expensive.

As tight as your budget may be, it's important to get started right away. If you are absolutely scraping by with every last penny going to bills, then start with just 5%, but move up to 10% as soon as you can. If you earn $500 a week, for example, put $25–$50 in your savings account each week. At first, this may mean clipping coupons, renting a movie instead of going to the theater, or pressing your own shirts instead of taking them to the cleaner. Think carefully about ways you can save just a few dollars—because just a few dollars from each paycheck is all it takes to build up a solid savings account.

The money you save will add up quickly. For example, if your annual salary is $40,000, each year you would put $4,000 into your savings account. That still leaves you with $36,000 to cover all your expenses. After ten years, you will have saved $40,000, plus interest. And the more money in your account, the more interest you earn, the larger your emergency fund, the more you can afford to relax later in your life.

Once you get in the habit of putting 10% of your money into savings, it won't feel like a sacrifice. The 90% that's left will be your working budget, and you won't even miss that 10% because you won't be used to spending it. Yet you will know that it is there, ready for an emergency, helping to keep you financially secure. So take my father's advice, and mine: Put a piece of each paycheck into your savings. It's a habit that's worth every penny.

15. Sample Response

Is your favorite place in the home sitting on the couch in front of the television? Do you spend hours and hours there each day, surrounded by bags of chips and cans of soda? Do you panic when you can't find the remote control and think that you might actually have to get up off the sofa to change the channel?

If you answered "yes" to any of these questions, you are not alone. In fact, you are one of the millions of Americans who are "couch potatoes": people who spend their days and nights "vegging out" in front of the "tube."

Well, spud, it's time to get up out of that armchair and get some exercise!

I know how seductive television can be. I know how easy it is to plop onto the sofa and lose yourself in the world of sports, reality shows, and good old make-believe. I know how mesmerizing MTV and other channels can be and how hard it can be to pull yourself away. But all that television spells disaster for your body because it needs to be active to be healthy. And it's no good for your mental health or social life, either.

Think about what all that time in front of the television is doing to your body. Think about what all that sagging muscle and growing belly is doing to your life. Think about how your lack of energy affects you at work.

Now think about how different things would be if you spent some of that TV time getting exercise instead: You would feel better during the day. You would sleep better at night. You would have more energy. You would look better. You would have more confidence. You would be more creative. You would be healthier and happier. And you would not even miss the television.

What sort of exercise can you do? Anything! Go for a walk. Ride a bike. Jog. Lift weights. Take an aerobics class. Do yoga. Join a basketball or hockey league. Swim. Rollerblade. Grab a friend, a fellow couch potato, and exercise together.

You can start with just 15 minutes a day, two or three days a week, and build up slowly. Before you know it, your couch potato days will be over, and you will wonder how on earth you ever spent so much time in front of the TV.

16. Sample Response

Why do top athletes earn such inflated salaries? Because they bring big bucks into their cities and franchises. But what sort of service do they provide to society? Do they save lives? No. Do they improve the standard of living or promote positive social change? No. Do they help keep our streets safe or educate our kids? No. True, many of the top athletes are good role models for our children. But seven-figure salaries don't always mean model behavior.

It is true that professional athletes work hard, and many have spent their lives pursuing their goals. It is also true that most professional athletes have a relatively short career span—a decade perhaps at the top of their game.

Limited as their professional sporting career may be, they don't deserve such high salaries. After their professional sports careers are over, they can certainly pursue other careers and work "regular" jobs like the rest of us.

Ending their stint as professional athletes doesn't mean they have to stop earning incomes. They just have to earn incomes in a different way. Why should they be any different from the rest of us who may need to switch careers?

It is also true that professional athletes may be injured while on the job; their work is indeed physical, and especially in contact sports like football, injuries are bound to happen. But, like the rest of us, they have insurance, and in nearly all cases, their exorbitant salaries more than cover their medical costs. And theirs is not the only high-risk job. What about miners, construction workers, or firefighters? They are at risk for physical injury every day, too—injuries that could likewise end their careers. But they sure aren't earning millions of dollars a year.

It is also true that professional athletes may spend years and years practicing with farm teams for a fraction of the salary they receive once they make it to the top. But in every career path, we start off with lower wages and must pay our dues and work our way up. Besides, farm team salaries are not always so low.

We're a sports-crazy country, a nation of fanatic sports fans and celebrity worshippers. We're awed and entertained by the best of them, but as much as they may inspire and amuse us, professional athletes do not deserve such high salaries. Those millions could be much more wisely spent.

17. Sample Response

Remember the last book that captured your imagination, that transported you to another place and time? Remember a book that made you fall in love with its characters, made you feel their pain and joy? Remember a story that taught you an important lesson, that helped you better understand others and make sense of the human condition? If so, then you can understand why the question "Is reading fiction a waste of time?" is such a silly question.

Fiction, unlike a user manual, a magazine article, or a newspaper editorial, probably won't offer you any practical knowledge that you can put to immediate use. It won't inform you of current events or give you advice on how to cultivate a better garden. It probably won't help you decide which candidate to vote for or which product to buy. But that certainly doesn't mean it's useless or impractical. Indeed, fiction serves three important functions for human beings: It helps us be more compassionate to others, it helps us better understand ourselves, and it cultivates our imaginations. It can also teach us about history, psychology, even biology and other sciences.

Compassion for others is rooted in understanding and acceptance, and a good story brings us into the inner world of its characters so that we can understand them. In Toni Morrison's novel *The Bluest Eye*, for example,

Morrison peels away the layers of her characters' histories piece by piece like an onion until we see into their core and understand what drives them.

They may still do awful things to each other, but she shows us *why* they do the things that they do, and we learn that we shouldn't judge others until we understand their pasts. Their stories are sad and painful, and we learn to love even the outcast Pecola. In fact, we learn that those outcasts are the ones who need our love the most.

Many stories and novels also help us better understand ourselves. Joseph Conrad's dark and powerful novel *Heart of Darkness* helps us see that all of us have a dark side and that we need to acknowledge this dark side in order to control it. It makes us question just how civilized we are and indeed what it means to be civilized in the first place.

Good fiction also cultivates our imagination, which is more important to us than some might think. Without imagination, we live a sad, empty life. Imagination is central to our emotional health and is a key factor in our level of intelligence. Facts are one thing, but facts can be of no real use unless coupled with imagination. Fiction can help us by keeping our imagination fresh and active. In a story like Franz Kafka's "Metamorphosis," for example, we are asked to imagine that Gregor, the main character, wakes up one morning and has turned into a giant bug. Crazy? Perhaps. But once we accept this premise and imagine Gregor as a five-foot-long cockroach, we can feel his family's horror and imagine his agony as he finds himself trapped in his room and abandoned by those he loves.

Is reading fiction a waste of time? That's like asking if laughing is a waste of time. We don't need fiction to survive, but we do need it

to be kinder, more understanding, and more creative human beings.

18. Sample Response

Not long ago, the nation was gripped by the horrifying news that a baby had been stolen from a car in a parking lot while her mother, who was returning a shopping cart, was just a few feet away. Thanks to the description of the kidnapper captured by surveillance cameras in the parking lot and broadcast over radios, television, and highway overpass signs, the kidnapper was quickly caught and the baby returned, unharmed, to her mother.

Had it not been for those surveillance cameras, that mother would probably never have seen her baby girl again.

I can't think of a much better argument for the use of surveillance cameras in public places. That baby's life was saved by those parking lot cameras. Many people worry about the use of surveillance cameras in public places such as parking lots, stores, parks, and roadways. They don't like the idea that they are being watched. They worry that the information captured on the surveillance tapes can somehow be used against them. But how? It seems to me that the only reason we should worry about being caught on surveillance cameras is if we are doing something wrong. If we are behaving lawfully in a public place, then why worry if it is captured on film?

Surveillance cameras can provide two immensely important services. One, they can help us find those who commit crimes, including thieves, kidnappers, vandals, and even murderers. Two, they can serve as a powerful deterrent to crime. A thief who plans to steal a car may think twice if he knows he will be caught on video. A woman who hopes to kidnap a child may abandon her plans if she knows she will be captured on film.

Surveillance cameras can also help us in less critical but nonetheless practical ways. In some towns in England, for example, radio dee-jays use information from surveillance cameras to announce the availability of parking spaces in crowded public parking lots. Problems of all shapes and sizes can also be noted and addressed through video surveillance. For example, imagine a video camera installed in a local town square. Reviewing the films, officials might realize that people who meet in the square move quickly into the shade of the one tree in the center of the square. This could move officials to plant more trees or provide tables with umbrellas so that people could meet and relax in the shade. Similarly, a video camera in a grocery store might reveal that aisle 7 is always overcrowded, prompting the manager to rearrange items to more evenly distribute shoppers.

Of course it's possible to have too much of a good thing, and if surveillance cameras cross the line and start being installed on private property—that is, in our offices and homes—then we will have the "Big Brother is watching" scenario opponents fear. If that were the case, I would be against surveillance cameras, too. But as long as surveillance cameras are limited to public places, they can help ensure our safety.

19. Sample Response

Just as there are many definitions of success, there are also many definitions of greatness. Alexander Smith said that a great person is someone who does a thing for the first time. He's right, and the list of those great people is long and includes the likes of Neil Armstrong, Jackie Robinson, and Thomas Edison. But Smith's definition isn't broad enough to include many other people who I believe are also great. In my opinion, greatness can also be attained by doing something to improve the lives of others.

Mother Teresa is the first person to come to mind under this broadened definition. Mother Teresa, who received the Nobel Peace Prize in 1979, dedicated her life to helping the poor, the sick, and the hungry. She left her homeland of Yugoslavia to work with the impoverished people of India, where she self-lessly served others for almost 70 years. She became a nun and founded the Missionaries of Charity sisterhood and the House for the Dying. She embraced those whom many in society chose to disdain and ignore: the crip-pled and diseased, the homeless and helpless. She gave them food, shelter, medical care, and the compassion that so many others denied them. She was certainly not the first to dedicate her life to the care of others, but she was cer-tainly a great woman.

Another great person who also won a Nobel Peace Prize was Dr. Albert Schweitzer, a German doctor who, like Mother Teresa, also selflessly served the poor and sick. Schweitzer dedicated himself to the people of Africa. There, he built a hospital and a leper colony, a refuge for those who had been rejected by society. Again, he was not the first to offer care and comfort for the sick and suffering. But he cer-tainly was great.

Harriet Tubman is also clearly a great woman. She led hundreds of American slaves to freedom along the Underground Railroad, risk-ing her life over and over again to bring her fel-low slaves to freedom. She gave them the greatest gift one can offer: freedom to live a bet-ter way of life. She wasn't the first to escape, and she wasn't the first to go back for others. But she was the one who kept going back. She knew that each time she returned for another, she was risking her life. But like Mother Teresa and Dr. Schweitzer, Harriet Tubman was utterly dedi-cated to improving the lives of others.

Greatness comes in many forms, and we are lucky to have many examples of greatness upon which to model our lives. Some great people are those who were able to be the first to accomplish something marvelous.

Others, like Mother Teresa, Albert Schweitzer, and Harriet Tubman, are great because they worked tirelessly to ease the suffering of their fellow human beings.

20. Sample Response

Planning to lease a car because you don't think you can afford to buy? Think again. Leasing can end up being just as expensive as buying—and you don't even get to keep the car. Even if you decide to buy the car at the end of your lease, you may end up paying considerably more money than if you'd decided to buy from the beginning.

Most people who are thinking about leasing are attracted to this option because they believe it will cost them less money. And they're right—it is cheaper, but only in the short term. For example, if you were to lease a 2002 Subaru Forester, with $2,500 down, you might pay $250 per month for the car. If you were to buy the same car, with $2,500 down, you would pay closer to $350 per month. Over a three-year lease, that's $3,600—a big savings. But after your lease is over, you have to give the car back. If you want to keep driving it, either you'll have to put another down payment on another lease, or, if you have the option to buy the car, you'll have to pay thousands of dollars to purchase the vehicle—dollars that won't be spread out in more manageable monthly payments.

Many people want to lease because they can then drive a nicer car than they might otherwise be able to afford. For example, if your monthly budget allowed you to spend $250 on your car, you might be able to lease a brand-new Ford Explorer. For the same price, you might have to buy an Explorer that was two or three years old with 50,000 miles, or buy a new but considerably less expensive make and model. A lease therefore allows you to drive the latest models of more expensive cars. But when your lease is over, you will have to return that Explorer. Whatever car you can afford to buy, you get to keep it, and it will always have a resale or trade-in value if you wanted to later upgrade to a newer car.

Furthermore, people who lease cars are often shocked by how much they must pay when the lease is over. Most leases limit you to a certain number of miles, and if you go over that allotment, you must pay for each mile. As a result, at the end of your lease, you may end up paying thousands of dollars in mileage fees. For example, if your lease covers you for 25,000 miles over three years, but you drive 40,000, that's an extra 15,000 miles. At $.11 per mile, that's $1,650 you'll have to pay. And you still won't have a car.

In addition, when you lease, you still have to pay for regular maintenance and repairs to the vehicle. Since you must return the car when your lease expires, you are paying to repair *someone else's car*. If you own the car, however, you know that every dollar you spend maintaining or repairing the car is an investment in a real piece of property—your property, not someone else's.

By now, the benefits of buying over leasing should be clear. But if you're still not convinced, remember this fundamental fact: If you lease, when your lease is up, after you've made all of your monthly payments, paid for extra mileage, and paid for repairs, *you must give the car back*. It isn't yours to keep, no matter how much the lease cost you. Whatever make or model you can afford to buy is yours to keep after you make your payments. There's no giving it back, and that makes all the difference.

21. Sample Response

Benjamin Franklin is one of the greatest figures in American history, and I have a great deal of respect for this incredible inventor, politician, and writer. But I must respectfully disagree with his claim that "Money never made a man happy yet, nor will it. There is nothing in its nature to produce happiness." I agree that money in and of itself does not make a person happy; but I believe that money can help provide one thing that is essential to happiness: good health.

While money can do nothing to change our genetic makeup and our physiological predisposition to illness and disease, it can give us access to better healthcare throughout our lives. This begins with prenatal care and childhood vaccinations. In impoverished third-world countries, infant mortality rates are three, four, even ten times higher than in the United States, and as many as one in four women still die in childbirth because they do not have access to modern medical care. Sadly, people who are too poor to afford vaccinations and routine healthcare for their children watch helplessly as many of those children succumb to illnesses and diseases that are rarely fatal here in the United States.

Money also enables us to afford better doctors and see specialists throughout our lives. If your child has difficulty hearing, for example, and you have insurance (which costs money) or cash, you can see a hearing specialist and pay for therapy. If you have migraines that make you miserable, you can see a headache specialist and afford medication and treatment. Having money also means being able to afford preventive measures, such as taking vitamins and getting regular checkups. It means being able to afford products and services that can enhance our health, such as gym memberships, organic foods, and acupuncture.

Another important thing money can do is enable us to live in a healthy environment. Many of the world's poorest people live in dirty, dangerous places—unsanitary slums crawling with diseases and health hazards of all sorts. In a particularly poor area of the Bronx, for example, children had an abnormally high rate of asthma because their families couldn't afford to move away from the medical waste treatment plant that was poisoning the air.

Money can also help us be healthy by enabling us to afford proper heating and cooling measures. This includes being able to afford a warm winter coat and the opportunity to cool off at a pool or in the ocean. On a more basic level, it means being able to afford heat in the winter and air-conditioning in the summer. During heat waves, victims of heat stroke are often those who are too poor to afford air-conditioning in their apartments. In extreme cold, the same is true: People who freeze to death or become gravely ill from the cold are often those who are unable to afford high heating bills.

Having money may not make people happy, but it sure goes a long way toward keeping them healthy. And as they say, if you haven't got your health, you haven't got anything.

A Final Word

Whew! Throughout this book, you've reviewed a number of reading comprehension strategies that will help you do your best on the GED® Reasoning through Language Arts test. In this chapter, you've learned some tips that will help you do your best as you put the writing strategies into practice. You are on your way to earning an outstanding score on the test and bringing home the ultimate prize—your GED® test credential!

Certainly, remembering all this information and facing the GED® test can be intimidating, but you are taking all the right steps toward doing your best. Review these strategies until you are comfortable and confident in your abilities with each. Take the practice tests in this book and monitor your own learning. If there are skills you need to brush up on, go back to that section of the book and review the information. When you find skills that you have mastered, give yourself a pat on the back. You've earned it!

Keep the test-taking, prewriting, draft, and revision tips in this book in mind any time you take a test, not just the GED® test! Read passages and answer choices carefully, pay attention to details, take time to plan out your writing, proofread thoroughly, and select the best answer choice for multiple-choice questions. These are all great ways to succeed in test taking.

And don't sweat it when you come across a question that seems tough or a prompt you have no idea how to answer. It happens to everyone, no matter how you prepare. Remember to map out your short answers and essay responses, to brainstorm or outline, and to revise thoughtfully. Don't waste your time trying to fill up the space with meaningless or nonsensical words. Take a deep breath, choose your strongest idea as a topic sentence, and, if nothing else, make a brief outline. Move on if you need to—you can always come back at the end if time allows, and having the extra time to think may be all the help you need.

Remember, you're on the right track. Taking charge of your own learning and being prepared are great first steps toward a successful GED® test experience. Good luck!

REVIEW

In this chapter, you have reviewed strategies for writing an effective essay.

1. An **essay** has three main parts:
   - an introduction
   - a body
   - a conclusion

   You can think of these three parts as the beginning, middle, and end.

2. The **introduction** catches the reader's attention and introduces the main idea of the essay in the form of a thesis statement. The **body** develops the thesis statement in two or three paragraphs. The **conclusion** restates the thesis statement and brings the essay to a close.

3. The **writing** process has three main steps:
   - planning
   - writing
   - revising

4. **Planning** is an important step in the writing process. It helps you decide what you want to write about and organize your ideas effectively. Planning includes writing a thesis statement, brainstorming ideas, and then organizing them into an outline. Once you've completed these three steps, writing your essay should go more smoothly.

5. **Revising** gives you one last chance to make sure your essay is as good as it can be. If you have planned well, you should not have to make any major changes during the revision process. Some things to check for include capitalization, punctuation, repetition, and clarity.

CHAPTER

9 ▶ GED® RLA PRACTICE TEST 1

This practice test is modeled on the format, content, and timing of the official GED® Reasoning through Language Arts test.

Part I

Like the official exam, this section presents a series of questions that assess your ability to read, write, edit, and understand standard written English. You'll be asked to answer questions based on informational and literary reading passages. Refer to the passages as often as necessary when answering the questions.

Work carefully, but do not spend too much time on any one question. Be sure you answer every question.

Set a timer for 95 minutes (1 hour and 35 minutes), and try to take this test uninterrupted, under quiet conditions.

Part II

The official GED® Reasoning through Language Arts test also includes an essay question, called the Extended Response. Set a timer for 45 minutes, and try to read the given passage and then brainstorm, write, and proofread your essay without interruption, under quiet conditions.

Complete answer explanations for every test question and sample essays at different scoring levels follow the exam. Good luck!

Part I

48 total questions
95 minutes to complete

Please use the following to answer questions 1–6.

Remarks by the First Lady on a Visit to Thank USDA Employees

May 3, 2013

1   Thank you for supporting our farmers and our ranchers and working tirelessly to market their products across the globe, which, by the way, helps to create jobs right here at home. Thank you for protecting our environment by promoting renewable energy sources that will power our country for generations to come. So that's an impact on not just us but our children and our grandchildren and their children. Thank you for that work. Thank you for lifting up rural communities. And thank you for keeping our food safe. And I think this is something most of the country doesn't realize—the work that you do here to protect the environment, you keep our food safe, working to end hunger, improve nutrition for families across this country.

2   And the nutrition issue, as Tom mentioned, as you all know, is something near and dear to my heart, not just as First Lady but as a mother. In fact, one of the first things that I did as, you know, as First Lady, was to plant the garden at the White House. And it's really pretty. [*Laughter.*] I hope you guys get a chance to see it—it's beautiful now. It rained a couple of days. Thank you. [*Laughter.*] And the idea with planting the garden wasn't just to encourage kids to eat more vegetables. I also wanted to teach them about where their food comes from.

3   I think you've known this—we see this as we traveled around the country—some kids have never seen what a real tomato looks like off the vine. They don't know where a cucumber comes from. And that really affects the way they view food. So a garden helps them really get their hands dirty, literally, and understand the whole process of where their food comes from. And I wanted them to see just how challenging and rewarding it is to grow your own food, so that they would better understand what our farmers are doing every single day across this country and have an appreciation for that work, that tradition—that American tradition of growing our own food and feeding ourselves.

4   And the garden helped spark a conversation in this country about healthy eating that led us to create Let's Move. As you know, it's a nationwide initiative to end childhood obesity in this country in a generation, so that all of our kids can grow up healthy. And all of you all at USDA, let me just tell you, have been such a critical part of this effort right from the very start. This would not happen—all the conversation, all the movement around health—that's all because of so many of you right here in this room and throughout this building, and in agencies and facilities all over this country. You helped to launch our new MyPlate icon, which is changing the way families serve their meals and gives them a really easy way to understand what a healthy plate looks like.

1. What is the likely overall purpose or intent of the passage?
   a. to discuss the programs Mrs. Obama began with the goal of inspiring kids to eat healthier
   b. to thank farmers for their work
   c. to introduce Mrs. Obama's nutrition initiative
   d. to emphasize the important role of USDA employees in creating good nutrition in the United States

2. Write your response in the box below.

   According to Mrs. Obama, [   ] mentioned that the nutrition issue is something near and dear to her heart.

3. Based on the passage, Mrs. Obama would most likely
   a. take her children to watch a professional basketball game.
   b. spend an evening teaching her children how to cook dinner.
   c. organize a family game night.
   d. spend an afternoon playing soccer with her husband, the president.

4. Which statement is NOT supporting evidence that the health of United States citizens is important to the First Lady?
   a. "Thank you for protecting our environment by promoting renewable energy sources that will power our country for generations to come."
   b. "And thank you for keeping our food safe."
   c. "And the nutrition issue, as Tom mentioned, as you all know, is something near and dear to my heart, not just as a First Lady but as a mother."
   d. "You helped to launch our new MyPlate icon, which is changing the way families serve their meals and gives them a really easy way to understand what a healthy plate looks like."

5. Which of the following is a synonym of the word **initiative** as it's used in this sentence: "[I]t's a nationwide initiative to end childhood obesity in this country in a generation, so that all of our kids can grow up healthy"?
   a. program
   b. enthusiasm
   c. disinterest
   d. involvement

6. How does the inclusion of paragraph 3 affect the overall theme of the passage?
   a. It damages Mrs. Obama's claim.
   b. It strengthens Mrs. Obama's position.
   c. It has no effect on the overall theme.
   d. It intentionally confuses the reader.

Please use the following to answer questions 7–11.

Excerpt from "The Cask of Amontillado," by Edgar Allan Poe

1 He had a weak point—this Fortunato—although in other regards he was a man to be respected and even feared. He prided himself on his connoisseurship in wine. Few Italians have the true virtuoso spirit. For the most part their enthusiasm is adopted to suit the time and opportunity, to practice imposture upon the British and Austrian millionaires. In painting and gemmary, Fortunato, like his countrymen, was a quack, but in the matter of old wines he was sincere. In this respect I did not differ from him materially—I was skillful in the Italian vintages myself, and bought largely whenever I could.

2 It was about dusk, one evening during the supreme madness of the carnival season, that I encountered my friend. He accosted me with excessive warmth, for he had been drinking much. The man wore motley. He had on a tight-fitting parti-striped dress, and his head was surmounted by the conical cap and bells. I was so pleased to see him that I thought I should never have done wringing his hand.

3 I said to him—"My dear Fortunato, you are luckily met. How remarkably well you are looking today. But I have received a pipe of what passes for Amontillado, and I have my doubts."

4 "How?" said he. "Amontillado, a pipe? Impossible! And in the middle of the carnival!"

5 "I have my doubts," I replied, "and I was silly enough to pay the full Amontillado price without consulting you in the matter. You were not to be found, and I was fearful of losing a bargain."

6 "Amontillado!"

7 "I have my doubts."

8 "Amontillado!"

9 "And I must satisfy them."

10 "Amontillado!"

11 "As you are engaged, I am on my way to Luchresi. If anyone has a critical turn it is he. He will tell me—"

12 "Luchresi cannot tell Amontillado from Sherry."

13 "And yet some fools will have it that his taste is a match for your own."

14 "Come, let us go."

15 "Whither?"

16 "To your vaults."

17 "My friend, no; I will not impose upon your good nature. I perceive you have an engagement. Luchresi—"

18 "I have no engagement—come."

19 "My friend, no. It is not the engagement but the severe cold with which I perceive you are afflicted. The vaults are insufferably damp. They are encrusted with nitre."

20 "Let us go, nevertheless. The cold is merely nothing. Amontillado! You have been imposed upon. And as for Luchresi, he cannot distinguish Sherry from Amontillado."

21 Thus speaking, Fortunato possessed himself of my arm; and putting on a mask of black silk and drawing a roquelaire closely about my person, I suffered him to hurry me to my palazzo.

7. Who are Fortunato's "countrymen"?
   a. Italians
   b. Britons
   c. Austrians
   d. Spaniards

8. What do Fortunato and the narrator have in common?
   a. an interest in Italian history
   b. they are wearing the same clothing
   c. a passion for wine
   d. a love of the carnival season

9. Which statement, in context, is NOT supporting evidence that Fortunato has a passion for wine?
   a. "[B]ut in the matter of old wines he was sincere."
   b. "I was so pleased to see him that I thought I should never have done wringing his hand."
   c. "Luchresi cannot tell Amontillado from Sherry."
   d. "The cold is merely nothing. Amontillado!"

10. In the context of the story, which of the following is an example of irony?
   a. "He prided himself on his connoisseurship in wine."
   b. "For most part their enthusiasm is adopted to suit the time and opportunity . . ."
   c. "My dear Fortunato, you are luckily met."
   d. "The vaults are insufferably damp."

11. Why does the narrator first insist that he will ask Luchresi's opinion of the Amontillado?
   a. because Luchresi has more expertise in wine than Fortunato does
   b. because Fortunato and the narrator are known enemies
   c. to gain the trust of Fortunato
   d. to prey on Fortunato's pride

Please use the following to answer questions 12–16.

Excerpt from "My First Lie, and How I Got Out of It," by Mark Twain

1 I do not remember my first lie, it is too far back; but I remember my second one very well. I was nine days old at the time, and had noticed that if a pin was sticking in me and I advertised it in the usual fashion, I was lovingly petted and coddled and pitied in a most agreeable way and got a ration between meals besides.

2 It was human nature to want to get these riches, and I fell. I lied about the pin—advertising one when there wasn't any. You would have done it; George Washington did it, anybody would have done it. During the first half of my life I never knew a child that was able to raise above that temptation and keep from telling that lie. Up to 1867 all the civilized children that were ever born into the world were liars—including George. Then the safety pin came in and blocked the game. But is that reform worth anything? No; for it is reform by force and has no virtue in it; it merely stops that form of lying, it doesn't impair the disposition to lie, by a shade. It is the cradle application of conversion by fire and sword, or of the temperance principle through prohibition.

3 To return to that early lie. They found no pin and they realized that another liar had been added to the world's supply. For by grace of a rare inspiration a quite commonplace but seldom noticed

(continues)

fact was borne in upon their understandings—that almost all lies are acts, and speech has no part in them. Then, if they examined a little further they recognized that all people are liars from the cradle onward, without exception, and that they begin to lie as soon as they wake in the morning, and keep it up without rest or refreshment until they go to sleep at night. If they arrived at that truth it probably grieved them—did, if they had been heedlessly and ignorantly educated by their books and teachers; for why should a person grieve over a thing which by the eternal law of his make he cannot help? He didn't invent the law; it is merely his business to obey it and keep it still; join the universal conspiracy and keep so still that he shall deceive his fellow-conspirators into imagining that he doesn't know that the law exists. It is what we all do—we that know. I am speaking of *the lie of silent assertion*; we can tell it without saying a word, and we all do it—we that know. In the magnitude of its territorial spread it is one of the most majestic lies that the civilizations make it their sacred and anxious care to guard and watch and propagate.

4   For instance. It would not be possible for a humane and intelligent person to invent a rational excuse for slavery; yet you will remember that in the early days of the emancipation agitation in the North the agitators got but small help or countenance from anyone. Argue and plead and pray as they might, they could not break the universal stillness that reigned, from pulpit and press all the way down to the bottom of society—the clammy stillness created and maintained by the lie of silent assertion—the silent assertion that there wasn't anything going on in which humane and intelligent people were interested.

12. Which of the following can be inferred from the first two paragraphs?
   a. The author grew up in the same state as George Washington.
   b. Before 1867, parents punished infants by poking them with pins.
   c. Before 1867, infants wore diapers fastened with straight pins.
   d. Safety pins were critical to eliminating a child's disposition to lie.

13. In the first two paragraphs, which of the following does the author present as evidence that humans are born liars?
   a. scientific data
   b. personal experience
   c. physical evidence
   d. historical documentation

14. Which of the following best expresses the author's position on lying?
   a. It should be forbidden.
   b. It should be forgiven, but only for children.
   c. It should be studied so that its cause can be found and eliminated.
   d. It should be accepted as a fundamental part of human nature.

15. Based on the fourth paragraph, why does the author think that slavery was allowed to continue for so long?
   a. because people acted as though it was not an important issue
   b. because people understood the economic importance of slaves to the South
   c. because slave owners lied to everyone else about how they treated their slaves
   d. because agitators in the North didn't state their case

16. Which of the following details does NOT support the main idea of the passage?

    a. Even babies have a disposition to lie.

    b. The introduction of the safety pin occurred in 1867.

    c. People often lie through acts rather than words.

    d. Early opponents of slavery faced indifference from society.

Please use the following to answer questions 17–20.

Rebecca Dyer, Executive Director
Abacus Childcare
2404 Bellevue Ave
Baton Rouge, LA 70810

(1) I would like to submit an application for the childcare position that was recently posted on your website. I have (2) with children in varying capacities for almost four years, and absolutely love kids of all ages. I have a high energy level and infinite amount of patience that blends well with successfully managing a group of children.

(3), I nannied two preschool-aged twins before they entered kindergarten. During that time, I learned to effectively develop entertaining and educational activities, manage disputes and disruptive behavior in a caring yet firm manner, and maintain a safe environment in the home. I also helped teach the children proper manners, personal cleanliness, and appropriate social skills. I believe the time I spent working with the family allowed me to develop excellent communication skills and management capabilities.

Outside of my work experience, I'm detail-oriented and very organized. I pride myself in (4) problem-solving abilities and love working hard to provide value to my work environment. I am dependable, always on time, and keep the promises that I make.

I would love to speak with you regarding the position if you feel like I would be a good fit on your team. I have attached my resume with contact information and have three references available upon request.

Thank you for your time,

Mallory Holloway

17. Which is the correct choice for (1)?
   a. Dear Ms. Dyer,
   b. dear ms. dyer,
   c. dear ms. Dyer,
   d. Dear ms. dyer,

18. What is the correct form of the verb "to work" in (2)?
   a. to work
   b. works
   c. worked
   d. work

19. Which transitional word fits best in the beginning of (3)?
   a. Recently
   b. Currently
   c. However
   d. In addition

20. Which of the following is a correct fit for (4)?
   a. your
   b. me
   c. my
   d. mine

Please use the following to answer questions 21–24.

John F. Kennedy's Inaugural Address, 1961

1 Vice President Johnson, Mr. Speaker, Mr. Chief Justice, President Eisenhower, Vice President Nixon, President Truman, Reverend Clergy, fellow citizens:

2 We observe today not a victory of party but a celebration of freedom—symbolizing an end as well as a beginning—signifying renewal as well as change. For I have sworn before you the same solemn oath our forebears prescribed nearly a century and three quarters ago.

3 The world is very different now. For man holds in his mortal hands the power to abolish all forms of human poverty and all forms of human life. And yet the same revolutionary beliefs for which our forebears fought are still at issue around the globe.

4 We dare not forget today that we are the heirs of that first revolution. Let the word go forth from this time and place, to friend and foe alike, that the torch has been passed to a new generation of Americans—born in this century, tempered by war, disciplined by a hard and bitter peace, proud of our ancient heritage—and unwilling to witness or permit the slow undoing of those human rights to which this nation has always been committed, and to which we are committed today at home and around the world.

5 Let every nation know, whether it wishes us well or ill, that we shall pay any price, bear any burden, meet any hardship, support any friend, oppose any foe, to assure the survival and the success of liberty.

6 This much we pledge—and more.

7 To those old allies whose cultural and spiritual origins we share, we pledge the loyalty of faithful friends. United, there is little we cannot do in a host of cooperative ventures. Divided, there is little we can do—for we dare not meet a powerful challenge at odds and split asunder.

(continues)

8 To those new states whom we welcome to the ranks of the free, we pledge our word that one form of colonial control shall not have passed away merely to be replaced by a far more iron tyranny. We shall not always expect to find them supporting our view. But we shall always hope to find them strongly supporting their own freedom—and to remember that, in the past, those who foolishly sought power by riding the back of the tiger ended up inside.

9 To those peoples in the villages of half the globe struggling to break the bonds of mass misery, we pledge our best efforts to help them help themselves, for whatever period is required—not because the communists may be doing it, not because we seek their votes, but because it is right. If a free society cannot help the many who are poor, it cannot save the few who are rich.

10 To our sister republics south of our border, we offer a special pledge—to convert our good words into good deeds—in a new alliance for progress—to assist free men and free governments in casting off the chains of poverty. But this peaceful revolution of hope cannot become the prey of hostile powers. Let all our neighbors know that we shall join with them to oppose aggression or subversion anywhere in the Americas. And let every other power know that this hemisphere intends to remain the master of its own house.

11 To that world assembly of sovereign states, the United Nations, our last best hope in an age where the instruments of war have far outpaced the instruments of peace, we renew our pledge of support—to prevent it from becoming merely a forum for invective—to strengthen its shield of the new and the weak—and to enlarge the area in which its writ may run.

12 Finally, to those nations who would make themselves our adversary, we offer not a pledge but a request: that both sides begin anew the quest for peace, before the dark powers of destruction unleashed by science engulf all humanity in planned or accidental self-destruction.

21. Which sentence best represents the theme of the speech?
   a. "We observe today not a victory of party but a celebration of freedom—symbolizing an end as well as a beginning—signifying renewal as well as change."
   b. "We dare not forget today that we are the heirs of that first revolution."
   c. "But this peaceful revolution of hope cannot become the prey of hostile powers."
   d. "Let all our neighbors know that we shall join with them to oppose aggression or subversion anywhere in the Americas."

22. What word or phrase signifies to the reader the meaning of the word **tyranny** in the following sentence? "To those new states whom we welcome to the ranks of the free, we pledge our word that one form of colonial control shall not have passed away merely to be replaced by a far more iron tyranny."
   a. new states
   b. ranks of the free
   c. colonial control
   d. iron

23. What is the purpose of repeating "little we cannot do" and "little we can do" in the following sentence? "United, there is little we cannot do in a host of cooperative ventures. Divided, there is little we can do—for we dare not meet a powerful challenge at odds and split asunder."

a. to contrast the difference between being united and being divided

b. to highlight the similarity of being united and being divided

c. to stress the United States' role in foreign politics

d. to promise what Kennedy wants to accomplish during his presidency

24. From the list of five choices below, circle *all* of the characteristics that Kennedy displays in this speech.

1. fear
2. a strong will
3. compassion
4. morality
5. aggression

Please use the following to answer questions 25–30.

Franklin Delano Roosevelt's Pearl Harbor Address to the Nation, 1941

1 Mr. Vice President, Mr. Speaker, Members of the Senate, and of the House of Representatives:

2 Yesterday, December 7, 1941—a date which will live in infamy—the United States of America was suddenly and deliberately attacked by naval and air forces of the Empire of Japan.

3 The United States was at peace with that nation and, at the solicitation of Japan, was still in conversation with its government and its emperor looking toward the maintenance of peace in the Pacific.

4 Indeed, one hour after Japanese air squadrons had commenced bombing in the American island of Oahu, the Japanese ambassador to the United States and his colleague delivered to our Secretary of State a formal reply to a recent American message. And while this reply stated that it seemed useless to continue the existing diplomatic negotiations, it contained no threat or hint of war or of armed attack.

5 It will be recorded that the distance of Hawaii from Japan makes it obvious that the attack was deliberately planned many days or even weeks ago. During the intervening time, the Japanese government has deliberately sought to deceive the United States by false statements and expressions of hope for continued peace.

6 The attack yesterday on the Hawaiian Islands has caused severe damage to American naval and military forces. I regret to tell you that very many American lives have been lost. In addition, American ships have been reported torpedoed on the high seas between San Francisco and Honolulu.

7 Yesterday, the Japanese government also launched an attack against Malaya.

(continues)

8 Last night, Japanese forces attacked Hong Kong.

9 Last night, Japanese forces attacked Guam.

10 Last night, Japanese forces attacked the Philippine Islands.

11 Last night, the Japanese attacked Wake Island.

12 And this morning, the Japanese attacked Midway Island.

13 Japan has, therefore, undertaken a surprise offensive extending throughout the Pacific area. The facts of yesterday and today speak for themselves. The people of the United States have already formed their opinions and well understand the implications to the very life and safety of our nation.

14 As Commander in Chief of the Army and Navy, I have directed that all measures be taken for our defense. But always will our whole nation remember the character of the onslaught against us.

15 No matter how long it may take us to overcome this premeditated invasion, the American people in their righteous might will win through to absolute victory.

16 I believe that I interpret the will of the Congress and of the people when I assert that we will not only defend ourselves to the uttermost but will make it very certain that this form of treachery shall never again endanger us.

17 Hostilities exist. There is no blinking at the fact that our people, our territory, and our interests are in grave danger.

18 With confidence in our armed forces, with the unbounding determination of our people, we will gain the inevitable triumph.

19 I ask that the Congress declare that since the unprovoked and dastardly attack by Japan on Sunday, December 7, 1941, a state of war has existed between the United States and the Japanese empire.

25. What is the tone of the address?
a. shocked but assertive
b. timid and fearful
c. surprised and scared
d. insecure yet aggressive

26. What purpose does the word **indeed** serve in the fourth paragraph?
a. to conclude his former idea
b. to alert the audience of a new premise
c. to emphasize the surprise of the attack
d. to introduce a new theme in the speech

27. What can be inferred from the first sentence in paragraph 5?
a. Japan is close to Hawaii.
b. Japan and Hawaii are a significant distance apart.
c. The United States mainland is as close to Hawaii as Japan is.
d. Japan announced that it was going to attack.

28. What is the purpose of repeating the phrase "Last night, Japanese forces attacked"?
  a. to show that Japanese forces were disorganized
  b. to emphasize that it is cowardly to attack at night
  c. to show how other countries are united against Japan
  d. to emphasize the extent of Japan's attack

29. Which of the following describes "the character of the onslaught against us"?
  a. expected
  b. aggressive
  c. regretful
  d. unintentional

30. Which of the following is NOT evidence that the attack came as a surprise?
  a. "The United States was at peace with that nation."
  b. "[O]ne hour after Japanese air squadrons had commenced bombing in the American island of Oahu, the Japanese ambassador to the United States and his colleague delivered to our Secretary of State a formal reply to a recent American message."
  c. "During the intervening time, the Japanese government has deliberately sought to deceive the United States by false statements and expressions of hope for continued peace."
  d. "Hostilities exist."

Please use the following to answer questions 31–34.

Memo to: All Employees
From: Alexandra Chandler
Subject: Work Hours

Hello all!

(1) Beginning next week, we will poll the office in order to receive everyone's input as we modify work hours.

The company (2) they want to change the schedule in order to better fit the needs of the employees. We will have three options to choose from. The first option is to keep the work schedule as it is currently: 9 to 5, Monday through Friday. The second option is to work one more hour per day on Monday through Thursday, but work only half a day on Friday. The third option is to work two extra hours on Monday through Thursday, and have Fridays off.

Although (3) completely open to all three options, the members of the executive board feel that the second option may fit the goals of the company and employees the best. Many of us already stay to work late at the beginning of the week, and the extra hour would not feel unnatural. We have also noticed that on (4). We understand this to be normal behavior and want to alter hours so that we can better serve you.

We think that the second option would fit well with the patterns we have already observed; however, we still want your opinions. We will be sending questionnaires via e-mail for you to fill out within the week. Please take some time to think about your responses before completing the survey as we want the possible change to best reflect the needs of the office.

Please keep a lookout for the questionnaire and return it to us by the end of next week.

Thank you for your time,

Alexandra Chandler

---

31. Which choice fits correctly in (1)?

   a. We are announcing some really big changes that might really affect us in the next few months.

   b. We would like to announce some potential changes affecting our team in the next few months.

   c. FYI, stuff might be different soon.

   d. PS: Thank you for your cooperation.

32. Choose the correct form of **decide** for (2).

   a. will decide

   b. has decided

   c. decides

   d. decide

33. Which choice fits correctly in (3)?

   a. there

   b. their

   c. they is

   d. they are

34. Which choice fits correctly in (4)?

   a. Friday, afternoons employee activity drops

   b. Friday afternoons employee, activity drops

   c. Friday afternoons, employee activity drops

   d. Friday afternoons employee activity, drops

Please use the following to answer questions 35–42.

Excerpt from Barack Obama's First Inaugural Address, January 20, 2009

1 In reaffirming the greatness of our nation we understand that greatness is never a given. It must be earned. Our journey has never been one of short-cuts or settling for less. It has not been the path for the faint-hearted, for those that prefer leisure over work, or seek only the pleasures of riches and fame. Rather, it has been the risk-takers, the doers, the makers of things—some celebrated, but more often men and women obscure in their labor—who have carried us up the long rugged path towards prosperity and freedom.

2 For us, they packed up their few worldly possessions and traveled across oceans in search of a new life. For us, they toiled in sweatshops, and settled the West, endured the lash of the whip, and plowed the hard earth. For us, they fought and died in places like Concord and Gettysburg, Normandy and Khe Sahn.

3 Time and again these men and women struggled and sacrificed and worked till their hands were raw so that we might live a better life. They saw America as bigger than the sum of our individual ambitions, greater than all the differences of birth or wealth or faction.

4 This is the journey we continue today. We remain the most prosperous, powerful nation on Earth. Our workers are no less productive than when this crisis began. Our minds are no less inventive, our goods and services no less needed than they were last week, or last month, or last year. Our capacity remains undiminished. But our time of standing pat, of protecting narrow interests and putting off unpleasant decisions—that time has surely passed. Starting today, we must pick ourselves up, dust ourselves off, and begin again the work of remaking America.

5 For everywhere we look, there is work to be done. The state of our economy calls for action, bold and swift. And we will act, not only to create new jobs but to lay a new foundation for growth. We

(continues)

will build the roads and bridges, the electric grids and digital lines that feed our commerce and bind us together. We'll restore science to its rightful place and wield technology's wonders to raise health care's quality and lower its cost. We will harness the sun and the winds and the soil to fuel our cars and run our factories. And we will transform our schools and colleges and universities to meet the demands of a new age. All this we can do. All this we will do.

6 Now, there are some who question the scale of our ambitions, who suggest that our system cannot tolerate too many big plans. Their memories are short, for they have forgotten what this country has already done, what free men and women can achieve when imagination is joined to common purpose and necessity to courage. What the cynics fail to understand is that the ground has shifted beneath them, that the stale political arguments that have consumed us for so long no longer apply.

7 The question we ask today is not whether our government is too big or too small, but whether it works—whether it helps families find jobs at a decent wage, care they can afford, a retirement that is dignified. Where the answer is yes, we intend to move forward. Where the answer is no, programs will end. And those of us who manage the public's dollars will be held to account, to spend wisely, reform bad habits, and do our business in the light of day, because only then can we restore the vital trust between a people and their government.

Excerpt from Barack Obama's Second Inaugural Address, January 21, 2013

1 We, the people, still believe that every citizen deserves a basic measure of security and dignity. We must make the hard choices to reduce the cost of health care and the size of our deficit. But we reject the belief that America must choose between caring for the generation that built this country and investing in the generation that will build its future. For we remember the lessons of our past, when twilight years were spent in poverty, and parents of a child with a disability had nowhere to turn. We do not believe that in this country, freedom is reserved for the lucky, or happiness for the few. We recognize that no matter how responsibly we live our lives, any one of us, at any time, may face a job loss, or a sudden illness, or a home swept away in a terrible storm. The commitments we make to each other—through Medicare, and Medicaid, and Social Security—these things do not sap our initiative; they strengthen us. They do not make us a nation of takers; they free us to take the risks that make this country great.

2 We, the people, still believe that our obligations as Americans are not just to ourselves, but to all posterity. We will respond to the threat of climate change, knowing that the failure to do so would betray our children and future generations. Some may still deny the overwhelming judgment of science, but none can avoid the devastating impact of raging fires, and crippling drought, and more powerful storms. The path towards sustainable energy sources will be long and sometimes difficult. But America cannot resist this transition; we must lead it. We cannot cede to other nations the technology that will power new jobs and new industries—we must claim its promise.

(continues)

That's how we will maintain our economic vitality and our national treasure—our forests and waterways; our croplands and snowcapped peaks. That is how we will preserve our planet, commanded to our care by God. That's what will lend meaning to the creed our fathers once declared.

3 We, the people, still believe that enduring security and lasting peace do not require perpetual war. Our brave men and women in uniform, tempered by the flames of battle, are unmatched in skill and courage. Our citizens, seared by the memory of those we have lost, know too well the price that is paid for liberty. The knowledge of their sacrifice will keep us forever vigilant against those who would do us harm. But we are also heirs to those who won the peace and not just the war, who turned sworn enemies into the surest of friends, and we must carry those lessons into this time as well.

4 We will defend our people and uphold our values through strength of arms and rule of law. We will show the courage to try and resolve our differences with other nations peacefully—not because we are naïve about the dangers we face, but because engagement can more durably lift suspicion and fear. America will remain the anchor of strong alliances in every corner of the globe; and we will renew those institutions that extend our capacity to manage crisis abroad, for no one has a greater stake in a peaceful world than its most powerful nation. We will support democracy from Asia to Africa, from the Americas to the Middle East, because our interests and our conscience compel us to act on behalf of those who long for freedom. And we must be a source of hope to the poor, the sick, the marginalized, the victims of prejudice—not out of mere charity, but because peace in our time requires the constant advance of those principles that our common creed describes: tolerance and opportunity; human dignity and justice.

---

35. Which best summarizes the main idea expressed in the first paragraph of Obama's First Inaugural Address?
   a. Luck made the United States a successful and great nation.
   b. Those who worked hard and took risks shaped America.
   c. The United States is a great nation and hard work will keep it so.
   d. Obama feels very fortunate to have been elected president.

36. Which sentence's meaning is strengthened by the "men and women [who] sacrificed and struggled" mentioned in the first three paragraphs in Obama's First Inaugural Address?
   a. "Our capacity remains undiminished."
   b. "For everywhere we look, there is work to be done."
   c. "We'll restore science to its rightful place and wield technology's wonders to raise health care's quality and lower its cost."
   d. "Their memories are short, for they have forgotten what this country has already done, what free men and women can achieve when imagination is joined to common purpose and necessity to courage."

37. From the list of five choices below, circle *all* of the phrases that support the main idea of Obama's First Inaugural Address.
1. "Our journey has never been one of short-cuts or settling for less."
2. "This is the journey we continue today."
3. "All this we can do. All this we will do."
4. "We will harness the sun and the winds and the soil to fuel our cars and run our factories."
5. "What the cynics fail to understand is that the ground has shifted beneath them, that the stale political arguments that have consumed us for so long no longer apply."

38. What is Obama's purpose in beginning each of three paragraphs of his Second Inaugural Address with "We, the people"?
a. to show American pride
b. to stress past successes in order to prove the country does not need to change
c. to quote the Preamble
d. to emphasize the theme of betterment in the United States of America

39. What is the effect of repeating the words **generation** and **build** to compare "the generation that built this country" with the "generation that will build its future"?
a. because Obama is talking about the same people
b. to create a connection between the past and the future
c. because he thinks the next generation will be better than the last
d. to emphasize that both generations still have work to do

40. Which of the following does NOT support Obama's claim in his Second Inaugural Address that Americans feel an obligation to future generations?
a. "For we remember the lessons of our past, when twilight years were spent in poverty, and parents of a child with a disability had nowhere to turn."
b. "We will respond to the threat of climate change, knowing that the failure to do so would betray our children and future generations."
c. "Time and again these men and women struggled and sacrificed and worked till their hands were raw so that we might live a better life."
d. "We will defend our people and uphold our values through strength of arms and rule of law."

41. Where will Obama support democracy, according to his Second Inaugural Address?
a. in the Americas
b. worldwide
c. in Europe
d. in the Middle East

42. Which of the following sentences from the Second Inaugural Address best fits into the theme of the First Inaugural Address?
a. "They do not make us a nation of takers; they free us to take the risks that make this country great."
b. "That's what will lend meaning to the creed our fathers once declared."
c. "We, the people, still believe that enduring security and a lasting peace do not require perpetual war."
d. "We must make the hard choices to reduce the cost of health care and the size of our deficit."

Please use the following to answer questions 43–48.

Remarks upon Signing the Civil Rights Bill (July 2, 1964), Lyndon Baines Johnson

1 My fellow Americans:

2 I am about to sign into law the Civil Rights Act of 1964. I want to take this occasion to talk to you about what that law means to every American.

3 One hundred and eighty-eight years ago this week a small band of valiant men began a long struggle for freedom. They pledged their lives, their fortunes, and their sacred honor not only to found a nation, but to forge an ideal of freedom—not only for political independence, but for personal liberty—not only to eliminate foreign rule, but to establish the rule of justice in the affairs of men.

4 That struggle was a turning point in our history. Today in far corners of distant continents, the ideals of those American patriots still shape the struggles of men who hunger for freedom.

5 This is a proud triumph. Yet those who founded our country knew that freedom would be secure only if each generation fought to renew and enlarge its meaning. From the minutemen at Concord to the soldiers in Viet-Nam, each generation has been equal to that trust.

6 Americans of every race and color have died in battle to protect our freedom. Americans of every race and color have worked to build a nation of widening opportunities. Now our generation of Americans has been called on to continue the unending search for justice within our own borders.

7 We believe that all men are created equal. Yet many are denied equal treatment.

8 We believe that all men have certain unalienable rights. Yet many Americans do not enjoy those rights.

9 We believe that all men are entitled to the blessings of liberty. Yet millions are being deprived of those blessings—not because of their own failures, but because of the color of their skin.

10 The reasons are deeply imbedded in history and tradition and the nature of man. We can understand—without rancor or hatred—how this all happened.

11 But it cannot continue. Our Constitution, the foundation of our Republic, forbids it. The principles of our freedom forbid it. Morality forbids it. And the law I will sign tonight forbids it.

43. Which sentence is NOT an example of an American ideal?

   a. "We believe that all men are created equal."

   b. "The principles of our freedom forbid it."

   c. "Not only for political independence, but for personal liberty."

   d. "Yet many are denied equal treatment."

44. Which sentence expresses the same idea as "Yet many are denied equal treatment"?

   a. "Yet many Americans do not enjoy those rights."

   b. "We believe that all men are entitled to the blessings of liberty."

   c. "We can understand—without rancor or hatred—how this all happened."

   d. "Americans of every race and color have died in battle to protect our freedom."

45. Based on Johnson's remarks, which is the best example of the United States' "unending search for justice within our own borders"?

   a. Civil War

   b. The Grand Canyon

   c. Civil Rights Act of 1964

   d. Vietnam War

46. Which answer best summarizes the main idea expressed in the paragraph that begins "One hundred and eighty-eight years ago"?

   a. The United States was formed a long time ago.

   b. The founding fathers worked hard to create a just nation.

   c. The country has always treated everyone fairly.

   d. Men of all races fought for freedom 188 years ago.

47. Which sentence best expresses the theme of President Johnson's remarks?

   a. American ideals include fair treatment for everyone.

   b. The United States is a great country.

   c. Everyone is treated the same in the United States.

   d. Lyndon B. Johnson was one of the best presidents.

48. Which of the following does NOT support Lyndon B. Johnson's stance that the Civil Rights Bill is in line with American values?

   a. "They pledged their lives, their fortunes, and their sacred honor not only to found a nation, but to forge an ideal of freedom."

   b. "Today in far corners of distant continents, the ideals of those American patriots still shape the struggles of men who hunger for freedom."

   c. "Americans of every race and color have died in battle to protect our freedom."

   d. "The reasons are deeply imbedded in history and tradition and the nature of man."

Part II

1 question
45 minutes to complete

This practice allows you to compose your response to the given task and then compare it with examples of responses at the different score levels. You will also get a scoring guide that includes a detailed explanation of how official GED® test graders will score your response. You may use this scoring guide to score your own response.

   It is important to note that on the official test this task must be completed in no more than 45 minutes. Before you begin planning and writing, read the two texts:

Page 227: excerpt from George W. Bush's First Inaugural Address

Page 228: excerpt from Barack Obama's First Inaugural Address

As you read the texts, think about the details from both texts that you might use in your argumentative essay. After reading the texts, plan your essay. Think about the ideas, facts, definitions, details, and other information and examples that you will want to use. Think about how you will introduce your topic and what the main topic will be for each paragraph.

As you write your argumentative essay, be sure to do the following:

- Introduce your claim.
- Support your claim with logical reasoning and relevant evidence from the texts.
- Acknowledge and address an alternative or opposing claim.
- Organize the reasons and evidence logically.
- Use words, phrases, and clauses to connect your ideas and to clarify the relationships among claims, counterclaims, reasons, and evidence.
- Establish and maintain a formal style.
- Provide a concluding statement or section that follows from and supports the argument presented.

Good luck!

Please use the following to answer the essay question.

George W. Bush's First Inaugural Address
January 20, 2001

1 We have a place, all of us, in a long story—a story we continue, but whose end we will not see. It is the story of a new world that became a friend and liberator of the old, a story of a slave-holding society that became a servant of freedom, the story of a power that went into the world to protect but not possess, to defend but not to conquer.

2 It is the American story—a story of flawed and fallible people, united across the generations by grand and enduring ideals.

3 The grandest of these ideals is an unfolding American promise that everyone belongs, that everyone deserves a chance, that no insignificant person was ever born.

4 Americans are called to enact this promise in our lives and in our laws. And though our nation has sometimes halted, and sometimes delayed, we must follow no other course.

5 Through much of the last century, America's faith in freedom and democracy was a rock in a raging sea. Now it is a seed upon the wind, taking root in many nations.

6 Our democratic faith is more than the creed of our country, it is the inborn hope of our humanity, an ideal we carry but do not own, a trust we bear and pass along. And even after nearly 225 years, we have a long way yet to travel.

7 While many of our citizens prosper, others doubt the promise, even the justice, of our own country. The ambitions of some Americans are limited by failing schools and hidden prejudice and the circumstances of their birth. And sometimes our differences run so deep, it seems we share a continent, but not a country.

(continues)

8 We do not accept this, and we will not allow it. Our unity, our union, is the serious work of leaders and citizens in every generation. And this is my solemn pledge: I will work to build a single nation of justice and opportunity.

9 And we are confident in principles that unite and lead us onward.

10 America has never been united by blood or birth or soil. We are bound by ideals that move us beyond our backgrounds, lift us above our interests and teach us what it means to be citizens. Every child must be taught these principles. Every citizen must uphold them. And every immigrant, by embracing these ideals, makes our country more, not less, American.

11 Today, we affirm a new commitment to live out our nation's promise through civility, courage, compassion and character.

12 America, at its best, matches a commitment to principle with a concern for civility. A civil society demands from each of us good will and respect, fair dealing and forgiveness.

Excerpt from Barack Obama's First Inaugural Address
January 20, 2009

1 In reaffirming the greatness of our nation we understand that greatness is never a given. It must be earned. Our journey has never been one of short-cuts or settling for less. It has not been the path for the faint-hearted, for those that prefer leisure over work, or seek only the pleasures of riches and fame. Rather, it has been the risk-takers, the doers, the makers of things—some celebrated, but more often men and women obscure in their labor—who have carried us up the long rugged path towards prosperity and freedom.

2 For us, they packed up their few worldly possessions and traveled across oceans in search of a new life. For us, they toiled in sweatshops, and settled the West, endured the lash of the whip, and plowed the hard earth. For us, they fought and died in places like Concord and Gettysburg, Normandy and Khe Sahn.

3 Time and again these men and women struggled and sacrificed and worked till their hands were raw so that we might live a better life. They saw America as bigger than the sum of our individual ambitions, greater than all the differences of birth or wealth or faction. This is the journey we continue today. We remain the most prosperous, powerful nation on Earth. Our workers are no less productive than when this crisis began. Our minds are no less inventive, our goods and services no less needed than they were last week, or last month, or last year. Our capacity remains undiminished. But our time of standing pat, of protecting narrow interests and putting off unpleasant decisions—that time has surely passed. Starting today, we must pick ourselves up, dust ourselves off, and begin again the work of remaking America.

(continues)

4   For everywhere we look, there is work to be done. The state of our economy calls for action, bold and swift. And we will act, not only to create new jobs, but to lay a new foundation for growth. We will build the roads and bridges, the electric grids and digital lines that feed our commerce and bind us together. We'll restore science to its rightful place, and wield technology's wonders to raise health care's quality and lower its cost. We will harness the sun and the winds and the soil to fuel our cars and run our factories. And we will transform our schools and colleges and universities to meet the demands of a new age. All this we can do. All this we will do.

5   Now, there are some who question the scale of our ambitions, who suggest that our system cannot tolerate too many big plans. Their memories are short, for they have forgotten what this country has already done, what free men and women can achieve when imagination is joined to common purpose, and necessity to courage. What the cynics fail to understand is that the ground has shifted beneath them, that the stale political arguments that have consumed us for so long no longer apply.

6   The question we ask today is not whether our government is too big or too small, but whether it works—whether it helps families find jobs at a decent wage, care they can afford, a retirement that is dignified. Where the answer is yes, we intend to move forward. Where the answer is no, programs will end. And those of us who manage the public's dollars will be held to account, to spend wisely, reform bad habits, and do our business in the light of day, because only then can we restore the vital trust between a people and their government.

PROMPT: There is ongoing debate in the political arena about what it means to be an American and what goals society should set.

Weigh the opinions and vision of two United States Presidents and then write an argumentative essay supporting either vision. Be sure to use relevant and specific evidence from both texts in your argumentative essay. Remember to take only 45 minutes to plan, draft, and edit your response.

_____

_____

_____

_____

_____

_____

_____

Answers and Explanations

Part I

1. **Choice d is correct.** This is the only answer that encompasses everything Mrs. Obama speaks on, from thanking the USDA employees to explaining how the healthy initiatives could not succeed without them.

   Choice **a** is incorrect. Although Mrs. Obama discusses different programs she has created with that goal, she uses those examples to demonstrate the greater theme.

   Choice **b** is incorrect. Mrs. Obama shows her appreciation for farmers, but this answer ignores many other ideas and information brought up throughout the passage.

   Choice **c** is incorrect. Mrs. Obama mentions the Let's Move initiative, but it is clear from her comments that the initiative is already underway; therefore, the purpose of Mrs. Obama's remarks is not to introduce Let's Move.

2. According to Mrs. Obama, a man named **Tom** mentioned that the nutrition issue is something near and dear to her heart. In the second paragraph, Mrs. Obama states: ". . . the nutrition issue, as Tom mentioned, as you all know, is something near and dear to my heart . . ."

3. **Choice b is correct.** Selecting this answer choice shows that the reader comprehends the importance Mrs. Obama places on family and healthy habits.

   Choice **a** is incorrect. This answer ignores the main topics of the passage, which include an emphasis on participating in an active lifestyle, not watching one.

   Choice **c** is incorrect. This answer choice only identifies one theme and ignores the focus on nutrition.

   Choice **d** is incorrect. Although this answer incorporates both the themes of family and having healthy habits, it disregards Mrs. Obama's emphasis on teaching children healthy habits.

4. **Choice a is correct.** Even though Mrs. Obama is stating another of the USDA's contributions, this answer does not focus on health or food, but rather renewable resources. Also, the other three answer choices clearly support the question's conclusion.

   Choice **b** is incorrect. This sentence demonstrates Mrs. Obama's concern through her gratitude.

   Choice **c** is incorrect. This statement explicitly states Mrs. Obama's personal interest in health in the United States.

   Choice **d** is incorrect. In this sentence, Mrs. Obama gives a specific example of the ways in which she, along with the USDA, has worked to teach citizens healthy habits.

5. **Choice a is correct.** If you replace the word "initiative" with the word "program," the sentence would retain its meaning.

   Choice **b** is incorrect. The word "enthusiasm" does not fit the context.

   Choice **c** is incorrect. "Disinterest" is an antonym of "initiative."

   Choice **d** is incorrect. Replacing "initiative" with "involvement" loses the meaning of the sentence.

6. **Choice b is correct.** It demonstrates the necessity of garden programs by highlighting the fact that some children don't know how food is grown or where their food comes from. Choice **a** is incorrect. This response neglects Mrs. Obama's emphasis on why nutritional programs are important. Choice **c** is incorrect. The paragraph supports the theme of the speech by providing information about why the programs and worker involvement are necessary. Choice **d** is incorrect. Mrs. Obama is very clear and explicitly states that children not only do not know about nutrition, but do not know where their food comes from. This ties into the overall theme of health and demonstrates why Mrs. Obama believes these programs are needed.

7. **Choice a is correct.** Two sentences before "countrymen," the narrator says, "Few Italians have the true virtuoso spirit." The next few sentences, including the one that uses "countrymen," are descriptions of traits that Italians do or do not have, according to the narrator. Choice **b** is incorrect. Two sentences before "countrymen," the narrator says "Few Italians have the true virtuoso spirit." The next few sentences discuss how the enthusiasm of many Italians is often a deception to take advantage of the British or Austrians, according to the narrator. Choice **c** is incorrect. Two sentences before "countrymen," the narrator says "Few Italians have the true virtuoso spirit." The next few sentences discuss how the enthusiasm of many Italians is often a deception to take advantage of the British or Austrians, according to the narrator. Choice **d** is incorrect. There is no mention or indication in the passage that Fortunato is a Spaniard.

8. **Choice c is correct.** The narrator states that Fortunato is "sincere" in his knowledge of "old wines," and "In this respect I did not differ from him materially." Choice **a** is incorrect. At no point does the narrator say anything about Italian history. Choice **b** is incorrect. The narrator describes Fortunato's "parti-striped dress," but does not describe his own clothing. Choice **d** is incorrect. The narrator states the events happened "one evening during the supreme madness of the carnival season," but makes no declarations about his feelings at the time.

9. **Choice b is correct.** This describes the narrator's reaction to finding Fortunato, not Fortunato's feelings about wine. Choice **a** is incorrect. The narrator is clearly stating Fortunato knows wine. Choice **c** is incorrect. Fortunato is attempting to prove that he knows wines and convince the narrator to take him to the cask of Amontillado instead of consulting their friend Luchresi. Choice **d** is incorrect. After the narrator warns Fortunato that his health would be in danger if they went to find the vault because of the cold, Fortunato dismisses the concern in favor of the wine.

10. **Choice c is correct.** Fortunato is actually quite unlucky as he has just stumbled across a man who wants to, and later does, kill him. Choice **a** is incorrect. The narrator is being sincere. Choice **b** is incorrect. This is a follow-up statement used to explain the narrator's claim that "[f]ew Italians have the true virtuoso spirit." Choice **d** is incorrect. Although the narrator does not actually mean to deter Fortunato from the journey to his death, there is no text-based reason to believe that the vaults are not cold and wet.

11. **Choice d is correct.** Early in the text, the narrator states that Fortunato "had a weak point—this Fortunato—although in other regards he was a man to be respected and even feared. He prided himself on his connoisseurship in wine."

Choice **a** is incorrect. There is nothing in the text that indicates Luchresi has more expertise in wine than Fortunato. As a matter of fact, the narrator himself states that "in the matter of old wines [Fortunato] was sincere."

Choice **b** is incorrect. On the contrary, if the narrator and Fortunato were known enemies, Fortunato would not trust him and follow him down to the vault.

Choice **c** is incorrect. The two men already know and trust each other, which is evidenced in their interactions and dialogue.

12. **Choice c is correct.** The author suggests that before 1867 many babies were poked by pins, and then the safety pin came along and eliminated the problem. It can be inferred that the reason the earlier babies were being poked was because their diapers were fastened with straight pins.

Choice **a** is incorrect. The only connection the author makes between himself and George Washington is that he, like Washington, was born into the world a liar.

Choice **b** is incorrect. Although the author suggests that before 1867 infants were often poked by pins, he does not imply that pin-poking was a form of parental punishment.

Choice **d** is incorrect. Although the author states that safety pins made children unable to "lie" by crying as if they had been poked by a pin, the author also states that this "doesn't impair the disposition to lie."

13. **Choice b is correct.** The author states, "During the first half of my life I never knew a child that was able to raise above that temptation and keep from telling that lie."

Choice **a** is incorrect. The author offers no scientific data to support his claim.

Choice **c** is incorrect. The author does not present any physical evidence to support his claim.

Choice **d** is incorrect. Although the author states that George Washington lied as a child, he offers no historical documentation to support this statement.

14. **Choice d is correct.** The author states that "all people are liars from the cradle onward" and also asks, "[W]hy should a person grieve over a thing which by the eternal law of his make he cannot help?"

Choice **a** is incorrect. The author does not suggest that lying should be forbidden and, in fact, argues that stopping a person from lying does not remove a person's disposition to lie.

Choice **b** is incorrect. The author does not suggest that different rules should be applied to adults and children.

Choice **c** is incorrect. The author does not suggest that eliminating lying is a goal toward which people should strive.

15. Choice a is correct. The author argues that those who didn't speak up about slavery implied "that there wasn't anything going on in which humane and intelligent people were interested," which was a quiet way of countering antislavery activists.

Choice **b** is incorrect. The author does not mention economics as an issue related to slavery.

Choice **c** is incorrect. The author does not suggest that slave owners lied to others; the main idea of the paragraph is that people lied to themselves about slavery.

Choice **d** is incorrect. The author says that anti-slavery agitators in the North would "[a]rgue and plead and pray," but they didn't get enough support in response.

16. Choice b is correct. While this detail is mentioned in the passage, it does not reflect the main idea of the passage, which is that lying is a part of human nature.

Choices **a**, **c**, and **d** are incorrect. These details support the main idea of the passage, which is that lying is a part of human nature.

17. Choice a is correct. All three words need to be capitalized. Beginning letters of sentences are always capitalized, and people's names and titles are capitalized.

Choice **b** is incorrect. This answer lacks all necessary capitalization. All three words need to be capitalized. Beginning letters of sentences are always capitalized, and people's names and titles are capitalized.

Choices **c** and **d** are incorrect. All three words must be capitalized.

18. Choice c is correct. This is the correct past tense for a singular subject.

Choice **a** is incorrect. "I have to work with children" does not make sense within the context. The author is explaining what she has done in the past.

Choices **b** and **d** are incorrect. These answer choices do not make sense in context.

19. Choice a is correct. This word correctly matches the past-tense verb "nannied."

Choice **b** is incorrect. This does not fit in context with the past-tense verb "nannied."

Choice **c** is incorrect. The word "however" indicates contrast with a previous statement. The ideas in the sentence complement previous sentences, and do not offer contrast.

Choice **d** is incorrect. This answer choice does not make sense in context. In order to keep with form, "recently" is a better answer.

20. Choice c is correct. "My" is the correct possessive pronoun.

Choice **a** is incorrect. This is not the correct possessive pronoun. The speaker is talking about her abilities.

Choice **b** is incorrect. "Me" is not a possessive pronoun. It is clear that the abilities belong to someone.

Choice **d** is incorrect. Although "mine" is possessive, one uses it to indicate objects that belong to them, and it would be awkward to say "mine abilities."

21. Choice a is correct. This choice summarizes the passage in totality, identifying Kennedy's emphasis on the past and the present as he accepts the presidency.
Choice **b** is incorrect. This choice neglects Kennedy's focus on the future of the nation and the world.
Choice **c** is incorrect. Kennedy stresses hope and good things to come throughout the text; however, this is just a small slice of everything he says and is not the main theme.
Choice **d** is incorrect. Although Kennedy speaks about the United States' and its allies' role in furthering peace and democracy, this choice ignores the weight Kennedy puts on how the past shaped the country.

22. Choice c is correct. The use of "replaced" and "more" signifies that "colonial control" and "tyranny" mean similar things.
Choice **a** is incorrect. The sentence is addressed to the "new states" to whom the promise of a guard against more tyranny is made.
Choice **b** is incorrect. This phrase represents the opposite of tyranny, the state to which the countries have been "welcomed." The second half of the sentence is a promise to protect them and guard against tyranny.
Choice **d** is incorrect. "Iron" is an adjective used to describe tyranny.

23. Choice a is correct. Kennedy is contrasting being united with being divided in order to make a point about why countries should cooperate (because they can accomplish anything "in a host of cooperative ventures").
Choice **b** is incorrect. This is the opposite of Kennedy's intention.
Choice **c** is incorrect. Kennedy is focusing on everyone working together and not on foreign policy.
Choice **d** is incorrect. Although Kennedy says that he is committed to peace and cooperation, this speech focuses on discussing the perils of not working together.

24. Choice 1 is incorrect. Kennedy makes a point of saying that the United States will "pay any price, bear any burden, meet any hardship, support any friend, oppose any foe, in order to assure the survival and the success of liberty." This does not show fear.
Choice 2 is correct. Many times Kennedy emphasizes doing what is necessary to help those in need and that the United States will "pay any price."
Choice 3 is correct. Kennedy stresses that he is committed to showing people who are "struggling" how to "help themselves," and wants to "assist free men and free governments in casting off the chains of poverty."
Choice 4 is correct. Kennedy states he pledges the United States' "best efforts" not for political reasons, "but because it is right." He also says he wants to "convert our good words into good deeds."
Choice 5 is incorrect. In the last paragraph, Kennedy explicitly asks "that both sides begin anew the quest for peace." He does not threaten his opponents but rather warns against the consequences of not working together.

25. Choice a is correct. Roosevelt emphasizes that the attack was a complete surprise because the two nations were not warring, yet states that he has "directed that all measures be taken for our defense." Even though he was not expecting the event, he knows that "hostilities exist" and has handled the situation.

Choice **b** is incorrect. Roosevelt says the United States has "confidence in our armed forces" and "determination of our people" and will "gain the inevitable triumph." These are not words of a timid or fearful person.

Choice **c** is incorrect. Although he asserts many times that the attack came as a surprise, he does not show fear through his words. Rather, he shows confidence in the country.

Choice **d** is incorrect. Some of what Roosevelt says is aggressive, like asking Congress to declare war, but he seems confident in the abilities of the nation rather than insecure.

26. Choice c is correct. Roosevelt is effectively stressing how "[t]he United States was at peace with that nation" by emphatically pointing out that the Japanese ambassador responded to the American message.

Choice **a** is incorrect. The fourth paragraph says that there were "existing diplomatic negotiations," an example of how Japan was "still in conversation," as stated in the previous paragraph.

Choice **b** is incorrect. The fourth paragraph supports the premise of the third paragraph.

Choice **d** is incorrect. The fourth paragraph supports the theme of the previous paragraphs.

27. Choice b is correct. Roosevelt is implying that the two islands are far enough apart that the attack had to have been "deliberately planned." Choice **a** is incorrect. The attack wouldn't have had to have been planned "days or even weeks ago" if the island was close and easy for the Japanese to attack.

Choice **c** is incorrect. The United States mainland is not mentioned and is irrelevant in this context.

Choice **d** is incorrect. There is no evidence in the speech to support this answer choice. The opposite is true.

28. Choice d is correct. The drumbeat rhythm of repetition emphasizes the great number of attacks on one country after another.

Choice **a** is incorrect. There is no evidence in the speech that Japan was disorganized. In fact, evidence in the speech supports the conclusion that the opposite was true.

Choice **b** is incorrect. There is no evidence in the speech to support this conclusion.

Choice **c** is incorrect. There is no mention of how the other countries handled or will handle the attack.

29. Choice b is correct. Roosevelt states many times the attack was an intentional move that put "our interests . . . in grave danger."

Choice **a** is incorrect. Contrary to this answer choice, evidence in the speech supports the conclusion that Japan launched a surprise attack on the United States.

Choice **c** is incorrect. There is no evidence in the speech to support this conclusion.

Choice **d** is incorrect. It is clear from the speech that the attack was planned.

30. Choice d is correct. This sentence comes after describing how the surprise attack was carried out, acknowledging resulting clear and present danger.

Choice **a** is incorrect. An attack is not expected from a nation in peaceful accord with the United States.

Choice **b** is incorrect. This sentence shows that the nations were working together to find a solution prior to the attack.

Choice **c** is incorrect. This sentence describes how Japan worked to make sure the attack was a surprise by deceiving the United States.

31. Choice b is correct. The tone is appropriate for a work e-mail.

Choice **a** is incorrect. The phrases "some really big" and "that might really affect" are informal and awkward.

Choice **c** is incorrect. The tone is too informal for a work e-mail.

Choice **d** is incorrect. A postscript (PS) comes at the end of a letter, not at the beginning.

32. Choice b is correct. This is the past participle verb. The decision "has" already been made.

Choice **a** is incorrect. This is the future tense, and the decision has already been made.

Choice **c** is incorrect. This is the present tense, and the action is not happening now.

Choice **d** is incorrect. This is the present tense of the verb.

33. Choice d is correct. The plural pronoun matches the plural form of the verb. The contraction of these two words is "they're" and is a homophone of "there" and "their."

Choice **a** is incorrect. The word "there" refers to location.

Choice **b** is incorrect. "Their" is a possessive pronoun.

Choice **c** is incorrect. Although this has the correct plural pronoun, "is" is for singular subjects.

34. Choice c is correct. This answer correctly closes off the thought from the first part of the sentence before introducing the second part of the sentence. It shows a natural pause.

Choice **a** is incorrect. "Friday" modifies "afternoons," so they cannot be broken up by a comma.

Choice **b** is incorrect. "Employee" serves as an adjective for "activity." They cannot be separated.

Choice **d** is incorrect. "Activity" is the noun and "drops" is the verb. They should not be separated.

35. Choice b is correct. Obama remarks that greatness is not a given and must be earned, implying that the United States is not great by luck, but by work and determination.

Choice **a** is incorrect. Luck is not mentioned as making a great nation.

Choice **c** is incorrect. The future is not mentioned in the first paragraph.

Choice **d** is incorrect. Obama does not discuss his personal feelings about being president in the address.

36. Choice d is correct. The sentence later in the passage recalls the men and women mentioned earlier to stress that the cynics are wrong in thinking great things cannot be accomplished.

Choice **a** is incorrect. Although this answer recognizes the theme of the sentence, that the United States has a large and historical "capacity" for greatness, it does not explicitly call on the image of the people working or modify that idea.

Choice **b** is incorrect. This choice neglects the connection Obama makes between the people who worked hard to shape America and the cynics who are ignoring their struggles by doubting change.

Choice **c** is incorrect. This phrase in the question has nothing to do with the cost of healthcare or technology.

37. Choice 1 is correct. The main idea in the address is that America was formed by hard work, and that attitude needs to and will be continued throughout this presidency. This phrase supports that by firmly stating that taking the easy way out is not what "our journey" has been about.

Choice 2 is correct. This phrase supports the theme of the future of the United States.

Choice 3 is correct. This phrase supports the idea that citizens and the government must work hard and will work hard.

Choice **4** is incorrect. This phrase is about renewable energy, which is used as a detail of what Obama wants to focus on and is not the main focus.

Choice **5** is incorrect. This phrase stresses the negative and opposition to progress; it does not support the idea of ambition.

38. Choice d is correct. Obama draws on the history of the United States, like "the creed our fathers once declared," to stress that citizens have an "obligation" to help "all posterity." Choice **a** is incorrect. Although Obama does carefully praise the country throughout, the point of the passage is to discuss the future challenges and how past successes enable us to face those challenges.

Choice **b** is incorrect. Choosing this answer shows the reader clearly does not comprehend that the main focus of the text is what Obama believes needs to change.

Choice **c** is incorrect. This is the tool Obama is utilizing, not the effect of utilizing that tool.

39. Choice b is correct. Obama uses words, or rhetoric, to show that he thinks the two are connected and that their interests both matter. Choice **a** is incorrect. This choice neglects the verb tense change of "built" to "will build." This shows he is talking about past people/actions and future people/actions.

Choice **c** is incorrect. This sentence makes no value judgment on either party, and does not state one is better than the other.

Choice **d** is incorrect. One generation's actions are in the past, as "built" is the past tense verb; their work is done.

40. Choice d is correct. Obama is stressing American might and willingness to use its power, not speaking of obligations to future generations.

Choice **a** is incorrect. In this sentence, Obama looks to the past for solutions to today's problems.

Choice **b** is incorrect. Obama is looking to the future, arguing that failure to act to halt climate change would "betray our children and future generations."

Choice **c** is incorrect. Here, Obama draws on the past as a reason United States citizens must fight for the future.

41. Choice b is correct. Specifically, Obama says, "We will support democracy from Asia to Africa; from the Americas to the Middle East . . ."

Choices **a**, **b**, and **c** are incorrect. Obama says, "We will support democracy from Asia to Africa; from the Americas to the Middle East . . ."

42. Choice b is correct. This sentence supports the first inaugural's theme of continuing the hard work of the past in order to secure prosperity and freedom for tomorrow.

Choice **a** is incorrect. This sentence refers to healthcare and taking care of the country's citizens; this is mentioned in the first address, but it is not the theme.

Choice **c** is incorrect. Obama's First Inaugural Address did not focus on war.

Choice **d** is incorrect. These details are not the theme of the first address.

43. Choice d is correct. It is not an American ideal to deny freedom. The opposite is true. Freedom is the theme of American ideals.

Choice **a** is incorrect. This American ideal is cited in paragraph 7.

Choice **b** is incorrect. This American ideal is cited in the last paragraph.

Choice **c** is incorrect. This American ideal is cited in paragraph 3.

44. Choice a is correct. People not having the same rights as others means roughly the same thing as the denial of equal treatment.

Choice **b** is incorrect. This means the opposite of the quotation in question.

Choice **c** is incorrect. In this sentence, Johnson is explaining that there were reasons for what happened rather than restating the problem of people being treated differently.

Choice **d** is incorrect. Johnson is affirming that Americans of all races have contributed to their country.

45. Choice c is correct. This is the best answer because one of the main points of the remarks is to explain that the Civil Rights Act will bring the United States closer to achieving its goals and values.

Choice **a** is incorrect. Johnson does not mention the Civil War in the passage.

Choice **b** is incorrect. The Grand Canyon is one of America's natural wonders, unrelated to America's unending search for justice domestically.

Choice **d** is incorrect. Johnson alludes to the Vietnam War in the text and uses it as an example of how American values are spanning the globe, but this is a small detail in the passage rather than a main idea. As well, Vietnam is outside of "our own borders."

46. Choice b is correct. Johnson talks about the values that the forefathers focused on when forming the nation in this paragraph.

Choice **a** is incorrect. This is a detail of the passage, but not the main theme.

Choice **c** is incorrect. This idea is not stated in the paragraph, and it also runs counter to the entire point of the speech.

Choice **d** is incorrect. There is no evidence to support this conclusion in the remarks.

47. Choice a is correct. Johnson expresses many times and in a variety of ways that equality is one of the cornerstones of American values.

Choice **b** is incorrect. Johnson talks about how he believes America is a great country, but this is not the main idea of his remarks.

Choice **c** is incorrect. Johnson's remarks are about America's ideal of ensuring equality, yet to be achieved.

Choice **d** is incorrect. Johnson makes no value judgment about himself.

48. Choice d is correct. This is Johnson's brief explanation of how inequality happened, rather than an explanation of how the law aligns with American values.

Choice **a** is incorrect. Johnson uses history and the vision of the forefathers to illustrate that freedom is a core American value and that freedom includes equality.

Choice **b** is incorrect. Johnson says that because American values are shaping foreign struggles, the United States must continue to make sure that it upholds its own values.

Choice **c** is incorrect. Johnson uses this sentence to say that all kinds of people, regardless of race, have fought for the country.

Part II

Your extended response will be scored based on three traits, or elements:

- **Trait 1:** Creation of arguments and use of evidence
- **Trait 2:** Development of ideas and organizational structure
- **Trait 3:** Clarity and command of standard English conventions

Your essay will be scored on a 6-point scale—each trait is worth up to 2 points. The final score is counted twice, so the maximum number of points you can earn is 12.

Trait 1 tests your ability to write an essay that takes a stance based on the information in the reading passages. To earn the highest score possible, you must carefully read the information and express a clear opinion on what you have read. You will be scored on how well you use the information from the passages to support your argument.

Your response will also be scored on how well you analyze the author's arguments in the passages. To earn the highest score possible, you should discuss whether you think the author is making a good argument, and why or why not.

For your reference, here is a table that readers will use when scoring your essay with a 2, 1, or 0.

TRAIT 1: CREATION OF ARGUMENTS AND USE OF EVIDENCE	
2	• Makes text-based argument(s) and establishes an intent connected to the prompt • Presents specific and related evidence from source text(s) to support argument (may include a few unrelated pieces of evidence or unsupported claims) • Analyzes the topic and/or the strength of the argument within the source text(s) (e.g., distinguishes between supported and unsupported claims, makes valid inferences about underlying assumptions, identifies false reasoning, evaluates the credibility of sources)
1	• Makes an argument with some connection to the prompt • Presents some evidence from source text(s) to support argument (may include a mix of related and unrelated evidence that may or may not cite the text) • Partly analyzes the topic and/or the strength of the argument within the source text(s); may be limited, oversimplified, or inaccurate
0	• May attempt to make an argument OR lacks an intent or connection to the prompt OR attempts neither • Presents little or no evidence from source text(s) (sections of text may be copied from source directly) • Minimally analyzes the topic and/or the strength of the argument within the source text(s); may present no analysis, or little or no understanding of the given argument
Non-scorable	• Response consists only of text copied from the prompt or source text(s) • Response shows that test-taker has not read the prompt or is entirely off-topic • Response is incomprehensible • Response is not in English • No response has been attempted (has been left blank)

Trait 2 tests whether you respond to the writing prompt with a well-structured essay. Support of your thesis must come from evidence in the passages, as well as personal opinions and experiences that build on your central idea. Your ideas must be fully explained and include specific details. Your essay should use words and phrases that allow your details and ideas to flow naturally. Here is a table that outlines what is involved in earning a score of 2, 1, or 0.

TRAIT 2: DEVELOPMENT OF IDEAS AND ORGANIZATIONAL STRUCTURE	
2	• Contains ideas that are generally logical and well-developed; most ideas are expanded upon • Contains a logical sequence of ideas with clear connections between specific details and main ideas • Develops an organizational structure that conveys the message and goal of the response; appropriately uses transitional devices • Develops and maintains an appropriate style and tone that signal awareness of the audience and purpose of the task • Uses appropriate words to express ideas clearly
1	• Contains ideas that are partially developed and/or may demonstrate vague or simplistic logic; only some ideas are expanded upon • Contains some evidence of a sequence of ideas, but specific details may be unconnected to main ideas • Develops an organizational structure that may partially group ideas or is partially effective at conveying the message of the response; inconsistently uses transitional devices • May inconsistently maintain an appropriate style and tone to signal an awareness of the audience and purpose of the task • May contain misused words and/or words that do not express ideas clearly
0	• Contains ideas that are ineffectively or illogically developed, with little or no elaboration of main ideas • Contains an unclear or no sequence of ideas; specific details may be absent or unrelated to main ideas • Develops an ineffective or no organizational structure; inappropriately uses transitional devices, or does not use them at all • Uses an inappropriate style and tone that signals limited or no awareness of audience and purpose • May contain many misused words, overuse of slang, and/or express ideas in an unclear or repetitious manner
Non-scorable	• Response consists only of text copied from the prompt or source text(s) • Response shows that test-taker has not read the prompt or is entirely off-topic • Response is incomprehensible • Response is not in English • No response has been attempted (has been left blank)

Trait 3 tests how you create the sentences that make up your essay. To earn a high score, you will need to write sentences with variety—some short, some long, some simple, some complex. You will also need to prove that you have a good handle on standard English, including correct word choice, grammar, and sentence structure.

Here is a table that outlines what is involved in attaining a score of 2, 1, or 0.

TRAIT 3: CLARITY AND COMMAND OF STANDARD ENGLISH CONVENTIONS	
2	• Demonstrates generally correct sentence structure and an overall fluency that enhances clarity with regard to the following skills: 1) Diverse sentence structure within a paragraph or paragraphs 2) Correct use of subordination, coordination, and parallelism 3) Avoidance of awkward sentence structures and wordiness 4) Use of transitional words, conjunctive adverbs, and other words that enhance clarity and logic 5) Avoidance of run-on sentences, sentence fragments, and fused sentences • Demonstrates proficient use of conventions with regard to the following skills: 1) Subject–verb agreement 2) Placement of modifiers and correct word order 3) Pronoun usage, including pronoun antecedent agreement, unclear pronoun references, and pronoun case 4) Frequently confused words and homonyms, including contractions 5) Use of apostrophes with possessive nouns 6) Use of punctuation (e.g., commas in a series or in appositives and other non-essential elements, end marks, and punctuation for clause separation) 7) Capitalization (e.g., beginnings of sentences, proper nouns, and titles) • May contain some errors in mechanics and conventions that do not impede comprehension; overall usage is at a level suitable for on-demand draft writing
1	• Demonstrates inconsistent sentence structure; may contain some choppy, repetitive, awkward, or run-on sentences that may limit clarity; demonstrates inconsistent use of skills 1–5 as listed under Trait 3, Score Point 2 • Demonstrates inconsistent use of basic conventions with regard to skills 1–7 as listed under Trait 3, Score Point 2 • May contain many errors in mechanics and conventions that occasionally impede comprehension; overall usage is at the minimum level acceptable for on-demand draft writing
0	• Demonstrates improper sentence structure to the extent that meaning may be unclear; demonstrates minimal use of skills 1–5 as listed under Trait 3, Score Point 2 • Demonstrates minimal use of basic conventions with regard to skills 1–7 as listed under Trait 3, Score Point 2 • Contains numerous significant errors in mechanics and conventions that impede comprehension; overall usage is at an unacceptable level for on-demand draft writing OR • Response is insufficient to show level of proficiency involving conventions and usage
Non-scorable	• Response consists only of text copied from the prompt or source text(s) • Response shows that test-taker has not read the prompt or is entirely off-topic • Response is incomprehensible • Response is not in English • No response has been attempted (has been left blank)

Sample Score 6 Essay

The inaugural addresses of Presidents Bush and Obama have one key difference that is immediately apparent: President Bush's address is focused on the past, while President Obama's speech is focused on the future.

Neither speaker gives an exact description of the historical context of his address, but even someone unfamiliar with the history of the past fifteen years can pick up a few clues. President Bush states: "A civil society demands from each of us good will and respect, fair dealing and forgiveness." Forgiveness is something offered for past wrongs. He also speaks of "civility" and "compassion." It seems clear that President Bush was assuming office at a time when people were angry and divided over an issue or issues, and that he feels the need to urge forgiveness.

President Obama, on the other hand, is a bit more explicit about his context, saying: "The state of our economy calls for action, bold and swift." Obviously, Obama is assuming office in the midst of an economic crisis. But in his speech, he frames that crisis as an opportunity to envision and create a better future. In the same paragraph in which he mentions the economy, Obama repeatedly refers to what "we will" do in the future: "we will act," "we will build," "we will restore," "we will harness," and "we will transform."

This is not to say that Obama does not mention the past at all. Both presidents pay homage to previous generations. However, Obama does so in more concrete and inclusive terms, mentioning experiences and events that resonate with a wide range of Americans—working in sweatshops, enduring slavery, and fighting in the Civil War, in World War II, and in Vietnam. In contrast, Bush speaks vaguely, though fondly, of our "democratic ideals."

Though, in essence, both speeches touch on many similar points—that America is a land of promise and that we should make sure all American enjoy the fruits of that promise, Obama's speech is more powerful because he seems to have a clear vision of how to move forward. Bush's speech seems like it was designed to soothe an angry electorate, not to lay out a clear agenda. His speech was fine, in that it was well organized and included the usual patriotic language. But in my opinion, any inaugural address should acknowledge the current state of the nation's affairs and lay out a plan for the future. Obama's speech does this, while Bush's does not.

About this essay:

This response is a six-point response because it is well organized, free of major grammatical or mechanical problems, and it uses details from both passages to make a coherent and even-handed argument that is based more on fact than on personal emotions.

Trait 1: Creation of Arguments and Use of Evidence

This response evaluates the arguments in the source texts, develops an effective position supported by the texts, and fulfills the criteria to earn 2 points for Trait 1.

This response establishes its stance in the first sentence (*President Bush's address is focused on the past, while President Obama's speech is focused on the future*) and develops it a step further in the conclusion (*But in my opinion, any inaugural address should acknowledge the current state of the nation's affairs and lay out a plan for the future. Obama's speech does this, while Bush's does not*).

The writer also provides a summary of support for that stance (*It seems clear that President Bush was assuming office at a time when people were angry and divided over an issue or issues, and that he feels the need to urge forgiveness. President Obama, on the other hand, is a bit more explicit about his context, saying: "The state of our economy calls for action, bold and swift."*)

Trait 2: Development of Ideas and Organizational Structure

This response is well developed and fulfills the criteria to earn 2 points for Trait 2. It is well organized, from the writer's clear point of view in the first paragraph, to the side-by-side comparison of the strengths of each speech.

The writer's vocabulary and sentence structures are sophisticated, and the tone shows an intensity of purpose.

Trait 3: Clarity and Command of Standard English Conventions

This response fulfills the criteria for draft writing and earns 2 points for Trait 3. Besides employing sophisticated sentence structure (*However, Obama does so in more concrete and inclusive terms, mentioning experiences and events that resonate with a wide range of Americans—working in sweatshops, enduring slavery, and fighting in the Civil War, in World War II, and in Vietnam.*), this response uses clear transitions in its compare and contrast construction (*In contrast, Bush speaks vaguely, though fondly, of our "democratic ideals."*)

Sample Score 4 Essay

People become president need to make sure they appeal to all Americans, not just a few. This is why President Bush's inaugural address was more effective than President Obama's. President Bush reminded listeners repeatedly of their common heritage. President Obama's speech seemed more self-centered because he talked about all the things he wanted to accomplish, but did not consider the concerns of average Americans.

President Bush talks about issues that all Americans are related to. For example he says "The grandest of these ideals is an unfolding American promise that everyone belongs, that everyone deserves a chance, that no insignificant person was ever born." He is talking about democracy here, and that is something all Americans agree with. But Obama seems to be picking a fight with political opponents when he says things like "What the cynics fail to understand is that the ground has shifted beneath them, that the stale political arguments that have consumed us for so long no longer apply." To me, Obama seems to be saying that people who don't agree with him are cynics with "stale" arguments. That could be denigrated to many people.

A president is president to all Americans, not just a few. That is why I think that the way President Bush talks about the need for all of us to practice "civility" is so important. Our country has many problems to solve, and we can't solve them without civility and being willing to forgive each other and operate with good will.

In conclusion, I believe President Bush did the best job in introducing himself and his plans as president to the country. He did so by appealing to everyone, not just to his supporters.

About this essay:

The essay is well structured, and the writer uses multiple quotes from the passages to back up key points. However, there are some minor grammatical/mechanical errors, and the writer uses opinion and emotion as much as supporting evidence from the passages.

Trait 1: Creation of Arguments and Use of Evidence

This response attempts to evaluate the arguments in the source texts, develops a position supported by the texts, and meets the criteria to earn 1 point for Trait 1. The writer establishes their perspective in the first sentence (*People become president need to make sure they appeal to all Americans, not just a few.*) and uses quotes to support their opinion (*Obama seems to be picking a fight with political opponents when he says things like "What the cynics fail to understand is that the ground has shifted beneath them, that the stale political arguments that have consumed us for so long no longer apply."*) though they also make leaps without textual evidence.

Trait 2: Development of Ideas and Organizational Structure

This response fulfills the criteria to earn 2 points for Trait 2. The writer begins by establishing their opinion, examines specific facets of each speech, and concludes by comparing the two speeches directly (*In conclusion, I believe President Bush did the best job in introducing himself and his plans as president to the country. He did so by appealing to everyone, not just to his supporters*).

Trait 3: Clarity and Command of Standard English Conventions

This response fulfills the criteria for draft writing and earns 1 point for Trait 3. There are some errors that make understanding the writer's meaning challenging (*That could be denigrated to many people.*)

Sample Score 3 Essay

If you look at President Bush's speech and compare and contrast it with President Obama's speech, you can see right away that Obama's is better.

Bush and Obama both talk about the path of America. But Obama makes Americans sound strong. He talks about the whip and the lash, and working your hands raw, and you can just feel how tough Americans are. But Bush just talks about how we are "flawed" and that sometimes we "halted." I don't think this is how people are aspired. It's not who we are.

Obama gets on a roll near the end of his speech with all the talk about "we will do this" and "we will do that," but all Bush does is say "be nice" and "be forgiving." Forgiving for what? Right away, you get your suspicious up.

That's why Obama's speech is better. He isn't afraid to call it like it is and he won't let anything stand in his way. All Bush seems to worry about is good manners.

About this essay:

This is a three-point response: although it does have a structure, it lacks a clear central argument and features scant support from the passages. It also has grammatical errors that interfere with meaning.

Trait 1: Creation of Arguments and Use of Evidence

This response attempts to evaluate the arguments in the source texts, though they struggle to develop a position supported by the texts, and so they earn 1 point for Trait 1.

Trait 2: Development of Ideas and Organizational Structure

This response has a structure but features little to no development of ideas, instead relying on a fairly straightforward recap of the texts. It meets the criteria to earn 1 point for Trait 2.

Trait 3: Clarity and Command of Standard English Conventions

This response attempts to fulfill the criteria for draft writing and earns 1 point for Trait 3. The spelling and syntactical errors reflect insufficient time revising or a lack of facility with written English (*aspired, "get your suspicious up"*).

Sample Score 0 Essay

President Bush knows what it means to be American. He talks about patriotism and civil society and about how immigrants can find opportunities to be American here. President Obama's speech is just scary. All that talk about the hard work people are supposed to like and the hard work we have to do. What about our government?

It's like Obama forgot that you have to talk like a president when you are giving a speech to the American people. This isn't a pep rally. You have to show you know yor stuff. That is what Bush does. He knows his American history. He quotes the facts.

Obama talks about what he wants to do and the work we are supposed to do. That's not facts. That's just wishes. Facts are what make speeches important.

About this essay:

This is a zero-point response because it is poorly structured, features multiple spelling and grammatical errors, and relies very little on evidence from the passages. Rather, it is based on the writer's unsupported emotions.

10 ▶ GED® RLA PRACTICE TEST 2

This practice test is modeled on the format, content, and timing of the official GED® Reasoning through Language Arts test.

Part I

Like the official exam, this section presents a series of questions that assess your ability to read, write, edit, and understand standard written English. You'll be asked to answer questions based on informational and literary reading passages. Refer to the passages as often as necessary when answering the questions.

Work carefully, but do not spend too much time on any one question. Be sure you answer every question.

Set a timer for 95 minutes (1 hour and 35 minutes), and try to take this test uninterrupted, under quiet conditions.

Part II

The official GED® Reasoning through Language Arts test also includes an Extended Response question—an essay question. Set a timer for 45 minutes and try to read the given passage and brainstorm, write, and proof-read your essay uninterrupted, under quiet conditions.

Complete answer explanations for every test question and sample essays at different scoring levels follow the exam. Good luck!

Part I

48 total questions
95 minutes to complete

Please use the following to answer questions 1–8.

This excerpt is from the Declaration of Independence.

1   When in the Course of human events, it becomes necessary for one people to dissolve the political bands which have connected them with another, and to assume among the powers of the earth, the separate and equal station to which the Laws of Nature and of Nature's God entitle them, a decent respect to the opinions of mankind requires that they should declare the causes which impel them to the separation.

2   We hold these truths to be self-evident, that all men are created equal, that they are endowed by their Creator with certain unalienable Rights, that among these are Life, Liberty and the pursuit of Happiness.—That to secure these rights, Governments are instituted among Men, deriving their just powers from the consent of the governed,—That whenever any Form of Government becomes destructive of these ends, it is the Right of the People to alter or to abolish it, and to institute new Government, laying its foundation on such principles and organizing its powers in such form, as to them shall seem most likely to effect their Safety and Happiness. Prudence, indeed, will dictate that Governments long established should not be changed for light and transient causes; and accordingly all experience hath shewn, that mankind are more disposed to suffer, while evils are sufferable, than to right themselves by abolishing the forms to which they are accustomed. But when a long train of abuses and usurpations, pursuing invariably the same Object evinces a design to reduce them under absolute Despotism, it is their right, it is their duty, to throw off such Government, and to provide new Guards for their future security.—Such has been the patient sufferance of these Colonies; and such is now the necessity which constrains them to alter their former Systems of Government. The history of the present King of Great Britain is a history of repeated injuries and usurpations, all having in direct object the establishment of an absolute Tyranny over these States. To prove this, let Facts be submitted to a candid world.

3   He has refused his Assent to Laws, the most wholesome and necessary for the public good. He has forbidden his Governors to pass Laws of immediate and pressing importance, unless suspended in their operation till his Assent should be obtained; and when so suspended, he has utterly neglected to attend to them. He has refused to pass other Laws for the accommodation of large districts of people, unless those people would relinquish the right of Representation in the Legislature, a right inestimable to them and formidable to tyrants only. He has called together legislative bodies at places unusual, uncomfortable, and distant from the depository of their public Records, for the sole purpose of fatiguing them into compliance with his measures. He has dissolved Representative Houses repeatedly, for opposing with manly firmness his invasions on the rights of the people.

1. Write your answers in the boxes below.

   Based on the excerpt, "He has dissolved Representative Houses repeatedly" is an example of an injustice committed by the ⬚ of ⬚ .

2. Paragraph 3 can be summed up as
   a. a list of laws for life in the colonies written by the King of Great Britain
   b. a list of laws created for the newly independent United States of America
   c. a list praising the many good acts carried out by the King of Great Britain
   d. a list of injustices committed by the King of Great Britain against the colonies

3. Which of the following quotations expresses the Declaration's main idea that the American colonies want independence from Great Britain?
   a. "We hold these truths to be self-evident, that all men are created equal"
   b. "it becomes necessary for one people to dissolve the political bands which have connected them with another"
   c. "He has refused to pass other Laws for the accommodation of large districts of people"
   d. "they are endowed by their Creator with certain unalienable Rights"

4. Which of the following quotations builds on the argument that governments should get their powers from the consent of the governed?
   a. "He has refused his Assent to Laws, the most wholesome and necessary for the public good"
   b. "whenever any Form of Government becomes destructive of these ends, it is the Right of the People to alter or to abolish it"
   c. "He has dissolved Representative Houses repeatedly"
   d. "He has called together legislative bodies at places unusual, uncomfortable, and distant from the depository of their public Records"

5. What evidence supports the claim that the King of Great Britain has wronged the colonists?
   a. a list of court rulings against the King in favor of the colonists
   b. a list of all his wrongdoings provided by other world leaders
   c. a list of the King's wrongdoings
   d. a list of names of colonists whom have been personally wronged

6. How would you evaluate the list of grievances given to support the claim that the King of England wronged the colonists?
   a. relevant and sufficient
   b. relevant and insufficient
   c. irrelevant and sufficient
   d. irrelevant and insufficient

7. Which of the following claims is supported by evidence?
   a. All men are equal.
   b. The King of Great Britain is a tyrannical leader.
   c. All men have certain unalienable rights.
   d. Governments should be controlled by the governed.

8. The quotation "to secure these rights, Governments are instituted among Men, deriving their just powers from the consent of the governed" is an example of which of the following?
a. an explanation
b. factual evidence
c. valid reasoning
d. false reasoning

Read the following excerpt and answer the next four questions.

What Was Her Life About?

(1) We were married and lived together for seventy years,
(2) Enjoying, working, raising twelve children,
(3) Eight of whom we lost
(4) Ere I had reached the age of sixty.
(5) I spun, wove, kept the house, nursed the sick,
(6) Made the garden, and for the holiday
(7) Rambled over the fields where sang many larks,
(8) And by the Spoon River gathering many a shell,
(9) And many a flower and medicinal weed—
(10) Shouting to the wooded hills, singing to the green valleys.
(11) At ninety-six I had lived enough, that is all,
(12) And passed a sweet repose.
 —Edgar Lee Masters, *Spoon River Anthology*

9. Based on the excerpt, what does the woman mean when she talks of passing "a sweet repose" (line 12)?
a. her death
b. her old age
c. how well she slept at night
d. needing to rest more as she grew older

10. Which of the following words best describes the overall mood of the poem?
a. joy
b. anger
c. acceptance
d. wonder

11. Which of the following is the most likely explanation of the line from the poem that reads, "Shouting to the wooded hills, singing to the green valleys" (line 10)?
a. The speaker had a fine singing voice.
b. The speaker loved the countryside.
c. The speaker preferred sounds to silence.
d. The speaker spent of a lot of time working in the fields.

12. Which can you infer about the couple's marriage?
a. They were never meant to be together.
b. They could not deal with the loss of their children.
c. They had an extremely happy marriage.
d. They had their sorrows and their joys.

Please use the following passage to answer questions 13 and 14.

This excerpt is from a speech by George W. Bush delivered on March 19, 2008.

1 Operation Iraqi Freedom was a remarkable display of military effectiveness. Forces from the UK, Australia, Poland, and other allies joined our troops in the initial operations. As they advanced, our troops fought their way through sandstorms so intense that they blackened the daytime sky. Our troops engaged in pitched battles with Fedayeen Saddam, death squads acting on the orders of Saddam Hussein that obeyed neither the conventions of war nor the dictates of conscience. These death squads hid in schools, and they hid in hospitals, hoping to draw fire against Iraqi civilians. They used women and children as human shields. They stopped at nothing in their efforts to prevent us from prevailing, but they couldn't stop the coalition advance.

2 Aided by the most effective and precise air campaign in history, coalition forces raced across 350 miles of enemy territory, destroying Republican Guard divisions, pushing through the Karbala Gap, capturing Saddam International Airport, and liberating Baghdad in less than one month. . . .

3 Because we acted, Saddam Hussein no longer fills fields with the remains of innocent men, women, and children. . . . Because we acted, Saddam's regime is no longer invading its neighbors or attacking them with chemical weapons and ballistic missiles.

13. Based on this speech excerpt about Operation Iraqi Freedom, take the following list of events and write them in the correct order of occurrence on the lines below.

coalition forces cross 350 miles of enemy territory

Operation Iraqi Freedom is launched

Baghdad is liberated

1. _____

2. _____

3. _____

14. In the excerpt from Bush's speech, what does the Middle Eastern setting, comprising "sandstorms so intense that they blackened the daytime sky," add to the first paragraph, which mentions troops fighting death squads?
a. a heightened sense of beauty
b. a heightened sense of contentment
c. a heightened sense of danger
d. a decreased sense of danger

Please use the following to answer questions 15–20.

The 1976 Democratic National Convention Keynote Address, delivered by Barbara Jordan

1   Throughout—throughout our history, when people have looked for new ways to solve their problems and to uphold the principles of this nation, many times they have turned to political parties. They have often turned to the Democratic Party. What is it? What is it about the Democratic Party that makes it the instrument the people use when they search for ways to shape their future? Well, I believe the answer to that question lies in our concept of governing. Our concept of governing is derived from our view of people. It is a concept deeply rooted in a set of beliefs firmly etched in the national conscience of all of us.

2   Now, what are these beliefs? First, we believe in equality for all and privileges for none. This is a belief—this is a belief that each American, regardless of background, has equal standing in the public forum—all of us. Because—because we believe this idea so firmly, we are an inclusive rather than an exclusive party. Let everybody come.

3   I think it no accident that most of those immigrating to America in the 19th century identified with the Democratic Party. We are a heterogeneous party made up of Americans of diverse backgrounds. We believe that the people are the source of all governmental power, that the authority of the people is to be extended, not restricted.

4   This—this can be accomplished only by providing each citizen with every opportunity to participate in the management of the government. They must have that, we believe. We believe that the government which represents the authority of all the people, not just one interest group, but all the people, has an obligation to actively—actively—seek to remove those obstacles which would block individual achievement—obstacles emanating from race, sex, economic condition. The government must remove them, seek to remove them.

5   We are a party—we are a party of innovation. We do not reject our traditions, but we are willing to adapt to changing circumstances, when change we must. We are willing to suffer the discomfort of change in order to achieve a better future. We have a positive vision of the future founded on the belief that the gap between the promise and reality of America can one day be finally closed. We believe that.

6   This, my friends is the bedrock of our concept of governing. This is a part of the reason why Americans have turned to the Democratic Party. These are the foundations upon which a national community can be built. Let all understand that these guiding principles cannot be discarded for short-term political gains. They represent what this country is all about. They are indigenous to the American idea. And these are principles which are not negotiable.

15. What is the main idea of the second paragraph?

   a. Every citizen is welcomed by the Democratic Party.

   b. Immigrants have often chosen to support the Democratic Party.

   c. Barbara Jordan approves of the Democratic Party.

   d. The Democratic Party accepts only the best of the best.

16. Which of the following statements supports Barbara Jordan's belief that the government must represent all people?

   a. "Because we believe this idea so firmly, we are an inclusive rather than an exclusive party."

   b. "This can be accomplished only by providing each citizen with every opportunity to participate in the management of the government."

   c. "We do not reject our traditions, but we are willing to adapt to changing circumstances, when change we must."

   d. "These are the foundations upon which a national community can be built."

17. Based on the text, which of the following scenarios would Barbara Jordan most likely support?

   a. A Democratic Party presidential candidate holding a private dinner for a select group of people.

   b. Members of a political party focusing on recruiting only those who can donate large amounts of money.

   c. A Democratic candidate running for the state senate.

   d. A local Democratic Party group holding an open forum for members of the community.

18. Which of the following statements best summarizes the main idea of the address?

   a. Many people have chosen to support the Democratic Party over the years.

   b. The values of the Democratic Party represent American ideals.

   c. The Democratic Party has evolved when necessary.

   d. all of the above

19. In which of the following phrases does Barbara Jordan criticize the Democratic Party?

   a. When she calls it "the instrument the people use when they search for ways to shape their future."

   b. When she says that those in the party "believe in equality for all and privileges for none."

   c. When she says that it is a "party of innovation."

   d. none of the above

20. From which statement can you infer that Barbara Jordan believes the government should enact laws against race and gender discrimination?

   a. "What is it about the Democratic Party that makes it the instrument the people use when they search for ways to shape their future?"

   b. "We believe that the people are the source of all governmental power, that the authority of the people is to be extended, not restricted."

   c. "We have a positive vision of the future founded on the belief that the gap between the promise and reality of America can one day be finally closed."

   d. "We believe that the government which represents the authority of all the people . . . has an obligation to actively—actively—seek to remove those obstacles which would block individual achievement."

Please use the following to answer questions 21–25.

> **To:** All Staff
> **From:** Allison Lewis, Manager
> **Date:** July 15, 2016
> **Subject:** Piles of Books
>
> It has come to our attention that there have been piles of books that (1) on the floor in the fiction, cooking, and teen sections of the bookstore by the end of every day. It has gotten so bad that some customers are complaining that they are in the way of a large portion of shelved books. (2), we are introducing a new policy that mandates employees check their assigned sections for piles every hour and that employees then shelf any books found out of place.
>
> (3) make sure to follow this procedure regularly. Even piles of a few books can cause unnecessary obstacles for customers.
>
> Thank you for (4) cooperation!
>
> (5)
>
> Allison Lewis

21. Choose the correct form of **accumulate** for (1).
   a. accumulate
   b. accumulates
   c. accumulated
   d. will accumulate

22. Which word fits correctly in (2)?
   a. Therefore
   b. However
   c. Meanwhile
   d. Instead

23. Which word fits correctly in (3)?
   a. please
   b. pleases
   c. Please
   d. Pleases

24. Which word fits correctly in (4)?
   a. my
   b. your
   c. their
   d. her

25. Which word fits correctly in (5)?
   a. Best.
   b. Best!
   c. Best'
   d. Best,

Please use the following to answer questions 26–29.

This excerpt is from *The Fall of the House of Usher*, by Edgar Allan Poe.

During the whole of a dull, dark, and soundless day in the autumn of the year, when the clouds hung oppressively low in the heavens, I had been passing alone, on horseback, through a singularly dreary tract of country; and at length found myself, as the shades of the evening drew on, within view of the melancholy House of Usher. I know not how it was; but, with the first glimpse of the building, a sense of insufferable gloom pervaded my spirit. I say insufferable; for the feeling was unrelieved by any of that half-pleasurable, because poetic, sentiment, with which the mind usually receives even the sternest natural images of the desolate or terrible. I looked upon the scene before me—upon the mere house, and the simple landscape features of the domain—upon the bleak walls—upon the vacant eye-like windows—upon a few rank sedges—and upon a few white trunks of decayed trees—with an utter depression of soul which I can compare to no earthly sensation more properly than to the after-dream of the reveler upon opium—the bitter lapse into everyday life—the hideous dropping off of the veil. There was an iciness, a sinking, a sickening of the heart—an unredeemed dreariness of thought which no goading of the imagination could torture into aught of the sublime. What was it—I paused to think—what was it that so unnerved me in the contemplation of the House of Usher? It was a mystery all insoluble; nor could I grapple with the shadowy fancies that crowded upon me as I pondered. I was forced to fall back upon the unsatisfactory conclusion that while, beyond doubt, there are combinations of very simple natural objects which have the power of thus affecting us, still the analysis of this power lies among considerations beyond our depth. It was possible, I reflected, that a mere different arrangement of the particulars of the scene, of the details of the picture, would be sufficient to modify, or perhaps to annihilate its capacity for sorrowful impression; and, acting upon this idea, I reined my horse to the precipitous brink of a black and lurid tarn that lay in unruffled luster by the dwelling, and gazed down—but with a shudder even more thrilling than before—upon the remodeled and inverted images of the gray sedge, and the ghastly tree stems, and the vacant and eye-like windows.

26. The words **sorrowful**, **sickening**, **melancholy**, and **dreary** serve to give the excerpt a
a. joyous tone.
b. foreboding tone.
c. courageous tone.
d. silly tone.

27. Based on this excerpt, take the following list of events and write them in the correct order of occurrence on the lines below.
   rides through the countryside
   feels a sense of gloom
   reins his horse near the house
   comes to the House of Usher

   1. _____
   2. _____
   3. _____
   4. _____

28. The phrase "vacant eye-like windows" is an example of
a. alliteration.
b. hyperbole.
c. onomatopoeia.
d. personification.

29. Replacing "insufferable gloom" with which of the following words changes the tone of the phrase "a sense of insufferable gloom pervaded my spirit"?
a. melancholy
b. joy
c. sadness
d. despair

Please use the following to answer questions 30–35.

From the personal memoirs of Ulysses S. Grant, LXX

1   Things began to quiet down, and as the certainty that there would be no more armed resistance became clearer, the troops in North Carolina and Virginia were ordered to march immediately to the capital, and go into camp there until mustered out. Suitable garrisons were left at the prominent places throughout the South to insure obedience to the laws that might be enacted for the government of the several States, and to insure security to the lives and property of all classes. I do not know how far this was necessary, but I deemed it necessary, at that time, that such a course should be pursued. I think now that these garrisons were continued after they ceased to be absolutely required; but it is not to be expected that such a rebellion as was fought between the sections from 1861 to 1865 could terminate without leaving many serious apprehensions in the mind of the people as to what should be done.

2   Sherman marched his troops from Goldsboro, up to Manchester, on the south side of the James River, opposite Richmond, and there put them in camp, while he went back to Savannah to see what the situation was there.

3   It was during this trip that the last outrage was committed upon him. Halleck had been sent to Richmond to command Virginia, and had issued orders prohibiting even Sherman's own troops from obeying his, Sherman's, orders. Sherman met the papers on his return, containing this order of Halleck, and very justly felt indignant at the outrage. On his arrival at Fortress Monroe returning from Savannah, Sherman received an invitation from Halleck to come to Richmond and be his guest. This he indignantly refused, and informed Halleck, furthermore, that he had seen his order. He also stated that he was coming up to take command of his troops, and as he marched through it would probably be as well for Halleck not to show himself, because he (Sherman) would not be responsible for what some rash person might do through indignation for the treatment he had received. Very soon after that, Sherman received orders from me to proceed to Washington City, and to go into camp on the south side of the city pending the mustering-out of the troops.

(continues)

4   The march of Sherman's army from Atlanta to the sea and north to Goldsboro, while it was not accompanied with the danger that was anticipated, yet was magnificent in its results, and equally magnificent in the way it was conducted. It had an important bearing, in various ways, upon the great object we had in view, that of closing the war. All the States east of the Mississippi River up to the State of Georgia, had felt the hardships of the war. Georgia, and South Carolina, and almost all of North Carolina, up to this time, had been exempt from invasion by the Northern armies, except upon their immediate sea coasts. Their newspapers had given such an account of Confederate success, that the people who remained at home had been convinced that the Yankees had been whipped from first to last, and driven from pillar to post, and that now they could hardly be holding out for any other purpose than to find a way out of the war with honor to themselves.

5   Even during this march of Sherman's the newspapers in his front were proclaiming daily that his army was nothing better than a mob of men who were frightened out of their wits and hastening, panic-stricken, to try to get under the cover of our navy for protection against the Southern people. As the army was seen marching on triumphantly, however, the minds of the people became disabused and they saw the true state of affairs. In turn they became disheartened, and would have been glad to submit without compromise.

30. Why were garrisons left in the South?
   a. Violence was still prevalent.
   b. The Civil War is brewing.
   c. Grant thought it was necessary at the time.
   d. Sherman made the order.

31. What historical event can you infer was drawing to a close at the time this was written?

   [   ]

32. How would the tone of the passage change if the word **outrage** was replaced with **injustice** in the sentence, "It was during this trip that the last outrage was committed upon him"?
   a. It would support Grant's disapproval of Sherman's March.
   b. It would strengthen Grant's support of Sherman's March as necessary.
   c. It would increase Grant's list of criticisms of Sherman.
   d. It would confirm Grant's claim that the Confederates believed they had succeeded.

33. Which of the following quotations reveals Grant's disagreement with the Confederate viewpoint after the Civil War?
   a. "[B]ut it is not to be expected that such a rebellion as was fought between the sections from 1861 to 1865 could terminate without leaving many serious apprehensions in the mind of the people as to what should be done."
   b. "It was during this trip that the last outrage was committed upon him."
   c. "Their newspapers had given such an account of Confederate success, that the people who remained at home had been convinced that the Yankees had been whipped from first to last, and driven from pillar to post. . . ."
   d. "In turn they became disheartened, and would have been glad to submit without compromise."

34. Put the events in chronological order.

    A—Sherman's men were ordered not to listen to him

    B—the Confederates "saw the true state of affairs"

    C—the Civil War

    D—Sherman's March

  a. C, A, D, B

  b. C, A, B, D

  c. A, C, D, B

  d. A, C, B, D

35. What does the word **triumphantly** mean in the following sentence: "As the army was seen marching on triumphantly, however, the minds of the people became disabused and they saw the true state of affairs"?

  a. sheepishly

  b. victoriously

  c. angrily

  d. defeatedly

Please use the following to answer questions 36–39.

"Watching Volcanoes," by Millie Ceron

1 Scientists who watch volcanoes bear a great responsibility. It is up to them to alert the public when they think that a volcano is about to erupt. But it is not always easy to tell when an eruption is imminent. I know, because my whole career as a scientist has been spent studying volcanoes. I've learned that predicting eruptions is a very inexact science. There often are certain warning signs, but they can be very difficult to interpret. What should you do when you see them? You certainly don't want to cause a panic or tell people to flee unless it is really necessary, yet you also don't want to underestimate the danger. Scientists like me usually try to steer a path between these two extremes. But we also try to err on the side of caution: It's always better to be safe than sorry!

2 What are the signs that an eruption may soon occur? The main ones are earthquakes beneath the mountain, bulges in the sides of the mountain, and the escape of volcanic gases.

3 **Watching for Earthquakes.** Earthquakes often occur for some time before an eruption of *magma* (molten rock) and volcanic gases force their way up through underground channels. Sometimes the force causes a continuous shaking called *tremor*. To record earthquakes, a device called a *seismometer* is used. Four to eight seismometers are typically installed close to or on the mountain. Only by being very close to the volcano can seismometers pick up the tiny earthquakes that may be the first sign that a volcano may erupt.

4 When an eruption is just about to take place, earthquakes often occur in "swarms." Scientists monitor these swarms around the clock. The reason is that variations in the type and strength of the quakes are often the best indication that an eruption is just about to happen.

(continues)

5 **Watching for Bulges in the Sides of the Mountain.** During the months or weeks prior to an eruption, magma rises inside a volcano. The pressure created by this magma often causes the sides of the mountain to "tilt." Sometimes it even causes visible bulges in the mountainside. To monitor these bulges, scientists use a sensitive instrument called a *tiltmeter*. Today they also use satellite-based technology to take precise measurements. By these methods scientists discovered that in the months before Mount Saint Helens erupted in 1982, one side of the mountain swelled by more than 100 meters.

6 **Watching for Volcanic Gases.** The gases dissolved in magma provide the main force in a volcanic eruption. Consequently, it is important to find out whether any gases are present and if so, what kinds of gases. However, collecting these gases is not easy. They are often found escaping from vents high up on the mountain or in the crater. Scientists may visit the vents themselves and collect the gases in bottles for analysis in the laboratory. But such visits are dangerous: the climb can be difficult, the gases themselves can be hazardous to breathe, and there is always the danger of an eruption. Scientists may also place automated gas monitors near the vents, but these devices are often destroyed by the acidic gases. Another way to collect the gases is by flying through the gas clouds above the volcano in specially equipped airplanes. But it is difficult to obtain good samples by this method, and bad weather can keep planes on the ground just when monitoring is most urgent. However, when scientists succeed in collecting volcanic gases, they can tell a lot about how a volcano works and what effects it may have on Earth's climate and environment.

"The 1992 Eruptions at Mt. Spurr, Alaska," by Ling Chen

1 Mt. Spurr is a small volcano located 80 miles west of Anchorage, Alaska. In August 1991, eight seismographs placed on the mountain began recording many very small earthquakes. Airborne gas sampling was used to check for the presence of volcanic gases.

2 In early June 1992, earthquake activity increased. Then on June 27 a "swarm" of earthquakes suggested magma moving at shallow depth. As the earthquakes grew stronger, scientists broadcast a warning that an eruption might be about to occur. Later that day, pilots reported ash plumes erupting from the mountain.

3 After the June 27 eruption, earthquake activity declined rapidly to its lowest level in months. Scientists concluded that the danger of further eruptions was low. During July, bad weather often grounded pilots, preventing airborne observation of the volcano and collection of volcanic gas samples. Weeks passed during which little occurred at the mountain.

(continues)

4   On August 18, however, a pilot suddenly reported a huge ash plume above the crater. Scientists immediately broadcast a warning that an eruption was occurring.

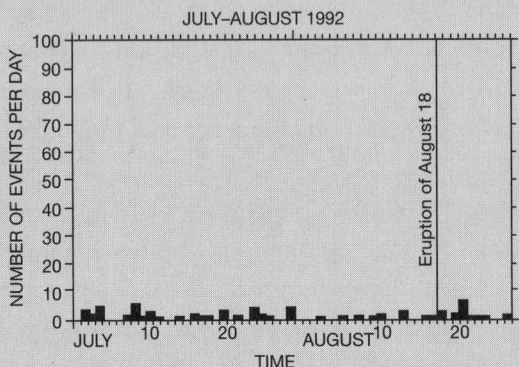

This graph shows earthquake activity recorded at Mt. Spurr before the eruption of August 18. The eruption ended after a few hours, and earthquake activity remained low, so the likelihood of further eruptions again seemed to be low.

5   That fall, however, earthquake activity increased once again beneath Mt. Spurr. "Swarms" of strong earthquakes were recorded in both early October and early November. Each time, scientists issued warnings that "a large eruption is likely within the next 24 to 48 hours." However, no eruption took place. When another "swarm" of earthquakes occurred in December, scientists decided not to issue an eruption warning.

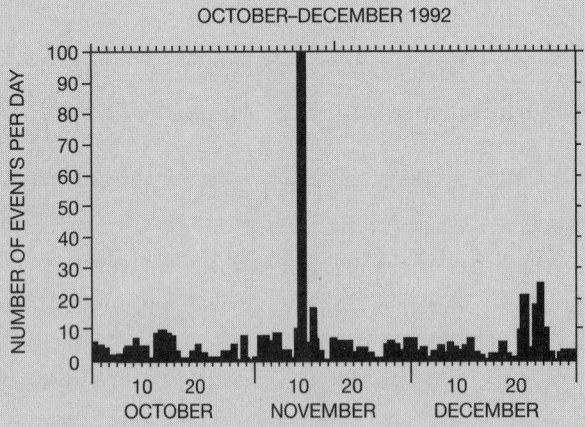

This graph shows earthquake activity recorded at Mt. Spurr from October through December 1992.

36. What is the main purpose of paragraph 3 in "Watching Volcanoes"?

a. to describe how scientists monitor earthquakes to predict volcanic eruptions

b. to define scientific terms, such as magma, tremor, and seismometer

c. to explain how scientists use seismometers to record earthquakes

d. to show how earthquakes cause volcanic gases to escape

37. Which of the following best summarizes "Watching Volcanoes"?

a. Scientists monitor bulges in the sides of mountains with tiltmeters because bulges may indicate a volcanic eruption will soon occur.

b. Scientists should not visit vents on mountaintops to collect and analyze gases because it is extremely dangerous.

c. Scientists were concerned enough about a small volcano near Anchorage, Alaska, to issue a warning it might erupt in June 1992.

d. Scientists who watch volcanoes monitor signs of eruption by various means to ensure the public is aware of possible dangers.

38. How are "Watching Volcanoes" and "The 1992 Eruptions at Mt. Spurr, Alaska" different?

a. "Watching Volcanoes" focuses on a particular eruption, and "The 1992 Eruptions at Mt. Spurr, Alaska" is about volcanoes in general.

b. "Watching Volcanoes" is a personal account, and "The 1992 Eruptions at Mt. Spurr, Alaska" is an objective report.

c. "Watching Volcanoes" discusses seismometers or seismographs, and "The 1992 Eruptions at Mt. Spurr, Alaska" does not.

d. "Watching Volcanoes" is a diary entry, and "The 1992 Eruptions at Mt. Spurr, Alaska" is a newspaper article.

39. Considering that there were never more than ten events in a single day from July to August 1992, why might the first graph allot space for as many as 100 events?

a. to illustrate how Mt. Spurr was not capable of erupting

b. to forecast a major rise of events in September

c. to contrast the dramatic number of events in November on the second graph

d. because this is the standard graph that all volcano-watching scientists use

Please use the following to answer questions 40–43.

This excerpt is from *Pride and Prejudice*, by Jane Austen.

1 It is a truth universally acknowledged that a single man in possession of a good fortune must be in want of a wife.

2 However little known the feelings or views of such a man may be on his first entering a neighbourhood, this truth is so well fixed in the minds of the surrounding families, that he is considered as the rightful property of someone or other of their daughters.

3 "My dear Mr. Bennet," said his lady to him one day, "have you heard that Netherfield Park is let at last?"

4 Mr. Bennet replied that he had not.

5 "But it is," returned she; "for Mrs. Long has just been here, and she told me all about it."

6 Mr. Bennet made no answer.

7 "Do not you want to know who has taken it?" cried his wife, impatiently.

8 "You want to tell me, and I have no objection to hearing it."

9 This was invitation enough.

10 "Why, my dear, you must know, Mrs. Long says that Netherfield is taken by a young man of large fortune from the north of England; that he came down on Monday in a chaise and four to see the place, and was so much delighted with it that he agreed with Mr. Morris immediately; that he is to take possession before Michaelmas, and some of his servants are to be in the house by the end of next week."

11 'What is his name?'

12 "Bingley."

13 "Is he married or single?"

14 "Oh, single, my dear, to be sure! A single man of large fortune; four or five thousand a year. What a fine thing for our girls!"

15 "How so? How can it affect them?"

16 "My dear Mr. Bennet," replied his wife, "how can you be so tiresome? You must know that I am thinking of his marrying one of them."

17 "Is that his design in settling here?"

18 "Design? Nonsense, how can you talk so! But it is very likely that he may fall in love with one of them, and therefore you must visit him as soon as he comes."

19 "I see no occasion for that. You and the girls may go, or you may send them by themselves, which perhaps will be still better, for, as you are as handsome as any of them, Mr. Bingley might like you the best of the party."

20 "My dear, you flatter me. I certainly *have* had my share of beauty, but I do not pretend to be anything extraordinary now. When a woman has five grown-up daughters, she ought to give over thinking of her own beauty."

21 "In such cases, a woman has not often much beauty to think of."

(continues)

22 "But, my dear, you must indeed go and see Mr. Bingley when he comes into the neighbour-hood."

23 "It is more than I engage for, I assure you."

24 "But consider your daughters. Only think what an establishment it would be for one of them. Sir William and Lady Lucas are determined to go, merely on that account; for in general, you know, they visit no newcomers. Indeed you must go, for it will be impossible for *us* to visit him, if you do not."

25 "You are over scrupulous, surely. I daresay Mr. Bingley will be very glad to see you; and I will send a few lines by you to assure him of my hearty consent to his marrying whichever he chooses of the girls; though I must throw in a good word for my little Lizzy."

26 "I desire you will do no such thing. Lizzy is not a bit better than the others: and I am sure she is not half so handsome as Jane, nor half so good-humoured as Lydia. But you are always giving *her* the preference."

27 "They have none of them much to recommend them," replied he: "they are all silly and ignorant like other girls; but Lizzy has something more of quickness than her sisters."

28 "Mr. Bennet, how can you abuse your own children in such a way? You take delight in vexing me. You have no compassion on my poor nerves."

29 "You mistake me, my dear. I have a high respect for your nerves. They are my old friends. I have heard you mention them with consideration these twenty years at least."

30 "Ah, you do not know what I suffer."

31 "But I hope you will get over it, and live to see many young men of four thousand a year come into the neighbourhood."

32 "It will be no use to us, if twenty such should come, since you will not visit them."

33 "Depend upon it, my dear, that when there are twenty, I will visit them all."

34 Mr. Bennet was so odd a mixture of quick parts, sarcastic humour, reserve, and caprice, that the experience of three-and-twenty years had been insufficient to make his wife understand his character. *Her* mind was less difficult to develop. She was a woman of mean understanding, little information, and uncertain temper. When she was discontented, she fancied herself nervous. The business of her life was to get her daughters married: its solace was visiting and news.

40. What is the number of the paragraph that supports the idea that a wealthy man is always looking for a wife?

Paragraph [   ]

41. What is the theme of the excerpt?
   a. travel
   b. divorce
   c. holidays
   d. marriage

42. In paragraph 14, what does "four or five thousand a year" refer to?

    a. the number of Mr. Bingley's annual trips to the Bennets' town

    b. Mr. Bingley's annual income

    c. Mr. Bennet's annual income

    d. Mrs. Long's annual income

43. What conclusion can you draw about Mrs. Bennet's wishes?

    a. She wants to marry Mr. Bingley for his money.

    b. She wants one of her daughters to marry Mr. Bingley.

    c. She doesn't want any of her daughters to marry Mr. Bingley.

    d. She wishes she had married someone with more money.

Please use the following to answer questions 44–48.

To: All Staff
From: Allison Lewis, Manager
Date: June 5, 2016
Subject: Bookstore Procedures

I am writing to clear up some issues dealing with our bookstores procedures. I have been getting a lot of questions about what procedures bookstore staff members are meant to follow on every shift. Recently, I have taken it upon myself to write a list of the procedures for reference.

1. at the beginning of a shift, all staff must sign in through our computer system.
2. Staff members assigned two the floor shift should check for misplaced books regularly and reshelf those books.
3. Staff members assigned to the stock shift should keep the warehouse clean and organized.
4. No staff member is allowed to give a discount to any customer without manager approval.
5. Staff members do not receive free and complimentary drinks at the in-store café.
6. Customers are not allowed to preorder books that are not yet on our preorder list.
7. Before leaving a shift, all staff members must perform one last check for cleanliness and organization of the store and must sign out though our computer system.
8. If a staff member forget to sign in or sign out, he or she must consult the manager before estimating his or her sign in and sign out times.

Thank you for your cooperation!

Best,
Allison Lewis

44. In the first sentence of the company memo, what should be added to make it correct?
   a. an apostrophe at the end of *procedures*
   b. an apostrophe at the end of *bookstores*
   c. an apostrophe between *bookstore* and *s*
   d. nothing

45. Reread the first list item:

1. at the beginning of a shift, all staff must sign in through our computer system.

Now, rewrite the sentence to correct any errors by writing it in the box below:

1. [   ]

46. In the second list item of the company memo, what should be changed to make it correct?
   a. change *two* to *to*
   b. change *for* to *four*
   c. change *and* to *or*
   d. no change

47. In the fifth list item, which of the following changes would improve the sentence?
   a. delete *and complimentary*
   b. delete *in-store café*
   c. insert *on the house* before *free*
   d. no change

48. In the eighth list item of the company memo, what should be changed in order to make it correct?
   a. change *forget* to *forgets*
   b. change *he or she* to *they*
   c. change *consult* to *consults*
   d. no change

Part II

1 question
45 minutes to complete

This practice allows you to compose your response to the given task and then compare it with examples of responses at the different score levels. You will also get a scoring guide that includes a detailed explanation of how official GED® test graders will score your response. You may use this scoring guide to score your own response.

Before you begin, it is important to note that on the official test this task must be completed in no more than 45 minutes. But don't rush to complete your response; take time to carefully read the passage(s) and the question prompt. Then think about how you would like to respond.

As you write your essay, be sure to:

- Decide which position presented in the passages is better supported by evidence.
- Explain why your chosen position has better support.
- Recognize that the position with better support may not be the position you agree with.
- Present multiple pieces of evidence from the passage to defend your assertions.
- Thoroughly construct your main points, organizing them logically, with strong supporting details.
- Connect your sentences, paragraphs, and ideas with transitional words and phrases.
- Express your ideas clearly and choose your words carefully.
- Use varied sentence structures to increase the clarity of your response.
- Reread and revise your response.

Good luck!

Please use the following passages to answer the essay question.

An Analysis of Stem Cell Research

1   Stem cell research is research using embryonic and "somatic" or "adult" stem cells for the purpose of advancing medicine. This research has been in existence since the beginning of the twentieth century, and over the years many breakthroughs have come from it. In 1998, scientists discovered methods to derive stem cells from human embryos. In 2006, researchers made another breakthrough, which involved reprogramming some adult cells in certain conditions to assume a stem-cell-like state. Stem cells themselves are useful in medical research because they are at the early state of reproduction, where the cell can either remain a stem cell or become a cell that would be involved in the formation of bones, brain cells, skin, the nervous system, organs, muscles, and every other part of the body.

Benefits of Stem Cell Research

2   Theoretically, research points to stem cell research being of great value in medical advancement. At this time, it is not yet clear how much can be done with stem cell research, and the possible benefits are incalculable. It could lead to cures for diabetes or heart disease. It is also seen as a potential resource to help cure cancer and Parkinson's disease, or even to regenerate a severed spinal cord and allow someone to walk who has been confined to a wheelchair. Although this sounds miraculous, it will not happen without extensive work and time.

3   Currently, adult stem cell therapies are used in the form of bone marrow transplants for treating leukemia. In 2006, researchers created artificial liver cells from umbilical cord blood stem cells. And in 2008, a study was published of the first successful cartilage regeneration in a human knee using adult stem cells. The variety of ways in which stem cell research could aid in curing many diseases has just begun to be explored.

4   While there are questions regarding human embryo stem cells for research, there are a variety of ways to acquire stem cells. As noted in a 2008 Stanford publication, regarding human embryo stem cell research specifically, a majority of the researchers are not actually touching newly derived stem cells, but are instead using the lineage and data of stem cells that have already been researched by other scientists. They have made these cell lines available for others to work with and learn from. Along with advances regarding adult stem cell research, this could be a fruitful direction for medical inquiry.

(continues)

Arguments against Stem Cell Research

5 Stem cell research is a risky endeavor that does not have clear-cut benefits, and a lot of moral questions are involved. While it seems clear that certain diseases are being treated by stem cell therapies, there are too many questions regarding further study and use.

6 With human embryo stem cells, a major concern is where they are coming from. One suggestion is for these stem cells to be taken from embryos that have been created for reproduction via in vitro fertilization. These embryos could be donated for scientific research after it is confirmed that they are not going to be used for reproduction. While this seems like a simple solution, there's also the question of the actual usefulness of those stem cells. With all stem cell therapies, *Consumer Reports* in 2010 noted the concern regarding transplanted cells forming tumors and becoming cancerous if the cell's division continued uncontrollably. There are also concerns of immune rejection by the patient being treated. While immunosuppressant drugs are used in organ transplant surgery, would this work on a body with new cells injected into it? There's also the additional question of whether the correct cell types can be induced in the stem cells, since the stem cells themselves are undifferentiated and can become many different kinds of cells.

7 While certain therapies have been successfully created, this research is still very untested. More conversations and clear education of the public are needed regarding this controversial form of medical therapy and the research behind it.

PROMPT:
While the first passage outlines the benefits of and identifies arguments for stem cell research, the second passage identifies arguments against stem cell research.

In your response, analyze both passages to determine which position is better supported. Use relevant and specific evidence from both sources to support your response.

Answers and Explanations

Part I

1. **The correct answer is the King of Great Britain.** The second to the last sentence in the second paragraph states, "The history of the present King of Great Britain is a history of repeated injuries and usurpations, all having in direct object the establishment of an absolute Tyranny over these States." The America colonists rebelled against the King of Great Britain's control of the colonies.

2. **Choice d is correct.** This paragraph incorporates a list of injustices that had been committed against the colonies by the King of Great Britain. The previous paragraphs describe suffering that the King caused the colonies, and paragraph 3 provides examples of those injuries.
   Choice **a** is incorrect. This paragraph incorporates a list of injustices that had been committed against the colonies by the King of Great Britain. It is not a list of laws written by the King, but a list of acts he committed.
   Choice **b** is incorrect. This paragraph incorporates a list of injustices that had been committed against the colonies by the King of Great Britain. It is not a list of laws for the newly independent United States of America because the colonies were not yet independent when the Declaration was written.
   Choice **c** is incorrect. This paragraph incorporates a list of injustices that had been committed against the colonies by the King of Great Britain. It is not a list of his good acts due to the fact that they are all negative things, and because the previous paragraphs mention that the King has committed repeated injuries against the colonies.

3. **Choice b is correct.** This quotation explicitly states that one group of people wishes to dissolve political ties with another group of people, meaning the colonies dissolving political ties with Great Britain.
   Choice **a** is incorrect. This quotation supports the idea of equality for all men, but does not express the desire to be free from Great Britain.
   Choice **c** is incorrect. This quotation expresses one of the grievances that the colonists have against the King of Great Britain. It is one of the reasons why the colonies want to split from Great Britain, but it does not express that desire itself.
   Choice **d** is incorrect. This quotation supports the idea of certain rights for all men, but does not express the desire to be free from Great Britain.

4. **Choice b is correct.** This quotation goes into more depth about what it means to have a government that gains its power from the consent of the governed and that is essentially controlled by the governed. This helps build the argument for popular sovereignty that this excerpt expresses.
   Choice **a** is incorrect. This quotation expresses a grievance that the colonists have against the King of Great Britain. It does not specifically help to build an argument for popular sovereignty.
   Choice **c** is incorrect. This quotation expresses a grievance that the colonists have against the King of Great Britain. It does not specifically help to build an argument for popular sovereignty.
   Choice **d** is incorrect. This quotation expresses a grievance that the colonists have against the King of Great Britain. It does not specifically help to build an argument for popular sovereignty.

5. Choice c is correct. The final paragraph of the excerpt is a list of the King's wrongdoings against the colonies.

Choice **a** is incorrect. The excerpt does not list court cases against the King.

Choice **b** is incorrect. The list of wrongdoings in the excerpt is by American colonists, not by other world leaders.

Choice **d** is incorrect. This excerpt does not name any specific individuals; it attempts to speak for the colonists as a whole.

6. Choice a is correct. The information given in the list of grievances is made up of examples of wrongdoings that the King has done against the colonists. This is definitely relevant to a claim that the King has carried out wrongs against the colonists. Furthermore, the list goes on for a long paragraph, making it more than sufficient to support the claim.

Choice **b** is incorrect. While the choice of relevancy is correct, the list goes on for a long paragraph, making it more than sufficient to support the claim. Therefore, the choice of insufficiency is incorrect.

Choice **c** is incorrect. While the choice of sufficiency is correct, the information given in the list of grievances is made up of examples of wrongdoings that are relevant to the claim. Therefore, the choice of irrelevancy is incorrect.

Choice **d** is incorrect. The information given in the list of grievances is made up of examples of wrongdoings that the King has done against the colonists. This is definitely relevant to a claim that the King has carried out wrongs against the colonists. Furthermore, the list goes on for a long paragraph, making it more than sufficient to support the claim.

7. Choice b is correct. The whole last paragraph of the excerpt is a list of tyrannical actions the King of Great Britain committed against the colonists.

Choice **a** is incorrect. The excerpt claims that "all men are created equal," but it does not provide evidence as to why this is true. No evidence is given to support this claim.

Choice **c** is incorrect. The excerpt claims that all men "are endowed by their Creator with certain unalienable Rights," but it does not provide evidence to support this claim.

Choice **d** is incorrect. The excerpt discusses the idea of popular sovereignty, but it provides no evidence to support this claim.

8. Choice d is correct. Factually, there is no validity to the claim that the only way to secure certain rights is through a government controlled by the governed. Logically, there is really no reason why this would be the only way to secure those rights. Therefore, this is an example of false reasoning.

Choice **a** is incorrect. This statement is not really an explanation of anything but rather an opinion that in order to secure certain rights, governments should derive their power from the governed.

Choice **b** is incorrect. This statement does not give any evidence based in actual fact. Instead, it expresses an opinion that in order to secure certain rights, governments should derive their power from the governed.

Choice **c** is incorrect. Factually, there is no validity to the claim that the only way to secure certain rights is through a government controlled by the governed. Logically, there is really no reason why this would be the only way to secure those rights. Therefore, this is an example of false reasoning, not valid reasoning.

9. a. Based on the excerpt, the reader can determine that the woman is talking about her death. The other choices do not fit in with the context of the poem.

10. c. This is the best answer. The speaker tells about her life in a matter-of-fact manner. She does not seem to be in a state of *wonder*. She certainly does not seem *angry* or particularly full of *joy*.

11. b. The line suggests that the speaker loved nature. It does not suggest that she worked in the fields or that she had a fine singing voice. No other choice is supported by the poem.

12. d. The poem recounts what occurred in their marriage, both good and bad, so this is the best answer. The other choices are not supported by the poem.

13. The correct order is:

1. Operation Iraqi Freedom is launched

2. coalition forces cross 350 miles of enemy territory

3. Baghdad is liberated.

This order is correct due to the implied order of events that Bush mentions in the excerpt. Operation Iraqi Freedom had to have been launched before coalition forces could cross 350 miles of enemy territory. The ultimate outcome of the operation was the liberation of Baghdad; therefore, that is the last event in the progression.

14. Choice c is correct. The setting is described as harsh and unforgiving. This technique is used to heighten the sense of danger to the troops fighting death squads, in order to persuade the audience of its truth.

Choice **a** is incorrect. The choice of describing an extreme climate with intense sandstorms in this paragraph is not meant to express beauty. This technique is used to heighten the sense of danger to the troops fighting death squads, in order to persuade the audience of its truth.

Choice **b** is incorrect. The choice of describing an extreme climate with intense sandstorms in this paragraph is not meant to express contentment. This technique is used to heighten the sense of danger to the troops fighting death squads, in order to persuade the audience of its truth.

Choice **d** is incorrect. The setting is described as having intense sandstorms and pitched battles. This technique is used to heighten the sense of danger to the troops fighting death squads, in order to persuade the audience of its truth.

15. Choice a is correct. In the paragraph, Jordan states that the party is "an inclusive rather than an exclusive party" and that "everybody" should come.

Choice **b** is incorrect. This is what the third paragraph is about, not the second paragraph.

Choice **c** is incorrect. Although it can be inferred that Jordan approves of the party, this is not the main point of the second paragraph.

Choice **d** is incorrect. This is the opposite of the meaning of the second paragraph.

16. **Choice b is correct.** Here, Jordan says that everyone should be able to participate in government. This is what the question is asking for.

    Choice **a** is incorrect. In this sentence, Jordan is stating that the Democratic Party accepts all people. It slightly fits the question, but there is a better answer.

    Choice **c** is incorrect. Jordan is speaking about how the party evolves, not about how the government represents all people.

    Choice **d** is incorrect. This is a summary of all the values that Jordan brings up and is too broad to be just about the representation of everyone.

17. **Choice d is correct.** Jordan says the party is for all people and that everyone should be represented in government. An open forum is an inclusive event that allows people to speak their mind.

    Choice **a** is incorrect. Jordan explicitly states that the Democratic Party is inclusive. This would be an exclusive event, contrary to what she states.

    Choice **b** is incorrect. This is an example of exclusivity, which is not in line with the values she expresses.

    Choice **c** is incorrect. Although this would be a logical choice, this is a broader answer, and there is a better choice. Jordan does not talk about senate races in the passage.

18. **Choice b is correct.** Throughout her address, Jordan compares American values to the party's values and claims that they are in line with each other. This is the best summary.

    Choice **a** is incorrect. This is a detail Jordan includes, but it does not represent the main idea of her address.

    Choice **c** is incorrect. This is another detail rather than a summary.

    Choice **d** is incorrect. This cannot be correct because choices **a** and **c** are wrong.

19. **Choice d is correct.** Jordan praises the Democratic Party throughout her speech.

    Choice **a** is incorrect. This phrase praises the party.

    Choice **b** is incorrect. Jordan is commending the party.

    Choice **c** is incorrect. Jordan is ascribing a positive quality, innovation, to her party's character.

20. **Choice d is correct.** Jordan does not come right out and say that the government should pass laws to combat racism and gender discrimination, which would block individual achievement, but she stresses the word "actively" in connection with the government's "obligation" to "remove those obstacles." Passing laws is "active" on the part of the government, and it is logical to infer that Jordan would support laws to curb discrimination.

    Choice **a** is incorrect. Jordan is asking why people are drawn to her party, not calling on government to enact anti-discrimination laws.

    Choice **b** is incorrect. Jordan is discussing political power in a democracy, not anti-discrimination law.

    Choice **c** is incorrect. Jordan is talking about the beliefs of the Democratic Party, not about laws the U.S. government should enact.

21. Choice a is correct. In order to make the verb agree with the plural subject, *piles of books*, the verb needs to be in present tense and not end in *s*.

Choice **b** is incorrect. In order to make the verb agree with the plural subject, *piles of books*, the verb needs to be in present tense and not end in *s* (*accumulate*), not the present tense ending in *s* (*accumulates*).

Choice **c** is incorrect. In order to make the verb agree with the plural subject, *piles of books*, the verb needs to be in present tense (*accumulate*), not in the past tense (*accumulated*).

Choice **d** is incorrect. In order to make the verb agree with the plural subject, *piles of books*, the verb needs to be in present tense (*accumulate*), not in the future tense (*will accumulate*).

22. Choice a is correct. *Therefore* is the correct transition word to use when describing a cause-and-effect relationship. And as the first word in the sentence, the word is correctly capitalized.

Choice **b** is incorrect. *However* is a transition word used to show contrast. Since the accumulating piles of books cause the effect of instituting a new policy, *Therefore* is the correct transition word to use when describing a cause-and-effect relationship.

Choice **c** is incorrect. *Meanwhile* denotes time. Since the accumulating piles of books cause the effect of instituting a new policy, *Therefore* is the correct transition word to use when describing a cause-and-effect relationship.

Choice **d** is incorrect. *Instead* is a transition word used to show contrast. Since the accumulating piles of books cause the effect of instituting a new policy, *Therefore* is the correct transition word to use when describing a cause-and-effect relationship.

23. Choice c is correct. Because this word starts a sentence, the first letter needs to be capitalized. Choice **a** is incorrect. Because this word starts a sentence, the first letter needs to be capitalized. Choice **b** is incorrect. Because this word starts a sentence, the first letter needs to be capitalized. Also, *please* is being used as a command, and the addition of an *s* at the end does not make sense in this context.

Choice **d** is incorrect. *Please* is being used as a command, and the addition of an *s* at the end does not make sense in this context.

24. Choice b is correct. Of the possessive pronouns listed, *your* in the second person is correct to address the reader.

25. Choice d is correct. The closing of a letter or memo ends with a comma, followed on the next line by the letter writer's name.

Choice **a** is incorrect. The closing of a letter or memo ends with a comma, followed on the next line by the letter writer's name.

Choice **b** is incorrect. The closing of a letter or memo ends with a comma, followed on the next line by the letter writer's name.

Choice **c** is incorrect. The closing of a letter or memo ends with a comma, followed on the next line by the letter writer's name.

26. Choice b is correct. The author chose these words to create a dark and foreboding tone.

27. The correct order is:
1. **rides through the countryside**
2. **comes to the House of Usher**
3. **feels a sense of gloom**
4. **reins his horse near the house**

This is based on the order of events recounted by the narrator in the excerpt.

28. Choice d is correct. Personification is giving human characteristics to inanimate objects. The phrase "vacant eye-like windows" gives the human quality of vacant eyes to windows.

Choice **a** is incorrect. Alliteration is a repetition of consonant sounds at the beginning of several words in a row. An example would be "brightly beautiful butterflies."

Choice **b** is incorrect. Hyperbole is extreme exaggeration, for example: "He walks louder than an elephant."

Choice **c** is incorrect. Onomatopoeia refers to words that mimic the sounds they describe, for example: "The fire hissed, crackled, and popped."

29. Choice b is correct. The word *joy* changes the tone and meaning of the phrase from an expression of unhappiness and gloom to a positive and happy expression.

Choice **a** is incorrect. *Melancholy* preserves the unhappy and negative tone of the original phrase.

Choice **c** is incorrect. *Sadness* preserves the unhappy and negative tone of the original phrase.

Choice **d** is incorrect. *Despair* preserves the unhappy and negative tone of the original phrase.

30. Choice c is correct. Grant admits that he did "not know how far this was necessary," but "deemed it necessary, at that time." He feels later that his decision was justified.

Choice **a** is incorrect. The passage opens with the statement "things began to quiet down," the opposite of widespread violence.

Choice **b** is incorrect. The first words in the first sentence report that the war was winding down.

Choice **d** is incorrect. Grant deemed the garrisons necessary "at that time."

31. The correct answer is the Civil War. It can be inferred from the passage that the Civil War had just concluded. The passage clearly describes the "rebellion as was fought between the sections from 1861 to 1865." There are many other context clues. In addition, the excerpt is from Grant's memoir after 1865 and Sherman's March through the South.

32. Choice b is correct. Grant refers to Sherman's March as "magnificent" and as signifying "closing the war."

Choice **a** is incorrect. Grant obviously approves of the march.

Choice **c** is incorrect. Grant is sympathizing with Sherman, not criticizing him.

Choice **d** is incorrect. The word change is unrelated to Grant's feelings about how "[t]heir newspapers had given such an account of Confederate success."

33. Choice c is correct. Grant is describing how the Confederate view is false.

Choice **a** is incorrect. Grant is expressing sympathy with the general consensus of feeling after the war.

Choice **b** is incorrect. This sentence comments on Sherman's March, not Grant's disagreement with the Confederate viewpoint.

Choice **d** is incorrect. This sentence describes how Grant assumed the Confederates felt upon seeing Sherman, not Grant's disagreement with the Confederate viewpoint.

34. Choice a is correct. The correct order is C—the Civil War, A—Sherman's men were ordered not to listen to him, D—Sherman's March, then B—the Confederates "saw the true state of affairs."

35. Choice b is correct. Grant is describing how seeing the victorious soldiers' march reminded the South of what really happened.

Choice **a** is incorrect. The opposite is true for the victorious army. For example, Grant emphasizes how the march was a positive thing because it set the Confederates straight on who won.

Choice **c** is incorrect. There is no evidence in the excerpt to support this conclusion.

Choice **d** is incorrect. The opposite is true for the victorious army.

36. Choice a is correct. Paragraph 3 is mainly about how scientists monitor earthquakes to predict volcanic eruptions.

Choice **b** is incorrect. Although these terms are defined in this paragraph, they are supporting details.

Choice **c** is incorrect. The paragraph does not explain how seismometers work.

Choice **d** is incorrect. Although the paragraph mentions that volcanic gases force their way up through underground channels, this is a small detail and not the paragraph's main idea.

37. Choice d is correct. This best summarizes the main ideas of "Watching Volcanoes" by referencing the scientists who watch volcanoes, the ways they monitor volcanoes, and why their work is important.

Choice **a** is incorrect. This is a good summary of the section titled "Watching for Bulges in the Sides of the Mountain," but it does not summarize the entire passage.

Choice **b** is incorrect. The article mentions that vents are dangerous, not that scientists should not visit them for study. This is a small detail and not a summary of the complete article.

Choice **c** is incorrect. This answer refers to the second article, "The 1992 Eruptions at Mt. Spurr, Alaska," not "Watching Volcanoes."

38. Choice b is correct. "Watching Volcanoes" is a first-person account of watching volcanoes from the perspective of a volcano-watching scientist. "The 1992 Eruptions at Mt. Spurr, Alaska" is an objective report without any indication that the journalist is involved in volcano science.

Choice **a** is incorrect. The opposite is true. "Watching Volcanoes" discusses volcanoes in general, and "The 1992 Eruptions at Mt. Spurr, Alaska" focuses on the volcano at Mt. Spurr, Alaska.

Choice **c** is incorrect. Both passages discuss seismometers or seismographs, the instruments that scientists use to measure earthquake magnitude.

Choice **d** is incorrect. Although "Watching Volcanoes" is written from the first-person point of view like a diary, it does not describe what the writer did on a particular day as a diary does. Although it is possible that "The 1992 Eruptions at Mt. Spurr, Alaska" was published in a newspaper, there is no way of knowing this based on the passage.

39. Choice c is correct. Having vertical axes to 100 incidents on both graphs dramatizes the explosion of 90 more incidents than on any day in the first graph occurring in November 1992 in the second graph.

Choice **a** is incorrect. Based on the dramatic rise in events in November 1992 shown in the second graph, the volcano was close to erupting, and the threat was serious enough that scientists warned, "a large eruption is likely within the next 24 to 48 hours."

Choice **b** is incorrect. September is not charted on either graph.

Choice **d** is incorrect. There is no evidence to support this claim.

40. **The correct answer is paragraph 1.** Paragraph 1 explicitly states that "a single man in possession of a good fortune must be in want of a wife."

41. **Choice d is correct.** The topic of marriage is the focus of the introductory paragraphs as well as the majority of the dialogue.

Choice **a** is incorrect. Travel is not the main topic of the excerpt.

Choice **b** is incorrect. Divorce is not a topic in the excerpt.

Choice **c** is incorrect. The Michaelmas holiday is a minor topic in the excerpt, not the main topic.

42. **Choice b is correct.** Mrs. Bennet is discussing Bingley's fortune—in other words, his income.

Choice **a** is incorrect. Mrs. Bennet is discussing Bingley's fortune—in other words, his income.

Choice **c** is incorrect. Mrs. Bennet is talking to Mr. Bennet in this dialogue, and she would not need to be telling her husband about his own money in the third person. Furthermore, they are just beginning to discuss Mr. Bingley when this number amount is mentioned.

Choice **d** is incorrect. Mrs. Bennet is discussing Bingley's fortune—in other words, his income.

43. **Choice b is correct.** This whole excerpt is about the supposition that wealthy men need to find wives and the topic of marriage in general. Mrs. Bennet spends most of the dialogue discussing the merits of Mr. Bingley and how he would be a good match for one of her daughters.

Choice **a** is incorrect. Mrs. Bennet is a married woman, and every time she mentions marriage it is in reference to her daughters.

Choice **c** is incorrect. This whole excerpt is about the supposition that wealthy men need to find wives and the topic of marriage in general.

Choice **d** is incorrect. The only time that Mrs. Bennet mentions money is in reference to the wealth of Mr. Bingley and how that makes him a good match for one of her daughters. She never implies that she wishes she had married someone wealthier.

44. **Choice c is correct.** The noun possessing *procedures* is singular.

Choice **a** is incorrect. *Procedures* is not being used as a possessive noun in this context. Therefore, an apostrophe is not needed.

Choice **b** is incorrect. There is one bookstore, so the possessive noun is singular, not plural.

Choice **d** is incorrect. The singular noun *bookstore* possesses *procedures*, so an apostrophe should be inserted between *bookstore* and *s*.

45. **The correct answer is: At the beginning of a shift, all staff must sign in through our computer system.** The first word in a sentence must always be capitalized.

46. Choice a is correct. This is a common homonym error. *Two* is a number designation, and in this context, the preposition *to* is necessary instead. This is to reference what the staff members are assigned to, not a number designation.

Choice **b** is incorrect. This change would cause a homonym error. The preposition *for* is needed to denote an action that the staff members should take. The homonym *four* denoting number does not make sense in this context.

Choice **c** is incorrect. The procedure listed here has two parts. The staff members need to look for misplaced books *and* reshelf them. The procedure does not imply that staff members can choose to do one thing or the other.

Choice **d** is incorrect. *Two* is a number designation, and in this context, the preposition *to* is necessary instead. This is to reference what the staff members are assigned to, not a number designation.

47. Choice a is correct. *Free* and *complimentary* mean essentially the same thing. *And complimentary* adds an unnecessary wordiness to the sentence and should be deleted.

Choice **b** is incorrect. *In-store café* is the object of the preposition *at* and is needed in order to make the prepositional phrase complete.

Choice **c** is incorrect. *Free, complimentary*, and *on the house* all mean the same thing. Therefore, the use of all three together causes unnecessary wordiness.

Choice **d** is incorrect. *Free* and *complimentary* mean essentially the same thing. *And complimentary* adds an unnecessary wordiness to the sentence and should be deleted.

48. Choice a is correct. In order for the subject *staff member* to agree with the verb, *forget* must end in an *s*. This is a common subject–verb agreement rule.

Choice **b** is incorrect. Since *he or she* is referencing a *staff member*, all the subjects in the sentence need to be singular. The change to *they* would change this number agreement, making the pronoun plural that is referencing a singular noun, which is incorrect.

Choice **c** is incorrect. In order for the subject *he or she* to agree with the verb, *consult* should not end in an *s*. This is a common subject-verb agreement rule.

Choice **d** is incorrect. In order for the subject *staff member* to agree with the verb, *forget* must end in an *s*. This is a common subject-verb agreement rule.

Part II

Your extended response will be scored based on three traits, or elements:

- **Trait 1:** Creation of arguments and use of evidence
- **Trait 2:** Development of ideas and organizational structure
- **Trait 3:** Clarity and command of standard English conventions

Your essay will be scored on a 6-point scale—each trait is worth up to 2 points. The final score is counted twice, so the maximum number of points you can earn is 12.

Trait 1 tests your ability to write an essay that takes a stance based on the information in the reading passages. To earn the highest score possible, you must carefully read the information and express a clear opinion on what you have read. You will be scored on how well you use the information from the passages to support your argument.

Your response will also be scored on how well you analyze the author's arguments in the passages. To earn the highest score possible, you should discuss whether or not you think the author is making a good argument, and why or why not.

For your reference, here is a table that readers will use when scoring your essay with a 2, 1, or 0.

TRAIT 1: CREATION OF ARGUMENTS AND USE OF EVIDENCE	
2	• Makes text-based argument(s) and establishes an intent connected to the prompt • Presents specific and related evidence from source text(s) to support argument (may include a few unrelated pieces of evidence or unsupported claims) • Analyzes the topic and/or the strength of the argument within the source text(s) (e.g., distinguishes between supported and unsupported claims, makes valid inferences about underlying assumptions, identifies false reasoning, evaluates the credibility of sources)
1	• Makes an argument with some connection to the prompt • Presents some evidence from source text(s) to support argument (may include a mix of related and unrelated evidence that may or may not cite the text) • Partly analyzes the topic and/or the strength of the argument within the source text(s); may be limited, oversimplified, or inaccurate
0	• May attempt to make an argument OR lacks an intent or connection to the prompt OR attempts neither • Presents little or no evidence from source text(s) (sections of text may be copied from source directly) • Minimally analyzes the topic and/or the strength of the argument within the source text(s); may present no analysis, or little or no understanding of the given argument
Non-scorable	• Response consists only of text copied from the prompt or source text(s) • Response shows that test-taker has not read the prompt or is entirely off-topic • Response is incomprehensible • Response is not in English • No response has been attempted (has been left blank)

Trait 2 tests whether you respond to the writing prompt with a well-structured essay. Support of your thesis must come from evidence in the passages, as well as personal opinions and experiences that build on your central idea. Your ideas must be fully explained and include specific details. Your essay should use words and phrases that allow your details and ideas to flow naturally. Here is a table that outlines what is involved in earning a score of 2, 1, or 0.

TRAIT 2: DEVELOPMENT OF IDEAS AND ORGANIZATIONAL STRUCTURE	
2	• Contains ideas that are generally logical and well-developed; most ideas are expanded upon • Contains a logical sequence of ideas with clear connections between specific details and main ideas • Develops an organizational structure that conveys the message and goal of the response; appropriately uses transitional devices • Develops and maintains an appropriate style and tone that signal awareness of the audience and purpose of the task • Uses appropriate words to express ideas clearly
1	• Contains ideas that are partially developed and/or may demonstrate vague or simplistic logic; only some ideas are expanded upon • Contains some evidence of a sequence of ideas, but specific details may be unconnected to main ideas • Develops an organizational structure that may partially group ideas or is partially effective at conveying the message of the response; inconsistently uses transitional devices • May inconsistently maintain an appropriate style and tone to signal an awareness of the audience and purpose of the task • May contain misused words and/or words that do not express ideas clearly
0	• Contains ideas that are ineffectively or illogically developed, with little or no elaboration of main ideas • Contains an unclear or no sequence of ideas; specific details may be absent or unrelated to main ideas • Develops an ineffective or no organizational structure; inappropriately uses transitional devices, or does not use them at all • Uses an inappropriate style and tone that signal limited or no awareness of audience and purpose • May contain many misused words, overuse of slang, and/or express ideas in an unclear or repetitious manner
Non-scorable	• Response consists only of text copied from the prompt or source text(s) • Response shows that test-taker has not read the prompt or is entirely off-topic • Response is incomprehensible • Response is not in English • No response has been attempted (has been left blank)

Trait 3 tests how you create the sentences that make up your essay. To earn a high score, you will need to write sentences with variety—some short, some long, some simple, some complex. You will also need to prove that you have a good handle on standard English, including correct word choice, grammar, and sentence structure.

Here is a table that outlines what is involved in attaining a score of 2, 1, or 0.

TRAIT 3: CLARITY AND COMMAND OF STANDARD ENGLISH CONVENTIONS	
2	• Demonstrates generally correct sentence structure and an overall fluency that enhances clarity with regard to the following skills: 1) Diverse sentence structure within a paragraph or paragraphs 2) Correct use of subordination, coordination, and parallelism 3) Avoidance of awkward sentence structures and wordiness 4) Use of transitional words, conjunctive adverbs, and other words that enhance clarity and logic 5) Avoidance of run-on sentences, sentence fragments, and fused sentences • Demonstrates proficient use of conventions with regard to the following skills: 1) Subject–verb agreement 2) Placement of modifiers and correct word order 3) Pronoun usage, including pronoun antecedent agreement, unclear pronoun references, and pronoun case 4) Frequently confused words and homonyms, including contractions 5) Use of apostrophes with possessive nouns 6) Use of punctuation (e.g., commas in a series or in appositives and other non-essential elements, end marks, and punctuation for clause separation) 7) Capitalization (e.g., beginnings of sentences, proper nouns, and titles) • May contain some errors in mechanics and conventions that do not impede comprehension; overall usage is at a level suitable for on-demand draft writing
1	• Demonstrates inconsistent sentence structure; may contain some choppy, repetitive, awkward, or run-on sentences that may limit clarity; demonstrates inconsistent use of skills 1–5 as listed under Trait 3, Score Point 2 • Demonstrates inconsistent use of basic conventions with regard to skills 1–7 as listed under Trait 3, Score Point 2 • May contain many errors in mechanics and conventions that occasionally impede comprehension; overall usage is at the minimum level acceptable for on-demand draft writing
0	• Demonstrates improper sentence structure to the extent that meaning may be unclear; demonstrates minimal use of skills 1–5 as listed under Trait 3, Score Point 2 • Demonstrates minimal use of basic conventions with regard to skills 1–7 as listed under Trait 3, Score Point 2 • Contains numerous significant errors in mechanics and conventions that impede comprehension; overall usage is at an unacceptable level for on-demand draft writing OR • Response is insufficient to show level of proficiency involving conventions and usage
Non-scorable	• Response consists only of text copied from the prompt or source text(s) • Response shows that test-taker has not read the prompt or is entirely off-topic • Response is incomprehensible • Response is not in English • No response has been attempted (has been left blank)

Sample Score 6 Essay

Stem cell research is a complicated topic to evaluate. While it is noted as having a lot of potential with regard to medical advancements, there are several elements of it that can cause moral quandaries, such as the use of human embryos in the research. At the same time, it is providing valuable therapies for diseases such as leukemia and could treat diseases like diabetes and heart disease. With that in mind and on reviewing the two passages, I find that I must argue in favor of stem cell research.

Since the passage against stem cell research makes several valid points, especially questioning the source of the stem cells used in the research, this is sure to inspire many readers to question the morality of the supporting argument. This concern does not actually have any evidence behind it, saying that only human embryo stem cells are being used, so it is difficult to know where this concern came from. In addition, the particular evidence noting that stem cell research itself is potentially harmful has no scientific basis and was simply based on concerns from the populace, as noted by Consumer Reports, *rather than actual research. At the end of the third paragraph, this passage even questions whether scientists could differentiate the cells properly to make them become what is needed for that specific stem cell therapy. Would the stem cells become actual brain cells or would they just become a bunch of organ cells and cause a tumorous growth? This is stated without any evidence to back up the concern at all. While it is clear that the reason stem cell research is interesting in any form is that the cells themselves can be formed into any other cell needed, this worry about differentiation seems to be idle speculation rather than something that would legitimately make this research impossible.*

In contrast, the passage supporting stem cell research is full of dates and specific examples. While the against passage only notes an article from Consumer Reports, *this passage notes research done in the 1900s, all the way through 2008. It points out some of the current research and medical benefits of stem cell research being used right now, including bone marrow transfu-*

sions to treat leukemia and the generation of artificial liver cells just in 2006. It also notes that the major concern regarding the source of the stem cells should be less of a concern due to a report from Stanford, a major research institute, about how researchers acquire the data of human embryo stem cells. It appears that not every single researcher is getting a new set of embryo stem cells to work off of. Instead, the information about one set is shared among all of the researchers. Also, the passage pointed to a 2008 article about medical advancements using adult stem cells. If stem cell research should be argued against, there needs to be more thorough and specific evidence provided to support that argument.

It is clear that the arguments against stem cell research are antiquated and have been addressed by the medical community. Perhaps there is research regarding why stem cell research should not be pursued, but it is unspecified in these passages. Overall, while the supporting passage addresses many of the same concerns as the "against" passage, it is better organized and supported throughout with actual referenced research.

About this essay:

This essay has earned the maximum number of points in each trait for a total of 6 points.

Trait 1: Creation of Arguments and Use of Evidence

This response evaluates the arguments in the source text, develops an effective position supported by the text, and fulfills the criteria to earn 2 points for Trait 1.

This response establishes its stance at the conclusion of the first paragraph (*I find that I must argue in favor of stem cell research*) and provides a summary of support for that stance in the second and third paragraphs.

In the second paragraph, the writer also weighs the validity of the evidence in the "against" argument, for example: "*the particular evidence noting that stem cell research itself is potentially harmful has no scientific basis and was simply based on concerns from the populace, as noted by* Consumer Reports, *rather than actual research."*

Trait 2: Development of Ideas and Organizational Structure

This response is well developed and fulfills the criteria to earn 2 points for Trait 2. It is well organized, opens with a definitive stance, offers a discussion of the pros and cons of stem cell research and the evidence provided, and then provides a summary in support of the chosen stance. The writer provides multiple, specific examples and then elaborates on them, using an appropriately formal tone throughout.

Trait 3: Clarity and Command of Standard English Conventions

This response also fulfills the criteria for draft writing and earns 2 points for Trait 3. Besides employing sophisticated sentence structure (*Since the passage against stem cell research makes several valid points, especially questioning the source of the stem cells used in the research, this is sure to inspire many readers to question the morality of the supporting argument. This concern does not actually have any evidence behind it, saying that only human embryo stem cells are being used, so it is difficult to know where this concern came from*), this response uses clear transitions in its "compare and contrast" construction (*In contrast, the passage supporting stem cell research is full of dates and specific examples*).

In addition, the writer adheres to proper grammar and usage.

Sample Score 4 Essay

It seems clear that we must not allow stem cell research. It may have been around since the early 1900s, but that does not outweigh the moral questions it raises.

I am against stem cell research for mainly the same reasons stated in the passage. Since stem cell research has been around, there is no clear answer

regarding where the human embryo stem cells come from. This was not answered in the supporting passage.

What's more, I also think the possibility that the cells could form tumors and become cancerous, as noted in the against passage, is pretty worrying. At the very least, more education and research into the risks of stem cells are very necessary.

Finally, while it may be true that the arguments for stem cell research list many favorable benefits, and those aspects of stem cell research seem intriguing, the arguments against the research are better than the ones for it. At the very least there needs to be more education on the dangers.

About this essay:
This essay earned 1 point each for Trait 1 and Trait 2, and 2 points for Trait 3.

Trait 1: Creation of Arguments and Use of Evidence
This response makes a simple argument, supports it with some evidence from the source text, and offers a partial analysis of the opposing argument, earning it 1 point for Trait 1.

The writer generates an argument against stem cell research and makes a clear statement of her position in the first paragraph (*It seems clear that we must not allow stem cell research*), in the second paragraph (*I am against stem cell research for mainly the same reasons*), and final paragraph (*the arguments against the research are better than the ones for it*).

The writer does cite some evidence from the source text to support her position (*Since stem cell research has been around, there is no clear answer regarding where the human embryo stem cells come from*). The writer offers a partial analysis of the issue (*At the very least, more education and research into the risks of stem cells are very necessary* and *it may be true that the arguments for stem cell research list many favorable benefits*); however, this analysis is simplistic and limited.

In addition, in the second paragraph the writer offers a partial evaluation of the validity of the "for" arguments (*there is no clear answer regarding where the human embryo stem cells come from. This was not answered in the supporting passage*).

Trait 2: Development of Ideas and Organizational Structure

Although this response has a general organization and focus, the supporting ideas are developed unevenly; thus, it earns only 1 point in this trait.

This response establishes a discernible organizational structure by introducing stance and a comparison of the source text's two positions (*It seems clear that we must not allow stem cell research. It may have been around since the early 1900s, but that does not outweigh the moral questions it raises*).

The second and third paragraphs focus on the troubling aspects of stem cell research, and the writer offers a clear progression of ideas. Her main points are clear but not sufficiently elaborated upon. Her argument is based solely on what is offered in the passage (*I am against stem cell research for mainly the same reasons stated in the passage*).

The concluding paragraph offers a very basic comparison of the "for" and "against" arguments, but not much development is offered (*while [the good] aspects of stem cell research seem intriguing, the arguments against the research are better than the ones for it*).

Trait 3: Clarity and Command of Standard English Conventions

This response earns the full 2 points for Trait 3. It employs sophisticated sentence structure (*Finally, while it may be true that the arguments for stem cell research list many favorable benefits, and those aspects of stem cell research seem intriguing, the arguments against the research are better than the ones for it*) and clear transitions (*What's more . . . Finally . . .*).

In addition, the writer adheres to proper grammar and usage.

Sample Score 0 Essay

Stem cell research is way too confusing and disturbing for a lot of people. While these scientists think that listing all of the accomplishemtns will mean that stem cell research should continue it's not clear at all whether that's true. If perhaps you had loukemia, then it would be ok for it to continue.

Also we don't know where the human embryo stem cells come from also some of them could become cancerous and that isn't a good idea either I thought Loukemia was some kind of cancer, that makes it even more confusing. Also the differentiation of cells. If you can't get the right kind of cells for your therapy, then those cells are useless and are a waste.

I think it's a better idea to not have stem cell research until we know more about what it could do. There are too many factors that seem harmful or dangerous in some way.

About this essay:

This essay earned 0 points in Trait 1, Trait 2, and Trait 3.

Trait 1: Creation of Arguments and Use of Evidence

In general, this response provides a minimal summary of the source text and lacks insight and topic analysis, earning this response 0 points for Trait 1.

The writer fails to summarize source texts in a coherent and organized structure. Though this response addresses the source material, the writer fails to cite evidence to support any arguments and does not take a firm stance until the final paragraph (*I think it's a better idea to not have stem cell research until we know more about what it could do*). She also seems to flip-flop on her stance (*While these scientists think that listing all of the accomplishemtns will mean that stem cell research should continue it's not clear at all whether that's true. If perhaps you had loukemia, then it would be ok for it to continue*).

Trait 2: Development of Ideas and Organizational Structure

Overall, the response is poorly developed, disorganized, and lacks any clear progression of ideas, earning it 0 points for Trait 2.

The writer uses informal and colloquial language (*Stem cell research is way too confusing and disturbing for a lot of people*) and fails to demonstrate awareness of audience and purpose. The response lacks organizational structure and a clear progression of ideas.

Trait 3: Clarity and Command of Standard English Conventions

Many sentences lack sense and fluency and are incorrect and awkward. The writer misuses and confuses words, punctuation, and usage as well as the conventions of English in general, making the response almost incomprehensible and earning it 0 points for Trait 3.

This short response shows flawed sentence structure, including run-on sentences (*Also we don't know where the human embryo stem cells come from also some of them could become cancerous and that isn't a good idea either I thought Loukemia was some kind of cancer, that makes it even more confusing*) and fragments (*Also the differentiation of cells*).

ADDITIONAL ONLINE PRACTICE

Using the codes below, you'll be able to log in and access additional online practice materials!

Your free online practice access codes are:
FVEQ1L73T11V3LD0R770
FVEOT2TSC0JT2376K7S8

Follow these simple steps to redeem your codes:

- Go to **www.learningexpresshub.com/affiliate** and have your access codes handy.

If you're a new user:

- Click the **New user? Register here** button and complete the registration form to create your account and access your products.
- Be sure to enter your unique access code only once. If you have multiple access codes, you can enter them all—just use a comma to separate each code.
- The next time you visit, simply click the **Returning user? Sign in** button and enter your username and password.
- Do not re-enter a previously redeemed access code. Any products you previously accessed are saved in the **My Account** section on the site. Entering a previously redeemed access code will result in an error message.

If you're a returning user:

- Click the **Returning user? Sign in** button, enter your username and password, and click **Sign In**.
- You will automatically be brought to the **My Account** page to access your products.
- Do not re-enter a previously redeemed access code. Any products you previously accessed are saved in the **My Account** section on the site. Entering a previously redeemed access code will result in an error message.

If you're a returning user with a new access code:

- Click the **Returning user? Sign in** button, enter your username, password, and new access code, and click **Sign In**.
- If you have multiple access codes, you can enter them all—just use a comma to separate each code.
- Do not re-enter a previously redeemed access code. Any products you previously accessed are saved in the **My Account** section on the site. Entering a previously redeemed access code will result in an error message.

If you have any questions, please contact Customer Support at Support@ebsco.com. All inquiries will be responded to within a 24-hour period during our normal business hours: 9:00 A.M.–5:00 P.M. Eastern Time. Thank you!

5/18/2016

PHP for
the Web

Fourth Edition

LARRY ULLMAN

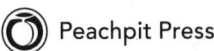
Peachpit Press

Visual QuickStart Guide
PHP for the Web, Fourth Edition
Larry Ullman

Peachpit Press
1249 Eighth Street
Berkeley, CA 94710
510/524-2178
510/524-2221 (fax)

Find us on the Web at: www.peachpit.com
To report errors, please send a note to: errata@peachpit.com
Peachpit Press is a division of Pearson Education.

Editor: Rebecca Gulick
Copyeditor: Liz Welch
Technical Reviewer: Jay Blanchard
Proofreader: Bob Campbell
Production Coordinator: Myrna Vladic
Compositor: Debbie Roberti
Indexer: Valerie Haynes-Perry
Cover Design: RHDG / Riezebos Holzbaur Design Group, Peachpit Press
Interior Design: Peachpit Press
Logo Design: MINE™ www.minesf.com

ISBN-13: 978-0-321-73345-0
ISBN-10:   0-321-73345-2

9 8 7 6 5 4

Printed and bound in the United States of America

Dedication

For Jessica, Gina, and Rich, with gratitude for all of their love and support.

Special Thanks to:

Many, many thanks to everyone at Peachpit Press for their assistance and hard work, especially:

The best darn editor in the world, Rebecca Gulick. Thanks for, well, just about everything.

Liz Welch, for her attention to detail.

Jay Blanchard, for the technical review and for his uncanny ability to predict what I'm going to say next.

Bob Campbell, for the sharp proofreading eye.

Deb Roberti and Myrna Vladic, who take a bunch of disparate stuff and turn it into a book. Valerie Haynes-Perry for the excellent indexing.

Everyone at Peachpit for doing what's required to create, publish, distribute, market, sell, and support these books.

My sincerest thanks to the readers of the other editions of this book and my other books. Thanks for your feedback and support and for keeping me in business.

Rasmus Lerdorf (who got the PHP ball rolling), the people at PHP.net and Zend.com, those who frequent the various newsgroups and mailing lists, and the greater PHP and open source communities for developing, improving upon, and supporting such wonderfully useful technology.

Karnesha, for entertaining the kids so that I can get some work done, even if I'd rather not.

Zoe and Sam, for continuing to be the kid epitome of awesomeness.

Jessica, for doing everything you do and everything you can. And for making all this mess work as well as it can, all things considered.

Table of Contents

Introduction ix

Chapter 1   Getting Started with PHP. 1

Basic HTML Syntax. 2
Basic PHP Syntax 7
Using FTP 10
Testing Your Script 12
Sending Text to the Browser 15
Using the PHP Manual 18
Sending HTML to the Browser 22
Adding Comments to Scripts. 25
Basic Debugging Steps. 28
Review and Pursue 30

Chapter 2   Variables 31

What Are Variables?. 32
Variable Syntax 36
Types of Variables. 38
Variable Values. 41
Understanding Quotation Marks 45
Review and Pursue 48

Chapter 3   HTML Forms and PHP 49

Creating a Simple Form 50
Choosing a Form Method 54
Receiving Form Data in PHP 57
Displaying Errors. 61
Error Reporting. 64
Manually Sending Data to a Page 67
Review and Pursue 72

Chapter 4   Using Numbers 73

Creating the Form 74
Performing Arithmetic 77
Formatting Numbers 81
Understanding Precedence 84
Incrementing and Decrementing a Number 86
Creating Random Numbers 88
Review and Pursue 90

Chapter 5   Using Strings 91

Creating the HTML Form 92
Concatenating Strings 95
Handling Newlines 98
HTML and PHP 100
Encoding and Decoding Strings 103
Finding Substrings 107
Replacing Parts of a String 111
Review and Pursue 114

Chapter 6   Control Structures 115

Creating the HTML Form 116
The if Conditional 119
Validation Functions 122
Using else 126
More Operators 129
Using elseif 138
The Switch Conditional 142
The for Loop 146
Review and Pursue 150

Chapter 7   Using Arrays 151

What Is an Array? 152
Creating an Array 154
Adding Items to an Array 158
Accessing Array Elements 161
Creating Multidimensional Arrays 164
Sorting Arrays 168
Transforming Between Strings and Arrays 172
Creating an Array from a Form 176
Review and Pursue 182

Chapter 8   Creating Web Applications. 183
Creating Templates. 184
Using External Files. 192
Using Constants. 197
Working with the Date and Time. 201
Handling HTML Forms with PHP, Revisited. 204
Making Forms Sticky 210
Sending Email 217
Output Buffering. 222
Manipulating HTTP Headers 225
Review and Pursue 230

Chapter 9   Cookies and Sessions. 231
What Are Cookies? 232
Creating Cookies 234
Reading from Cookies 239
Adding Parameters to a Cookie 242
Deleting a Cookie 245
What Are Sessions? 248
Creating a Session 249
Accessing Session Variables. 252
Deleting a Session 254
Review and Pursue 256

Chapter 10   Creating Functions 257
Creating and Using Simple Functions. 258
Creating and Calling Functions That
    Take Arguments. 265
Setting Default Argument Values 271
Creating and Using Functions That Return a Value. . . . 274
Understanding Variable Scope 279
Review and Pursue 286

Chapter 11   Files and Directories 287
File Permissions 288
Writing to Files. 293
Locking Files 301
Reading from Files. 304
Handling File Uploads 307
Navigating Directories 315
Creating Directories. 320
Reading Files Incrementally 327
Review and Pursue 332

Chapter 12   Intro to Databases 333

Introduction to SQL 334
Connecting to MySQL. 336
MySQL Error Handling 340
Creating and Selecting a Database 343
Creating a Table 347
Inserting Data into a Database. 352
Securing Query Data 358
Retrieving Data from a Database 361
Deleting Data in a Database 366
Updating Data in a Database. 372
Review and Pursue 378

Chapter 13   Putting It All Together 379

Getting Started 380
Connecting to the Database 382
Writing the User-Defined Function 383
Creating the Template 385
Logging In 388
Logging Out 392
Adding Quotes. 393
Listing Quotes 397
Editing Quotes 400
Deleting Quotes 406
Creating the Home Page 410
Review and Pursue 414

Appendix A   Installation and Configuration 415

Appendix B   Resources and Next Steps 437

Index 447

Introduction

When I began the first edition of this book in 2000, PHP was a little-known *open source* project. It was adored by technical people in the know but not yet recognized as the popular choice for Web development that it is today. When I taught myself PHP, very little documentation was available on the language—and that was my motivation for writing this book in the first place.

Today things are different. The Internet has gone through a boom and a bust and has righted itself. Furthermore, PHP is now the reigning king of dynamic Web design tools and has expanded somewhat beyond the realm of just Web development. But despite PHP's popularity and the increase in available documentation, sample code, and examples, a good book discussing the language is still relevant. Although PHP is in the midst of its fifth major release, a book such as this—which teaches the language in simple but practical terms— can still be your best guide in learning the information you need to know.

This book will teach you PHP, providing both a solid understanding of the fundamentals and a sense of where to look for more advanced information. Although it isn't a comprehensive programming reference, through demonstrations and real-world examples, this book provides the knowledge you need to begin building dynamic Web sites and Web applications using PHP.

What Is PHP?

PHP originally stood for *Personal Home Page*. It was created in 1994 by Rasmus Lerdorf to track the visitors to his online résumé. As its usefulness and capabilities grew (and as it began to be utilized in more professional situations), PHP came to mean *PHP: Hypertext Preprocessor*. (The definition basically means that PHP handles data before it becomes HTML—which stands for Hypertext Markup Language.)

According to the official PHP Web site, found at www.php.net 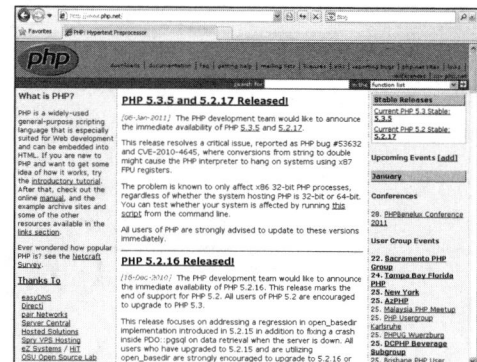, PHP is a "widely-used general-purpose scripting language that is especially suited for Web development and can be embedded into HTML." I'll explain the two key parts of this definition in more detail.

To say that PHP *can be embedded into HTML* means that PHP code can be written within your HTML code—HTML being the code with which all Web pages are built. Therefore, programming with PHP starts off as only slightly more complicated than hand-coding HTML.

Also, PHP is a *scripting language*, as opposed to *a compiled language*. This means that PHP is designed to do something *only after an event occurs*—for example, when a user submits a form or goes to a URL (Uniform Resource Locator—the technical term for a Web address). Another popular example of a scripting language is JavaScript, which commonly handles events that occur within the Web browser. These two languages can also be described as *interpreted*, because the code must be run through an executable, such as the PHP module or the browser's JavaScript component. Conversely, compiled languages such as C and C++ can be used to write stand-alone applications that can act independent of any event.

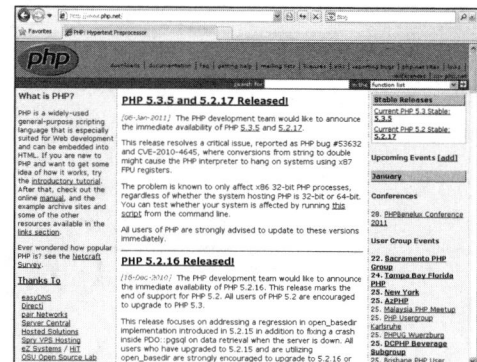

A As of this writing, this is the appearance of the official PHP Web site, located at www.php.net. Naturally, this should be the first place you look to address most of your PHP questions and curiosities.

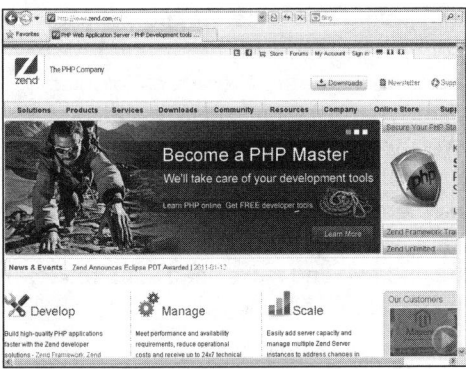

B This is the home page of Zend, creators of the programming at the heart of PHP. The site contains useful software as well as a code gallery and well-written tutorials.

What PHP Is Not

The thing about PHP that confuses most new learners is what PHP *can't do*. Although you can use the language for an amazing array of tasks, its main limitation is that PHP cannot be used for client-side features found in some Web sites.

Using a client-side technology like JavaScript, you can create a new browser window, add mouseovers, make pop-up alerts, resize the browser window, find out the screen size on the user's machine, and dynamically generate and alter forms. None of these tasks can be accomplished using PHP (because PHP is server-side, whereas those are client-side issues). But, you can use PHP to create JavaScript, just as you can use PHP to create HTML.

When it comes time to develop your own PHP projects, remember that you can only use PHP to send information (HTML and such) to the Web browser. You can't do anything else within the Web browser until another request from the server has been made (a form has been submitted or a link has been clicked).

You should also understand that PHP is a *server-side* technology. This refers to the fact that everything PHP does occurs on the server (as opposed to on the *client*, which is the computer being used by the person viewing the Web site). A *server* is just a computer set up to provide the pages you see when you go to a Web address with your browser (for example, Firefox, Microsoft Internet Explorer, or Safari). I'll discuss this process in more detail later (see "How PHP Works").

Finally, PHP is *cross-platform*, meaning that it can be used on machines running Unix, Windows, Macintosh, and other operating systems. Again, we're talking about the *server's* operating system, not the client's. Not only can PHP run on almost any operating system, but, unlike many other programming languages, it enables you to switch your work from one platform to another with few or no modifications.

At the time this book was written, PHP was simultaneously in versions 5.3.5 and 5.2.17. (There are slight differences between versions 5.3 and 5.2, so 5.2 continues to be supported for a while.) Although this book was written using a stable version of PHP 5.3, all of the code is backward compatible, at least to PHP version 5.*x*, if not to 4.*x*. In a couple of situations where a feature requires a more current version of PHP, or where older versions might have slight variations, a note in a sidebar or a tip will indicate how you can adjust the code accordingly.

More information can be found at PHP.net and www.zend.com, the minds behind the core of PHP **B**.

Why Use PHP?

Put simply, PHP is better, faster, and easier to learn than the alternatives. All Web sites must begin with just HTML, and you can create an entire site using a number of static HTML pages. But basic HTML is a limited approach that does not allow for flexibility or responsiveness. Visitors accessing HTML-only sites see simple pages with no level of customization or dynamic behavior. With PHP, you can create exciting and original pages based on whatever factors you want to consider. PHP can also interact with databases and files, handle email, and do many other things that HTML alone cannot.

Webmasters learned a long time ago that HTML alone won't produce enticing and lasting Web sites. Toward this end, server-side technologies such as PHP have become the norm. These technologies allow Web page designers to create Web applications that are dynamically generated, taking into account whichever elements the programmer desires. Often database-driven, these advanced sites can be updated and maintained more readily than static HTML pages.

When it comes to choosing a server-side technology, the primary alternatives to PHP are CGI scripts (Common Gateway Interface, commonly, but not necessarily written in Perl), ASP.NET (Active Server Pages), Adobe's ColdFusion, JSP (JavaServer Pages), and Ruby on Rails. And although there are some server-side JavaScript tools now available, JavaScript isn't truly an alternative to PHP (or vice versa).

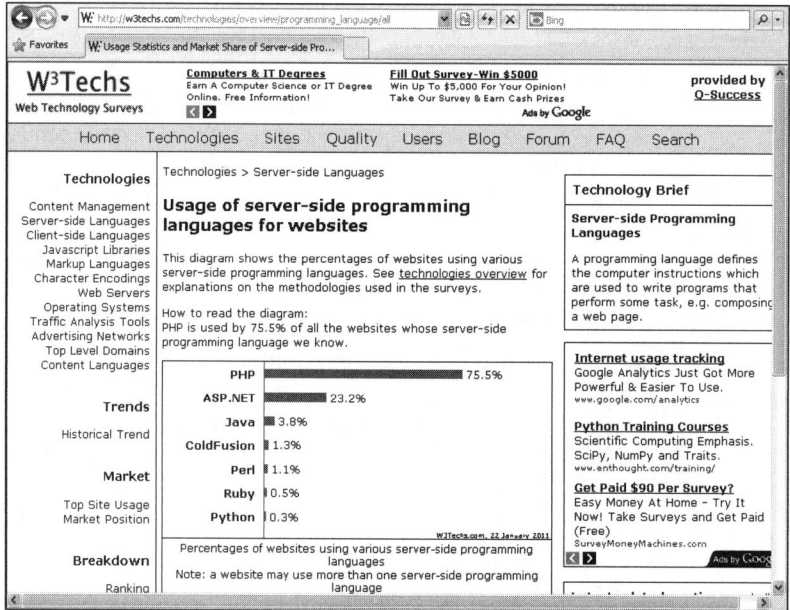

Ⓐ The Web Technology Surveys site says that PHP is running on 75% of all Web sites (http://w3techs.com/technologies/overview/programming_language/all).

So the question is, why should a Web designer use PHP instead of CGI, ASP.NET, JSP, or whatever to make a dynamic Web site?

- **PHP is much easier to learn and use.** People—perhaps like you—without any formal programming training can write PHP scripts with ease after reading this one book. In comparison, ASP.NET requires an understanding of VBScript, C#, or another language; and CGI requires Perl (or C). These are more complex languages and are much more difficult to learn.

- **PHP was written specifically for dynamic Web page creation.** Perl (and VBScript and Java and Ruby) were not, and this fact suggests that, by its very intent, PHP can do certain tasks faster and more easily than the alternatives. I'd like to make it clear, however, that although I'm suggesting PHP is *better for certain things* (specifically those it was created to do), PHP isn't a "better" programming language than Java or Perl—they can do things PHP can't.

- **PHP is both free and cross-platform.** Therefore, you can learn and use PHP on nearly any computer and at no cost. Furthermore, its open source nature means that PHP's users are driving its development, not some corporate entity.

- **PHP is the most popular tool available for developing dynamic Web sites.** As of this writing, PHP is in use on over 75% of all Web sites **Ⓐ** and is the fourth most popular programming language overall **Ⓑ**. Many of the biggest Web sites—Yahoo!, Wikipedia, and Facebook, just to name three—and content management tools, such as WordPress, Drupal, Moodle, and Joomla, use PHP. By learning this one language, you'll provide yourself with either a usable hobby or a lucrative skill.

Position Jan 2011	Position Jan 2010	Delta in Position	Programming Language	Ratings Jan 2011	Delta Jan 2010	Status
1	1	=	Java	17.773%	+0.29%	A
2	2	=	C	15.822%	-0.39%	A
3	4	↑	C++	8.783%	-0.93%	A
4	3	↓	PHP	7.835%	-2.24%	A
5	7	↑↑	Python	6.265%	+1.81%	A
6	6	=	C#	6.226%	+0.46%	A
7	5	↓↓	(Visual) Basic	5.867%	-1.49%	A
8	12	↑↑↑↑	Objective-C	3.011%	+1.63%	A
9	8	↓	Perl	2.857%	-0.71%	A
10	10	=	Ruby	1.784%	-0.69%	A
11	9	↓↓	JavaScript	1.589%	-1.12%	A

Ⓑ The Tiobe Index (http://www.tiobe.com/index.php/content/paperinfo/tpci/index.html) uses a combination of factors to rank the popularity of programming languages.

How PHP Works

PHP is a server-side language, which means the code you write in PHP resides on a host computer that serves Web pages to Web browsers. When you go to a Web site (www.LarryUllman.com, for example), your Internet service provider (ISP) directs your request to the server that holds the www.LarryUllman.com information. That server reads the PHP code and processes it according to its scripted directions. In this example, the PHP code tells the server to send the appropriate Web page data to your browser in the form of HTML **A**. In short, PHP creates an HTML page on the fly based on parameters of your choosing.

This differs from an HTML-generated site in that when a request is made, the server merely sends the HTML data to the Web browser—no server-side interpretation

occurs **B**. Hence, to the end user's browser, there may or may not be an obvious difference between what **home. html** and **home.php** look like, but how you arrive at that point is critically altered. The major difference is that by using PHP, you can have the server *dynamically* generate the HTML code. For example, different information could be presented if it's Monday as opposed to Tuesday or if the user has visited the page before. Dynamic Web page creation sets apart the less appealing, static sites from the more interesting and, therefore, more visited, interactive ones.

The central difference between using PHP and using straight HTML is that PHP does everything on the server and then sends the appropriate information to the browser. This book covers how to use PHP to send the right data to the browser.

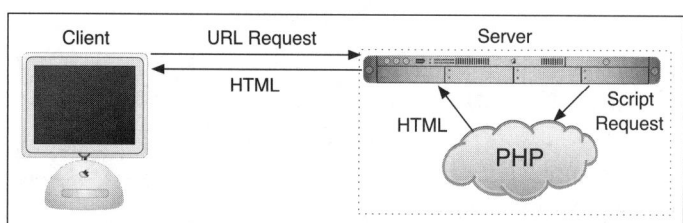

A This graphic demonstrates (albeit in very simplistic terms) how the process works between a client, the server, and a PHP module (an application added to the server to increase its functionality) to send HTML back to the browser.

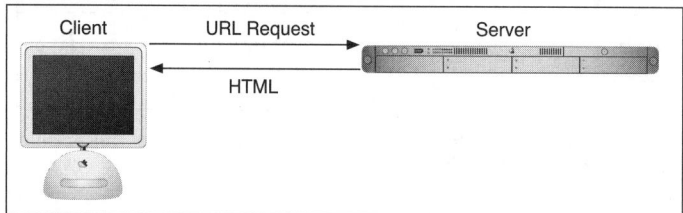

B Compare this direct relationship of how a server works handles basic HTML to **A**. This is also why HTML pages can be viewed in your browser from your own computer—they don't need to be "served," but dynamically generated pages need to be accessed through a server that handles the processing.

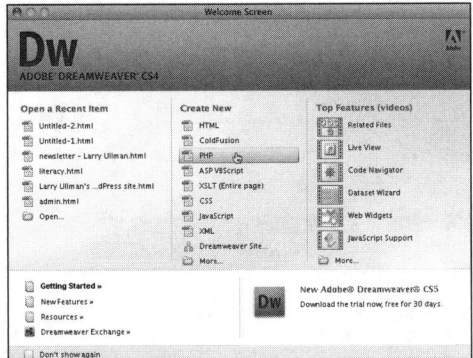

A The popular Dreamweaver application supports PHP development, among other server-side technologies.

What You'll Need

The most important requirement for working with PHP—because it's a server-side scripting language—is access to a PHP-enabled server. Considering PHP's popularity, your ISP or Web host most likely has this option available to you on their servers. You'll need to contact them to see what technology they support.

Your other option is to install PHP and a Web server application (like Apache) on your own computer. Users of Windows, Mac OS X, or Linux can easily install and use PHP for no cost. Directions for installing PHP are available in Appendix A, "Installation and Configuration." If you're up to the task of using your own PHP-installed server, you can take some consolation in knowing that PHP is available for free from the PHP Web site (www.php.net) and comes in easy-to-install packages. If you take this approach, and I recommend that you do, then your computer will act as both the client and the server.

The second requirement is almost a given: You must have a text editor on your computer. Crimson Editor, SciTE, TextWrangler, and similar freeware applications are all sufficient for your purposes; and BBEdit, TextPad, TextMate, and other commercial applications offer more features that you may appreciate. If you're accustomed to using a graphical interface (also referred to as WYSIWYG— What You See Is What You Get) like Adobe Dreamweaver **A** or Aptana Studio, you can consult that application's manual to see how to program within it.

continues on next page

Third, you need a method of getting the scripts you write to the server. If you've installed PHP on your own computer, you can save the scripts to the appropriate directory. However, if you're using a remote server with your ISP or Web host, you'll need an FTP (File Transfer Protocol) program to send the script to the server. There are plenty of FTP applications available; in Chapter 1, "Getting Started with PHP," I use the free FileZilla (http://filezilla-project.org 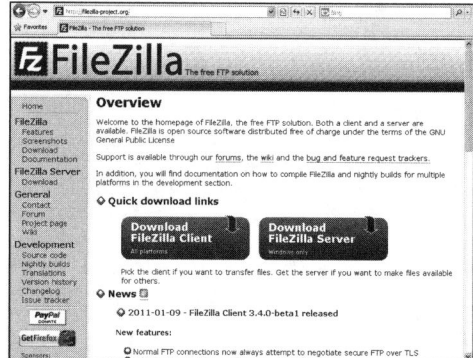) for an example.

Finally, if you want to follow the examples in Chapter 12, "Intro to Databases," you need access to MySQL (www.mysql.com ) or another database application. MySQL is available in a free version that you can install on your own computer.

This book assumes only a basic knowledge of HTML, although the more comfortable you are handling raw HTML code *without* the aid of a WYSIWYG application such as Dreamweaver, the easier the transition to using PHP will be. Every programmer will eventually turn to an HTML reference at some time or other, regardless of how much you know, so I encourage you to keep a good HTML book by your side. One such introduction to HTML is Elizabeth Castro's *HTML, XHTML, and CSS: Visual QuickStart Guide* (Peachpit Press, 2007).

Previous programming experience is certainly not required. However, it may expedite your learning, because you'll quickly see numerous similarities between, for example, Perl and PHP or JavaScript and PHP.

B The FileZilla application can be used on many different operating systems to move PHP scripts and other files to a remote server.

C MySQL's Web site (as of this writing).

Script i.1 A sample PHP script, with line numbers and bold emphasis on a specific section of code.

```
1    <!DOCTYPE html PUBLIC "-//W3C//DTD XHTML
     1.0 Transitional//EN"
2        "http://www.w3.org/TR/xhtml1/DTD/
         xhtml1-transitional.dtd">
3    <html xmlns="http://www.w3.org/1999/
     xhtml" xml:lang="en" lang="en">
4    <head>
5        <meta http-equiv="Content-Type"
         content="text/html; charset=utf-8"/>
6        <title>Hello, World!</title>
7    </head>
8    <body>
9    <?php print "Hello, World!"; ?>
10   </body>
11   </html>
```

About This Book

This book attempts to convey the fundamentals of programming with PHP while hinting at some of the more advanced features you may want to consider in the future, without going into overwhelming detail. It uses the following conventions to do so.

The step-by-step instructions indicate what coding you're to add to your scripts and where. The specific text you should type is printed in a unique type style to separate it from the main body text. For example:

```
<?php print "Hello, World!"; ?>
```

The PHP code is also written as its own complete script and is numbered by line for reference (**Script i.1**). You shouldn't insert these numbers yourself, because doing so will render your work inoperable.

continues on next page

What's New in This Book?

I would consider this fourth edition to be a modest revision of an already solid book. The biggest change in this edition is the removal of the previous version of Chapter 13, covering regular expressions. The type of regular expressions being discussed in earlier versions of the book have since been *deprecated*, meaning support for them is being dropped from the language. A more complex way of addressing regular expressions is beyond what's appropriate for beginning readers, and is covered in detail in my *PHP 6 and MySQL 5 for Dynamic Web Sites: Visual QuickPro Guide* (Peachpit Press, 2008).

As a replacement for the excised material, the new Chapter 13, "Putting It All Together," walks you through the creation of a fully functioning Web site, using almost everything discussed in the entire book (while still teaching a couple of tricks). I hope you'll find this added chapter to be an illuminating demonstration of how to apply your new knowledge.

Second, each chapter in this edition of the book now concludes with a "Review and Pursue" section. Over a page or two, you'll be asked questions meant to reinforce some of the chapter's key points. Prompts will direct you toward ways you can learn related, additional information, or try similar exercises. Help with the questions and prompts can be found in the book's corresponding forum (at www.LarryUllman.com/forum/).

Finally, I tweaked some of the examples mostly to satisfy my own drive for perfection.

I recommend using a text editor that automatically displays the line numbers for you—the numbers will help when you're debugging your work. In the scripts you'll sometimes see particular lines highlighted in bold, in order to draw attention to new or relevant material.

Because of the nature of how PHP works, you need to understand that there are essentially three views of every script: the PHP code (e.g., Script i.1), the code that's sent to the browser (primarily HTML), and what the browser displays to the end user. Where appropriate, sections of or all of the browser window are revealed, showing the end result of the exercise **A**. Occasionally, you'll also see an image displaying the HTML source that the browser received **B**. You can normally access this view by choosing View Source or View Page Source from the appropriate Web browser menu. To summarize, **B** displays the HTML the browser receives, and **A** demonstrates how the browser interprets that HTML. Using PHP, you'll create the HTML that's sent to the browser.

Because the column in this book is narrower than the common text editor screen, sometimes lines of PHP code printed in the steps have to be broken where they would not otherwise break in your editor. A small gray arrow indicates when this kind of break occurs. For example:

```
print "This is going to be a longer
→ line of code.";
```

You should continue to use one line in your scripts, or else you'll encounter errors when executing them. (The gray arrow isn't used in scripts that are numbered.)

While demonstrating new features and techniques, I'll do my best to explain the why's and how's of them as I go. Between reading about and using a function, you should clearly comprehend it. Should something remain confusing, though, this book contains a number of references where you can find answers to any questions (see Appendix B, "Resources and Next Steps"). If you're confused by a particular function or example, your best bet will be to check the online PHP manual or the book's supporting Web site (and its user support forum).

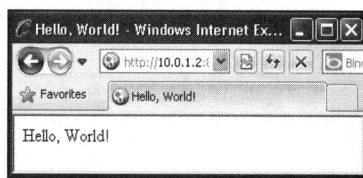

A This is a sample view you'll see of the browser window. For the purposes of this book, it won't make any difference which Web browser or operating system you use.

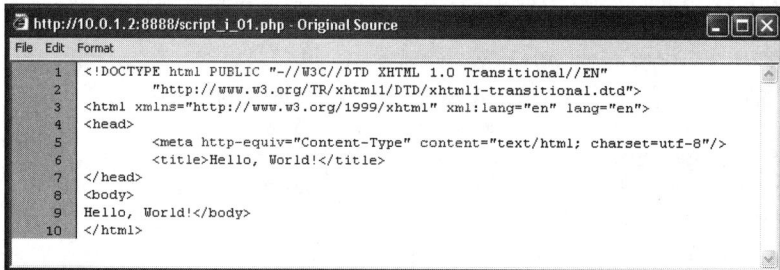

B By viewing the source code received by the Web browser, you can see the HTML created by PHP and sent by the server.

Which Book Is Right for You?

This is the fourth edition of my first book on PHP. Like the original, it's written with the beginner or nonprogrammer in mind. If you have little or no programming experience, prefer a gentler pace, or like to learn things in bite-sized pieces, this is the book for you. Make no mistake: This book covers what you need to know to begin develop dynamic Web sites (while using practical examples), but it does so without any in-depth theory or advanced applications.

Conversely, if you pick up new technologies really quickly or already have some experience developing Web sites, you may find this to be too basic. In that case, you should consider my *PHP 6 and MySQL 5 for Dynamic Web Sites: Visual QuickPro Guide* instead (Peachpit Press, 2008). It discusses SQL and MySQL in much greater detail and goes through several more complex examples, but it does so at a quick jog.

Companion Web Site

While you're reading this book, you may also find it helpful to visit the *PHP for the Web: Visual QuickStart Guide, 4th Edition* Web site, found within www.LarryUllman.com. There you'll find every script in this book available in a downloadable form. (However, I strongly encourage you to type the scripts yourself in order to become more familiar with the structure and syntax of PHP.)

The site also includes a more detailed reference section with links to numerous useful Web pages where you can continue learning PHP. In addition, the site provides an errata page listing any mistakes made in this text.

What many users find most helpful, though, is the book's supporting forum, found through the Web site or more directly at www.LarryUllman.com/forum/. Using the forum, you can:

- Find answers to problems you're having
- Receive advice on how to approach an idea you have
- Get debugging help
- See how changes in the technologies have affected the examples in the book
- Learn what other people are doing with PHP
- Confirm the answers to review questions
- Receive a faster reply from me than if you send me a direct email

Questions, comments, or suggestions?

If you have a PHP-specific question, there are newsgroups, mailing lists, and question-and-answer sections available on PHP-related Web sites for you to turn to. These are discussed in more detail in Appendix B. Browsing through these references or searching the Internet will almost always provide you with the fastest answer.

You can also direct your questions, comments, and suggestions to me. You'll get the fastest reply using the book's corresponding forum (I always answer those questions first). If you'd rather email me, you can do so through the contact page on the Web site. I do try to answer every email I receive, but it will probably take a week or two (whereas you'll likely get a reply in the forum within a couple of days).

For more tips and an enlightening read, see the sidebar and Eric Steven Raymond's "How to Ask Questions the Smart Way" at www.catb.org/~esr/faqs/smart-questions.html. The 10 minutes you spend on it will save you hours in the future. Those people who will answer your questions, like myself, will be most appreciative!

How to Ask Questions the Smart Way

Whether you're posting a message to the book's supporting forum, sending me an email, or asking a question in a newsgroup, knowing how to most effectively ask a question improves the quality of the response you'll receive as well as the speed with which you'll get your answer. To receive the best answer in the shortest amount of time, follow these steps:

1. Search the Internet, read the manuals, and browse any applicable documentation.

2. Ask your question in the most appropriate forum (newsgroup, mailing list, and so on).

3. Use a clear and concise subject.

4. Describe your problem in detail, show any relevant code, say what went wrong, indicate what version of PHP you're using, and state what operating system you're running.

Getting Started with PHP

When learning any new programming language, you should always begin with an understanding of the basic syntax and functionality, which is what you'll learn in this chapter. The focus here is on the fundamentals of both HTML and PHP, and how the two languages work together. The chapter also covers some recommended programming and debugging techniques, the mastery of which will improve your work in the long run.

If you've never programmed before, a focused reading of this chapter will start you on the right track. If you have some programming experience, you'll be able to breeze through these pages, gaining a perspective for the book's remaining material in the meantime. By the end of this chapter you will have successfully written and executed your first PHP scripts and be on your way to developing dynamic Web applications.

In This Chapter

Basic HTML Syntax	2
Basic PHP Syntax	7
Using FTP	10
Testing Your Script	12
Sending Text to the Browser	15
Using the PHP Manual	18
Sending HTML to the Browser	22
Adding Comments to Scripts	25
Basic Debugging Steps	28
Review and Pursue	30

Basic HTML Syntax

All Web pages are made using HTML (Hypertext Markup Language). Every Web browser, be it Microsoft's Internet Explorer, Apple's Safari, Mozilla's Firefox, or Google's Chrome, turns HTML code—

```
<h1>Hello, World!</h1>
I just wanted to say <em>Hello</em>.
```

—into the stylized Web page seen by the user Ⓐ.

As of this writing, the most current version of HTML is 4.01. The next major release, HTML 5, is being actively developed and discussed, but is not production ready (again, as of this writing). This book uses a slight variant of HTML called XHTML (eXtensible HTML). XHTML is almost exactly like HTML, with the following differences:

- All tags are written in lowercase.

- Nested tags must be *well formed*.

  This rule isn't as complicated as it sounds. It means that you can't write **<div><p>text</div></p>**; instead you use **<div><p>text</p></div>**.

- All tag attributes must be quoted.

  In HTML, you might write **<table border=2>**, but in XHTML, you must use **<table border="2">**.

- All tags must be closed.

  This rule is the most confusing for most people. Many HTML tags have both an open and a close, like **<div class="someclass">text</div>**. However, a few don't have implicit closing tags. These include **<hr>**, **
, **<img>, and **<input>**. To make these valid XHTML tags, you need to close

---

Hello, World!

I just wanted to say *Hello*.

Ⓐ How one Web browser renders the HTML code.

them by adding a space and a slash at the end, like this:

```
<hr />
<br />
<img src="image.png" />
<input type="text" name="age" />
```

Basic CSS

The HTML and XHTML elements define a page's content, but formatting the look and behavior of such content is best left to CSS (Cascading Style Sheets). As with HTML and XHTML, this book does not teach CSS in any detail, but as some of the book's code will use CSS, you should be familiar with its basic syntax, too.

You can add CSS to a Web page in a couple of ways. The first, and recommended, method is to use HTML **style** tags:

```
<style type="text/css">
rules
</style>
```

Between the opening and closing tags, the CSS rules are defined. You can also use the **link** HTML tag to incorporate CSS rules defined in an external file:

```
<link href="styles.css" rel="stylesheet" type="text/css" />
```

CSS rules are applied to combinations of general page elements, CSS classes, and specific items:

```
img   { border: 0px; }
.error { color: red; }
#about { background-color: #ccc; }
```

The first rule applies to every image tag. The second applies to any element that has a class of *error*:

```
<p class="error">Error!</p>
```

The third rule applies to just the specific element that has an ID value of *about*:

```
<p id="about">About...</p>
```

(Not all elements need to have an **id** attribute, but no two elements can have the same **id** value.)

For the most part, this book will just use CSS to do simple things, such as changing the color or background color of an element or some text.

Even though using a separate CSS section or file is best, in order to keep things simple, this book will occasionally apply CSS inline:

```
<p style="color: red;">Error!</p>
```

For more on CSS, search the Web or see a dedicated book on the subject.

Before getting into the syntax of PHP, let's create one simple but valid XHTML document that will act as a template for almost all of this book's examples.

To create an XHTML page:

1. Open your text editor or Integrated Development Environment (IDE).

   You can use pretty much any application to create HTML, XHTML, and PHP pages. Popular choices include Adobe's Dreamweaver (www. adobe.com), which runs on Windows and Mac OS X; EditPlus (www.editplus. com) and Crimson Editor (www. crimsoneditor.com) for Windows; and Bare Bones' BBEdit (www.barebones. com) or MacroMates' TextMate (www. macromates.com) for the Mac.

2. Choose File > New to create a new, blank document.

   Some text editors allow you to start by creating a new document of a certain type—for example, a new XHTML file **B**. If your application has this option, use it.

3. Start with the XHTML header lines (**Script 1.1**):

   ```
   <!DOCTYPE html PUBLIC "-//W3C//DTD
   → XHTML 1.0 Transitional//EN"
     "http://www.w3.org/TR/xhtml1/DTD/
     → xhtml1-transitional.dtd">
   <html xmlns="http://www.w3.org/
   → 1999/xhtml" xml:lang="en"
   → lang="en">
   ```

   A valid XHTML document begins with these lines. They tell the Web browser what type of document to expect. For this template, and in the entire book, *XHTML 1.0 Transitional* pages will be created.

B BBEdit and most other Web development applications will create the basics of an XHTML document for you.

Script 1.1 This sample document shows the basics of XHTML code.

```
1    <!DOCTYPE html PUBLIC "-//W3C//DTD XHTML
     1.0 Transitional//EN"
2    "http://www.w3.org/TR/xhtml1/DTD/
     xhtml1-transitional.dtd">
3    <html xmlns="http://www.w3.org/1999/
     xhtml" xml:lang="en" lang="en">
4    <head>
5        <meta http-equiv="content-type"
         content="text/html; charset=utf-8" />
6        <title>Welcome to this Page!</title>
7    </head>
8    <body>
9    <h1>This is a basic XHTML page!</h1>
10   <br />
11   <p>Even with <span style="font-size:
     150%;">some</span> decoration, it's still
     not very exciting.</p>
12   </body>
13   </html>
```

Understanding Encoding

Encoding is a huge subject, but what you most need to understand is this: *the encoding you use in a file dictates what characters can be represented* (and therefore, what languages can be used). To select an encoding, you must first confirm that your text editor or IDE can save documents using that encoding. Some applications let you set the encoding in the preferences or options area; others set the encoding when you save the file.

To indicate to the Web browser the encoding being used, there's the corresponding **meta** tag:

```
<meta http-equiv="content-type"
→ content="text/html;
→ charset=utf-8" />
```

The **charset=utf-8** part says that UTF-8 (short for *8-bit Unicode Transformation Format*) encoding is being used. Unicode is a way of reliably representing every symbol in every alphabet. Version 6 of Unicode—the current version as of this writing—supports over 99,000 characters! The most commonly used Unicode encoding is UTF-8.

If you want to create a multilingual Web page, UTF-8 is the way to go and I'll be using it in this book's examples. You don't have to, of course. But whatever encoding you do use, make sure that the encoding indicated by the XHTML page matches the actual encoding used by the text editor or IDE. If you don't, you'll likely see odd characters when you view the page in a Web browser.

This means adherence to XHTML 1.0 standards. The *Transitional* part means the page can use *deprecated* (no longer recommended) tags (as opposed to *Strict* mode, which isn't forgiving).

4. Create the head section of the page:

```
<head>
  <meta http-equiv="content-type"
  → content="text/html;
  → charset=utf-8"/>
  <title>Welcome to this Page!
  → </title>
</head>
```

The head of an XHTML page includes the **content-type meta** tag, required for valid XHTML. The "Understanding Encoding" sidebar discusses what the **charset** part of the tag means.

The head also contains the page's title, which will appear at the top of the browser window, as well as in the browser's bookmarks and history. You can also place JavaScript and CSS references in the head.

5. Create the body section:

```
<body>
<h1>This is a basic XHTML page!
→ </h1>
<br />
<p>Even with <span style=
→ "font-size: 150%;">some</span>
→ decoration, it's still not very
→ exciting.</p>
</body>
```

continues on next page

The page's content—what is seen in the Web browser—goes between opening and closing **body** tags. Per XHTML rules, the break tag (**
**) includes a space before the slash that closes it. All the other tags are similar to their standard HTML counterparts except that they're in lowercase. CSS is used to increase the font size for the word *some*.

6. Type **</html>** to complete the HTML page.

7. Choose File > Save As. In the dialog box that appears, choose Text Only (or ASCII) for the format, if you're given the option.

   XHTML and PHP documents are just plain text files (unlike, for example, a Microsoft Word document, which is stored in a proprietary format). You may also need to indicate the encoding when you save the file (again, see the sidebar).

8. Navigate to the location where you wish to save the script.

   You can place this script anywhere you'd like on your computer, although using one dedicated folder for every script in this book, perhaps with subfolders for each chapter, makes sense.

9. Save the file as **welcome.html**.

   Even though you're coding with XHTML, the page will still use the standard **.html** extension.

10. Test the page by viewing it in your Web browser **C**.

   Unlike with PHP scripts (as you'll soon discover), you can test XHTML and HTML pages by opening them directly in a Web browser.

TIP Use the book's support forum (www.LarryUllman.com/forum/) or search the Web to find a good HTML and PHP editor or IDE.

TIP The book uses XHTML, but that doesn't mean you have to. If you're more comfortable with HTML, stick with what you know. It won't affect the operability of your PHP scripts.

TIP For more information on XHTML and HTML, check out Elizabeth Castro's excellent book, *HTML, XHTML, and CSS, Sixth Edition: Visual QuickStart Guide* (Peachpit Press, 2006).

TIP I'll use the terms HTML and XHTML interchangeably throughout the book. In fact, you'll probably see just HTML the majority of the time, but understand that I mean XHTML as well.

C The XHTML page, as interpreted by the Web browser.

Basic PHP Syntax

Now that you've seen how HTML will be handled in this book, it's time to begin PHP scripting. To create your first PHP page, you'll start exactly as you would if you were creating an HTML document from scratch. Understanding the reason for this is vitally important: Web browsers are client applications that understand HTML; *PHP is a server-side technology*, which cannot be run in the client. To bridge this gap, PHP will be used on the server to generate HTML that's run in a Web browser (refer to the book's Introduction for a visual representation of this relationship).

There are three main differences between a standard HTML document and a PHP document. First, PHP scripts should be saved with the **.php** file extension (for example, **index.php**). Second, you place PHP code within **<?php** and **?>** tags, normally within the context of some HTML:

```
...
<body><h1>This is HTML.</h1>
<?php PHP code! ?>
<p>More HTML</p>
...
```

The PHP tags indicate the parts of the page to be run through the PHP processor on the server. This leads to the third major difference: *PHP scripts must be run on a PHP-enabled Web server* (whereas HTML pages can be viewed on any computer, directly in a browser). This means that *PHP scripts must always be run through a URL* (i.e., http://*something*/page.php). If you're viewing a PHP script in a Web browser and the address does not begin with *http*, the PHP script will not work.

continues on next page

To make this first PHP script do something without too much programming fuss, you'll use the **phpinfo()** function. This function, when called, sends a table of information to the Web browser. That table lists the specifics of the PHP installation on that particular server. It's a great way to test your PHP installation, and it has a high "bang for your buck" quality.

To create a new PHP script on your computer:

1. Create a new HTML document in your text editor or IDE, to be named **phpinfo.php** (Script 1.2):

```
<!DOCTYPE html PUBLIC "-//W3C//
→ DTD XHTML 1.0 Transitional//EN"
→ "http://www.w3.org/TR/xhtml1/DTD/
→ xhtml1-transitional.dtd">
<html xmlns="http://www.w3.org/
→ 1999/xhtml" xml:lang="en"
→ lang="en">
<head>
  <meta http-equiv="content-type"
  → content="text/html;
  → charset=utf-8" />
  <title>First PHP Script</title>
</head>
<body>
</body>
</html>
```

This particular HTML is largely irrelevant to the overall point of creating a PHP page—but, for consistency's sake, this is the same template as in the basic XHTML example (Script 1.1).

Script 1.2 This first PHP script takes a typical HTML page, adds the PHP tags, and invokes a PHP function.

```
1    <!DOCTYPE html PUBLIC "-//W3C//DTD XHTML
     1.0 Transitional//EN"
2        "http://www.w3.org/TR/xhtml1/DTD/
         xhtml1-transitional.dtd">
3    <html xmlns="http://www.w3.org/1999/
     xhtml" xml:lang="en" lang="en">
4    <head>
5       <meta http-equiv="content-type"
        content="text/html; charset=utf-8" />
6       <title>First PHP Script</title>
7    </head>
8    <body>
9    <?php
10   phpinfo();
11   ?>
12   </body>
13   </html>
```

2. Create some blank lines between the opening and closing **body** tags by pressing Return (Mac) or Enter (PC).

3. Type **<?php** on its own line, just after the opening **body** tag.

   This initial PHP tag tells the server that the following code is PHP and should be handled as such.

4. Add the following on the next line:

   ```
   phpinfo();
   ```

   The syntax will be explained in detail later, but in short, this is just a call to an existing PHP function named *phpinfo*. You must use the opening and closing parentheses, with nothing between them, and the semicolon.

5. Type **?>** on its own line, just before the closing body tag.

   The closing PHP tag tells the server that the PHP section of the script is over. Any text outside of the PHP tags is immediately sent to the Web browser as HTML and isn't treated as PHP code.

6. Save the script as **phpinfo.php**.

   Not to overstate the point, but remember that PHP scripts must use a valid file extension. Most likely you'll have no problems if you save your files as *filename*.**php**.

   You also need to be certain that the application or operating system is not adding a hidden extension to the file. Notepad on Windows, for example, will attempt to add **.txt** to uncommon file extensions, which will render the PHP script unusable.

TIP Just as a file's extension on your computer tells the operating system in what application to open the file, a Web page's extension tells the server how to process the file: *file*.php goes through the PHP module, *file*.aspx is processed as ASP.NET, and *file*.html is a static HTML document (normally). The extension associations are determined by the Web server's settings.

TIP If you're developing PHP scripts for a hosted Web site, check with your hosting company to learn which file extensions you can use for PHP documents. In this book you'll see .php, the most common extension.

TIP You'll occasionally see PHP's *short tags*—simply <? and ?>—used in other people's scripts, although it's best to stick with the formal tags. In fact, support for the short tags is being dropped from the language.

TIP You'll find it handy to have a copy of the phpinfo.php file around. As you'll soon see, this script will report upon PHP's capabilities, settings, and other features of your server. In fact, this book will frequently suggest you return to this script for those purposes.

TIP PHP scripts can also be executed without a Web browser, using a command-line interface and a stand-alone PHP executable. But that topic is well outside the scope of this book (and it's a much less common use of PHP regardless).

Using FTP

Unlike HTML, which can be tested directly in a Web browser, PHP scripts need to be run from a PHP-enabled server in order for you to see the results. Specifically, PHP is run through a *Web server application*, like Apache (http://httpd.apache.org), Abyss (www.aprelium.com), or Internet Information Server (IIS, www.iis.net).

There are two ways you can obtain a PHP-enabled server:

1. Install the software on your computer.

2. Acquire Web hosting.

PHP is open source software (meaning, in part, that it's free) and is generally easy to install (with no adverse effect on your computer as a whole). If you want to install PHP and a Web server on your computer, follow the directions in Appendix A, "Installation and Configuration." Once you've done so, you can skip ahead to the next section of the chapter, where you'll learn how to test your first PHP script.

If you're not running PHP on your own computer, you'll need to transfer your

PHP scripts to the PHP-enabled server using FTP (File Transfer Protocol). The Web hosting company or server's administrator will provide you with FTP access information, which you'll enter into an FTP client. There are many FTP client applications available; in this next sequence of steps, I'll use the free FileZilla (http://filezilla-project.org/), which runs on many operating systems.

To FTP your script to the server:

1. Open your FTP application.

2. In the application's connection window, enter the information provided by your Web host **A**.

   FTP access requires a hostname (e.g., the domain name or an IP address), username, and password.

3. Click Quickconnect (or your FTP client's equivalent).

   If you've provided the correct information, you should be able to connect. If not, you'll see error messages at the top of the FileZilla window **B**.

A The connection section of FileZilla's main window (as it appears on the Mac).

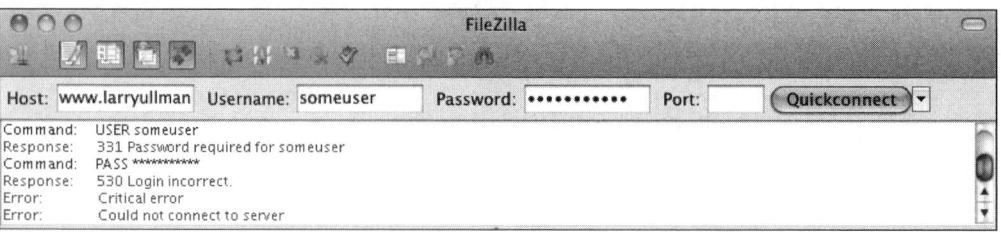

B The reported error says that the login information is incorrect.

4. Navigate to the proper directory for your Web pages (for example, **www**, **htdocs**, or **httpdocs**).

The FTP application won't necessarily drop you off in the appropriate directory. You may need to do some navigation to get to the *Web document root*. The Web document root is the directory on the server to which a URL directly points (for example, www.larryullman. com). If you're unsure of what the Web document root is for your setup, see the documentation provided by the hosting company (or ask them for support).

In FileZilla, the right-hand column represents the files and directories on the server; the left-hand column represents the files and directories on your computer **C**. Just double-click on folders to enter them.

5. Upload your script—**phpinfo.php**—to the server.

To do this in FileZilla, you just need to drag the file from the left column—your computer—to the right column—the server.

TIP Some text editors and IDEs have built-in FTP capability, allowing you to save your scripts directly to the server. Some, like Dreamweaver and TextMate, can run PHP scripts without leaving the application at all.

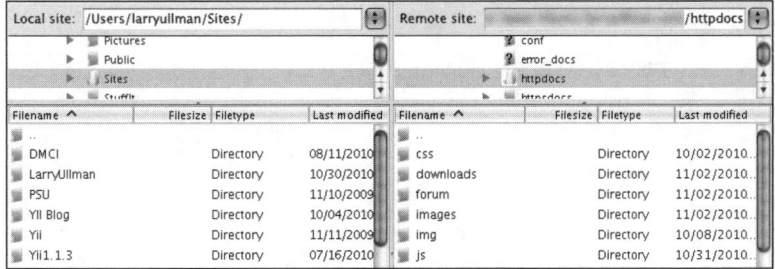

Local site: /Users/larryullman/Sites/				Remote site:			/httpdocs
▶ Pictures				conf			
▶ Public				error_docs			
▶ Sites				▶ httpdocs			
Stuffit				httpdocs			

Filename ^	Filesize	Filetype	Last modified	Filename ^	Filesize	Filetype	Last modified
..				..			
DMCI		Directory	08/11/2010	css		Directory	10/02/2010...
LarryUllman		Directory	10/30/2010	downloads		Directory	11/02/2010...
PSU		Directory	11/10/2009	forum		Directory	11/02/2010...
YII Blog		Directory	10/04/2010	images		Directory	11/02/2010...
Yii		Directory	11/11/2009	img		Directory	10/08/2010...
Yii1.1.3		Directory	07/16/2010	js		Directory	10/31/2010...

C I've successfully connected to the remote server and navigated into the **httpdocs** directory (aka the *Web document root*).

Testing Your Script

Testing a PHP script is a two-step process. First you must put the PHP script in the appropriate directory for the Web server. Second, you run the PHP script in your Web browser by loading the correct URL.

If you're using a separate Web server, like one provided by a hosting company, you just need to use an FTP application to upload your PHP script to it (as in the previous steps). If you have installed PHP on your personal computer, then you can test your PHP scripts by saving them in, or moving them to, the Web document root. This is normally

- **~/Sites** for Mac OS X users (where ~ stands for your home directory)
- *AbyssDir*/htdocs on any operating system, where *AbyssDir* is the directory in which the Abyss Web Server was installed
- **C:\Inetpub\wwwroot** for Windows users running IIS
- **C:\xampp\htdocs** for Windows users running XAMPP (www.apachefriends.com)
- **/Applications/MAMP/htdocs** for Mac users running MAMP (www.mamp.info)

If you're not sure what the Web document root for your setup is, see the documentation for the Web server application or operating system (if the Web server application is built-in).

Once you've got the PHP script in the right place, use your browser to execute it.

To test your script in the browser:

1. Open your favorite Web browser.

   For the most part, PHP doesn't behave differently on different browsers (because PHP runs on the server), so use whichever browser you prefer. In this book, you'll see that I primarily use Firefox and Safari, regardless of the operating system.

2. In the browser's address bar, enter the URL of the site where your script has been saved.

   In my case, I enter *www.larryullman.com*, but your URL will certainly be different.

   If you're running PHP on your own computer, the URL is http://localhost (Windows); or http://localhost/*~username* (Mac OS X), where you should replace *username* with your username. Some all-in-one packages, such as MAMP and XAMPP, may also use a *port* as part of the URL: http://localhost:8888.

   If you're not sure what URL to use, see the documentation for the Web server application you installed.

3. Add **/phpinfo.php** to the URL.

   If you placed the script within a subdirectory of the Web document root, you would add that subdirectory name to the URL as well (e.g., **/ch01/phpinfo.php**).

4. Press Return/Enter to load the URL.

   The page should load in your browser window **A**.

continues on next page

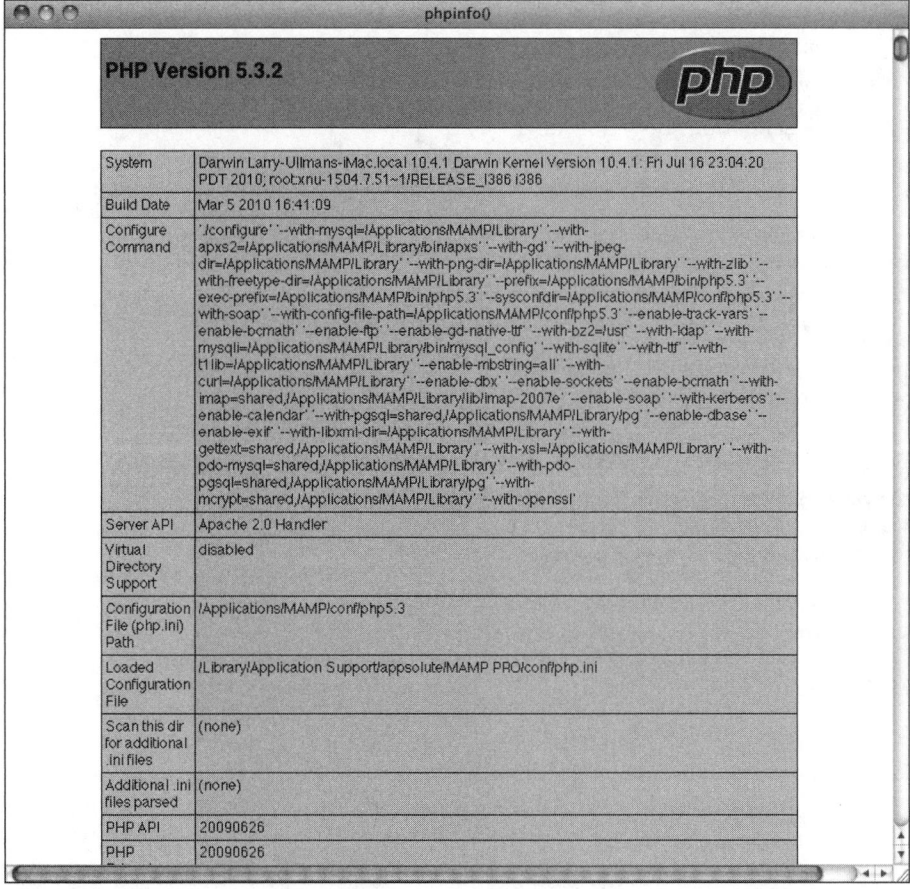

A If the script has been executed correctly, the browser result should look like this (woohoo!).

If you see the PHP code 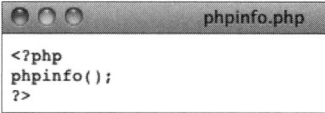 **B** or a blank page, it could mean many things:

- You are not loading the PHP script through a URL (i.e., the address does not begin with *http*).
- PHP has not been enabled on the server.
- You are not using the proper extension.

If you see a *file not found* or similar error **C**, it could be because

- You entered the incorrect URL.
- The PHP script is not in the proper directory.
- The PHP script does not have the correct name or extension.

> **TIP** It's very important to remember that you can't open a PHP file directly in a Web browser as you would open HTML pages or files in other applications. PHP scripts must be processed by the Web server, which means you must access them via a URL (an address that starts with *http://*).

> **TIP** Even if you aren't a seasoned computer professional, you should consider installing PHP on your computer. Doing so isn't too difficult, and PHP is free. Again, see Appendix A for instructions.

> **TIP** Technically speaking, you don't need to add any HTML to a `phpinfo()` script. If you don't, the `phpinfo()` function will still generate a complete HTML page.

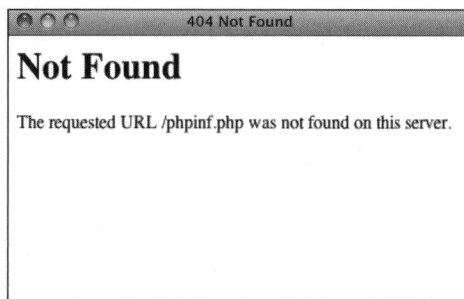

B If you see the raw PHP code, then the PHP code is not being executed.

Not Found

The requested URL /phpinf.php was not found on this server.

C This server response indicates a mismatch between the URL attempted and the files that actually exist on the server.

Sending Text to the Browser

PHP wouldn't be very useful if all you could do was see that it works (although that confirmation is critical). You'll use PHP most frequently to send information to the browser in the form of plain text and HTML tags. To do so, use `print`:

```
print "something";
```

Just type the word `print`, followed by what you want to display: a simple message, the value of a variable, the result of a calculation, and so forth. In the previous example, the message is a string of text, so it must be surrounded with quotation marks (in comparison, numbers are not quoted).

To be clear, `print` doesn't actually *print* anything; it just outputs data. When a PHP script is run through a Web browser, that PHP output is received by the browser itself.

Also notice that the line is terminated with a semicolon (`;`). Every statement in PHP code must end with a semicolon, and forgetting this requirement is a common cause of errors. A *statement* in PHP is an executable line of code, like

```
print "something";
```

or

```
phpinfo();
```

Conversely, comments, PHP tags, control structures (conditionals, loops, and so on), and certain other constructs discussed in this book don't require semicolons.

Finally, you should know about a minor technicality: whereas `phpinfo()` is a *function*, `print` is actually a *language construct*. Although it's still standard to refer to `print` as a function, because `print` is a language construct, no parentheses are required when using it, as in the `phpinfo()` example.

To print a simple message:

1. Begin a new HTML document in your text editor or IDE, to be named **hello.php** (Script 1.3):

```
<!DOCTYPE html PUBLIC "-//W3C//DTD
→ XHTML 1.0 Transitional//EN"
→ "http://www.w3.org/TR/xhtml1/DTD/
→ xhtml1-transitional.dtd">
<html xmlns="http://www.w3.org/
→ 1999/xhtml" xml:lang="en"
→ lang="en">
<head>
  <meta http-equiv="content-type"
  → content="text/html;
  → charset=utf-8" />
  <title>Hello, World!</title>
</head>
<body>
<p>The following was created
→ by PHP:
```

Most of this code is the standard HTML. The last line will be used to distinguish between the hard-coded HTML and the PHP-generated HTML.

2. On the next line, type **<?php** to create the initial PHP tag.

3. Add

```
print "Hello, world!";
```

Printing the phrase *Hello, world!* is the first step most programming references teach. Even though it's a trivial reason to use PHP, you're not really a programmer until you've made at least one *Hello, world!* application.

Script 1.3 By putting the **print** statement between the PHP tags, the server will dynamically send the *Hello, world!* greeting to the browser.

```
1   <!DOCTYPE html PUBLIC "-//W3C//DTD XHTML
    1.0 Transitional//EN"
2        "http://www.w3.org/TR/xhtml1/DTD/
         xhtml1-transitional.dtd">
3   <html xmlns="http://www.w3.org/1999/xhtml"
    xml:lang="en" lang="en">
4   <head>
5     <meta http-equiv="content-type"
      content="text/html; charset=utf-8" />
6     <title>Hello, World!</title>
7   </head>
8   <body>
9   <p>The following was created by PHP:
10  <?php
11  print "Hello, world!";
12  ?>
13  </p>
14  </body>
15  </html>
```

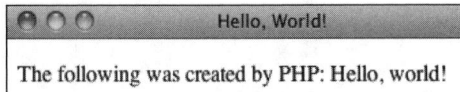

The following was created by PHP: Hello, world!

A A simple *Hello, world!* example: your first foray into PHP programming.

4. Close the PHP section and complete the HTML page:

```
?>
</p>
</body>
</html>
```

5. Save the file as **hello.php**, place it on your PHP-enabled server, and test it in your browser **A**.

If you're running PHP on your own computer, remember that you can save the file to the proper directory and access the script via http://localhost/.

If you see an error or a blank page instead of the results shown in the figure, see the debugging section at the end of this chapter.

TIP PHP is case-insensitive when it comes to calling functions like `phpinfo()` and `print`: `print`, `Print`, and `PRINT` net the same results. Later in the book you'll see examples where case makes a crucial difference.

TIP You can use other functions to send text to the browser, including `echo` and `printf()`, but this book primarily uses `print`.

TIP You can—and commonly will—use `print` over multiple lines:

```
print "This is a longer
sentence of text.";
```

The closing quotation mark terminates the message being printed and the semicolon is placed only at the end of that line.

Using the PHP Manual

The PHP manual—accessible online at www.php.net/manual—lists every function and feature of the language. The manual is organized with general concepts (installation, syntax, variables) discussed first and ends with the functions by topic (MySQL, string functions, and so on).

To quickly look up any function in the PHP manual, go to www.php.net/*functionname* in your Web browser (for example, www.php.net/print).

To understand how functions are described, look at the start of the **print** function's page **A**.

The first line is the name of the function itself, followed by the versions of PHP in which it's available. As the language grows, new functions are added and, occasionally, older functions are removed. Then there's a textual description of the function along with the function's basic usage. The usage is the most important and confusing part.

In this example, the first value, **int**, says that **print** returns an integer value (specifically, **print** returns 1, always).

---

print

(PHP 4, PHP 5)

print — Output a string

⊟ **Description**   Report a bug

```
int print ( string $arg )
```

Outputs *arg*.

print() is not actually a real function (it is a language construct) so you are not required to use parentheses with its argument list.

A The PHP manual's page for the **print** construct.

Within the parentheses, **string $arg**
states that the function takes one required
argument, which should be in the form of a
string. You've already seen this in action.

As a comparison, check out the manual's
listing for the **nl2br()** function **B**. This
function converts newlines found within
text (the equivalent of pressing Return/
Enter) into HTML break tags. This function,
which returns a string, takes a string as its
first argument and an optional Boolean
(**true/false**) as its second. Whenever you
see the square brackets, that indicates
optional arguments, which are always
listed last. When a function takes multiple
arguments, they are separated by commas.
Hence, this function can be called like so:

```
nl2br("Some text");
nl2br("Some text", false);
```

As the definition also indicates, the second
argument has a default value of **true**,
meaning it'll create XHTML **
** tags
unless the function is passed a second
argument value of **false**. In that case, the
function will create HTML **
** tags instead.

If you're ever confused by a function or
how it is properly used, check the PHP
manual's reference page for it.

---

nl2br

(PHP 4, PHP 5)

nl2br — Inserts HTML line breaks before all newlines in a string

⊟ **Description**   Report a bug

```
string nl2br ( string $string [, bool $is_xhtml = true ] )
```

Returns *string* with '<br />' or '<br>' inserted before all newlines.

B The PHP manual's page for the **nl2br()** function.

To look up a function definition:

1. Head to www.php.net/*functionname* in your Web browser.

   If the PHP manual doesn't have a matching record for the function you tried, check the spelling or look at the recommended alternatives that the manual presents **C**.

2. Compare the versions of PHP that the function exists in with the version of PHP you're using.

   Use the `phpinfo()` function, already demonstrated, to know for certain what version of PHP you are running. If a function was added in a later version of PHP, you'll either need to upgrade the version you have or use a different approach.

3. Examine what type of data the function returns.

   Sometimes you may be having a problem with a function because it returns a different type of value than you expect it to.

PHP Function List

Sorry, but the function **n2br** is not in the online manual. Perhaps you misspelled it, or it is a relatively new function that hasn't made it into the online documentation yet. The following are the 20 functions which seem to be closest in spelling to **n2br** (really good matches are in bold). Perhaps you were looking for one of these:

nl2br	bcsqrt	long2ip
png2wbmp	finfo_buffer	bzerrno
atan2	iconv_substr	natsort
mongodbref	bzerror	opendir
substr	bin2hex	strpbrk
hebrev	deg2rad	mongodb
bzread	scandir	

If you want to search the entire PHP website for the string **"n2br"**, then click here.

For a quick overview over all documented PHP functions, click here.

C The manual will present alternative functions if the entered URL doesn't directly match a reference.

4. Examine how many and what types of arguments the function requires or can take.

The most common mistake when using functions is sending the wrong number or type of arguments when the function is called.

5. Read the user comments, when present, to learn more.

Sometimes the user comments can be quite helpful (other times not).

TIP If you see a message saying that a function has been deprecated **D**, that means the function will be dropped from future versions of PHP and you should start using the newer, better alternative (there almost always is one, and it will be identified).

---

ereg

(PHP 4, PHP 5)

ereg — Regular expression match

⊟ Description   Report a bug

```
int ereg ( string $pattern , string $string [, array &$regs ] )
```

Searches a *string* for matches to the regular expression given in *pattern* in a case-sensitive way.

Warning

This function has been ***DEPRECATED*** as of PHP 5.3.0. Relying on this feature is highly discouraged.

D Deprecated functions should be avoided in your code.

Sending HTML to the Browser

As those who first learned HTML quickly discovered, viewing plain text in a Web browser leaves a lot to be desired. Indeed, HTML was created to make plain text more appealing and useful. Because HTML works by adding tags to text, you can use PHP to also send HTML tags to the browser, along with other data:

```
print "<b>Hello, world!</b>";
```

There is one situation where you have to be careful, though. HTML tags that require double quotation marks, like `<a href="page.php">link</a>,` will cause problems when printed by PHP, because the `print` function uses quotation marks as well **A**:

```
print "<a href="page.php">link</a>";
```

One workaround is to *escape* the quotation marks within the HTML by preceding them with a backslash (\):

```
print "<a href=\"page.php\">link</a>";
```

By escaping each quotation mark within the `print` statement, you tell PHP to print the mark itself instead of treating the quotation mark as either the beginning or end of the string to be printed.

To send HTML to the browser:

1. Open the hello.php script (Script 1.3) in your text editor or IDE, if it is not already open.

2. Edit the *Hello, world!* text on line 11 by adding HTML tags, making it read (**Script 1.4**) as follows:

   ```
   print "<span style=\"font-weight:
   → bold;\">Hello, world!</span>";
   ```

A Attempting to print double quotation marks will create errors, as they conflict with the `print` statement's primary double quotation marks.

Script 1.4 With the `print` function, you can send HTML tags along with text to the browser, where the formatting will be applied.

```
1   <!DOCTYPE html PUBLIC "-//W3C//DTD XHTML
    1.0 Transitional//EN"
2       "http://www.w3.org/TR/xhtml1/DTD/
        xhtml1-transitional.dtd">
3   <html xmlns="http://www.w3.org/1999/xhtml"
    xml:lang="en" lang="en">
4   <head>
5       <meta http-equiv="content-type"
        content="text/html; charset=utf-8" />
6       <title>Hello, World!</title>
7   </head>
8   <body>
9   <p>The following was created by PHP:
10  <?php
11  print "<span style=\"font-weight:
    bold;\">Hello, world!</span>";
12  ?>
13  </p>
14  </body>
15  </html>
```

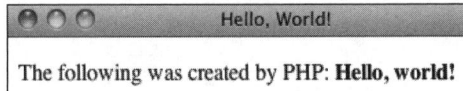

The following was created by PHP: **Hello, world!**

B The new version of the *Hello, world!* page, with a little more decoration and appeal.

To make the PHP-generated part of the message stand out, CSS styling will embolden the greeting. For this to work, you must escape the quotation marks within the **span** tag so that they don't conflict with the **print** statement's quotation mark.

3. Save the script as **hello2.php**, place it on your PHP-enabled server, and run the page in your browser **B**.

continues on next page

Using White Space

When you're programming in PHP, you should understand that white space is generally (but not universally) ignored. Any blank line (just one or several in a row) in PHP code is irrelevant to the end result. Likewise, tabs and spaces are normally inconsequential to PHP. And as PHP code is not visible in the Web browser (unless there's a problem with the server), white space in your PHP files has no impact on what the end user sees.

The spacing of HTML code shows up in the HTML source of a Web page but has only a minimal effect on what's viewed in the Web browser. For example, all of a Web page's HTML source code could be placed on one line without changing what the end user sees. If you had to hunt for a problem in the HTML source, however, you would not like the long, single line of HTML. You can affect the spacing of dynamically generated HTML code by printing it in PHP over multiple lines, or by using the newline character (**\n**) within double quotation marks:

```
print "Line 1\nLine 2";
```

Again, use of the newline character affects the *HTML source code* of the Web page, not what the end user will see rendered in the browser.

To adjust the spacing in the rendered Web page, you'll use CSS, plus paragraph, div, and break tags, among others.

4. View the HTML page source to see the code that was sent to the browser **C**.

How you do this depends upon the browser: select View > Page Source in Firefox, View > Source in Internet Explorer, or View > View Source in Safari.

This is a step you'll want to be in the habit of taking, particularly when problems occur. Remember that PHP is primarily used to generate HTML, sent to and interpreted by the Web browser. Often, confirming what was sent to the Web browser (by viewing the source) will help explain the problem you're seeing in the browser's interpretation (or visible result).

TIP Understanding the role of quotation marks and how to escape problematic characters is crucial to programming with PHP. These topics will be covered in more detail in the next two chapters.

TIP The HTML you send to the Web browser from PHP doesn't need to be this simple. You can create tables, JavaScript, and much, much more.

TIP Remember that any HTML outside of the PHP tags will automatically go to the browser. Within the PHP tags, `print` statements are used to send HTML to the Web browser.

```
Source of http://phpvqs4:8888/hello2.php

<!DOCTYPE html PUBLIC "-//W3C//DTD XHTML 1.0 Transitional//EN"
        "http://www.w3.org/TR/xhtml1/DTD/xhtml1-transitional.dtd">
<html xmlns="http://www.w3.org/1999/xhtml" xml:lang="en" lang="en">
<head>
        <meta http-equiv="content-type" content="text/html; charset=utf-8" />
        <title>Hello, World!</title>
</head>
<body>
<p>The following was created by PHP:
<span style="font-weight: bold;">Hello, world!</span></p>
</body>
</html>
```

C The resulting HTML source code of **hello2.php** **B** on page 22.

Adding Comments to Scripts

Comments are integral to programming, not because they do anything but because they help you remember why *you* did something. The computer ignores these comments when it processes the script. Furthermore, PHP comments are never sent to the Web browser and therefore remain your secret.

PHP supports three ways of adding comments. You can comment out one line of code by putting either **//** or **#** at the beginning of the line you want ignored:

```
// This is a comment.
```

You can also use **//** or **#** to begin a comment at the end of a PHP line, like so:

```
print "Hello"; // Just a greeting.
```

Although it's largely a stylistic issue, **//** is much more commonly used in PHP than **#**.

You can comment out multiple lines by using **/*** to begin the comment and ***/** to conclude it:

```
/* This is a
multi-line comment. */
```

Some programmers also prefer this comment style as it contains both open and closing "tags," providing demarcation for where the comment begins and ends.

To add comments to a script:

1. Open the hello2.php (Script 1.4) in your text editor or IDE.

2. After the initial PHP tag, add some comments to your script (**Script 1.5**):

   ```
   /*
    *Filename: hello3.php
    *Book reference: Script 1.5
    *Created by: Larry Ullman
    */
   ```

   This is just a sample of the kind of comments you can write. You should document what the script does, what information it relies on, who created it, when, and so forth. Stylistically, such comments are often placed at the top of a script (as the first thing within the PHP section, that is), using formatting like this. The extra asterisks aren't required; they just draw attention to the comments.

3. On line 17, in front of the **print** statement, type **//**.

   By preceding the **print** statement with two slashes, the function call is "commented out," meaning it will never be executed.

4. After the closing PHP tag (on line 19), add an HTML comment:

   ```
   <!-- This is an HTML comment. -->
   ```

   This line of code will help you distinguish among the different comment types and where they appear. This comment will only appear within the HTML source code.

5. Save the script as **hello3.php**, place it on your PHP-enabled server, and run the page in your Web browser .

Script 1.5 PHP and HTML comments are added to the script to document it and to render a line of PHP code inert.

```
1   <!DOCTYPE html PUBLIC "-//W3C//DTD XHTML
    1.0 Transitional//EN"
2        "http://www.w3.org/TR/xhtml1/DTD/
         xhtml1-transitional.dtd">
3   <html xmlns="http://www.w3.org/1999/xhtml"
    xml:lang="en" lang="en">
4   <head>
5       <meta http-equiv="content-type"
        content="text/html; charset=utf-8" />
6       <title>Hello, World!</title>
7   </head>
8   <body>
9   <p>The following was created by PHP: <br />
10  <?php
11  /*
12   * Filename: hello3.php
13   * Book reference: Script 1.5
14   * Created by: Larry Ullman
15   */
16
17  //print "<span style=\"font-weight:
    bold;\">Hello, world!</span>\n";
18
19  ?>
20  <!-- This is an HTML comment. -->
21  </p>
22  </body>
23  </html>
```

```
● ● ○                    Hello, World!

The following was created by PHP:
```

A With the **print** statement commented out, the page looks just as it would if the **print** function weren't there.

6. View the source of the page to see the HTML comment **B**.

TIP You can comment out just one line of code or several using the /* and */ method. With // or #, you can negate only one line at a time.

TIP Different programmers prefer to comment code in different ways. The important thing is to find a system that works for you and stick to it.

TIP Note that you cannot use HTML comment characters (<!-- and -->) within PHP to comment out code. You could have PHP print those tags to the browser, but in that case you'd create a comment that appeared in the HTML source code on the client's computer (but not in the browser window). PHP comments never make it as far as a user's computer.

TIP Despite my strong belief that you can't over-comment your scripts, the scripts in this book aren't as documented as they should be, in order to save space. But the book will document each script's name and number, for cross-reference purposes.

TIP When you change a script's code, be certain to update its comments as well. It's quite confusing to see a comment that suggests a script or a line of code does something other than what it actually does.

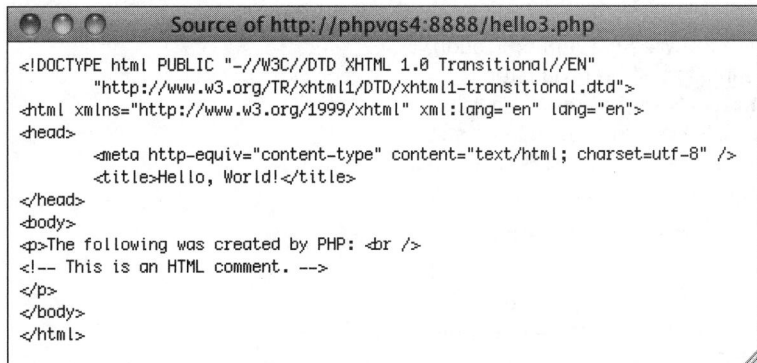

```
Source of http://phpvqs4:8888/hello3.php

<!DOCTYPE html PUBLIC "-//W3C//DTD XHTML 1.0 Transitional//EN"
        "http://www.w3.org/TR/xhtml1/DTD/xhtml1-transitional.dtd">
<html xmlns="http://www.w3.org/1999/xhtml" xml:lang="en" lang="en">
<head>
        <meta http-equiv="content-type" content="text/html; charset=utf-8" />
        <title>Hello, World!</title>
</head>
<body>
<p>The following was created by PHP: <br />
<!-- This is an HTML comment. -->
</p>
</body>
</html>
```

B HTML comments don't appear in the Web browser but are in the HTML source. PHP comments remain in the PHP script on the server.

Basic Debugging Steps

Debugging is by no means a simple concept to grasp, and unfortunately, it's one that is only truly mastered by doing. The next 50 pages could be dedicated to the subject and you'd still only be able to pick up a fraction of the debugging skills that you'll eventually acquire and need.

The reason I introduce debugging in this somewhat harrowing way is that it's important not to enter into programming with delusions. Sometimes code won't work as expected, you'll inevitably create careless errors, and some days you'll want to pull your hair out, even when using a comparatively user-friendly language such as PHP. In short, *prepare to be perplexed and frustrated at times*. I've been coding in PHP since 1999, and occasionally I still get stuck in the programming muck. But debugging is a very important skill to have, and one that you will eventually pick up out of necessity and experience. As you begin your PHP programming adventure, I can offer the following basic but concrete debugging tips.

To debug a PHP script:

- **Make sure you're always running PHP scripts through a URL!**

    This is perhaps the most common beginner's mistake. PHP code must be run through the Web server application, which means it must be requested through **http://something**. When you see actual PHP code instead of the result of that code's execution, most likely you're not running the PHP script through a URL.

- **Know what version of PHP you're running.**

    Some problems will arise from the version of PHP in use. Before you ever use any PHP-enabled server, run the **phpinfo.php** file (Script 1.2) to confirm the version of PHP in use.

- **Make sure `display_errors` is on.**

  This is a basic PHP configuration setting (discussed in Appendix A). You can confirm this setting by executing the `phpinfo()` function (just use your browser to search for `display_errors` in the resulting page). For security reasons, PHP may not be set to display the errors that occur. If that's the case, you'll end up seeing blank pages when problems occur. To debug most problems, you'll need to see the errors, so turn this setting on while you're learning. You'll find instructions for doing so in Appendix A and Chapter 3, "HTML Forms and PHP."

- **Check the HTML source code.**

  Sometimes the problem is hidden in the HTML source of the page. In fact, sometimes the PHP error message can be hidden there!

- **Trust the error message.**

  Another very common beginner's mistake is to not fully read or trust the error that PHP reports. Although an error message can often be cryptic and may seem meaningless, it can't be ignored. At the very least, PHP is normally correct as to the line on which the problem can be found. And if you need to relay that error message to someone else (like when you're asking me for help), do include the entire error message!

- **Take a break!**

  So many of the programming problems I've encountered over the years, and the vast majority of the toughest ones, have been solved by stepping away from my computer for a while. It's easy to get frustrated and confused, and in such situations, any further steps you take are likely to only make matters worse.

TIP These are just some general debugging techniques, specifically tailored to the beginning PHP programmer. They should suffice for now, though, as the examples in this book are relatively simple. More complex coding requires more advanced debugging techniques, so my *PHP 6 and MySQL 5 for Dynamic Web Sites: Visual QuickPro Guide* (Peachpit Press, 2007) dedicates a whole chapter to this subject.

Review and Pursue

New in this edition of the book, each chapter ends with a "Review and Pursue" section. In these sections you'll find questions regarding the material just covered and prompts for ways to expand your knowledge and experience on your own. If you have any problems with these sections, either in answering the questions or pursuing your own endeavors, turn to the book's supporting forum (www.LarryUllman.com/forum/).

Review

- What is HTML? What is XHTML? Name two differences between HTML and XHTML.

- What encoding is your text editor or IDE set to use? Does that match the encoding specified in your generated HTML pages?

- What is CSS and what is it used for?

- What file extension should PHP scripts have for your particular server?

- What is meant by "Web root directory"? What is the Web root directory for your server?

- How do you test PHP scripts? What happens when PHP scripts are not run through a URL?

- Name two ways comments can be added to PHP code. Identify some ways you would use comments.

Pursue

- If you have access to more than one server, confirm what version of PHP is running on another server.

- Create a static HTML page that displays some information. Then replace some of the static content with content created by PHP.

- Create a template to use for your own work. The template should contain the HTML shell, the opening and closing PHP tags, and some basic comments.

- Confirm, using the **phpinfo()** function, that **display_errors** is enabled on your server. If it's not, change your server's configuration to enable it (see Chapter 3 and Appendix A).

- In subsequent chapters, occasionally check the PHP manual's page when a new function is mentioned in the book.

2

Variables

In the previous chapter, you learned how to use PHP to send simple text and HTML to a Web browser—in other words, something for which you don't need PHP at all! Don't worry, though; this book will teach you how to use **print** in conjunction with other PHP features to do great and useful things with your Web site.

To make the leap from creating simple, static pages to dynamic Web applications and interactive Web sites, you need *variables*. Understanding what variables are, the types that a language supports, and how to use them is critical.

This chapter discusses the fundamentals of variables used in PHP, and later chapters cover the different types in greater detail. If you've never dealt with variables before, this chapter will be a good introduction. If you're familiar with the concept, then you should be able to work through this chapter with ease.

In This Chapter

What Are Variables?	32
Variable Syntax	36
Types of Variables	38
Variable Values	41
Understanding Quotation Marks	45
Review and Pursue	48

What Are Variables?

A *variable* is a container for data. Once data has been stored in a variable (or, stated more accurately, once a variable has been assigned a value), that data can be altered, printed to the Web browser, saved to a database, emailed, and so forth.

Variables in PHP are, by their nature, flexible: You can put data into a variable, retrieve that data from it (without affecting the value of the variable), put new data in, and continue this cycle as long as necessary. But variables in PHP are largely temporary: *Most only exist*—that is, they only have a value—*for the duration of the script's execution on the server*. Once the execution passes the final closing PHP tag, those variables cease to exist. Furthermore, after users click a link or submit a form, they are taken to a new page that may have an entirely separate set of variables.

Before getting too deep into the discussion of variables, let's write a quick script that reveals some of PHP's *predefined* variables. These are variables that PHP automatically creates when a script runs. Over the course of the book you'll be introduced to many different predefined variables. For this particular example, let's look at the predefined **$_SERVER** variable. It contains lots of information about the computer on which PHP is running.

The **print_r()** function offers an easy way to display any variable's value:

```
print_r($variable_name);
```

Just provide the name of the variable you'd like to inspect as a single argument to the **print_r()** function (you'll learn more about a variable's syntax throughout this chapter).

```
1    <!DOCTYPE html PUBLIC "-//W3C//DTD XHTML
     1.0 Transitional//EN"
2       "http://www.w3.org/TR/xhtml1/DTD/
        xhtml1-transitional.dtd">
3    <html xmlns="http://www.w3.org/1999/xhtml"
     xml:lang="en" lang="en">
4    <head>
5       <meta http-equiv="Content-Type"
        content="text/html; charset=utf-8"/>
6       <title>Predefined Variables</title>
7    </head>
8    <body>
9    <pre>
10   <?php // Script 2.1 - predefined.php
11
12   // Show the value of the $_SERVER
     variable:
13   print_r ($_SERVER);
14
15   ?>
16   </pre>
17   </body>
18   </html>
```

To print PHP's predefined variables:

1. Create a new PHP script in your text editor or IDE, to be named **predefined.php** (Script 2.1).

2. Create the initial HTML tags:

   ```
   <!DOCTYPE html PUBLIC "-//W3C//DTD
   → XHTML 1.0 Transitional//EN"
      "http://www.w3.org/TR/xhtml1/DTD/
      → xhtml1-transitional.dtd">
   <html xmlns="http://www.w3.org/
   → 1999/xhtml" xml:lang="en"
   → lang="en">
   <head>
      <meta http-equiv="Content-Type"
      → content="text/html;
      → charset=utf-8"/>
      <title>Predefined Variables
      → </title>
   </head>
   <body>
   <pre>
   ```

   This code repeats the XHTML template created in the preceding chapter. Within the body of the page, the **<pre>** tags are being used to make the generated PHP information more legible. Without using the **<pre>** tags, the **print_r()** function's output would be quite messy.

3. Add the PHP code:

   ```
   <?php // Script 2.1 - predefined.php
   print_r($_SERVER);
   ?>
   ```

   The PHP code contains just one function call. The function should be provided with the name of a variable.

   continues on next page

In this example, the variable is **$_SERVER**, which is special in PHP. **$_SERVER** stores all sorts of data about the server: its name and operating system, the name of the current user, information about the Web server application (Apache, Abyss, IIS, etc.), and more. It also reflects the PHP script being executed: its name, where it's stored on the server, and so forth.

Note that you must type **$_SERVER** exactly as it is here, in all uppercase letters.

4. Complete the HTML page:

```
</pre>
</body>
</html>
```

5. Save the file as **predefined.php**, upload it to your server (or save it to the appropriate directory on your computer), and test it in your Web browser **Ⓐ**.

Once again, remember that you must run all PHP scripts through a URL (i.e., http://*something*).

```
Array
(
    [HTTP_HOST] => phpvqs4:8888
    [HTTP_USER_AGENT] => Mozilla/5.0 (Macintosh; U; Intel Mac OS X 10.6;
    [HTTP_ACCEPT] => text/html,application/xhtml+xml,application/xml;q=0
    [HTTP_ACCEPT_LANGUAGE] => en-us,en;q=0.5
    [HTTP_ACCEPT_ENCODING] => gzip,deflate
    [HTTP_ACCEPT_CHARSET] => ISO-8859-1,utf-8;q=0.7,*;q=0.7
    [HTTP_KEEP_ALIVE] => 115
    [HTTP_CONNECTION] => keep-alive
    [PATH] => /usr/bin:/bin:/usr/sbin:/sbin
    [SERVER_SIGNATURE] =>
    [SERVER_SOFTWARE] => Apache
    [SERVER_NAME] => phpvqs4
    [SERVER_ADDR] => 127.0.0.1
    [SERVER_PORT] => 8888
    [REMOTE_ADDR] => 127.0.0.1
    [DOCUMENT_ROOT] => /Users/larryullman/Sites/phpvqs4
    [SERVER_ADMIN] => you@example.com
    [SCRIPT_FILENAME] => /Users/larryullman/Sites/phpvqs4/predefined.php
    [REMOTE_PORT] => 51149
    [GATEWAY_INTERFACE] => CGI/1.1
    [SERVER_PROTOCOL] => HTTP/1.1
    [REQUEST_METHOD] => GET
    [QUERY_STRING] =>
    [REQUEST_URI] => /predefined.php
    [SCRIPT_NAME] => /predefined.php
    [PHP_SELF] => /predefined.php
    [REQUEST_TIME] => 1289831848
    [argv] => Array
        (
        )

    [argc] => 0
)
```

Ⓐ The **$_SERVER** variable, as printed out by this script, is a master list of values pertaining to the server and the PHP script.

6. If possible, transfer the file to another computer or server running PHP and execute the script in your Web browser again **B**.

TIP Printing out the value of any variable as you've done here is one of the greatest debugging tools. Scripts often don't work as you expect them to because one or more variables do not have the values you assume they should, so confirming their actual values is extremely helpful.

TIP If you don't use the HTML `<pre></pre>` tags, the result will be like the mess in **C**.

```
Array
(
    [HTTP_HOST] => larryullman.com
    [HTTP_USER_AGENT] => Mozilla/5.0 (Macintosh; U; Intel Mac OS X 10_6_5; en-us
    [HTTP_ACCEPT] => application/xml,application/xhtml+xml,text/html;q=0.9,text/
    [HTTP_ACCEPT_LANGUAGE] => en-us
    [HTTP_ACCEPT_ENCODING] => gzip, deflate
    [HTTP_CONNECTION] => keep-alive
    [PATH] => /sbin:/usr/sbin:/bin:/usr/bin:/usr/X11R6/bin
    [SERVER_SIGNATURE] =>
Apache/2.0.63 (CentOS) Server at larryullman.com Port 80

    [SERVER_SOFTWARE] => Apache/2.0.63 (CentOS)
    [SERVER_NAME] => larryullman.com
    [SERVER_ADDR] => 207.58.187.78
    [SERVER_PORT] => 80
    [REMOTE_ADDR] => 71.58.97.51
    [DOCUMENT_ROOT] => ███████████████████httpdocs
    [SERVER_ADMIN] => Larry@DMCInsights.com
    [SCRIPT_FILENAME] => ███████████████████httpdocs/predefined.php
    [REMOTE_PORT] => 44766
    [GATEWAY_INTERFACE] => CGI/1.1
    [SERVER_PROTOCOL] => HTTP/1.1
    [REQUEST_METHOD] => GET
    [QUERY_STRING] =>
    [REQUEST_URI] => /predefined.php
    [SCRIPT_NAME] => /predefined.php
    [PHP_SELF] => /predefined.php
    [REQUEST_TIME] => 1289832083
)
```

B With the **predefined.php** page, different servers will generate different results (compare with Figure **A**).

```
Array ( [HTTP_HOST] => phpvqs4:8888 [HTTP_USER_AGENT] => Mozilla/5.0 (Macintosh; U; Intel Mac OS X 10.6; en-US; rv:1.9.2.12) Gecko
/*:q=0.8 [HTTP_ACCEPT_LANGUAGE] => en-us,en;q=0.5 [HTTP_ACCEPT_ENCODING] => gzip,deflate [HTTP_ACCEPT_CHARSET] => I
[HTTP_CACHE_CONTROL] => max-age=0 [PATH] => /usr/bin:/bin:/usr/sbin:/sbin [SERVER_SIGNATURE] => [SERVER_SOFTWARE] => Ap
[REMOTE_ADDR] => 127.0.0.1 [DOCUMENT_ROOT] => /Users/larryullman/Sites/phpvqs4 [SERVER_ADMIN] => you@example.com [SCRIP
[GATEWAY_INTERFACE] => CGI/1.1 [SERVER_PROTOCOL] => HTTP/1.1 [REQUEST_METHOD] => GET [QUERY_STRING] => [REQUE
[REQUEST_TIME] => 1289832176 [argv] => Array ( ) [argc] => 0 )
```

C With large, complex variables such as **$_SERVER**, not using the HTML preformatting tags with **print_r()** creates an incomprehensible mess (compare to Figures **A** and **B**).

Variable Syntax

Now that you've had a quick dip in the variable pool, it's time to investigate the subject further. In the preceding example, the script reported upon PHP's predefined **$_SERVER** variable. You can also create your own variables, once you understand the proper syntax. To create appropriate variable names, you must follow these rules:

- All variable names must be preceded by a dollar sign (**$**).

- Following the dollar sign, the variable name must begin with either a letter (A–Z, a–z) or an underscore (_). It can't begin with a number.

- The rest of the variable name can contain any combination of letters, underscores, and numbers.

- You may not use spaces within the name of a variable. (Instead, the underscore is commonly used to separate words.)

- Each variable must have a unique name.

- Variable names are *case-sensitive*! Consequently, **$variable** and **$Variable** are two different constructs, and it would be a bad idea to use two variables with such similar names.

This last point is perhaps the most important: variable names in PHP are case-sensitive. Using the wrong letter case is a very common cause of bugs. (If you used, for example, **$_server** or **$_Server** in the previous script, you'd see either an error message or nothing at all **A**.)

```
Notice:  Undefined variable: _server in /Users/larryullman/Sites/phpvqs4/predefined.php on line 13
```

A Misspelling a variable's name, including its case, will create undesired and unpredictable results.

Script 2.2 Properly documenting the purposes of variables, along with using meaningful names, is a hallmark of a professional programmer.

```
1   <!DOCTYPE html PUBLIC "-//W3C//DTD XHTML
    1.0 Transitional//EN"
2       "http://www.w3.org/TR/xhtml1/DTD/
        xhtml1-transitional.dtd">
3   <html xmlns="http://www.w3.org/1999/xhtml"
    xml:lang="en" lang="en">
4   <head>
5       <meta http-equiv="Content-Type"
        content="text/html; charset=utf-8"/>
6       <title>Variables and Comments</title>
7   </head>
8   <body>
9   <?php // Script 2.2
10
11  // Define my variables....
12
13  $year = 2011; // The current year.
14  $june_avg = 88; // The average
    temperature for the month of June.
15  $page_title = 'Weather Reports';
    // A title for the page.
16
17  // ... and so forth.
18
19  ?>
20  </body>
21  </html>
```

TABLE 2.1 Valid Variables in PHP

Name
`$first_name`
`$person`
`$address1`
`$_SERVER`

TABLE 2.2 Invalid Variables in PHP

Name	Reason
`$first name`	Has a space
`$first.name`	Has a period
`first_name`	Does not begin with **$**
`$1address`	A number cannot follow **$**

To help minimize bugs, I recommend the following policies:

- Always use all lowercase variable names.
- Make your variable names descriptive (e.g., **`$first_name`** is better than **`$fn`**).
- Use comments to indicate the purpose of variables (**Script 2.2**), redundant as that may seem.
- Above all, be consistent with whatever naming convention you choose!

Table 2.1 lists some sample valid variables; **Table 2.2** lists some invalid variables and the rules they violate.

TIP Unlike some other languages, PHP generally doesn't require you to *declare* or *initialize* a variable prior to use. In other words, you *can* refer to variables without first defining them. But it's best not to do that; I try to write my scripts so that every variable is defined or validated before use.

TIP There are two main variable naming conventions, determined by how you delineate words. These are the so-called *camel-hump* or *camel-case* (named because of the way capital letters break up the word—for example, `$FirstName`) and *underscore* (`$first_name`) styles. This book uses the latter convention.

Types of Variables

This book covers the three main PHP variable types: *numbers*, *strings*, and *arrays*. I'll introduce them quickly here, and later chapters will discuss them in more detail:

- Chapter 4, "Using Numbers"
- Chapter 5, "Using Strings"
- Chapter 7, "Using Arrays"

A fourth variable type, *objects*, is introduced in Appendix B, "Resources and Next Steps," but isn't covered in this book. That particular subject is just too advanced for a beginner's guide—in fact, basic coverage of the subject in my *PHP 5 Advanced: Visual QuickPro Guide* (Peachpit Press, 2007) requires over 150 pages!

Numbers

Technically speaking, PHP breaks numbers into two types: *integers* and *floating-point* (also known as *double-precision floating-point* or *doubles*). Due to the lax way PHP handles variables, it won't affect your programming to group the two categories of numbers into one all-inclusive membership. Still, let's briefly discuss the differences between the two, for clarity's sake.

The first type of numbers—integers—are the same as whole numbers. They can be positive or negative but include neither fractions nor decimals. Numbers that use a decimal point (even something like 1.0) are floating-point numbers. You must also use floating-point numbers to refer to fractions, because the only way to express a fraction in PHP is to convert it to its decimal equivalent. Hence, $1\frac{1}{4}$ is written as 1.25. **Table 2.3** lists some sample valid numbers and their formal type; **Table 2.4** lists invalid numbers and the rules they violate.

TIP As you'll soon see, you can quote invalid numbers to turn them into valid strings.

TABLE 2.3 Valid Numbers in PHP

Number	Type
1	Integer
1.0	Floating-point
1972	Integer
19.72	Floating-point
–1	Integer
–1.0	Floating-point

TABLE 2.4 Invalid Numbers in PHP

Number	Reason
1/3	Contains a slash
1996a	Contains a letter
08.02.06	Contains multiple decimals

Strings

A string is any number of characters enclosed within a pair of either single (') or double (") quotation marks. Strings can contain any combination of letters, numbers, symbols, and spaces. Strings can also contain variables.

Here are examples of valid string values:

```
"Hello, world!"
"Hello, $first_name!"
"1/3"
'Hello, world! How are you today?'
"08.02.06"
"1996"
''
```

That last one is an *empty string*—a string that contains no characters.

In short, to create a string, just wrap something within quotation marks. There are cases, however, where you may run into problems. For example:

```
"I said, "How are you?""
```

This string will be tricky and I hinted at the same problem in Chapter 1, "Getting Started with PHP," with respect to printing HTML code. When PHP hits the second quotation mark in the above, it assumes the string ends there; the continuing text (*How...*) causes an error. To use a quotation mark within a string you can *escape* the quotation mark by putting a backslash (\) before it:

```
"I said, \"How are you?\""
```

The backslash tells PHP to treat each escaped quotation mark as part of the *value* of the string, rather than using it as the string's opening or closing indicators.

You can similarly circumvent this problem by using different quotation mark types:

```
'I said, "How are you?"'
"I said, 'How are you?'"
```

TIP Notice that "1996" converts an integer into a string, simply by placing the number within quotes. Essentially, the string contains the characters *1996*, whereas the number (a nonquoted value) would be equal to 1996. It's a fine distinction, and one that won't matter in your code, because you can perform mathematical calculations with the string *1996* just as you can with the number.

TIP Chapter 1 also demonstrated how to create a new line by printing the \n character within double quotation marks. Although escaping a quotation mark prints the quotation mark, escaping an *n* prints a new line, escaping an *r* creates a carriage return, and escaping a *t* creates a tab.

TIP Understanding strings, variables, and the single and double quotation marks is critical to programming with PHP. For this reason, a section at the end of this chapter is dedicated to the subject.

Arrays

Arrays are covered more thoroughly in Chapter 7, but let's look at them briefly here. Whereas a string or a number contains a single value (both are said to be *scalar*), an array can have more than one value assigned to it. You can think of an array as a list or table of values: you can put multiple strings and/or numbers into one array.

Arrays use *keys* to create and retrieve the values they store. The resulting structure—a list of key-value pairs—looks similar to a two-column spreadsheet. Unlike arrays in other programming languages, the array structure in PHP is so flexible that it can use either numbers or strings for both the keys and the values. The array doesn't even need to be consistent in this respect. (All of this will make more sense in Chapter 7, when you start working with specific examples.)

PHP has two different types of arrays, based on the format of the keys. If the array uses numbers for the keys (**Table 2.5**), it's called an *indexed* array. If it uses strings for the keys (**Table 2.6**), it's an *associative* array. In either case, the values in the array can be of any variable type (string, number, and so on).

TIP The array's key is also called its *index*. You'll see these two terms used interchangeably.

TIP An array can, and frequently will, contain other arrays, creating what is called a *multi-dimensional* array.

TIP What PHP calls an *associative array* is called a *hash* in Perl and Ruby, among other languages.

TABLE 2.5 Indexed Array

Key	Value
0	Don
1	Betty
2	Roger
3	Jane

TABLE 2.6 Associative Array

Key	Value
VT	Vermont
NH	New Hampshire
IA	Iowa
PA	Pennsylvania

```
Number is 1
String is Hello, world!
```

A The result of printing the values of two variables.

```
_SERVER is Array
```

B Using the **print** statement on a complex variable type, such as an array, will not have the results you desire.

Variable Values

To assign a value to a variable, regardless of the variable type, you use the equals sign (**=**). Therefore, the equals sign is called the *assignment operator*, because it assigns the value on the right to the variable on the left. For example:

```
$number = 1;
$floating_number = 1.2;
$string = "Hello, world!";
```

As each of these lines represents a complete statement (i.e., an executable action), they each conclude with a semicolon.

To print out the value of a variable, you can use the **print** function:

```
print $number;
print $string;
```

If you want to print a variable's value within a context, you can place the variable's name in the printed string, as long as you use double quotation marks **A**:

```
print "Number is $number";
print "String is $string";
```

Using **print** in this way works for the scalar (single-valued) variable types—numbers and strings. For complex variable types—arrays and objects—you cannot just use **print** **B**:

```
print "SERVER is $_SERVER";
```

As you've already seen, **print_r()** can handle these nonscalar types, and you'll learn other approaches later in the book.

continues on next page

Whether you're dealing with scalar or nonscalar variables, don't forget that printing out their values is an excellent debugging technique when you're having problems with a script!

Because variable types aren't locked in (PHP is referred to as a *weakly typed* language), they can be changed on the fly:

```
$variable = 1;
$variable = "Greetings";
```

If you were to print the value of **$variable** now, the result would be *Greetings*. The following script better demonstrates the concept of assigning values to variables and then accessing those values.

To assign values to and access variables:

1. Create a new PHP script in your text editor or IDE, to be named **variables.php** (Script 2.3).

2. Create the initial HTML tags:

```
<!DOCTYPE html PUBLIC "-//W3C//DTD
→ XHTML 1.0 Transitional//EN"
   "http://www.w3.org/TR/xhtml1/DTD/
   → xhtml1-transitional.dtd">
<html xmlns="http://www.w3.org/
→ 1999/xhtml" xml:lang="en"
→ lang="en">
<head>
   <meta http-equiv="Content-Type"
   → content="text/html;
   → charset=utf-8"/>
   <title>Variables</title>
</head>
<body>
```

Script 2.3 Some basic variables are defined and their values printed by this script.

```
1    <!DOCTYPE html PUBLIC "-//W3C//DTD XHTML
     1.0 Transitional//EN"
2         "http://www.w3.org/TR/xhtml1/DTD/
     xhtml1-transitional.dtd">
3    <html xmlns="http://www.w3.org/1999/xhtml"
     xml:lang="en" lang="en">
4    <head>
5        <meta http-equiv="Content-Type"
         content="text/html; charset=utf-8"/>
6        <title>Variables</title>
7    </head>
8    <body>
9    <?php // Script 2.3 - variables.php
10
11   // An address:
12   $street = "100 Main Street";
13   $city = "State College";
14   $state = "PA";
15   $zip = 16801;
16
17   // Print the address:
18   print "<p>The address is:<br />$street
     <br />$city $state $zip</p>";
19
20   ?>
21   </body>
22   </html>
```

3. Begin the PHP code:

```
<?php // Script 2.3 - variables.php
```

4. Define some number and string variables:

```
$street = "100 Main Street";
$city = "State College";
$state = "PA";
$zip = 16801;
```

These lines create four different variables of both string and number types. The strings are defined using quotation marks, and each variable name follows the syntactical naming rules.

Remember that each statement must conclude with a semicolon and that the variable names are case-sensitive.

5. Print out the values of the variables within some context:

```
print "<p>The address is:<br />
→ $street <br />$city $state
→ $zip</p>";
```

Here a single **print** statement can access all the variables. The entire string to be printed (consisting of text, HTML tags, and variables) is enclosed within double quotation marks. The HTML **
** tags make the text flow over multiple lines in the browser window (remember, the extra space and slash in the break tag are there for sake of XHTML compliance).

continues on next page

6. Complete the PHP section and the HTML page:

```
?>
</body>
</html>
```

7. Save the file as **variables.php**, upload it to your server (or save it to the appropriate directory on your computer), and test it in your Web browser .

TIP If you see a parse error **D** when you run this script, you probably either omitted a semicolon or have an imbalance in your quotation marks.

TIP If one of the variable's values isn't printed out or you see an *Undefined variable* error **E**, you most likely failed to spell a variable name the same way twice.

TIP If you see a blank page, you most likely have an error but PHP's `display_errors` configuration is set to off. See Chapter 3, "HTML Forms and PHP," for details.

● ● ●   Variables

The address is:
100 Main Street
State College PA 16801

C Some variables are assigned values, and then printed within a context.

Parse error: syntax error, unexpected T_VARIABLE in **/Users/larryullman/Sites/phpvqs4/variables.php** on line **15**

D Parse errors are the most common type of PHP error, as you'll discover. They're frequently caused by missing semicolons or an imbalance of quotation marks or parentheses.

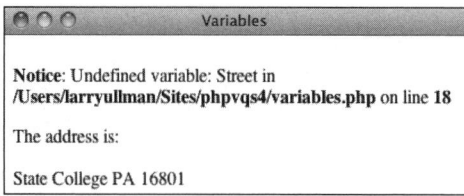

● ● ●   Variables

Notice: Undefined variable: Street in **/Users/larryullman/Sites/phpvqs4/variables.php** on line **18**

The address is:

State College PA 16801

E The *Undefined variable* error indicates that you used a variable with no value (it hasn't been defined). This can happen with misspellings and capitalization inconsistencies.

Script 2.4 This script simply demonstrates how the type of quotation mark you use with variables affects the end result.

```
1    <!DOCTYPE html PUBLIC "-//W3C//DTD XHTML
     1.0 Transitional//EN"
2       "http://www.w3.org/TR/xhtml1/DTD/
        xhtml1-transitional.dtd">
3    <html xmlns="http://www.w3.org/1999/xhtml"
     xml:lang="en" lang="en">
4    <head>
5       <meta http-equiv="content-type"
        content="text/html; charset=utf-8" />
6       <title>Quotes</title>
7    </head>
8    <body>
9    <?php // Script 2.4 - quotes.php
10
11   // Single or double quotation marks
     won't matter here:
12   $first_name = 'Larry';
13   $last_name = "Ullman";
14
15   // Single or double quotation marks DOES
     matter here:
16   $name1 = '$first_name $last_name';
17   $name2 = "$first_name $last_name";
18
19   // Single or double quotation marks DOES
     matter here:
20   print "<h1>Double Quotes</h1><p>name1
     is $name1 <br />
21   name2 is $name2</p>";
22
23   print '<h1>Single Quotes</h1><p>name1
     is $name1 <br />
24   name2 is $name2</p>';
25
26   ?>
27   </body>
28   </html>
```

Understanding Quotation Marks

Now that you know the basics of variables and how to create them, I want to make sure you completely understand how to properly use quotation marks. PHP, like most programming languages, allows you to use both double (") and single (') quotation marks—but they give vastly different results. It's critical that you comprehend the distinction, so the next example will run tests using both types.

The rule to remember is: *Items within single quotation marks are treated literally; items within double quotation marks are extrapolated.* This means that within double quotation marks, a variable's name is replaced with its value, as in Script 2.3, but the same is not true for single quotation marks.

This rule applies anywhere in PHP you might use quotation marks, including uses of the **print** function and the assignment of values to string variables. An example is the best way to demonstrate this critical concept.

To use quotation marks:

1. Begin a new PHP script in your text editor or IDE, to be named **quotes.php** (**Script 2.4**).

2. Create the initial HTML tags:

```
<!DOCTYPE html PUBLIC "-//W3C//DTD
→ XHTML 1.0 Transitional//EN"
  "http://www.w3.org/TR/xhtml1/
  → DTD/xhtml1-transitional.dtd">
<html xmlns="http://www.w3.org/
→ 1999/xhtml" xml:lang="en"
→ lang="en">
```

continues on next page

```
<head>
  <meta http-equiv="content-type"
  → content="text/html;
  → charset=utf-8" />
  <title>Quotes</title>
</head>
<body>
```

3. Begin the PHP code:

```
<?php // Script 2.4 - quotes.php
```

4. Create two string variables:

```
$first_name = 'Larry';
$last_name = "Ullman";
```

It doesn't matter whether you use single or double quotation marks for these two variables, as each string can be treated literally. However, if you're using your own name here (and feel free to do so) and it contains an apostrophe, you'll need to either use double quotation marks or escape the apostrophe within single quotation marks:

```
$last_name = "O'Toole";
$last_name = 'O\'Toole';
```

5. Create two different *name* variables, using the existing first- and last-name variables:

```
$name1 = '$first_name $last_name';
$name2 = "$first_name
→ $last_name";
```

In these lines it makes a huge difference which quotation marks you use. The **$name1** variable is now literally equal to *$first_name $last_name*, because no extrapolation occurs. Conversely, **$name2** is equal to *Larry Ullman*, presumably the intended result.

6. Print out the variables using both types of quotation marks:

```
print "<h1>Double Quotes
→ </h1><p>name1 is $name1 <br />
name2 is $name2</p>";
print '<h1>Single Quotes
→ </h1><p>name1 is $name1 <br />
name2 is $name2</p>';
```

Again, the quotation marks make all the difference here. The first **print** statement, using double quotation marks, prints out the values of the **$name1** and **$name2** variables, whereas the second, using single quotation marks, prints out *$name1* and *$name2* literally.

The HTML in the **print** statements makes them more legible in the browser, and each statement is executed over two lines, which is perfectly acceptable.

7. Complete the PHP section and the HTML page:

```
?>
</body>
</html>
```

Double Quotes

name1 is $first_name $last_name
name2 is Larry Ullman

Single Quotes

name1 is $name1
name2 is $name2

A The different quotation marks (single versus double) dictate whether the variable's name or value is printed.

8. Save the file as **quotes.php**, upload it to your server (or save it to the appropriate directory on your computer), and test it in your Web browser **A**.

TIP If you're still confused about the distinction between the two types of quotation marks, stick with double quotation marks and you'll be safer.

TIP Arguably, using single quotation marks when you can is marginally preferable, as PHP won't need to search the strings looking for variables. But, at best, this is a minor point.

TIP The shortcuts for creating newlines (\n), carriage returns (\r), and tabs (\t) must also be used within double quotation marks to have the desired effect.

TIP Remember that you don't always need to use quotation marks at all. When assigning a numeric value or when only printing a variable, you can omit them:

```
$num = 2;
print $num;
```

Review and Pursue

If you have any problems with the review questions or the pursue prompts, turn to the book's supporting forum (www.LarryUllman.com/forum/).

Review

- What kind of variable is **$_SERVER** an example of?
- What character must all variables begin with?
- What characters can be used first in a variable's name? What other characters can be used in a variable's name, after the first character?
- Are variable names case-sensitive or case-insensitive?
- What does it mean to say that a variable is *scalar*? What are examples of scalar variable types? What is an example of a nonscalar variable type?
- What is the assignment operator?
- What great debugging technique—with respect to variables—was introduced in this chapter?
- What is the difference between using single or double quotation marks?

Pursue

- Create another PHP script that defines some variables and prints their values. Try using variables of different scalar types.
- Create a PHP script that prints the value of some variables within some HTML. More sophisticated practice might involve using PHP and variables to create a link or image tag.

3
HTML Forms and PHP

The previous chapter provided a brief introduction to the topic of variables. Although you'll often create your own variables, you'll also commonly use variables in conjunction with HTML forms. Forms are a fundamental unit of today's Web sites, enabling such features as registration and login systems, search capability, and online shopping. Even the simplest site will find logical reasons to incorporate HTML forms. And with PHP, it's stunningly simple to receive and handle data generated by them.

With that in mind, this chapter will cover the basics of creating HTML forms and explain how the submitted form data is available to a PHP script. This chapter will also introduce several key concepts of real PHP programming, including how to manage errors in your scripts.

In This Chapter

Creating a Simple Form	50
Choosing a Form Method	54
Receiving Form Data in PHP	57
Displaying Errors	61
Error Reporting	64
Manually Sending Data to a Page	67
Review and Pursue	72

Creating a Simple Form

For the HTML form example in this chapter, you'll create a feedback page that takes the user's salutation, name, email address, response, and comments **Ⓐ**. The code that generates a form goes between opening and closing **form** tags:

```
<form>
form elements
</form>
```

The **form** tags dictate where a form begins and ends. Every element of the form must be entered between these two tags. The opening **form** tag also contains an **action** attribute. It indicates the page to which the form data should be submitted. This value is one of the most important considerations when you're creating a form. In this book, the **action** attributes will always point to PHP scripts:

```
<form action="somepage.php">
```

Before creating this next form, let's briefly revisit the topic of XHTML. As stated in the first chapter, XHTML has some rules that result in a significantly different syntax than HTML. For starters, the code needs to be in all lowercase letters, and every tag attribute must be enclosed in quotes. Further, every tag must be closed; those that don't have formal closing tags, like **input**, are closed by adding a blank space and a slash at the end. Thus, in HTML you might write

```
<INPUT TYPE=TEXT NAME=address
 ⇢ SIZE=40>
```

but in XHTML you'd write

```
<input type="text" name="address"
 ⇢ size="40" />
```

Ⓐ The HTML form that will be used in this chapter's examples.

```
1   <!DOCTYPE html PUBLIC "-//W3C//DTD XHTML
    1.0 Transitional//EN"
2       "http://www.w3.org/TR/xhtml1/DTD/
        xhtml1-transitional.dtd">
3   <html xmlns="http://www.w3.org/1999/
    xhtml" xml:lang="en" lang="en">
4   <head>
5       <meta http-equiv="Content-Type"
        content="text/html; charset=utf-8"/>
6       <title>Feedback Form</title>
7   </head>
8   <body>
9   <!-- Script 3.1 - feedback.html -->
10  <div><p>Please complete this form to
    submit your feedback:</p>
11
12  <form action="handle_form.php">
13
14      <p>Name: <select name="title">
15      <option value="Mr.">Mr.</option>
16      <option value="Mrs.">Mrs.</option>
17      <option value="Ms.">Ms.</option>
18      </select> <input type="text"
        name="name" size="20" /></p>
19
20      <p>Email Address: <input
        type="text" name="email"
        size="20" /></p>
21
22      <p>Response: This is...
23      <input type="radio"
        name="response" value="excellent" />
        excellent
24      <input type="radio"
        name="response" value="okay" />
        okay
25      <input type="radio"
        name="response" value="boring" />
        boring</p>
26
27      <p>Comments: <textarea
        name="comments" rows="3"
        cols="30"></textarea></p>
28
29      <input type="submit" name="submit"
        value="Send My Feedback" />
30
31  </form>
32  </div>
33  </body>
34  </html>
```

Hopefully this quick explanation will help you understand the XHTML in the following script.

Finally, in both HTML and XHTML, each form element needs to have its own unique name. Stick to a consistent naming convention when naming elements, using only letters, numbers, and the underscore (_). The result should be names that are also logical and descriptive.

To create a basic HTML form:

1. Begin a new document in your text editor or IDE, to be named **feedback.html** (Script 3.1):

   ```
   <!DOCTYPE html PUBLIC "-//W3C//DTD
   → XHTML 1.0 Transitional//EN"
     "http://www.w3.org/TR/xhtml1/
     → DTD/xhtml1-transitional.dtd">
   <html xmlns="http://www.w3.org/
   → 1999/xhtml" xml:lang="en"
   → lang="en">
   <head>
     <meta http-equiv="Content-Type"
     → content="text/html;
     → charset=utf-8"/>
     <title>Feedback Form</title>
   </head>
   <body>
   <!-- Script 3.1 - feedback.html -->
   <div><p>Please complete this form
   → to submit your feedback:</p>
   ```

2. Add the opening **form** tag:

   ```
   <form action="handle_form.php">
   ```

   The **form** tag indicates that this form will be submitted to the page **handle_form. php**, found within the same directory as this HTML page. You can use a full URL to the PHP script, if you'd prefer to be explicit (e.g., **http://www.example.com/ handle_form.php**).

   continues on next page

3. Add a select menu plus a text input for the person's name:

```
<p>Name: <select name="title">
<option value="Mr.">Mr.</option>
<option value="Mrs.">Mrs.</option>
<option value="Ms.">Ms.</option>
</select> <input type="text"
name="name" size="20" /></p>
```

The inputs for the person's name will consist of two elements 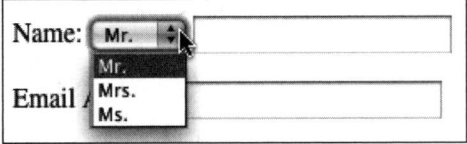. The first is a drop-down menu of common titles: *Mr.*, *Mrs.*, and *Ms.* Each option listed between the **select** tags is an answer the user can choose **B**. The second element is a basic text box for the person's full name.

4. Add a text input for the user's email address:

```
<p>Email Address: <input
→ type="text" name="email"
→ size="20" /></p>
```

5. Add radio buttons for a response:

```
<p>Response: This is...
<input type="radio" name="response"
→ value="excellent" /> excellent
<input type="radio" name="response"
→ value="okay" /> okay
<input type="radio" name="response"
→ value="boring" /> boring</p>
```

This HTML code creates three radio buttons (clickable circles, **A**). Because they all have the same **name** value, only one of the three can be selected at a time. Per XHTML rules, the code is in lowercase except for the values, and an extra space and slash are added to the end of each input to close the tag.

B The **select** element creates a drop-down menu of options.

6. Add a **textarea** to record the comments:

```
<p>Comments: <textarea
→ name="comments" rows="3"
→ cols="30"></textarea></p>
```

A **textarea** gives users more space to enter their comments than a text input would. However, the text input lets you limit how much information users can enter, which you can't do with the **textarea** (not without using JavaScript, that is). When you're creating a form, choose input types appropriate to the information you wish to retrieve from the user.

Note that a **textarea** *does* have a closing tag.

7. Add the submit button:

```
<input type="submit" name="submit"
→ value="Send My Feedback" />
```

The **value** attribute of a submit element is what appears on the button in the Web browser **Ⓐ**. You could also use *Go!* or *Submit*, for example.

8. Close the form:

```
</form>
```

9. Complete the page:

```
</div>
</body>
</html>
```

10. Save the page as **feedback.html** and view it in your browser.

Because this is an HTML page, not a PHP script, you could view it in your Web browser directly from your computer.

TIP Note that feedback.html uses the HTML extension because it's a standard HTML page (not a PHP script). You could use the .php extension without a problem, even though there's no actual PHP code. (Remember that in a PHP page, anything not within the PHP tags—<?php and ?>—is assumed to be HTML.)

TIP Be certain that your action attribute correctly points to an existing file on the server, or your form won't be processed properly. In this case, the form will be submitted to handle_form.php, to be located in the same directory as the feedback.html page.

TIP In this example, an HTML form is created by hand-coding the HTML, but you can do this in a Web page application (such as Adobe Dreamweaver) if you're more comfortable with that approach.

TIP One welcome addition in the forthcoming HTML 5 specification are new form elements, such as email, url, and number.

Choosing a Form Method

The experienced HTML developer will notice that the feedback form just created is missing one thing: The initial **form** tag has no **method** attribute. The **method** attribute tells the server how to transmit the data from the form to the handling script.

You have two choices with **method**: GET and POST. With respect to forms, the difference between using GET and POST is squarely in how the information is passed from the form to the processing script. The GET method sends all the gathered information along as part of the URL. The POST method transmits the information invisibly to the user. For example, upon submitting a form, if you use the GET method, the resulting URL will be something like

```
http://www.example.com/page.php?
→ some_var=some_value&age=20&...
```

Following the name of the script, **page.php**, is a question mark, followed by one *name=value* pair for each piece of data submitted.

When using the POST method, the end user will only see

```
http://www.example.com/page.php
```

When deciding which method to use, keep in mind these four factors:

- With the GET method, a limited amount of information can be passed.

- The GET method sends the data to the handling script publicly (which means, for example, that a password entered in a form would be viewable by anyone within eyesight of the Web browser, creating a larger security risk).

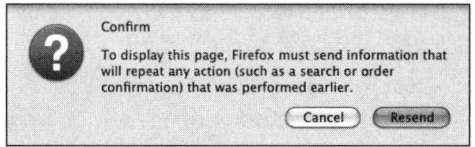

A If users refresh a PHP script that data has been sent to via the POST method, they will be asked to confirm the action (the specific message will differ using other browsers).

Script 3.2 The **method** attribute with a value of *post* is added to complete the form.

```
1    <!DOCTYPE html PUBLIC "-//W3C//DTD XHTML
     1.0 Transitional//EN"
2        "http://www.w3.org/TR/xhtml1/DTD/
     xhtml1-transitional.dtd">
3    <html xmlns="http://www.w3.org/1999/
     xhtml" xml:lang="en" lang="en">
4    <head>
5        <meta http-equiv="Content-Type"
         content="text/html; charset=utf-8"/>
6        <title>Feedback Form</title>
7    </head>
8    <body>
9    <!-- Script 3.2 - feedback.html -->
10   <div><p>Please complete this form to
     submit your feedback:</p>
11
12   <form action="handle_form.php"
     method="post">
13
14       <p>Name: <select name="title">
15       <option value="Mr.">Mr.</option>
16       <option value="Mrs.">Mrs.</option>
17       <option value="Ms.">Ms.</option>
18       </select> <input type="text"
         name="name" size="20" /></p>
19
20       <p>Email Address: <input type="text"
         name="email" size="20" /></p>
21
22       <p>Response: This is...
23       <input type="radio" name="response"
         value="excellent" /> excellent
24       <input type="radio" name="response"
         value="okay" /> okay
25       <input type="radio" name="response"
         value="boring" /> boring</p>
26
27       <p>Comments: <textarea name="comments"
         rows="3" cols="30"></textarea></p>
28
29       <input type="submit" name="submit"
         value="Send My Feedback" />
30
31   </form>
32   </div>
33   </body>
34   </html>
```

- A page generated by a form that used the GET method can be bookmarked, but one based on POST can't be.

- Users will be prompted if they attempt to reload a page accessed via POST Ⓐ, but will not be prompted for pages accessed via GET.

Generally speaking, GET requests are used when asking for information from the server. Search pages almost always use GET (check out the URLs the next time you use a search engine), as do sites that paginate results (like the ability to browse categories of products). Conversely, POST is normally used to trigger a server-based action. This might be the submission of a contact form (result: an email gets sent) or the submission of a blog's comment form (result: a comment is added to the database and therefore the page).

This book uses POST almost exclusively for handling forms, although you'll also see a useful technique involving the GET method (see "Manually Sending Data to a Page" at the end of this chapter).

To add a method to a form:

1. Open **feedback.html** (Script 3.1) in your text editor or IDE, if it is not already open.

2. Within the initial **form** tag, add **method="post"** (Script 3.2, line 12).

   The form's **method** attribute tells the browser how to send the form data to the receiving script. Because there may be a lot of data in the form's submission (including the comments), and because it wouldn't make sense for the user to bookmark the resulting page, POST is the logical method to use.

continues on next page

3. Save the script and reload it in your Web browser.

   It's important that you get in the habit of reloading pages in the Web browser after you make changes. It's quite easy to forget the reloading step and find yourself flummoxed when your changes are not being reflected.

4. View the source of the page to make sure all the required elements are present and have the correct attributes **B**.

TIP In the discussion of the methods, **GET** and **POST** are written in capital letters to make them stand out. However, the form in the script uses *post* for XHTML compliance. Don't worry about this inconsistency (if you caught it at all)—the method will work regardless of case.

```
<!DOCTYPE html PUBLIC "-//W3C//DTD XHTML 1.0 Transitional//EN"
        "http://www.w3.org/TR/xhtml1/DTD/xhtml1-transitional.dtd">
<html xmlns="http://www.w3.org/1999/xhtml" xml:lang="en" lang="en">
<head>
        <meta http-equiv="Content-Type" content="text/html; charset=utf-8"/>
        <title>Feedback Form</title>
</head>
<body>
<!-- Script 3.2 - feedback.html -->
<div><p>Please complete this form to submit your feedback:</p>

<form action="handle_form.php" method="post">

        <p>Name: <select name="title">
        <option value="Mr.">Mr.</option>
        <option value="Mrs.">Mrs.</option>
        <option value="Ms.">Ms.</option>
        </select> <input type="text" name="name" size="20" /></p>

        <p>Email Address: <input type="text" name="email" size="20" /></p>

        <p>Response: This is...
        <input type="radio" name="response" value="excellent" /> excellent
        <input type="radio" name="response" value="okay" /> okay
        <input type="radio" name="response" value="boring" /> boring</p>

        <p>Comments: <textarea name="comments" rows="3" cols="30"></textarea></p>

        <input type="submit" name="submit" value="Send My Feedback" />

</form>
</div>
</body>
</html>
```

B With forms, much of the important information, such as the **action** and **method** values or element names, can only be seen within the HTML source code.

Receiving Form Data in PHP

Now that you've created a basic HTML form capable of taking input from a user, you need to write the PHP script that will receive and process the submitted form data. For this example, the PHP script will simply repeat what the user entered into the form. In later chapters, you'll learn how to take this information and store it in a database, send it in an email, write it to a file, and so forth.

To access the submitted form data, you need to refer to a particular *predefined variable*. Chapter 2, "Variables," already introduced one predefined variable: **$_SERVER**. When it comes to handling form data, the specific variable the PHP script would refer to is either **$_GET** or **$_POST**. If an HTML form uses the GET method, the submitted form data will be found in **$_GET**. When an HTML form uses the POST method, the submitted form data will be found in **$_POST**.

$_GET and **$_POST**, besides being predefined variables (i.e., ones you don't need to create), are *arrays*, a special variable type (**$_SERVER** is also an array). This means that both **$_GET** and **$_POST** may contain numerous values, making the printing of those values more challenging. You cannot treat arrays like so (also see Figure B under "Variable Values" in Chapter 2):

```
print $_POST; // Will not work!
```

Instead, to access a specific value, you must refer to the array's *index* or *key*. Chapter 7, "Using Arrays," goes into this subject in detail, but the premise is simple. Start with a form element whose **name** attribute has a value of *something*:

```
<input type="text" name="something" />
```

Then, assuming that the form uses the POST method, the value entered into that form element would be available in **$_POST['something']**:

```
print $_POST['something'];
```

Unfortunately, there is one little hitch here: When used within double quotation marks, the single quotation marks around the key will cause parse errors Ⓐ:

```
print "Thanks for saying:
→ $_POST['something']";
```

There are a couple of ways you can avoid this problem. This chapter will use the solution that's syntactically the simplest: just assign the particular **$_POST** element to another variable first:

```
$something = $_POST['something'];
print "Thanks for saying: $something";
```

Two final notes before implementing this information in a new PHP script: First, as with all variables in PHP, **$_POST** is case-sensitive: it must be typed exactly as you see it here (a dollar sign, one underscore, then all capital letters). Second, the indexes in **$_POST**—*something* in the preceding example—must exactly match the **name** attributes values in the corresponding form element.

```
Parse error: syntax error, unexpected
T_ENCAPSED_AND_WHITESPACE, expecting T_STRING or
T_VARIABLE or T_NUM_STRING in /Users/larryullman/Sites
/phpvqs4/handle_form.php on line 19
```

Ⓐ This ugly parse error is created by attempting to use **$_POST['something']** within double quotation marks.

To handle an HTML form:

1. Begin a new document in your text editor or IDE, to be named **handle_form.php** (Script 3.3):

```
<!DOCTYPE html PUBLIC "-//W3C//DTD
→XHTML 1.0 Transitional//EN"
  "http://www.w3.org/TR/xhtml1/DTD/
  →xhtml1-transitional.dtd">
<html xmlns="http://www.w3.org/
→1999/xhtml" xml:lang="en"
→lang="en">
<head>
  <meta http-equiv="Content-Type"
  →content="text/html;
  →charset=utf-8"/>
  <title>Your Feedback</title>
</head>
<body>
```

2. Add the opening PHP tag and any comments:

```
<?php // Script 3.3 handle_form.php
// This page receives the data
→from feedback.html.
// It will receive: title, name,
→email, response, comments, and
→submit in $_POST.
```

Comments are added to the script to make the script's purpose clear. Even though the **feedback.html** page indicates where the data is sent (via the **action** attribute), a comment here indicates the reverse (where this script is getting its data). It also helps to spell out the exact form element names, in a case-sensitive manner.

3. Assign the received data to new variables:

```
$title = $_POST['title'];
$name = $_POST['name'];
$response = $_POST['response'];
$comments = $_POST['comments'];
```

Script 3.3 This script displays the form data submitted to it by referencing the associated **$_POST** variables.

```
1   <!DOCTYPE html PUBLIC "-//W3C//DTD XHTML
    1.0 Transitional//EN"
2       "http://www.w3.org/TR/xhtml1/DTD/
    xhtml1-transitional.dtd">
3   <html xmlns="http://www.w3.org/1999/
    xhtml" xml:lang="en" lang="en">
4   <head>
5       <meta http-equiv="Content-Type"
    content="text/html; charset=utf-8"/>
6       <title>Your Feedback</title>
7   </head>
8   <body>
9   <?php // Script 3.3 handle_form.php
10
11  // This page receives the data from
    feedback.html.
12  // It will receive: title, name, email,
    response, comments, and submit in $_POST.
13
14  // Create shorthand versions of the
    variables:
15  $title = $_POST['title'];
16  $name = $_POST['name'];
17  $response = $_POST['response'];
18  $comments = $_POST['comments'];
19
20  // Print the received data:
21  print "<p>Thank you, $title $name,
    for your comments.</p>
22  <p>You stated that you found this
    example to be '$response' and
    added:<br />$comments</p>";
23
24  ?>
25  </body>
26  </html>
```

Magic Quotes

Earlier versions of PHP had a feature called *Magic Quotes*, which has since been deprecated (meaning you shouldn't use it and it will be removed from the language in time). Magic Quotes—when enabled—automatically escapes single and double quotation marks found in submitted form data. So the string *I'd like more information* would be turned into *I\'d like more information*.

The escaping of potentially problematic characters can be useful and even necessary in some situations. But if the Magic Quotes feature is enabled on your PHP installation, you'll see these backslashes when the PHP script prints out the form data. You can undo its effect using the **stripslashes()** function. To apply it to the **handle_form.php** script, you would do this, for example:

```
$comments = stripslashes
→ ($_POST['comments']);
```

instead of just this:

```
$comments = $_POST['comments'];
```

That will have the effect of converting an escaped submitted string back to its original, non-escaped value.

If you're not seeing extraneous slashes added to submitted form data, you don't need to worry about Magic Quotes.

Again, since the form uses the POST method, the submitted data can be found in the **$_POST** array. The individual values are accessed using the syntax **$_POST['*name_attribute_value*']**. This works regardless of the form element's type (input, select, checkbox, etc.).

To make it easier to use these values in a **print** statement in Step 4, each value is assigned to a new variable in this step. Neither **$_POST['email']** nor **$_POST['submit']** is being addressed, but you can create variables for those values if you'd like.

4. Print out the user information:

```
print "<p>Thank you, $title $name,
→ for your comments.</p>
<p>You stated that you found this
→ example to be '$response' and
→ added:<br />$comments</p>";
```

This one **print** statement uses the four variables within a context to show the user what data the script received.

5. Close the PHP section and complete the HTML page:

```
?>
</body>
</html>
```

6. Save the script as **handle_form.php**.

Note that the name of this file must exactly match the value of the **action** attribute in the form.

7. Upload the script to the server (or store it in the proper directory on your computer if you've installed PHP), making sure it's saved in the same directory as **feedback.html**.

continues on next page

8. Load **feedback.html** in your Web browser through a URL (*http://something*).

   You must load the HTML form through a URL so that when it's submitted to the PHP script, that PHP script is also run through a URL. *PHP scripts must always be run through a URL!*

   Failure to load a form through a URL is a common beginner's mistake.

9. Fill out **B**, and then submit the form **C**.

   If you see a blank page, read the next section of the chapter for how to display the errors that presumably occurred.

   If you see an error notice **D** or see that a variable does not have a value when printed, you likely misspelled either the form element's **name** value or the **$_POST** array's index (or you filled out the form incompletely).

> **TIP** If you want to pass a preset value along to a PHP script, use the *hidden* type of input within your HTML form. For example, the line

```
<input type="hidden" name="form_page"
value="feedback.html" />
```

inserted between the form tags will create a variable in the handling script called **$_POST['form_page']** with the value **feedback.html**.

> **TIP** Notice that the value of radio button and certain menu variables is based on the **value** attribute of the selected item (for example, *excellent* from the radio button). This is also true for checkboxes. For text boxes, the value of the variable is what the user typed.

> **TIP** If the **handle_form.php** script displays extra slashes in submitted strings, see the "Magic Quotes" sidebar for an explanation and solution.

> **TIP** You can also access form data, regardless of the form's method, in the **$_REQUEST** pre-defined variable. **$_GET** and **$_POST** are more precise, however, and therefore preferable.

Please complete this form to submit your feedback:

Name: (Mr. ♦) Larry Ullman

Email Address: larry@example.com

Response: This is... ⦿ excellent ○ okay ○ boring

Comments: No problems so far!

(Send My Feedback)

B Whatever the user enters into the HTML form should be printed out to the Web browser by the **handle_form.php** script **C**.

Thank you, Mr. Larry Ullman, for your comments.

You stated that you found this example to be 'excellent' and added: No problems so far!

C This is another application of the **print** statement discussed in Chapter 1, but it constitutes your first dynamically generated Web page.

Notice: Undefined index: Name in **/Users/larryullman/Sites /phpvqs4/handle_form.php** on line **16**

Thank you, Mr. , for your comments.

D Notices like these occur when a script refers to a variable that doesn't exist. In this particular case, the cause is erroneously referring to **$_POST['Name']** when it should be **$_POST['name']**.

Displaying Errors

One of the very first issues that arise when it comes to debugging PHP scripts is that you may or may not even see the errors that occur. After you install PHP on a Web server, it will run under a default configuration with respect to security, performance, how it handles data, and so forth. One of the default settings is to not display any errors. In other words, the **display_errors** setting will be off **A**. When that's the case, what you might see when a script has an error is a blank page. (This is the norm on fresh installations of PHP; most hosting companies will enable **display_errors**.)

The reason that errors should not be displayed on a live site is that it's a security risk. Simply put, PHP's errors often give away too much information for the public at large to see (not to mention showing PHP errors looks unprofessional). But you, the developer, *do need* to see these errors in order to fix them!

To have PHP display errors, you can do one of the following:

- Turn **display_errors** back on for PHP as a whole. (See the "Configuring PHP" section of Appendix A, "Installation and Configuration," for more information.)

- Turn **display_errors** back on for an individual script.

continues on next page

display_errors	Off	Off
display_startup_errors	On	On
doc_root	*no value*	*no value*
docref_ext	*no value*	*no value*
docref_root	*no value*	*no value*
enable_dl	On	On
error_append_string	*no value*	*no value*
error_log	/Applications/MAMP/logs/php_error.log	/Applications/MAMP/logs/php_error.log
error_prepend_string	*no value*	*no value*
error_reporting	32767	32767

A Run a `phpinfo()` script (e.g., Script 1.2) to view your server's **display_errors** setting.

While developing a site, the first option is by far preferred. However, it's only a possibility for those with administrative control over the server. Anyone can use the second option by including this line in a script:

```
ini_set ('display_errors', 1);
```

The **ini_set()** function allows a script to temporarily override a setting in PHP's configuration file (many, but not all, settings can be altered this way). The previous example changes the **display_errors** setting to *on*, which is represented by the number 1.

Although this second method can be implemented by anyone, the downside is that if your script contains certain kinds of errors (discussed next), the script cannot be executed. In that situation, this line of code won't be executed, and the particular error—or any that prevents a script from running at all—still results in a blank page.

To display errors in a script:

1. Open **handle_form.php** in your text editor or IDE, if it is not already open.

2. As the first line of PHP code, enter the following (**Script 3.4**):

   ```
   ini_set ('display_errors', 1);
   ```

   Again, this line tells PHP you'd like to see any errors that occur. You should call it first thing in your PHP section so the rest of the PHP code will abide by this new setting.

3. Save the file as **handle_form.php**.

Script 3.4 This addition to the PHP script turns on the **display_errors** directive so that errors will be shown.

```
1   <!DOCTYPE html PUBLIC "-//W3C//DTD XHTML
    1.0 Transitional//EN"
2       "http://www.w3.org/TR/xhtml1/DTD/
    xhtml1-transitional.dtd">
3   <html xmlns="http://www.w3.org/1999/
    xhtml" xml:lang="en" lang="en">
4   <head>
5       <meta http-equiv="Content-Type"
    content="text/html; charset=utf-8"/>
6       <title>Your Feedback</title>
7   </head>
8   <body>
9   <?php // Script 3.4 - handle_form.php #2
10
11  ini_set ('display_errors', 1);
    // Let me learn from my mistakes!
12
13  // This page receives the data from
    feedback.html.
14  // It will receive: title, name, email,
    response, comments, and submit in
    $_POST.
15
16  // Create shorthand versions of the
    variables:
17  $title = $_POST['title'];
18  $name = $_POST['name'];
19  $response = $_POST['response'];
20  $comments = $_POST['comments'];
21
22  // Print the received data:
23  print "<p>Thank you, $title $name, for
    your comments.</p>
24  <p>You stated that you found this
    example to be '$response' and added:
    <br />$comments</p>";
25
26  ?>
27  </body>
28  </html>
```

Please complete this form to submit your feedback:

Name: [Mr. ⬍] [Larry Ullman]

Email Address: [   ]

Response: This is... ⊙ excellent ⊙ okay ⊙ boring

Comments: [   ]

(Send My Feedback)

B Incompletely filling out the form...

Notice: Undefined index: response in **/Users/larryullman/Sites/phpvqs4/handle_form.php** on line 19

Thank you, Mr. Larry Ullman, for your comments.

You stated that you found this example to be " and added:

C ...results in error messages. These notices are generated by references to form elements for which there are no values.

4. Upload the file to your Web server and test it in your Web browser (**B** and **C**).

If the resulting page has no errors in it, then the script will run as it did before. If you saw a blank page when you ran the form earlier, you should now see messages like those in **C**. Again, if you see such errors, you likely misspelled the name of a form element, misspelled the index in the **$_POST** array, or didn't fill out the form completely.

TIP Make sure `display_errors` is enabled any time you're having difficulties debugging a script. If you installed PHP on your computer, I *highly* recommend enabling it in your PHP configuration while you learn (again, see Appendix A).

TIP If you see a blank page when running a PHP script, also check the HTML source code for errors or other problems.

TIP Remember that the `display_errors` directive only controls whether error messages are sent to the Web browser. It doesn't create errors or prevent them from occurring in any way.

TIP Failure to use an equals sign after *name* in a form element will also cause problems:

```
<input name"something" />
```

Error Reporting

Another PHP configuration issue you should be aware of, along with `display_errors`, is *error reporting*. There are eleven different types of errors in PHP, plus four user-defined types (which aren't covered in this book). **Table 3.1** lists the four most important general error types, along with a description and example of each.

You can set what errors PHP reports on in two ways. First, you can adjust the `error_reporting` level in PHP's configuration file (again, see Appendix A). If you are running your own PHP server, you'll probably want to adjust that global setting while developing your scripts.

The second option is to use the `error_reporting()` function in a script. The function takes either a number or one or more *constants* (nonquoted strings with predetermined meanings) to adjust the levels. The most important of these constants are listed in **Table 3.2**.

TABLE 3.1 PHP Error Types

Type	Description	Example
Notice	Nonfatal error that may or may not be indicative of a problem	Referring to a variable that has no value
Warning	Nonfatal error that is most likely problematic	Misusing a function
Parse error	Fatal error caused by a syntactical mistake	Omission of a semicolon or an imbalance of quotation marks, braces, or parentheses
Error	A general fatal error	Memory allocation problem

TABLE 3.2 Error Reporting Constants

Name
E_NOTICE
E_WARNING
E_PARSE
E_ERROR
E_ALL
E_STRICT
E_DEPRECATED

Script 3.5 Adjust a script's level of error reporting to give you more or less feedback on potential and existing problems. In my opinion, more is always better.

```
1   <!DOCTYPE html PUBLIC "-//W3C//DTD XHTML
    1.0 Transitional//EN"
2      "http://www.w3.org/TR/xhtml1/DTD/
       xhtml1-transitional.dtd">
3   <html xmlns="http://www.w3.org/1999/
    xhtml" xml:lang="en" lang="en">
4   <head>
5      <meta http-equiv="Content-Type"
       content="text/html; charset=utf-8"/>
6      <title>Your Feedback</title>
7   </head>
8   <body>
9   <?php // Script 3.5 - handle_form.php #3
10
11  ini_set ('display_errors', 1);
    // Let me learn from my mistakes!
12  error_reporting (E_ALL | E_STRICT);
    // Show all possible problems!
13
14  // This page receives the data from
    feedback.html.
15  // It will receive: title, name, email,
    response, comments, and submit in
    $_POST.
16
17  // Create shorthand versions of the
    variables:
18  $title = $_POST['title'];
19  $name = $_POST['name'];
20  $response = $_POST['response'];
21  $comments = $_POST['comments'];
22
23  // Print the received data:
24  print "<p>Thank you, $title $name, for
    your comments.</p>
25  <p>You stated that you found this
    example to be '$response' and added:
    <br />$comments</p>";
26
27  ?>
28  </body>
29  </html>
```

Using this information, you could add any of the following to a script:

```
error_reporting (0);
error_reporting (E_ALL);
error_reporting (E_ALL & ~E_NOTICE);
```

The first line says that no errors should be reported. The second requests that all errors be reported. The last example states that you want to see all error messages except notices (the **&** ~ means *and not*). Keep in mind that adjusting this setting doesn't prevent or create errors; it just affects whether or not errors are reported.

It's generally best to develop and test PHP scripts using the highest level of error reporting possible. To accomplish that, declare that you want *all errors plus strict* error reporting:

```
error_reporting (E_ALL | E_STRICT);
```

The **E_ALL** setting does not include **E_STRICT**, which is why that line says that all errors should be shown *or* (the vertical bar, called the *pipe*) strict errors should be shown. This latter setting takes reporting a step further, also raising notices for things that could be a problem in future versions of PHP. Let's apply this setting to the **handle_form.php** page.

To adjust error reporting in a script:

1. Open **handle_form.php** (Script 3.4) in your text editor or IDE, if it is not already.

2. After the **ini_set()** line, add the following (**Script 3.5**):

   ```
   error_reporting (E_ALL | E_STRICT);
   ```

3. Save the file as **handle_form.php**.

continues on next page

4. Place the file in the proper directory for your PHP-enabled server and test it in your Web browser by submitting the form (**A** and **B**).

At this point, if the form is filled out completely and the **$_POST** indexes exactly match the names of the form elements, you shouldn't see any errors (as in the figures). If any problems exist, including any potential problems (thanks to **E_STRICT**), they should be displayed and reported.

> **TIP** The PHP manual lists all the error-reporting levels, but those listed here are the most important.

> **TIP** The code in this book was tested using the highest level of error reporting: **E_ALL | E_STRICT**.

Please complete this form to submit your feedback:

Name: [Ms. ▼] Blankenship

Email Address: [ida@example.edu]

Response: This is... ○ excellent ○ okay ◉ boring

Comments: [Enough already!]

(Send My Feedback)

A Try the form one more time...

Thank you, Ms. Blankenship, for your comments.

You stated that you found this example to be 'boring' and added: Enough already!

B ...and here's the result (if filled out completely and without any programmer errors).

Manually Sending Data to a Page

The last example for this chapter is a slight tangent to the other topics but plays off the idea of handling form data with PHP. As discussed in the section "Choosing a Form Method," if a form uses the GET method, the resulting URL is something like

```
http://www.example.com/page.php?
→ some_var=some_value&age=20&...
```

The receiving page (here, **page.php**) is sent a series of *name=value* pairs, each of which is separated by an ampersand (**&**). The whole sequence is preceded by a question mark (immediately after the handling script's name).

To access the values passed to the page in this way, turn to the **$_GET** variable. Just as you would when using **$_POST**, refer to the specific name as an index in **$_GET**. In that example, **page.php** receives a **$_GET['some_var']** variable with a value of *some_value*, a **$_GET['age']** variable with a value of *20*, and so forth.

You can pass data to a PHP script in this way by creating an HTML form that uses the GET method. But you can also use this same idea to send data to a PHP page *without* the use of the form. Normally you'd do so by creating links:

```
<a href="page.php?id=22">Some Link</a>
```

That link, which could be dynamically generated by PHP, will pass the value *22* to **page.php**, accessible in **$_GET['id']**.

To try this for yourself, the next pair of scripts will easily demonstrate this concept, using a hard-coded HTML page.

To create the HTML page:

1. Begin a new document in your text editor or IDE, to be named **hello.html** (Script 3.6):

```
<!DOCTYPE html PUBLIC "-//W3C//DTD
→ XHTML 1.0 Transitional//EN"
  "http://www.w3.org/TR/xhtml1/
  → DTD/xhtml1-transitional.dtd">
<html xmlns="http://www.w3.org/
→ 1999/xhtml" xml:lang="en"
→ lang="en">
<head>
  <meta http-equiv="Content-Type"
  → content="text/html;
  → charset=utf-8"/>
  <title>Greetings!</title>
</head>
<body>
<!-- Script 3.6 - hello.html -->
<div><p>Click a link to say
→ hello:</p>
```

2. Create links to a PHP script, passing values along in the URL:

```
<ul>
  <li><a href="hello.php?
  → name=Michael">Michael</a></li>
  <li><a href="hello.php?
  → name=Celia">Celia</a></li>
  <li><a href="hello.php?
  → name=Jude">Jude</a></li>
  <li><a href="hello.php?
  → name=Sophie">Sophie</a></li>
</ul>
```

Script 3.6 This HTML page uses links to pass values to a PHP script in the URL (thereby emulating a form that uses the GET method).

```
1   <!DOCTYPE html PUBLIC "-//W3C//DTD XHTML
    1.0 Transitional//EN"
2       "http://www.w3.org/TR/xhtml1/DTD/
    xhtml1-transitional.dtd">
3   <html xmlns="http://www.w3.org/1999/
    xhtml" xml:lang="en" lang="en">
4   <head>
5       <meta http-equiv="Content-Type"
    content="text/html; charset=utf-8"/>
6       <title>Greetings!</title>
7   </head>
8   <body>
9   <!-- Script 3.6 - hello.html -->
10  <div><p>Click a link to say hello:</p>
11
12  <ul>
13      <li><a href="hello.php?
        name=Michael">Michael</a></li>
14      <li><a href="hello.php?
        name=Celia">Celia</a></li>
15      <li><a href="hello.php?
        name=Jude">Jude</a></li>
16      <li><a href="hello.php?
        name=Sophie">Sophie</a></li>
17  </ul>
18
19  </div>
20  </body>
21  </html>
```

Click a link to say hello:

- Michael
- Celia
- Jude
- Sophie

A The simple HTML page, with four links to the PHP script.

The premise here is that the user will see a list of links, each associated with a specific name **A**. When the user clicks a link, that name is passed to **hello.php** in the URL **B**.

If you want to use different names, that's fine, but stick to one-word names without spaces or punctuation (or else they won't be passed to the PHP script properly, for reasons that will be explained in time).

3. Complete the HTML page:

```
</div>
</body>
</html>
```

4. Save the script as **hello.html** and place it within the proper directory on your PHP-enabled server.

5. Load the HTML page through a URL in your Web browser.

Although you can view HTML pages without going through a URL, you'll click links in this page to access the PHP script, so you'll need to start off using a URL here. Don't click any of the links yet, as the PHP script doesn't exist!

```
<!-- Script 3.6 - hello.html -->
<div><p>Click a link to say hello:</p>

<ul>
        <li><a href="hello.php?name=Michael">Michael</a></li>
        <li><a href="hello.php?name=Celia">Celia</a></li>
        <li><a href="hello.php?name=Jude">Jude</a></li>
        <li><a href="hello.php?name=Sophie">Sophie</a></li>
</ul>

</div>
```

B The HTML source of the page shows how values are being passed along in the URL for the four links.

To create the PHP script:

1. Begin a new document in your text editor or IDE, to be named **hello.php** (Script 3.7):

```
<!DOCTYPE html PUBLIC "-//W3C//DTD
→ XHTML 1.0 Transitional//EN"
  "http://www.w3.org/TR/xhtml1/
  → DTD/xhtml1-transitional.dtd">
<html xmlns="http://www.w3.org/
→ 1999/xhtml" xml:lang="en"
→ lang="en">
<head>
  <meta http-equiv="Content-Type"
  → content="text/html;
  → charset=utf-8"/>
  <title>Greetings!</title>
</head>
<body>
```

2. Begin the PHP code:

```
<?php // Script 3.7 - hello.php
```

3. Address the error management, if desired:

```
ini_set ('display_errors', 1);
error_reporting (E_ALL | E_STRICT);
```

These two lines, which configure how PHP responds to errors, are explained in the pages leading up to this section. They may or may not be necessary for your situation but can be helpful.

4. Use the **name** value passed in the URL to create a greeting:

```
$name = $_GET['name'];
print "<p>Hello, <span
style=\"font-weight:
bold;\">$name</span>!</p>";
```

The **name** variable is sent to the page through the URL (see Script 3.6). To access that value, refer to **$_GET['name']**. Again, you would use **$_GET** (as opposed to **$_POST**) because the value is coming from a GET request.

Script 3.7 This PHP page refers to the **name** value passed in the URL in order to print a greeting.

```
1   <!DOCTYPE html PUBLIC "-//W3C//DTD XHTML
    1.0 Transitional//EN"
2       "http://www.w3.org/TR/xhtml1/DTD/
        xhtml1-transitional.dtd">
3   <html xmlns="http://www.w3.org/1999/
    xhtml" xml:lang="en" lang="en">
4   <head>
5       <meta http-equiv="Content-Type"
        content="text/html; charset=utf-8"/>
6       <title>Greetings!</title>
7   </head>
8   <body>
9   <?php // Script 3.7 - hello.php
10
11  ini_set ('display_errors', 1);
    // Let me learn from my mistakes!
12  error_reporting (E_ALL | E_STRICT);
    // Show all possible problems!
13
14  // This page should receive a name value
    in the URL.
15
16  // Say "Hello":
17  $name = $_GET['name'];
18  print "<p>Hello, <span
    style=\"font-weight: bold;\">$name
    </span>!</p>";
19
20  ?>
21  </body>
22  </html>
```

C By clicking the first link, *Michael* is passed along in the URL and is greeted by name.

D By clicking the second link, *Celia* is sent along in the URL and is also greeted by name.

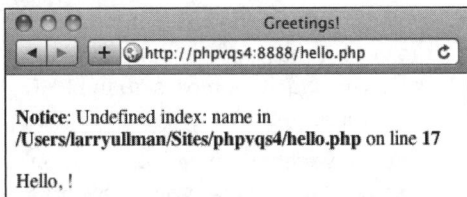

E If the **$_GET['name']** variable isn't assigned a value, the browser prints out this awkward message, along with the error notice.

F Any value assigned to **name** (lowercase) in the URL is used by the PHP script.

As with earlier PHP scripts, the value in the predefined variable (**$_GET**) is first assigned to another variable, to simplify the syntax in the **print** statement.

5. Complete the PHP code and the HTML page:

```
?>
</body>
</html>
```

6. Save the script as **hello.php** and place it within the proper directory on your PHP-enabled server.

   It should be saved in the same directory as **hello.html** (Script 3.6).

7. Click the links in **hello.html** to view the result **C** and **D**.

TIP If you run **hello.php** directly (i.e., without clicking any links), you'll get an error notice because no name value would be passed along in the URL **E**.

TIP Because **hello.php** reads a value from the URL, it actually works independently of **hello.html**. For example, you can directly edit the **hello.php** URL to greet anyone, even if **hello.html** does not have a link for that name **F**.

TIP If you want to use a link to send multiple values to a script, separate the *name=value* pairs (for example, first_name=Larry) with the ampersand (&). So, another link may be hello.php? first_name=Larry&last_name=Ullman. You should continue to use only single words, without punctuation or spaces, however (until you later learn about the urlencode() function).

TIP Although the example here—setting the value of a person's name—may not be very practical, this basic technique is useful on many occasions. For example, a PHP script might constitute a template, and the content of the resulting Web page would differ based on the values the page received in the URL.

Review and Pursue

If you have any problems with the review questions or the pursue prompts, turn to the book's supporting forum (www.LarryUllman.com/forum/).

Review

- What is the significance of a form's **action** attribute?

- What is the significance of a form's **method** attribute? Is it more secure to use GET or POST? Which method type can be bookmarked in the browser?

- What predefined variable will contain the data from a form submission? Note: There are multiple answers.

- Why must an HTML page that contains a form that's being submitted to a PHP script be loaded through a URL?

- Under what circumstances will attempts to enable **display_errors** in a script not succeed? Why is it not secure to enable **display_errors** on live sites?

Pursue

- Load **feedback.html** in your Web browser without going through a URL (i.e., the address bar would likely start with *file://*). Fill out and submit the form. Observe the result so that you can recognize this problem, and understand its cause, in case you see similar results in the future.

- If you have not already, and if you can, make sure that **display_errors** is enabled on your development environment.

- If you have not already, and if you can, make sure that **error_reporting** is set to **E_ALL | E_STRICT** on your development environment.

- Try introducing different errors in a PHP script—by improperly balancing quotation marks, failing to use semicolons, referring to variables improperly, and so on—to see the result.

- Experiment with the **hello.html** and the **hello.php** pages to send different values, including numbers, to the PHP script through the URL.

- Create a variation on **hello.html** that sends multiple *name=value* pairs to a PHP script. Have the PHP script then print all the received values.

- If you're the inquisitive type, and don't mind waiting for answers, try passing more complicated values to a page through the URL. Try using spaces and punctuation to see what happens.

- Create a new HTML form that performs a task you envision yourself needing (or a lighter-weight version of that functionality). Then create the PHP script that handles the form, printing just the received data.

Using Numbers

Chapter 2, "Variables," briefly discussed the various types of variables, how to assign values to them, and how they're generally used. In this chapter, you'll work specifically with number variables—both integers (whole numbers) and floating-point numbers (aka floats or decimals).

The chapter begins by creating an HTML form that will be used to generate number variables. Then you'll learn how to perform basic arithmetic, how to format numbers, and how to cope with *operator precedence*. The last two sections of this chapter cover incrementing and decrementing numbers, plus generating random numbers. Throughout the chapter, you'll also learn about other useful number-related PHP functions.

In This Chapter

Creating the Form	74
Performing Arithmetic	77
Formatting Numbers	81
Understanding Precedence	84
Incrementing and Decrementing a Number	86
Creating Random Numbers	88
Review and Pursue	90

Creating the Form

Most of the PHP examples in this chapter will perform various calculations based on an e-commerce premise. A form will take price, quantity, discount amount, tax rate, and shipping cost **Ⓐ**, and the PHP script that handles the form will return a total cost. That cost will also be broken down by the number of payments the user wants to make in order to generate a monthly cost value **Ⓑ**.

To start, let's create an HTML page that allows the user to enter the values.

To create the HTML form:

1. Begin a new HTML document in your text editor or IDE, to be named `calculator.html` (Script 4.1):

```
<!DOCTYPE html PUBLIC "-//W3C//DTD
→ XHTML 1.0 Transitional//EN"
  "http://www.w3.org/TR/xhtml1/DTD/
  → xhtml1-transitional.dtd">
<html xmlns="http://www.w3.org/
  → 1999/xhtml" xml:lang="en"
  → lang="en">
<head>
  <meta http-equiv="Content-Type"
  → content="text/html;
  → charset=utf-8"/>
  <title>Product Cost Calculator
  → </title>
</head>
<body><!-- Script 4.1 -
→ calculator.html -->
<div><p>Fill out this form to
→ calculate the total cost:</p>
```

Fill out this form to calculate the total cost:

Price: 5.00

Quantity: 100

Discount: 10.00

Tax: 7.5 (%)

Shipping method: Slow and steady

Number of payments to make: 10

Calculate!

Ⓐ This form takes numbers from the user and sends them to a PHP page.

You have selected to purchase:
100 widget(s) at
$5.00 price each plus a
$5.00 shipping cost and a
7.5 percent tax rate.
After your $10.00 discount, the total cost is $532.13.
Divided over 10 monthly payments, that would be $53.21 each.

Ⓑ The PHP script performs a series of calculations on the submitted data and outputs the results. The results should look like this by the end of the chapter.

Script 4.1 This basic HTML form will be the origination of the numbers on which mathematical calculations will be performed in several PHP scripts.

```
1   <!DOCTYPE html PUBLIC "-//W3C//DTD
    XHTML 1.0 Transitional//EN"
2       "http://www.w3.org/TR/xhtml1/DTD/
    xhtml1-transitional.dtd">
3   <html xmlns="http://www.w3.org/1999/
    xhtml" xml:lang="en" lang="en">
4   <head>
5       <meta http-equiv="Content-Type"
    content="text/html;
    charset=utf-8"/>
6       <title>Product Cost Calculator
    </title>
7   </head>
8   <body><!-- Script 4.1 -
    calculator.html -->
9   <div><p>Fill out this form to
    calculate the total cost:</p>
10
11  <form action="handle_calc.php"
    method="post">
12
13  <p>Price: <input type="text"
    name="price" size="5" /></p>
14
15  <p>Quantity: <input type="text"
    name="quantity" size="5" /></p>
16
17  <p>Discount: <input type="text"
    name="discount" size="5" /></p>
18
19  <p>Tax: <input type="text" name="tax"
    size="3" /> (%)</p>
20
21  <p>Shipping method: <select
    name="shipping">
22  <option value="5.00">Slow and steady
    </option>
23  <option value="8.95">Put a move on
    it.</option>
24  <option value="19.36">I need it
    yesterday!</option>
25  </select></p>
26
27  <p>Number of payments to make:
    <input type="text" name="payments"
    size="3" /></p>
28
29  <input type="submit" name="submit"
    value="Calculate!" />
30
31  </form>
32
33  </div>
34  </body>
35  </html>
```

2. Create the initial **form** tag:

```
<form action="handle_calc.php"
→ method="post">
```

This **form** tag begins the HTML form. Its **action** attribute indicates that the form data will be submitted to a page named **handle_calc.php**. The tag's **method** attribute tells the page to use POST to send the data. See Chapter 3, "HTML Forms and PHP," for more details.

3. Create the inputs for the price, quantity, discount, and tax:

```
<p>Price: <input type="text"
→ name="price" size="5" /></p>
<p>Quantity: <input type="text"
→ name="quantity" size="5" /></p>
<p>Discount: <input type="text"
→ name="discount" size="5" /></p>
<p>Tax: <input type="text"
→ name="tax" size="3" /> (%)</p>
```

XHTML has no input type for numbers, so you create text boxes for these values. A parenthetical indicates that the tax should be entered as a percent.

Also remember that the names used for the inputs have to correspond to valid PHP variable names (letters, numbers, and the underscore only; doesn't start with a number, and so forth).

continues on next page

4. Add a field in which the user can select a shipping method:

```
<p>Shipping method: <select
→ name="shipping">
<option value="5.00">Slow and
→ steady</option>
<option value="8.95">Put a move
→ on it.</option>
<option value="19.36">I need it
→ yesterday!</option>
</select></p>
```

The shipping selection is made using a drop-down menu. The value of the selected option is the cost for that option. If the user selects, for example, the *Put a move on it.* option, the value of `$_POST['shipping']` in `handle_calc.php` will be *8.95*.

5. Complete the HTML form:

```
<p>Number of payments to make:
→ <input type="text"
→ name="payments" size="3" /></p>
<input type="submit" name="submit"
→ value="Calculate!" />
</form>
```

The final two input types take a number for how many payments are required and then create a submit button (labeled *Calculate!*). The closing **form** tag marks the end of the form section of the page.

6. Complete the HTML page:

```
</div>
</body>
</html>
```

7. Save the script as `calculator.html` and view it in your Web browser.

Because this is an HTML page, you can view it directly in a Web browser.

```
1   <!DOCTYPE html PUBLIC "-//W3C//DTD XHTML
    1.0 Transitional//EN"
2       "http://www.w3.org/TR/xhtml1/DTD/
    xhtml1-transitional.dtd">
3   <html xmlns="http://www.w3.org/1999/
    xhtml" xml:lang="en" lang="en">
4   <head>
5       <meta http-equiv="Content-Type"
    content="text/html; charset=utf-8"/>
6       <title>Product Cost Calculator</title>
7       <style type="text/css" media="screen">
8       .number { font-weight: bold; }
9       </style>
10  </head>
11  <body>
12  <?php // Script 4.2 - handle_calc.php
13  /* This script takes values from
    calculator.html and performs
14  total cost and monthly payment
    calculations. */
15
16  // Address error handling, if you want.
17
18  // Get the values from the $_POST array:
19  $price = $_POST['price'];
20  $quantity = $_POST['quantity'];
21  $discount = $_POST['discount'];
22  $tax = $_POST['tax'];
23  $shipping = $_POST['shipping'];
24  $payments = $_POST['payments'];
25
26  // Calculate the total:
27  $total = $price * $quantity;
28  $total = $total + $shipping;
29  $total = $total - $discount;
30
31  // Determine the tax rate:
32  $taxrate = $tax/100;
33  $taxrate = $taxrate + 1;
34
35  // Factor in the tax rate:
36  $total = $total * $taxrate;
37
38  // Calculate the monthly payments:
39  $monthly = $total / $payments;
40
```

code continues on next page

Performing Arithmetic

Just as you learned in grade school, basic mathematics involves the principles of addition, subtraction, multiplication, and division. These are performed in PHP using the most obvious operators:

- Addition (**+**)
- Subtraction (**-**)
- Multiplication (*****)
- Division (**/**)

To use these operators, you'll create a PHP script that calculates the total cost for the sale of some widgets. This handling script could be the basis of a shopping cart application—a very practical Web page feature (although in this case the relevant number values will come from **calculator.html**).

When you're writing this script, be sure to note the use of comments (**Script 4.2**) to illuminate the different lines of code and the reasoning behind them.

To create your sales cost calculator:

1. Create a new document in your text editor or IDE, to be named **handle_calc.php** (Script 4.2):

```
<!DOCTYPE html PUBLIC "-//W3C//DTD
→ XHTML 1.0 Transitional//EN"
  "http://www.w3.org/TR/xhtml1/DTD/
→ xhtml1-transitional.dtd">
<html xmlns="http://www.w3.org/
→ 1999/xhtml" xml:lang="en"
→ lang="en">
<head>
  <meta http-equiv="Content-Type"
→ content="text/html;
→ charset=utf-8"/>
  <title>Product Cost Calculator
→ </title>
```

continues on next page

```
<style type="text/css"
→ media="screen">
   .number { font-weight: bold; }
</style>
</head>
<body>
```

The head of the document defines one CSS class called *number*. Any element within the page that has that class value will be given extra font weight. In other words, when the numbers from the form, and the results of the various calculations, are printed in the script's output, they'll be made more obvious.

2. Insert the PHP tags and address error handling, if desired:

```
<?php // Script 4.2 -
→ handle_calc.php
```

Depending on your PHP configuration, you may or many not want to add a couple of lines that turn on **display_errors** and adjust the level of error reporting. See Chapter 3 for specifics.

3. Assign the **$_POST** elements to local variables:

```
$price = $_POST['price'];
$quantity = $_POST['quantity'];
$discount = $_POST['discount'];
$tax = $_POST['tax'];
$shipping = $_POST['shipping'];
$payments = $_POST['payments'];
```

The script will receive all the form data in the predefined **$_POST** variable. To access individual form values, refer to **$_POST['*index*']**, replacing *index* with the corresponding form element's **name** value. These values are assigned to individual local variables here, to make it easier to use them throughout the rest of the script.

Note that each variable is given a descriptive name and is written entirely in lowercase letters.

Script 4.2 *continued*

```
41   // Print out the results:
42   print "<p>You have selected to
     purchase:<br />
43   <span class=\"number\">$quantity
     </span> widget(s) at <br />
44   $<span class=\"number\">$price</span>
     price each plus a <br />
45   $<span class=\"number\">$shipping
     </span> shipping cost and a <br />
46   <span class=\"number\">$tax</span>
     percent tax rate.<br />
47   After your $<span class=\"number\">
     $discount</span> discount, the total
     cost is
48   $<span class=\"number\">$total
     </span>.<br />
49   Divided over <span class=\"number\">
     $payments</span> monthly payments,
     that would be $<span class=\"number\">
     $monthly</span> each.</p>";
50
51   ?>
52   </body>
53   </html>
```

4. Begin calculating the total cost:

```
$total = $price * $quantity;
$total = $total + $shipping;
$total = $total - $discount;
```

The asterisk (*) indicates multiplication in PHP, so the total is first calculated as the number of items purchased (**$quantity**) multiplied by the price. Then the shipping cost is added to the total value (remember that the shipping cost correlates to the **value** attribute of each shipping drop-down menu's **option** tags), and the discount is subtracted.

Note that it's perfectly acceptable to determine a variable's value in part by using that variable's existing value (as is done in the last two lines).

5. Calculate the tax rate and the new total:

```
$taxrate = $tax/100;
$taxrate = $taxrate + 1;
$total = $total * $taxrate;
```

The tax rate should be entered as a percent—for example, 8 or 5.75. This number is then divided by 100 to get the decimal equivalent of the percent (.08 or .0575). Finally, you calculate how much something costs with tax by adding 1 to the percent and then multiplying that new rate by the total. This is the mathematical equivalent of multiplying the decimal tax rate times the total and then adding this result to the total (for example, a 5 percent tax on $100 is $5, making the total $105, which is the same as multiplying $100 times 1.05).

6. Calculate the monthly payment:

```
$monthly = $total / $payments;
```

As an example of division, assume that the widgets can be paid for over the course of many months. Hence, you divide the total by the number of payments to find the monthly payment.

7. Print the results:

```
print "<p>You have selected to
→ purchase:<br />
<span class=\"number\">$quantity
→ </span> widget(s) at <br />
$<span class=\"number\">$price
→ </span> price each plus a <br />
$<span class=\"number\">$shipping
→ </span> shipping cost and a <br />
<span class=\"number\">$tax</span>
→ percent tax rate.<br />
After your $<span class=\"number\">
→ $discount</span> discount, the
→ total cost is
$<span class=\"number\">$total
→ </span>.<br />
Divided over <span class=\"number\">
→ $payments</span> monthly
→ payments, that would be $<span
→ class=\"number\">$monthly</span>
→ each.</p>";
```

The **print** statement sends every value to the Web browser along with some text. To make it easier to read, **
** tags are added to format the browser result; in addition, the **print** function operates over multiple lines to make the PHP code cleaner. Each variable's value will be highlighted in the browser by wrapping it within **span** tags that have a **class** attribute of *number* (see Step 1).

8. Close the PHP section and complete the HTML page:

```
?>
</body>
</html>
```

9. Save the script as **handle_calc.php** and place it in the proper directory for your PHP-enabled server.

Make sure that **calculator.html** is in the same directory.

continues on next page

10. Test the script in your Web browser by filling out **A** and submitting **B** the form.

Not to belabor the point, but make sure you start by loading the HTML form through a URL (*http://something*) so that when it's submitted, the PHP script is also run through a URL.

You can experiment with these values to see how effectively your calculator works. If you omit any values, the resulting message will just be a little odd but the calculations should still work **C**.

TIP As you'll certainly notice, the calculator comes up with numbers that don't correspond well to real dollar values (see **B** and **C**). In the next section, "Formatting Numbers," you'll learn how to address this issue.

TIP If you want to print the value of the total before tax or before the discount (or both), you can do so in two ways. You can insert the appropriate `print` statements immediately after the proper value has been determined but before the `$total` variable has been changed again. Or, you can use new variables to represent the values of the subsequent calculations (for example, `$total_with_tax` and `$total_less_discount`).

TIP Attempting to print a dollar sign followed by the value of a variable, such as $10 (where 10 comes from a variable), has to be handled carefully. You can't use the syntax `$$variable`, because the combination of two dollar signs creates a type of variable that's too complex to discuss in this book. One solution is to put something—a space or an HTML tag, as in this example—between the dollar sign and the variable name. Another option is to escape the first dollar sign:

```
print "The total is \$$total";
```

A third option is to use concatenation, which is introduced in the next chapter.

Fill out this form to calculate the total cost:
Price: 19.95
Quantity: 6
Discount: 10.00
Tax: 6 (%)
Shipping method: Slow and steady
Number of payments to make: 12
[Calculate!]

A The HTML form...

You have selected to purchase:
6 widget(s) at
$19.95 price each plus a
$5.00 shipping cost and a
6 percent tax rate.
After your $10.00 discount, the total cost is $121.582.
Divided over 12 monthly payments, that would be $10.1318333333 each.

B ...and the resulting calculations.

You have selected to purchase:
6 widget(s) at
$19.95 price each plus a
$5.00 shipping cost and a
percent tax rate.
After your $ discount, the total cost is $124.7.
Divided over 12 monthly payments, that would be $10.3916666667 each.

C You can omit or change any value and rerun the calculator. Here the tax and discount values have been omitted.

TIP This script performs differently, depending on whether the various fields are submitted. The only truly problematic field is the number of monthly payments: If this is omitted, you'll see a division-by-zero warning. Chapter 6, "Control Structures," will cover validating form data before it's used.

TIP HTML 5 is expected to have one or more inputs that restrict the user to entering numeric values.

Formatting Numbers

Although the calculator is on its way to being practical, it still has one legitimate problem: You can't ask someone to make a monthly payment of $10.13183333! To create more usable numbers, you need to format them.

There are two appropriate functions for this purpose. The first, **round( )**, rounds a value to a specified number of decimal places. The function's first argument is the number to be rounded. This can be either a number or a variable that has a numeric value. The second argument is optional; it represents the number of decimal places to which to round. If omitted, the number will be rounded to the nearest integer. For example:

```
round (4.30); // 4
round (4.289, 2); // 4.29
$num = 236.26985;
round ($num); // 236
```

The other function you can use in this situation is **number_format( )**. It works like **round( )** in that it takes a number (or a variable with a numeric value) and an optional decimal specifier. This function has the added benefit of formatting the number with commas, the way it would commonly be written:

```
number_format (428.4959, 2); // 428.50
number_format (428, 2); // 428.00
number_format (123456789);
→ // 123,456,789
```

Let's rewrite the PHP script to format the numbers appropriately.

To format numbers:

1. Open **handle_calc.php** in your text editor or IDE, if it is not already open (Script 4.2).

2. After all the calculations but before the **print** statement, add the following (**Script 4.3**):

   ```
   $total = number_format ($total, 2);
   $monthly = number_format
   → ($monthly, 2);
   ```

   To format these two numbers, apply this function after every calculation has been made but before they're sent to the Web browser. The second argument (the 2) indicates that the resulting number should have exactly two decimal places; this setting rounds the numbers and adds zeros at the end, as necessary.

Script 4.3 The `number_format()` function is applied to the values of two number variables, so they are more appropriate.

```
1   <!DOCTYPE html PUBLIC "-//W3C//DTD XHTML
    1.0 Transitional//EN"
2     "http://www.w3.org/TR/xhtml1/DTD/
    xhtml1-transitional.dtd">
3   <html xmlns="http://www.w3.org/1999/
    xhtml" xml:lang="en" lang="en">
4   <head>
5     <meta http-equiv="Content-Type"
    content="text/html; charset=utf-8"/>
6     <title>Product Cost Calculator</title>
7     <style type="text/css" media="screen">
8       .number { font-weight: bold;}
9     </style>
10  </head>
11  <body>
12  <?php // Script 4.3 - handle_calc.php #2
13  /* This script takes values from
    calculator.html and performs
14  total cost and monthly payment
    calculations. */
15
16  // Address error handling, if you want.
17
18  // Get the values from the $_POST array:
19  $price = $_POST['price'];
20  $quantity = $_POST['quantity'];
21  $discount = $_POST['discount'];
22  $tax = $_POST['tax'];
23  $shipping = $_POST['shipping'];
24  $payments = $_POST['payments'];
25
26  // Calculate the total:
27  $total = $price * $quantity;
28  $total = $total + $shipping;
29  $total = $total - $discount;
30
31  // Determine the tax rate:
32  $taxrate = $tax/100;
33  $taxrate = $taxrate + 1;
34
35  // Factor in the tax rate:
36  $total = $total * $taxrate;
37
38  // Calculate the monthly payments:
39  $monthly = $total / $payments;
40
41  // Apply the proper formatting:
42  $total = number_format ($total, 2);
43  $monthly = number_format ($monthly, 2);
44
```

code continues on next page

```
45    // Print out the results:
46    print "<p>You have selected to
      purchase:<br />
47    <span class=\"number\">$quantity</span>
      widget(s) at <br />
48    $<span class=\"number\">$price</span>
      price each plus a <br />
49    $<span class=\"number\">$shipping</span>
      shipping cost and a <br />
50    <span class=\"number\">$tax</span> percent
      tax rate.<br />
51    After your $<span class=\"number\">
      $discount</span> discount, the total
      cost is
52    $<span class=\"number\">$total</span>.<br />
53    Divided over <span class=\"number\">
      $payments</span> monthly payments, that
      would be $<span class=\"number\">$monthly
      </span> each.</p>";
54
55    ?>
56    </body>
57    </html>
```

Fill out this form to calculate the total cost:

Price: 99.00

Quantity: 4

Discount: 25.00

Tax: 5.5 (%)

Shipping method: Put a move on it.

Number of payments to make: 24

[Calculate!]

Ⓐ Another form entry.

You have selected to purchase:
4 widget(s) at
$99.00 price each plus a
$8.95 shipping cost and a
5.5 percent tax rate.
After your **$25.00** discount, the total cost is **$400.85**.
Divided over **24** monthly payments, that would be **$16.70** each.

Ⓑ The updated version of the script returns more appropriate number values thanks to the **number_format()** function.

---

3. Save the file, place it in the same directory as **calculator.html**, and test it in your browser **Ⓐ** and **Ⓑ**.

TIP Another, much more complex way to format numbers is to use the `printf()` and `sprintf()` functions. Because of their tricky syntax, they're not discussed in this book; see the PHP manual for more information.

TIP Non-Windows versions of PHP also have a `money_format()` function, which can be used in lieu of `number_format()`.

TIP For complicated reasons, the `round()` function rounds exact halves (.5, .05, .005, and so on) down half the time and up half the time.

TIP In PHP, function calls can have spaces between the function name and its parentheses or not. Both of these are fine:

```
round ($num);
round($num);
```

TIP The `number_format()` function takes two other optional arguments that let you specify what characters to use to indicate a decimal point and break up thousands. This is useful, for example, for cultures that write 1,000.89 as 1.000,89. See the PHP manual for the correct syntax, if you want to use this option.

Understanding Precedence

Inevitably, after a discussion of the various sorts of mathematical operators comes the discussion of precedence. *Precedence* refers to the order in which a series of calculations are executed. For example, what is the value of the following variable?

`$number = 10 - 4 / 2;`

Is `$number` worth 3 (10 minus 4 equals 6, divided by 2 equals 3) or 8 (4 divided by 2 equals 2, subtracted from 10 equals 8)? The answer here is 8, because division takes precedence over subtraction.

Appendix B, "Resources and Next Steps," shows the complete list of operator precedence for PHP (including operators that haven't been covered yet). However, instead of attempting to memorize a large table of peculiar characters, you can bypass the whole concept by using parentheses. Parentheses always take precedence over any other operator. Thus:

```
$number = (10 - 4) / 2; // 3
$number = 10 - (4 / 2); // 8
```

Using parentheses in your calculations ensures that you never see peculiar results due to precedence issues. Parentheses can also be used to rewrite complex calculations in fewer lines of code. Let's rewrite the **handle_calc.php** script, combining multiple lines into one by using parentheses, while maintaining accuracy.

Script 4.4 By using parentheses, calculations made over multiple lines (see Script 4.3) can be condensed without affecting the script's mathematical accuracy.

```
1   <!DOCTYPE html PUBLIC "-//W3C//DTD XHTML
    1.0 Transitional//EN"
2      "http://www.w3.org/TR/xhtml1/DTD/
       xhtml1-transitional.dtd">
3   <html xmlns="http://www.w3.org/1999/
    xhtml" xml:lang="en" lang="en">
4   <head>
5      <meta http-equiv="Content-Type"
       content="text/html; charset=utf-8"/>
6      <title>Product Cost Calculator</title>
7      <style type="text/css" media="screen">
8         .number { font-weight: bold;}
9      </style>
10  </head>
11  <body>
12  <?php // Script 4.4 - handle_calc.php #3
13  /* This script takes values from
    calculator.html and performs
14  total cost and monthly payment
    calculations. */
15
16  // Address error handling, if you want.
17
18  // Get the values from the $_POST array:
19  $price = $_POST['price'];
20  $quantity = $_POST['quantity'];
21  $discount = $_POST['discount'];
22  $tax = $_POST['tax'];
23  $shipping = $_POST['shipping'];
24  $payments = $_POST['payments'];
25
26  // Calculate the total:
27  $total = (($price * $quantity) +
    $shipping) - $discount;
28
29  // Determine the tax rate:
30  $taxrate = ($tax/100) + 1;
31
32  // Factor in the tax rate:
33  $total = $total * $taxrate;
34
35  // Calculate the monthly payments:
36  $monthly = $total / $payments;
37
38  // Apply the proper formatting:
39  $total = number_format ($total, 2);
40  $monthly = number_format ($monthly, 2);
41
```

code continues on next page

```
42    // Print out the results:
43    print "<p>You have selected to
      purchase:<br />
44    <span class=\"number\">$quantity</span>
      widget(s) at <br />
45    $<span class=\"number\">$price</span>
      price each plus a <br />
46    $<span class=\"number\">$shipping</span>
      shipping cost and a <br />
47    <span class=\"number\">$tax</span> percent
      tax rate.<br />
48    After your $<span class=\"number\">$discount
      </span> discount, the total cost is
49    $<span class=\"number\">$total</span>.<br />
50    Divided over <span class=\"number\">
      $payments</span> monthly payments, that
      would be $<span class=\"number\">$monthly
      </span> each.</p>";
51
52    ?>
53    </body>
54    </html>
```

Fill out this form to calculate the total cost:

Price: 1.50

Quantity: 250

Discount: 0

Tax: 6   (%)

Shipping method: I need it yesterday!

Number of payments to make: 2

Calculate!

A Testing the form one more time.

You have selected to purchase:
250 widget(s) at
$1.50 price each plus a
$19.36 shipping cost and a
6 percent tax rate.
After your **$0** discount, the total cost is **$418.02**.
Divided over **2** monthly payments, that would be **$209.01** each.

B Even though the calculations have been condensed, the math works out the same. If you see different results or get an error message, double-check your parentheses for balance (an equal number of opening and closing parentheses).

To manage precedence:

1. Open **handle_calc.php** in your text editor or IDE, if it is not already open (Script 4.3).

2. Replace the three lines that initially calculate the order total with the following (**Script 4.4**):

   ```
   $total = (($price * $quantity) +
   → $shipping) - $discount;
   ```

   There's no reason not to make all the calculations in one step, as long as you use parentheses to ensure that the math works properly. The other option is to memorize PHP's rules of precedence for multiple operators, but using parentheses is a lot easier.

3. Change the two lines that calculate and add in the tax to this:

   ```
   $taxrate = ($tax/100) + 1;
   ```

   Again, the tax calculations can be made in one line instead of two separate ones.

4. Save the script, place it in the same directory as **calculator.html**, and test it in your browser **A** and **B**.

TIP Be sure that you match your parentheses consistently as you create your formulas (every opening parenthesis requires a closing parenthesis). Failure to do so will cause parse errors.

TIP Granted, using the methods applied here, you could combine all the total calculations into just one line of code (instead of three)—but there is such a thing as oversimplifying.

Incrementing and Decrementing a Number

PHP, like Perl and most other programming languages, includes some shortcuts that let you avoid ugly constructs such as

`$tax = $tax + 1;`

When you need to increase the value of a variable by 1 (called an *incremental* adjustment) or decrease the value of a variable by 1 (a *decremental* adjustment), you can use **++** and **--**, respectively:

```
$var = 20; // 20
$var++; // 21
$var++; // 22
$var--; // 21
```

Solely for the sake of testing this concept, you'll rewrite the **handle_calc.php** script one last time.

To increment the value of a variable:

1. Open **handle_calc.php** in your text editor or IDE, if it is not already open (Script 4.4).

2. Change the tax rate calculation from Script 4.3 to read as follows (**Script 4.5**):

   ```
   $taxrate = $tax/100;
   $taxrate++;
   ```

   The first line calculates the tax rate as the **$tax** value divided by 100. The second line increments this value by 1 so that it can be multiplied by the total to determine the total with tax.

Script 4.5 Incrementing or decrementing a number is a common operation using **++** or **--**, respectively.

```
1    <!DOCTYPE html PUBLIC "-//W3C//DTD XHTML
     1.0 Transitional//EN"
2        "http://www.w3.org/TR/xhtml1/DTD/
         xhtml1-transitional.dtd">
3    <html xmlns="http://www.w3.org/1999/
     xhtml" xml:lang="en" lang="en">
4    <head>
5        <meta http-equiv="Content-Type"
         content="text/html; charset=utf-8"/>
6        <title>Product Cost Calculator
         </title>
7        <style type="text/css" media="screen">
8            .number { font-weight: bold;}
9        </style>
10   </head>
11   <body>
12   <?php // Script 4.3 - handle_calc.php #4
13   /* This script takes values from
     calculator.html and performs
14   total cost and monthly payment
     calculations. */
15
16   // Address error handling, if you want.
17
18   // Get the values from the $_POST array:
19   $price = $_POST['price'];
20   $quantity = $_POST['quantity'];
21   $discount = $_POST['discount'];
22   $tax = $_POST['tax'];
23   $shipping = $_POST['shipping'];
24   $payments = $_POST['payments'];
25
26   // Calculate the total:
27   $total = (($price * $quantity) +
     $shipping) - $discount;
28
29   // Determine the tax rate:
30   $taxrate = $tax/100;
31   $taxrate++;
32
33   // Factor in the tax rate:
34   $total = $total * $taxrate;
35
36   // Calculate the monthly payments:
37   $monthly = $total / $payments;
38
39   // Apply the proper formatting:
40   $total = number_format ($total, 2);
41   $monthly = number_format ($monthly, 2);
42
```

code continues on next page

```
43    // Print out the results:
44    print "<p>You have selected to
      purchase:<br />
45    <span class=\"number\">$quantity</span>
      widget(s) at <br />
46    $<span class=\"number\">$price</span>
      price each plus a <br />
47    $<span class=\"number\">$shipping</span>
      shipping cost and a <br />
48    <span class=\"number\">$tax</span>
      percent tax rate.<br />
49    After your $<span class=\"number\">
      $discount</span> discount, the total
      cost is
50    $<span class=\"number\">$total</span>.<br />
51    Divided over <span class=\"number\">
      $payments</span> monthly payments, that
      would be $<span class=\"number\">
      $monthly</span> each.</p>";
52
53    ?>
54    </body>
55    </html>
```

Fill out this form to calculate the total cost:

Price: 5.00

Quantity: 100

Discount: 10.00

Tax: 7.5 (%)

Shipping method: Slow and steady ▾

Number of payments to make: 10

[Calculate!]

A The last execution of the form.

You have selected to purchase:
100 widget(s) at
$5.00 price each plus a
$5.00 shipping cost and a
7.5 percent tax rate.
After your **$10.00** discount, the total cost is **$532.13**.
Divided over **10** monthly payments, that would be **$53.21** each.

B It won't affect your calculations if you use the long or short version of incrementing a variable (compare Scripts 4.4 and 4.5).

---

3. Save the script, place it in the same directory as **calculator.html**, and test it in your browser **A** and **B**.

TIP Although functionally it doesn't matter whether you code $taxrate = $taxrate + 1; or the abbreviated $taxrate++, the latter method (using the increment operator) is more professional and common.

TIP In Chapter 6, "Control Structures," you'll see how the increment operator is commonly used in conjunction with loops.

Arithmetic Assignment Operators

PHP also supports a combination of mathematical and assignment operators. These are +=, -=, *=, and /=. Each will assign a value to a variable by performing a calculation on it. For example, these next two lines both add 5 to a variable:

```
$num = $num + 5;
$num += 5;
```

This means the **handle_calc.php** script could determine the tax rate using this:

```
$tax = $_POST['tax']; // Say, 5
$tax /= 100; // Now $tax is .05
$tax += 1; // 1.05
```

You'll frequently see these shorthand ways of performing arithmetic.

Creating Random Numbers

The last function you'll learn about in this chapter is **rand()**, a random-number generator. All it does is output a random number:

```
$n = rand(); // 31
$n = rand(); // 87
```

The **rand()** function can also take minimum and maximum parameters, if you prefer to limit the generated number to a specific range:

```
$n = rand (0, 10);
```

These values are inclusive, so in this case 0 and 10 are feasible returned values.

As an example of generating random numbers, let's create a simple "Lucky Numbers" script.

To generate random numbers:

1. Begin a new document in your text editor or IDE, to be named **random.php** (**Script 4.6**):

   ```
   <!DOCTYPE html PUBLIC "-//W3C//DTD
   → XHTML 1.0 Transitional//EN"
      "http://www.w3.org/TR/xhtml1/
      → DTD/xhtml1-transitional.dtd">
   <html xmlns="http://www.w3.org/
   → 1999/xhtml" xml:lang="en"
   → lang="en">
   <head>
     <meta http-equiv="Content-Type"
     → content="text/html;
     → charset=utf-8"/>
     <title>Lucky Numbers</title>
   </head>
   <body>
   ```

2. Include the PHP tags and address error management, if you need to:

   ```
   <?php // Script 4.6 - random.php
   ```

Script 4.6 The **rand()** function generates a random number.

```
1    <!DOCTYPE html PUBLIC "-//W3C//DTD XHTML
     1.0 Transitional//EN"
2       "http://www.w3.org/TR/xhtml1/DTD/
        xhtml1-transitional.dtd">
3    <html xmlns="http://www.w3.org/1999/
     xhtml" xml:lang="en" lang="en">
4    <head>
5       <meta http-equiv="Content-Type"
        content="text/html; charset=utf-8"/>
6       <title>Lucky Numbers</title>
7    </head>
8    <body>
9    <?php // Script 4.6 - random.php
10   /* This script generates 3 random
     numbers. */
11
12   // Address error handling, if you want.
13
14   // Create three random numbers:
15   $n1 = rand (1, 99);
16   $n2 = rand (1, 99);
17   $n3 = rand (1, 99);
18
19   // Print out the numbers:
20   print "<p>Your lucky numbers are:<br />
21   $n1<br />
22   $n2<br />
23   $n3</p>";
24
25   ?>
26   </body>
27   </html>
```

Your lucky numbers are:
32
68
71

A The three random numbers created by invoking the **rand()** function.

Your lucky numbers are:
23
81
2

B Running the script again produces different results.

Other Mathematical Functions

PHP has a number of built-in functions for manipulating mathematical data. This chapter introduced **round()**, **number_format()**, and **rand()**.

PHP has broken **round()** into two other functions. The first, **ceil()**, rounds every number to the next highest integer. The second, **floor()**, rounds every number to the next lowest integer.

Another function the calculator page could make good use of is **abs()**, which returns the absolute value of a number. In case you don't remember your absolute values, the function works like this:

```
$number = abs(-23); // 23
$number = abs(23); // 23
```

In layman's terms, the absolute value of a number is always a positive number.

Beyond these functions, PHP supports all the trigonometry, exponent, base conversion, and logarithm functions you'll ever need. See the PHP manual for more information.

3. Create three random numbers:

```
$n1 = rand (1, 99);
$n2 = rand (1, 99);
$n3 = rand (1, 99);
```

This script prints out a person's lucky numbers, like those found on the back of a fortune cookie. These numbers are generated by calling the **rand()** function three separate times and assigning each result to a different variable.

4. Print out the numbers:

```
print "<p>Your lucky numbers
are:<br />
$n1<br />
$n2<br />
$n3</p>";
```

The **print** statement is fairly simple. The numbers are printed, each on its own line, by using the HTML break tag.

5. Close the PHP code and the HTML page:

```
?>
</body>
</html>
```

6. Save the file as **random.php**, place it in the proper directory for your PHP-enabled server, and test it in your Web browser **A**. Refresh the page to see different numbers **B**.

TIP The getrandmax() function returns the largest possible random number that can be created using rand(). This value differs by operating system.

TIP PHP has another function that generates random numbers: mt_rand(). It works similarly to (but, arguably, better than) rand() and is the smarter choice for sensitive situations like cryptography. Also see the PHP manual's page for the mt_rand() function for more discussion of generating random numbers as a whole.

Review and Pursue

If you have any problems with the review questions or the pursue prompts, turn to the book's supporting forum (www. LarryUllman.com/forum/).

Review

- What are the four primary arithmetic operators?

- Why will the following code not work:

  ```
  print "The total is $$total";
  ```

  What must be done instead?

- Why must an HTML page that contains a form that's being submitted to a PHP script be loaded through a URL?

- What functions can be used to format numerical values? How do you format numbers to a specific number of decimals?

- What is the importance of operator precedence?

- What are the incremental and decremental operators?

- What are the arithmetic assignment operators?

Pursue

- Look up the PHP manual page for one of the new functions mentioned in this chapter. Use the links on that page to investigate a couple of other number-related functions PHP has.

- Create another HTML form for taking numeric values. Then create the PHP script that receives the form data, performs some calculations, formats the values, and prints the results.

5

Using Strings

As introduced in Chapter 2, "Variables," a second category of variables used by PHP is strings—a collection of characters enclosed within either single or double quotation marks. A string variable may consist of a single letter, a word, a sentence, a paragraph, HTML code, or even a jumble of nonsensical letters, numbers, and symbols (which might represent a password). Strings may be the most common variable type used in PHP.

This chapter covers PHP's most basic built-in functions and operators for manipulating string data, regardless of whether the string originates from a form or is first declared within the script. Some common techniques will be introduced—joining strings together, trimming strings, and encoding strings. Other uses for strings are illustrated in subsequent chapters.

In This Chapter

Creating the HTML Form	92
Concatenating Strings	95
Handling Newlines	98
HTML and PHP	100
Encoding and Decoding Strings	103
Finding Substrings	107
Replacing Parts of a String	111
Review and Pursue	114

Creating the HTML Form

As in Chapter 3, let's begin by creating an HTML form that sends different values—in the form of string variables—to a PHP script. The theoretical example being used is an online bulletin board or forum where users can post a message, their email address, and their first and last names **Ⓐ**.

To create the HTML form:

1. Begin a new HTML document in your text editor or IDE, to be named **posting.html** (Script 5.1):

   ```
   <!DOCTYPE html PUBLIC "-//W3C//DTD
   → XHTML 1.0 Transitional//EN"
     "http://www.w3.org/TR/xhtml1/
   → DTD/xhtml1-transitional.dtd">
   <html xmlns="http://www.w3.org/
   → 1999/xhtml" xml:lang="en"
   → lang="en">
   <head>
     <meta http-equiv="Content-Type"
   → content="text/html;
   → charset=utf-8"/>
     <title>Forum Posting</title>
   </head>
   <body>
   <!-- Script 5.1 - posting.html -->
   <div><p>Please complete this form
   → to submit your posting:</p>
   ```

2. Create the initial **form** tag:

   ```
   <form action="handle_post.php"
   → method="post">
   ```

   This form will send its data to the **handle_post.php** script and will use the POST method.

Please complete this form to submit your posting:

First Name:

Last Name:

Email Address:

Posting:

Send My Posting

Ⓐ This HTML form is the basis for most of the examples in this chapter.

Script 5.1 This form sends string data to a PHP script.

```
1   <!DOCTYPE html PUBLIC "-//W3C//DTD
    XHTML 1.0 Transitional//EN"
2       "http://www.w3.org/TR/xhtml1/DTD/
    xhtml1-transitional.dtd">
3   <html xmlns="http://www.w3.org/1999/
    xhtml" xml:lang="en" lang="en">
4   <head>
5       <meta http-equiv="Content-Type"
    content="text/html; charset=utf-8"/>
6       <title>Forum Posting</title>
7   </head>
8   <body>
9   <!-- Script 5.1 - posting.html -->
10  <div><p>Please complete this form to
    submit your posting:</p>
11
12  <form action="handle_post.php"
    method="post">
13
14      <p>First Name: <input type="text"
    name="first_name" size="20" /></p>
15
16      <p>Last Name: <input type="text"
    name="last_name" size="20" /></p>
17
18      <p>Email Address: <input type="text"
    name="email" size="30" /></p>
19
20      <p>Posting: <textarea name="posting"
    rows="9" cols="30"></textarea></p>
21
22      <input type="submit" name="submit"
    value="Send My Posting" />
23
24  </form>
25  </div>
26  </body>
27  </html>
```

3. Add inputs for the first name, last name, and email address:

```
<p>First Name: <input type="text"
→ name="first_name" size="20" /></p>
<p>Last Name: <input type="text"
→ name="last_name" size="20" /></p>
<p>Email Address: <input type=
→ "text" name="email"
→ size="30" /></p>
```

These are all basic text input types, which were covered in Chapter 3. Remember that the various inputs' name values should adhere to the rules of PHP variable names (no spaces; must not begin with a number; must consist only of letters, numbers, and the underscore).

4. Add an input for the posting:

```
<p>Posting: <textarea
→ name="posting" rows="9"
→ cols="30"></textarea></p>
```

The posting field is a **textarea**, which is a larger type of text input box.

5. Create a submit button and close the form:

```
<input type="submit" name="submit"
→ value="Send My Posting" />
</form>
```

Every form must have a submit button (or a submit image).

6. Complete the HTML page:

```
</div>
</body>
</html>
```

continues on next page

7. Save the file as **posting.html**, place it in the appropriate directory on your PHP-enabled server, and view it in your Web browser **Ⓐ**.

This is an HTML page, so it doesn't have to be on a PHP-enabled server in order for you to view it. But because it will eventually send data to a PHP script, it's best to go ahead and place the file on your server.

TIP Technically speaking, all form data, aside from uploaded files, is sent to the handling script as strings. This includes numeric data entered into text boxes, options selected from drop-down menus, checkbox or radio button values, and so forth. Even the form in Chapter 4, "Using Numbers," sent strings with numeric values to the handling script.

TIP Many forum systems written in PHP are freely available for your use. This book doesn't discuss how to fully develop one, but a multilingual forum is developed in my *PHP 6 and MySQL 5 for Dynamic Web Sites: Visual QuickPro Guide* (Peachpit Press, 2007).

TIP This book's Web site has a forum where readers can post questions and other readers (and the author) answer questions. You can find it at www.LarryUllman.com/forum/list.php?30.

Concatenating Strings

Concatenation is an unwieldy term but a useful concept. It refers to the appending of one item onto another. Specifically, in programming, you concatenate *strings*. The period (**.**) is the operator for performing this action, and it's used like so:

```
$s1 = 'Hello, ';
$s2 = 'world!';
$greeting = $s1 . $s2;
```

The end result of this concatenation is that the **$greeting** variable has a value of *Hello, world!*.

Because of the way PHP deals with variables, the same effect could be accomplished using

```
$greeting = "$s1$s2";
```

This code works because PHP replaces variables within double quotation marks with their value. However, the formal method of using the period to concatenate strings is more commonly used and is recommended (it will be more obvious what's occurring in your code).

Another way of performing concatenation involves the *concatenation assignment operator*:

```
$greeting = 'Hello, ';
$greeting .= 'world!';
```

This second line roughly means "assign to **$greeting** its current value plus the concatenation of *world!*" The end result is **$greeting** having the value *Hello, world!* once again.

The **posting.html** script sends several string variables to the **handle_post.php** page. Of those variables, the first and last names could logically be concatenated. It's quite common, and even recommended, to take a user's first and last names as separate inputs, as this form does. On the other hand, it would be advantageous to be able to refer to the two together as one name. You'll write the PHP script with this in mind.

To use concatenation:

1. Begin a new document in your text editor or IDE, to be named **handle_post.php** (Script 5.2):

```
<!DOCTYPE html PUBLIC "-//W3C//DTD
→ XHTML 1.0 Transitional//EN"
   "http://www.w3.org/TR/xhtml1/
      → DTD/xhtml1-transitional.dtd">
<html xmlns="http://www.w3.org/
→ 1999/xhtml" xml:lang="en"
→ lang="en">
<head>
   <meta http-equiv="Content-Type"
      → content="text/html;
charset=utf-8"/>
   <title>Forum Posting</title>
</head>
<body>
```

2. Create the initial PHP tag, and address error management, if necessary:

```
<?php // Script 5.2 -
→ handle_post.php
```

If you don't have **display_errors** enabled, or if **error_reporting** is set to the wrong level, see Chapter 3 for the lines to include here to alter those settings.

3. Assign the form data to local variables:

```
$first_name = $_POST['first_name'];
$last_name = $_POST['last_name'];
$posting = $_POST['posting'];
```

The form uses the POST method, so all the form data will be available in **$_POST**.

This example doesn't have a line for the email address because you won't be using it yet, but you can replicate this code to reference that value as well.

4. Create a new **$name** variable using concatenation:

```
$name = $first_name . ' ' .
→ $last_name;
```

Script 5.2 This PHP script demonstrates *concatenation*, one of the most common manipulations of a string variable. Think of it as addition for strings.

```
1    <!DOCTYPE html PUBLIC "-//W3C//DTD
     XHTML 1.0 Transitional//EN"
2        "http://www.w3.org/TR/xhtml1/DTD/
         xhtml1-transitional.dtd">
3    <html xmlns="http://www.w3.org/1999/
     xhtml" xml:lang="en" lang="en">
4    <head>
5        <meta http-equiv="Content-Type"
         content="text/html; charset=utf-8"/>
6        <title>Forum Posting</title>
7    </head>
8    <body>
9    <?php // Script 5.2 - handle_post.php
10   /* This script receives five values
     from posting.html:
11   first_name, last_name, email, posting,
     submit */
12
13   // Address error management, if you
     want.
14
15   // Get the values from the $_POST
     array:
16   $first_name = $_POST['first_name'];
17   $last_name = $_POST['last_name'];
18   $posting = $_POST['posting'];
19
20   // Create a full name variable:
21   $name = $first_name . ' ' .
     $last_name;
22
23   // Print a message:
24   print "<div>Thank you, $name, for
     your posting:
25   <p>$posting</p></div>";
26
27   ?>
28   </body>
29   </html>
```

Please complete this form to submit your posting:

First Name: Jeremy

Last Name: Messersmith

Email Address: jm@example.org

This is my posting. It could be more original.

Posting:

Send My Posting

A The HTML form in use...

Thank you, Jeremy Messersmith, for your posting:

This is my posting. It could be more original.

B ...and the resulting PHP page.

TIP You can link as many strings as you want using concatenation. You can even join numbers to strings:

```
$new_string = $s1 . $s2 . $number;
```

This works because PHP is *weakly typed*, meaning that its variables aren't locked in to one particular format. Here, the $number variable will be turned into a string and appended to the value of the $new_string variable.

TIP Concatenation can be used in many ways, even when you're feeding arguments to a function. An uncommon but functional example would be

```
$text = nl2br($heading . $body);
```

The nl2br() function, first mentioned in Chapter 1, "Getting Started with PHP," will be discussed in detail next.

This act of concatenation takes two variables plus a space and joins them all together to create a new variable, called **$name**. Assuming you entered *Elliott* and *Smith* as the names, then **$name** would be equal to *Elliott Smith*.

5. Print out the message to the user:

```
print "<div>Thank you, $name, for
→ your posting:
<p>$posting</p></div>";
```

This message reports back to the user what was entered in the form.

6. Close the PHP section and complete the HTML page:

```
?>
</body>
</html>
```

7. Save your script as **handle_post.php**, place it in the same directory as **posting.html** (on your PHP-enabled server), and test both the form and the script in your Web browser **A** and **B**.

As a reminder, you must load the form through a URL (*http://something*) so that, when the form is submitted, the handling PHP script is also run through a URL.

TIP If you used quotation marks of any kind in your form and saw extraneous slashes in the printed result, see the sidebar "Magic Quotes" in Chapter 3 for an explanation of the cause and for the fix.

TIP As a reminder, it's important to understand the difference between single and double quotation marks in PHP. Characters within single quotation marks are treated literally; characters within double quotation marks are interpreted (for example, a variable's name will be replaced by its value). See Chapter 3 for a refresher.

Handling Newlines

A common question beginning PHP developers have involves handling newlines in strings. The **textarea** form element allows a user to enter text over multiple lines by pressing Return/Enter. Each use of Return/Enter equates to a newline in the resulting string. These newlines work within a **textarea** but have no effect on a rendered PHP page **A** and **B**.

To create the equivalent of newlines in a rendered Web page, you use the break tag: **
. Fortunately, PHP has the **nl2br() function, which automatically converts newlines into break tags:

$var = nl2br($var);

Let's apply this function to **handle_post.php** so that the user's posting retains its formatting.

To convert newlines to breaks:

1. Open **handle_post.php** (Script 5.2) in your text editor or IDE, if it is not already open.

2. Apply the **nl2br()** function when assigning a value to the **$posting** variable (**Script 5.3**):

   $posting = nl2br($_POST['posting']);

   Now **$posting** will be assigned the value of **$_POST['posting']**, with any newlines converted to HTML break tags.

Please complete this form to submit your posting:

First Name: Rocky

Last Name: Votolato

Email Address: rv@example.edu

    Here's one line.

    Here's another line.

    Here's a third line.

Posting:

[Send My Posting]

A Newlines in form data like text areas…

Thank you, Rocky Votolato, for your posting:

Here's one line. Here's another line. Here's a third line.

B …are not rendered by the Web browser.

Thank you, Rocky Votolato, for your posting:

Here's one line.

Here's another line.

Here's a third line.

C Now the same submitted data **A** is properly displayed over multiple lines in the Web browser.

```
<div>Thank you, Rocky Votolato, for your posting:
<p>Here's one line.

Here's another line.

Here's a third line.</p></div></body>
</html>
```

D The HTML source, corresponding to **B**, shows the effect that newlines have in the Web browser (i.e., they add spacing within the HTML source code).

```
1    <!DOCTYPE html PUBLIC "-//W3C//DTD
     XHTML 1.0 Transitional//EN"
2       "http://www.w3.org/TR/xhtml1/DTD/
        xhtml1-transitional.dtd">
3    <html xmlns="http://www.w3.org/1999/
     xhtml" xml:lang="en" lang="en">
4    <head>
5       <meta http-equiv="Content-Type"
        content="text/html; charset=utf-8"/>
6       <title>Forum Posting</title>
7    </head>
8    <body>
9    <?php // Script 5.3 - handle_post.php #2
10   /* This script receives five values
     from posting.html:
11   first_name, last_name, email, posting,
     submit */
12
13   // Address error management, if you
     want.
14
15   // Get the values from the $_POST
     array:
16   $first_name = $_POST['first_name'];
17   $last_name = $_POST['last_name'];
18   $posting = nl2br($_POST['posting']);
19
20   // Create a full name variable:
21   $name = $first_name . ' ' . $last_name;
22
23   // Print a message:
24   print "<div>Thank you, $name, for your
     posting:
25   <p>$posting</p></div>";
26
27   ?>
28   </body>
29   </html>
```

3. Save the file, place it in the same directory as **posting.html** (on your PHP-enabled server), and test again in your Web browser **C**.

TIP Newlines can also be inserted into strings by placing the newline character—\n—between double quotation marks.

TIP Other HTML tags, like paragraph tags, also affect spacing in the rendered Web page. You can turn newlines (or any character) into paragraph tags using a replace function, but the code for doing so is far more involved than just invoking nl2br().

TIP Newlines present in strings sent to the browser will have an effect, but only in the HTML source of the page **D**.

HTML and PHP

As stated several times over by now, PHP is a server-side technology that's frequently used to send data to the Web browser. This data can be in the form of plain text, HTML code, or, more commonly, both.

In this chapter's primary example, data is entered in an HTML form and then printed back to the Web browser using PHP. A potential problem is that the user can enter HTML characters in the form, which can affect the resulting page's formatting  and **B**—or, worse, cause security problems.

You can use a couple of PHP functions to manipulate HTML tags within PHP string variables:

- **htmlspecialchars()** converts *certain* HTML tags into their *entity versions*.

- **htmlentities()** turns *all* HTML tags into their *entity versions*.

- **strip_tags()** removes all HTML and PHP tags.

The first two functions turn an HTML tag (for example, **<span>**) into an entity version like **<span>**. The entity version appears in the output but isn't rendered. You might use either of these if you wanted to display code without enacting it. The third function, **strip_tags()**, removes HTML and PHP tags entirely.

You ought to watch for special tags in user-provided data for two reasons. First, as already mentioned, submitted HTML would likely affect the rendered page (e.g., mess up a table, tweak the CSS, or just add formatting where there shouldn't be any). The second concern is more important. Because JavaScript is placed within HTML **script** tags, a malicious user could submit JavaScript that would be executed when it's redisplayed on the page **C**. This is how *cross-site scripting* (XSS) attacks are performed.

A If the user enters HTML code in the posting...

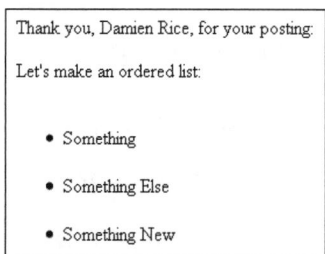

B ...it's rendered by the Web browser when reprinted.

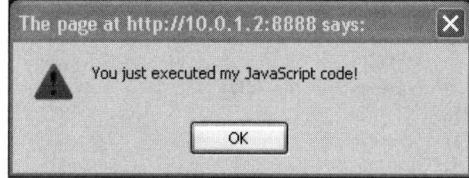

C Displaying HTML submitted by a user in the Web browser can have terrible consequences, such as the execution of JavaScript.

Script 5.4 This version of the PHP script addresses HTML tags in two different ways.

```
1    <!DOCTYPE html PUBLIC "-//W3C//DTD
     XHTML 1.0 Transitional//EN"
2        "http://www.w3.org/TR/xhtml1/DTD/
         xhtml1-transitional.dtd">
3    <html xmlns="http://www.w3.org/1999/
     xhtml" xml:lang="en" lang="en">
4    <head>
5        <meta http-equiv="Content-Type"
         content="text/html; charset=utf-8"/>
6        <title>Forum Posting</title>
7    </head>
8    <body>
9    <?php // Script 5.4 - handle_post.php #3
10   /* This script receives five values
     from posting.html:
11   first_name, last_name, email, posting,
     submit */
12
13   // Address error management, if you
     want.
14
15   // Get the values from the $_POST
     array:
16   $first_name = $_POST['first_name'];
17   $last_name = $_POST['last_name'];
18   $posting = nl2br($_POST['posting']);
19
20   // Create a full name variable:
21   $name = $first_name . ' ' . $last_name;
22
23   // Adjust for HTML tags:
24   $html_post = htmlentities($_POST
     ['posting']);
25   $strip_post = strip_tags($_POST
     ['posting']);
26
27   // Print a message:
28   print "<div>Thank you, $name, for
     your posting:
29   <p>Original: $posting</p>
30   <p>Entity: $html_post</p>
31   <p>Stripped: $strip_post</p></div>";
32
33   ?>
34   </body>
35   </html>
```

To see the impact these functions have, this next rewrite of **handle_post.php** will use them each and display the respective results.

To address HTML in PHP:

1. Open **handle_post.php** (Script 5.3) in your text editor or IDE, if it is not already open.

2. Before the **print** line, add (**Script 5.4**):

   ```
   $html_post = htmlentities
   → ($_POST['posting']);
   $strip_post = strip_tags
   → ($_POST['posting']);
   ```

   To clarify the difference between how these two functions work, apply them both to the posting text, creating two new variables in the process. Refer to **$_POST['posting']** here and not **$posting** because **$posting** already reflects the application of the **nl2br()** function, which means that break tags may have been introduced that were not explicitly entered by the user.

3. Alter the **print** statement to read as follows:

   ```
   print "<div>Thank you, $name, for
   → your posting:
   <p>Original: $posting</p>
   <p>Entity: $html_post</p>
   <p>Stripped: $strip_post</p></div>";
   ```

   To highlight the different results, print out the three different versions of the posting text. First is the original posting as it was entered, after being run through **nl2br()**. Next is the **htmlentities()** version of the posting, which will show the HTML tags without rendering them. Finally, the **strip_tags()** version will be printed; it doesn't include any HTML (or PHP) tags.

   continues on next page

4. Save the file, place it in the same directory as **posting.html** (on your PHP-enabled server), and test it again in your Web browser **D** and **E**.

If you view the HTML source code of the resulting PHP page **F**, you'll also see the effect that applying these functions has.

TIP For security purposes, it's almost always a good idea to use htmlentities(), htmlspecialchars(), or strip_tags() to any user-provided data that's being printed to the Web browser. I don't do so through the course of this book only to minimize clutter.

TIP The html_entity_decode() function does just the opposite of htmlentities(), turning HTML entities into their respective HTML code.

TIP Another useful function for outputting strings in the Web browser is wordwrap(). This function wraps a string to a certain number of characters.

TIP To turn newlines into breaks while still removing any HTML or PHP tags, apply nl2br() after strip_tags():

```
$posting =
nl2br(strip_tags($_POST['posting']));
```

In that line, the strip_tags() function will be called first, and its result will be sent to the nl2br() function.

Please complete this form to submit your posting:

First Name: `Laura`

Last Name: `Burhenn`

Email Address: `lb@example.com`

```
I don't understand why it says
<em>something</em>.
```

Posting:

`Send My Posting`

D The HTML characters entered as part of a posting will now be addressed by PHP.

Thank you, Laura Burhenn, for your posting:

Original: I don't understand why it says *something*.

Entity: I don't understand why it says something.

Stripped: I don't understand why it says something.

E The resulting PHP page shows the original post as it would look if printed without modification, the effect of **htmlentities()**, and the effect of **strip_tags()**.

```
<p>Original: I don't understand why it says <em>something</em>.</p>
<p>Entity: I don't understand why it says &lt;em&gt;something&lt;/em&gt;.</p>
<p>Stripped: I don't understand why it says something.</p></div></body>
```

F The HTML source for the content displayed in **E**.

```
1    <!DOCTYPE html PUBLIC "-//W3C//DTD
     XHTML 1.0 Transitional//EN"
2       "http://www.w3.org/TR/xhtml1/DTD/
     xhtml1-transitional.dtd">
3    <html xmlns="http://www.w3.org/1999/
     xhtml" xml:lang="en" lang="en">
4    <head>
5       <meta http-equiv="Content-Type"
        content="text/html; charset=utf-8"/>
6       <title>Forum Posting</title>
7    </head>
8    <body>
9    <?php // Script 5.5 - handle_post.php #4
10   /* This script receives five values
     from posting.html:
11   first_name, last_name, email, posting,
     submit */
12
13   // Address error management, if you
     want.
14
15   // Get the values from the $_POST
     array:
16   $first_name = $_POST['first_name'];
17   $last_name = $_POST['last_name'];
18   $posting = nl2br($_POST['posting']);
19
20   // Create a full name variable:
21   $name = $first_name . ' ' . $last_name;
22
23   // Print a message:
24   print "<div>Thank you, $name, for your
     posting:
25   <p>$posting</p></div>";
26
27   // Make a link to another page:
28   $name = urlencode($name);
29   $email = urlencode($_POST['email']);
30   print "<p>Click <a href=\"   thanks.php?
     name=$name&email=$email   \">here
     </a> to continue.</p>";
31
32   ?>
33   </body>
34   </html>
```

Encoding and Decoding Strings

At the end of Chapter 3, the section "Manually Sending Data to a Page" demonstrated how to use the thinking behind the GET form method to send data to a page. In that example, instead of using an actual form, data was appended to the URL, making it available to the receiving script. I was careful to say that only single words could be passed this way, without spaces or punctuation. But what if you want to pass several words as one variable value or use special characters?

To safely pass any value to a PHP script through the URL, apply the **urlencode()** function. As its name implies, this function takes a string and *encodes* it (changes its format) so that it can properly be passed as part of a URL. Among other things, the function replaces spaces with plus signs (**+**) and translates special characters (for example, the apostrophe) into less problematic versions. To use this function, you might code

$string = urlencode($string);

To demonstrate one application of **urlencode()**, let's update the **handle_post.php** page so that it also creates a link that passes the user's name and email address to a third page.

To use urlencode():

1. Open **handle_post.php** (Script 5.4) in your text editor or IDE, if it is not already open.

2. Delete the **htmlentities()** and **strip_tags()** lines added in the previous set of steps (**Script 5.5**).

continues on next page

3. Revert to the older version of the **print** invocation:

```
print "<div>Thank you, $name, for
→ your posting:
<p>$posting</p></div>";
```

4. After the **print** statement, add the following:

```
$name = urlencode($name);
$email = urlencode($_POST['email']);
```

This script will pass these two variables to a second page. In order for it to do so, they must both be encoded.

Because the script has not previously referred to or used the **$email** variable, the second line both retrieves the email value from the **$_POST** array and encodes it in one step. This is the same as having these two separate lines:

```
$email = $_POST['email'];
$email = urlencode($email);
```

5. Add another **print** statement that creates the link:

```
print "<p>Click <a href=\"thanks.
→ php?name=$name&email=$email\">
→ here</a> to continue.</p>";
```

The primary purpose of this **print** statement is to create an HTML link in the Web page, the source code of which would be something like

```
<a href="thanks.php?name=Larry+
→ Ullman&email=larry%40example.
→ com">here</a>
```

To accomplish this, begin by hard-coding most of the HTML and then include the appropriate variable names. Because the HTML code requires that the URL for the link be in double quotation marks—and the **print** statement already uses double quotation marks—you must escape them (by preceding them with backslashes) in order for them to be printed.

Please complete this form to submit your posting:

First Name: Christopher

Last Name: O'Reilly

Email Address: chris.oreilly@example.com

Nothing like a piano cover of
Radiohead or Elliott Smith!

Posting:

Send My Posting

A Another use of the form.

Thank you, Christopher O'Reilly, for your posting:

Nothing like a piano cover of Radiohead or Elliott Smith!

Click here to continue.

B The handling script now displays a link to another page.

6. Save the file, place it in the proper directory of your PHP-enabled server, and test it again in your Web browser **A** and **B**.

Note that clicking the link will result in a server error, as the **thanks.php** script hasn't yet been written.

7. View the HTML source code of the handling page to see the resulting link in the HTML code **C**.

TIP Values sent directly from a form are automatically URL-encoded prior to being sent and decoded upon arrival at the receiving script. You only need the `urlencode()` function to manually encode data (as in the example).

TIP The `urldecode()` function does just the opposite of `urlencode()`—it takes an encoded URL and turns it back into a standard form. You'll use it less frequently, though, as PHP will automatically decode most values it receives.

continues on next page

```
<p>Click <a href="thanks.php?name=Christopher+O%27Reilly&email=chris.oreilly%40example.com">here</a>
```

C The HTML source code of the page **B** shows the dynamically generated link.

TIP Since you can use concatenation with functions, the new `print` statement could be written as follows:

```
print 'Click <a href="thanks.php?
 name=' . $name . '&email=' .
 $email . '">here</a> to continue.';
```

This method has two added benefits over the original approach. First, it uses single quotation marks to start and stop the statement, meaning you don't need to escape the double quotation marks. Second, the variables used are more obvious—they aren't buried in a lot of other code.

TIP You do not need to encode numeric PHP values in order to use them in a URL, as they do not contain problematic characters. That being said, it won't hurt to encode them either.

TIP At the end of the chapter you'll be prompted to create `thanks.php`, which greets the user by name and email address **D**.

Thank you, Christopher O'Reilly.
We will contact you at chris.oreilly@example.com.

D The third page in this process—to be created by you at the end of the chapter—prints a message based on values it receives in the URL.

Encrypting and Decrypting Strings

Frequently, in order to protect data, programmers *encrypt* it—alter its state by transforming it to a form that's more difficult, if not impossible, to discern. Passwords are an example of a value you might want to encrypt. Depending on the level of security you want to establish, usernames, email addresses, and phone numbers are likely candidates for encryption, too.

You can use the **crypt()** function to encrypt data, but be aware that no decryption option is available (it's known as *one-way* encryption). So, a password may be encrypted using it and then stored, but the decrypted value of the password can never be determined. Using this function in a Web application, you might encrypt a user's password upon registration; then, when the user logged in, the password they entered at that time would also be encrypted, and the two protected versions of the password would be compared. The syntax for using **crypt()** is

`$data = crypt($data);`

A second encryption function is **mcrypt_encrypt()**, which can be decrypted using the appropriately named **mcrypt_decrypt()** function. Unfortunately, in order for you to be able to use these two functions, the Mcrypt extension must be installed with the PHP module. Its usage and syntax is also more complex (I discuss it in my *PHP 5 Advanced: Visual QuickPro Guide* [Peachpit Press, 2007]).

If the data is being stored in a database, you can also use functions built into the database application (for example, MySQL, PostgreSQL, Oracle, or SQL Server) to perform encryption and decryption. Depending on the technology you're using, it most likely provides both one- and two-way encryption tools.

Comparing Strings

To compare two strings, you can always use the equality operator, which you'll learn about in the next chapter. Otherwise, you can use these functions:

- **strcmp()** indicates how two strings compare by returning a whole number.

- **strnatcmp()** is similar but linguistically more precise.

These also have case-insensitive companions, **strcasecmp()** and **strnatcasecmp()**.

To see if a substring is contained within another string (i.e., to find a needle in a haystack), you'll use these functions:

- **strstr()** returns the haystack from the first occurrence of a needle to the end.

- **strpos()** searches through a haystack and returns the numeric location of a particular needle.

Both of these functions also have a case-insensitive alternative: **stristr()** and **stripos()**, respectively. Each of these functions is normally used in a conditional to test whether the substring was found.

Finding Substrings

PHP has a few functions you can use to pull apart strings, search through them, and perform comparisons. Although these functions are normally used with conditionals, discussed in Chapter 6, "Control Structures," they are important enough that they'll be introduced here; later chapters will use them more formally.

Earlier in this chapter you learned how to join strings using concatenation. Along with making larger strings out of smaller pieces, PHP easily lets you extract subsections from a string. The trick to using any method to pull out a subsection of a string is that you must know something about the string itself in order to know how to break it up.

The **strtok()** function creates a substring, referred to as a *token*, from a larger string by using a predetermined separator (such as a comma or a space). For example, if you have users enter their full name in one field (presumably with their first and last names separated by a space), you can pull out their first name with this code:

```
$first = strtok($_POST['name'], ' ');
```

That line tells PHP to extract everything from the beginning of **$_POST['name']** until it finds a blank space.

If you have users enter their full name in the format *Surname, First*, you can find their surname by writing

```
$last = strtok($_POST['name'], ', ');
```

A second way to pull out sections of a string is by referring to the *indexed position* of the characters within the string. The indexed position of a string is the numerical location of a character, counting from the beginning. However, PHP—like most programming languages—begins all indexes with the number 0. For example, to index the string *Larry*, you begin with the L at position 0, followed by *a* at 1, *r* at 2, the second *r* at 3, and *y* at 4. Even though the string length of *Larry* is 5, its index goes from 0 to 4 (i.e., indexes always go from 0 to the string's length minus 1).

With this in mind, you can call on the **substr()** function to create a substring based on the index position of the substring's characters:

```
$sub = substr($string, 0, 10);
```

The first argument is the master string from which the substring will be derived. Second, indicate where the substring begins, as its indexed position (0 means that you want to start with the first character). Third, from that starting point, state how many characters the substring should contain (10). If the master string does not have that many characters in it, the resulting substring will end with the end of the master string. This argument is optional; if omitted, the substring will also go until the end of the master string.

You can also use negative numbers to count backward from the end of the string:

```
$string = 'ardvark';
$sub = substr($string, -3, 3); // ark
```

The second line says that three characters should be returned starting at the third character from the end. With that particular example, you can again omit the third argument and have the same result:

```
$sub = substr($string, -3); // ark
```

Script 5.6 This version of **handle_post.php** counts the number of words in the posting and trims the displayed posting down to just the first 50 characters.

```
1    <!DOCTYPE html PUBLIC "-//W3C//DTD
     XHTML 1.0 Transitional//EN"
2        "http://www.w3.org/TR/xhtml1/DTD/
     xhtml1-transitional.dtd">
3    <html xmlns="http://www.w3.org/1999/
     xhtml" xml:lang="en" lang="en">
4    <head>
5        <meta http-equiv="Content-Type"
     content="text/html; charset=utf-8"/>
6        <title>Forum Posting</title>
7    </head>
8    <body>
9    <?php // Script 5.6 - handle_post.php #5
10   /* This script receives five values
     from posting.html:
11   first_name, last_name, email, posting,
     submit */
12
13   // Address error management, if you
     want.
14
15   // Get the values from the $_POST
     array:
16   $first_name = $_POST['first_name'];
17   $last_name = $_POST['last_name'];
18   $posting = nl2br($_POST['posting']);
19
20   // Create a full name variable:
21   $name = $first_name . ' ' . $last_name;
22
23   // Get a word count:
24   $words = str_word_count($posting);
25
26   // Get a snippet of the posting:
27   $posting = substr($posting, 0, 50);
28
29   // Print a message:
30   print "<div>Thank you, $name, for
     your posting:
31   <p>$posting...</p>
32   <p>($words words)</p></div>";
33
34   ?>
35   </body>
36   </html>
```

To see how many characters are in a string, use **strlen()**:

print strlen('Hello, world!'); // 13

The count will include spaces and punctuation. To see how many *words* are in a string, use **str_word_count()**. This function, along with **substr()**, will be used in this next revision of the **handle_post.php** script.

To create substrings:

1. Open **handle_post.php** (Script 5.5) in your text editor or IDE, if it is not already open.

2. Before the **print** statement, add the following (**Script 5.6**):

   $words = str_word_count($posting);

   This version of the script will do two new things with the user's posting. One will be to display the number of words it contains. That information is gathered here and assigned to the **$words** variable.

3. On the next line (also before the **print** statement), add

   $posting = substr($posting, 0, 50);

   The second new thing this script will do is limit the displayed posting to its first 50 characters. You might use this, for example, if one page shows the beginning of a post, then a link takes the user to the full posting. To implement this limit, the **substr()** function is called.

continues on next page

4. Update the **print** statement to read

```
print "<div>Thank you, $name, for
→ your posting:
<p>$posting...</p>
<p>($words words)</p></div>";
```

There are two changes here. First, ellipses are added after the posting to indicate that this is just part of the whole posting. Then, within another paragraph, the number of words is printed.

5. Delete the two **urlencode()** lines and the corresponding **print** line.

I'm referring specifically to the code added in the previous incarnation of the script, linking to **thanks.php**.

6. Save the file, place it in the proper directory of your PHP-enabled server, and test it again in your Web browser **A** and **B**.

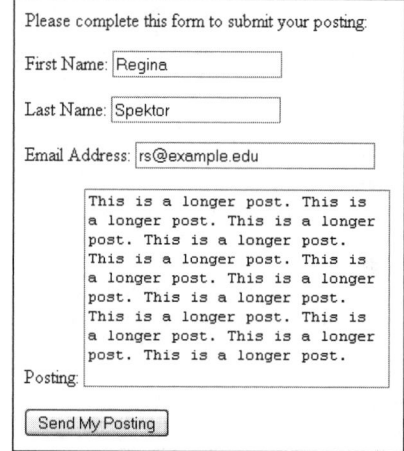

Please complete this form to submit your posting:

First Name: Regina

Last Name: Spektor

Email Address: rs@example.edu

This is a longer post. This is a longer post. This is a longer post. This is a longer post. This is a longer post. This is a longer post. This is a longer post. This is a longer post. This is a longer post. This is a longer post. This is a longer post. This is a longer post.

Posting:

Send My Posting

A Postings longer than 50 characters...

Thank you, Regina Spektor, for your posting:

This is a longer post. This is a longer post. This...

(60 words)

B ...will be cut short. The word count is also displayed.

Replacing Parts of a String

Instead of just finding substrings within a string, as the previous section discusses, you might find that you need to *replace substrings* with new values. You can do so using the **str_ireplace()** function:

```
$string = str_ireplace($needle,
→ $replacement, $haystack);
```

This function replaces every occurrence of **$needle** found in **$haystack** with **$replacement**. For example:

```
$me = 'Larry E. Ullman';
$me = str_ireplace('E.', 'Edward',
→ $me);
```

The **$me** variable now has a value of *Larry Edward Ullman*.

That function performs a *case-insensitive* search. To be more restrictive, you can perform a *case-sensitive* search using **str_replace()**. In this next script, **str_ireplace()** will be used to eliminate "bad words" in submitted text.

There's one last string-related function I want to discuss: **trim()**. This function removes any white space—spaces, newlines, and tabs—from the beginning and end of a string. It's quite common for extra spaces to be added to a string variable, either because a user enters information carelessly or due to sloppy HTML code. For purposes of clarity, data integrity, and Web design, it's worth your while to delete those spaces from the strings before you use them. Extra spaces sent to the Web browser could make the page appear oddly, and those sent to a database or cookie could have unfortunate consequences at a later date (for example, if a password has a superfluous space, it might not match when it's entered without the space).

The **trim()** function automatically strips away any extra spaces from both the beginning and the end of a string (but not the middle). The format for using **trim()** is as follows:

```
$string = ' extra space before and
→after text ';
$string = trim($string);
// $string is now equal to 'extra
→space before and after text'.
```

To use str_ireplace( ) and trim():

1. Open **handle_post.php** (Script 5.6) in your text editor or IDE, if it is not already open.

2. Apply **trim()** to the form data (**Script 5.7**):

```
$first_name =
→trim($_POST['first_name']);
$last_name =
→trim($_POST['last_name']);
$posting = trim($_POST['posting']);
```

Just in case the incoming data has extraneous white space at its beginning or end, the **trim()** function is applied.

3. Remove the use of **substr()**:

```
$posting = substr($posting, 0, 50);
```

You'll want to see the entire posting for this example, so remove this invocation of **substr()**.

4. Before the **print** statement, add

```
$posting = str_ireplace('badword',
→'XXXXX', $posting);
```

This specific example flags the use of a bad word in a posting by crossing it out. Rather than an actual curse word, the code uses **badword**. (You can use whatever you want, of course.)

Script 5.7 This final version of the handling script applies the **trim()** function and then replaces uses of **badword** with a bunch of Xs.

```
1   <!DOCTYPE html PUBLIC "-//W3C//DTD
    XHTML 1.0 Transitional//EN"
2      "http://www.w3.org/TR/xhtml1/DTD/
    xhtml1-transitional.dtd">
3   <html xmlns="http://www.w3.org/1999/
    xhtml" xml:lang="en" lang="en">
4   <head>
5      <meta http-equiv="Content-Type"
    content="text/html; charset=utf-8"/>
6      <title>Forum Posting</title>
7   </head>
8   <body>
9   <?php // Script 5.7 - handle_post.php #6
10  /* This script receives five values
    from posting.html:
11  first_name, last_name, email, posting,
    submit */
12
13  // Address error management, if you
    want.
14
15  // Get the values from the $_POST
    array.
16  // Strip away extra spaces using
    trim():
17  $first_name = trim($_POST
    ['first_name']);
18  $last_name = trim($_POST
    ['last_name']);
19  $posting = trim($_POST['posting']);
20
21  // Create a full name variable:
22  $name = $first_name . ' ' . $last_name;
23
24  // Get a word count:
25  $words = str_word_count($posting);
26
27  // Take out the bad words:
28  $posting = str_ireplace('badword',
    'XXXXX', $posting);
29
30  // Print a message:
31  print "<div>Thank you, $name, for your
    posting:
32  <p>$posting</p>
33  <p>($words words)</p></div>";
34
35  ?>
36  </body>
37  </html>
```

Please complete this form to submit your posting:

First Name: Bad

Last Name: Poster

Email Address: faker@bad.example.com

I feel like using a BADWORD in my post!

Posting:

Send My Posting

Ⓐ If a user enters a word you'd prefer they not use...

Thank you, Bad Poster, for your posting:

I feel like using a XXXXX in my post!

(9 words)

Ⓑ ...you can have PHP replace it.

If you'd like to catch many bad words, you can use multiple lines, like so:

```
$posting = str_ireplace
→('badword1', 'XXXXX', $posting);
$posting = str_ireplace
→('badword2', 'XXXXX', $posting);
$posting = str_ireplace
→('badword3', 'XXXXX', $posting);
```

5. Update the **print** statement so that it no longer uses the ellipses:

```
print "<div>Thank you, $name, for
→your posting:
<p>$posting</p>
<p>($words words)</p></div>";
```

6. Save the file, place it in the proper directory of your PHP-enabled server, and test again in your Web browser **Ⓐ** and **Ⓑ**.

TIP The str_ireplace() function will even catch bad words in context. For example, if you entered *I feel like using badwords*, the result would be *I feel like using XXXXXs*.

TIP The str_ireplace() function can also take an array of needle terms, an array of replacement terms, and even an array as the haystack. Because you may not know what an array is yet, this technique isn't demonstrated here.

TIP If you need to trim excess spaces from the beginning or the end of a string but not both, PHP breaks the trim() function into two more specific functions: rtrim() removes spaces found at the end of a string variable (on its right side), and ltrim() handles those at the beginning (its left). They're both used just like trim():

```
$string = rtrim($string);
$string = ltrim($string);
```

Review and Pursue

If you have any problems with the review questions or the pursue prompts, turn to the book's supporting forum (www.LarryUllman.com/forum/).

Review

- How do you create a string?

- What are the differences between using *single* and *double* quotation marks?

- What is the *concatenation* operator? What is the *concatenation assignment* operator?

- What is the impact of having a newline in a string printed to the browser? How do you convert a newline character to a break tag?

- What problems can occur when HTML is entered into form elements whose values will later be printed back to the Web browser? What steps can be taken to sanctify submitted form data?

- What function makes data safe to pass in a URL?

- How do you escape problematic characters within a string? What happens if you do not escape them?

- The characters in a string are indexed beginning at what number?

- What does the **trim()** function do?

Pursue

- Look up the PHP manual page for one of the new functions mentioned in this chapter. Use the links on that page to examine a couple of other string-related functions PHP has.

- Check out the PHP manual page specifically for the **substr()** function. Read the other examples found on that page to get a better sense of how **substr()** can be used.

- Write the **thanks.php** script that goes along with Script 5.5. If you need help, revisit the **hello.php** script from Chapter 3 (Script 3.7).

- Rewrite the **print** statement in the final version of **handle_post.php** (Script 5.7), so that it uses single quotation marks and concatenation instead of double quotation marks.

- Create another HTML form for taking string values. Then create the PHP script that receives the form data, addresses any HTML or PHP code, manipulates the data in some way, and prints out the results.

6

Control Structures

Control structures—*conditionals* and *loops*—are a staple of programming languages. PHP has two conditionals—**if** and **switch**—both of which you'll master in this chapter. Conditionals allow you to establish a test and then perform actions based on the results. This functionality provides the ability to make Web sites even more dynamic.

The discussion of **if** conditionals requires introduction of two last categories of operators: *comparison* and *logical* (you've already seen the arithmetic and assignment operators in the previous chapters). You'll commonly use these operators in your conditionals, along with the Boolean concepts of *TRUE* and *FALSE*.

Finally, this chapter introduces loops, which allow you to repeat an action for a specified number of iterations. Loops can save you programming time and help you get the most functionality out of arrays, as you'll see in the next chapter.

In This Chapter

Creating the HTML Form	116
The if Conditional	119
Validation Functions	122
Using else	126
More Operators	129
Using elseif	138
The Switch Conditional	142
The for Loop	146
Review and Pursue	150

Creating the HTML Form

As with the previous chapters, the examples in this chapter are based on an HTML form that sends data to a PHP page. In this case, the form is a simple registration page that requests the following information **Ⓐ**:

- Email address
- Password
- Confirmation of the password
- Year of birth (to verify age)
- Favorite color (for customization purposes)
- Agreement to the site's terms (a common requirement)

The following steps walk through the creation of this form before getting into the PHP code.

To create the HTML form:

1. Begin a new HTML document in your text editor or IDE, to be named **register.html** (Script 6.1):

```
<!DOCTYPE html PUBLIC "-//W3C//DTD
→ XHTML 1.0 Transitional//EN"
  "http://www.w3.org/TR/xhtml1/
  → DTD/xhtml1-transitional.dtd">
<html xmlns="http://www.w3.org/
→ 1999/xhtml" xml:lang="en"
→ lang="en">
<head>
  <meta http-equiv="Content-Type"
  → content="text/html;
  → charset=utf-8"/>
  <title>Registration Form</title>
</head>
<body>
<!-- Script 6.1 - register.html -->
<div><p>Please complete this form
→ to register:</p>
```

Ⓐ The HTML form used in this chapter.

Script 6.1 This pseudo-registration form is the basis for the examples in this chapter.

```
1   <!DOCTYPE html PUBLIC "-//W3C//DTD
    XHTML 1.0 Transitional//EN"
2      "http://www.w3.org/TR/xhtml1/DTD/
       xhtml1-transitional.dtd">
3   <html xmlns="http://www.w3.org/1999/
    xhtml" xml:lang="en" lang="en">
4   <head>
5      <meta http-equiv="Content-Type"
       content="text/html; charset=utf-8"/>
6      <title>Registration Form</title>
7   </head>
8   <body>
9   <!-- Script 6.1 - register.html -->
10  <div><p>Please complete this form to
    register:</p>
11
12  <form action="handle_reg.php"
    method="post">
13
14     <p>Email Address: <input type="text"
       name="email" size="30" /></p>
15
16     <p>Password: <input type="password"
       name="password" size="20" /></p>
17
18     <p>Confirm Password: <input
       type="password" name="confirm"
       size="20" /></p>
19
```

code continues on next page

```
20      <p>Year You Were Born: <input
        type="text" name="year"
        value="YYYY" size="4" /></p>
21
22      <p>Favorite Color:
23      <select name="color">
24      <option value="">Pick One</option>
25      <option value="red">Red</option>
26      <option value="yellow">Yellow
        </option>
27      <option value="green">Green</option>
28      <option value="blue">Blue</option>
29      </select></p>
30
31      <p><input type="checkbox"
        name="terms" value="Yes" /> I agree
        to the terms (whatever they may
        be).</p>
32
33      <input type="submit" name="submit"
        value="Register" />
34
35      </form>
36
37      </div>
38      </body>
39      </html>
```

Password: ●●●●●●●●●●●●●

B A password input type, as it's being filled out.

2. Create the initial **form** tag:

   ```
   <form action="handle_reg.php"
   → method="post">
   ```

   As with many of the previous examples, this page uses the POST method. The handling script, identified by the **action** attribute, will be **handle_reg.php**, found in the same directory as the HTML form.

3. Create inputs for the email address and passwords:

   ```
   <p>Email Address: <input
   → type="text" name="email"
   → size="30" /></p>
   <p>Password: <input
   → type="password" name="password"
   → size="20" /></p>
   <p>Confirm Password: <input
   → type="password" name="confirm"
   → size="20" /></p>
   ```

   These lines should be self-evident. Each line is wrapped in HTML **<p></p>** tags to improve the spacing in the Web browser. Also, note that two password inputs are created—the second is used to confirm the text entered in the first. Password input types don't reveal what the user enters **B**, so it's a standard policy to require the user to enter passwords twice (thereby ensuring that users know exactly what password they provided).

4. Create an input for the user's birth year:

   ```
   <p>Year You Were Born: <input
   → type="text" name="year"
   → value="YYYY" size="4" /></p>
   ```

   Rather than use a drop-down menu that displays 50 or 100 years, have users enter their birth year in a text box. By presetting the **value** attribute of the input, you make the text box indicate the proper format for the year **A**.

continues on next page

5. Create a drop-down menu for the user's favorite color:

```
<p>Favorite Color:
<select name="color">
<option value="">Pick One</option>
<option value="red">Red</option>
<option value="yellow">Yellow
→ </option>
<option value="green">Green</option>
<option value="blue">Blue</option>
</select></p>
```

The truth is that I'm adding this input so that it can be used for a specific example later in the chapter, but it might be used to customize the look of the site after the user logs in. Naturally, you can add as many colors as you want here.

6. Create a check box for the user to agree to the site's terms:

```
<p><input type="checkbox"
→ name="terms" value="Yes" />
→ I agree to the terms (whatever
→ they may be).</p>
```

Many sites have some sort of terms or licensing that the user must indicate acceptance of, normally by checking a box. This particular form doesn't have a link to where the user can read the terms, but it probably doesn't matter as no one reads them (and this is just a hypothetical example anyway). In any case, using this element, you'll be able to see how checkboxes are treated by the handling PHP script.

7. Add a submit button and close the form:

```
    <input type="submit" name=
    → "submit" value="Register" />
</form>
```

8. Complete the HTML page:

```
</div>
</body>
</html>
```

9. Save the file as **register.html**, place it in the proper directory for your PHP-enabled server, and load the page in your Web browser.

TIP Registration pages should always have users confirm their password and possibly their username or email address (whatever information will be used to log in).

TIP Most registration pages use either a nickname or an email address for the username. If you use the email address as a username, it's easier for your users to remember their registration information (a user may have only a couple of email addresses but a gazillion usernames for different sites around the Web). Furthermore, email addresses are, by their nature, unique to an individual, whereas usernames are not.

The if Conditional

The basic programming conditional is the standard **if** (what used to be called an **if-then** conditional—the **then** is now implied). The syntax for this kind of conditional is simple:

```
if (condition) {
    statement(s);
}
```

The *condition* must go within parentheses; then the *statement(s)* are placed within curly brackets. The statements are commands to be executed (for example, printing a string or adding two numbers together). Each separate statement (or command) must have its own semicolon indicating the end of the line, but there is no limit on the number of statements that can be associated with a conditional.

Programmers commonly indent these statements from the initial **if** line to indicate that they're the result of a conditional, but that format isn't syntactically required. You'll also see people use this syntax:

```
if (condition)
{
    statement(s);
}
```

How you arrange your curly brackets is a matter of personal preference—and the source of minor online skirmishes. Just pick a style you like and stick to it.

Failure to use a semicolon after each statement, forgetting an opening or closing parenthesis or curly bracket, or using a semicolon after either of the braces will cause errors to occur. Be mindful of your syntax as you code with conditionals!

PHP uses the Boolean concepts of TRUE and FALSE when determining whether to execute the statements. If the condition is TRUE, the statements are executed; if it's FALSE, they are not executed **Ⓐ**.

continues on next page

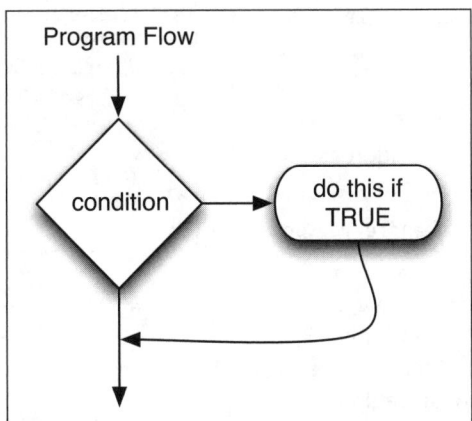

Ⓐ How an **IF** conditional affects the program flow of a script.

Over the course of this chapter (most of it, anyway), a PHP script will be developed until it fully validates the **register.html** form data. To start, this first version of the script will just create the basic shell of the validation process, defining and using a variable with a Boolean value that will track the success of the validation process.

To create an if conditional:

1. Begin a new document in your text editor or IDE, to be named **handle_reg.php** (Script 6.2):

```
<!DOCTYPE html PUBLIC "-//W3C//DTD
→ XHTML 1.0 Transitional//EN"
   "http://www.w3.org/TR/xhtml1/
   → DTD/xhtml1-transitional.dtd">
<html xmlns="http://www.w3.org/
→ 1999/xhtml" xml:lang="en"
→ lang="en">
<head>
   <meta http-equiv="Content-Type"
   → content="text/html;
   → charset=utf-8"/>
   <title>Registration</title>
</head>
<body>
<h1>Registration Results</h1>
```

2. Begin the PHP section and address error management, if necessary:

```
<?php // Script 6.2 - handle_reg.php
```

If you don't have **display_errors** enabled, or if **error_reporting** is set to the wrong level, see Chapter 3, "HTML Forms and PHP," for the lines to include here to alter those settings.

3. Create a *flag* variable:

```
$okay = TRUE;
```

To validate the form data, a *flag* variable will be used to represent whether or not the form was properly

Script 6.2 This shell of a PHP script will be expanded to completely validate the form data.

```
1   <!DOCTYPE html PUBLIC "-//W3C//DTD
    XHTML 1.0 Transitional//EN"
2      "http://www.w3.org/TR/xhtml1/DTD/
       xhtml1-transitional.dtd">
3   <html xmlns="http://www.w3.org/1999/
    xhtml" xml:lang="en" lang="en">
4   <head>
5      <meta http-equiv="Content-Type"
       content="text/html;
       charset=utf-8"/>
6      <title>Registration</title>
7   </head>
8   <body>
9   <h1>Registration Results</h1>
10  <?php // Script 6.2 - handle_reg.php
11  /* This script receives seven values
    from register.html:
12  email, password, confirm, year, terms,
    color, submit */
13
14  // Address error management, if you
    want.
15
16  // Flag variable to track success:
17  $okay = TRUE;
18
19  // If there were no errors, print a
    success message:
20  if ($okay) {
21      print '<p>You have been
        successfully registered (but
        not really).</p>';
22  }
23  ?>
24  </body>
25  </html>
```

completed. It's called a "flag" variable because the variable stores a simple value that indicates a status. For example: yes, the form was filled out entirely or no, it was not.

The variable is initialized with a Boolean value of *TRUE*, meaning that the assumption is that the form was completed properly. Understand that Booleans are *case-insensitive* in PHP, so you could also write *True* or *true*.

4. Print a message if everything is all right:

```
if ($okay) {
    print '<p>You have been
    ➝ successfully registered
    ➝ (but not really).</p>';
}
```

Over the course of this chapter, validation routines will be added to this script, checking the submitted form data. If any data fails a routine, then **$okay** will be set to FALSE. In that case, this conditional will also be FALSE, so the message won't be printed. However, if the data passes every validation routine, then **$okay** will still be TRUE, in which case this message will be printed.

5. Complete the PHP section and the HTML page:

```
?>
</body>
</html>
```

6. Save the file as **handle_reg.php**, place it in the proper directory for your PHP-enabled server (in the same directory as **register.html**), and test both in your Web browser **B** and **C**.

Of course, the fact is that this particular script will always print the success message, as no code will set **$okay** to **FALSE**. You can even run the script directly and see the same result.

TIP If the statement area of your conditional is only one line long, you technically don't need the curly brackets. In that case, you can write the conditional using either of these formats:

```
if (condition) statement;
```

or

```
if (condition)
    statement;
```

You may run across code in these formats. However, I think it's best to always use the multiline format, with the curly brackets (as demonstrated in the syntax introduction) to improve consistency and minimize errors.

Please complete this form to register:

Email Address: [   ]

Password: [••••••••••••]

Confirm Password: [   ]

Year You Were Born: [YYYY]

Favorite Color: [Yellow ▼]

☑ I agree to the terms (whatever they may be).

(Register)

B Filling out the HTML form to any degree...

Registration Results

You have been successfully registered (but not really).

C ...results in just this.

Validation Functions

PHP has dozens of functions commonly used to validate form data. Of these functions, the three most important ones are used in this chapter's examples.

First up is the **empty()** function, which checks to see if a given variable has an "empty" value. A variable is considered to have an empty value if the variable has no value, has a value of 0, or has a value of FALSE. In any of these cases, the function returns TRUE; otherwise, it returns FALSE:

```
$var1 = 0;
$var2 = 'something';
$var3 = ' '; // An empty string
empty($var); // TRUE, no defined value
empty($var1); // TRUE, empty value
empty($var2); // FALSE, non-empty value
empty($var3); // TRUE, empty value
```

This function is perfect for making sure that text boxes in forms have been filled out. For example, if you have a text input named *email* and the user doesn't enter anything in it before submitting the form, then the **$_POST['email']** variable will exist but will have an empty value.

Next is the **isset()** function, which is almost the opposite of **empty()**, albeit with a slight difference. The **isset()** function returns TRUE if a variable has any value (including 0, FALSE, or an empty string). If the variable does not have a value, **isset()** returns FALSE:

```
$var1 = 0;
$var2 = 'something';
$var3 = ' '; // An empty string
isset($var); // FALSE, no defined
value
isset($var1); // TRUE
isset($var2); // TRUE
isset($var3); // TRUE
```

```
1   <!DOCTYPE html PUBLIC "-//W3C//DTD
    XHTML 1.0 Transitional//EN"
2       "http://www.w3.org/TR/xhtml1/DTD/
    xhtml1-transitional.dtd">
3   <html xmlns="http://www.w3.org/1999/
    xhtml" xml:lang="en" lang="en">
4   <head>
5       <meta http-equiv="Content-Type"
    content="text/html;
    charset=utf-8"/>
6       <title>Registration</title>
7       <style type="text/css"
    media="screen">
8           .error { color: red; }
9       </style>
10  </head>
11  <body>
12  <h1>Registration Results</h1>
13  <?php // Script 6.3 - handle_reg.php #2
14  /* This script receives seven values
    from register.html:
15  email, password, confirm, year, terms,
    color, submit */
16
17  // Address error management, if you want.
18
19  // Flag variable to track success:
20  $okay = TRUE;
21
22  // Validate the email address:
23  if (empty($_POST['email'])) {
24      print '<p class="error">Please
    enter your email address.</p>';
25      $okay = FALSE;
26  }
27
28  // Validate the password:
29  if (empty($_POST['password'])) {
30      print '<p class="error">Please
    enter your password.</p>';
31      $okay = FALSE;
32  }
33
34  // If there were no errors, print a
    success message:
35  if ($okay) {
36      print '<p>You have been successfully
    registered (but not really).</p>';
37  }
38  ?>
39  </body>
40  </html>
```

The **isset()** function is commonly used to validate nontext form elements like checkboxes, radio buttons, and select menus.

Finally, the **is_numeric()** function returns TRUE if the submitted variable has a valid numerical value and FALSE otherwise. Integers, decimals, and even strings (if they're a valid number) can all pass the **is_numeric()** test:

```
$var1 = 2309;
$var2 = '80.23';
$var3 = 'Bears';
is_numeric($var1); // TRUE
is_numeric($var2); // TRUE
is_numeric($var3); // FALSE
```

Let's start applying these functions to the PHP script to perform data validation.

To validate form data:

1. Open **handle_reg.php** (Script 6.2) in your text editor or IDE, if it is not already open.

2. Within the document's head, define a CSS class (**Script 6.3**):

   ```
   <style type="text/css"
   → media="screen">
     .error { color: red; }
   </style>
   ```

   This CSS class will be used to format any printed registration errors.

3. Validate the email address:

   ```
   if (empty($_POST['email'])) {
     print '<p class="error">Please
     → enter your email address.</p>';
     $okay = FALSE;
   }
   ```

continues on next page

This **if** conditional uses the code **empty($_POST['email'])** as its condition. If that variable is empty, meaning it has no value, a value of 0, or a value of an empty string, the conditional is TRUE. In that case, the **print** statement will be executed and the **$okay** variable will be assigned a value of FALSE (indicating that everything is not okay).

If the variable isn't empty, then the conditional is FALSE, the **print** function is never called, and **$okay** will retain its original value.

4. Repeat the validation for the password:

```
if (empty($_POST['password'])) {
  print '<p class="error">Please
→ enter your password.</p>';
  $okay = FALSE;
}
```

This is a repeat of the email validation, but with the variable name and **print** statement changed accordingly. The other form inputs will be validated in time.

All of the printed error messages are placed within HTML paragraph tags that have a **class** value of *error*. By doing so, the CSS formatting will be applied (i.e., the errors will be printed in red, not that it'll be apparent in this book's figures).

5. Save the file as **handle_reg.php**, place it in the same directory as **register. html** (on your PHP-enabled server), and test both the form and the script in your Web browser **A** and **B**.

Please complete this form to register:

Email Address: [   ]

Password: [   ]

Confirm Password: [••••••   ]

Year You Were Born: [1901]

Favorite Color: [Green   ⬍]

☐ I agree to the terms (whatever they may be).

(Register)

A If you omit the email address or password form input...

Registration Results

Please enter your email address.

Please enter your password.

B ...you'll see messages like these.

6. Resubmit the form in different states of completeness to test the results some more.

If you do provide both email address and password values, the result will be exactly like that in Figure C in the section "The if Conditional," because the **$okay** variable will still have a value of TRUE.

TIP When you use functions within conditionals, as with empty() here, it's easy to forget a closing parenthesis and see a parse error. Be extra careful with your syntax when you're coding any control structure.

TIP One use of the isset() function is to avoid referring to a variable unless it exists. If PHP is set to report notices (see "Error Reporting" in Chapter 3), then, for example, using $var if it has not been defined will cause an error. You can avoid this by coding

```
if (isset($var)) {
    // Do whatever with $var.
}
```

TIP Even though almost all form data is sent to a PHP script as strings, the is_numeric() function can still be used for values coming from a form because it can handle strings that contain only numbers.

TIP The isset() function can take any number of variables as arguments:

```
if (isset($var1, $var2)) {
    print 'Both variables exist.';
}
```

If all the named variables are set, the function returns **TRUE**; if any variable is not set, the function returns **FALSE**.

Using else

The next control structure we'll discuss is the **if-else** conditional. This control structure allows you to execute one or more statements when a condition is TRUE and execute one or more other statements when the condition is FALSE:

```
if (condition) {
      statement(s);
} else {
      other_statement(s);
}
```

The important thing to remember when using this construct is that unless the condition is explicitly met, the **else** statement will be executed. In other words, the statements after the **else** constitute the *default action*, whereas the statements after the **if** condition are the exception to the rule **A**.

Let's rewrite the **handle_reg.php** page, incorporating an **if-else** conditional to validate the birth year. In the process, a new variable will be created, representing the user's age.

To use else:

1. Open **handle_reg.php** (Script 6.3) in your text editor or IDE, if it is not already open.

2. After the password validation but before the **$okay** conditional, begin a new conditional (**Script 6.4**):

   ```
   if (is_numeric($_POST['year'])) {
   ```

   Because the **year** variable should be a number, you can use the **is_numeric()** function to check its value, rather than **empty()**. This is a basic start to this particular form element's validation; later scripts will expand on this.

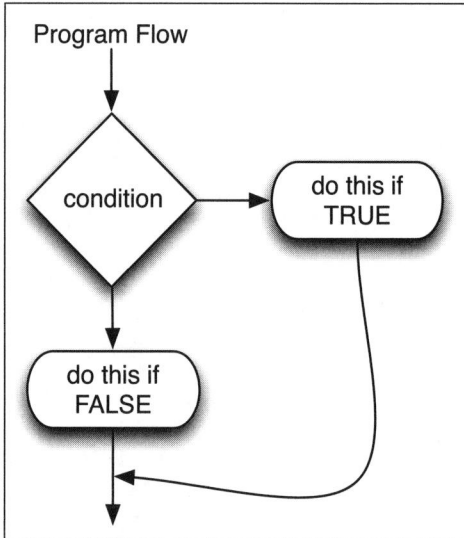

A How an **IF-ELSE** conditional affects the program flow of a script.

Script 6.4 By adding an **if-else** conditional, this script validates the birth year and creates a new variable in the process.

```
1   <!DOCTYPE html PUBLIC "-//W3C//DTD
    XHTML 1.0 Transitional//EN"
2      "http://www.w3.org/TR/xhtml1/DTD/
    xhtml1-transitional.dtd">
3   <html xmlns="http://www.w3.org/1999/
    xhtml" xml:lang="en" lang="en">
4   <head>
5      <meta http-equiv="Content-Type"
    content="text/html;
    charset=utf-8"/>
6      <title>Registration</title>
7      <style type="text/css"
    media="screen">
8         .error { color: red; }
9      </style>
10  </head>
11  <body>
12  <h1>Registration Results</h1>
13  <?php // Script 6.4 - handle_reg.php #3
14  /* This script receives seven values
    from register.html:
15  email, password, confirm, year, terms,
    color, submit */
16
```

code continues on next page

```
17   // Address error management, if you
     want.
18
19   // Flag variable to track success:
20   $okay = TRUE;
21
22   // Validate the email address:
23   if (empty($_POST['email'])) {
24       print '<p class="error">Please
         enter your email address.</p>';
25       $okay = FALSE;
26   }
27
28   // Validate the password:
29   if (empty($_POST['password'])) {
30       print '<p class="error">Please
         enter your password.</p>';
31       $okay = FALSE;
32   }
33
34   // Validate the birth year:
35   if (is_numeric($_POST['year'])) {
36       $age = 2011 - $_POST['year'];
         // Calculate age this year.
37   } else {
38       print '<p class="error">Please
         enter the year you were born as
         four digits.</p>';
39       $okay = FALSE;
40   }
41
42   // If there were no errors, print a
     success message:
43   if ($okay) {
44       print '<p>You have been successfully
         registered (but not really).</p>';
45       print "<p>You will turn $age
         this year.</p>";
46   }
47   ?>
48   </body>
49   </html>
```

3. Create a new variable:

$age = 2011 - $_POST['year'];

If the **$_POST['year']** variable has a numeric value (meaning that the conditional is TRUE), then the **$age** variable is assigned the value of the current year minus the provided year. For now, without knowledge of PHP's date functions, just hard-code the current year into the equation.

4. Add an **else** clause:

```
} else {
    print '<p class="error">Please
    → enter the year you were born
    → as four digits.</p>';
    $okay = FALSE;
}
```

If the year does not have a numeric value, an error message is printed and the **$okay** variable is set to FALSE (as is the case if any validation routine fails).

5. After the final **print** statement but within the same **$okay** conditional, also print out the value of **$age**:

print "<p>You will turn $age this → year.</p>";

If the **$okay** variable still has a value of TRUE, then the submitted data passed every validation routine. This means that the user's age has been calculated (in the sense of how old they'll be at some point this year), and it can be printed, too.

continues on next page

6. Save your script, place it in the same directory as **register.html** (on your PHP-enabled server), and test it in your Web browser again **B**, **C**, and **D**.

TIP Another good validation function is `checkdate()`, which you can use to confirm that a date exists (or existed in the past). You would use it like so:

```
if (checkdate($month, $day, $year)) {…
```

Please complete this form to register:

Email Address: me@example.com

Password: ••••••••

Confirm Password: ••••••••

Year You Were Born: YYYY

Favorite Color: Green

☑ I agree to the terms (whatever they may be).

Register

B Test the form again, without providing a year value, and...

Registration Results

Please enter the year you were born as four digits.

C ...you'll see this.

Registration Results

You have been successfully registered (but not really).

You will turn 57 this year.

D If the user provides a numeric value for their birth year, the user's age will now be calculated and printed (assuming that an email address and password was also provided).

TABLE 6.1 PHP's Operators

Operator	Usage	Type
+	Addition	Arithmetic
-	Subtraction	Arithmetic
*	Multiplication	Arithmetic
/	Division	Arithmetic
%	Modulus (remainder of a division)	Arithmetic
++	Incrementation	Arithmetic
--	Decrementation	Arithmetic
=	Assigns a value to a variable	Assignment
==	Equality	Comparison
!=	Inequality	Comparison
<	Less than	Comparison
>	Greater than	Comparison
<=	Less than or equal to	Comparison
>=	Greater than or equal to	Comparison
!	Negation	Logical
AND	And	Logical
&&	And	Logical
OR	Or	Logical
||	Or	Logical
XOR	Or not	Logical
.	Concatenation	String

More Operators

Previous chapters discussed most of PHP's operators along with the variable types that use them. These operators include *arithmetic* for numbers: addition (**+**), subtraction (**-**), multiplication (*****), and division (**/**), along with the incremental (**++**) and decremental (**--**) shortcuts for increasing or decreasing the value of a number by 1. Then there is the *assignment* operator (**=**), which is used to set the value of a variable, regardless of type. You've also learned about *concatenation* (**.**), which appends one string to another.

When it comes to creating conditionals, the *comparison* and *logical* operators are the most important. **Table 6.1** lists the operators to be discussed, along with those you've already seen.

Comparison

When the assignment operator (the equals sign) was introduced in Chapter 2, "Variables," you learned that its meaning isn't exactly what you'd conventionally think it to be. The line

```
$var = 5;
```

doesn't state that **$var** *is equal to* 5 but that it *is assigned the value of* 5. This is an important distinction.

When you're writing conditionals, you'll often want to see if a variable is equal to a specific value (to match usernames or passwords, perhaps), which you can't do with the equals sign alone (because that operator is used for assigning a value, not equating values). Instead, for comparisons, use the equality operator (**==**):

```
$var = 5;
if ($var == 5) { ...
```

continues on next page

These two lines of code together first establish the value of **$var** as 5 and then make a TRUE conditional that checks if **$var** is equal to 5. This example demonstrates the significant difference one more equals sign makes in your PHP code and why *you must distinguish carefully between the assignment and comparison operators*.

The next comparison operator—*not equal to*—is represented by an exclamation mark coupled with an equals sign (**!=**). The remaining comparison operators are identical to their mathematical counterparts: less than (**<**), greater than (**>**), less than or equal to (**< =**), and greater than or equal to (**> =**).

As a demonstration of comparison operators, you'll check that the user's birth year is before 2011 and that the confirmed password matches the original password.

To use comparison operators:

1. Open **handle_reg.php** (Script 6.4) in your text editor or IDE, if it is not already.

2. After the password validation, check that the two passwords match (**Script 6.5**):

```
if ($_POST['password']
→ != $_POST['confirm']) {
  print '<p class="error">Your
  → confirmed password does
  → not match the original
  → password.</p>';
  $okay = FALSE;
}
```

To compare these two string values, use the inequality operator. Alternatively, you could use one of the string comparison functions (see Chapter 5, "Using Strings"), but **!=** is just fine.

Script 6.5 This version of the form-handling script uses comparison operators to validate the password and year values.

```
1   <!DOCTYPE html PUBLIC "-//W3C//DTD XHTML
    1.0 Transitional//EN"
2       "http://www.w3.org/TR/xhtml1/DTD/
        xhtml1-transitional.dtd">
3   <html xmlns="http://www.w3.org/1999/
    xhtml" xml:lang="en" lang="en">
4   <head>
5       <meta http-equiv="Content-Type"
        content="text/html; charset=utf-8"/>
6       <title>Registration</title>
7       <style type="text/css" media="screen">
8           .error { color: red; }
9       </style>
10  </head>
11  <body>
12  <h1>Registration Results</h1>
13  <?php // Script 6.5 - handle_reg.php #4
14  /* This script receives seven values
    from register.html:
15  email, password, confirm, year, terms,
    color, submit */
16
17  // Address error management, if you want.
18
19  // Flag variable to track success:
20  $okay = TRUE;
21
22  // Validate the email address:
23  if (empty($_POST['email'])) {
24      print '<p class="error">Please enter
        your email address.</p>';
25      $okay = FALSE;
26  }
27
28  // Validate the password:
29  if (empty($_POST['password'])) {
30      print '<p class="error">Please enter
        your password.</p>';
31      $okay = FALSE;
32  }
33
34  // Check the two passwords for equality:
35  if ($_POST['password'] !=
    $_POST['confirm']) {
36      print '<p class="error">Your
        confirmed password does not match
        the original password.</p>';
```

code continues on next page

Script 6.5 *continued*

```
37        $okay = FALSE;
38    }
39
40    // Validate the birth year:
41    if (is_numeric($_POST['year'])) {
42        $age = 2011 - $_POST['year'];
          // Calculate age this year.
43    } else {
44        print '<p class="error">Please enter
          the year you were born as four
          digits.</p>';
45        $okay = FALSE;
46    }
47
48    // Check that they were born before
      this year:
49    if ($_POST['year'] >= 2011) {
50        print '<p class="error">Either you
          entered your birth year wrong or
          you come from the future!</p>';
51        $okay = FALSE;
52    }
53
54    // If there were no errors, print a
      success message:
55    if ($okay) {
56        print '<p>You have been successfully
          registered (but not really).</p>';
57        print "<p>You will turn $age this
          year.</p>";
58    }
59
60    ?>
61    </body>
62    </html>
```

3. After the year validation, report an error if the year is greater than or equal to 2011:

```
if ($_POST['year'] >= 2011) {
    print '<p class="error">Either
    → you entered your birth year
    → wrong or you come from the
    → future!</p>';
    $okay = FALSE;
}
```

If the user entered their year of birth as 2011 or later, it's presumably a mistake. (If you're reading this book after 2011, change the year accordingly).

continues on next page

4. Save your script, place it in the same directory as `register.html` (on your PHP-enabled server), and test it in your Web browser again **A** and **B**.

TIP Before you compare two string values that come from a form (like the password and confirmed password), it's a good idea to apply the `trim()` function to both, to get rid of any errant spaces. I didn't do so here, so as not to overcomplicate matters, but this habit is recommended.

TIP Another method of checking that a text input type has been filled out (as opposed to using the `empty()` function) is this:

```
if (strlen($var) > 0 ) {
    // $var is okay.
}
```

TIP In an `if` conditional, if you make the mistake of writing `$var = 5` in place of `$var == 5`, you'll see that the corresponding conditional statements are always executed. This happens because although the condition `$var == 5` may or may not be TRUE, the condition `$var = 5` is always TRUE.

TIP Some programmers advocate *reverse conditionals*—for example, writing

```
if (5 == $var) {
```

Although it looks awkward, if you inadvertently code `5 = $var`, an error results (allowing you to catch the mistake more easily) because the number 5 can't be assigned another value.

Please complete this form to register:

Email Address: `me@example.com`

Password: ••••••••••••••••••••

Confirm Password: ••••

Year You Were Born: 2023

Favorite Color: Green ◆

☑ I agree to the terms (whatever they may be).

(Register)

A Run the form once again…

Registration Results

Your confirmed password does not match the original password.

Either you entered your birth year wrong or you come from the future!

B …with two new validation checks in place.

Nesting Conditionals

Besides using logical operators to create more complex conditionals, you can use *nesting* for this purpose (the process of placing one control structure inside another). The key to doing so is to place the interior conditional as the *statement(s)* section of the exterior conditional. For example:

```
if (condition1) {
        if (condition2) {
                statement(s)2;
        } else { // condition2
else

other_statement(s)2;
        } // End of 2
} else { // condition1 else
        other_statement(s)1;
} // End of 1
```

As you can see from this example, you can cut down on the complexity of these structures by using extensive indentations and comments. As long as every conditional is syntactically correct, there are no rules as to how many levels of nesting you can have, whether you use an **else** clause or even whether a sub-conditional is part of the **if** or the **else** section of the main conditional.

Logical

Writing conditions in PHP comes down to identifying TRUE or FALSE situations. You can do this by using functions and comparative operators, as you've already seen. *Logical* operators—the final operator type discussed in this chapter—help you create more elaborate or obvious constructs.

In PHP, one example of a TRUE condition is simply a variable name that has a value that isn't zero, an empty string, or FALSE, such as

```
$var = 5;
if ($var) { ...
```

You've already seen this with the **$okay** variable being used in the handling PHP script.

A condition is also TRUE if it makes logical sense:

```
if (5 >= 3) { ...
```

A condition will be FALSE if it refers to a variable and that variable has no value (or a value of 0 or an empty string), or if you've created an illogical construct. The following condition is always FALSE:

```
if (5 <= 3) { ...
```

In PHP, the exclamation mark (!) is the *not* operator. You can use it to invert the TRUE/FALSE status of a statement. For example:

```
$var = 'value';
if ($var) {... // TRUE
if (!$var) {... // FALSE
if (isset($var)) {... // TRUE
if (!isset($var)) {... // FALSE
if (!empty($var)) {... // TRUE
```

To go beyond simple one-part conditions, PHP supports five more types of logical operators: two versions of *and* (**AND** and **&&**), two versions of *or* (**OR** and **||**—a character called the *pipe*, put together twice), and

continues on next page

or not (**XOR**). When you have two options for one operator (as with *and* and *or*), they differ only in precedence. For almost every situation, you can use either version of *and* or either version of *or* interchangeably.

Using parentheses and logical operators, you can create even more complex **if** conditionals. For an **AND** conditional, every conjoined part must be TRUE in order for the whole conditional to be TRUE. With **OR**, at least one subsection must be TRUE to render the whole condition TRUE. These conditionals are TRUE:

```
if ( (5 <= 3) OR (5 >= 3) ) { ...
if ( (5 > 3) AND (5 < 10) ) { ...
```

These conditionals are FALSE:

```
if ( (5 != 5) AND (5 > 3) ) { ...
if ( (5 != 5) OR (5 < 3) ) { ...
```

As you construct your conditionals, remember two important things: first, in order for the statements that are the result of a conditional to be executed, the entire conditional must have a TRUE value; second, by using parentheses, you can ignore rules of precedence and ensure that your operators are addressed in the order of your choosing.

To demonstrate logical operators, let's add more conditionals to the **handle_reg.php** page. You'll also nest one of the year conditionals inside another conditional (see the sidebar "Nesting Conditionals" for more).

To use logical operators:

1. Open **handle_reg.php** (Script 6.5) in your text editor or IDE, if it is not already open.

2. Delete the existing year validations (**Script 6.6**).

   You'll entirely rewrite these conditionals as one nested conditional, so it's best to get rid of the old versions entirely.

Script 6.6 Here the handling PHP script is changed so that the year validation routine uses both multiple and nested conditions. Also, the terms of agreement check box is now validated.

```
1   <!DOCTYPE html PUBLIC "-//W3C//DTD XHTML
    1.0 Transitional//EN"
2       "http://www.w3.org/TR/xhtml1/DTD/
        xhtml1-transitional.dtd">
3   <html xmlns="http://www.w3.org/1999/
    xhtml" xml:lang="en" lang="en">
4   <head>
5       <meta http-equiv="Content-Type"
        content="text/html; charset=utf-8"/>
6       <title>Registration</title>
7       <style type="text/css" media="screen">
8           .error { color: red; }
9       </style>
10  </head>
11  <body>
12  <h1>Registration Results</h1>
13  <?php // Script 6.6 - handle_reg.php #5
14  /* This script receives seven values
    from register.html:
15  email, password, confirm, year, terms,
    color, submit */
16
17  // Address error management, if you want.
18
19  // Flag variable to track success:
20  $okay = TRUE;
21
22  // Validate the email address:
23  if (empty($_POST['email'])) {
24      print '<p class="error">Please enter
        your email address.</p>';
25      $okay = FALSE;
26  }
27
28  // Validate the password:
29  if (empty($_POST['password'])) {
30      print '<p class="error">Please enter
        your password.</p>';
31      $okay = FALSE;
32  }
33
34  // Check the two passwords for equality:
35  if ($_POST['password'] !=
    $_POST['confirm']) {
36      print '<p class="error">Your confirmed
        password does not match the original
        password.</p>';
```

code continues on next page

```
37        $okay = FALSE;
38    }
39
40    // Validate the year:
41    if ( is_numeric($_POST['year']) AND
        (strlen($_POST['year']) == 4) ) {
42
43        // Check that they were born
          before 2011.
44        if ($_POST['year'] < 2011) {
45            $age = 2011 - $_POST['year'];
              // Calculate age this year.
46        } else {
47            print '<p class="error">Either
              you entered your birth year
              wrong or you come from the
              future!</p>';
48            $okay = FALSE;
49        } // End of 2nd conditional.
50
51    } else { // Else for 1st conditional.
52
53        print '<p class="error">Please
          enter the year you were born as
          four digits.</p>';
54        $okay = FALSE;
55
56    } // End of 1st conditional.
57
58    // Validate the terms:
59    if (!isset($_POST['terms'])) {
60        print '<p class="error">You must
          accept the terms.</p>';
61        $okay = FALSE;
62    }
63
64    // If there were no errors, print a
      success message:
65    if ($okay) {
66        print '<p>You have been successfully
          registered (but not really).</p>';
67        print "<p>You will turn $age this
          year.</p>";
68    }
69    ?>
70    </body>
71    </html>
```

3. Check that the year variable is a four-digit number:

```
if ( is_numeric($_POST['year']) AND
→ (strlen($_POST['year']) == 4) ) {
```

This conditional has two parts. The first you've already seen—it tests for a valid numeric value. The second part gets the length of the year variable (using the **strlen()** function) and checks if the length value is equal to 4. Because of the **AND**, this conditional is TRUE only if both conditions are met.

4. Create a subconditional to check if the year value is before 2011:

```
if ($_POST['year'] < 2011) {
    $age = 2011 - $_POST['year'];
} else {
    print '<p class="error">Either
    → you entered your birth year
    → wrong or you come from the
    → future!</p>';
    $okay = FALSE;
} // End of 2nd conditional.
```

This **if-else** conditional acts as the *statements* part of the main conditional, and is thus executed only if that condition is TRUE. This **if-else** checks whether the year variable is less than 2011 (i.e., the user must have been born before the current year). If that condition is TRUE, the user's age is calculated as before. Otherwise, an error message is printed and the **$okay** variable is set to FALSE (indicating a problem occurred).

Note that this conditional is just the opposite of the previous version: verifying that a value is less than some number instead of greater than or equal to that number.

continues on next page

5. Complete the main year conditional:

```
} else { // Else for 1st
→ conditional.
  print '<p class="error">Please
  → enter the year you were born
  → as four digits.</p>';
  $okay = FALSE;
} // End of 1st conditional.
```

This **else** section completes the conditional begun in Step 3. If at least one of the conditions set forth there is FALSE, this message is printed and **$okay** is set to FALSE.

6. Confirm that the terms checkbox wasn't ignored:

```
if (!isset($_POST['terms'])) {
  print '<p class="error">You must
  → accept the terms.</p>';
  $okay = FALSE;
}
```

If the **$_POST['terms']** variable is not set, then the user failed to check that box and an error should be reported. To be more exact, this conditional could be

```
if ( !isset($_POST['terms']) AND
→ ($_POST['terms'] == 'Yes') ) {
```

7. Those are the only changes to the script, so you can now save it again, place it in the same directory as **register.html** (on your PHP-enabled server), and test it in your Web browser again **C** and **D**.

Please complete this form to register:

Email Address: me@example.com

Password: ••••••••

Confirm Password: ••••••••

Year You Were Born: 15

Favorite Color: Green

☐ I agree to the terms (whatever they may be).

(Register)

C The PHP script now catches if the year isn't a four-digit number, as will be the case with this form submission.

Registration Results

Please enter the year you were born as four digits.

You must accept the terms.

D Error messages are printed if fields are incorrectly filled out or if the terms checkbox is not checked.

8. If desired, change your **year** value to be in the future and submit the form again **E**.

TIP It's another common programming convention—which is maintained in this book—to write the terms **TRUE** and **FALSE** in all capitals. This isn't a requirement of PHP, though. For example, the following conditional is **TRUE**:

```
if (true) {...
```

TIP It's very easy in long, complicated conditionals to forget an opening or closing parenthesis or curly bracket, which will produce either error messages or unexpected results. Find a system (like spacing out your conditionals and using comments) to help clarify your code. Another good technique is to create the entire conditional's structure first, and then go back to add the details.

TIP If you have problems getting your if-else statements to execute, print out the values of your variables to help debug the problem. A conditional may not be **TRUE** or **FALSE** because a variable doesn't have the value you think it does.

Registration Results

Either you entered your birth year wrong or you come from the future!

E The year validation still checks that the date is before 2011.

Using elseif

Similar to the **if-else** conditional is **if-elseif** (or **if-elseif-else**). This conditional acts like a running **if** statement and can be expanded to whatever complexity you require:

```
if (condition1) {
      statement(s);
} elseif (condition2) {
      other_statement(s);
}
```

Here's another example 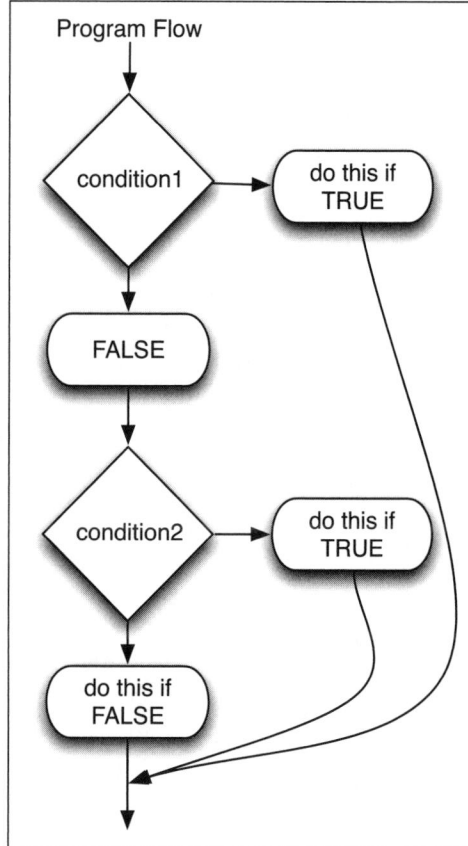:

```
if (condition1) {
      statement(s);
} elseif (condition2) {
      other_statement(s);
} else {
      other_other_statement(s);
}
```

If present, you must always make the **else** the last part of a conditional because it's executed unless one of the conditions to that point has been met (again, **else** represents the *default* behavior). You can, however, continue to use **elseif**s as many times as you want as part of one **if** conditional. You may also forego an **else** clause, if you don't need a default response.

As an example of this, let's create a conditional that prints a message based on the selected color value.

Ⓐ How an **IF-ELSEIF-ELSE** conditional affects the program flow of a script.

Script 6.7 This multiline **if-elseif-else** conditional validates that a submitted color has an allowed value and is used to determine what type of color the selection is.

```
1    <!DOCTYPE html PUBLIC "-//W3C//DTD XHTML
     1.0 Transitional//EN"
2       "http://www.w3.org/TR/xhtml1/DTD/
        xhtml1-transitional.dtd">
3    <html xmlns="http://www.w3.org/1999/
     xhtml" xml:lang="en" lang="en">
4    <head>
5       <meta http-equiv="Content-Type"
        content="text/html; charset=utf-8"/>
6       <title>Registration</title>
7       <style type="text/css" media="screen">
8          .error { color: red; }
9       </style>
10   </head>
11   <body>
12   <h1>Registration Results</h1>
13   <?php // Script 6.7 - handle_reg.php #6
14   /* This script receives seven values
     from register.html:
15   email, password, confirm, year, terms,
     color, submit */
16
17   // Address error management, if you want.
18
19   // Flag variable to track success:
20   $okay = TRUE;
21
22   // Validate the email address:
23   if (empty($_POST['email'])) {
24      print '<p class="error">Please enter
        your email address.</p>';
25      $okay = FALSE;
26   }
27
28   // Validate the password:
29   if (empty($_POST['password'])) {
30      print '<p class="error">Please enter
        your password.</p>';
31      $okay = FALSE;
32   }
33
34   // Check the two passwords for equality:
35   if ($_POST['password'] !=
     $_POST['confirm']) {
36      print '<p class="error">Your confirmed
        password does not match the original
        password.</p>';
```

code continues on next page

To use elseif:

1. Open **handle_reg.php** (Script 6.6) in your text editor or IDE, if it is not already open.

2. Before the **$okay** conditional, begin a new conditional (**Script 6.7**):

   ```
   if ($_POST['color'] == 'red') {
      $color_type = 'primary';
   ```

   The color value comes from a select menu with four possible options: *red*, *yellow*, *green*, and *blue*. This conditional will determine whether the user has selected a primary—red, yellow, or blue—or secondary (all others) color. The first condition checks if the value of **$_POST['color']** is equal to the string *red*.

   Be certain to use the *equality* operator—two equals signs—and not the *assignment* operator—one—in the conditional.

3. Add an **elseif** clause for the second color:

   ```
   } elseif ($_POST['color'] ==
   → 'yellow') {
      $color_type = 'primary';
   ```

   The **elseif** continues the main conditional begun in Step 2. The condition itself is a replication of the condition in Step 2, using a new color comparison.

continues on next page

4. Add **elseif** clauses for the other two colors:

```
} elseif ($_POST['color'] ==
→ 'green') {
  $color_type = 'secondary';
} elseif ($_POST['color'] ==
→ 'blue') {
  $color_type = 'primary';
```

Once you understand the main concept, it's just a matter of repeating the **elseif**s for every possible color value.

5. Add an **else** clause:

```
} else {
  print '<p class="error">Please
  → select your favorite
  → color.</p>';
  $okay = FALSE;
}
```

If the user didn't select a color, or if they manipulated the form to submit a different color value (other than *red*, *yellow*, *green*, or *blue*), none of the conditions will be TRUE, meaning this **else** clause will take effect. That clause prints an error and assigns a value of FALSE to **$okay**, indicating a problem.

It doesn't matter in what order the colors are checked, so long as the **else** clause comes last.

Script 6.7 *continued*

```
37      $okay = FALSE;
38    }
39
40    // Validate the year:
41    if ( is_numeric($_POST['year']) AND
      (strlen($_POST['year']) == 4) ) {
42
43      // Check that they were born before
        2011.
44      if ($_POST['year'] < 2011) {
45        $age = 2011 - $_POST['year'];
          // Calculate age this year.
46      } else {
47        print '<p class="error">Either you
          entered your birth year wrong or
          you come from the future!</p>';
48        $okay = FALSE;
49      } // End of 2nd conditional.
50
51    } else { // Else for 1st conditional.
52
53      print '<p class="error">Please enter
        the year you were born as four
        digits.</p>';
54      $okay = FALSE;
55
56    } // End of 1st conditional.
57
58    // Validate the terms:
59    if ( !isset($_POST['terms']) AND
      ($_POST['terms'] == 'Yes') ) {
60      print '<p class="error">You must
        accept the terms.</p>';
61      $okay = FALSE;
62    }
63
64    // Validate the color:
65    if ($_POST['color'] == 'red') {
66      $color_type = 'primary';
67    } elseif ($_POST['color'] == 'yellow') {
68      $color_type = 'primary';
69    } elseif ($_POST['color'] == 'green') {
70      $color_type = 'secondary';
71    } elseif ($_POST['color'] == 'blue') {
72      $color_type = 'primary';
73    } else { // Problem!
74      print '<p class="error">Please
        select your favorite color.</p>';
75      $okay = FALSE;
76    }
```

code continues on next page

```
77
78   // If there were no errors, print a
     success message:
79   if ($okay) {
80       print '<p>You have been successfully
         registered (but not really).</p>';
81       print "<p>You will turn $age this
         year.</p>";
82       print "<p>Your favorite color is a
         $color_type color.</p>";
83   }
84   ?>
85   </body>
86   </html>
```

Registration Results

You have been successfully registered (but not really).

You will turn 12 this year.

Your favorite color is a secondary color.

B The script now prints a message acknowledging the user's color choice.

Registration Results

Please select your favorite color.

C Failure to select a color results in this error message.

6. Within the **$okay** conditional, print the user's favorite color type:

```
print "<p>Your favorite color is
 a $color_type color.</p>";
```

7. Save the script, place it in the same directory as **register.html** (on your PHP-enabled server), and test it in your Web browser again, using different color options **B** and **C**.

TIP One thing most beginner developers don't realize is that it's possible—in fact, quite easy—for a hacker to submit data to your PHP script without using your intended HTML form. For this reason, it's important that you validate the existence of expected variables (i.e., that they are set), their type, and their values.

TIP PHP also allows you to write `elseif` as two words, if you prefer:

```
if (condition1) {
    statement(s);
} else if (condition2) {
    statement(s)2;
}
```

The Switch Conditional

Once you get to the point where you have longer **if-elseif-else** conditionals, you may find that you can save programming time and clarify your code by using a **switch** conditional instead. The **switch** conditional takes only one possible condition, normally just a variable:

```
switch ($var) {
    case value1:
        statement(s)1;
        break;
    case value2:
        statement(s)2;
        break;
    default:
        statement(s)3;
        break;
}
```

You must understand how a **switch** conditional works in order to use it properly. After the keyword **switch**, a variable is identified within parentheses. PHP will then look at each case in order, trying to identify a matching value. Note that, as with any other use of strings and numbers in PHP, numeric values would not be quoted; string values should be. After the **case value** section, a *colon* (not a semicolon) prefaces the associated statements, which are normally indented beginning on the following line.

Once PHP finds a case that matches the value of the conditional variable, it executes the subsequent statements. Here's the tricky part: once PHP has found a matching case, it will continue going through the **switch** until it either comes to the end of the **switch** conditional (the closing curly bracket) or hits a **break** statement, at which point it exits the **switch** construct. Thus, it's imperative that you

Script 6.8 Switch conditionals can simplify complicated **if-elseif** conditionals.

```
1    <!DOCTYPE html PUBLIC "-//W3C//DTD XHTML
     1.0 Transitional//EN"
2        "http://www.w3.org/TR/xhtml1/DTD/
         xhtml1-transitional.dtd">
3    <html xmlns="http://www.w3.org/1999/
     xhtml" xml:lang="en" lang="en">
4    <head>
5        <meta http-equiv="Content-Type"
         content="text/html; charset=utf-8"/>
6        <title>Registration</title>
7        <style type="text/css" media="screen">
8            .error { color: red; }
9        </style>
10   </head>
11   <body>
12   <h1>Registration Results</h1>
13   <?php // Script 6.8 - handle_reg.php #7
14   /* This script receives seven values
     from register.html:
15   email, password, confirm, year, terms,
     color, submit */
16
17   // Address error management, if you want.
18
19   // Flag variable to track success:
20   $okay = TRUE;
21
22   // Validate the email address:
23   if (empty($_POST['email'])) {
24       print '<p class="error">Please enter
         your email address.</p>';
25       $okay = FALSE;
26   }
27
28   // Validate the password:
29   if (empty($_POST['password'])) {
30       print '<p class="error">Please enter
         your password.</p>';
31       $okay = FALSE;
32   }
33
34   // Check the two passwords for equality:
35   if ($_POST['password'] !=
     $_POST['confirm']) {
36       print '<p class="error">Your confirmed
         password does not match the original
         password.</p>';
37       $okay = FALSE;
38   }
```

code continues on next page

```
39
40    // Validate the year:
41    if ( is_numeric($_POST['year']) AND
      (strlen($_POST['year']) == 4) ) {
42
43       // Check that they were born before
         2011.
44       if ($_POST['year'] < 2011) {
45          $age = 2011 - $_POST['year'];
            // Calculate age this year.
46       } else {
47          print '<p class="error">Either you
            entered your birth year wrong or
            you come from the future!</p>';
48          $okay = FALSE;
49       } // End of 2nd conditional.
50
51    } else { // Else for 1st conditional.
52
53       print '<p class="error">Please enter
         the year you were born as four
         digits.</p>';
54       $okay = FALSE;
55
56    } // End of 1st conditional.
57
58    // Validate the terms:
59    if ( !isset($_POST['terms']) AND
      ($_POST['terms'] == 'Yes') ) {
60       print '<p class="error">You must
         accept the terms.</p>';
61       $okay = FALSE;
62    }
63
64    // Validate the color:
65    switch ($_POST['color']) {
66       case 'red':
67          $color_type = 'primary';
68          break;
69       case 'yellow':
70          $color_type = 'primary';
71          break;
72       case 'green':
73          $color_type = 'secondary';
74          break;
75       case 'blue':
76          $color_type = 'primary';
77          break;
78       default:
```

code continues on next page

close every case —even the **default** case, for consistency's sake—with a **break** (the sidebar "Break, Exit, Die, and Continue" discusses this keyword in more detail).

This previous **switch** conditional is like a rewrite of:

```
if ($var == value1) {
      statement(s)1;
} elseif ($variable == value2) {
      statement(s)2;
} else {
      statement(s)3;
}
```

Because the **switch** conditional uses the value of **$var** as its condition, it first checks to see if **$var** is equal to *value1* and, if so, executes *statement(s)1*. If not, it checks to see if **$var** is equal to *value2* and, if so, executes *statement(s)2*. If neither condition is met, the default action of the **switch** conditional is to execute *statement(s)3*.

With this in mind, let's rewrite the colors conditional as a **switch**.

To use a switch conditional:

1. Open **handle_reg.php** (Script 6.7) in your text editor or IDE, if it is not already open.

2. Delete the extended colors conditional (**Script 6.8**).

3. Begin the **switch**:

   switch ($_POST['color']) {

   As mentioned earlier, a **switch** conditional takes only one condition: a variable's name. In this example, it's **$_POST['color']**.

   continues on next page

4. Create the first case:

```
case 'red':
  $color_type = 'primary';
  break;
```

The first case checks to see if $_POST['color'] has a value of *red*. If so, then, the same statement is executed as before. Next you include a **break** statement to exit the **switch**.

5. Add a case for the second color:

```
case 'yellow':
  $color_type = 'primary';
  break;
```

6. Add cases for the remaining colors:

```
case 'green':
  $color_type = 'secondary';
  break;
case 'blue':
  $color_type = 'primary';
  break;
```

Script 6.8 *continued*

```
79        print '<p class="error">Please
          select your favorite color.</p>';
80        $okay = FALSE;
81        break;
82  } // End of switch.
83
84  // If there were no errors, print a
    success message:
85  if ($okay) {
86      print '<p>You have been successfully
        registered (but not really).</p>';
87      print "<p>You will turn $age this
        year.</p>";
88      print "<p>Your favorite color is a
        $color_type color.</p>";
89  }
90  ?>
91  </body>
92  </html>
```

Break, Exit, Die, and Continue

PHP includes many *language constructs*—tools that aren't functions but still do something in your scripts. For example, **print** is a language construct. Another example is **break**, which is demonstrated in the **switch**. **break** exits the current structure, be it a **switch**, an **if-else** conditional, or a loop.

Similar to this is **continue**, which terminates the current iteration of a loop. Any remaining statements within the loop aren't executed, but the loop's condition is checked again to see if the loop should be entered.

exit and **die** are more potent versions of **break** (and they're synonymous). Instead of exiting the current structure, these two language constructs terminate the execution of the PHP script. Therefore, all PHP code after a use of **exit** or **die** is never executed. For that matter, any HTML after these constructs is never sent to the Web browser. You'll see **die** used most frequently as a heavy-handed error handling tool. **exit** is often used in conjunction with the **header()** function.

Registration Results

You have been successfully registered (but not really).

You will turn 47 this year.

Your favorite color is a primary color.

A The handling script still works the same, whether the user selects a color...

Registration Results

Please select your favorite color.

B ...or fails to.

7. Add a **default** case and complete the switch:

```
default:
    print '<p class="error">Please
    → select your favorite
    → color.</p>';
    $okay = FALSE;
    break;
} // End of switch.
```

This **default** case is the equivalent of the **else** clause used in the original conditional.

8. Save your script, place it in the same directory as **register.html** (on your PHP-enabled server), and test it in your Web browser again **A** and **B**.

TIP A **default** case isn't required in your **switch** conditional (you could set it up so that if the value isn't explicitly met by one of the cases, nothing happens), but if it's used, it should be the last case.

TIP If you're using a string in your **switch** conditional as the case value, keep in mind that it's case sensitive, meaning that *Value* won't match *value*.

The for Loop

Loops are the final type of control structure discussed in this chapter. As suggested earlier, loops are used to execute a section of code repeatedly. You may want to print something a certain number of times, or you may want to do something with each value in an array (i.e., a list of values). For either of these cases, and many more, you can use a loop. (The latter example is demonstrated in the next chapter.)

PHP supports three kinds of loops: **for**, **while**, and **foreach**. The **while** loop is similar to **for**, but it's used most frequently when retrieving values from a database or reading from a text file (it's introduced in the sidebar). The **foreach** loop is related to using arrays and is introduced in the next chapter.

The **for** loop is designed to perform specific statements for a determined number of iterations (unlike **while**, which runs until a condition is FALSE—similar, but significantly different, concepts). You normally use a dummy variable in the loop for this purpose:

```
for (initial expression; condition;
→ closing expression) {
    statement(s);
}
```

The initial expression is executed once: the first time the loop is called. Then the condition is used to determine whether to execute the statements. The closing expression is executed each time the condition is found to be TRUE, but only after the statements are executed **A**.

Here's a simple loop that prints out the numbers 1 through 10:

```
for ($i = 1; $i <= 10; $i++) {
    print $i;
}
```

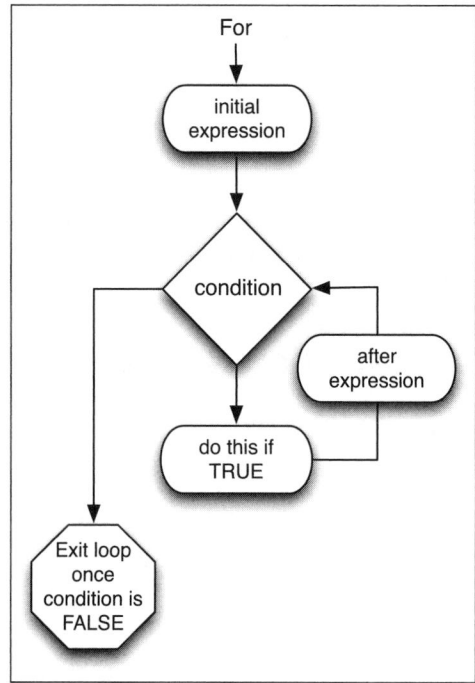

A This flowchart represents how a **for** loop is executed in PHP.

```
1    <!DOCTYPE html PUBLIC "-//W3C//DTD XHTML
     1.0 Transitional//EN"
2       "http://www.w3.org/TR/xhtml1/DTD/
     xhtml1-transitional.dtd">
3    <html xmlns="http://www.w3.org/1999/
     xhtml" xml:lang="en" lang="en">
4    <head>
5       <meta http-equiv="Content-Type"
     content="text/html; charset=utf-8"/>
6       <title>Registration Form</title>
7    </head>
8    <body>
9    <!-- Script 6.9 - register.php -->
10   <div><p>Please complete this form to
     register:</p>
11
12   <form action="handle_reg.php"
     method="post">
13
14      <p>Email Address: <input type="text"
     name="email" size="30" /></p>
15
16      <p>Password: <input type="password"
     name="password" size="20" /></p>
17
18      <p>Confirm Password: <input
     type="password" name="confirm"
     size="20" /></p>
19
20      <p>Date Of Birth:
21      <select name="month">
22      <option value="">Month</option>
23      <option value="1">January</option>
24      <option value="2">February</option>
25      <option value="3">March</option>
26      <option value="4">April</option>
27      <option value="5">May</option>
28      <option value="6">June</option>
29      <option value="7">July</option>
30      <option value="8">August</option>
31      <option value="9">September</option>
32      <option value="10">October</option>
33      <option value="11">November</option>
34      <option value="12">December</option>
35      </select>
36      <select name="day">
37      <option value="">Day</option>
38      <?php // Print out 31 days:
```

code continues on next page

To practice with the **for** loop, let's expand the registration form so that it asks the user for their complete birthday. A **for** loop can be used to easily create a day drop-down menu in the HTML form.

To write a for loop:

1. Open **register.html** (Script 6.1) in your text editor or IDE, if it is not already open.

2. Remove the existing birth year prompt and input (**Script 6.9**).

    You'll replace this one prompt with three separate elements to represent the entire birthday: month, day, and year.

3. Where the birth year prompt was, after the password confirmation and before the color option, add a prompt and a list of months:

    ```
    <p>Date Of Birth:
    <select name="month">
    <option value="">Month</option>
    <option value="1">January</option>
    <option value="2">February</option>
    <option value="3">March</option>
    <option value="4">April</option>
    <option value="5">May</option>
    <option value="6">June</option>
    <option value="7">July</option>
    <option value="8">August</option>
    <option value="9">September</option>
    <option value="10">October</option>
    <option value="11">November</option>
    <option value="12">December</option>
    </select>
    ```

    First is a textual prompt, telling the user to supply their entire date of birth. Next comes a select menu in which the user can pick their birth month. The value for each option is numeric; the viewed text is a string (the month's name).

continues on next page

4. Begin a select menu for the birth day:

```
<select name="day">
<option value="">Day</option>
```

This code starts the **select** form element for the user's birth day of the month. The list of possible values will be generated using PHP.

5. Create a new PHP section:

```
<?php
```

Because PHP can be embedded within HTML, you'll use it to populate the drop-down menu. Begin with the standard PHP tag.

6. Create a **for** loop to print out 31 days as select menu options:

```
for ($i = 1; $i <= 31; $i++) {
  print "<option value=\"$i\">$i
  → </option>\n";
}
```

The loop begins by creating a dummy variable called **$i**. On the first use of the loop, this variable is set to 1. Then, as long as **$i** is less than or equal to 31, the contents of the loop are executed. These contents are the **print** line, which creates code like

```
<option value="1">1</option>
```

followed by a return (created with **\n**). After this statement is executed, the **$i** variable is incremented by 1. Then the condition (**$i <= 31**) is checked again, and the process is repeated.

7. Close the PHP section:

```
?>
```

8. Save the file as **register.php**.

You must save the file with the **.php** extension now, in order for the PHP code to be executed.

Script 6.9 continued

```
39      for ($i = 1; $i <= 31; $i++) {
40          print "<option value=\"$i\">$i
            </option>\n";
41      }
42      ?>
43      </select>
44      <input type="text" name="year"
            value="YYYY" size="4" /></p>
45
46      <p>Favorite Color:
47      <select name="color">
48      <option value="">Pick One</option>
49      <option value="red">Red</option>
50      <option value="yellow">Yellow</option>
51      <option value="green">Green</option>
52      <option value="blue">Blue</option>
53      </select></p>
54
55      <p><input type="checkbox"
            name="terms" value="Yes" /> I agree to
            the terms (whatever they may be).</p>
56
57      <input type="submit" name="submit"
            value="Register" />
58
59  </form>
60
61  </div>
62  </body>
63  </html>
```

Please complete this form to register:

Email Address: [   ]

Password: [   ]

Confirm Password: [   ]

Date Of Birth: [Month ▼] [Day ▼] [YYYY]

Favorite Color: [Pick One ▼]

☐ I agree to the terms (whatever they may be).

(Register)

B The new version of the HTML form, with some dynamically generated content.

```
        <option value="11">November</option>
        <option value="12">December</option>
        </select>
        <select name="day">
        <option value="">Day</option>
        <option value="1">1</option>
<option value="2">2</option>
<option value="3">3</option>
<option value="4">4</option>
<option value="5">5</option>
<option value="6">6</option>
<option value="7">7</option>
```

C If you view the HTML source code for the form, you'll see the data generated by the **for** loop.

The while Loop

The second of the three types of loops that exist in PHP—the **while** loop—is designed to continue working as long as the condition you establish is TRUE. Like the **for** loop, it checks the value of the condition before each iteration. Once the condition becomes FALSE, the **while** loop is exited:

```
while (condition) {
        statement(s);
}
```

The main difference between **for** and **while** is that **while** doesn't include a system for setting initial conditions or for executing closing expressions.

You also have the option of using the **do...while** loop, which guarantees that the statements are executed at least once (this isn't necessarily true of the **while** loop):

```
do {
        statement(s);
} while (condition);
```

Although there is a fair amount of overlap regarding when you can use the two major loop constructs (**while** and **for**), you'll discover as you program that sometimes one is more logical than the other. The **while** loop is frequently used in the retrieval of data from a database (see Chapter 12, "Intro to Databases").

9. Place the file in the proper directory for your PHP-enabled server and test it in your Web browser **B**.

   As long as this script is in the same directory as **handle_reg.php**, you can even fill out and submit the form as you would with the plain HTML version.

10. If desired, view the HTML source code to see the PHP-generated options **C**.

TIP It's conventional to use simple variables as the counters within **for** loops: $i, $j, $k, etc.

TIP Just as you can write the **if** conditional on one line if you have only one statement, you can do the same with the **while** and **for** loops. Again, though, this isn't recommended.

TIP Loops can be nested inside each other. You can also place conditionals within loops, loops within conditionals, and so forth.

TIP Pay close attention to your loop's condition so that the loop ends at some point. Otherwise, you'll create an infinite loop, and the script will run and run and run.

Review and Pursue

If you have any problems with the review questions or the pursue prompts, turn to the book's supporting forum (www.LarryUllman.com/forum/).

Review

- Why is it important to have a user confirm their password during the registration process?

- What is the basic structure of an **if** conditional in PHP? An **if-else** conditional? An **if-elseif**? An **if-elseif-else**?

- What are the differences between the **empty()** and **isset()** functions?

- What is the *assignment* operator? What is the *equality* operator?

- Without knowing anything about **$var**, will the following conditional be TRUE or FALSE? Why?

  ```
  if ($var = 'donut') {
  ```

- What do these operators mean?

  - **&&**

  - **||**

  - **!**

- What is the syntax of a **switch** conditional? When is a **switch** most commonly used?

- What is the syntax of a **for** loop?

Pursue

- Check out the PHP manual's pages for the various operators.

- Rewrite **handle_reg.php** so that it uses a variable for the current year, instead of hard-coding that value.

- For debugging purposes, add code to the beginning of the **handle_reg.php** script that prints out the values of the received variables. Hint: There's a short and a long way to do this.

- Rewrite one of the versions of **handle_reg.php** so that it prints the user's favorite color selection in the user's favorite color. Hint: You'll want to use CSS and concatenation.

- Update **handle_reg.php** so that it validates the user's birthday by looking at the three individual form elements: month, day, and year. Create a variable that represents the user's birthday in the format *XX/DD/YYYY* (again, you'll use concatenation for this).

Using Arrays

The next—and last—variable type you'll learn about in this book is the *array*. Arrays are significantly different from numbers or strings, and you can't make the most of programming in PHP without understanding them.

Because of their unique nature, this chapter will cover arrays more deliberately and slowly than the other variable types. The chapter begins with an introduction to the concept, along with the basics of creating and using arrays. Then it covers multidimensional arrays and some of the array-related functions. The chapter concludes with array-string conversions and a demonstration on how to create an array from an HTML form.

In This Chapter

What Is an Array?	152
Creating an Array	154
Adding Items to an Array	158
Accessing Array Elements	161
Creating Multidimensional Arrays	164
Sorting Arrays	168
Transforming Between Strings and Arrays	172
Creating an Array from a Form	176
Review and Pursue	182

What Is an Array?

Arrays constitute a complicated but very useful notion. Whereas numbers and strings are *scalar* variables (meaning they always have only a single value), an array is a collection of multiple values assembled into one overriding variable. An array can consist of numbers and/or strings (and/or other arrays), which allows this one variable to hold exponentially more information than a simple string or number can. For example, if you wanted to create a grocery list using strings, your code would look something like this:

```
$item1 = 'apples';
$item2 = 'bananas';
$item3 = 'oranges';
```

For each added item, you'd need to create a new string. This approach is cumbersome, and it makes it difficult to refer back to the entire list or any specific value later in your code. You can greatly simplify matters by placing your entire list into one array (say, **$items**), which contains everything you need (**Table 7.1**).

As an array, your list can be added to, sorted, searched, and so forth. With this context in mind, let's look into the syntax of arrays.

TABLE 7.1 Grocery List Array

Item Number	Item
1	apples
2	bananas
3	oranges

Syntactical rules for arrays

The other variable types you've dealt with—numbers and strings—have a variable name and a corresponding value (for example, **$first_name** could be equal to *Larry*). Arrays also have a name, derived using the same conventions:

- They begin with a dollar sign.
- They continue with a letter or underscore.
- They finish with any combination of letters, numbers, or the underscore.

But arrays differ in that they contain multiple *elements* (think of each row in Table 7.1 as an element). An element consists of an *index* or *key* (the two words can be used interchangeably) and a value. In Table 7.1, the Item Number is the key, and the Item is the value.

An array's index is used as a reference point to the values. An array can use either numbers or strings as its keys (or both), depending on how you set it up.

Generally, when you use an array it looks the same as any other variable, except that you include a key in square brackets (**[]**) to reference particular values. Whereas **$items** refers to the array as a whole, **$items[1]** points to a specific element in the array (in this example, *apples*).

Creating an Array

The formal method of creating an array is to use the **array()** function. Its syntax is:

```
$list = array ('apples', 'bananas',
→'oranges');
```

Arrays automatically begin their indexing at 0, unless otherwise specified. In that example—which doesn't specify an index for the elements—the first item, *apples*, is automatically indexed at 0, the second item at 1, and the third at 2.

You can assign the index when using **array()**:

```
$list = array (1 => 'apples', 2 =>
→'bananas', 3 => 'oranges');
```

Because PHP is very liberal when it comes to blank space in your scripts, you can make this structure easier to read by writing it over multiple lines:

```
$list = array (
1 => 'apples',
2 => 'bananas',
3 => 'oranges'
);
```

Finally, the index value you specify doesn't have to be a number—you can use strings as well. This indexing technique is practical for making more meaningful lists. As an example, you could create an array that records the soup of the day for each day of the week, as in the following script. This example will also demonstrate how you can, and cannot, print out an array (which has already been demonstrated but is worth rehashing).

```
1    <!DOCTYPE html PUBLIC "-//W3C//DTD
     XHTML 1.0 Transitional//EN"
2        "http://www.w3.org/TR/xhtml1/DTD/
     xhtml1-transitional.dtd">
3    <html xmlns="http://www.w3.org/1999/
     xhtml" xml:lang="en" lang="en">
4    <head>
5        <meta http-equiv="Content-Type"
     content="text/html;
     charset=utf-8"/>
6        <title>No Soup for You!</title>
7    </head>
8    <body>
9    <h1>Mmm...soups</h1>
10   <?php // Script 7.1 - soups1.php
11   /* This script creates and prints out
     an array. */
12   // Address error management, if you
     want.
13
14   // Create the array:
15   $soups = array (
16   'Monday' => 'Clam Chowder',
17   'Tuesday' => 'White Chicken Chili',
18   'Wednesday' => 'Vegetarian'
19   );
20
21   // Try to print the array:
22   print "<p>$soups</p>";
23
24   // Print the contents of the array:
25   print_r ($soups);
26
27   ?>
28   </body>
29   </html>
```

To create an array:

1. Begin a new document in your text editor or IDE, to be named **soups1.php** (Script 7.1):

   ```
   <!DOCTYPE html PUBLIC "-//W3C//DTD
   → XHTML 1.0 Transitional//EN"
     "http://www.w3.org/TR/xhtml1/
     → DTD/xhtml1-transitional.dtd">
   <html xmlns="http://www.w3.org/
   → 1999/xhtml" xml:lang="en"
   → lang="en">
   <head>
     <meta http-equiv="Content-Type"
     → content="text/html;
     → charset=utf-8"/>
     <title>No Soup for You!</title>
   </head>
   <body>
   <h1>Mmm...soups</h1>
   ```

2. Begin the PHP section of the script and address error handling, if necessary:

   ```
   <?php // Script 7.1 - soups1.php
   ```

   If you don't have **display_errors** enabled, or if **error_reporting** is set to the wrong level, see Chapter 3, "HTML Forms and PHP," for the lines to include here to alter those settings.

3. Use the **array()** function to create an array:

   ```
   $soups = array (
   'Monday' => 'Clam Chowder',
   'Tuesday' => 'White Chicken Chili',
   'Wednesday' => 'Vegetarian'
   );
   ```

continues on next page

This is the proper format for initializing (creating and assigning a value to) an array in PHP, using strings as the indices. Because both the keys and values are strings, you surround them with quotation marks. As with all strings, you can use either single or double quotation marks, so long as you're mindful of other quotation marks that might be found within the string.

4. Attempt to print the array:

```
print "<p>$soups</p>";
```

As you've already seen, arrays are also different in that they can't be printed the way you'd print other (scalar) variables.

5. Use the `print_r()` function to print out the array differently:

```
print_r ($soups);
```

In Chapter 2, "Variables," you learned how to use `print_r()` to show the contents and structure of any variable. Use it here so that you can see the difference between the way this function and `print` work with arrays.

6. Close the PHP and the HTML sections:

```
?>
</body>
</html>
```

7. Save your document as **soups1.php**, place it in the proper directory for your PHP-enabled server, and test it in your Web browser Ⓐ.

Remember to run the PHP script through a URL.

Mmm...soups

Array

Array ([Monday] => Clam Chowder [Tuesday] => White Chicken Chili [Wednesday] => Vegetarian)

Ⓐ Because an array is structured differently than other variable types, a request to print an array results in the word *Array*. On the other hand, the `print_r()` function prints the array's contents and structure.

TIP The practice of beginning any index at 0 is standard in PHP and most other programming languages. As unnatural as this counting system may seem, it's here to stay, so you have two possible coping techniques. First, manually start all your arrays indexed at position 1. Second, unlearn a lifetime of counting from 1. You can decide which is easier, but most programmers just get used to this odd construct.

TIP You must refer to an array's elements via the same index used to create the array. In the $soups example, $soups[0] has no value even though the array obviously has a first element (the first element normally being indexed at 0 numerically).

TIP If you use the array() function to define an index, you can associate the first index, and the others will follow sequentially. For example:

```
$list = array (1 => 'apples',
'bananas', 'oranges');
```

Now *bananas* is indexed at 2 and oranges at 3.

TIP The range() function can also be used to create an array of items based on a range of values. Here are two examples:

```
$ten = range (1, 10);
$alphabet = range ('a', 'z');
```

TIP As of PHP version 5, the range() function includes a *step* parameter that lets you specify increments:

```
$evens = range (0, 100, 2);
```

TIP If you use the var_dump() function in your script in lieu of print_r(), it shows not only the contents of the array but also its structure in a more detailed format **B**.

TIP An array whose keys are numbers is called an *indexed* array. If the keys are strings, it's referred to as an *associative* array. Other languages refer to associative arrays as *hashes*.

```
array(3) { ["Monday"]=> string(12) "Clam Chowder" ["Tuesday"]=>
string(19) "White Chicken Chili" ["Wednesday"]=> string(10)
"Vegetarian" }
```

B The var_dump() function (used with Script 7.1 instead of the print_r() function) shows how many elements are in an array and how long each string value is.

Adding Items to an Array

In PHP, once an array exists, you can add extra elements to the array with the assignment operator (the equals sign), in a way similar to how you assign a value to a string or a number. When doing so, you can specify the key of the added element or not specify it, but in either case, you must refer to the array with the square brackets. To add two items to the existing **$list** array, you'd write

```
$list[] = 'pears';
$list[] = 'tomatoes';
```

If you don't specify the key, each element is appended to the existing array, indexed with the next sequential number. Assuming this is the same array from the preceding section, which was indexed at 1, 2, and 3, *pears* is now located at 4 and *tomatoes* at 5.

If you do specify the index, the value is assigned at that location. Any existing value already indexed at that point is overwritten, like so:

```
$list[3] = 'pears';
$list[4] = 'tomatoes';
```

Now, the value of the element in the fourth position of the array is *tomatoes*, and no element of **$list** is equal to *oranges* (that value was overwritten by *pears*). With this in mind, unless you intend to overwrite any existing data, you'll be better off not naming a specific key when adding values to your arrays. However, if the array uses strings for indices, you'll probably want to specify keys so that you don't end up with an unusual combination of string and numeric keys.

To test this process, in the following task you'll rewrite **soups1.php** to add more elements to the array. To see the difference adding more elements makes, you'll print out the number of elements in the array before and after the new additions. Just as you can find the length of a string—how

Deleting Arrays and Array Elements

You won't frequently need to delete an individual item from an array, but it's possible to do using the **unset()** function. This function eliminates a variable and frees up the memory it used. When applied to an array element, that element is deleted:

```
unset($array[4]);
unset($array['name']);
```

If you apply **unset()** to an entire array or any other variable type, the whole variable is deleted:

```
unset($array);
unset($string);
```

You can also *reset* an array (empty it without deleting the variable altogether) using the **array()** function:

```
$array = array();
```

This has the effect of initializing the variable: making it exist and defining its type without assigning a value.

```
1    <!DOCTYPE html PUBLIC "-//W3C//DTD
     XHTML 1.0 Transitional//EN"
2      "http://www.w3.org/TR/xhtml1/DTD/
     xhtml1-transitional.dtd">
3    <html xmlns="http://www.w3.org/1999/
     xhtml" xml:lang="en" lang="en">
4    <head>
5        <meta http-equiv="Content-Type"
         content="text/html; charset=utf-8"/>
6        <title>No Soup for You!</title>
7    </head>
8    <body>
9    <h1>Mmm...soups</h1>
10   <?php // Script 7.2 - soups2.php
11   /* This script creates and prints out
     an array. */
12   // Address error management, if you want.
13
14   // Create the array:
15   $soups = array (
16   'Monday' => 'Clam Chowder',
17   'Tuesday' => 'White Chicken Chili',
18   'Wednesday' => 'Vegetarian'
19   );
20
21   // Count and print the current number
     of elements:
22   $count1 = count ($soups);
23   print "<p>The soups array originally
     had $count1 elements.</p>";
24
25   // Add three items to the array:
26   $soups['Thursday'] = 'Chicken
     Noodle';
27   $soups['Friday'] = 'Tomato';
28   $soups['Saturday'] = 'Cream of Broccoli';
29
30   // Count and print the number of
     elements again:
31   $count2 = count ($soups);
32   print "<p>After adding 3 more soups,
     the array now has $count2 elements.</p>";
33
34   // Print the contents of the array:
35   print_r ($soups);
36
37   ?>
38   </body>
39   </html>
```

many characters it contains—by using **strlen()**, you can determine the number of elements in an array by using **count()**:

```
$how_many = count($array);
```

To add elements to an array:

1. Open **soups1.php** in your text editor or IDE, if it is not already.

2. After the array is initialized using **array()**, add the following (**Script 7.2**, to be named **soups2.php**):

   ```
   $count1 = count ($soups);
   print "<p>The soups array originally
   → had $count1 elements.</p>";
   ```

   The **count()** function determines how many elements are in **$soups**. By assigning that value to a variable, you can easily print out the number.

3. Add three more elements to the array:

   ```
   $soups['Thursday'] = 'Chicken Noodle';
   $soups['Friday'] = 'Tomato';
   $soups['Saturday'] = 'Cream of
   → Broccoli';
   ```

   This code adds three more soups—indexed at *Thursday*, *Friday*, and *Saturday*—to the existing array.

4. Recount how many elements are in the array, and print this value:

   ```
   $count2 = count ($soups);
   print "<p>After adding 3 more
   → soups, the array now has
   → $count2 elements.</p>";
   ```

   This second **print** call is a repetition of the first, showing how many elements the array now contains.

5. Delete this line:

   ```
   print "<p>$soups</p>";
   ```

   This line isn't needed anymore, so you can get rid of it (you now know that you can't print an array that easily).

continues on next page

6. Save your script as **soups2.php**, place it in the proper directory for your PHP-enabled server, and test it in your Web browser **A**.

Merging Arrays

PHP has a function that allows you to append one array onto another. Think of it as concatenation for arrays. The function, **array_merge()**, works like so:

```
$new_array = array_merge
  ($array1, $array2);
```

You could also write the **soups2.php** page using this function:

```
$soups2 = array (
'Thursday'  => 'Chicken Noodle',
'Friday'  => 'Tomato',
'Saturday'  => 'Cream of
  Broccoli'
);
$soups = array_merge($soups,
  $soups2);
```

You could even accomplish this result with the plus sign (thus adding two arrays together):

```
$soups = $soups + $soups2;
```

or

```
$soups += $soups2;
```

TIP Be very careful when you directly add elements to an array. There's a correct way to do it—

```
$array[] = 'Add This';
```

or

```
$array[1] = 'Add This';
```

—and an incorrect way:

```
$array = 'Add This';
```

If you forget to use the brackets, the new value will replace the entire existing array, leaving you with a simple string or number.

TIP The code

```
$array[] = 'Value';
```

creates the **$array** variable if it doesn't yet exist.

TIP While working with these arrays, I'm using single quotation marks to enclose both the keys and the values. Nothing needs to be interpolated (like a variable), so double quotation marks aren't required. It's perfectly acceptable to use double quotation marks, though, if you want to.

TIP You don't (and, in fact, shouldn't) quote your keys if they're numbers, variables, or constants (you'll learn about constants in Chapter 8, "Creating Web Applications"). For example:

```
$day = 'Sunday';
$soups[$day] = 'Mushroom';
```

TIP The **sizeof()** function is an alias to **count()**. It also returns the number of elements in an array.

Mmm...soups

The soups array originally had 3 elements.

After adding 3 more soups, the array now has 6 elements.

Array ([Monday] => Clam Chowder [Tuesday] => White Chicken Chili [Wednesday] => Vegetarian [Thursday] => Chicken Noodle [Friday] => Tomato [Saturday] => Cream of Broccoli)

A A direct way to ensure that the new elements were successfully added to the array is to count the number of elements before and after you make the additions.

Accessing Array Elements

Regardless of how you establish an array, there's only one way to retrieve a specific element (or value) from it, and that is to refer to its index:

```
print "The first item is $array[0]";
```

If the array uses strings for indexes, which should be quoted, you must adjust for the quotation marks you'd use around the index, because they conflict with the **print** syntax. This line will cause problems **A**:

```
print "<p>Monday's soup is
→ $soups['Monday'].</p>";
```

To combat this issue, you can wrap the whole array construct within curly brackets **B**:

```
print "<p>Monday's soup is
→ {$soups['Monday']}.</p>";
```

Ironically, the feature that makes arrays so useful—being able to store multiple values in one variable—also gives it a limitation the other variable types don't have: You must know the keys of the array in order to access its elements. If the array was set using strings, like the **$soups** array, then referring to **$soups[1]** points to nothing **C**. For that matter, because *indexes are case-sensitive*, **$soups['monday']** is meaningless because *Clam Chowder* was indexed at **$soups['Monday']**.

The fastest and easiest way to access all the values of an array is to use a **foreach** loop. This construct loops through every element of an array:

```
foreach ($array as $key => $value) {
        print "<p>Key is $key. Value
            → is $value</p>";
}
```

With each iteration of the loop, the current array element's key will be assigned to the **$key** variable and the value to **$value**. Note that you can use any variable here: **$k** and **$v** are likely choices, too.

You can now write a new soups script to use this knowledge.

> **Parse error**: syntax error, unexpected T_ENCAPSED_AND_WHITESPACE, expecting T_STRING or T_VARIABLE or T_NUM_STRING in **/Users /larryullman/Sites/phpvqs4/soups2.php** on line **37**

A Referencing a specific element in an associative array will cause parse errors within double quotation marks.

> Monday's soup is Clam Chowder.

B Wrapping an array element reference in curly brackets is one way to avoid parse errors.

> **Notice**: Undefined offset: 1 in **/Users/larryullman/Sites/phpvqs4/soups2.php** on line **37**

C Referring to an array index that does not exist will create an *Undefined offset* or *Undefined Index* notice.

To print the values of any array:

1. Begin a new document in your text editor or IDE (**Script 7.3, to be named soups3.php**):

```
<!DOCTYPE html PUBLIC "-//W3C//DTD
→ XHTML 1.0 Transitional//EN"
   "http://www.w3.org/TR/xhtml1/
   → DTD/xhtml1-transitional.dtd">
<html xmlns="http://www.w3.org/
→ 1999/xhtml" xml:lang="en" lang="en">
<head>
   <meta http-equiv="Content-Type"
   → content="text/html;
   → charset=utf-8"/>
   <title>No Soup for You!</title>
</head>
<body>
<h1>Mmm...soups</h1>
```

2. Start the PHP section of the page and address error management, if you need:

```
<?php // Script 7.3 - soups3.php
```

3. Create the **$soups** array:

```
$soups = array (
'Monday' => 'Clam Chowder',
'Tuesday' => 'White Chicken Chili',
'Wednesday' => 'Vegetarian',
'Thursday' => 'Chicken Noodle',
'Friday' => 'Tomato',
'Saturday' => 'Cream of Broccoli'
);
```

Here the entire array is created at once, although you could use the same method (creating the array in steps) as in the preceding script, if you'd rather.

Script 7.3 A **foreach** loop is the easiest way to access every element in an array.

```
1   <!DOCTYPE html PUBLIC "-//W3C//DTD
       XHTML 1.0 Transitional//EN"
2        "http://www.w3.org/TR/xhtml1/DTD/
         xhtml1-transitional.dtd">
3    <html xmlns="http://www.w3.org/1999/
       xhtml" xml:lang="en" lang="en">
4    <head>
5        <meta http-equiv="Content-Type"
         content="text/html;
         charset=utf-8"/>
6        <title>No Soup for You!</title>
7    </head>
8    <body>
9    <h1>Mmm...soups</h1>
10   <?php // Script 7.3 - soups3.php
11   /* This script creates and prints out
     an array. */
12
13   // Address error management, if you
     want.
14
15   // Create the array:
16   $soups = array (
17   'Monday' => 'Clam Chowder',
18   'Tuesday' => 'White Chicken Chili',
19   'Wednesday' => 'Vegetarian',
20   'Thursday' => 'Chicken Noodle',
21   'Friday' => 'Tomato',
22   'Saturday' => 'Cream of Broccoli'
23   );
24
25   // Print each key and value:
26   foreach ($soups as $day => $soup) {
27       print "<p>$day: $soup</p>\n";
28   }
29
30   ?>
31   </body>
32   </html>
```

4. Create a **foreach** loop to print out each day's soup:

```
foreach ($soups as $day => $soup)
{
    print "<p>$day: $soup</p>\n";
}
```

The **foreach** loop iterates through every element of the **$soups** array, assigning each index to **$day** and each value to **$soup**. These values are then printed out within HTML paragraph tags. The **print** statement concludes with a newline character (created by **\n**), which will make the HTML source code of the page more legible.

5. Close the PHP section and the HTML page:

```
?>
</body>
</html>
```

6. Save the page as **soups3.php**, place it in the proper directory for your PHP-enabled server, and test it in your Web browser **D**.

Mmm…soups

Monday: Clam Chowder

Tuesday: White Chicken Chili

Wednesday: Vegetarian

Thursday: Chicken Noodle

Friday: Tomato

Saturday: Cream of Broccoli

TIP One option for working with arrays is to assign a specific element's value to a separate variable using the assignment operator:

```
$total = $array[1];
```

By doing this, you can preserve the original value in the array and still manipulate the value separately as a variable.

TIP If you only need to access an array's values (and not its keys), you can use this **foreach** structure:

```
foreach ($array as $value) {
    // Do whatever.
}
```

TIP Another way to access all of an array's elements is to use a **for** loop:

```
for ($n = 0; $n < count($array); $n++) {
    print "The value is $array[$n]";
}
```

TIP The curly brackets are used to avoid errors when printing array values that have strings for keys. Here are two examples where using quotation marks is not problematic, so the curly brackets aren't required:

```
$name = trim ($array['name']);
$total = $_POST['qty'] *
$_POST['price'];
```

TIP Curly brackets can also be used to separate a variable reference from a dollar sign or other characters:

```
print "The total is ${$total}.";
```

D The execution of the loop for every element in the array generates this page. The **foreach** construct allows the script to access each key and value without prior knowledge of what they are.

Creating Multidimensional Arrays

Multidimensional arrays are both simple and complicated at the same time. The structure and concept may be somewhat difficult to grasp, but creating and accessing multidimensional arrays in PHP is surprisingly easy.

You use a multidimensional array to create an array containing more information than a standard array. You accomplish this by using other arrays for values instead of just strings and numbers. For example:

```
$fruits = array ('apples', 'bananas',
→'oranges');
$meats = array ('steaks',
→'hamburgers', 'pork chops');
$groceries = array (
'fruits' => $fruits,
'meats' => $meats,
'other' => 'peanuts',
'cash' => 30.00
);
```

This array, **$groceries**, now consists of one string (*peanuts*), one floating-point number (*30.00*), and two arrays (**$fruits** and **$meats**).

Pointing to an element in an array within an array can seem tricky. The key (pardon the pun) is to continue adding indices in square brackets as necessary, working from the outer array inward. With that example, *bananas* is at **$groceries['fruits'][1]**. First, you point to the element (in this case, an array) in the **$groceries** array by using **['fruits']**. Then, you point to the element in that array based on its position—it's the second item, so you use the index **[1]**.

In this next task, you'll write a script that creates another multidimensional array example.

Script 7.4 The multidimensional **$books** array stores a lot of information in one big variable.

```
1    <!DOCTYPE html PUBLIC "-//W3C//DTD
     XHTML 1.0 Transitional//EN"
2       "http://www.w3.org/TR/xhtml1/DTD/
        xhtml1-transitional.dtd">
3    <html xmlns="http://www.w3.org/1999/
     xhtml" xml:lang="en" lang="en">
4    <head>
5       <meta http-equiv="Content-Type"
        content="text/html;
        charset=utf-8"/>
6       <title>Larry Ullman's Books and
        Chapters</title>
7    </head>
8    <body>
9    <h1>Some of Larry Ullman's Books</h1>
10   <?php // Script 7.4 - books.php
11   /* This script creates and prints out
     a multidimensional array. */
12   // Address error management, if you
     want.
13
14   // Create the first array:
15   $phpvqs = array (1 => 'Getting Started
     with PHP', 'Variables', 'HTML Forms
     and PHP', 'Using Numbers');
16
17   // Create the second array:
18   $phpadv = array (1 => 'Advanced
     PHP Techniques', 'Developing Web
     Applications', 'Advanced Database
     Concepts', 'Security Techniques');
19
20   // Create the third array:
21   $phpmysql = array (1 => 'Introduction
     to PHP', 'Programming with PHP',
     'Creating Dynamic Web Sites',
     'Introduction to MySQL');
22
23   // Create the multidimensional array:
24   $books = array (
25   'PHP VQS' => $phpvqs,
26   'PHP Advanced VQP' => $phpadv,
27   'PHP and MySQL VQP' => $phpmysql
28   );
29
```

code continues on next page

```
30   // Print out some values:
31   print "<p>The third chapter of
     my first book is <i>{$books['PHP
     VQS'][3]}</i>.</p>";
32   print "<p>The first chapter of my
     second book is <i>{$books['PHP
     Advanced VQP'][1]}</i>.</p>";
33   print "<p>The fourth chapter of
     my fourth book is <i>{$books['PHP
     and MySQL VQP'][4]}</i>.</p>";
34
35   // See what happens with foreach:
36   foreach ($books as $key => $value) {
37       print "<p>$key: $value</p>\n";
38   }
39
40   ?>
41   </body>
42   </html>
```

To use multidimensional arrays:

1. Begin a new document in your text editor or IDE, to be named **books.php** (Script 7.4):

   ```
   <!DOCTYPE html PUBLIC "-//W3C//DTD
   → XHTML 1.0 Transitional//EN"
      "http://www.w3.org/TR/xhtml1/
      → DTD/xhtml1-transitional.dtd">
   <html xmlns="http://www.w3.org/
   → 1999/xhtml" xml:lang="en" lang="en">
   <head>
      <meta http-equiv="Content-Type"
      → content="text/html;
      → charset=utf-8"/>
      <title>Larry Ullman's Books and
      → Chapters</title>
   </head>
   <body>
   <h1>Some of Larry Ullman's
   → Books</h1>
   ```

2. Create the initial PHP tags, and address error management, if necessary:

   ```
   <?php // Script 7.4 - books.php
   ```

3. Create the first array:

   ```
   $phpvqs = array (1 => 'Getting
   → Started with PHP', 'Variables',
   → 'HTML Forms and PHP', 'Using
   → Numbers');
   ```

   To build up the multidimensional array, you'll create three standard arrays and then use them as the values for the larger array. This array (called **$phpvqs**, which is short for *PHP for the Web: Visual QuickStart Guide*) uses numbers for the keys and strings for the values. The numbers begin with 1 and correspond to the chapter numbers. The values are the chapter titles.

   continues on next page

4. Create the next two arrays:

```
$phpadv = array (1 => 'Advanced
→ PHP Techniques', 'Developing Web
→ Applications', 'Advanced
→ Database Concepts', 'Security
→ Techniques');
$phpmysql = array (1 =>
→ 'Introduction to PHP',
→ 'Programming with PHP',
→ 'Creating Dynamic Web Sites',
→ 'Introduction to MySQL');
```

For each array, add only the book's first four chapters for simplicity's sake.

5. Create the main, multidimensional array:

```
$books = array (
'PHP VQS' => $phpvqs,
'PHP Advanced VQP' => $phpadv,
'PHP and MySQL VQP' => $phpmysql
);
```

The **$books** array is the master array for this script. It uses strings for keys (which are shortened versions of the book titles) and arrays for values. Use the **array()** function to create it, as you would any other array.

6. Print out the name of the third chapter of the *PHP Visual QuickStart Guide* book:

```
print "<p>The third chapter of
→ my first book is <i>{$books['PHP
→ VQS'][3]}</i>.</p>";
```

Following the rules stated earlier, all you need to do to access any individual chapter name is to begin with **$books**, follow that with the first index (**['PHP VQS']**), and follow that with the next index (**[3]**). Because you're placing this in a **print** call, you enclose the whole construct in curly brackets to avoid parse errors.

7. Print out two more examples:

```
print "<p>The first chapter of
→ my second book is <i>{$books
→ ['PHP Advanced VQP'][1]}</i>.</p>";
print "<p>The fourth chapter of
→ my fourth book is <i>{$books
→ ['PHP and MySQL VQP'][4]}</i>.</p>";
```

8. Run the **$books** array through a **foreach** loop to see the results:

```
foreach ($books as $key => $value)
{
    print "<p>$key: $value</p>\n";
}
```

Some of Larry Ullman's Books

The third chapter of my first book is *HTML Forms and PHP*.

The first chapter of my second book is *Advanced PHP Techniques*.

The fourth chapter of my fourth book is *Introduction to MySQL*.

PHP VQS: Array

PHP Advanced VQP: Array

PHP and MySQL VQP: Array

Ⓐ The first three lines are generated by **print** statements. The last three show the results of the **foreach** loop (and the notices come from attempting to print an array).

```
PHP VQS
Chapter 1 is Getting Started with PHP
Chapter 2 is Variables
Chapter 3 is HTML Forms and PHP
Chapter 4 is Using Numbers

PHP Advanced VQP
Chapter 1 is Advanced PHP Techniques
Chapter 2 is Developing Web Applications
Chapter 3 is Advanced Database Concepts
Chapter 4 is Security Techniques

PHP and MySQL VQP
Chapter 1 is Introduction to PHP
Chapter 2 is Programming with PHP
Chapter 3 is Creating Dynamic Web Sites
Chapter 4 is Introduction to MySQL
```

B One **foreach** loop within another can access every element of a two-dimensional array.

```
Array
(
    [PHP VQS] => Array
        (
            [1] => Getting Started with PHP
            [2] => Variables
            [3] => HTML Forms and PHP
            [4] => Using Numbers
        )

    [PHP Advanced VQP] => Array
        (
            [1] => Advanced PHP Techniques
            [2] => Developing Web Applications
            [3] => Advanced Database Concepts
            [4] => Security Techniques
        )

    [PHP and MySQL VQP] => Array
        (
            [1] => Introduction to PHP
            [2] => Programming with PHP
            [3] => Creating Dynamic Web Sites
            [4] => Introduction to MySQL
        )

)
```

C The **print_r()** function shows the structure and contents of the **$books** array.

The **$key** variable will be assigned each abbreviated book title, and the **$value** variable ends up containing each chapter array.

9. Close the PHP section and complete the HTML page:

```
?>
</body>
</html>
```

10. Save the file as **books.php**, place it in the proper directory for your PHP-enabled server, and test it in your browser **A**.

TIP To access every element of every array, you can nest two **foreach** loops like this **B**:

```
foreach ($books as $title =>
→ $chapters) {
    print "<p>$title";
    foreach ($chapters as $number =>
    → $chapter) {
        print "<br />Chapter $number
        → is $chapter";
    }
    print '</p>';
}
```

TIP Using the **print_r()** or **var_dump()** function (preferably enclosed in HTML **<pre>** tags for better formatting), you can view an entire multidimensional array **C**.

TIP You can create a multidimensional array in one statement by using a series of nested **array()** calls (instead of using several steps as in this example). However, doing so isn't recommended, because it's all too easy to make syntactical errors as a statement becomes more and more nested.

TIP Although all the subarrays in this example have the same structure (numbers for indexes and four elements), that isn't required with multidimensional arrays.

TIP To learn about the greater "Larry Ullman Collection," including the three books referenced here, head to www.LarryUllman.com.

Sorting Arrays

PHP supports a variety of ways to sort an array (*sort* refers to an alphabetical sort if the values being sorted are strings, or a numerical sort if the values being sorted are numbers). When you're sorting an array, you must keep in mind that an array consists of pairs of *keys and values*. Thus, an array can be sorted based on the keys or the values. This is further complicated by the fact that you can sort the values and keep the corresponding keys aligned, or you can sort the values and have them be assigned new keys.

To sort the values without regard to the keys, you use **sort()**. To sort these values (again, without regard to the keys) in reverse order, you use **rsort()**. The syntax for every sorting function is:

function($array);

So, **sort()** and **rsort()** are used as follows:

```
sort($array);
rsort($array);
```

To sort the values while maintaining the correlation between each value and its key, you use **asort()**. To sort the values in reverse while maintaining the key correlation, you use **arsort()**.

To sort by the keys while maintaining the correlation between the key and its value, you use **ksort()**. Conversely, **krsort()** sorts the keys in reverse. **Table 7.2** lists all these functions.

Finally, **shuffle()** randomly reorganizes the order of an array.

As an example of sorting arrays, you'll create a list of students and the grades they received on a test, and then sort this list first by grade and then by name.

TABLE 7.2 Array Sorting Functions

Function	Sorts By	Maintains Key-Values?
sort()	Values	No
rsort()	Values (inverse)	No
asort()	Values	Yes
arsort()	Values (inverse)	Yes
ksort()	Keys	Yes
krsort()	Keys (inverse)	Yes

```
1    <!DOCTYPE html PUBLIC "-//W3C//DTD
     XHTML 1.0 Transitional//EN"
2        "http://www.w3.org/TR/xhtml1/DTD/
         xhtml1-transitional.dtd">
3    <html xmlns="http://www.w3.org/1999/
     xhtml" xml:lang="en" lang="en">
4    <head>
5        <meta http-equiv="Content-Type"
         content="text/html;
         charset=utf-8"/>
6        <title>My Little Gradebook</title>
7    </head>
8    <body>
9    <?php // Script 7.5 - sort.php
10   /* This script creates, sorts, and
     prints out an array. */
11
12   // Address error management, if you
     want.
13
14   // Create the array:
15   $grades = array(
16   'Richard' => 95,
17   'Sherwood' => 82,
18   'Toni' => 98,
19   'Franz' => 87,
20   'Melissa' => 75,
21   'Roddy' => 85
22   );
23
24   // Print the original array:
25   print '<p>Originally the array looks
     like this: <br />';
26   foreach ($grades as $student =>
     $grade) {
27       print "$student: $grade<br />\n";
28   }
29   print '</p>';
30
31   // Sort by value in reverse order,
     then print again:
32   arsort ($grades);
33   print '<p>After sorting the array by
     value using arsort(), the array looks
     like this: <br />';
```

code continues on next page

To sort an array:

1. Begin a new document in your text editor or IDE, to be named **sort.php** (Script 7.5):

   ```
   <!DOCTYPE html PUBLIC "-//W3C//DTD
   → XHTML 1.0 Transitional//EN"
     "http://www.w3.org/TR/xhtml1/
   → DTD/xhtml1-transitional.dtd">
   <html xmlns="http://www.w3.org/
   → 1999/xhtml" xml:lang="en"
   → lang="en">
   <head>
     <meta http-equiv="Content-Type"
   → content="text/html;
   charset=utf-8"/>
     <title>My Little Gradebook</
   title>
   </head>
   <body>
   ```

2. Begin the PHP section, and address error handling, if desired:

   ```
   <?php // Script 7.5 - sort.php
   ```

3. Create the array:

   ```
   $grades = array(
   'Richard' => 95,
   'Sherwood' => 82,
   'Toni' => 98,
   'Franz' => 87,
   'Melissa' => 75,
   'Roddy' => 85
   );
   ```

   The **$grades** array consists of six students' names along with their corresponding grades. Because the grades are numbers, they don't need to be quoted when assigning them.

   continues on next page

4. Print a caption, and then print each element of the array using a **foreach** loop:

```
print '<p>Originally the array
→ looks like this: <br />';
foreach ($grades as $student =>
→ $grade) {
  print "$student: $grade<br />\n";
}
print '</p>';
```

As the **$grades** array will be printed three times, captions indicating each state of the array will be useful. At first, the script prints the array in the original order. To do that, use a **foreach** loop, where each index (the student's name) is assigned to **$student**, and each value (the student's grade) is assigned to **$grade**. The final **print** call closes the HTML paragraph.

5. Sort the array in reverse order by value to determine who has the highest grade:

```
arsort ($grades);
```

To determine who has the highest grade, you need to use **arsort()** instead of **asort()**. The latter, which sorts the array in numeric order, would order the grades 75, 82, 85, and so on, rather than the desired 98, 95, 87.

You also must use **arsort()** and not **rsort()** in order to maintain the key-value relationship (**rsort()** would eliminate the student's name associated with each grade).

6. Print the array again (with a caption), using another loop:

```
print '<p>After sorting the array
→ by value using arsort(), the
→ array looks like this: <br />';
foreach ($grades as $student =>
→ $grade) {
  print "$student: $grade<br />\n";
}
print '</p>';
```

Script 7.5 *continued*

```
34   foreach ($grades as $student =>
     $grade) {
35       print "$student: $grade<br />\n";
36   }
37   print '</p>';
38
39   // Sort by key, then print again:
40   ksort ($grades);
41   print '<p>After sorting the array by
     key using ksort(), the array looks
     like this: <br />';
42   foreach ($grades as $student =>
     $grade) {
43       print "$student: $grade<br />\n";
44   }
45   print '</p>';
46
47   ?>
48   </body>
49   </html>
```

```
Originally the array looks like this:
Richard: 95
Sherwood: 82
Toni: 98
Franz: 87
Melissa: 75
Roddy: 85

After sorting the array by value using arsort(), the array looks like this:
Toni: 98
Richard: 95
Franz: 87
Roddy: 85
Sherwood: 82
Melissa: 75

After sorting the array by key using ksort(), the array looks like this:
Franz: 87
Melissa: 75
Richard: 95
Roddy: 85
Sherwood: 82
Toni: 98
```

A You can sort an array in a number of ways with varied results. Pay close attention to whether you want to maintain your key-value association when choosing a sort function.

7. Sort the array by key to put the array in alphabetical order by student name:

```
ksort ($grades);
```

The **ksort()** function organizes the array by key (in this case, alphabetically) while maintaining the key-value correlation.

8. Print a caption and the array one last time:

```
print '<p>After sorting the array
→ by key using ksort(), the array
→ looks like this: <br />';
foreach ($grades as $student =>
→ $grade) {
   print "$student: $grade<br />\n";
}
print '</p>';
```

9. Complete the script with the standard PHP and HTML tags:

```
?>
</body>
</html>
```

10. Save your script as **sort.php**, place it in the proper directory for your PHP-enabled server, and test it in your Web browser **A**.

TIP Because each element in an array must have its own unique key, the $grades array will only work using unique student names.

TIP The natsort() and natcasesort() functions sort a string (while maintaining key-value associations) using *natural order*. The most obvious example of natural order sorting is that it places *name2* before *name12*, whereas sort() orders them *name12* and then *name2*.

TIP The usort(), uasort(), and ursort() functions let you sort an array using a user-defined comparison function. These functions are most often used with multidimensional arrays.

Transforming Between Strings and Arrays

Now that you have an understanding of both strings and arrays, this next section introduces two functions for switching between the formats. The first, **implode()**, turns an array into a string. The second, **explode()**, does just the opposite. Here are some reasons to use these functions:

- To turn an array into a string in order to pass that value appended to a URL (which you can't do as easily with an array)

- To turn an array into a string in order to store that information in a database

- To turn a string into an array to convert a comma-delimited text field (say a keyword search area of a form) into its separate parts

The syntax for using **explode()** is as follows:

```
$array = explode(separator, $string);
```

The *separator* refers to whatever character(s) define where one value ends and another begins. Commonly this is a comma, a tab, or a blank space. Thus your code might be

```
$array = explode(',', $string);
```

or

```
$array = explode(' ', $string);
```

To go from an array to a string, you need to define what the separator (aka the *glue*) should be, and PHP does the rest:

```
$string = implode(glue, $array);
$string = implode(',', $array);
```

or

```
$string = implode(' ', $array);
```

To demonstrate how to use **explode()** and **implode()**, you'll create an HTML form that takes a space-delimited string of names from the user **A**. The PHP script will then turn the string into an array so that it can sort the list. Finally, the code will create and return the alphabetized string **B**.

Enter the words you want alphabetized with each individual word separated by a space:

| Brian Sommar Eric Mark Shauna Allison Mike | (Alphabetize!) |

A This HTML form takes a list of words, which is then alphabetized by the **list.php** script **B**.

An alphabetized version of your list is:
Allison
Brian
Eric
Mark
Mike
Shauna
Sommar

B Here's the same list, alphabetized for the user. This process is quick and easy to code, but doing so would be impossible without arrays.

Script 7.6 This is a simple HTML form where a user can submit a list of words. Including detailed instructions for how the form should be used is a prudent Web design policy.

```
1   <!DOCTYPE html PUBLIC "-//W3C//DTD
    XHTML 1.0 Transitional//EN"
2       "http://www.w3.org/TR/xhtml1/DTD/
    xhtml1-transitional.dtd">
3   <html xmlns="http://www.w3.org/1999/
    xhtml" xml:lang="en" lang="en">
4   <head>
5       <meta http-equiv="Content-Type"
    content="text/html;
    charset=utf-8"/>
6       <title>I Must Sort This Out!</title>
7   </head>
8   <body>
9   <!-- Script 7.6 - list.html -->
10  <div><p>Enter the words you want
    alphabetized with each individual word
    separated by a space:</p>
11
12  <form action="list.php" method="post">
13
14      <input type="text" name="words"
    size="60" />
15      <input type="submit" name="submit"
    value="Alphabetize!" />
16
17  </form>
18  </div>
19  </body>
20  </html>
```

To create the HTML form:

1. Begin a new document in your text editor or IDE, to be named `list.html` (Script 7.6):

```
<!DOCTYPE html PUBLIC "-//W3C//DTD
→ XHTML 1.0 Transitional//EN"
    "http://www.w3.org/TR/xhtml1/
    → DTD/xhtml1-transitional.dtd">
<html xmlns="http://www.w3.org/
→ 1999/xhtml" xml:lang="en"
→ lang="en">
<head>
    <meta http-equiv="Content-Type"
    → content="text/html;
    → charset=utf-8"/>
    <title>I Must Sort This Out!
    → </title>
</head>
<body>
<!-- Script 7.6 - list.html -->
```

2. Create an HTML form with a text input:

```
<div><p>Enter the words you
→ want alphabetized with each
→ individual word separated by
→ a space:</p>
<form action="list.php"
→ method="post">
    <input type="text" name="words"
    → size="60" />
```

It's important in cases like this to instruct the user. For example, if the user enters a comma-delimited list, the PHP script won't be able to handle the string properly (after completing both scripts, try using commas in lieu of spaces and see what happens).

continues on next page

3. Create a submit button, and then close the form and the HTML page:

```
<input type="submit" name=
→ "submit" value="Alphabetize!" />
</form>
</div>
</body>
</html>
```

4. Save your script as **list.html** and place it in the proper directory for your PHP-enabled server.

Now you'll write the **list.php** page to process the data generated by **list.html**.

To convert between strings and arrays:

1. Begin a new document in your text editor or IDE, to be named **list.php** (Script 7.7):

```
<!DOCTYPE html PUBLIC "-//W3C//DTD
→ XHTML 1.0 Transitional//EN"
   "http://www.w3.org/TR/xhtml1/
    → DTD/xhtml1-transitional.dtd">
<html xmlns="http://www.w3.org/
→ 1999/xhtml" xml:lang="en"
→ lang="en">
<head>
  <meta http-equiv="Content-Type"
   → content="text/html;
   → charset=utf-8"/>
  <title>I Have This Sorted Out
   → </title>
</head>
<body>
<?php // Script 7.7 - list.php
```

2. Turn the incoming string, **$_POST['words']**, into an array:

```
$words_array = explode(' ' ,
→ $_POST['words']);
```

This line of code creates a new array, **$words_array**, out of the string

Script 7.7 Because the `explode()` and `implode()` functions are so simple and powerful, you can quickly and easily sort a submitted list of words (of practically any length) in just a couple of lines.

```
1    <!DOCTYPE html PUBLIC "-//W3C//DTD
     XHTML 1.0 Transitional//EN"
2        "http://www.w3.org/TR/xhtml1/DTD/
         xhtml1-transitional.dtd">
3    <html xmlns="http://www.w3.org/1999/
     xhtml" xml:lang="en" lang="en">
4    <head>
5      <meta http-equiv="Content-Type"
       content="text/html;
       charset=utf-8"/>
6      <title>I Have This Sorted Out</title>
7    </head>
8    <body>
9    <?php // Script 7.7 - list.php
10   /* This script receives a string in
     $_POST['words']. It then turns it into
     an array,
11   sorts the array alphabetically, and
     reprints it. */
12
13   // Address error management, if you
     want.
14
15   // Turn the incoming string into an
     array:
16   $words_array = explode(' ' ,
     $_POST['words']);
17
18   // Sort the array:
19   sort($words_array);
20
21   // Turn the array back into a string:
22   $string_words = implode('<br />',
     $words_array);
23
24   // Print the results:
25   print "<p>An alphabetized
     version of your list is: <br />
     $string_words</p>";
26
27   ?>
28   </body>
29   </html>
```

$_POST['words']. Each space between the words in $_POST['words'] indicates that the next word should be a new array element. Hence the first word becomes $words_array[0], then there is a space in $_POST['words'], then the second word becomes $words_array[1], and so forth, until the end of $_POST['words'].

3. Sort the array alphabetically:

```
sort($words_array);
```

Because you don't need to maintain key-value associations in the $words_array, you can use sort() instead of asort().

4. Create a new string out of the sorted array:

```
$string_words = implode('<br />',
→ $words_array);
```

Arrays don't print as easily as strings, so turn $words_array into a string called $string_words. The resulting string starts with the value of $words_array[0], followed by the HTML <br /> tag, the value of $words_array[1], and so on. Using <br /> instead of a space or comma gives the list a more readable format when it's printed to the browser.

5. Print the new string to the browser:

```
print "<p>An alphabetized
→ version of your list is:
→ <br />$string_words</p>";
```

6. Close the PHP section and the HTML page:

```
?>
</body>
</html>
```

7. Save your page as list.php, place it in the same directory as list.html, and test both scripts in your Web browser Ⓐ and Ⓑ.

TIP You'll also run across code written using the join() function, which is synonymous with implode().

Creating an Array from a Form

Throughout this chapter, you've established arrays entirely from within a PHP page. You can, however, send an array of data to a PHP script via an HTML form. In fact, every time you use **$_POST**, this is the case. But you can take this one step further by creating arrays using an HTML form. Such arrays will then be a part of the greater **$_POST** array (thereby making **$_POST** a multidimensional array).

A logical use of this capability is in dealing with checkboxes, where users might need to select multiple options from a group **A**. The HTML source code for a checkbox is as follows:

```
<input type="checkbox"
name="topping" value="Ham" />
```

The problem in this particular case is that each form element must have a unique name. If you created several checkboxes, each with a name of *topping*, only the value of the last checked box would be received in the PHP script. If you were to create unique names for each checkbox—*ham*, *tomato*, *black_olives*, etc.—working with the selected values would be tedious.

The workaround is to use array syntax, as demonstrated in the next example.

Pizza Toppings: ☐ Extra Tomato ☐ Ham ☐ Sausage ☐ Pepperoni ☐ Black Olives ☐ Turnips ☐ Kumquats

A Checkboxes in an HTML form, presenting several possible options.

Script 7.8 This HTML form has an array for the checkbox input names.

```
1   <!DOCTYPE html PUBLIC "-//W3C//DTD
    XHTML 1.0 Transitional//EN"
2       "http://www.w3.org/TR/xhtml1/DTD/
    xhtml1-transitional.dtd">
3   <html xmlns="http://www.w3.org/1999/
    xhtml" xml:lang="en" lang="en">
4   <head>
5       <meta http-equiv="Content-Type"
    content="text/html;
    charset=utf-8"/>
6       <title>Add an Event</title>
7   </head>
8   <body>
9   <!-- Script 7.8 - event.html -->
10  <div><p>Use this form to add an
    event:</p>
11
12  <form action="event.php" method="post">
13
14      <p>Event Name: <input type="text"
    name="name" size="30" /></p>
15      <p>Event Days:
16      <input type="checkbox" name=
    "days[]" value="Sunday" /> Sun
17      <input type="checkbox" name=
    "days[]" value="Monday" /> Mon
18      <input type="checkbox" name=
    "days[]" value="Tuesday" /> Tue
19      <input type="checkbox" name=
    "days[]" value="Wednesday" /> Wed
20      <input type="checkbox" name=
    "days[]" value="Thursday" /> Thu
21      <input type="checkbox" name=
    "days[]" value="Friday" /> Fri
22      <input type="checkbox" name=
    "days[]" value="Saturday" /> Sat
23      </p>
24      <input type="submit" name="submit"
    value="Add the Event!" />
25
26  </form>
27  </div>
28  </body>
29  </html>
```

To create an array with an HTML form:

1. Begin a new document in your text editor or IDE, to be named **event.html** (Script 7.8):

   ```
   <!DOCTYPE html PUBLIC "-//W3C//DTD
   → XHTML 1.0 Transitional//EN"
      "http://www.w3.org/TR/xhtml1/
   → DTD/xhtml1-transitional.dtd">
   <html xmlns="http://www.w3.org/
   → 1999/xhtml" xml:lang="en"
   → lang="en">
   <head>
      <meta http-equiv="Content-Type"
   → content="text/html;
   → charset=utf-8"/>
      <title>Add an Event</title>
   </head>
   <body>
   <!-- Script 7.8 - event.html -->
   <div><p>Use this form to add an
   → event:</p>
   ```

2. Begin the HTML form:

   ```
   <form action="event.php"
   → method="post">
   ```

   This form will be submitted to **event.php**, found in the same directory as this HTML page.

3. Create a text input for an event name:

   ```
   <p>Event Name: <input type="text"
   → name="name" size="30" /></p>
   ```

   This example allows the user to enter an event name and the days of the week when it takes place.

   continues on next page

4. Create the days checkboxes:

```
<p>Event Days:
<input type="checkbox" name=
→"days[]" value="Sunday" /> Sun
<input type="checkbox" name=
→"days[]" value="Monday" /> Mon
<input type="checkbox" name=
→"days[]" value="Tuesday" /> Tue
<input type="checkbox" name=
→"days[]" value="Wednesday" /> Wed
<input type="checkbox" name=
→"days[]" value="Thursday" /> Thu
<input type="checkbox" name=
→"days[]" value="Friday" /> Fri
<input type="checkbox" name=
→"days[]" value="Saturday" /> Sat
</p>
```

All of these checkboxes use *days[ ]* as the **name** value, which creates a **$_POST['days']** array in the PHP script. The **value** attributes differ for each checkbox, corresponding to the day of the week.

5. Complete the HTML form:

```
<input type="submit" name=
→"submit" value="Add the
→Event!" />
</form>
```

6. Complete the HTML page:

```
</div>
</body>
</html>
```

7. Save your page as **event.html** and place it in the proper directory for your PHP-enabled server.

You also need to write the **event.php** page to handle this HTML form.

Script 7.9 This PHP script receives an array of values in **$_POST['days']**.

```
1    <!DOCTYPE html PUBLIC "-//W3C//DTD
     XHTML 1.0 Transitional//EN"
2       "http://www.w3.org/TR/xhtml1/DTD/
     xhtml1-transitional.dtd">
3    <html xmlns="http://www.w3.org/1999/
     xhtml" xml:lang="en" lang="en">
4    <head>
5       <meta http-equiv="Content-Type"
     content="text/html;
     charset=utf-8"/>
6       <title>Add an Event</title>
7    </head>
8    <body>
9    <?php // Script 7.9 - event.php
10   /* This script handle the event form. */
11
12   // Address error management, if you
     want.
13
14   // Print the text:
15   print "<p>You want to add an event
     called <b>{$_POST['name']}</b> which
     takes place on: <br />";
16
17   // Print each weekday:
18   if (isset($_POST['days']) AND
     is_array($_POST['days'])) {
19
20       foreach ($_POST['days'] as $day) {
21           print "$day<br />\n";
22       }
23
24   } else {
25       print 'Please select at least one
     weekday for this event!';
26   }
27
28   // Complete the paragraph:
29   print '</p>';
30   ?>
31   </body>
32   </html>
```

To handle the HTML form:

1. Begin a new document in your text editor or IDE, to be named **event.php** (**Script 7.9**):

   ```
   <!DOCTYPE html PUBLIC "-//W3C//DTD
   → XHTML 1.0 Transitional//EN"
      "http://www.w3.org/TR/xhtml1/
      → DTD/xhtml1-transitional.dtd">
   <html xmlns="http://www.w3.org
   → /1999/xhtml" xml:lang="en" lang="en">
   <head>
      <meta http-equiv="Content-Type"
      → content="text/html;
      → charset=utf-8"/>
      <title>Add an Event</title>
   </head>
   <body>
   ```

2. Create the initial PHP tag, address error management (if need be), and print an introductory message:

   ```
   <?php // Script 7.9 - event.php
   print "<p>You want to add an event
   → called <b>{$_POST['name']}</b>
   → which takes place on: <br />";
   ```

   The **print** line prints out the value of the event's name. In a real-world version of this script, you would add a conditional to check that a name value was entered first (see Chapter 6, "Control Structures").

3. Begin a conditional to check that at least one weekday was selected:

   ```
   if (isset($_POST['days']) AND
   → is_array($_POST['days'])) {
   ```

   If no checkbox was clicked, then **$_POST['days']** won't be an existing variable. To avoid an error caused by referring to a variable that does not exist, the first part of the conditional checks that **$_POST['days']** is set.

   continues on next page

The second part of the condition—and both must be **TRUE** for the entire condition to be **TRUE**—confirms that **$_POST['days']** is an array. This is a good step to take because a **foreach** loop will create an error if it receives a variable that isn't an array **B**.

4. Print each selected weekday:

```
foreach ($_POST['days'] as $day) {
    print "$day<br />\n";
}
```

To print out each checked weekday, run the **$_POST['days']** array through a **foreach** loop. The array contains the values (from the HTML form inputs, for example, *Monday*, *Tuesday*, and so on) for every box that was selected.

5. Complete the **is_array()** conditional:

```
} else {
    print 'Please select at least
    → one weekday for this event!';
}
```

If no weekday was selected, then the **isset()** AND **is_array()** condition is **FALSE**, and this message is printed.

> **Warning**: Invalid argument supplied for foreach() in **/Users /larryullman/Sites/phpvqs4/event.php** on line **16**

B Attempting to use **foreach** on a variable that is not an array is a common cause of errors.

6. Complete the main paragraph, the PHP section, and the HTML page:

```php
print '</p>';
?>
</body>
</html>
```

7. Save the page as **event.php**, place it in the same directory as **event.html**, and test both pages in your Web browser **C**, **D**, and **E**.

TIP The same technique demonstrated here can be used to allow a user to select multiple options in a drop-down menu. Just give the menu a name with a syntax like *something*[], then the PHP script will receive every selection in $_POST['*something*'].

Use this form to add an event:

Event Name: Training Seminar

Event Days: ☐ Sun ☐ Mon ☑ Tue ☑ Wed ☑ Thu ☐ Fri ☐ Sat

(Add the Event!)

C The HTML form with its checkboxes.

You want to add an event called **Training Seminar** which takes place on:
Tuesday
Wednesday
Thursday

D The results of the HTML form.

You want to add an event called **Training Seminar** which takes place on:
Please select at least one weekday for this event!

E If users don't check any of the day boxes, they'll see this message.

Review and Pursue

If you have any problems with the review questions or the pursue prompts, turn to the book's supporting forum (www.LarryUllman.com/forum/).

Review

- What's the difference between an *indexed* array and an *associative* array?

- When should you use quotation marks for an array's key or value? When shouldn't you?

- How do you print a specific array element? How do you print every element in an array?

- What happens if you don't use the square brackets when adding an element to an array?

- What function returns the number of elements in an array?

- When must you use curly brackets for printing array elements?

- What is the difference between the **sort()** and **asort()** functions? Between **sort()** and **rsort()**?

- What is the syntax for **explode()**? For **implode()**? If you don't remember, check out the PHP manual page for either function.

Pursue

- Check out the PHP manual's pages for the array-related functions. Look into some of the other available array functions. In particular I'd recommend familiarizing yourself with **array_key_exists()**, **array_search()**, and **in_array()**.

- Rewrite **soups2.php** so that it displays the number of elements in the array without using a separate variable. Hint: You'll need to concatenate the **count()** function call into the **print** statement.

- Create another script that creates and displays a multidimensional array (or some of it, anyway).

- Rewrite **list.php** so that it uses **foreach** instead of **implode()**, but still prints each sorted word on its own line in the browser. Also add some form validation so that it only attempts to parse and sort the string if it has a value.

8

Creating Web Applications

The book to this point has covered the fundamentals of programming with PHP; now it's time to begin tying it all together into actual Web applications. In this chapter, you'll learn a number of functions and techniques for making your Web sites more professional, more feature-rich, and easier to maintain.

First, you'll learn how to use external files to break Web pages into individual pieces, allowing you to separate the logic from the presentation. Then you'll tinker with *constants*, a special data type in PHP. After that, you'll be introduced to some of the date- and time-related functions built into PHP.

Two of the chapter's topics discuss useful techniques: having the same page both display and handle an HTML form, and having a form remember user-submitted values. After that, you'll see how easy it can be to send email from PHP. The chapter concludes with the slightly more advanced topics of *output buffering* and *HTTP headers*.

In This Chapter

Creating Templates	184
Using External Files	192
Using Constants	197
Working with the Date and Time	201
Handling HTML Forms with PHP, Revisited	204
Making Forms Sticky	210
Sending Email	217
Output Buffering	222
Manipulating HTTP Headers	225
Review and Pursue	230

Creating Templates

Every example thus far has been a one-page script that handles an HTML form, sorts arrays, performs calculations, and so on. As you begin to develop multiple-page Web sites (which is to say, *Web applications*), it quickly becomes impractical to repeat common elements on multiple pages.

On more sophisticated Web sites, many features, such as the HTML design, will be used by every, or almost every, page within the site. You can put these elements into each individual page, but when you need to make a change, you'll be required to make that change over and over again. You can save time by creating *templates* that separate out the repeating content from the page-specific materials. For example, a Web site may have navigation, copyright, and other features that repeat across multiple pages and .

When you first start doing dynamic Web development, creating and using templates can be daunting. The key is to start with a basic prototype, as if you were creating a static Web page, and then divide that prototype into reusable parts. Using the PHP functions introduced in the next section of this chapter, the repeating parts can be easily included in each page while the new content is generated on a page-by-page basis. To create the template in use by this chapter's examples, let's start with the prototype. This example's layout 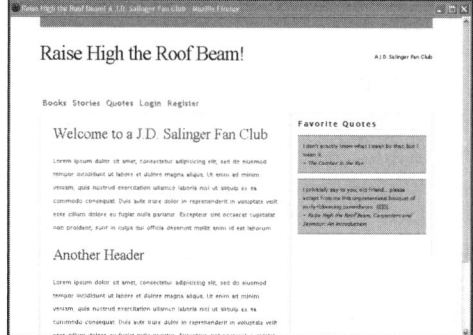 was created by James Koster of Six Shooter Media (www.sixshootermedia.com), and used with his kind permission.

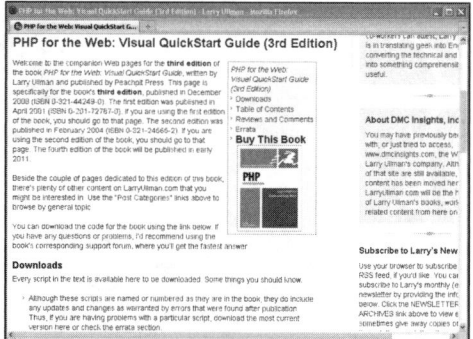

A The home page for the third edition of this book has its page-specific content in the left column and common elements in the right.

B The table of contents page uses some of the same common elements as the home page **A**, thanks to the templates.

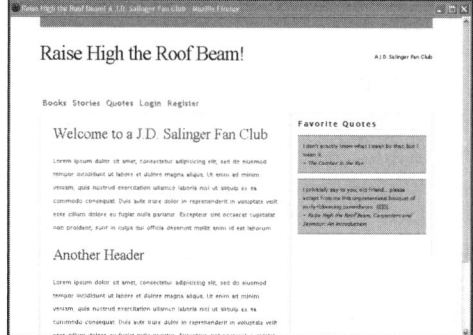

C The design for this chapter's examples, as a single, static HTML page.

Script 8.1 This script represents the basic look each page in the site should have.

```
1    <!DOCTYPE html PUBLIC "-//W3C//DTD XHTML
     1.1//EN" "http://www.w3.org/TR/xhtml11/
     DTD/xhtml11.dtd">
2    <html xmlns="http://www.w3.org/1999/
     xhtml" xml:lang="en">
3    <head>
4        <title>Raise High the Roof Beam!
         A J.D. Salinger Fan Club</title>
5        <meta http-equiv="content-type"
         content="text/html; charset=utf-8" />
6        <link rel="stylesheet"
         href="css/1.css" type="text/css"
         media="screen,projection" />
7    </head>
8    <body>
9    <div id="wrapper">
10
11       <div id="header">
12           <p class="description">A J.D.
             Salinger Fan Club</p>
13           <h1><a href="index.php">Raise High
             the Roof Beam!</a></h1>
14           <ul id="nav">
15               <li><a href="books.php">
                 Books</a></li>
16               <li><a href="#">Stories</a></li>
17               <li><a href="#">Quotes</a></li>
18               <li><a href="login.php">
                 Login</a></li>
19               <li><a href="register.php">
                 Register</a></li>
20           </ul>
21       </div><!-- header -->
22
23       <div id="sidebar">
24           <h2>Favorite Quotes</h2>
25               <p class="news">I don't exactly
                 know what I mean by that, but
                 I mean it.<br />- <em>The
                 Catcher in the Rye</em></p>
26               <p class="news">I privately say
                 to you, old friend... please
                 accept from me this unpretentious
                 bouquet of early-blooming
                 parentheses: (((()))).<br />- <em>
                 Raise High the Roof Beam,
                 Carpenters and Seymour: An
                 Introduction</em></p>
27       </div><!-- sidebar -->
28
```

code continues on next page

To create the layout model:

1. Begin a new HTML document in your text editor or IDE, to be named **template.html** (Script 8.1):

```
<!DOCTYPE html PUBLIC "-//W3C//DTD
→ XHTML 1.1//EN" "http://www.
→ w3.org/TR/xhtml11/DTD/xhtml11.dtd">
<html xmlns="http://www.w3.org/
→ 1999/xhtml" xml:lang="en">
<head>
   <title>Raise High the Roof
→ Beam! A J.D. Salinger Fan
→ Club</title>
   <meta http-equiv="content-type"
→ content="text/html;
→ charset=utf-8" />
```

The first step in developing any template system is to create a model document—an example of what a basic page should look like. Once you've created this, you can break it down into its parts.

2. Add the CSS code:

```
<link rel="stylesheet"
→ href="css/1.css" type="text/css"
→ media="screen,projection" />
```

This example uses CSS for most of the formatting and layout controls. The CSS itself is stored in an external file that becomes part of this page through the **link** tag. The file itself is named simply *1.css*, and is to be stored in a folder named *css*.

Note that you'll need to download the CSS file from the book's corresponding Web site (www.LarryUllman.com). You'll find it as part of the book's downloadable code.

continues on next page

3. Close the HTML head, begin the body, and create a *wrapper* **div** tag:

```
</head>
<body>
<div id="wrapper">
```

Many of today's designs wrap the entire page content within a primary **div**, so that all of the content can easily be formatted within the browser window.

4. Create the page's header:

```
<div id="header">
  <p class="description">A J.D.
  → Salinger Fan Club</p>
  <h1><a href="index.php">Raise
  → High the Roof Beam!</a></h1>
  <ul id="nav">
    <li><a href="books.php">
    → Books</a></li>
    <li><a href="#">Stories</a></li>
    <li><a href="#">Quotes</a></li>
    <li><a href="login.php">
    → Login</a></li>
    <li><a href="register.php">
    → Register</a></li>
  </ul>
</div><!-- header -->
```

The *header* area (also defined in the CSS code) creates the banner and the primary navigation links to the other pages in the Web application. The specific links reference four PHP scripts, all of which will be developed in this chapter.

Script 8.1 *continued*

```
29      <div id="content">
30          <!-- BEGIN CHANGEABLE CONTENT. -->
31          <h2>Welcome to a J.D. Salinger Fan
            Club</h2>
32          <p>Lorem ipsum dolor sit amet,
            consectetur adipisicing elit, sed
            do eiusmod tempor incididunt ut
            labore et dolore magna aliqua. Ut
            enim ad minim veniam, quis nostrud
            exercitation ullamco laboris
            nisi ut aliquip ex ea commodo
            consequat. Duis aute irure dolor
            in reprehenderit in voluptate
            velit esse cillum dolore eu fugiat
            nulla pariatur. Excepteur sint
            occaecat cupidatat non proident,
            sunt in culpa qui officia deserunt
            mollit anim id est laborum.</p>
33          <h2>Another Header</h2>
34          <p>Lorem ipsum dolor sit amet,
            consectetur adipisicing elit, sed
            do eiusmod tempor incididunt ut
            labore et dolore magna aliqua. Ut
            enim ad minim veniam, quis nostrud
            exercitation ullamco laboris
            nisi ut aliquip ex ea commodo
            consequat. Duis aute irure dolor
            in reprehenderit in voluptate
            velit esse cillum dolore eu fugiat
            nulla pariatur. Excepteur sint
            occaecat cupidatat non proident,
            sunt in culpa qui officia deserunt
            mollit anim id est laborum.</p>
35          <!-- END CHANGEABLE CONTENT. -->
36      </div><!-- content -->
37
38      <div id="footer">
39          <p>Template design by <a
            href="http://www.sixshootermedia.
            com">
            Six Shooter Media</a>.</p>
40          <p>&copy; 2011</p>
41      </div><!-- footer -->
42
43  </div><!-- wrapper -->
44  </body>
45  </html>
```

5. Create the page's sidebar:

```
<div id="sidebar">
  <h2>Favorite Quotes</h2>
    <p class="news">I don't
    → exactly know what I mean
    → by that, but I mean it.
    → <br />- <em>The Catcher in
    → the Rye</em></p>
    <p class="news">I privately
    → say to you, old friend...
    → please accept from me this
    → unpretentious bouquet of
    → early-blooming parentheses:
    → (((()))).<br />- <em>Raise
    → High the Roof Beam,
    → Carpenters and Seymour:
    → An Introduction</em></p>
</div><!-- sidebar -->
```

In the original template, the sidebar can be used for latest news, secondary links, a search box, and so forth. In this site's template, a couple of quotes are highlighted.

6. Begin, and mark, the start of the page-specific content:

```
<div id="content">
<!-- BEGIN CHANGEABLE CONTENT. -->
```

Everything up until this comment will remain the same for every page in the Web application. To indicate where the page-specific content begins (for your own benefit), include an HTML comment. In fact, looking back at the template so far, you'll see a number of HTML comments, helping to indicate what each piece of the page is for. You cannot over-comment your HTML or PHP code!

Just before that, the *content* area is begun. This area is defined in the CSS code and properly formats the main content part of the page. In other words, on every page, that page's content will go within the one **div** that has an **id** of **content**.

7. Create the page's content:

```
<h2>Welcome to a J.D. Salinger
→ Fan Club</h2>
<p>Lorem ipsum dolor sit
→ amet...</p>
```

For the prototype, the content is just a couple of headers and a whole lot of text (there's more in the actual script than I've included in this step).

8. Mark the end of the changeable content:

```
<!-- END CHANGEABLE CONTENT. -->
</div><!-- content -->
```

The code in Step 7 is the only text that will change on a page-by-page basis. Just as an HTML comment indicates where that section starts, one here indicates where it ends.

9. Add the footer:

```
<div id="footer">
  <p>Template design by <a href=
  → "http://www.sixshootermedia.
  → com">Six Shooter Media</a>.</p>
  <p>&copy; 2011</p>
</div><!-- footer -->
```

The footer includes a credit and an indication of copyright.

10. Finish the HTML page:

```
</div><!-- wrapper -->
</body>
</html>
```

To make the template easier to modify and maintain, you'll notice that HTML comments indicate which **div**s are being closed.

11. Save the file as **template.html** and test it in your Web browser **C**.

Once you've completed a prototype that you like, you can break it into its various parts to generate the template system.

To create the header file:

1. Open **template.html** (Script 8.1) in your text editor or IDE, if it isn't already open.

2. Select everything from the initial HTML code to the **<!-- BEGIN CHANGEABLE CONTENT -->** HTML comment 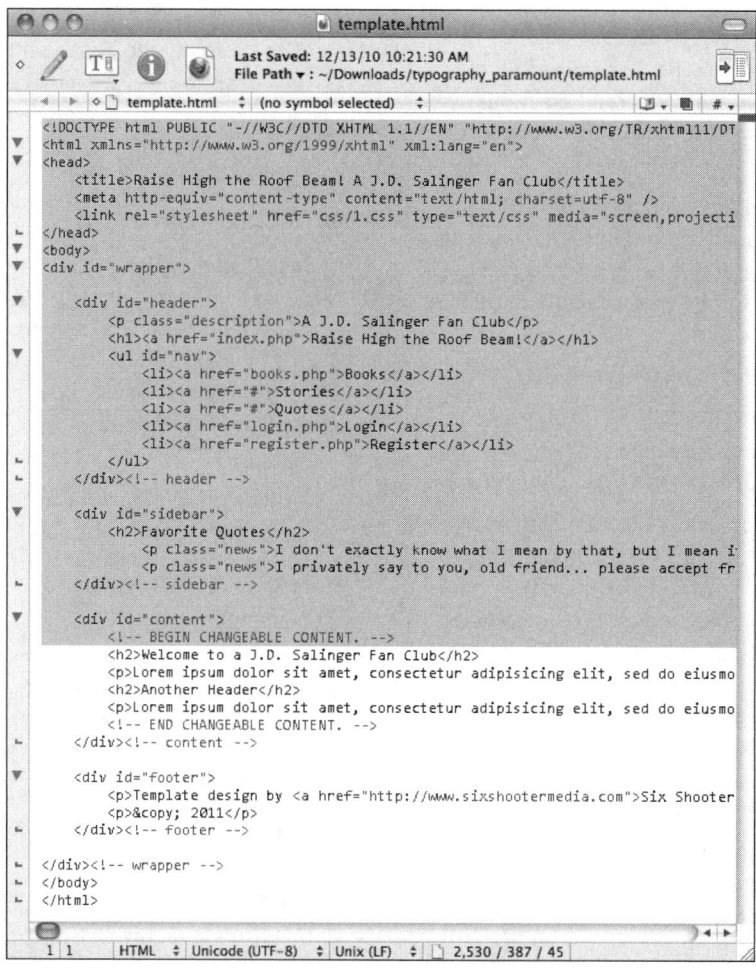.

   Part of the benefit of identifying the start of the page-specific content with an HTML comment is that it simplifies breaking the model into its parts.

D Using the prototype file, select and copy the initial lines of code to create the header.

Script 8.2 This is a basic header file that creates the HTML head information, includes the CSS file, and begins the body.

```
1   <!DOCTYPE html PUBLIC "-//W3C//DTD XHTML
    1.1//EN" "http://www.w3.org/TR/xhtml11/
    DTD/xhtml11.dtd">
2   <html xmlns="http://www.w3.org/1999/
    xhtml" xml:lang="en">
3   <head>
4       <title>Raise High the Roof Beam!
        A J.D. Salinger Fan Club</title>
5       <meta http-equiv="content-type"
        content="text/html; charset=utf-8" />
6       <link rel="stylesheet"
        href="css/1.css" type="text/css"
        media="screen,projection" />
7   </head>
8   <body>
9   <div id="wrapper">
10
11      <div id="header">
12          <p class="description">A J.D.
            Salinger Fan Club</p>
13          <h1><a href="index.php">Raise High
            the Roof Beam!</a></h1>
14          <ul id="nav">
15              <li><a href="books.php">Books
                </a></li>
16              <li><a href="#">Stories</a></li>
17              <li><a href="#">Quotes</a></li>
18              <li><a href="login.php">Login
                </a></li>
19              <li><a href="register.php">
                Register</a></li>
20          </ul>
21      </div><!-- header -->
22
23      <div id="sidebar">
24          <h2>Favorite Quotes</h2>
25              <p class="news">I don't exactly
                know what I mean by that,
                but I mean it.<br />- <em>The
                Catcher in the Rye</em></p>
26              <p class="news">I privately say to
                you, old friend... please accept
                from me this unpretentious
                bouquet of early-blooming
                parentheses: ((((())))).<br />-
                <em>Raise High the Roof Beam,
                Carpenters and Seymour: An
                Introduction</em></p>
27      </div><!-- sidebar -->
28
29      <div id="content">
30          <!-- BEGIN CHANGEABLE CONTENT. -->
31          <!-- Script 8.2 - header.html -->
```

3. Copy this code.

Using your Edit menu or keyboard shortcut (Ctrl+C on Windows, Command+C on the Macintosh), copy all of the highlighted code to your computer's temporary memory (the clipboard).

4. Create a new, blank document in your text editor or IDE, to be named **header.html**.

5. Paste the copied text into the document (**Script 8.2**).

Using your Edit menu or keyboard shortcut (Ctrl+V on Windows, Command+V on the Macintosh), paste all of the highlighted code into this new document.

6. Save the file as **header.html**.

Now that the header file has been created, you'll make the footer file using the same process.

To create the footer file:

1. Open **layout.html** (Script 8.1) in your text editor or IDE, if it isn't already open.

2. Select everything from the **<!-- END CHANGEABLE CONTENT -->** HTML comment to the end of the script 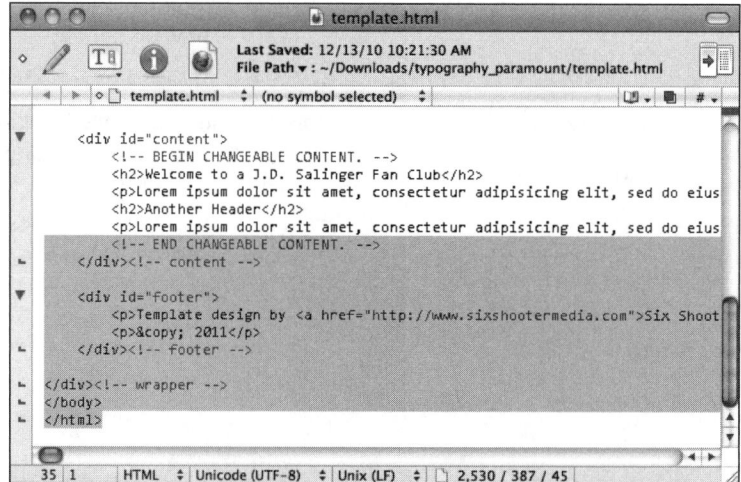.

3. Copy this code.

4. Create a new, blank document in your text editor, to be named **footer.html**.

5. Paste the copied text into the document (**Script 8.3**).

6. Save the file as **footer.html**.

Script 8.3 This is a basic footer file that concludes the HTML page.

```
1              <!-- Script 8.3 - footer.html -->
2              <!-- END CHANGEABLE CONTENT. -->
3      </div><!-- content -->
4
5      <div id="footer">
6          <p>Template design by <a
           href="http://www.sixshootermedia.
           com">Six Shooter Media</a>.</p>
7          <p>&copy; 2011</p>
8      </div><!-- footer -->
9
10     </div><!-- wrapper -->
11     </body>
12     </html>
```

Ⓔ Again using the prototype file, select and copy the concluding lines of code for the footer.

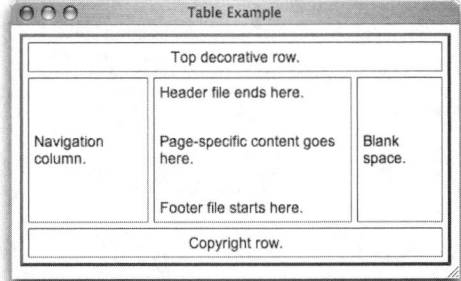

Table Example

Top decorative row.

| Navigation column. | Header file ends here.

Page-specific content goes here.

Footer file starts here. | Blank space. |

Copyright row.

F This mundane example shows how a table can be used with template files to create a design.

TIP There are many far more complex template systems you can use in PHP to separate the design from the logic. The best known of these is probably Smarty (www.smarty.net).

TIP Although this example uses CSS for its layout, you can certainly use tables instead **F**. Your header file might begin the HTML page and the table. Each content page would then create its own specific content, and the footer file would complete the table and the HTML page. To turn such a design into a template, copy all of the code up to *Page-specific content goes here.* into a header file and everything after that into a footer file.

CSS Templates

Cascading Style Sheets (CSS) have been an increasingly important part of the World Wide Web for some time. Their initial usage was focused on cosmetics (font sizes, colors, and so on), but now CSS is frequently used in lieu of tables to control the layout of pages. The Web application in this chapter uses this approach.

This example defines four areas of the page—*header, sidebar, content,* and *footer*. The *content* area will change for each page. The other areas contain standard items, such as navigation links, that appear on each page of the site.

Just to be clear: The relationship between PHP and CSS is the same as that between PHP and HTML—PHP runs on the server and HTML and CSS are significant to the browser. As with HTML, you *can* use PHP to generate CSS, but in this example, the CSS is hard-coded into a separate file.

Using External Files

As the preceding section stated, you can save development time by creating separate pages for particular elements and then incorporating them into the main PHP pages using specific functions. Two of these functions are **include()** and **require()**:

```
include ('file.php');
require ('file.html');
```

Both functions work the same way, with one relatively insignificant difference: If an **include()** function fails, the PHP script generates a warning  but continues to run. Conversely, if **require()** fails, it terminates the execution of the script **B**.

But what do these two functions do? Both **include()** and **require()** incorporate the referenced file into the main file (for clarity's sake, the file that has the **include()** or **require()** line is the *including* or *parent* file). The result is the same as if the included code were part of the parent file in the first place.

Understanding that basic idea—including a file makes it as if that file's contents were in the parent script to begin with—is key to making the most out of this feature. This means that any code within the included file not within PHP tags is treated as HTML. And this is true regardless of what extension the included file has (because it's the extension of the *including* file that counts).

There are many reasons to use included files. You could put your own defined functions into a common file (see Chapter 10, "Creating Functions," for information on writing your own functions). You might also want to place your database access information into a configuration file. First, however, let's include the template files created in the preceding section of the chapter in order to make pages abide by a consistent design.

A When an **include()** fails, warnings are issued, but the script continues to execute.

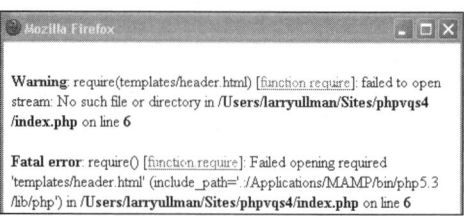

B When a **require()** function call fails, warnings and errors are issued, and the script stops running.

Script 8.4 Once the two included files have been created, the `include()` function incorporates them into the parent file to create the complete HTML page on the fly.

```
1   <?php // Script 8.4 - index.php
2   /* This is the home page for this site.
3   It uses templates to create the
    layout. */
4
5   // Include the header:
6   include('templates/header.html');
7   // Leave the PHP section to display lots
    of HTML:
8   ?>
9
10  <h2>Welcome to a J.D. Salinger Fan Club</
    h2>
11  <p>Lorem ipsum dolor sit amet,
    consectetur adipisicing elit, sed do
    eiusmod tempor incididunt ut labore
    et dolore magna aliqua. Ut enim ad
    minim veniam, quis nostrud exercitation
    ullamco laboris nisi ut aliquip ex ea
    commodo consequat. Duis aute irure dolor
    in reprehenderit in voluptate velit esse
    cillum dolore eu fugiat nulla pariatur.
    Excepteur sint occaecat cupidatat non
    proident, sunt in culpa qui officia
    deserunt mollit anim id est laborum.</p>
12  <h2>Another Header</h2>
13  <p>Lorem ipsum dolor sit amet,
    consectetur adipisicing elit, sed do
    eiusmod tempor incididunt ut labore
    et dolore magna aliqua. Ut enim ad
    minim veniam, quis nostrud exercitation
    ullamco laboris nisi ut aliquip ex ea
    commodo consequat. Duis aute irure dolor
    in reprehenderit in voluptate velit esse
    cillum dolore eu fugiat nulla pariatur.
    Excepteur sint occaecat cupidatat non
    proident, sunt in culpa qui officia
    deserunt mollit anim id est laborum.</p>
14
15  <?php // Return to PHP.
16  include('templates/footer.html');
    // Include the footer.
17  ?>
```

To use external files:

1. Create a new document in your text editor or IDE, to be named **index.php**.

2. Start with the initial PHP tags and add any comments (**Script 8.4**):

   ```
   <?php // Script 8.4 - index.php
   /* This is the home page for
   → this site.
   It uses templates to create the
   → layout. */
   ```

   Notice that, with the template system, the very first line of the script is the PHP tag. There's no need to begin with the initial HTML, because that is now stored in the **header.html** file.

3. Address error management, if necessary.

   This topic is discussed in Chapter 3, "HTML Forms and PHP," and may or may not need to be addressed in your scripts. See that chapter for more; this will be the last time I specifically mention it in this chapter.

4. Include the header file:

   ```
   include('templates/header.html');
   ```

   To use the template system, you include the header file here by invoking the **include()** function. Because the header file contains only HTML, all of its contents will be immediately sent to the Web browser as if they were part of this file. This line uses a *relative path* to refer to the included file (see the "File Navigation and Site Structure" sidebar) and assumes that the file is stored in the **templates** directory.

   continues on next page

5. Close the PHP section and create the page-specific content:

```
?>
<h2>Welcome to a J.D. Salinger
→ Fan Club</h2>
<p>Lorem ipsum dolor sit
→ amet...</p>
```

Because the bulk of this page is standard HTML, it's easier to just exit out of the PHP section and then add the HTML (rather than using **print** to send it to the Web browser). Again, there's more blather in the actual script than I've included here.

6. Create another PHP section and require the footer file:

```
<?php
include('templates/footer.html');
?>
```

To finish the page, you need to include the footer file (which displays the footer and closes the HTML code). To do this, you create a new section of PHP—you can have multiple sections of PHP code within a script—and call the **include()** function again.

7. Save the file as **index.php**.

8. Create a folder called **templates** within the main Web document directory on your PHP-enabled computer or Web server.

   To further separate the design elements from the main content, the header and footer files go within their own directory.

9. Place **header.html** and **footer.html** in the **templates** directory you just created.

File Navigation and Site Structure

To be able to use external files, you need to understand file navigation on your computer or server. Just as you must correctly refer to other pages in HTML links or images in Web sites, you must properly point a parent file to the included scripts. You can do this by using *absolute* or *relative* paths. An absolute path is a complete, specific address, like the following:

```
include('C:\inetpub\wwwfiles\
→ file.php');
include('/Users/larry/Sites/
→ file.php');
```

As long as the included file isn't moved, an absolute path will always work.

A relative path indicates where the included file is in relation to the parent file. These examples assume both are within the same directory:

```
include('file.php');
include('./file.php');
```

The included file can also be in a directory below the parent one, as in this chapter's example (also see **C**):

```
include('templates/header.html');
```

Or, the included file could be in the directory above the parent:

```
include('../file.php');
```

Finally, a note on site structure: Once you divvy up your Web application into multiple pieces, you should begin thinking about arranging the files in appropriate folders. Complex sites might have the main folder, another for images, one for administration files, and a special directory for templates and included files. As long as you properly reference the files in your **include()** or **require()** statements, structuring your applications will work fine and give the added benefit of making them easier to maintain.

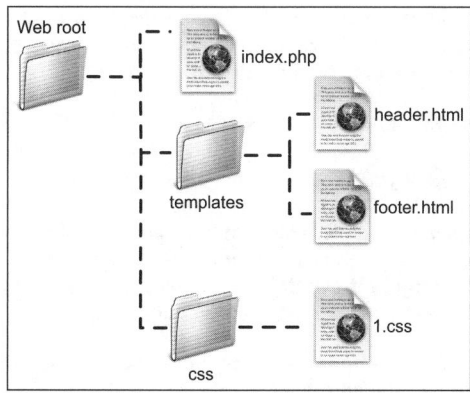

C How the four files and two folders should be organized on your PHP-enabled server.

10. Place `index.php` in the same directory as the `templates` folder.

    The relative locations on the computer between the index page and the two HTML pages must be correct in order for the code to work.

11. Create a folder called `css` within the main Web document directory on your PHP-enabled computer or Web server.

    The CSS script will need to go in this directory.

12. Place the `1.css` script, available as part of the book's downloadable code, in the `css` directory **C**.

    Even though the header file includes the CSS script, the reference to that script must be relative to `index.php`. It's that page, after all, that will include `header.html`.

13. Run `index.php` in your Web browser **D**.

    The resulting page should look exactly like the original layout (**C** in the previous section of the chapter).

continues on next page

D This page has been dynamically generated using included files.

14. View the page's source code in your Web browser.

The source code should be exactly like the source code of the **template.html** script (Script 8.1), aside from the added comments for the script names and numbers.

TIP All three files in this template system—`header.html`, `footer.html`, and `index.php`—must use the same *encoding* in order to avoid problems (see Chapter 1, "Getting Started with PHP," for more on encoding). Each file's encoding must also match the encoding established in the HTML code.

TIP The `require()` and `include()` functions can be used with or without parentheses:

```
require 'filename.html';
```

TIP You might sometimes use a variable that stores the name of the file to be included:

```
require $filename;
```

TIP Both `include()` and `require()` have variations: `include_once()` and `require_once()`. Each is identical to its counterpart except that it ensures that the same file can be included only one time (in a parent script). You should generally avoid using these, as they'll adversely affect the script's performance.

TIP If a section of PHP only executes a single command, it's common to place both it and the PHP tags on a single line:

```
<?php include 'filename.html'; ?>
```

TIP If you see error messages like those in Ⓐ and Ⓑ, the parent script can't locate an included file. This problem is most likely caused by a misspelled included filename or an error in the path (for example, using *header.html* instead of *templates/header.html*).

TIP If the rendered Web page does not seem to be reflecting the CSS styling, the HTML page can't find the corresponding file. Make sure you've stored the file in the proper folder, with the correct name, and that the reference is correct relative to `index.php`.

TIP A file's extension is less important for included files because they aren't intended to be run directly. As a general rule of thumb, you'll be safe using `.html` for an included file containing only or mostly HTML (in which case the extension indicates it's an HTML-related file) and `.php` for included files containing only or mostly PHP. Some programmers use an `.inc` extension (for include), but security risks can arise with this practice. For that reason, use the `.php` extension for any file containing sensitive information (like database access parameters). And, of course, always use the `.php` extension for any PHP script that will be executed directly.

TIP Another good use of an external file is to place your error settings code there so that those changes are applied to every page in the Web site.

Using Constants

Many of PHP's data types have already been discussed in this book: primarily numbers, strings, and arrays. *Constants* are another data type, but unlike variables, their values cannot change.

Whereas variables are assigned values via the assignment operator (=), constants are assigned values using the **define()** function:

```
define('CONSTANT_NAME', value);
```

Notice that—as a rule of thumb—constants are named using all capital letters, although doing so isn't required. Most important, constants don't use the initial dollar sign as variables do (because constants are not variables). Here are two constants:

```
define ('PI', 3.14);
define ('CURRENCY', 'euros');
```

As with any value, quote those that are strings, not those that are numbers.

Referring to constants is generally straightforward:

```
print CURRENCY;
number_format(PI, 1);
```

But using constants within quotation marks is more complicated. You can't print constants within single or double quotation marks, like this **A**:

```
print "The cost is 468 CURRENCY";
print 'The cost is 468 CURRENCY';
```

Instead, concatenation or multiple **print** statements are required:

```
print 'The cost is 468 ' . CURRENCY;
```

or

```
print 'The cost is 468 ';
print CURRENCY;
```

Along with the **define()** function for creating constants is the **defined()** function, which returns **TRUE** if the submitted constant has been defined. It's often used as the basis for a conditional:

```
if (defined('CONSTANT_NAME')) { …
```

As an example of working with constants, you'll give the sample application the ability to display a different title (which appears at the top of the browser window) for each page. To accomplish this, you'll define a constant in the parent script that will then be printed by the header file. This technique works because any variables or constants that exist in the parent document before the **include()** or **require()** call are available to the included file (it's as if the included file were part of the parent file).

The cost is 468 CURRENCY

A The value of a constant cannot be printed using the constant's name within quotation marks.

To use constants:

1. Create a new PHP document in your text editor or IDE, to be named **books.php** (Script 8.5):

   ```
   <?php // Script 8.5 - books.php
   ```

2. Define the page title as a constant:

   ```
   define ('TITLE', 'Books by J.D.
   → Salinger');
   ```

   Here one constant is defined, named **TITLE**, and given the value *Books by J.D. Salinger*.

3. Include the header file:

   ```
   include('templates/header.html');
   ```

   This script uses the same header file as all the others, although you'll modify that file shortly to take the constant into account.

4. Close the PHP section and create the HTML:

   ```
   ?>
   <h2>J.D. Salinger's Books</h2>
   <ul>
      <li>The Catcher in the Rye</li>
      <li>Nine Stories</li>
      <li>Franny and Zooey</li>
      <li>Raise High the Roof Beam,
      → Carpenters and Seymour: An
      → Introduction</li>
   </ul>
   ```

   The content here is simple but serves the page's purpose nicely.

5. Create a new PHP section that includes the footer file:

   ```
   <?php include('templates/
   → footer.html'); ?>
   ```

   As mentioned earlier in a tip, since the remaining PHP code consists of just

Script 8.5 This script uses the same template system as **index.php** (Script 8.4) but also uses a constant to identify the page's title.

```
1    <?php // Script 8.5 - books.php
2    /* This page lists J.D. Salinger's
     bibliography. */
3
4    // Set the page title and include the
     header file:
5    define ('TITLE', 'Books by J.D.
     Salinger');
6    include('templates/header.html');
7
8    // Leave the PHP section to display lots
     of HTML:
9    ?>
10
11   <h2>J.D. Salinger's Books</h2>
12   <ul>
13      <li>The Catcher in the Rye</li>
14      <li>Nine Stories</li>
15      <li>Franny and Zooey</li>
16      <li>Raise High the Roof Beam,
             Carpenters and Seymour: An
             Introduction</li>
17   </ul>
18
19   <?php include('templates/footer.html');
     ?>
```

Script 8.6 The `header.html` file is modified so that it can set the page title value based on the existence and value of a constant.

```
1    <!DOCTYPE html PUBLIC "-//W3C//DTD XHTML
     1.1//EN" "http://www.w3.org/TR/xhtml11/
     DTD/xhtml11.dtd">
2    <html xmlns="http://www.w3.org/1999/
     xhtml" xml:lang="en">
3    <head>
4        <title><?php // Print the page
         title.
5        if (defined('TITLE')) { // Is the
         title defined?
6            print TITLE;
7        } else { // The title is not
         defined.
8            print 'Raise High the Roof
             Beam! A J.D. Salinger Fan Club';
9        }
10       ?></title>
11       <meta http-equiv="content-type"
         content="text/html; charset=utf-8" />
12       <link rel="stylesheet"
         href="css/1.css" type="text/css"
         media="screen,projection" />
13   </head>
14   <body>
15   <div id="wrapper">
16
17       <div id="header">
18           <p class="description">A J.D.
             Salinger Fan Club</p>
19           <h1><a href="index.php">Raise High
             the Roof Beam!</a></h1>
20           <ul id="nav">
21               <li><a href="books.php">Books
                 </a></li>
22               <li><a href="#">Stories</a></li>
23               <li><a href="#">Quotes</a></li>
24               <li><a href="login.php">Login
                 </a></li>
25               <li><a href="register.php">
                 Register</a></li>
26           </ul>
27       </div><!-- header -->
28
29       <div id="sidebar">
30           <h2>Favorite Quotes</h2>
31               <p class="news">I don't exactly
                 know what I mean by that,
                 but I mean it.<br />- <em>The
                 Catcher in the Rye</em></p>
```

code continues on next page

one line it can all be written on a single line, including the opening and closing PHP tags. Just be certain to leave a space between the executed code—the `include()`—and the tags.

6. Save the file as **books.php**.

To take advantage of the constant, you now need to modify the **header.html** file.

To print out a constant:

1. Open **header.html** (Script 8.2) in your text editor or IDE.

2. Delete the *Raise High the Roof Beam! A J.D. Salinger Fan Club* text that appears between the **title** tags (line 4).

Now that the page title will be determined on a page-by-page basis, you don't need it to be hard-coded into the page.

3. In the place of the deleted text (between the **title** tags), add the following (**Script 8.6**):

```
<?php
if (defined('TITLE')) {
    print TITLE;
} else {
    print 'Raise High the Roof
→ Beam! A J.D. Salinger Fan
→ Club';
}
?>
```

To have PHP create the page title, you need to begin by starting a section of PHP code between the **title** tags. Then you use a conditional to see if the **TITLE** constant has been defined. If it has, print its value as the page title. If **TITLE** hasn't been defined, print a default title.

4. Save the file as **header.html**.

continues on next page

5. Upload **books.php** and **header.html** to your PHP-enabled server. The new PHP script, **books.php**, should go in the same directory as **index.php**; **header.html** should replace the previous version, in the same directory— **templates**—as **footer.html**.

6. Run **books.php** in your Web browser .

7. View **index.php** (the home page) in your Web browser 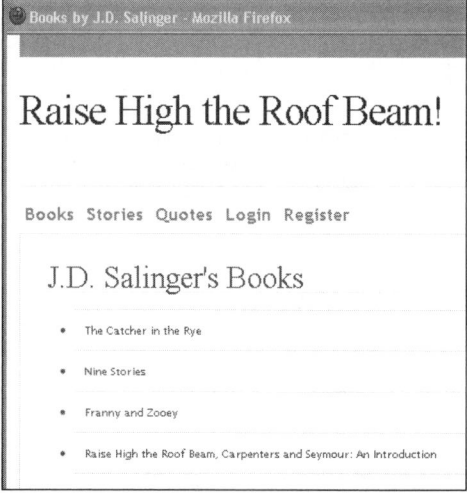.

8. If you want, add the constant definition line to **index.php** to change its title.

TIP The formal rules for naming constants are exactly like those for variables except for the omission of a dollar sign. Constant names must begin with a letter; can contain any combination of letters, numbers, and the underscore; and are case-sensitive.

TIP PHP runs with several predefined constants. These include PHP_VERSION (the version of PHP running) and PHP_OS (the operating system of the server).

TIP In Chapter 9, "Cookies and Sessions," you'll learn about another constant, SID (which stands for *session ID*).

TIP An added benefit of using constants is that they're *global in scope*. This concept will mean more to you after you read the section "Understanding Variable Scope" in Chapter 10.

TIP Not only can the value of a constant never be changed, a constant can't be deleted (*unset*, technically). Also, unlike arrays, a constant can only ever contain a single value, like a string or a number.

Script 8.6 *continued*

```
32              <p class="news">I privately say
                to you, old friend... please
                accept from me this unpretentious
                bouquet of early-blooming
                parentheses: (((()))).<br />-
                <em>Raise High the Roof Beam,
                Carpenters and Seymour: An
                Introduction</em></p>
33          </div><!-- sidebar -->
34
35          <div id="content">
36              <!-- BEGIN CHANGEABLE CONTENT. -->
37              <!-- Script 8.6 - header.html -->
```

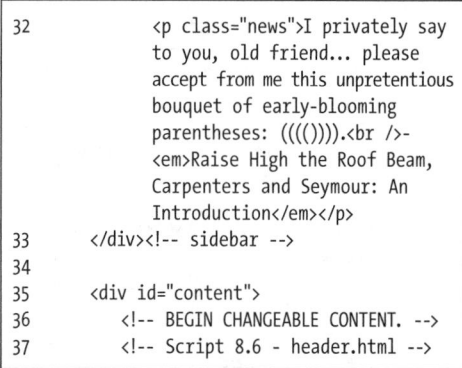

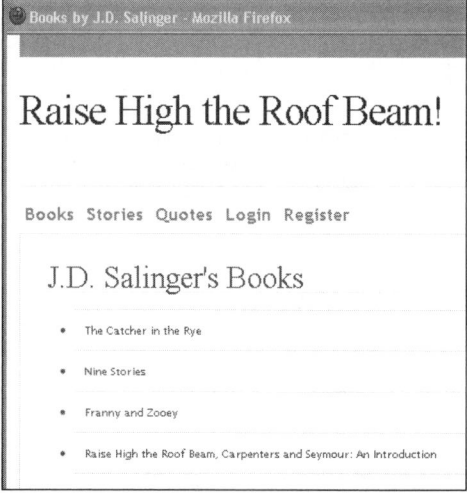

B The books page uses a PHP constant to create its title.

C Because the index page didn't have a **TITLE** constant defined in it, the default page title is used (thanks to the conditional in Script 8.6).

Working with the Date and Time

PHP has a few functions for working with the date and time, the most important of which is **date()**. The only thing the **date()** function does is return date and time information in a format based on the arguments it's fed, but you'd be surprised how useful that can be! The basic usage of the **date()** function is just

`date('`*formatting*`');`

A long list of possible options is available for formatting, as indicated in **Table 8.1** (the PHP manual lists a few more). These parameters can also be combined—for example, **date('l F j, Y')** returns *Wednesday January 26, 2011*.

TABLE 8.1 Date() Function Formatting

Character	Meaning	Example
Y	Year as 4 digits	2011
y	Year as 2 digits	11
L	Is it a leap year?	1 (for yes)
n	Month as 1 or 2 digits	2
m	Month as 2 digits	02
F	Month	February
M	Month as 3 letters	Feb
j	Day of the month as 1 or 2 digits	8
d	Day of the month as 2 digits	08
l (lowercase L)	Day of the week	Monday
D	Day of the week as 3 letters	Mon
w	Day of the week as a single digit	0 (Sunday)
z	Day of the year: 0 to 365	189
t	Number of days in the month	31
S	English ordinal suffix for a day, as 2 characters	rd
g	Hour; 12-hour format as 1 or 2 digits	6
G	Hour; 24-hour format as 1 or 2 digits	18
h	Hour; 12-hour format as 2 digits	06
H	Hour; 24-hour format as 2 digits	18
i	Minutes	45
s	Seconds	18
u	Microseconds	1234
a	am or pm	am
A	AM or PM	PM
U	Seconds since the epoch	1048623008
e	Timezone	UTC
I (capital i)	Is it daylight savings?	1 (for yes)
O	Difference from GMT	+0600

The **date()** function can take a second argument called a *timestamp*. A timestamp is a number representing how many seconds have passed since midnight on January 1, 1970—a moment referred to as the *epoch*. The **time()** function returns the timestamp for the current moment. The **mktime()** function can return a timestamp for a particular time and date:

```
mktime(hour, minute, second, month,
→ day, year);
```

So the code

```
$ts = mktime(12, 30, 0, 11, 5, 2011);
```

assigns to **$ts** the number of seconds from the epoch to 12:30 on November 5, 2011. That number can then be fed into the **date()** function like so:

```
date('D', $ts);
```

This returns *Sat*, which is the three-letter format for that day of the week.

As of PHP 5.1, you should establish the server's time zone prior to calling any date- or time-related function. To do so, use

```
date_default_timezone_set(timezone);
```

The *timezone* value is a string like *America/New_York* or *Pacific/Auckland*. There are too many to list here (Africa alone has over 50), but see the PHP manual for them all. If you don't take this step, you might see errors **Ⓐ**.

To demonstrate the **date()** function, let's update the header file so that it shows the current date and time in the sidebar **Ⓑ**.

To use date():

1. Open **header.html** (Script 8.6) in your text editor or IDE.

2. Before the closing **sidebar </div>** tag, add the following (**Script 8.7**):

   ```
   <p><?php
   ```

Warning: date() [function.date]: It is not safe to rely on the system's timezone settings. You are *required* to use the date.timezone setting or the date_default_timezone_set() function. In case you used any of those methods and you are still getting this warning, you most likely misspelled the timezone identifier. We selected 'America/New_York' for 'EST/-5.0/no DST' instead in /Users/larryullman/Sites/phpvqs4/templates/header.html on line 38

Ⓐ As of PHP 5.1, notices will be generated when a date or time function is used without the time zone being set.

Favorite Quotes

I don't exactly know what I mean by that, but I mean it.
– *The Catcher in the Rye*

I privately say to you, old friend... please accept from me this unpretentious bouquet of early-blooming parentheses: (((()))).
– *Raise High the Roof Beam, Carpenters and Seymour: An Introduction*

11:58 am Monday December 13

Ⓑ The Web site now displays the date and time in the sidebar, thanks to the **date()** function.

Script 8.7 The altered **header.html** file uses the **date()** function to print the current date and time.

```
1    <!DOCTYPE html PUBLIC "-//W3C//DTD XHTML
     1.1//EN" "http://www.w3.org/TR/xhtml11/
     DTD/xhtml11.dtd">
2    <html xmlns="http://www.w3.org/1999/
     xhtml" xml:lang="en">
3    <head>
4        <title><?php // Print the page title.
5        if (defined('TITLE')) { // Is the title
         defined?
6            print TITLE;
7        } else { // The title is not defined.
8            print 'Raise High the Roof Beam!
             A J.D. Salinger Fan Club';
9        }
10       ?></title>
11       <meta http-equiv="content-type"
         content="text/html; charset=utf-8" />
```

code continues on next page

Script 8.7 *continued*

```
12      <link rel="stylesheet"
        href="css/1.css" type="text/css"
        media="screen,projection" />
13  </head>
14  <body>
15  <div id="wrapper">
16
17      <div id="header">
18          <p class="description">A J.D.
            Salinger Fan Club</p>
19          <h1><a href="index.php">Raise High
            the Roof Beam!</a></h1>
20          <ul id="nav">
21              <li><a href="books.php">
                Books</a></li>
22              <li><a href="#">Stories</a></li>
23              <li><a href="#">Quotes</a></li>
24              <li><a href="login.php">
                Login</a></li>
25              <li><a href="register.php">
                Register</a></li>
26          </ul>
27      </div><!-- header -->
28
29      <div id="sidebar">
30          <h2>Favorite Quotes</h2>
31              <p class="news">I don't exactly
                know what I mean by that,
                but I mean it.<br />- <em>The
                Catcher in the Rye</em></p>
32              <p class="news">I privately say
                to you, old friend... please
                accept from me this unpretentious
                bouquet of early-blooming
                parentheses: ((((())))).<br />-
                <em>Raise High the Roof Beam,
                Carpenters and Seymour: An
                Introduction</em></p>
33              <p><?php // Print the current
                date and time...
34              // Set the timezone:
35              date_default_timezone_set
                ('America/New_York');
36
37              // Now print the date and time:
38              print date('g:i a l F j');
39              ?></p>
40      </div><!-- sidebar -->
41
42      <div id="content">
43          <!-- BEGIN CHANGEABLE CONTENT. -->
44          <!-- Script 8.7 - header.html -->
```

The initial HTML paragraph tag will wrap the date and time. Then open a PHP section so that you can call the **date()** function.

3. Establish the time zone:

date_default_timezone_set → **('America/New_York');**

Before calling **date()**, the time zone has to be set. To find yours, see www.php. net/timezones.

4. Use the **date()** function to print out the current date and time:

print date('g:i a l F j');

Using the formatting parameters from Table 8.1, the **date()** function will return a value like *4:15 pm Tuesday February 22*. This value will immediately be printed.

5. Close the PHP section and finish the HTML code:

?></p>

6. Save the file as **header.html**, place it in the **templates** directory of your PHP-enabled server, and test it in your Web browser **B**.

TIP Because PHP is a server-side technology, these functions reflect the date and time on the server. To get the time on the client (in other words, on the computer where the Web browser viewing the page is located), you must use JavaScript.

TIP The server's time zone can also be set in the PHP configuration file (see Appendix A, "Installation and Configuration"). Establishing the time zone there is generally a better idea than doing so on a script-by-script basis.

TIP Added to PHP 5.3 are new ways to create and manipulate dates and times using the DateTime class. While useful, this new tool requires familiarity with object-oriented programming, therefore making it beyond the scope of this beginner's book.

Handling HTML Forms with PHP, Revisited

All the examples in this book so far have used two separate scripts for handling HTML forms: one that displayed the form and another that received and processed the form's data. There's certainly nothing wrong with this method, but there are advantages to coding the entire process in one script. To make a page both display and handle a form, use a conditional **A**:

```
if (/* form has been submitted */) {
        // Handle the form.
} else {
        // Display the form.
}
```

There are many ways to determine if a form has been submitted. One option is to check whether any of the form's variables are set:

```
if (isset($_POST['something'])) { …
```

However, if the user submitted the form without completing it, that variable may not be set (depending on the corresponding form element type). A more reliable solution I've used in the past is to add a hidden input to a form so that it can be checked:

```
<input type="hidden"
→ name="submitted" value="true" />
```

Again, the only purpose of this hidden input is to reliably indicate that the form has been submitted, even if the user did nothing to complete the form. To check for that, the handling PHP code would use this conditional:

```
if (isset($_POST['submitted'])) { …
```

```
<?php
include('template/header.html');

if (/* form has been submitted */) {
```

validation

```
} else {
```

form

```
}
include('template/footer.html');
?>
```

Script

A This flowchart represents how the same PHP script can both display and handle an HTML form.

Another way of checking for a form's submission is to examine *how the page was accessed*. When you have a form that will be submitted back to the same page, two different types of requests will be made of that script **B**. The first request, which loads the form, will be a GET request. This is the standard request made of most Web pages. When the form is submitted, and its **action** attribute points to the same page, a second request of the script will be made, this time a POST request (assuming the form uses the POST method). With this in mind, you can test for a form's submission by checking the request type, found in the **$_SERVER** array:

```
if ($_SERVER['REQUEST_METHOD'] ==
→ 'POST') { …
```

As an example of this, you'll create the basics of a login form.

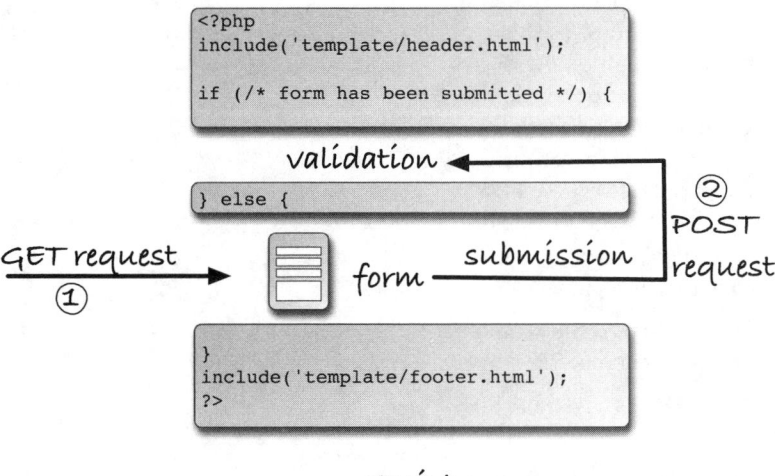

```php
<?php
include('template/header.html');

if (/* form has been submitted */) {
```

validation ←

```
} else {
```

GET request ①

form — *submission*

② POST request

```
}
include('template/footer.html');
?>
```

Script

B When the same PHP script both displays and handles an HTML form, the script will be requested using two different methods.

To use one page to display and handle a form:

1. Begin a new PHP document in your text editor or IDE, to be named **login.php** (**Script 8.8**):

   ```
   <?php // Script 8.8 - login.php
   ```

2. Define the page title as a constant and include the header file:

   ```
   define('TITLE', 'Login');
   include('templates/header.html');
   ```

   Using the constant system developed earlier in the chapter, give this page its own unique page title.

3. Add some introductory text:

   ```
   print '<h2>Login Form</h2>
     <p>Users who are logged in can
     → take advantage of certain
     → features like this, that, and
     → the other thing.</p>';
   ```

   This text, which appears outside of the main conditional, will always show in the Web browser, whether the form is being displayed or has been submitted. Because the core of this script revolves around a PHP conditional, it's arguably clearer to print out HTML from PHP rather than exit out of the PHP code as you did in the previous two examples (**index.php** and **books.php**).

4. Begin the conditional to check whether the form has been submitted:

   ```
   if ($_SERVER['REQUEST_METHOD'] ==
   → 'POST') {
   ```

   To test whether the form has been submitted, check whether **$_SERVER ['REQUEST_METHOD']** equals *POST* (case-sensitive).

Script 8.8 The login page serves two purposes: It displays the login form and handles its submission.

```
1   <?php // Script 8.8 - login.php
2   /* This page lets people log into the
    site (in theory). */
3
4   // Set the page title and include the
    header file:
5   define('TITLE', 'Login');
6   include('templates/header.html');
7
8   // Print some introductory text:
9   print '<h2>Login Form</h2>
10      <p>Users who are logged in can take
        advantage of certain features like
        this, that, and the other thing.</p>';
11
12  // Check if the form has been submitted:
13  if ($_SERVER['REQUEST_METHOD'] ==
    'POST') {
14
15      // Handle the form:
16      if ( (!empty($_POST['email'])) &&
        (!empty($_POST['password'])) ) {
17
18          if ( (strtolower($_POST
            ['email']) == 'me@example.com')
            && ($_POST['password'] ==
            'testpass') ) { // Correct!
19
20              print '<p>You are logged
                in!<br />Now you can blah,
                blah, blah...</p>';
21
22          } else { // Incorrect!
23
24              print '<p>The submitted
                email address and password
                do not match those on
                file!<br />Go back and try
                again.</p>';
25
26          }
27
28      } else { // Forgot a field.
29
30          print '<p>Please make sure you
            enter both an email address
            and a password!<br />Go back
            and try again.</p>';
31
```

code continues on next page

```
32        }
33
34    } else { // Display the form.
35
36        print '<form action="login.php"
          method="post">
37        <p>Email Address: <input
          type="text" name="email"
          size="20" /></p>
38        <p>Password: <input
          type="password" name="password"
          size="20" /></p>
39        <p><input type="submit" name=
          "submit" value="Log In!" /></p>
40        </form>';
41
42    }
43
44    include('templates/footer.html');
      // Need the footer.
45    ?>
```

5. Create a nested pair of conditionals to process the form data:

```
if ( (!empty($_POST['email'])) &&
→ (!empty($_POST['password'])) ) {
  if ( (strtolower($_POST['email'])
  → == 'me@example.com') &&
  → ($_POST['password'] ==
  → 'testpass') ) {
    print '<p>You are logged
    → in!<br />Now you can blah,
    → blah, blah...</p>';
  } else { // Incorrect!
    print '<p>The submitted email
    → address and password do not
    → match those on file!<br />
    → Go back and try again.</p>';
  }
} else {
  print '<p>Please make sure you
  → enter both an email address
  → and a password!<br />Go back
  → and try again.</p>';
}
```

These conditionals handle the form data. The first conditional checks that both the email address and password variables have values. If they don't, a message is displayed (*Please make sure...*). Within that first conditional, another conditional checks whether the email address is equal to *me@example.com* and the password is equal to *testpass*. If so, let's say the user is logged in (it would be too advanced at this juncture to store and retrieve user information to create a real login system). Otherwise, a message indicates that the wrong values were entered.

continues on next page

Be certain to use the equals operator (==) here and not the assignment operator (=) in this conditional, which is a common mistake. Also, in case the user enters their address as *Me@example.com*, or any other capitalized permutation, the **strtolower()** function is first applied to the email address, prior to checking for equality.

6. Complete the main conditional:

```
} else { // Display the form.
  print '<form action="login.php"
  → method="post">
  <p>Email Address: <input
  → type="text" name="email"
  → size="20" /></p>
  <p>Password: <input type=
  → "password" name="password"
  → size="20" /></p>
  <p><input type="submit" name=
  → "submit" value="Log In!" /></p>
  </form>';

}
```

This concludes the main conditional, which checks whether the form has been submitted. If it hasn't been, then the form is displayed. The form itself is very simple **C**.

To clarify a point of possible confusion, even though the form's **method** attribute has a value of *post* (all lowercase), to check for the form's submission, the request method value is still *POST* (all uppercase).

Login Form

Users who are logged in can take advantage of certain features like this, that, and the other thing.

Email Address: [   ]

Password: [   ]

[Log In!]

C This simple login page takes an email address and a password.

Login Form

Users who are logged in can take advantage of certain features like this, that, and the other thing.

You are logged in!
Now you can blah, blah, blah...

D Upon successfully logging in, the user sees this message.

Login Form

Users who are logged in can take advantage of certain features like this, that, and the other thing.

Please make sure you enter both an email address and a password!
Go back and try again.

E Failure to submit either an email address or a password results in this message.

Login Form

Users who are logged in can take advantage of certain features like this, that, and the other thing.

The submitted email address and password do not match those on file!
Go back and try again.

F If either the email address or the password doesn't match that in the script, the user sees this error message.

7. Require the footer file and complete the PHP page:

   ```
   include('templates/footer.html');
   ?>
   ```

8. Save the file as **login.php**, place it in the same directory as **index.php**, and test it in your Web browser **D**, **E**, and **F**.

TIP In the real world, you would add some CSS formatting to the error messages so that they stand out. The next section of the chapter will include this feature.

TIP This trick of checking for the presence of a hidden input can be confusing. It works because the same script—login.php—will be accessed twice by the user. The first time the form will not have been submitted, so a conditional checking if $_POST['submitted'] is set will be FALSE and the form will be displayed. Then the page will be accessed again after the user clicks submit, at which point the conditional becomes TRUE.

TIP If you want a page to handle a form and then immediately display the form again, use this:

```
if ($_SERVER['REQUEST_METHOD'] ==
→ 'POST') {
    // Handle the form.
}
// Display the form.
```

Making Forms Sticky

A *sticky* form remembers values entered into it. A common example is a search engine, which often displays your terms in the search box, even when showing the results of the search. You might also want to use sticky forms on occasions where the user failed to complete a form accurately and therefore must resubmit it **Ⓐ**.

From a technological standpoint, sticky forms work by having their form element values predetermined. You can make this happen by setting the **value** attribute of text inputs:

```
<input type="text" name="first_name"
→ value="Stephanie" />
```

To have PHP preset that value, print the appropriate variable between the quotation marks:

```
<input type="text" name="first_name"
→ value="<?php print $_POST
→ ['first_name']; ?>" />
```

The first time the form is run, the PHP code prints nothing (because the variable has no value). If the form is displayed again after submission, values that the user originally entered in the form input will be displayed there automatically. That's the basic idea, but a more professional implementation would address two things...

Registration Form

Register so that you can take advantage of certain features like this, that, and the other thing.

Please enter your last name!

Please enter your email address!

Please enter a password!

Please try again!

First Name: Larry

Last Name:

Ⓐ Creating sticky forms makes it easier for users to correct omissions in incomplete form submissions.

```
        <p>First Name: <input type="text" name="first_name" size="20" value="<br />
<b>Notice</b>:  Undefined index: first_name in <b>/Users/larryullman/Sites/phpvqs4/register.php</b>
" /></p>
```

Ⓑ The HTML source of the page shows the PHP error caused by referring to a variable that does not exist.

Registration Form

Register so that you can take advantage of certain features like this, that, and the other thing.

First Name: [   ]

Last Name: [   ]

Email Address: [   ]

Password: [   ]

Confirm Password: [   ]

[Register!]

C The registration form as the user first sees it.

First, it's best not to refer to variables that don't exist. Doing so creates PHP warnings, and with the PHP code buried in a form element's attribute, the warning itself will only be fully visible in the HTML source code **B**. To avoid that, check that the variable is set before printing it:

```
<input type="text" name="first_name"
→ value="<?php if (isset($_POST
→ ['first_name']) { print $_POST
→ ['first_name']; } ?>" />
```

Second, certain characters that could be in a submitted value will cause problems if printed as a form element's value. To prevent such problems, apply the **htmlspecialchars()** function (discussed in Chapter 5, "Using Strings"). With this in mind, a longer but better version of this code is as follows:

```
<input type="text" name="first_name"
→ value="<?php if (isset($_POST
→ ['first_name']) { print
→ htmlspecialchars($_POST['first_
→ name']); } ?>" />
```

To demonstrate, you'll create the shell of a registration form **C**.

To make a sticky form:

1. Create a new PHP script in your text editor or IDE, to be named **register. php** (Script 8.9):

   ```
   <?php // Script 8.9 - register.php
   ```

2. Set the page title and include the HTML header:

   ```
   define('TITLE', 'Register');
   include('templates/header.html');
   ```

3. Add some introductory text and define a CSS class:

   ```
   print '<h2>Registration Form</h2>
     <p>Register so you can
   → take advantage of certain
   → features like this, that, and
   → the other thing.</p>';
   print '<style type="text/css"
   → media="screen">
     .error { color: red; }
   </style>';
   ```

   So that the error messages, generated by improperly completing the registration form, stand out, a CSS class is defined that colors the applicable text in red. Although CSS is normally defined in the page's head, you can put it anywhere.

4. Check whether the form has been submitted:

   ```
   if ($_SERVER['REQUEST_METHOD'] ==
   → 'POST') {
   ```

   Like the login page, this one script both displays and handles the registration form. To check if the form has been submitted, the same code previously explained is used here.

Script 8.9 The registration form uses a so-called *sticky* feature so that it recalls the values previously entered into it

```
1    <?php // Script 8.9 - register.php
2    /* This page lets people register for
     the site (in theory). */
3
4    // Set the page title and include the
     header file:
5    define('TITLE', 'Register');
6    include('templates/header.html');
7
8    // Print some introductory text:
9    print '<h2>Registration Form</h2>
10       <p>Register so that you can take
         advantage of certain features like
         this, that, and the other thing.</p>';
11
12   // Add the CSS:
13   print '<style type="text/css"
     media="screen">
14       .error { color: red; }
15   </style>';
16
17   // Check if the form has been submitted:
18   if ($_SERVER['REQUEST_METHOD'] == 'POST') {
19
20       $problem = FALSE; // No problems
         so far.
21
22       // Check for each value...
23       if (empty($_POST['first_name'])) {
24           $problem = TRUE;
25           print '<p class="error">Please
             enter your first name!</p>';
26       }
27
28       if (empty($_POST['last_name'])) {
29           $problem = TRUE;
30           print '<p class="error">Please
             enter your last name!</p>';
31       }
32
33       if (empty($_POST['email'])) {
34           $problem = TRUE;
35           print '<p class="error">Please
             enter your email address!</p>';
36       }
37
38       if (empty($_POST['password1'])) {
```

code continues on next page

```
39          $problem = TRUE;
40          print '<p class="error">Please
            enter a password!</p>';
41      }
42
43      if ($_POST['password1'] != $_POST
        ['password2']) {
44          $problem = TRUE;
45          print '<p class="error">Your
            password did not match your
            confirmed password!</p>';
46      }
47
48      if (!$problem) { // If there weren't
        any problems...
49
50          // Print a message:
51          print '<p>You are now registered!
            <br />Okay, you are not really
            registered but...</p>';
52
53          // Clear the posted values:
54          $_POST = array();
55
56      } else { // Forgot a field.
57
58          print '<p class="error">Please try
            again!</p>';
59
60      }
61
62  } // End of handle form IF.
63
64  // Create the form:
65  ?>
66  <form action="register.php"
    method="post">
67
68      <p>First Name: <input type="text"
        name="first_name" size="20"
        value="<?php if (isset($_POST
        ['first_name'])) { print
        htmlspecialchars($_POST['first_
        name']); } ?>" /></p>
69
70      <p>Last Name: <input type="text"
        name="last_name" size="20"
        value="<?php if (isset($_POST
        ['last_name'])) { print
        htmlspecialchars($_POST['last_
        name']); } ?>" /></p>
```

code continues on next page

5. Create a flag variable:

$problem = FALSE;

The **$problem** variable will be used to indicate whether a problem occurred. Specifically, you want to make sure that every form input has been filled out before you formally register the user. Initially, this variable is set to **FALSE**, because no problems have occurred.

This is the same approach used in Chapter 6, "Control Structures."

6. Check that a first name was entered:

```
if (empty($_POST['first_name'])) {
    $problem = TRUE;
    print '<p class="error">Please
    → enter your first name!</p>';
}
```

As a simple test to determine whether the user has entered a first name value, check that the variable isn't empty. (This technique was first discussed in Chapter 6.) If the variable is empty, then indicate a problem by setting that variable to **TRUE** and print an error message. The error message has a class type of *error*, so that the CSS formatting is applied.

7. Repeat the validation for the last name and email address:

```
if (empty($_POST['last_name'])) {
    $problem = TRUE;
    print '<p class="error">Please
    → enter your last name!</p>';
}
if (empty($_POST['email'])) {
    $problem = TRUE;
    print '<p class="error">Please
    → enter your email address!</p>';
}
```

Both of these checks are variations on the username validation routine.

continues on next page

8. Validate the passwords:

```php
if (empty($_POST['password1'])) {
    $problem = TRUE;
    print '<p class="error">Please
    enter a password!</p>';
}
if ($_POST['password1'] != $_POST
['password2']) {
    $problem = TRUE;
    print '<p class="error">Your
    password did not match your
    confirmed password!</p>';
}
```

The password validation requires two conditionals. The first checks whether the **$_POST['password1']** variable is empty. The second checks whether the **$_POST['password1']** variable isn't equal to the **$_POST['password2']** variable. You don't need to see if **$_POST['password2']** is empty because if it is and **$_POST['password1']** isn't, the second conditional will catch that problem. If **$_POST['password1']** and **$_POST['password2']** are both empty, the first conditional will catch the mistake.

9. Check whether a problem occurred:

```php
if (!$problem) {
    print '<p>You are now
    registered!<br />Okay,
    you are not really registered
    but...</p>';
    $_POST = array();
```

If there were no problems, the **$problem** variable is still **FALSE**, and the initial condition here is **TRUE** (the condition is that **$problem** has a value of **FALSE**). In that case, the registration process would take place. The formal registration process, where the data is stored in a file or database, has not yet been developed, so a simple message appears in its stead here.

Script 8.9 *continued*

```
71
72      <p>Email Address: <input
        type="text" name="email"
        size="20" value="<?php if
        (isset($_POST['email'])) { print
        htmlspecialchars($_POST['email']);
        } ?>" /></p>
73
74      <p>Password: <input
        type="password" name="password1"
        size="20" value="<?php if
        (isset($_POST['password1']))
        { print htmlspecialchars($_POST
        ['password1']); } ?>" /></p>
75      <p>Confirm Password: <input
        type="password" name="password2"
        size="20" value="<?php if
        (isset($_POST['password2']))
        { print htmlspecialchars($_POST
        ['password2']); } ?>" /></p>
76
77      <p><input type="submit" name="submit"
        value="Register!" /></p>
78
79  </form>
80
81  <?php include('templates/footer.html');
    // Need the footer. ?>
```

Next, the **$_POST** variable is assigned the value of **array()**. This line has the effect of wiping out the contents of the **$_POST** variable (i.e., resetting it as an empty array). This step is taken only upon a successful (theoretical) registration so that the values are not redisplayed in the registration form (e.g., see Step 12).

10. Complete the conditionals:

```
  } else { // Forgot a field.
    print '<p class="error">
    → Please try again!</p>';
  }
} // End of handle form IF.
```

The **else** clause applies if a problem occurred, in which case the user is asked to complete the form again.

11. Begin the HTML form:

```
?>
<form action="register.php"
→ method="post">
```

Unlike the login example, this page always displays the form. Therefore, the form isn't part of any conditional. Also, because there's a lot of HTML to be generated, it'll be easier to leave the PHP section of the page and just output the HTML directly.

12. Create the sticky first name input:

```
<p>First Name: <input type="text"
→ name="first_name" size="20"
→ value="<?php if (isset($_POST
→ ['first_name'])) { print
→ htmlspecialchars($_POST
→ ['first_name']); } ?>" /></p>
```

To make the first name input sticky, preset its **value** attribute by printing out the **$_POST['first_name']** variable, but only if it's set. The conditional is therefore put within PHP tags within the HTML's **value** section of the form element. As already mentioned, the **htmlspecialchars()** function is used to handle any potentially problematic characters.

Note that if the user filled out the form properly, the entire **$_POST** array will have been reset, making this PHP conditional false.

13. Repeat the process for the last name and email address:

```
<p>Last Name: <input type="text"
→ name="last_name" size="20"
→ value="<?php if (isset($_POST
→ ['last_name'])) { print
→ htmlspecialchars($_POST
→ ['last_name']); } ?>" /></p>
<p>Email Address: <input
→ type="text" name="email"
→ size="20" value="<?php if
→ (isset($_POST['email'])) { print
→ htmlspecialchars($_POST
→ ['email']); } ?>" /></p>
```

These are variations on Step 12, switching the variable names as appropriate.

14. Add the rest of the form:

```
<p>Password: <input type=
→ "password" name="password1"
→ size="20" value="<?php if
→ (isset($_POST['password1']))
→ { print htmlspecialchars
→ ($_POST['password1']); } ?>" /></p>
<p>Confirm Password: <input
→ type="password" name="password2"
→ size="20" value="<?php if
→ (isset($_POST['password2']))
→ { print htmlspecialchars
→ ($_POST['password2']); }
→ ?>" /></p>
<p><input type="submit" name=
→ "submit" value="Register!" /></p>
</form>
```

It used to be the case that you couldn't preset a value for a password input, but some browsers now support this feature. Then there is the submit button and the closing **form** tag.

continues on next page

15. Complete the PHP page:

```
<?php include('templates/
→ footer.html'); ?>
```

The last step is to include the HTML footer.

16. Save the file as **register.php**, place it in the proper directory on your PHP-enabled server, and test it in your Web browser **D** and **E**.

TIP According to (X)HTML rules, you must quote all attributes in form inputs. Specifically, you should use double quotation marks. If you don't quote your values, any spaces in them mark the end of the value (for example, *Larry Ullman* will display as just *Larry* in the form input). Although quoting attributes will not be a requirement of HTML5, I still recommend doing so.

TIP To preset the status of radio buttons or check boxes as checked, add the code checked="checked" to the input tag:

```
<input type="checkbox" name=
→ "interests[]" value="Skiing"
→ checked="checked" />
```

Of course, you'd need to use a PHP conditional to see if that text should be added to the element's definition.

TIP To preselect a pull-down menu, use select-ed="selected":

```
<select name="year">
<option value="2011">2011</option>
<option value="2012" select-ed=
→ "selected">2012</option>
</select>
```

Again, you'd need to use a PHP conditional to see if that text should be added to the element's definition.

TIP To preset the value of a text area, place the value between the textarea tags:

```
<textarea name="comments" rows="10"
→ cols="50">preset value</textarea>
```

D The registration form indicates any problems and retains the form values.

E The registration form after the user successfully fills it out.

Email Address:

me@example.com,you@example.edu,whomever@example.net

A A user could easily attempt to send emails to multiple recipients through a form like this.

Sending Email

Sending email using PHP is *theoretically* simple, merely requiring only PHP's `mail()` function. This function uses the server's email application (such as **sendmail** on Unix or Mac OS X) or an SMTP (Simple Mail Transfer Protocol) server to send out the messages. The basic usage of this function is as follows:

```
mail(to, subject, body);
```

The first argument is the email address (or *addresses*, separated by commas) to which the email should be sent. The second argument establishes the message's subject line, and the third argument creates the message's content.

This function can take another argument through which you can add more details (*additional headers*) to the email, including a *From* address, email priority, and carbon-copy addresses:

```
mail('someone@example.com', 'Test
→Email', 'This is a test email',
→'From: 'email@example.com');
```

Although doing so is easy in theory, using this function in real-world code can be far more complex. For starters, setting up your own computer to send out email can be a challenge (see the sidebar "Configuring Your Server to Send Email").

Second, you should take steps to prevent malicious people from using your forms to send out spam. In our next example, an email will be sent to the provided email address. If a conniving user supplies multiple addresses **A**, an email will be sent to each one. There are many ways of safeguarding against this. For the level of this book, one simple option is to confirm

continues on next page

that there's only a single @ present in the provided address (i.e., it's only one email address). You can count how many times a substring is present in a string using the aptly named **substr_count()** function:

```
if (substr_count($_POST['email'],
→ '@') == 1) {…
```

With those caveats, let's add a **mail()** function call to the registration page so that you get a sense of how the function might be used.

To send email with PHP:

1. Open **register.php** (Script 8.9) in your text editor or IDE.

2. Change the email validation so that it also checks for a single "at" symbol (**Script 8.10**):

```
if (empty($_POST['email']) ||
→ (substr_count($_POST['email'],
→ '@') != 1) ) {
```

Now the email address validation fails if the value is empty or if it doesn't contain exactly one @. This doesn't constitute thorough validation—far from it—but the emails address becomes less of a security risk to use. See the tips for ways to improve upon this.

3. After the registration message (line 51), add the following:

```
$body = "Thank you for registering
→ with the J.D. Salinger fan
→ club! Your password is
→ '{$_POST['password1']}'.";
mail($_POST['email'], 'Registration
→ Confirmation', $body, 'From:
→ admin@example.com');
```

continues on page 220

Script 8.10 In PHP, you can send email by calling the **mail()** function.

```
1    <?php // Script 8.10 - register.php #2
2    /* This page lets people register for
     the site (in theory). */
3
4    // Set the page title and include the
     header file:
5    define('TITLE', 'Register');
6    include('templates/header.html');
7
8    // Print some introductory text:
9    print '<h2>Registration Form</h2>
10       <p>Register so that you can take
         advantage of certain features like
         this, that, and the other thing.</p>';
11
12   // Add the CSS:
13   print '<style type="text/css" media="screen">
14       .error { color: red; }
15   </style>';
16
17   // Check if the form has been submitted:
18   if ($_SERVER['REQUEST_METHOD'] == 'POST')
     {
19
20       $problem = FALSE; // No problems so far.
21
22       // Check for each value...
23       if (empty($_POST['first_name'])) {
24           $problem = TRUE;
25           print '<p class="error">Please
             enter your first name!</p>';
26       }
27
28       if (empty($_POST['last_name'])) {
29           $problem = TRUE;
30           print '<p class="error">Please
             enter your last name!</p>';
31       }
32
33       if (empty($_POST['email']) ||
         (substr_count($_POST['email'],
         '@') != 1) ) {
34           $problem = TRUE;
35           print '<p class="error">Please
             enter your email address!</p>';
36       }
37
38       if (empty($_POST['password1'])) {
39           $problem = TRUE;
```

code continues on next page

Script 8.10 *continued*

```
40          print '<p class="error">Please enter a password!</p>';
41      }
42
43      if ($_POST['password1'] != $_POST['password2']) {
44          $problem = TRUE;
45          print '<p class="error">Your password did not match your confirmed password!</p>';
46      }
47
48      if (!$problem) { // If there weren't any problems...
49
50          // Print a message:
51          print '<p>You are now registered!<br />Okay, you are not really registered but...</p>';
52
53          // Send the email:
54          $body = "Thank you for registering with the J.D. Salinger fan club! Your password
            is '{$_POST['password1']}'.";
55          mail($_POST['email'], 'Registration Confirmation', $body, 'From: admin@example.com');
56
57          // Clear the posted values:
58          $_POST = array();
59
60      } else { // Forgot a field.
61
62          print '<p class="error">Please try again!</p>';
63
64      }
65
66  } // End of handle form IF.
67
68  // Create the form:
69  ?>
70  <form action="register.php" method="post">
71
72      <p>First Name: <input type="text" name="first_name" size="20" value="<?php if (isset($_POST
        ['first_name'])) { print htmlspecialchars($_POST['first_name']); } ?>" /></p>
73
74      <p>Last Name: <input type="text" name="last_name" size="20" value="<?php if (isset($_POST
        ['last_name'])) { print htmlspecialchars($_POST['last_name']); } ?>" /></p>
75
76      <p>Email Address: <input type="text" name="email" size="20" value="<?php if (isset($_POST
        ['email'])) { print htmlspecialchars($_POST['email']); } ?>" /></p>
77
78      <p>Password: <input type="password" name="password1" size="20" value="<?php if (isset($_POST
        ['password1'])) { print htmlspecialchars($_POST['password1']); } ?>" /></p>
79      <p>Confirm Password: <input type="password" name="password2" size="20" value="<?php if
        (isset($_POST['password2'])) { print htmlspecialchars($_POST['password2']); } ?>" /></p>
80
81      <p><input type="submit" name="submit" value="Register!" /></p>
82
83  </form>
84
85  <?php include('templates/footer.html'); // Need the footer. ?>
```

Sometimes the easiest way to use this function is to establish the body as a variable and then feed it into the **mail()** function (as opposed to writing the email's body within the function call). The message itself is sent to the address with which the user registered, with the subject *Registration Confirmation*, from the address *admin@example.com*. If you'll be running this script on a live server, you should use an actual email address for that site as the *from* value.

4. Save the file, place it in the proper directory of your PHP- and email-enabled server, and test it in your Web browser 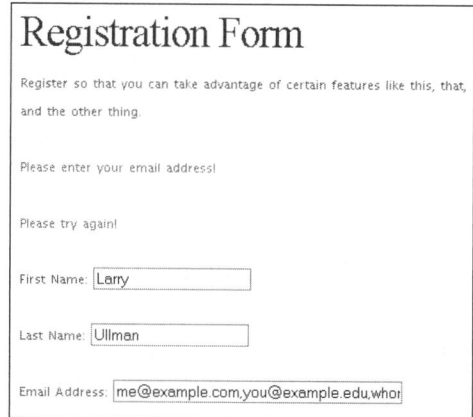.

5. Upon successfully completing the form, check your email for the message **C**.

TIP The "Review and Pursue" section at the end of this chapter points you in the direction of an excellent tool for validating email addresses, provided you're using version 5.2 or later of PHP.

TIP In my *PHP 6 and MySQL 5 for Dynamic Web Sites: Visual QuickPro Guide* (Peachpit Press, 2007) and online in my forums (www.LarryUllman.com/forum/), I discuss other ways to secure the emails that get sent by a PHP script.

TIP If you have problems receiving the PHP-sent email, start by confirming that the mail server works on its own without involving PHP. Then make sure you're using a valid *from* address. Finally, try using different recipient addresses and keep an eye on your spam folder to see that the message isn't getting put there (if applicable).

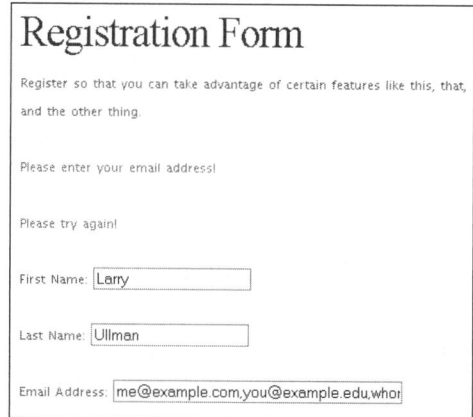

B If the user provides multiple email addresses **A**, they'll see an error message.

C This email was sent by the PHP script upon successful pseudo-registration.

Configuring Your Server to Send Email

Sending email with PHP is easy, as long as your Web server (or computer) is set up to send email. If you're using a Web hosting service or your own Unix computer (like Linux), this shouldn't be a problem at all. If you do have a problem, contact the hosting company for support.

If you're running your own server (e.g., if you're developing locally), the ability to send email could be a sticking point. If you're using an all-in-one installer, such as MAMP or XAMPP (see Appendix A), it should also have an email server as part of the package. If you don't receive the email after registering, check the associated software's documentation for what you may need to do to enable email.

If you're using a Web server built into the operating system, such as Apache on Mac OS X, you may or may not already be set up to send email. To start, go ahead and try this example using a valid email address. If you don't receive the email, see Appendix A for information about getting `mail()` to work.

I'll also add that I almost never worry about getting PHP on my own computer to send out emails because I'll never be running live Web sites from my computer. In other words, why waste time getting something to work that you'll never end up using (whereas getting PHP to send out email on a live server does matter)?

TIP It's possible to send email with attachments or HTML email, although doing so requires far more sophisticated coding (normally involving classes and objects). Fortunately, a number of programmers have already developed workable solutions that are available for use. See Appendix B, "Resources and Next Steps," for Web sites that may be of assistance.

TIP The `mail()` function returns a value (1 or 0) indicating its successful use. This value only indicates whether PHP was able to attempt to send the email (by using whatever email system is in place). There's no easy way to use PHP to see whether an email address is valid or whether the end user received the message.

TIP To send an email to multiple addresses, either use the *CC* parameter or separate each *TO* address with a comma.

TIP To create new lines within the email body, either create the message over multiple lines or use the newline character (\n) within double quotation marks.

TIP If you want to send multiple headers in addition to the *From* address, separate them with a combination of \r\n:

```
mail ('email@example.com', 'Testing',
→ $body, "From:email@example.org\r\
→ nBcc:hidden@example.net,third@
→ example.com");
```

Output Buffering

There are a handful of functions that you'll use in this chapter and the next that can only be called if nothing has been sent to the Web browser. These functions include `header()`, `setcookie()`, and `session_start()`. If you use them after the Web browser has already received some text, HTML, or even a blank space, you'll get a dreaded "*headers already sent*" error message **A**.

One solution that I recommend for beginning PHP developers is to make use of *output buffering* (also called *output control*). In a normal PHP script, any HTML outside of the PHP tags is immediately sent to the Web browser. This is also true when any **print** statement is executed. With output buffering, the HTML and printed data—the output—will instead be placed into a buffer (i.e., memory). At the end of the script, the buffer will then be sent to the Web browser, or if appropriate, the buffer can be cleared without being sent to the Web browser. There are many reasons to use output buffering, but for beginners, one benefit is that you can use certain functions without worrying about *headers already sent* errors. Although you haven't dealt with any of the named functions yet, this chapter

introduces output buffering now. Using this feature will greatly reduce errors when you begin using headers (in the next section of this chapter), cookies (in the next chapter), and sessions (also in the next chapter).

To begin output buffering, use the `ob_start()` function at the very top of your page. Once you call it, every **print** and similar function will send data to a memory buffer rather than to the Web browser. Conversely, HTTP calls, like `header()` and `setcookie()`, won't be buffered and will operate as usual.

At the conclusion of the script, call the `ob_end_flush()` function to send the accumulated buffer to the Web browser. Or use the `ob_end_clean()` function to delete the buffered data without passing it along. Both functions also turn off output buffering for that script.

From a programmer's perspective, output buffering allows you to structure a script in a more linear form, without concern for HTTP headers. Let's remake `header.html` and `footer.html` so that every page uses output buffering. You won't appreciate the benefits yet, but the number of errors you *won't see* over the rest of this book will go a long way toward preserving your programming sanity.

> **Warning**: Cannot modify header information – headers already sent by (output started at /Users/larryullman/Sites/phpvqs4/templates/header.html:4) in **/Users/larryullman /Sites/phpvqs4/login.php** on line **22**

A If the browser receives any HTML prior to a **header()** call, you'll see this error message.

Script 8.11 Add output buffering to the Web application by calling the **ob_start()** function at the top of the **header.html** script.

```
1    <?php // Script 8.11 - header.html #4
2
3    // Turn on output buffering:
4    ob_start();
5
6    ?><!DOCTYPE html PUBLIC "-//W3C//DTD XHTML
     1.1//EN" "http://www.w3.org/TR/xhtml11/
     DTD/xhtml11.dtd">
7    <html xmlns="http://www.w3.org/1999/
     xhtml" xml:lang="en">
8    <head>
9        <title><?php // Print the page title.
10       if (defined('TITLE')) { // Is the title
         defined?
11           print TITLE;
12       } else { // The title is not defined.
13           print 'Raise High the Roof Beam! A
             J.D. Salinger Fan Club';
14       }
15       ?></title>
16       <meta http-equiv="content-type"
         content="text/html; charset=utf-8" />
17       <link rel="stylesheet"
         href="css/1.css" type="text/css"
         media="screen,projection" />
18   </head>
19   <body>
20   <div id="wrapper">
21
22       <div id="header">
23           <p class="description">A J.D.
             Salinger Fan Club</p>
24           <h1><a href="index.php">Raise High
             the Roof Beam!</a></h1>
25           <ul id="nav">
26               <li><a href="books.php">
                 Books</a></li>
27               <li><a href="#">Stories</a></li>
28               <li><a href="#">Quotes</a></li>
29               <li><a href="login.php">
                 Login</a></li>
30               <li><a href="register.php">
                 Register</a></li>
31           </ul>
32       </div><!-- header -->
33
34       <div id="sidebar">
35           <h2>Favorite Quotes</h2>
36               <p class="news">I don't exactly
                 know what I mean by that,
                 but I mean it.<br />- <em>The
                 Catcher in the Rye</em></p>
```

To use output buffering:

1. Open **header.html** (Script 8.7) in your text editor or IDE.

2. At the very top of the page, before any HTML code, add the following (**Script 8.11**):

   ```
   <?php
   ob_start();
   ?>
   ```

   The key to using output buffering is to call the **ob_start()** function as early as possible in a script. In this example, you create a special section of PHP prior to any HTML and call **ob_start()** there. By turning on output buffering in your header file and turning it off in your footer file, you buffer every page in the Web application.

3. Open **footer.html** (Script 8.8) in your text editor or IDE.

continues on next page

Script 8.11 *continued*

```
37               <p class="news">I privately say
                 to you, old friend... please
                 accept from me this unpretentious
                 bouquet of early-blooming
                 parentheses: ((((())))).<br />-
                 <em>Raise High the Roof Beam,
                 Carpenters and Seymour: An
                 Introduction</em></p>
38               <p><?php // Print the current
                 date and time...
39               // Set the timezone:
40               date_default_timezone_set
                 ('America/New_York');
41
42               // Now print the date and time:
43               print date('g:i a l F j');
44               ?></p>
45       </div><!-- sidebar -->
46
47       <div id="content">
48           <!-- BEGIN CHANGEABLE CONTENT. -->
```

4. At the end of the script, after all of the HTML, add (**Script 8.12**):

```php
<?php
ob_end_flush();
?>
```

This code turns off output buffering and sends the accumulated buffer to the Web browser. In other words, all the HTML is sent at this point.

5. Save both files and place them in the **templates** directory of your PHP-enabled server.

6. Test any page in your Web browser 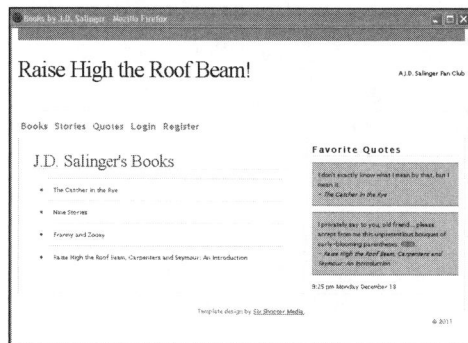.

TIP As a reminder, PHP code can be placed in a file with an `.html` extension—as in these two examples here—if that file is being included by a PHP script (like `index.php`).

TIP For some time now, output buffering has been automatically enabled in PHP's default configuration.

TIP You can set the maximum buffer size in `php.ini` (PHP's configuration file). The default is 4,096 bytes.

TIP The `ob_get_length()` function returns the length (in number of characters) of the current buffer contents.

TIP The `ob_get_contents()` function returns the current buffer so that it can be assigned to a variable, should the need arise.

TIP The `ob_flush()` function sends the current contents of the buffer to the Web browser and then discards them, allowing a new buffer to be started. This function lets your scripts maintain more moderate buffer sizes.

TIP The `ob_clean()` function deletes the current contents of the buffer without stopping the buffer process.

TIP PHP automatically runs `ob_end_flush()` at the conclusion of a script if it isn't otherwise done. But it's still a good idea to call it yourself.

Script 8.12 Output buffering is completed at the end of the footer file using **ob_end_flush()**, which sends the accumulated buffer to the Web browser.

```
1          <!-- END CHANGEABLE CONTENT. -->
2      </div><!-- content -->
3
4      <div id="footer">
5          <p>Template design by <a href=
           "http://www.sixshootermedia.com">
           Six Shooter Media</a>.</p>
6          <p>&copy; 2011</p>
7      </div><!-- footer -->
8
9  </div><!-- wrapper -->
10 </body>
11 </html><?php // Script 8.12 - footer.html #2
12
13 // Send the buffer to the browser and
   turn off buffering:
14 ob_end_flush();
15 ?>
```

 The site works the same as it did previously, but it will be easier to work with when you use HTTP headers in the next section of this chapter.

Manipulating HTTP Headers

Most interactions between a server and a Web browser (the client) take place over HTTP (Hypertext Transfer Protocol). This is why the addresses for Web pages begin with *http://*. But the Web server often needs to communicate with a browser in other ways, beyond just sending HTML, images, and the like. These additional communications can be accomplished using HTTP *headers*. There are dozens of uses for HTTP headers, all of which you can do using PHP's **header()** function.

Here, you'll learn a very common use of the **header()** function: redirecting the user from one page to another. To redirect the user's browser with PHP, you send a *location* header:

```
header('Location: page.php');
```

Normally, the **header()** function is followed by **exit()**, to cancel the execution of the script (because the browser has been redirected to another page):

```
header('Location: page.php');
exit();
```

The most important thing to understand about using **header()** is that the function must be called before anything else is sent to the Web browser—otherwise, you'll see the all-too-common "*headers already sent*" error message (see Ⓐ in the section "Output Buffering"). If your Web page receives *any* HTML or even blank space, the **header()** function won't work.

continues on next page

Fortunately, you learned about output buffering in the previous section. Because output buffering is turned on in the Web application, nothing is sent to the Web browser until the very last line of the footer script (when **ob_end_flush()** is called). By using this method, you can avoid the dreaded "*headers already sent*" error message.

To practice redirection, you'll rewrite the login page to take the user to a welcome page upon successful login.

To use the header() function:

1. Open **login.php** in your text editor or IDE (Script 8.8).

2. Delete the *You are logged in...* **print** statement (**Script 8.13**).

   Because the user is redirected to another page, there's no need to include this message.

Script 8.13 The new version of the login page redirects the user to another page using the **header()** function.

```
1   <?php // Script 8.13 - login.php #2
2   /* This page lets people log into the
    site (in theory). */
3
4   // Set the page title and include the
    header file:
5   define('TITLE', 'Login');
6   include('templates/header.html');
7
8   // Print some introductory text:
9   print '<h2>Login Form</h2>
10      <p>Users who are logged in can take
        advantage of certain features like
        this, that, and the other thing.</p>';
11
12  // Check if the form has been submitted:
13  if ($_SERVER['REQUEST_METHOD'] == 'POST') {
14
15      // Handle the form:
16      if ( (!empty($_POST['email'])) &&
        (!empty($_POST['password'])) ) {
17
18          if ( (strtolower($_POST['email'])
            == 'me@example.com') && ($_
            POST['password'] == 'testpass') ) {
            // Correct!
19
20              // Redirect the user to the
                welcome page!
21              ob_end_clean(); // Destroy
                the buffer!
22              header ('Location:
                welcome.php');
23              exit();
24
25          } else { // Incorrect!
26
27              print '<p>The submitted email
                address and password do not
                match those on file!<br />Go
                back and try again.</p>';
28
29          }
30
```

code continues on next page

```
31      } else { // Forgot a field.
32
33          print '<p>Please make sure you
            enter both an email address and
            a password!<br />Go back and try
            again.</p>';
34
35      }
36
37  } else { // Display the form.
38
39      print '<form action="login.php"
        method="post">
40      <p>Email Address: <input type="text"
        name="email" size="20" /></p>
41      <p>Password: <input type="password"
        name="password" size="20" /></p>
42      <p><input type="submit" name="submit"
        value="Log In!" /></p>
43      </form>';
44
45  }
46
47  include('templates/footer.html');
    // Need the footer.
48  ?>
```

3. Where the **print** statement was, add the following:

```
ob_end_clean();
header ('Location: welcome.php');
exit();
```

The first line destroys the page buffer (because the accumulated buffer won't be used). This isn't strictly required but is a good idea. The next line redirects the user to **welcome.php**. The third line terminates the execution of the rest of the script.

4. Save the file and place it in the proper directory for your PHP-enabled server (along with the other scripts from this chapter).

Now you need to create the **welcome.php** page to which the user will be redirected.

To write welcome.php:

1. Begin a new PHP document in your text editor or IDE, to be named **welcome.php** (**Script 8.14**):

```
<?php // Script 8.14 - welcome.php
```

2. Define the page title and include the header:

```
define('TITLE', 'Welcome to the
→J.D. Salinger Fan Club!');
include('templates/header.html');
```

3. Create the page content:

```
?>
<h2>Welcome to the J.D. Salinger
→ Fan Club!</h2>
<p>You've successfully logged
→ in and can now take advantage
→ of everything the site has to
→ offer.</p>
```

Script 8.14 The welcome page greets the user after they've logged in.

```
1    <?php // Script 8.14 - welcome.php
2    /* This is the welcome page. The user is redirected here
3    after they successfully log in. */
4
5    // Set the page title and include the header file:
6    define('TITLE', 'Welcome to the J.D. Salinger Fan Club!');
7    include('templates/header.html');
8
9    // Leave the PHP section to display lots of HTML:
10   ?>
11
12   <h2>Welcome to the J.D. Salinger Fan Club!</h2>
13   <p>You've successfully logged in and can now take advantage of everything the site has to
     offer.</p>
14   <p>Lorem ipsum dolor sit amet, consectetur adipisicing elit, sed do eiusmod tempor incididunt
     ut labore et dolore magna aliqua. Ut enim ad minim veniam, quis nostrud exercitation ullamco
     laboris nisi ut aliquip ex ea commodo consequat. Duis aute irure dolor in reprehenderit in
     voluptate velit esse cillum dolore eu fugiat nulla pariatur. Excepteur sint occaecat cupidatat
     non proident, sunt in culpa qui officia deserunt mollit anim id est laborum.</p>
15
16   <?php include('templates/footer.html'); // Need the footer. ?>
```

Login Form

Users who are logged in can take advantage of certain features like this, that, and the other thing.

Email Address: me@example.com

Password: ●●●●●●●●

[Log In!]

A The login form...

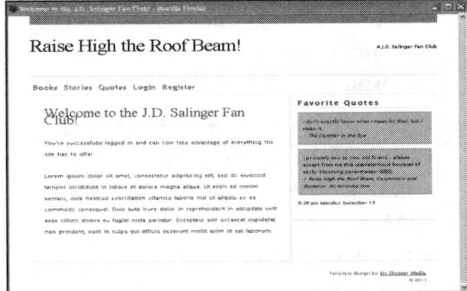

B ...and the redirection if the user properly logged in.

Login Form

Users who are logged in can take advantage of certain features like this, that, and the other thing.

The submitted email address and password do not match those on file! Go back and try again.

C If the user didn't properly log in, they remain on the login page.

---

4. Return to PHP and include the footer:

```
<?php include('templates/
→ footer.html'); ?>
```

5. Save the script as **welcome.php**, place it in the same directory as the new version of **login.php**, and test it in your Web browser **A**, **B**, and **C**.

TIP The `headers_sent()` function returns TRUE if the page has already received HTTP headers and the `header()` function can't be used.

TIP Using the GET method trick, you can pass values from one page to another using `header()`:

```
$var = urlencode('Pass this text');
header ("Location: page.php?
→ message=$var");
```

TIP The `header()` function should technically use a full path to the target page when redirecting. For example, it should be

```
header ('Location: http://www.
→ example.com/welcome.php');
```

or

```
header ('Location: http://localhost/
→ welcome.php');
```

TIP In my book *PHP 6 and MySQL 5 for Dynamic Web Sites: Visual QuickPro Guide*, I show some code for dynamically generating an absolute URL based on the location of the current script.

Review and Pursue

If you have any problems with the review questions or the pursue prompts, turn to the book's supporting forum (www.LarryUllman.com/forum/).

Review

- What is the difference between `include()` and `required()`?

- Why can you put PHP code into an included file even when it uses an `.html` extension?

- What are the differences between *relative* and *absolute* references to a file?

- How do you define a constant? Are constant names case-sensitive or case-insensitive? How do you check if a constant has been defined?

- What is the *epoch*? What is a *timestamp*?

- What is the significance of `$_SERVER['REQUEST_METHOD']`?

- How do you have a form element "remember" previously submitted values?

- How can you see a PHP error that occurs within a form element (e.g., when presetting a form's element's value)?

- What does the "*headers already sent*" error mean? How can it be prevented?

Pursue

- Create a new prototype design for this chapter's examples, and then create new header and footer files. View any of the site's pages again (you should not need to change any of the PHP scripts).

- Change the parameters to the `date()` function in `header.html` to display the date and/or time in a different manner.

- Rewrite the password conditionals found in `register.php` as a nested pair of conditionals. Hint: See Chapter 6 for examples.

- If you're using PHP 5.2 or later, check out the PHP manual pages for the *Filter* extension. Then incorporate the `filter_var()` function to validate the email address in `register.php`.

- Change the subject and body of the email sent upon (pseudo-) registration to something more interesting and informative.

Cookies and Sessions

Chapter 8, "Creating Web Applications," covered a number of techniques for developing more fully realized Web sites. One missing piece—the focus of this chapter—is how to maintain "state" as the user traverses a multipage Web site. The Hypertext Transfer Protocol (HTTP) is a *stateless* technology, meaning that it has no built-in method for tracking a user or remembering data from one page of an application to the next. This is a serious problem, because e-commerce applications, user registration and login systems, and other common online services rely on being able to follow the same user from page to page. Fortunately, maintaining state is quite simple with PHP.

This chapter discusses the two primary methods for tracking data: *cookies* and *sessions*. You'll start by learning how to create, read, modify, and delete cookies. Then you'll see how easy it is to master sessions, a more potent option for maintaining state.

In This Chapter

What Are Cookies?	232
Creating Cookies	234
Reading from Cookies	239
Adding Parameters to a Cookie	242
Deleting a Cookie	245
What Are Sessions?	248
Creating a Session	249
Accessing Session Variables	252
Deleting a Session	254
Review and Pursue	256

What Are Cookies?

Prior to the existence of cookies, traversing a Web site was a trip without a history. Although the browser tracks the pages you visit, allowing you to use the Back button to return to previously visited pages and indicating visited links in a different color, the server does not follow what individual users see and do. This is still true for sites that don't use cookies, as well as for users who have disabled cookies in their Web browsers 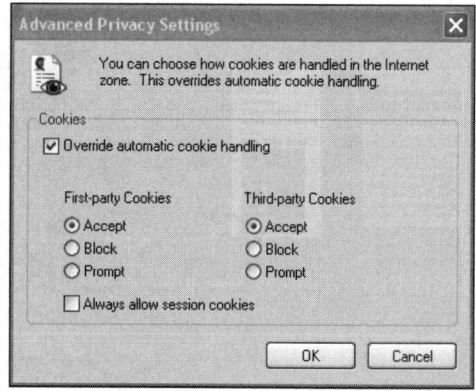.

Why is that a problem? If the server can't track a user, there can be no shopping carts for making purchases online. If cookies didn't exist (or if they're disabled in the Web browser), people wouldn't be able to use popular sites that require user registration. In short, without cookies, there would be no Amazon or Facebook or any of the other most popular or useful sites (not in their current incarnations, at least).

Cookies are simply a way for a server to store information on the user's computer. By doing so, the server can remember the user over the course of a visit or through several visits. Think of a cookie like a name tag: You tell the server your name, and it gives you a name tag. Then it can know who you are by referring back to the name tag.

This brings up another point about the security issues involved with cookies. Cookies have gotten a bad rap because users believe cookies allow a server to know too much about them. However, a cookie can only be used to store information that you give it, so it's as secure as you want it to be. And, as previously mentioned, it's very easy in modern browsers to customize the cookie handling as desired.

Ⓐ Most Web browsers let users set the cookie-handling preferences. This is Internet Explorer 8's Advanced Privacy Settings tab.

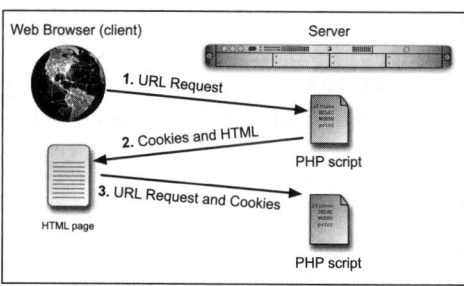

Ⓑ How cookies are sent back and forth between the server and the client.

PHP has very good support for cookies. In this chapter, you'll learn how to set a cookie, retrieve information from a cookie, and then delete the cookie. You'll also see some of the optional parameters you can use to apply limits to a cookie's existence.

Before moving on, there are two more things you ought to know about cookies. The first is how to debug cookie-related problems. You'll inevitably need to know how to do that, so the topic is discussed in the sidebar "Debugging Cookies." The second is how a cookie is transmitted and received **B**. Cookies are stored in the Web browser, but only the site that originally sent a cookie can read it. Also, the cookies are read by the site when the page on that site is requested by the Web browser. In other words, when the user enters a URL in the address bar and clicks Go (or whatever), the site reads any cookies it has access to and then serves up the requested page. This order is important because it dictates when and how cookies can be accessed.

TIP The ability to send, read, and delete cookies is one of the few overlaps between server-side PHP and browser-side JavaScript.

Debugging Cookies

When you begin working with cookies in PHP, you'll need to know how to debug your cookie-related scripts when difficulties arise. Three areas might cause you problems:

- Sending the cookie with PHP
- Receiving the cookie in your Web browser
- Accessing a cookie in a PHP script

The first and last issues can be debugged by printing out the variable values in your PHP scripts (as you'll soon learn). The second issue requires that you know how to work with cookies in your Web browser. For debugging purposes, you'll want your Web browser to notify you when a cookie is being sent.

With Internet Explorer on Windows, you can do this by choosing Internet Options under the Tools menu. Then click the Privacy tab, followed by the Advanced button under Settings. Click "Override automatic cookie handling," **A** and then choose Prompt for both First-party and Third-party Cookies (you can actually block the third-party cookies, if you'd rather). Other versions of Internet Explorer may use different variations on this process. Internet Explorer also has a Developer Tools window (linked under the Tools menu) that can be useful.

The best way to debug cookies when using Firefox on any platform is to install one of the many cookie-related extensions, like *Firecookie*. The *Firebug* extension, which every developer must use, also shows cookie-related information. But at the very least, if you select "Use custom settings for history" on the Privacy panel (in the Options/Preferences window), you'll be able to establish custom cookie behavior, such as being prompted.

Safari on Mac OS X and Windows doesn't give you as many cookie choices; you can find the available options on the Security tab of the Preferences window.

Some browsers also let you browse through the existing cookies to see their names and values. Doing so is a great asset in the debugging war.

Creating Cookies

An important thing to understand about cookies is that *they must be sent from the server to the client prior to any other information*. This means a script should send cookies before any **print** statement, before including an external file that contains HTML, and so forth.

Should the server attempt to send a cookie after the Web browser has already received HTML—even an extraneous white space—an error message will result and the cookie won't be sent . This is by far the most common cookie-related error.

Cookies are sent using the **setcookie()** function:

```
setcookie(name, value);
setcookie('CookieName', 'This is the
→ cookie value.');
```

That line of code sends to the browser a cookie with the name *CookieName* and the value *This is the cookie value.* 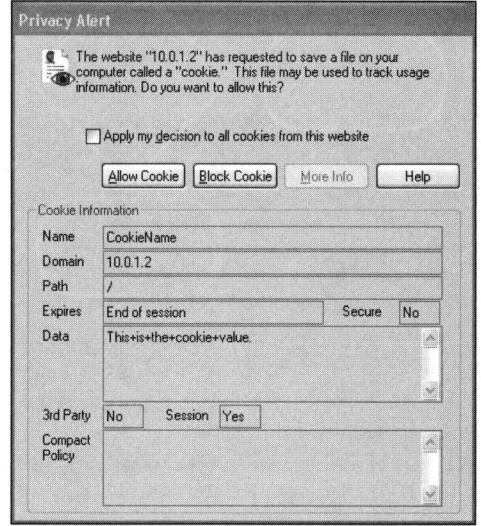.

You can continue to send more cookies to the browser with subsequent uses of the **setcookie()** function, although you're limited by the Web browser as to how many cookies can be sent from the same site:

```
setcookie('name2', 'some value');
setcookie('name3', 'another value');
```

Finally, when creating cookies, you can—as you'll see in this example—use a variable for the name or value attribute of your cookies:

```
setcookie($cookie_name, $cookie_value);
```

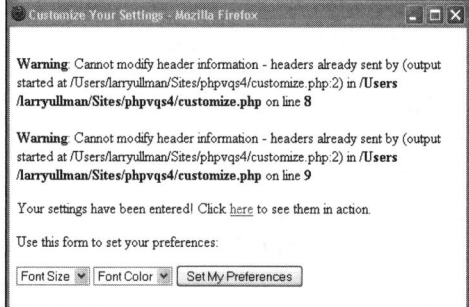

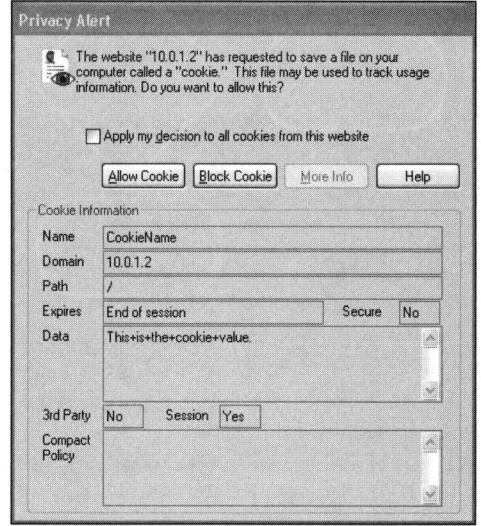

A A message like this is what you'll see if the **setcookie()** function is called after anything, even a blank line or space, has already been sent to the Web browser.

B If the browser is set to prompt the user for cookies, a message like this will appear for each cookie sent. (Note that the window, from Internet Explorer 8, shows the value in a URL-encoded format.)

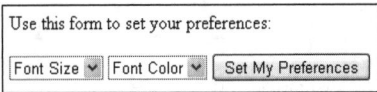

Use this form to set your preferences:

Font Size ▾ Font Color ▾ Set My Preferences

ⓒ This form is used to select the font size and color for use on another PHP page.

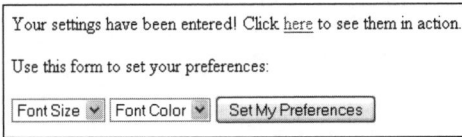

Your settings have been entered! Click here to see them in action.

Use this form to set your preferences:

Font Size ▾ Font Color ▾ Set My Preferences

ⓓ After submitting the form, the page shows a message and a link to another page (where the user's preferences will be used). That page will be created next.

Script 9.1 Two cookies will be used to store the user's choices for the font size and color. This page both displays and handles the form.

```
1    <?php // Script 9.1 - customize.php
2
3    // Handle the form if it has been
     submitted:
4    if (isset($_POST['font_size'],
     $_POST['font_color'])) {
5
6       // Send the cookies:
7       setcookie('font_size',
        $_POST['font_size']);
8       setcookie('font_color',
        $_POST['font_color']);
9
10      // Message to be printed later:
11      $msg = '<p>Your settings have
        been entered! Click <a href=
        "view_settings.php">here</a>
        to see them in action.</p>';
12
13   } // End of submitted IF.
14   ?><!DOCTYPE html PUBLIC "-//W3C//DTD XHTML
     1.0 Transitional//EN"
15      "http://www.w3.org/TR/xhtml1/DTD/
        xhtml1-transitional.dtd">
16   <html xmlns="http://www.w3.org/1999/
     xhtml" xml:lang="en" lang="en">
```

code continues on next page

For an example of setting cookies, you'll create a script that allows the user to specify the default font size and color for a page. The page displays a form for choosing these values **ⓒ** and then handles the form submission **ⓓ**. A separate page, created in the next section of this chapter, will use these settings.

To send cookies:

1. Create a new PHP document in your text editor or IDE, to be named **customize.php** (Script 9.1):

   <?php // Script 9.1 - customize.php

   The most critical issue with cookies is that they're created before anything is sent to the Web browser. To accomplish this, the script begins with a PHP section that handles the sending of cookies.

   Also be certain not to have any extraneous spaces or lines before the initial PHP tag.

2. Check whether the form has been submitted:

   **if (isset($_POST['font_size'],
   → $_POST['font_color'])) {**

   This page will both display and handle the form. It could use the same method explained in the previous chapter—checking if the **$_SERVER['REQUEST_ METHOD']** variable has a value of *POST*, but as an alternative approach, the script will perform basic, minimal validation as the test for a form submission. The conditional checks for the existence of two variables: **$_POST['font_size']** and **$_POST['font_color']**. If both are set, the form submission will be addressed.

   continues on next page

3. Create the cookies:

```
setcookie('font_size',
→ $_POST['font_size']);
setcookie('font_color',
→ $_POST['font_color']);
```

These two lines create two separate cookies. One is named *font_size* and the other *font_color*. Their values will be based on the selected values from the HTML form, which are stored in the $_POST['font_size'] and $_POST['font_color'] variables.

In a more fully developed application, you should first confirm that the variables both have acceptable values.

4. Create a message and complete the conditional and the PHP section:

```
$msg = '<p>Your settings
→ have been entered! Click
→ <a href="view_settings.
→ php">here</a> to see them in
→ action.</p>';
} // End of submitted IF.
?>
```

When the form has been submitted, the cookies will be sent and the **$msg** variable will be assigned a string value. This variable will be used later in the script to print a message. This approach is necessary, as you can't print the message at this juncture (because not even the HTML head has been created).

5. Create the HTML head and opening body tag:

```
<!DOCTYPE html PUBLIC "-//W3C//DTD
→ XHTML 1.0 Transitional//EN"
  "http://www.w3.org/TR/xhtml1/
  → DTD/xhtml1-transitional.dtd">
<html xmlns="http://www.w3.org/
→ 1999/xhtml" xml:lang="en"
→ lang="en">
```

Script 9.1 *continued*

```
17    <head>
18        <meta http-equiv="Content-Type"
          content="text/html; charset=utf-8"/>
19        <title>Customize Your Settings
          </title>
20    </head>
21    <body>
22    <?php // If the cookies were sent, print
      a message.
23    if (isset($msg)) {
24        print $msg;
25    }
26    ?>
27
28    <p>Use this form to set your
      preferences:</p>
29
30    <form action="customize.php"
      method="post">
31        <select name="font_size">
32        <option value="">Font Size</option>
33        <option value="xx-small">xx-small
          </option>
34        <option value="x-small">x-small
          </option>
35        <option value="small">small
          </option>
36        <option value="medium">medium
          </option>
37        <option value="large">large
          </option>
38        <option value="x-large">x-large
          </option>
39        <option value="xx-large">xx-large
          </option>
40        </select>
41        <select name="font_color">
42        <option value="">Font Color
          </option>
43        <option value="999">Gray</option>
44        <option value="0c0">Green</option>
45        <option value="00f">Blue</option>
46        <option value="c00">Red</option>
47        <option value="000">Black</option>
48        </select>
49        <input type="submit" name="submit"
          value="Set My Preferences" />
50    </form>
51
52    </body>
53    </html>
```

```
<head>
  <meta http-equiv="Content-Type"
  → content="text/html;
  → charset=utf-8"/>
  <title>Customize Your Settings
  → </title>
</head>
<body>
```

All of this code must come after the **setcookie()** lines. Not to overstate the fact, but no text, HTML, or blank spaces can be sent to the Web browser prior to the **setcookie()** calls.

6. Create another PHP section to report on the cookies being sent:

```
<?php
if (isset($msg)) {
  print $msg;
}
?>
```

This code prints out a message if the cookies have been sent. The first time the user comes to the page, the cookies haven't been sent, so **$msg** is not set, making this conditional **FALSE**, and this **print** invocation never runs. Once the form has been submitted, **$msg** has been set by this point, so this conditional is **TRUE** **D**.

7. Begin the HTML form:

```
<p>Use this form to set your
→ preferences:</p>
<form action="customize.php"
→ method="post">
  <select name="font_size">
  <option value="">Font Size
  → </option>
  <option value="xx-small">
  → xx-small</option>
  <option value="x-small">
  → x-small</option>
  <option value="small">small
  → </option>
```

```
<option value="medium">medium
→ </option>
<option value="large">large
→ </option>
<option value="x-large">x-large
→ </option>
<option value="xx-large">
→ xx-large</option>
</select>
```

The HTML form itself is very simple **C**. The user is given one drop-down menu to select the font size. The value for each corresponds to the CSS code used to set the document's font size: from *xx-small* to *xx-large*.

Because this script both displays and handles the form, the form's **action** attribute points to the same file.

8. Complete the HTML form:

```
<select name="font_color">
<option value="">Font Color
→ </option>
<option value="999">Gray</option>
<option value="0c0">Green</option>
<option value="00f">Blue</option>
<option value="c00">Red</option>
<option value="000">Black</option>
</select>
<input type="submit" name=
→ "submit" value="Set My
→ Preferences" />
</form>
```

The second drop-down menu is used to select the font color. The menu displays the colors in text form, but the values are HTML color values. Normally such values are written using six characters plus a pound sign (e.g., *#00cc00*), but CSS allows you to use just a three-character version and the pound sign will be added on the page that uses these values.

continues on next page

9. Complete the HTML page:

```
</body>
</html>
```

10. Save the file as **customize.php** and place it in the proper directory for your PHP-enabled server.

11. Make sure you've set your Web browser to prompt for each cookie, if applicable.

    To guarantee that the script is working, you want the browser to prompt you for each cookie, if you can. See the "Debugging Cookies" sidebar.

12. Run the script in your Web browser 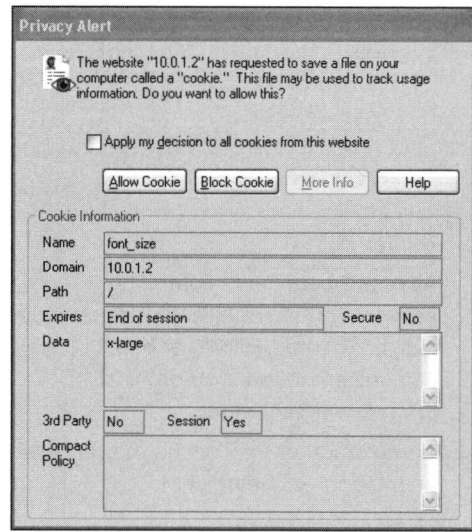 and .

TIP Cookies are one of the few areas in PHP that can behave differently from browser to browser or operating system to operating system. You should test your cookie-based applications on as many browsers and operating systems as you can.

TIP If you use the output buffering technique taught in Chapter 8, then you can place your setcookie() calls anywhere within the script (because the Web browser won't receive the data until the ob_end_flush() function is called).

TIP Cookies are limited to approximately 4 KB of total data. This is more than sufficient for most applications.

TIP To test whether it's safe to send a cookie, use the headers_sent() function. It reports on whether HTTP headers have already been sent to the Web browser.

E The user sees this message when the first **setcookie()** call is made, if they've opted to be prompted before accepting a cookie. This cookie is storing the value of *x-large* in a cookie named *font_size*.

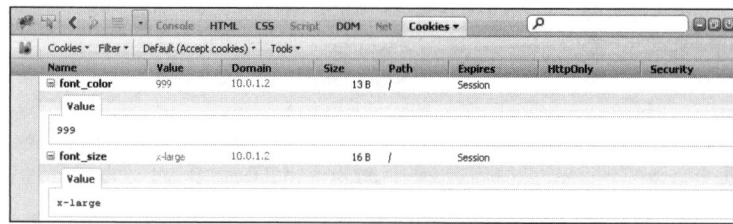

F The Firebug extension for Firefox shows the cookies received by the browser. The second cookie that's sent by the PHP script is called *font_color* and has a value of *999*, representing the color gray.

```
1    <!DOCTYPE html PUBLIC "-//W3C//DTD XHTML
     1.0 Transitional//EN"
2        "http://www.w3.org/TR/xhtml1/DTD/
         xhtml1-transitional.dtd">
3    <html xmlns="http://www.w3.org/1999/
     xhtml" xml:lang="en" lang="en">
4    <head>
5        <meta http-equiv="content-type"
         content="text/html; charset=utf-8" />
6        <title>View Your Settings</title>
7        <style type="text/css">
8            body {
9    <?php // Script 9.2 - view_settings.php
10
11   // Check for a font_size value:
12   if (isset($_COOKIE['font_size'])) {
13       print "\t\tfont-size: " .
         htmlentities($_COOKIE['font_
         size']) . ";\n";
14   } else {
15       print "\t\tfont-size: medium;";
16   }
17
18   // Check for a font_color value:
19   if (isset($_COOKIE['font_color'])) {
20       print "\t\tcolor: #" .
         htmlentities($_COOKIE['font_
         color']) . ";\n";
21   } else {
22       print "\t\tcolor: #000;";
23   }
24
25   ?>
26           }
27       </style>
28   </head>
29   <body>
30   <p><a href="customize.php">Customize Your
     Settings</a></p>
31   <p><a href="reset.php">Reset Your
     Settings</a></p>
32
33   <p>yadda yadda yadda yadda yadda
34   yadda yadda yadda yadda yadda
35   yadda yadda yadda yadda yadda
36   yadda yadda yadda yadda yadda
37   yadda yadda yadda yadda yadda</p>
38
39   </body>
40   </html>
```

Reading from Cookies

Just as form data is stored in the **$_POST** array (assuming it used the POST method) and values passed to a script in the URL are stored in the **$_GET** array, the **setcookie()** function places cookie data in the **$_COOKIE** array. To retrieve a value from a cookie, you only need to refer to the cookie name as the index of this array. For example, to retrieve the value of the cookie established with the line

setcookie('user', 'trout');

you would use the variable **$_COOKIE['user']**.

Unless you change the cookie's parameters (as you'll see later in this chapter), the cookie will automatically be accessible to every other page in your Web application. You should understand, however, that a cookie is never accessible to a script immediately after it's been sent. You can't do this:

setcookie('user', 'trout');
print $_COOKIE['user']; // No value.

The reason for this is the order in which cookies are read and sent (see **B** in the first section of this chapter).

To see how simple it is to access cookie values, let's write a script that uses the preferences set in **customize.php** to specify the page's text size and color. The script relies on CSS to achieve this effect.

To retrieve cookie data with PHP:

1. Begin a new PHP document in your text editor or IDE, to be named **view_settings.php** (Script 9.2):

   <!DOCTYPE html PUBLIC "-//W3C//
   → DTD XHTML 1.0 Transitional//EN"
   "http://www.w3.org/TR/xhtml1/
   → DTD/xhtml1-transitional.dtd">

continues on next page

```html
<html xmlns="http://www.w3.org/
→ 1999/xhtml" xml:lang="en"
→ lang="en">
<head>
  <meta http-equiv="content-type"
  → content="text/html;
  → charset=utf-8" />
  <title>View Your Settings
  → </title>
```

2. Start the CSS section:

```css
<style type="text/css">
  body {
```

The page will use CSS to enact the user's preferences. The aim is to create code like

```css
body {
    font-size: x-large;
    color: #999;
}
```

The two values will differ based on what the user selected in the **customize.php** page. In this step, you create the initial CSS tag.

3. Open a section of PHP code:

```php
<?php // Script 9.2 -
→ view_settings.php
```

The script will now use PHP to print out the remaining CSS, based on the cookies.

4. Use the font size cookie value, if it exists:

```php
if (isset($_COOKIE['font_size'])) {
  print "\t\tfont-size: " .
  → htmlentities($_COOKIE
  → ['font_size']) . ";\n";
} else {
  print "\t\tfont-size: medium;";
}
```

If the script can access a cookie with a name of *font_size*, it will print out that cookie's value as the CSS **font-size** value. The **isset()** function is

sufficient to see if the cookie exists. If no such cookie exists, PHP will print out a default size, *medium*.

For security purposes, the cookie's value is not directly printed. Instead, it's run through the **htmlentities()** function, discussed in Chapter 5, "Using Strings." This function will prevent bad things from happening should the user manipulate the value of the cookie (which is easy to do).

Also note that two tabs (**\t**) and a newline (**\n**) are added to the **print** statements so that the resulting CSS code is formatted properly. Not that this affects the functionality of the page, but...

5. Repeat this process for the font color cookie:

```php
if (isset($_COOKIE['font_color'])) {
  print "\t\tcolor: #" .
  → htmlentities($_COOKIE
  → ['font_color']) . ";\n";
} else {
  print "\t\tcolor: #000;";
}
```

Here the CSS's **color** attribute is being assigned a value. The cookie itself is used the same as in Step 4.

6. Close the PHP section, complete the CSS code, and finish the HTML head:

```php
?>
    }
  </style>
</head>
```

7. Start the HTML body and create links to two other pages:

```html
<body>
<p><a href="customize.php">
→ Customize Your Settings</a></p>
<p><a href="reset.php">Reset Your
→ Settings</a></p>
```

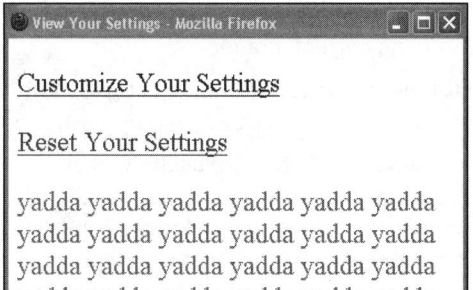

Customize Your Settings

Reset Your Settings

yadda yadda

A This page reflects the customized font choices made using the other PHP script.

B By viewing the source code of the page, you can also track how the CSS values change.

These two links take the user to two other PHP pages. The first, **customize. php**, has already been written and lets the user define their settings. The second, **reset.php**, will be written later in the chapter and lets the user delete their customized settings.

8. Add some text:

```
<p>yadda yadda yadda yadda yadda
yadda yadda yadda yadda yadda
yadda yadda yadda yadda yadda
yadda yadda yadda yadda yadda
yadda yadda yadda yadda yadda</p>
```

This text exists simply to show the effects of the cookie changes.

9. Complete the HTML page:

```
</body>
</html>
```

10. Save the file as **view_settings.php**, place it in the same directory as **customize.php**, and test it in your Web browser **A** by clicking the link on **customize.php**.

11. View the source of the page to see the resulting CSS code **B**.

12. Use the customize page to change your settings and return to this script.

Each submission of the form will create two new cookies storing the form values, thereby replacing the existing cookies.

TIP The value of a cookie is automatically encoded when it's sent and decoded on being received by the PHP page. The same is true of values sent by HTML forms.

Adding Parameters to a Cookie

Although passing just the **name** and **value** arguments to the **setcookie()** function will suffice for most of your cookie uses, you ought to be aware of the other arguments available. The function can take up to five more parameters, each of which limits the operation of the cookie:

```
setcookie(name, value, expiration,
  path, domain, secure, httponly);
```

The **expiration** argument is used to set a specific length of time for a cookie to exist. If it isn't specified, the cookie will continue to be functional until the user closes the browser. Normally, you set the expiration time by adding a particular number of minutes or hours to the current time. You can find the current time in PHP by using the **time()** function (it returns a timestamp; see Chapter 8). Therefore, this line of code sets the expiration time of the cookie to be one hour (60 seconds times 60 minutes) from the current moment:

```
setcookie(name, value, time()+3600);
```

Because the expiration time will be calculated as the value of **time()** plus 3600, that argument isn't put in quotes (you don't want to literally pass *time() + 3600* as the expiration but rather the result of that calculation).

The **path** and **domain** arguments are used to limit a cookie to a specific folder in a Web site (the path) or to a specific domain. Using the **path** option, you could limit a cookie to exist only while a user is in a specific subfolder of the domain:

```
setcookie(name, value, time()+3600,
  '/subfolder/');
```

Cookies are already specific to a domain, so the **domain** argument might be used to limit a cookie to a subdomain, such as **forum.example.com**.

```
setcookie(name, value, time()+3600, '',
  'forum.example.com');
```

Script 9.3 When you add the *expiration* arguments to the two cookies, the cookies will persist even after the user has closed out of and later returned to their browser.

```
1    <?php // Script 9.3 - customize.php #2
2
3    // Handle the form if it has been submitted:
4    if (isset($_POST['font_size'], $_POST['font_color'])) {
5
6        // Send the cookies:
7        setcookie('font_size', $_POST['font_size'], time()+10000000, '/');
8        setcookie('font_color', $_POST['font_color'], time()+10000000, '/');
9
10       // Message to be printed later:
11       $msg = '<p>Your settings have been entered! Click <a href="view_settings.php">here</a> to see
         them in action.</p>';
12
13   } // End of submitted IF.
14   ?><!DOCTYPE html PUBLIC "-//W3C//DTD XHTML 1.0 Transitional//EN"
15       "http://www.w3.org/TR/xhtml1/DTD/xhtml1-transitional.dtd">
16   <html xmlns="http://www.w3.org/1999/xhtml" xml:lang="en" lang="en">
```

code continues on next page

```
17    <head>
18        <meta http-equiv="Content-Type"
          content="text/html; charset=utf-8"/>
19        <title>Customize Your Settings
          </title>
20    </head>
21    <body>
22    <?php // If the cookies were sent, print
      a message.
23    if (isset($msg)) {
24        print $msg;
25    }
26    ?>
27
28    <p>Use this form to set your
      preferences:</p>
29
30    <form action="customize.php"
      method="post">
31        <select name="font_size">
32        <option value="">Font Size</option>
33        <option value="xx-small">xx-small
          </option>
34        <option value="x-small">x-small
          </option>
35        <option value="small">small
          </option>
36        <option value="medium">medium
          </option>
37        <option value="large">large
          </option>
38        <option value="x-large">x-large
          </option>
39        <option value="xx-large">xx-large
          </option>
40        </select>
41        <select name="font_color">
42        <option value="">Font Color</option>
43        <option value="999">Gray</option>
44        <option value="0c0">Green</option>
45        <option value="00f">Blue</option>
46        <option value="c00">Red</option>
47        <option value="000">Black</option>
48        </select>
49        <input type="submit" name="submit"
          value="Set My Preferences" />
50    </form>
51
52    </body>
53    </html>
```

The *secure* value dictates that a cookie should only be sent over a secure HTTPS connection. A value of 1 indicates that a secure connection must be used, whereas 0 indicates that a secure connection isn't necessary. You could ensure a secure cookie transmission for e-commerce sites:

```
setcookie('cart', '82ABC3012',
→ time()+3600, ', 'shop.example.com', 1);
```

As with all functions that take arguments, you must pass all the values in order. In the preceding example, if there's no need to specify (or limit) the path, you use empty quotes. With the **path** argument, you can also use a single slash (*/*) to indicate the root folder (i.e., no path restriction). By doing so, you maintain the proper number of arguments and can still indicate that an HTTPS connection is necessary.

The final argument—*httponly*—was added in PHP 5.2. It can be used to restrict access to the cookie (for example, preventing a cookie from being read using JavaScript) but isn't supported by all browsers.

Let's add an expiration date to the existing **customize.php** page so that the user's preferences will remain even after they've closed their browser and then returned to the site later.

To set a cookie's expiration date:

1. Open **customize.php** (Script 9.1) in your text editor or IDE.

2. Change the two **setcookie()** lines to read as follows (**Script 9.3**):

   ```
   setcookie('font_size', $_POST
   →['font_size'], time()+10000000,
   →'/', '', 0);
   setcookie('font_color', $_POST
   →['font_color'], time()+10000000,
   →'/', '', 0);
   ```

continues on next page

To make these cookies persist for a long time (specifically, for a couple of months), set the expiration time to be 10,000,000 seconds from now. While you're at it, set the **path** argument to the root of the site (*/*). Doing so may improve the consistency of sending these cookies across the various browsers.

Because the expiration date of the cookies is set months into the future, the user's preferences, which are stored in the cookies, will be valid even after the user has closed and reopened the browser. Without this expiration date, users would see the default font size and color and have to reassign their preferences with every new browser session.

3. Save the file, place it in the proper directory for your PHP-enabled server, and test it again in your Web browser **A** and **B**.

TIP Not all browsers acknowledge a cookie's adjusted expiration time when the cookie is being sent from your own computer (i.e., from *localhost*).

TIP Here are some general guidelines for what kind of expiration date to use with your cookies: If the cookie should last as long as the user browses through the site, don't set an expiration time. If the cookie should continue to exist after the user has closed and reopened the browser, set an expiration time that's weeks or months in the future. And if the cookie can constitute a security risk, set an expiration time of an hour or a fraction thereof so that the cookie doesn't continue to exist too long after a user has left the browser.

TIP For security purposes, you can set a 5- or 10-minute expiration time on a cookie and have the cookie re-sent with every new page the user visits. This way, the cookie will continue to persist as long as the user is active but will automatically die 5 or 10 minutes after the user's last action.

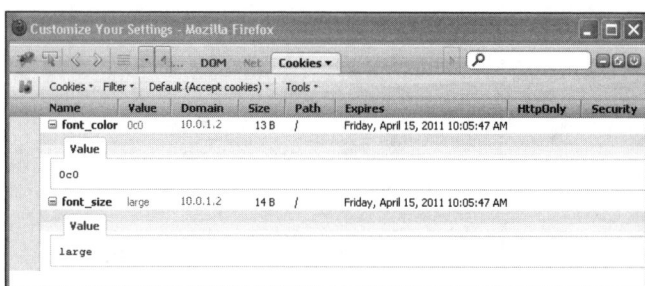

A The browser's cookie reporting tools (here, Firebug on Firefox) now reflects the cookie expiration dates.

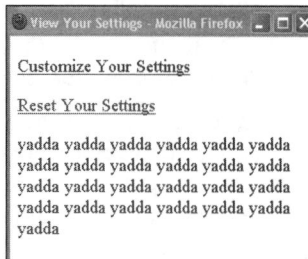

B The new cookie parameters don't adversely affect the functionality of the application.

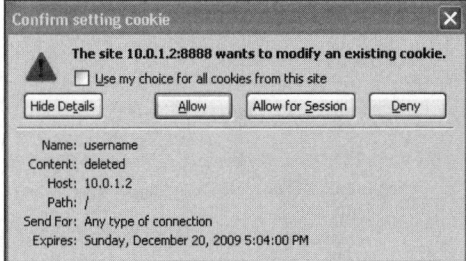

A How Firefox displays the cookie information when a deletion cookie is sent.

Deleting a Cookie

The final thing to know about cookies is how to delete them. Although a cookie automatically expires when the user's browser is closed or when the expiration date/time is met, sometimes you'll want to manually delete the cookie as well. For example, Web sites that have registered users and login capabilities generally delete any cookies when the user logs out.

The **setcookie()** function can take up to seven arguments, but only one is required—the name. If you send a cookie that consists of a name without a value, it will have the same effect as deleting the existing cookie of the same name. For example, to create the cookie *username*, you use this line:

```
setcookie('username', 'Larry');
```

To delete the *username* cookie, you code

```
setcookie('username', '');
```

or

```
setcookie('username', FALSE);
```

As an added precaution, you can also set an expiration date that's in the past **A**:

```
setcookie('username', FALSE,
→ time() - 600);
```

The only caveat when it comes to deleting a cookie is that you must use the same argument values that were used to set the cookie in the first place (aside from the value and expiration). For example, if you set a cookie while providing a **domain** value, you must also provide that value when deleting the cookie:

```
setcookie('user', 'larry', time() +
→ 3600, '', 'forums.example.com');
setcookie('user', '', time() -
→ 600, '', 'forums.example.com');
```

continues on next page

To demonstrate this feature, let's add a *reset* page to the Web application. This PHP script will destroy the sent cookies, so that the user's preferences are forgotten.

To delete a cookie:

1. Begin a new PHP script in your text editor or IDE, to be named **reset.php** (**Script 9.4**):

```
<?php // Script 9.4 - reset.php
```

2. Delete the existing cookies by sending blank cookies. Then complete the PHP code:

```
setcookie('font_size', '',
→ time() - 600, '/');
setcookie('font_color', '',
→ time() - 600, '/');
?>
```

These two lines send cookies named *font_size* and *font_color*, each with no value and an expiration time of 10 minutes ago. As you did when creating cookies, you must call the **setcookie()** function before anything else is sent to the Web browser.

3. Create the HTML head:

```
<!DOCTYPE html PUBLIC "-//W3C//DTD
→ XHTML 1.0 Transitional//EN"
  "http://www.w3.org/TR/xhtml1/
  → DTD/xhtml1-transitional.dtd">
<html xmlns="http://www.w3.org/
→ 1999/xhtml" xml:lang="en"
→ lang="en">
<head>
  <meta http-equiv="Content-Type"
  → content="text/html;
  → charset=utf-8"/>
  <title>Reset Your Settings
  → </title>
</head>
```

Script 9.4 To delete the existing cookies, send new cookies with the same names, empty values, and expirations in the past.

```
1    <?php // Script 9.4 - reset.php
2
3    // Delete the cookies:
4    setcookie('font_size', '', time()
     -  600, '/');
5    setcookie('font_color', '', time()
     - 600, '/');
6
7    ?><!DOCTYPE html PUBLIC "-//W3C//DTD XHTML
     1.0 Transitional//EN"
8        "http://www.w3.org/TR/xhtml1/DTD/
         xhtml1-transitional.dtd">
9    <html xmlns="http://www.w3.org/1999/
     xhtml" xml:lang="en" lang="en">
10   <head>
11       <meta http-equiv="Content-Type"
         content="text/html; charset=utf-8"/>
12       <title>Reset Your Settings</title>
13   </head>
14   <body>
15
16   <p>Your settings have been reset! Click
     <a href="view_settings.php">here</a> to
     go back to the main page.</p>
17
18   </body>
19   </html>
```

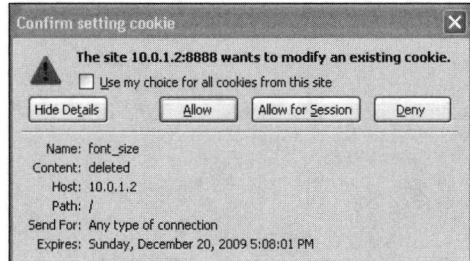

B When the `setcookie()` function is used with a name but no value, the existing cookie of that name is deleted. The expiration date in the past also guarantees proper destruction of the existing cookie.

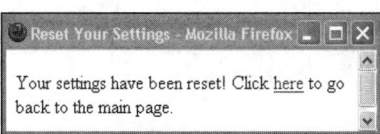

C The reset page sends two blank cookies and then displays this message.

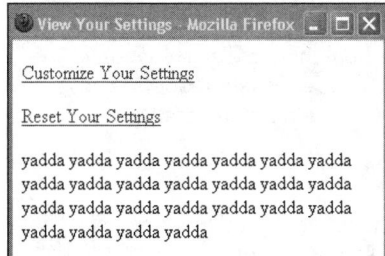

D After accessing the reset page, PHP destroys the cookies **B**, which will have the effect of resetting the `view_settings.php` page to its default formatting.

4. Add the page's body:

```
<body>
<p>Your settings have been reset!
→ Click <a href="view_settings.php">
→ here</a> to go back to the main
→ page.</p>
</body>
```

The body of this script merely tells users that their settings have been reset. A link is then provided to return to the main page.

5. Complete the HTML:

```
</html>
```

6. Save the page as `reset.php`, place it in the proper directory for your PHP-enabled server, and test it in your Web browser **B**, **C**, and **D**.

To test this page, either click the appropriate link in `view_settings.php` (Script 9.2) or just go to this page directly.

TIP Just as creating a cookie doesn't take effect until another page is loaded, deleting a cookie doesn't take effect until another page. This is to say that you can delete a cookie on a page but still access that cookie on it (because the cookie was received by the page before the delete cookie was sent).

TIP Just as creating cookies has mixed results using different browsers, the same applies to deleting them. Test your scripts on many browsers and play with the `setcookie()` settings to ensure the best all-around compatibility.

What Are Sessions?

A session, like a cookie, provides a way for you to track data for a user over a series of pages. The difference between the two—and this is significant—is that a cookie stores the data on the client (in the Web browser), whereas the session data is stored on the server. Because of this difference, sessions have numerous benefits over cookies:

- Sessions are generally more secure, because the data isn't transmitted back and forth between the client and server repeatedly.

- Sessions allow you to store more information than you can in a cookie.

- Sessions can be made to work even if the user doesn't accept cookies in their browser.

When you start a session, PHP generates a random session ID. Each user's session will have its own session ID, corresponding to the name of the text file on the server that stores the user's session data (**Script 9.5**). So that every PHP script on a site can associate the same session data with a particular user, the session ID must be tracked as well. By default, this session ID is sent to the Web browser as a cookie **Ⓐ**. Subsequent PHP pages will use this cookie to retrieve the session ID and access the session information.

Over the next few pages, you'll see just how easy sessions are to work with in PHP.

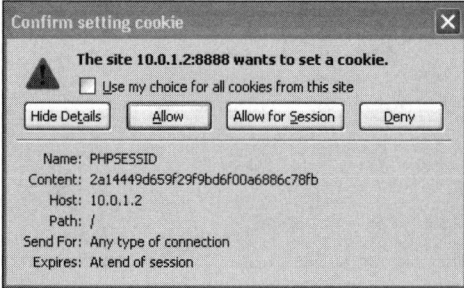

Ⓐ A session cookie being sent to the Web browser.

Script 9.5 How session data is stored in a file on the server.

```
1    email|s:14:"me@example.com";
     loggedin|i:1292883103;
```

Choosing Between Sessions and Cookies

Sessions have many benefits over cookies, but there are still reasons why you would use the latter. Cookies have these advantages over sessions:

- Marginally easier to create and retrieve

- Require slightly less work from the server

- Normally persist over a longer period of time

As a rule of thumb, you should use cookies in situations where security is less of an issue and only a minimum of data is being stored. If security's a concern and there will be oodles of information to remember, you're best off with sessions. Understand, though, that using sessions may require a little more effort in writing your scripts.

Creating a Session

Creating, accessing, or deleting a session begins with the **session_start()** function. This function will attempt to send a cookie the first time a session is started, so it absolutely must be called prior to any HTML or white space being sent to the Web browser. Therefore, on pages that use sessions, you should call the **session_start()** function as one of the very first lines in your script:

```php
<?php
session_start();
```

The first time a session is started, a random session ID is generated and a cookie is sent to the Web browser with a name of **PHPSESSID** (the session name) and a value like **4bcc48dc87cb4b54d63f99da23fb41e1** (see Ⓐ in the previous section).

Once the session has been started, you can record data to it by assigning values to the **$_SESSION** array:

```php
$_SESSION['first_name'] = 'Sam';
$_SESSION['age'] = 4;
```

Unlike with other arrays you might use in PHP, you should always treat this array as an associative array. In other words, you should explicitly use strings for the keys, such as *first_name* and *age*.

Each time a value is assigned to the **$_SESSION** array, PHP writes that data to a temporary file stored on the server (see Script 9.5).

To begin, you'll rewrite the login script from Chapter 8, this time storing the email address in a session.

To create a session:

1. Open **login.php** (Script 8.13) in your text editor or IDE.

2. Before the **ob_end_clean()** line, add the following (**Script 9.6**):

```
session_start();
$_SESSION['email'] = $_POST['email'];
$_SESSION['loggedin'] = time();
```

To store values in a session, begin by calling the **session_start()** function. Although you normally have to call this function first thing in a script (because it may attempt to send a cookie), that's not required here because the header file for this script begins output buffering (see Chapter 8).

The session first stores the user's submitted email address in **$_SESSION ['email']**. Then the timestamp of when the user logged in is assigned to **$_SESSION['loggedin']**. This value is determined by calling the **time()** function, which returns the number of seconds that have elapsed since the *epoch* (midnight on January 1, 1970).

3. Save the file as **login.php** and place it in the appropriate directory on your PHP-enabled computer.

This script should be placed in the same directory used in Chapter 8, as it requires some of those other files.

Script 9.6 This script stores two values in the session and then redirects the user to another page, where the session values can be accessed.

```
1   <?php // Script 9.6 - login.php #3
2   /* This page lets people log into the
    site (almost!). */
3
4   // Set the page title and include the
    header file:
5   define('TITLE', 'Login');
6   include('templates/header.html');
7
8   // Print some introductory text:
9   print '<h2>Login Form</h2>
10      <p>Users who are logged in can
        take advantage of certain features
        like this, that, and the other
        thing.</p>';
11
12  // Check if the form has been
    submitted:
13  if ($_SERVER['REQUEST_METHOD'] == 'POST') {
14
15      // Handle the form:
16      if ( (!empty($_POST['email'])) &&
        (!empty($_POST['password'])) ) {
17
18          if ( (strtolower($_POST
            ['email']) == 'me@example.com')
            && ($_POST['password'] ==
            'testpass') ) { // Correct!
19
20              // Do session stuff:
21              session_start();
22              $_SESSION['email'] =
                $_POST['email'];
23              $_SESSION['loggedin'] =
                time();
24
25              // Redirect the user to the
                welcome page!
26              ob_end_clean();
                // Destroy the buffer!
27              header ('Location: welcome.php');
28              exit();
29
30          } else { // Incorrect!
31
32              print '<p>The submitted email
                address and password do not
                match those on file!<br />Go
                back and try again.</p>';
```

code continues on next page

Script 9.6 *continued*

```
33
34          }
35
36      } else { // Forgot a field.
37
38          print '<p>Please make sure you
            enter both an email address and
            a password!<br />Go back and try
            again.</p>';
39
40      }
41
42  } else { // Display the form.
43
44      print '<form action="login.php"
        method="post">
45      <p>Email Address: <input type="text"
        name="email" size="20" /></p>
46      <p>Password: <input type="password"
        name="password" size="20" /></p>
47      <p><input type="submit" name=
        "submit" value="Log In!" /></p>
48      </form>';
49
50  }
51
52  include('templates/footer.html');
    // Need the footer.
53  ?>
```

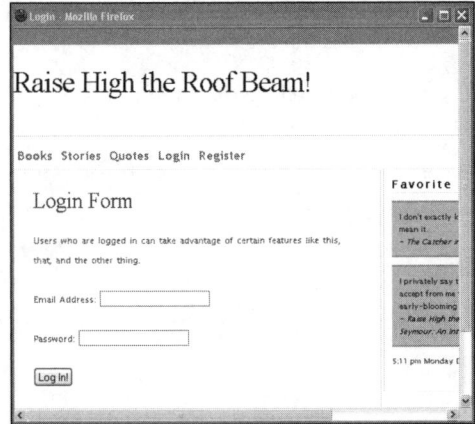

Ⓐ The login form.

4. Load the form in your Web browser to ensure that it has no errors **Ⓐ**.

Don't complete and submit the login form yet, as the welcome page needs to be updated prior to logging in.

TIP The `php.ini` configuration file includes many session-related settings that you can tinker with if you have administrative-level control over your server. Open the `php.ini` file in a text editor and see the manual for more information.

TIP You can also alter some of the session settings using the `ini_set()` function.

TIP The `session_name()` function lets you change the name of the session (instead of using the default *PHPSESSID*). It must be used before every `session_start()` call, like so:

```
session_name('YourVisit');
session_start();
```

TIP The `session_set_cookie_params()` function alters the session cookie settings, like the expiration time, the path, and the domain.

TIP The constant SID, short for *Session ID*, stores a string in the format *name=ID*. An example is *PHPSESSID=4bcc48dc87cb4b54d 63f99da23fb41e1*.

TIP You can store any type of value—number, string, array, or object—or any combination thereof in your sessions.

Accessing Session Variables

Now that you've stored values in a session, you need to know how to access them. The first step is to invoke the **session_start()** function. This is necessary on every page that will make use of sessions, whether it's creating a new session or accessing an existing one.

From there it's simply a matter of referencing the **$_SESSION** variable as you would any other array. With this in mind, you'll write another welcome page—similar to the one from Chapter 8—that accesses the stored *email* and *loggedin* values.

To access session variables:

1. Create a new PHP document in your text editor or IDE, to be named **welcome.php** (Script 9.7):

   ```php
   <?php // Script 9.7 - welcome.php
   ```

2. Begin the session:

   ```php
   session_start();
   ```

   Even when you're accessing session values, you should call the **session_start()** function before any data is sent to the Web browser.

3. Define a page title, and include the HTML header:

   ```php
   define('TITLE', 'Welcome to the
   →J.D. Salinger Fan Club!');
   include('templates/header.html');
   ```

   Because this page uses the same template system developed in Chapter 8, it also uses the same header system.

Script 9.7 You can access stored session values using the **$_SESSION** array, as long as your script uses **session_start()** first.

```php
1   <?php // Script 9.7 - welcome.php #2
2   /* This is the welcome page. The user is
    redirected here
3   after they successfully log in. */
4
5   // Need the session:
6   session_start();
7
8   // Set the page title and include the
    header file:
9   define('TITLE', 'Welcome to the J.D.
    Salinger Fan Club!');
10  include('templates/header.html');
11
12  // Print a greeting:
13  print '<h2>Welcome to the J.D.
    Salinger Fan Club!</h2>';
14  print '<p>Hello, ' . $_SESSION
    ['email'] . '!</p>';
15
16  // Print how long they've been
    logged in:
17  date_default_timezone_set('America/
    New_York');
18  print '<p>You have been logged
    in since: ' . date('g:i a',
    $_SESSION['loggedin']) . '</p>';
19
20  // Make a logout link:
21  print '<p><a href="logout.php">Click here
    to logout.</a></p>';
22
23  include('templates/footer.html');
    // Need the footer.
24  ?>
```

4. Greet the user by email address:

```
print '<h2>Welcome to the J.D.
→ Salinger Fan Club!</h2>';
print '<p>Hello, ' . $_SESSION
→ ['email'] . '!</p>';
```

To access the stored user's address, refer to **$_SESSION['email']**. Here, that value is concatenated to the rest of the string that's being printed out.

5. Show how long the user has been logged in:

```
date_default_timezone_set
→ ('America/New_York');
print '<p>You have been logged
→ in since: ' . date('g:i a',
→ $_SESSION['loggedin']) . '</p>';
```

To show how long the user has been logged in, refer to the **$_SESSION ['loggedin']** variable. By using this as the second argument sent to the **date()** function, along with the appropriate formatting parameters, you make the PHP script create text like *11:22 pm*.

Before using the **date()** function, however, you need to set the default time zone (this is also discussed in Chapter 8). If you want, after setting the time zone here, you can remove the use of the same function from the footer file.

6. Complete the content:

```
print '<p><a href="logout.php">
→ Click here to logout.</a></p>';
```

The next script will provide logout functionality, so a link to it is added here.

7. Include the HTML footer, and complete the HTML page:

```
include('templates/footer.html');
?>
```

8. Save the file as **welcome.php**, place it in the proper directory for your PHP-enabled server, and test it (starting with **login.php**, Script 9.6) in your Web browser **A**.

TIP To see whether a particular session variable exists, use isset($_SESSION['*var*']) as you would to check if any other variable is set.

TIP Always remember that the data stored in a session is being stored as plain text in an openly readable text file. Don't be cavalier about what gets stored in a session and never store really sensitive information, such as credit card data, there.

TIP For added security, data can be encrypted prior to storing it in a session and decrypted upon retrieval. Doing so requires the Mcrypt library and more advanced PHP knowledge, however.

Welcome to the J.D. Salinger Fan Club!

Hello, me@example.com!

You have been logged in since: 5:11 pm

Click here to logout.

A After successfully logging in (using *me@ example.com* and *testpass* in the form), the user is redirected to this page, which greets them using the session values.

Deleting a Session

It's important to know how to delete a session, just as it's important to know how to delete a cookie: Eventually you'll want to get rid of the data you've stored. Session data exists in two places—in an array during the execution of the script and in a text file, so you'll need to delete both. But first you must begin with the **session_start()** function, as always:

```
session_start();
```

Then, you clear the session variables by resetting the **$_SESSION** array:

```
$_SESSION = array();
```

Finally, remove the session data from the server (where it's stored in temporary files). To do this, use

```
session_destroy();
```

With that in mind, let's write **logout.php**, which will delete the session, effectively logging out the user.

To delete a session:

1. Start a new PHP script in your text editor or IDE, to be named **logout.php** (Script 9.8).

   ```
   <?php // Script 9.8 - logout.php
   ```

2. Begin the session:

   ```
   session_start();
   ```

   Remember that you can't delete a session until you activate the session using this function.

3. Reset the session array:

   ```
   $_SESSION = array();
   ```

   As explained in Chapter 7, "Using Arrays," the **array()** function creates a new, empty array. By assigning the result of this function call to **$_SESSION**, all the existing key-value pairs in **$_SESSION** will be erased.

Script 9.8 Deleting a session is a three-step process: start the session, reset the array, and destroy the session data.

```
1   <?php // Script 9.8 - logout.php
2   /* This is the logout page. It
    destroys the session information. */
3
4   // Need the session:
5   session_start();
6
7   // Delete the session variable:
8   unset($_SESSION);
9
10  // Reset the session array:
11  $_SESSION = array();
12
13  // Define a page title and include the
    header:
14  define('TITLE', 'Logout');
15  include('templates/header.html');
16
17  ?>
18
19  <h2>Welcome to the J.D. Salinger Fan
    Club!</h2>
20  <p>You are now logged out.</p>
21  <p>Thank you for using this site. We
    hope that you liked it.<br />
22  Blah, blah, blah...
23  Blah, blah, blah...</p>
24
25  <?php include('templates/
    footer.html'); ?>
```

Welcome to the J.D. Salinger Fan
Club!

You are now logged out.

Thank you for using this site. We hope that you liked it.
Blah, blah, blah... Blah, blah, blah...

Ⓐ The logout page destroys the session data.

4. Destroy the session data on the server:

```
session_destroy();
```

This step tells PHP to remove the actual session file on the server.

5. Include the HTML header, and complete this PHP section:

```
define('TITLE', 'Logout');
include('templates/header.html');
?>
```

6. Make the page content:

```
<h2>Welcome to the J.D. Salinger
Fan Club!</h2>
<p>You are now logged out.</p>
<p>Thank you for using this site.
We hope that you liked it.<br />
Blah, blah, blah...
Blah, blah, blah...</p>
```

7. Include the HTML footer:

```
<?php include('templates/footer.
html'); ?>
```

8. Save the file as **logout.php**, place it in the proper directory for your PHP-enabled server, and test it in your Web browser by clicking the link in **welcome.php Ⓐ**.

TIP To delete an individual session value, use:

```
unset($_SESSION['var']);
```

TIP The PHP module on the server will automatically perform *garbage collection* based on settings in its configuration. PHP uses garbage collection to manually delete session files from the server, with the assumption that they're no longer needed.

TIP You can have PHP use sessions without cookies, in which case the session ID must be appended to every link in your site (so that each page receives the session ID). If you enable the use_trans_sid setting (in the php.ini file), PHP will handle this for you.

Review and Pursue

If you have any problems with the review questions or the pursue prompts, turn to the book's supporting forum (www. LarryUllman.com/forum/).

Review

- Where does a cookie store data? Where does a session store data? Which is generally more secure?

- Name two debugging techniques when trying to solve issues involving cookies.

- How do the **path** and **domain** arguments to the **setcookie()** function affect the accessibility of the cookie?

- How do you delete a cookie?

- What function must every page call if it needs to assign or access session data?

- Why do sessions also use cookies (by default)?

Pursue

- Install the Firebug extension for Firefox, if you have not already. Install Firefox first, if you haven't!

- Look up the PHP manual page for the **setcookie()** function. Review the information and user comments there for added instructions on cookies.

- Rewrite **customize.php** so that the script also applies the user's preferences. Hint: You need to take into account the fact that the cookies aren't available immediately after they've been set. Instead, you would write the CSS code using the **$_GET** values after the form has been submitted, the **$_COOKIE** values upon first arriving at the page (if the cookies exist), and the default values otherwise.

- Make the form in **customize.php** *sticky*, so that it reflects the user's current choices.

- Rewrite **welcome.php** so that the **print** statement that greets the user by email address uses double quotation marks.

- For an added challenge, rewrite **welcome.php** so that the **print** statement that indicates how long the user has been logged in also uses double quotation marks. Hint: You'll need to use a variable.

- Rewrite the last three scripts so that the session uses a custom name.

Creating Functions

Throughout this book, you've used dozens of functions that provide much-needed functionality, such as **date()**, **setcookie()**, and **number_format()**. Whereas those functions have already been defined by PHP, here you'll be creating your own. However, once created, functions you've written and built-in PHP functions are used in the same manner.

Creating functions can save you oodles of time as a programmer. In fact, they constitute a strong step in the process of creating Web applications and building a solid library of PHP code to use in future projects.

In this chapter, you'll see how to write your own functions that perform specific tasks. After that, you'll learn how to pass information to a function, use default values in a function, and have a function return a value. You'll also learn how functions and variables work together.

In This Chapter

Creating and Using Simple Functions	258
Creating and Calling Functions That Take Arguments	265
Setting Default Argument Values	271
Creating and Using Functions That Return a Value	274
Understanding Variable Scope	279
Review and Pursue	286

Creating and Using Simple Functions

As you program, you'll discover that you use certain sections of code frequently, either within a single script or over the course of several scripts. Placing these routines into a self-defined function can save you time and make your programming easier, especially as your Web sites become more complex. Once you create a function, the actions of that function take place each time the function is called, just as **print** sends text to the browser with each use.

The syntax for creating a user-defined function is

```
function function_name () {
      statement(s);
}
```

For example:

```
function whatever() {
      print 'whatever';
}
```

You can use roughly the same naming conventions for functions as you do for variables, just without the initial dollar sign. Second to that is the suggestion that you create *meaningful* function names, just as you ought to write representative variable names (**create_header** would be a better function name than **function1**). Remember not to use spaces, though— doing so constitutes two separate words for the function name, which will result in error messages (the underscore is a logical replacement for the space). Unlike variables, function names in PHP are *not case-sensitive*, but you should still stick with a consistent naming scheme.

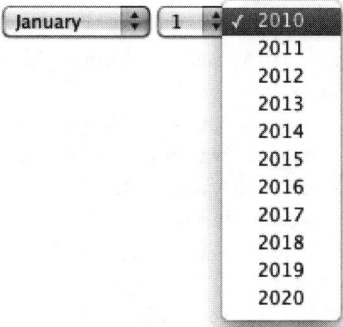

A These pull-down menus are created by a user-defined PHP function.

Any valid PHP code can go within the statement(s) area of the function, including calls to other functions. There is also no limit on the number of statements a function contains, but make sure each statement ends with a semicolon, just as you would within the rest of the PHP script. Functions can also contain any combination of control structures: conditionals and loops.

The exact formatting of a function isn't important as long as the requisite elements are there. These elements include the word *function*, the function's name, the opening and closing parentheses, the opening and closing brackets, and the statement(s). It's conventional to indent a function's statement(s) from the `function` keyword line, for clarity's sake, as you would with a loop or conditional. In any case, select a format style that you like (which is both syntactically correct and logically sound) and stick to it.

You call (or invoke) the function by referring to it just as you do any built-in function. The line of code

```
whatever();
```

will cause the statement part of the previously defined function—the `print` command—to be executed.

Let's begin by creating a function that generates month, day, and year pull-down menus for a form **A**.

To create and call a basic function:

1. Start a new PHP document in your text editor or IDE, to be named **menus.php** (Script 10.1):

```
<!DOCTYPE html PUBLIC "-//W3C//DTD
→ XHTML 1.0 Transitional//EN"
  "http://www.w3.org/TR/xhtml1/
  → DTD/xhtml1-transitional.dtd">
<html xmlns="http://www.w3.org/
→ 1999/xhtml" xml:lang="en"
→ lang="en">
<head>
  <meta http-equiv="content-type"
  → content="text/html;
  → charset=utf-8" />
  <title>Date Menus</title>
</head>
<body>
```

2. Begin the PHP section:

```
<?php // Script 10.1 - menus.php
```

3. Start defining a function:

```
function make_date_menus() {
```

The name of this function is *make_date_menus*, which is both descriptive of what the function does and easy to remember.

4. Create the month pull-down menu:

```
$months = array (1 => 'January',
→ 'February', 'March', 'April',
→ 'May', 'June', 'July', 'August',
→ 'September', 'October',
→ 'November', 'December');
print '<select name="month">';
foreach ($months as $key =>
→ $value) {
  print "\n<option value=
  → \"$key\">$value</option>";
}
print '</select>';
```

To generate a list of months, first create an array of the month names, indexed numerically beginning at 1 for *January*. When you specify the index for the first array element, the others will follow sequentially without the need to be explicit in naming them.

After the array has been created, the initial **select** tag is printed out. Then, a **foreach** loop runs through the **$months** array. For each element in the array, the HTML **option** tag is printed, using each element's key (the numbers 1 through 12) as the **option** value and each element's value (*January* through *December*) as the displayed text. Each line is also preceded by a newline character (**\n**) so that each option ends up on its own line within the HTML source.

continues on page 262

Script 10.1 The function defined in this script creates three pull-down menus for a form.

```
1   <!DOCTYPE html PUBLIC "-//W3C//DTD XHTML 1.0 Transitional//EN"
2       "http://www.w3.org/TR/xhtml1/DTD/xhtml1-transitional.dtd">
3   <html xmlns="http://www.w3.org/1999/xhtml" xml:lang="en" lang="en">
4   <head>
5       <meta http-equiv="content-type" content="text/html; charset=utf-8" />
6       <title>Date Menus</title>
7   </head>
8   <body>
9   <?php // Script 10.1 - menus.php
10  /* This script defines and calls a function. */
11
12  // This function makes three pull-down menus for the months, days, and years.
13  function make_date_menus() {
14
15      // Array to store the months:
16      $months = array (1 => 'January', 'February', 'March', 'April', 'May', 'June', 'July', 'August',
         'September', 'October', 'November', 'December');
17
18      // Make the month pull-down menu:
19      print '<select name="month">';
20      foreach ($months as $key => $value) {
21          print "\n<option value=\"$key\">$value</option>";
22      }
23      print '</select>';
24
25      // Make the day pull-down menu:
26      print '<select name="day">';
27      for ($day = 1; $day <= 31; $day++) {
28          print "\n<option value=\"$day\">$day</option>";
29      }
30      print '</select>';
31
32      // Make the year pull-down menu:
33      print '<select name="year">';
34      $start_year = date('Y');
35      for ($y = $start_year; $y <= ($start_year + 10); $y++) {
36          print "\n<option value=\"$y\">$y</option>";
37      }
38      print '</select>';
39
40  } // End of make_date_menus() function.
41
42  // Make the form:
43  print '<form action="" method="post">';
44  make_date_menus();
45  print '</form>';
46
47  ?>
48  </body>
49  </html>
```

5. Create the day pull-down menu:

```php
print '<select name="day">';
for ($day = 1; $day <= 31; $day++) {
  print "\n<option value=
    \"$day\">$day</option>";
}
print '</select>';
```

The day menu is a lot easier to create. To do so, use a simple **for** loop, running through the numbers 1 through 31.

6. Create the year pull-down menu:

```php
print '<select name="year">';
$start_year = date('Y');
for ($y = $start_year; $y
  <= ($start_year + 10); $y++) {
  print "\n<option value=
    \"$y\">$y</option>";
}
print '</select>';
```

To create the year pull-down menu, start by using the **date()** function to get the current year. Then create options for this year plus the next 10, using a **for** loop.

7. Close the function:

```php
} // End of make_date_menus()
  function.
```

When you're creating functions, it's easy to create parse errors by forgetting the closing curly bracket. You may want to add comments to help you remember this final step.

8. Make the **form** tags, and call the function:

```php
print '<form action="" method=
  "post">';
make_date_menus();
print '</form>';
```

The **print** statements are used to create the HTML **form** tags. Without a form, the date pull-down menus won't appear properly in the script.

Once you've created your function, you simply have to call it by name (being careful to use the exact spelling) to make the function work. Be sure to include the parentheses as well.

9. Complete the PHP and HTML:

```
?>
</body>
</html>
```

10. Save the file as **menus.php**, place it in the proper directory for your PHP-enabled server, and run it in your Web browser Ⓐ.

11. If you want, check out the HTML source of the page to see what was dynamically generated Ⓑ.

continues on next page

```
<form action="" method="post"><select name="month">
<option value="1">January</option>
<option value="2">February</option>
<option value="3">March</option>
<option value="4">April</option>
<option value="5">May</option>
<option value="6">June</option>
<option value="7">July</option>
<option value="8">August</option>
<option value="9">September</option>
<option value="10">October</option>
<option value="11">November</option>
<option value="12">December</option></select><select name="day">
<option value="1">1</option>
<option value="2">2</option>
<option value="3">3</option>
<option value="4">4</option>
<option value="5">5</option>
<option value="6">6</option>
<option value="7">7</option>
<option value="8">8</option>
<option value="9">9</option>
```

Ⓑ The source of the page shows the HTML created by the **print** statements in the **make_date_menus()** function.

TIP If you see a *"Call to undefined function: some_function..."* error message, it means you're trying to call a function that doesn't exist **C**. If you're trying to call a PHP function, either you misspelled the name or it's not supported on your version of PHP. Check the PHP manual for more. If you're calling a user-defined function when you see this error, either it hasn't been defined or you've misspelled it. Recheck your spelling in both the definition of the function and its usage to see if you made a mistake.

TIP The `function_exists()` function returns TRUE or FALSE based on whether a function exists in PHP. This applies to both user-defined functions and those that can be built into PHP:

```
if (function_exists('some_function'))
→ { …
```

TIP Although you aren't required to, I recommend that you habitually define your functions at the beginning of a script (or in an included file), rather than at the end of the script.

TIP Some people prefer this syntax for laying out their functions:

```
function function_name()
{
    statement(s);
}
```

TIP User-defined functions add extra memory requirements to your PHP scripts, so you should be judicious in using them. If you find that your function merely calls another PHP function or has but one line of code, it's probably not the best use of this capability.

> **Fatal error**: Call to undefined function make_date_menu() in /Users/larryullman/Sites/phpvqs4/menus.php on line **44**

C This error means that the PHP script does not have access to a function defined under the given name. In this case, the problem is due to a missing "s" in the function call: `make_date_menus()` vs. `make_date_menu()`.

Creating and Calling Functions That Take Arguments

Although being able to create a simple function is useful, writing one that takes input and does something with that input is even better. The input a function takes is called an *argument* (or a *parameter*). This is a concept you've seen before: the **sort()** function takes an array as an argument, which the function then sorts.

The syntax for writing functions that take arguments is as follows:

```
function function_name($arg1,
→ $arg2, …){
    statement(s);
}
```

The function's arguments are in the form of variables that are assigned the values sent to the function when you call it. The variables are defined using the same naming rules as any other variable in PHP:

```
function make_full_name($first,
→ $last) {
    print $first . ' ' . $last;
}
```

Functions that take input are called much like those that don't—you just need to remember to pass along the necessary values. You can do this either by passing variables:

```
make_full_name($fn, $ln);
```

or by sending literal values, as in

```
make_full_name('Larry', 'Ullman');
```

or some combination thereof:

```
make_full_name('Larry', $ln);
```

continues on next page

The important thing to note is that arguments are passed quite literally: The first variable in the function definition is assigned the first value in the call line, the second function variable is assigned the second call value, and so forth **A**. Functions aren't smart enough to intuitively understand how you meant the values to be associated. This is also true if you fail to pass a value, in which case the function will assume that value is null (*null* isn't the mathematical 0, which is actually a value, but closer to the idea of the word *nothing*). The same thing applies if a function takes four arguments and you pass three—the fourth will be null, which may create an error **B**.

```php
function make_full_name($first, $last) {
    print $first . ' ' . $last;
}

make_full_name($fn, $ln);

make_full_name('Larry', 'Ullman');

make_full_name('Larry', $ln);
```

A How values in function calls are assigned to function arguments.

Warning: Missing argument 2 for make_text_input(), called in /Users /larryullman/Sites/phpvqs4/sticky1.php on line 38 and defined in **/Users /larryullman/Sites/phpvqs4/sticky1.php** on line **14**

B As with any function (user-defined or built into PHP), passing an incorrect number of arguments when calling it yields warnings.

C These three form elements are created by a user-defined function.

D The form elements reflect the values entered by the user.

To demonstrate functions that take arguments, let's create a more interesting example. In Chapter 8, "Creating Web Applications," you learned how to make forms "sticky": having them remember their values from previous submissions. The code for a sticky text input might be

```
First Name: <input type="text"
→ name="first_name" size="20"
→ value="<?php if (isset($_POST
→ ['first_name'])) { print
→ htmlspecialchars($_POST
→ ['first_name']); } ?>" />
```

Since many forms, such as **register.php** from Chapter 8, repeatedly use similar code, you have a good candidate for a user-defined function.

This next script will define and call a function that creates sticky text inputs. The function will take one argument for the input's name, and another for the input's label (its textual prompt). The function will be called multiple times by the script to generate multiple inputs **C**. Upon form submission, the previously entered values will be remembered **D**.

To create and call a function that takes an argument:

1. Start a new PHP document in your text editor or IDE, to be named **sticky1.php** (**Script 10.2**):

```
<!DOCTYPE html PUBLIC "-//W3C//DTD
→ XHTML 1.0 Transitional//EN"
   "http://www.w3.org/TR/xhtml1/
   → DTD/xhtml1-transitional.dtd">
<html xmlns="http://www.w3.org
→ /1999/xhtml" xml:lang="en"
→ lang="en">
<head>
  <meta http-equiv="content-type"
  → content="text/html;
  → charset=utf-8" />
  <title>Sticky Text Inputs
  → </title>
</head>
<body>
```

2. Begin the PHP section:

```
<?php // Script 10.2 - sticky1.php
```

3. Start defining a function:

```
function make_text_input($name,
→ $label) {
```

The **make_text_input()** function requires two arguments, which will be assigned to the **$name** and **$label** variables.

4. Print an opening paragraph and a **label** tag:

```
print '<p><label>' . $label . ': ';
```

The code being generated by this function will be essentially like that just indicated (and in Chapter 8), but it will be wrapped in a paragraph tag and the input's label will be formally placed within **label** tags. The value of the label (e.g., *First Name*) will be passed to the function when the function is called.

continues on page 270

Script 10.2 The `make_text_input()` function takes two arguments, for the input's name and label.

```
1   <!DOCTYPE html PUBLIC "-//W3C//DTD XHTML 1.0 Transitional//EN"
2       "http://www.w3.org/TR/xhtml1/DTD/xhtml1-transitional.dtd">
3   <html xmlns="http://www.w3.org/1999/xhtml" xml:lang="en" lang="en">
4   <head>
5       <meta http-equiv="content-type" content="text/html; charset=utf-8" />
6       <title>Sticky Text Inputs</title>
7   </head>
8   <body>
9   <?php // Script 10.2 - sticky1.php
10  /* This script defines and calls a function that creates a sticky text input. */
11
12  // This function makes a sticky text input.
13  // This function requires two arguments be passed to it.
14  function make_text_input($name, $label) {
15
16      // Begin a paragraph and a label:
17      print '<p><label>' . $label . ': ';
18
19      // Begin the input:
20      print '<input type="text" name="' . $name . '" size="20" ';
21
22      // Add the value:
23      if (isset($_POST[$name])) {
24          print ' value="' . htmlspecialchars($_POST[$name]) . '"';
25      }
26
27      // Complete the input, the label and the paragraph:
28      print ' /></label></p>';
29
30  } // End of make_text_input() function.
31
32  // Make the form:
33  print '<form action="" method="post">';
34
35  // Create some text inputs:
36  make_text_input('first_name', 'First Name');
37  make_text_input('last_name', 'Last Name');
38  make_text_input('email', 'Email Address');
39
40  print '<input type="submit" name="submit" value="Register!" /></form>';
41
42  ?>
43  </body>
44  </html>
```

5. Begin the text input:

```
print '<input type="text"
→ name="' . $name . '" size="20" ';
```

The PHP **print** statement just creates the HTML **input** tag, but the value of the tag's **name** attribute will come from the **$name** variable (assigned a value when the function is called, such as *first_name*).

6. If applicable, add the input's preset value:

```
if (isset($_POST[$name])) {
  print ' value="' .
  vhtmlspecialchars($_POST
  → [$name]) . '"';
}
```

The code in Step 5 didn't actually complete the text input (the closing **/>** wasn't created), so another clause—specifically **value="whatever"**—can still be added. But that clause should only be added if **$_POST['input_name']** is set, so the conditional checks for that. As with the code in Chapter 8, the value is printed only after being run through **htmlspecialchars()**.

7. Complete the input, the label, the paragraph, and the function:

```
print ' /></label></p>';
} // End of make_text_input()
→ function.
```

8. Make the **form** tags and call the function:

```
print '<form action=""
→ method="post">';
make_text_input('first_name',
→ 'First Name');
```

It's important that the form uses the POST method, as the function checks for existing values in **$_POST**. You can actually omit an **action** value, in which case the form will automatically be submitted back to the same page.

To create a "first name" input, call the **make_text_input()** function, passing it the name the input should have and an appropriate label.

9. Create two more inputs:

```
make_text_input('last_name', 'Last
→ Name');
make_text_input('email', 'Email
→ Address');
```

Now the script has used the same function three times, in three different ways. The result will be three distinct text inputs.

10. Complete the form:

```
print '<input type="submit"
→ name="submit" value=
→ "Register!" /></form>';
```

The form needs a submit button in order to test the sticky feature.

11. Complete the PHP and HTML:

```
?>
</body>
</html>
```

12. Save the file as **sticky1.php**, place it in the proper directory for your PHP-enabled server, and run it in your Web browser **C** and **D**.

TIP You can define as many functions as you want, not just one per script as the examples in this chapter portray.

TIP There are no limits on how many arguments a function can take.

TIP Once you've defined your own functions like this, you can place them in an external file and then require that file when you need access to the functions.

Setting Default Argument Values

PHP allows functions to have *default argument values*: just assign a value to the argument in the function definition:

```
function greeting($who = 'world') {
    print "<p>Hello, $who!</p>";
}
```

Such a function will use the preset values unless it receives a value that then overwrites the default. In other words, by setting a default value for an argument, you render that particular argument optional when calling the function. You'd set an argument's default value if you wanted to assume a certain value but still allow for other possibilities **Ⓐ**:

```
greeting();
greeting('Zoe');
```

(Note: This isn't really a good use of a user-defined function, or a default argument value, but it's easily understood as an example.)

The default arguments must always be written after the other standard arguments (those without default values). This is because PHP directly assigns values to arguments in the order they're received from the call line. Thus, it isn't possible to omit a value for the first argument but include one for the second. For example, suppose you have

```
function calculate_total($qty,
→ $price = 20.00, $tax = 0.06) {...
```

If you call the function with the line

```
calculate_total(3, 0.07);
```

with the intention of setting **$qty** to 3, leaving **$price** at 20.00, and changing the **$tax** to 0.07, there will be problems.

The end result will be that **$qty** is set to 3, **$price** is set to 0.07, and **$tax** remains at 0.06 **Ⓑ**, which isn't the desired outcome. The proper way to achieve that effect would be to code

```
calculate_total(3, 20.00, 0.07);
```

Let's rework the **make_text_input()** function to incorporate the notion of setting default argument values.

Hello, world!

Hello, Zoe!

Ⓐ Calling the function without any arguments uses the default value (the first greeting); calling it with an argument provided means that value will be used instead (the second).

```
function calculate_total($qty, $price = 20.00, $tax = 0.06) {
    // Make the calculations.
}

calculate_total(3, 0.07);
```

Ⓑ Because of the way function arguments work, you cannot "skip" an argument when calling a function.

To write a function that uses default values:

1. Open **sticky1.php** (Script 10.2) in your text editor or IDE, if it isn't open already.

2. Add a third argument with a default value to the **make_text_input()** function (**Script 10.3**):

   ```
   function make_text_input($name,
   → $label, $size = 20) {
   ```

   Although I like the cleanliness of having all text inputs be the same size, a person's last name and email address is often longer than their first name, so an adjustable size would be better. By taking the input's size as an argument, this will be possible. But the size will have a default value, making it an optional argument. If three arguments are sent to the function, then **$size** will be set to the third value instead of the default.

Script 10.3 The function now takes three arguments, but only two of them are required. If no **$size** is passed to the function, its value will be 20.

```
1    <!DOCTYPE html PUBLIC "-//W3C//DTD XHTML 1.0 Transitional//EN"
2        "http://www.w3.org/TR/xhtml1/DTD/xhtml1-transitional.dtd">
3    <html xmlns="http://www.w3.org/1999/xhtml" xml:lang="en" lang="en">
4    <head>
5        <meta http-equiv="content-type" content="text/html; charset=utf-8" />
6        <title>Sticky Text Inputs</title>
7    </head>
8    <body>
9    <?php // Script 10.3 - sticky2.php
10   /* This script defines and calls a function that creates a sticky text input. */
11
12   // This function makes a sticky text input.
13   // This function requires two arguments be passed to it.
14   // A third argument is optional (it has a default value).
15   function make_text_input($name, $label, $size = 20) {
16
17       // Begin a paragraph and a label:
18       print '<p><label>' . $label . ': ';
19
```

code continues on next page

Script 10.3 *continued*

```
20      // Begin the input:
21      print '<input type="text" name="' .
        $name . '" size="' . $size . '" ';
22
23      // Add the value:
24      if (isset($_POST[$name])) {
25          print ' value="' . htmlspecialchars
            ($_POST[$name]) . '"';
26      }
27
28      // Complete the input, the label and
        the paragraph:
29      print ' /></label></p>';
30
31  } // End of make_text_input() function.
32
33  // Make the form:
34  print '<form action="" method="post">';
35
36  // Create some text inputs:
37  make_text_input('first_name', 'First
    Name');
38  make_text_input('last_name', 'Last
    Name', 30);
39  make_text_input('email', 'Email
    Address', 50);
40
41  print '<input type="submit" name="submit"
    value="Register!" /></form>';
42
43  ?>
44  </body>
45  </html>
```

3. Change the creation of the input so that it uses the **$size** variable:

```
print '<input type="text"
→ name="' . $name . '"
→ size="' . $size . '" ';
```

4. Change the function calls to vary the sizes:

```
make_text_input('first_name',
→ 'First Name');
make_text_input('last_name',
→ 'Last Name', 30);
make_text_input('email', 'Email
→ Address', 50);
```

Now the first input will use the default size, and the others will be longer.

5. Save the script as **sticky2.php**, place it in the proper directory of your PHP-enabled server, and test it in your Web browser **C**.

TIP To pass no value to a function for a particular argument, use an empty string (") or the word NULL (without quotes). Either of these values will override the default value, if one is established.

TIP As mentioned way back in Chapter 1, "Getting Started with PHP," the PHP manual marks optional function arguments using square brackets. For example, when you use the number_format() function, the number of decimals to round to is optional:

```
string number_format(float number
→ [, int decimals])
```

First Name: Peter

Last Name: O'Toole

Email Address: me@example.com

Register!

C Now the function is capable of changing the size of the input, based on an argument. If no value is provided for that argument, the default size is used instead (the first input).

Creating and Using Functions That Return a Value

Functions do more than take arguments; they can also return values. Doing so requires just two more steps. First, you use the **return** statement within the function. Second, you use the output somehow when you call the function. Commonly, you'll assign the returned value to a variable, but you can also, for example, directly print the output. Here is the basic format for a function that takes two arguments and returns a value:

```
function make_full_name($first,
→ $last) {
        $name = $first . ' ' . $last;
        return $name;
}
```

This function could be used like so:

```
$full_name = make_full_name($fn, $ln);
```

There the returned value of the function is assigned to a variable. Here it's printed immediately:

```
print make_full_name($fn, $ln)
```

To best demonstrate this concept, let's create a function that performs a simple calculation and formats the result. This script will display an HTML form where a user enters a quantity and price Ⓐ. When the form is submitted (back to this same page), a total value will be calculated and printed Ⓑ.

Ⓐ This simple form takes two values on which calculations will be made.

Ⓑ The result of the calculation, which takes place within a user-defined function.

To create and use a function that returns a value:

1. Create a new PHP document in your text editor or IDE, to be named **calculator.php** (Script 10.4):

```
<!DOCTYPE html PUBLIC "-//W3C//DTD
→ XHTML 1.0 Transitional//EN"
  "http://www.w3.org/TR/xhtml1/
  → DTD/xhtml1-transitional.dtd">
<html xmlns="http://www.w3.org/
→ 1999/xhtml" xml:lang="en"
→ lang="en">
<head>
  <meta http-equiv="Content-Type"
  → content="text/html;
  → charset=utf-8"/>
  <title>Cost Calculator</title>
</head>
<body>
```

continues on next page

Script 10.4 This script both displays and handles an HTML form in order to perform some basic calculations. The script uses a function that takes two arguments and returns a single value.

```
1    <!DOCTYPE html PUBLIC "-//W3C//DTD XHTML 1.0 Transitional//EN"
2        "http://www.w3.org/TR/xhtml1/DTD/xhtml1-transitional.dtd">
3    <html xmlns="http://www.w3.org/1999/xhtml" xml:lang="en" lang="en">
4    <head>
5        <meta http-equiv="Content-Type" content="text/html; charset=utf-8"/>
6        <title>Cost Calculator</title>
7    </head>
8    <body>
9    <?php // Script 10.4 - calculator.php
10   /* This script displays and handles an HTML form.
11   It uses a function to calculate a total from a quantity and price. */
12
13   // This function performs the calculations.
14   function calculate_total ($quantity, $price) {
15
16       $total = $quantity * $price; // Calculation
17       $total = number_format ($total, 2); // Formatting
18
19       return $total; // Return the value.
20
21   } // End of function.
22
```

code continues on next page

2. Begin the PHP code:

```php
<?php // Script 10.4 -
→ calculator.php
```

3. Define the function:

```php
function calculate_total
→ ($quantity, $price) {
  $total = $quantity * $price;
  $total = number_format
  → ($total, 2);
  return $total;
}
```

This function takes two arguments—a quantity and a price—and multiplies them to create a total. The total value is then formatted before it's returned by the function.

Although this may seem like a silly use of a function, the benefits of putting even a one-step calculation into a function are twofold: First, the

Script 10.4 *continued*

```
23   // Check for a form submission:
24   if ($_SERVER['REQUEST_METHOD'] == 'POST') {
25
26       // Check for values:
27       if ( is_numeric($_POST['quantity']) AND is_numeric($_POST['price']) ) {
28
29           // Call the function and print the results:
30           $total = calculate_total($_POST['quantity'], $_POST['price']);
31           print "<p>Your total comes to $<span style=\"font-weight: bold;\">$total</span>.</p>";
32
33       } else { // Inappropriate values entered.
34           print '<p style="color: red;">Please enter a valid quantity and price!</p>';
35       }
36
37   }
38   ?>
39   <form action="calculator.php" method="post">
40       <p>Quantity: <input type="text" name="quantity" size="3" /></p>
41       <p>Price: <input type="text" name="price" size="5" /></p>
42       <input type="submit" name="submit" value="Calculate!" />
43   </form>
44   </body>
45   </html>
```

calculation will be easier to find and modify at a later date with your function located at the beginning of your script instead of hidden in the rest of the code; and second, should you want to repeat the action again in a script, you can do so without duplicating code.

4. Begin the conditional to see if the form was submitted:

```
if ($_SERVER['REQUEST_METHOD'] ==
→ 'POST') {
```

Because this page both displays and handles the HTML form, it has a conditional that checks how the page is being requested. If it's a POST request, that means the form has been submitted.

5. Validate the form data and use the function:

```
if ( is_numeric($_POST['quantity'])
→ AND is_numeric($_POST['price']) ) {
  $total = calculate_total
  → ($_POST['quantity'],
  → $_POST['price']);
  print "<p>Your total comes
  → to $<span style=\"font-weight:
  → bold;\">$total</span>.</p>";
```

This part of the PHP code—which handles the form if it has been submitted—first checks that a numeric quantity and price were entered. If so, the total is determined by calling the **calculate_total()** function and assigning the result to the **$total** variable. This result is then printed out.

continues on next page

---

6. Complete the conditionals:

```
} else {
    print '<p style="color:
    → red;">Please enter a valid
    → quantity and price!</p>';
}
}
```

If either of the form variables was not properly submitted, a message is printed indicating that. The final curly bracket closes the form submission conditional.

A little CSS is applied to both printed messages (here and in Step 5).

7. Display the HTML form:

```
?>
<form action="calculator.php"
→ method="post">
    <p>Quantity: <input type="text"
    → name="quantity" size="3" /></p>
    <p>Price: <input type="text"
    → name="price" size="5" /></p>
    <input type="submit"
    → name="submit"
    → value="Calculate!" />
</form>
```

The form itself is quite simple, requesting two different values from the user **A**. Because this form is created outside of the main submission conditional, the form will always be displayed by the page **B**.

8. Complete the HTML page:

```
</body>
</html>
```

9. Save the page as **calculator.php**, place it in the proper directory for your PHP-enabled server, and test it in your Web browser **B**.

TIP You can have only one return statement *executed* in a function, but the same function can have multiple return statements. As an example, you may want to write a function that checks for a condition and returns a value indicating whether the condition was satisfied. In such a case, the function might contain:

```
if (condition) {
    return TRUE;
} else {
    return FALSE;
}
```

TIP The result returned by the function is either **TRUE** or **FALSE**, indicating whether the stated condition was met.

Understanding Variable Scope

The concept of *variable scope* wasn't introduced earlier because without an understanding of functions, scope makes little sense. Now that you are acquainted with functions, this section will revisit the topic of variables and discuss in some detail just how variables and functions work together.

As you saw in the second section of this chapter, "Creating and Calling Functions That Take Arguments," you can send variables to a function by passing them as arguments. However, you can also reference an external variable from within a function using the **global** statement. This is possible because of variable scope. The *scope* of a variable is the realm in which it exists. By default, the variables you write in a script exist for the life of that script. Conversely, environment variables, such as **$_SERVER['PHP_SELF']**, exist throughout every PHP script on the server.

Functions, though, create a new level of scope. Function variables—the arguments of a function as well as any variables defined within the function—exist only within that function and aren't accessible outside of it (that is, they're *local variables* with *local scope*). Likewise, a variable from outside a function is not available within the function, by default **A**. Even when a variable is used as an argument to a function call, that variable's *value* is being passed to the function, not the variable itself.

You can, however, make a variable external to a function available within the function by using the **global** statement. The **global** statement roughly means, "I want this variable within the function to refer to the same named variable outside of the function." In other words, the **global** statement turns a local variable with local scope into a global variable with global scope. Any changes made to the variable within the function are also reflected by the variable outside of the function, without using the **return** command (assuming the function is called, that is).

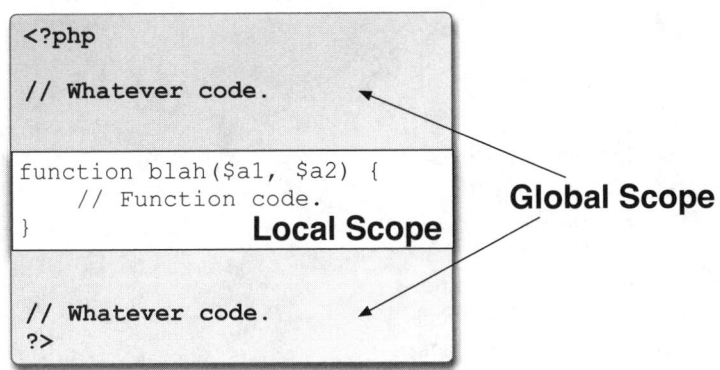

```php
<?php

// Whatever code.


function blah($a1, $a2) {
    // Function code.
}              Local Scope


// Whatever code.
?>
```

Global Scope

A Adding function definitions to a script adds another area of variable scope.

The syntax of the **global** statement is as follows:

```
function function_name($args) {
        global $variable;
        statement(s);
}
```

There is another issue regarding functions and variables: Because of variable scope, a local variable within a function is a different entity (perhaps with a different value) than a variable outside of the function, *even if the two variables use the exact same name*. Let's look at this more explicitly...

Say you have:

```
function test($arg) {
        // Do whatever.
}
$var = 1;
test($var);
```

When the function is called, the value of **$var** will be assigned **$arg**, so their values are the same but their names are different and they are different variables. However, if the name of the argument in the function is also **$var**—

```
function test($var) {
        // Do whatever.
}
$var = 1;
test($var);
```

—then the **$var** variable within the function is assigned the same value as the original **$var** outside of the function—but *they're still two separate variables*. The one has a scope within the function, and the other has a scope outside of it. This means that you can use the same name for variables in the function as exist outside of the function without conflict. Just remember they aren't the same variable. What happens

```
$n equals 1
Added one!
$n equals 1
```

B Changes to a local variable inside a function have no effect on a similarly named global variable.

```
$n equals 1
Added one!
$n equals 2
```

C Changes made to a global variable inside of a function will impact the variable outside of that function.

to a variable's value within a function only affects that variable within the function. As an example **B**:

```php
function add_one($n) {
        $n++;
        print 'Added one!<br />';
}
$n = 1;
print "\$n equals $n<br />";
add_one($n);
print "\$n equals $n<br />";
```

This is all true unless you use the **global** statement, which does make the two variables the same **C**:

```php
function add_one() {
        global $n; // Same!
$n++;
        print 'Added one!<br />';
}
$n = 1;
print "\$n equals $n<br />";
add_one();
print "\$n equals $n<br />";
```

Note that in this case, the variable's value no longer needs to be passed to the function either.

To demonstrate variable scope, let's rework the **calculator.php** script using the **global** statement.

To use the global statement:

1. Open **calculator.php** (Script 10.4) in your text editor or IDE, if it is not already open.

2. Before the function definition, add the following (**Script 10.5**):

   $tax = 8.75;

   This line creates a **$tax** variable with a set value that will be used in the cost calculations. It's assigned a value outside of the function because it will be used later in the main body of the script.

Script 10.5 The function in this script can use the **$tax** variable—even though it hasn't been passed to the function—thanks to the **global** statement.

```
1    <!DOCTYPE html PUBLIC "-//W3C//DTD XHTML 1.0 Transitional//EN"
2       "http://www.w3.org/TR/xhtml1/DTD/xhtml1-transitional.dtd">
3    <html xmlns="http://www.w3.org/1999/xhtml" xml:lang="en" lang="en">
4    <head>
5       <meta http-equiv="Content-Type" content="text/html; charset=utf-8"/>
6       <title>Cost Calculator</title>
7    </head>
8    <body>
9    <?php // Script 10.5 - calculator.php #2
10   /* This script displays and handles an HTML form.
11   It uses a function to calculate a total from a quantity, price, and tax rate. */
12
13   // Define a tax rate:
14   $tax = 8.75;
15
16   // This function performs the calculations.
17   function calculate_total ($quantity, $price) {
18
19       global $tax;
20
21       $total = $quantity * $price; // Calculation
22       $taxrate = ($tax / 100) + 1;
23       $total = $total * $taxrate; // Add the tax.
24       $total = number_format ($total, 2); // Formatting
25
26       return $total; // Return the value.
27
28   } // End of function.
29
```

code continues on next page

3. Within the function definition, add a **global** statement:

global $tax;

This statement tells the function to incorporate the same **$tax** variable as the one that exists outside of the function.

4. Before the **$total** in the function is formatted, recalculate the value using the tax rate:

$taxrate = ($tax / 100) + 1;
$total = $total * $taxrate;

To add the tax to the total value, you start by dividing the tax by 100 to create a percentage. Then you add 1 to this value to get a multiplier. This result is then multiplied by the total to come up with the new, final total.

continues on next page

Script 10.5 *continued*

```
30   // Check for a form submission:
31   if (isset($_POST['submitted'])) {
32
33       // Check for values:
34       if ( is_numeric($_POST['quantity']) AND is_numeric($_POST['price']) ) {
35
36           // Call the function and print the results:
37           $total = calculate_total($_POST['quantity'], $_POST['price']);
38           print "<p>Your total comes to $<span style=\"font-weight: bold;\">$total</span>,
             including the $tax percent tax rate.</p>";
39
40       } else { // Inappropriate values entered.
41           print '<p style="color: red;">Please enter a valid quantity and price!</p>';
42       }
43
44   }
45   ?>
46   <form action="calculator.php" method="post">
47       <p>Quantity: <input type="text" name="quantity" size="3" /></p>
48       <p>Price: <input type="text" name="price" size="5" /></p>
49       <input type="submit" name="submit" value="Calculate!" />
50       <input type="hidden" name="submitted" value="true" />
51   </form>
52   </body>
53   </html>
```

Notice that you use a **$taxrate** variable (based on **$tax**) to perform these calculations. This is because you'll print out the value of **$tax** later, and any changes made to it here will be reflected (because it's a global variable).

Quantity: 15

Price: 129.63

Calculate!

D Run the form again...

5. Alter the main **print** line (after the function call) so that it prints the tax rate as well:

```
print "<p>Your total comes to
→ $<span style=\"font-weight:
→ bold;\">$total</span>, including
→ the $tax percent tax rate.</p>";
```

The **$tax** variable defined at the beginning of the script is printed out at the end. If you hadn't used the **$taxrate** variable within the function and made the alterations to the global **$tax** instead, those calculations would be reflected in the value printed here.

6. Save the script, place it in the proper directory for your PHP-enabled server, and test it in your Web browser **D** and **E**.

Your total comes to **$2,114.59**, including the 8.75 percent tax rate.

Quantity:

Price:

Calculate!

E ...and the calculation now makes use of a global **$tax** variable.

Function Design Theory

Understanding the syntax for defining your own functions is important, but you also need to understand good function design theory. A proper user-defined function should be easily reusable, and be likely to be reused (i.e., if a Web site only ever calls a function once, there's no need for it). There should also be a "black box" mentality about the function: A programmer shouldn't need to know about the internals of a function in order to use it properly. As an example of this, think of any PHP function: You probably don't know what the underlying function code does specifically, but you can still tap into its power.

In support of the "black box" approach, proper function design suggests that you should be extremely cautious when using global variables. Arguably (pun!), a function should be passed all the information it needs, so that global variables—including the superglobals and constants—are not required.

Functions should also not make assumptions either, like `make_text_input()`, which assumes the form was submitted using the POST method.

By writing functions that neither rely upon global variables nor make assumptions as to what outside of the function is true, you make the function more independent and portable—in short, better.

TIP Constants and the superglobal arrays (`$_GET`, `$_POST`, `$_COOKIE`, and `$_SESSION`) have the added benefit that they're always available inside functions without requiring the `global` statement (which is why they are called *superglobals*).

TIP Each function has its own, separate local scope.

Review and Pursue

If you have any problems with the review questions or the pursue prompts, turn to the book's supporting forum (www.LarryUllman.com/forum/).

Review

- What is the basic syntax of a user-defined function?

- What naming rules must your own functions abide by?

- What naming rules must function arguments abide by?

- How do you provide a default value for a function's argument?

- In the example code in the "Understanding Variable Scope" section of the chapter, why does the code use \\$n? What would happen if that backslash wasn't there?

- What is variable scope? What scope does a function argument variable have?

- What scope does a variable in an included file have? Note: This is a tricky one!

Pursue

- Make the function in **menus.php** take arguments to indicate the starting year and the number of years to generate. Make the later argument have a default value. Then rewrite the function body so that it uses these values in the year **for** loop.

- Rewrite the **make_text_input()** function so that it can be told whether to look for an existing value in either **$_POST** or **$_GET**.

- Create a variation on the **make_text_input()** function that can create a text input or a password input, depending upon how the function is called.

- Come up with an idea for, create, and use your own custom function.

Files and Directories

Taking your Web applications to the next level requires a method of storing and retrieving data. You have two primary options in PHP: using files (and directories) or databases. This chapter will discuss the former, and the next chapter will introduce the latter. It's worth your time to learn both methods: Although a database can be more powerful and secure than a file-based system, you may be surprised at what's possible by writing and reading simple text documents on the server.

In this chapter, you'll learn about file permissions, a topic that you must grasp first. Then you'll learn to write to, read from, and lock files. After that, you'll see how to handle file uploads with PHP, how to create directories, and an alternate method for reading data from a file. These last two examples will also demonstrate a simple file-based registration and login system that you can use in your Web applications.

In This Chapter

File Permissions	288
Writing to Files	293
Locking Files	301
Reading from Files	304
Handling File Uploads	307
Navigating Directories	315
Creating Directories	320
Reading Files Incrementally	327
Review and Pursue	332

File Permissions

Before attempting to write to and read from a file, you must have an understanding of *file permissions*. The topic is large enough that you may want to pursue it further, but this quick introduction will get you started. Up front I will say that most of the information in this chapter applies to only non-Windows users. In my experience, the preparatory steps to be taken aren't necessary when running PHP on a Windows computer (although such things can change from one version of an operating system to the next). Still, having an understanding of permissions as a whole is a good idea, especially if you might later be running your PHP scripts on a non-Windows server.

Permissions identify who can do what with a file or directory. The options are *read*, *write*, and *execute* (actually, files can be designated *executable,* whereas directories are made *searchable*). Each of these options can be set for three types of users:

- The *owner* of the file (the person who created it or put it on the server)
- Members of a particular *group*, which a server administrator determines and which includes the owner
- *Others* (those who don't fall into the previous two categories)

There is also the implied *everyone* level, which includes all three user types.

As an example, if you use FTP to transfer a file to a server, the account used to connect to the server will be the owner of the file. The default file permissions will likely be that everyone can read the file but that only the owner can modify it (i.e., write to it).

The Web Root Directory

When discussing files, directories, and security, an important concept is that of the *Web root directory*. To grasp this concept, first consider that a file on a Web server is available in two ways. First, it exists in the file system. For example, this might be **C:\inetpub\wwwroot\filename.php** on your own computer, or **/var/web/sitename/htdocs/filename.php** on a remote server (that path would be applicable to *nix systems).

Second, files placed within the proper directories for a Web server are also available through HTTP, such as **http://www.example.com/filename.php** or **http://localhost/filename.php**.

With this in mind, the *Web root directory* is the folder in the file system where the base URL—such as **www.example.com**—points. Without further restrictions imposed, a Web browser can access all the files found within the Web root directory and below (i.e., in subfolders). A Web browser cannot, however, access files found outside of the Web root directory.

When creating writable files and directories, it's more secure to place them outside of the Web directory. In other words, if your Web pages go in **C:\inetpub\wwwroot** or **/Users/username/Sites**, then if you place items in **C:\inetpub** or **/Users/username**, they should be accessible to the locally running PHP but not to others over the Internet. The examples in this chapter follow this structure, and you should do so as well.

In general, the security concern here is more important for directories than for files.

A catch is that in most cases, PHP will be running through a Web server application, which counts as a different server user. Therefore, PHP and the Web server would be able to read files you put onto the server (and consequently make them available for viewing in a Web browser), but PHP would not, by default, be able to modify those files.

For the examples in this chapter, PHP needs to be able to write to some files and directories. This means that you must know how, and be able, to adjust the permissions a file or directory has. That being said, making a file or directory writable (i.e., making the permissions less restrictive) can be a security issue and should be done only when absolutely necessary.

Finally, a common point of confusion has to do with what, exactly, a "user" is. A user is an account created on a computer. On your own computer, there may be just one user—you—or several. Servers normally have multiple users, although most user accounts aren't associated with people who will log in, but rather with different processes running on the server. For example, there may be one user whose processes handle all Web requests and another user through which the database application runs. Most importantly, know that a "user" is not a person on another computer and that "everyone" means "everyone on the server." Just because you've made a file or directory writable by any user doesn't mean it's writable by anyone over the Internet. The user must be a recognized account on the server.

Creating the text file

In the chapter's first example, you'll work with a text file, **quotes.txt**, that's located on the server. If the file doesn't have the correct permissions to do what your PHP script is asking it to, you might see an error message like **A**. Before proceeding, you should create **quotes.txt** on the server and establish its permissions.

> **Warning**: fopen(../quotes.txt) [function.fopen]: failed to open stream: Permission denied in **/Users/larryullman/Sites/phpvqs4/add_quote.php** on line 20

A The ...*failed to open stream: Permission denied...* message is the result of attempting to do something to a file that isn't allowed by the server. Here the server is denying the **fopen()** function that is attempting to open **quotes.txt** for the purpose of writing to it.

To create quotes.txt:

1. Open your text editor or IDE and create a new, blank document.

2. Without typing anything into the file, save it as **quotes.txt**.

3. Move the file just outside of the Web root directory of your PHP-enabled server **B**.

   The sidebar "The Web Root Directory" explains where you should put the file with respect to your Web directory and why.

TIP The `file_exists()` function returns TRUE if a provided file or directory exists on the server. This can be used to test for the presence of a file before doing anything with it:

```
if (file_exists('somefile.ext')) { …
```

TIP Assuming that PHP has write permissions on a directory, you can create a blank document within that directory using PHP. This is accomplished using the `touch()` function:

```
touch('somefile.ext');
```

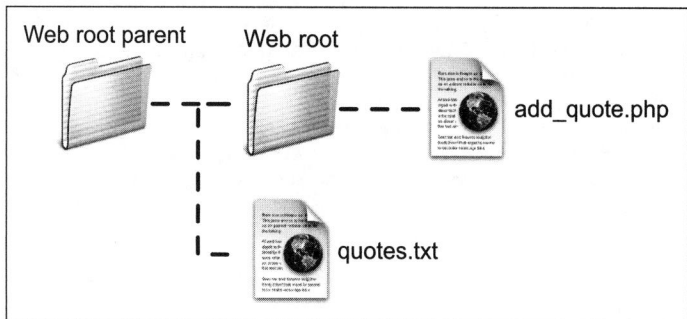

B The **quotes.txt** file should ideally be placed in the same directory as your Web documents folder (i.e., not in the directory with the actual Web documents).

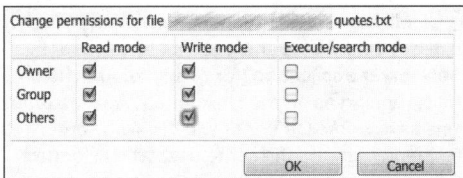

This control panel, provided by a hosting company, lets you adjust a file's permissions.

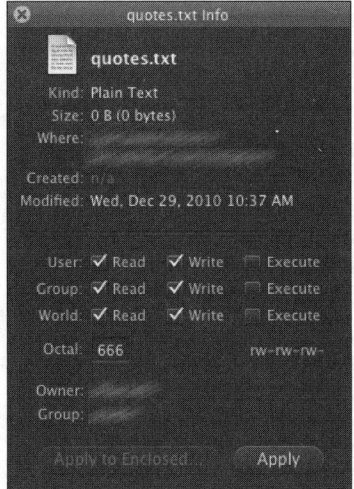

The Transmit FTP application uses this pop-up window to allow you to set a file's permissions.

Setting a file's permissions

The preceding sequence may seem like an odd series of steps, but in order to set the permissions on a file, the file must first exist. You do want the file to be blank, though, because you'll use PHP to write data to it later.

The desired end result for this example is to give either *others* or *everyone* permission to *read* and *write* (but not *execute*) `quotes.txt`. How you accomplish this depends on:

- Whether you're running PHP on your own computer or on a remote server
- The operating system of the PHP-enabled computer

Unfortunately, it would be impossible to offer steps for how every user should set the permissions under any circumstances, but here are some rough guidelines and steps to get you going.

To set a file's permissions on a remote server:

- Most ISPs offer users a Web-based control panel where they can set file permissions **C** as well as set other hosting parameters.
- You may be able to change a file's permissions using your FTP client **D**.

To set a file's permissions on your computer:

- If you're working on your own Windows computer, you may not need to change the permissions. To test this theory, try each example first. If a PHP script can't write to the file or directory in question, use the next suggestion to rework the permissions.

- Windows users who need to change the permissions can do so by viewing the file's or directory's properties. The resulting panel will differ for each version of Windows, but basically you just need to tweak who can access the file and how.

- Mac OS X users must select the file in the Finder and choose Get Info from the File menu. From there, use the Ownership & Permissions subpanel to adjust the file's permissions ⓔ.

- On Unix (including users of Linux and Mac OS X), you can also use the command line `chmod 0666 quotes.txt` in a terminal window, assuming that you have authority to do so.

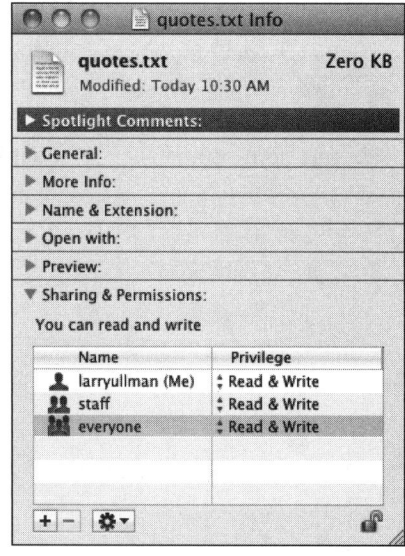

ⓔ The Mac OS X Get Info panel lets you adjust a file's ownership and permissions, among other things.

TIP Most operating systems have no *PHP* user. Instead, the *PHP* user is essentially the user the Web server application (for example, Apache or IIS) is running as. In the Unix family, Apache often runs as *nobody*. On Windows, the Web server frequently runs as the same user who is logged in (and who probably created the file), meaning there will be no need to alter a file's permissions.

TIP If you're already familiar with Telnet and `chmod`, you probably also understand what the **0666** number means, but here's an explanation for those of you who aren't familiar with it. The 0 is just a prefix indicating the number is written in an *octal* format. Each 6 corresponds to *read* (4) plus *write* (2) permission—first assigning 6 to the owner, then to the group, and then to others. Comparatively, 0777 allows *read* (4) plus *write* (2) plus *execute* (1) permission to all three types of users. This numbering is applicable for Unix variant operating systems (Linux, Solaris, and Mac OS X).

TIP PHP has several functions for changing a file or directory's permissions, including `chgrp()`, `chmod()`, and `chown()`. However, they will only work if PHP already has permission to modify the file or directory in question.

TIP A Web site running on a shared hosting environment has greater security risks than one running on a dedicated server as there are literally more users. For example, if you make a file or directory writable by every user, then anyone with access to that server can manipulate that file (assuming they know it exists and that other restrictions are not in place).

Writing to Files

Because you need to write something to a file in order to read something from it, this chapter explores writing first. The easiest way to write to a file is to use the **file_put_contents()** function:

```
file_put_contents($file, $data);
```

This function, added in PHP 5, will open the file and write the data there. The first argument is the name of the file. This can be an *absolute* or *relative* path (see the sidebar "File Paths"). The second argument is the data, which can be a string, number, or array (one-dimensional, not multidimensional). Neither the file nor the data has to be represented by a variable, but it's common to do so.

If the file doesn't exist, the function will attempt to create it. If the file does exist, the file's current contents will be replaced with the new data. If you'd prefer to have the new data appended to what's already in the file, add the **FILE_APPEND** constant as a third argument:

```
file_put_contents($file, $data,
→ FILE_APPEND);
```

When appending data to a file, you normally want each piece of data to be written on its own line, so each submission should conclude with the appropriate line break for the operating system of the computer running PHP. This would be

- **\n** on Unix and Mac OS X

- **\r\n** on Windows

As with any meaningful escape sequence, these must be placed within double quotation marks in order to work.

continues on next page

Alternatively, you can use the special PHP constant **PHP_EOL**, which represents the correct end-of-line character sequence (e.g., **\n** or **\r\n**) for the current operating system:

```
file_put_contents($file,
⇥$data . PHP_EOL, FILE_APPEND);
```

If you're not using PHP 5 or later, then the **file_put_contents()** function won't be available for you and you must use the legacy approach: first, open the file; second, write your data to it; and third, close the file:

```
$fp = fopen($file, mode);
fwrite($fp, $data . PHP_EOL);
fclose($fp);
```

To write to a file, you must create a *file pointer* when opening it. The file pointer returned by the **fopen()** function will be used by PHP to refer to the open file.

The most important consideration when opening the file is what *mode* you use. Depending on what you intend to do with the file, the mode dictates how to open it. The most forgiving mode is **a+**, which allows you to read or write to a file. It creates the file if it doesn't exist, and it appends—hence *a*—new data to the end of the file automatically. Conversely, **r** only allows you to read from a file. **Table 11.1** lists all the possible modes. Each mode can also be appended with a **b** flag, which forces files to be opened in binary mode. This is a safer option for files that might be read on multiple operating systems.

TABLE 11.1 fopen() Modes

Mode	Meaning
r	Reading only; begin reading at the start of the file.
r+	Reading or writing; begin at the start of the file.
w	Writing only; create the file if it doesn't exist, and overwrite any existing contents.
w+	Reading or writing; create the file if it doesn't exist, and overwrite any existing contents (when writing).
a	Writing only; create the file if it doesn't exist, and append the new data to the end of the file (retain any existing data and add to it).
a+	Reading or writing; create the file if it doesn't exist, and append the new data to the end of the file (when writing).
x	Writing only; create the file if it doesn't exist, but do nothing (and issue a warning) if the file does exist.
x+	Reading or writing; create the file if it doesn't exist, but do nothing (and issue a warning) if the file already exists (when writing).

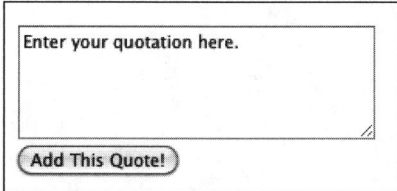

```
Enter your quotation here.


                                    //
( Add This Quote! )
```

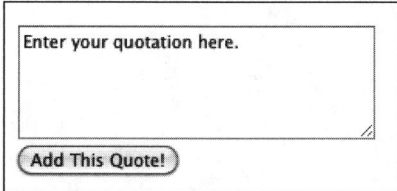 **A** This very simple form lets a user submit a quotation that will be written to a text file.

The **fwrite()** function writes the new data (sent as the second argument in the function call) to the file in accordance with the selected mode.

As the last step of the writing process, you close the file by once again referring to the file pointer while calling the **fclose()** function:

```
fclose($fp);
```

With this in mind, let's create a form that stores user-submitted quotations in a plain-text file **A**. Later in this chapter, another PHP script will retrieve and randomly display these quotations. Before we get into the code, however, there's one more function to be introduced: **is_writable()**. This function returns a Boolean value indicating the writability of the named file:

```
if (is_writable($file)) {…
```

Invoking this function prior to attempting to write to a file (or directory) is a simple way to avoid permissions errors.

To write to an external file:

1. Create a new PHP document in your text editor or IDE, to be named **add_quote.php** (Script 11.1):

```
<!DOCTYPE html PUBLIC "-//W3C//DTD
→ XHTML 1.0 Transitional//EN"
  "http://www.w3.org/TR/xhtml1/
  → DTD/xhtml1-transitional.dtd">
<html xmlns="http://www.w3.org/
→ 1999/xhtml" xml:lang="en"
→ lang="en">
<head>
  <meta http-equiv="content-type"
  → content="text/html;
  → charset=utf-8" />
  <title>Add A Quotation</title>
</head>
<body>
```

Script 11.1 This script takes a user-submitted quotation and stores it in a text file.

```
1   <!DOCTYPE html PUBLIC "-//W3C//DTD XHTML 1.0 Transitional//EN"
2       "http://www.w3.org/TR/xhtml1/DTD/xhtml1-transitional.dtd">
3   <html xmlns="http://www.w3.org/1999/xhtml" xml:lang="en" lang="en">
4   <head>
5       <meta http-equiv="content-type" content="text/html; charset=utf-8" />
6       <title>Add A Quotation</title>
7   </head>
8   <body>
9   <?php // Script 11.1 - add_quote.php
10  /* This script displays and handles an HTML form. This script takes text input and stores it
    in a text file. */
11
12  // Identify the file to use:
13  $file = '../quotes.txt';
14
15  // Check for a form submission:
16  if ($_SERVER['REQUEST_METHOD'] == 'POST') { // Handle the form.
17
18      if ( !empty($_POST['quote']) && ($_POST['quote'] != 'Enter your quotation here.') ) { // Need
        some thing to write.
19
20          if (is_writable($file)) { // Confirm that the file is writable.
21
22              file_put_contents($file, $_POST['quote'] . PHP_EOL, FILE_APPEND);
                // Write the data.
```

code continues on next page

2. Create a section of PHP code and identify the file to be used:

```php
<?php // Script 11.1 - add_quote.php
$file = '../quotes.txt';
```

As this script will reference the same file twice, it's a good idea to identify the file as a variable. This way, should you later need to change the name or location of the file, only one line of code will need to be edited.

The file identified is **quotes.txt**, which should be located in the directory above this script (which is presumably in the Web directory root; see **B** in the previous section of the chapter). See the sidebar "File Paths" for more on this syntax.

continues on next page

Script 11.1 *continued*

```
23
24          // Print a message:
25          print '<p>Your quotation has been stored.</p>';
26
27      } else { // Could not open the file.
28          print '<p style="color: red;">Your quotation could not be stored due to a system
            error.</p>';
29      }
30
31    } else { // Failed to enter a quotation.
32        print '<p style="color: red;">Please enter a quotation!</p>';
33    }
34
35  } // End of submitted IF.
36
37  // Leave PHP and display the form:
38  ?>
39
40  <form action="add_quote.php" method="post">
41      <textarea name="quote" rows="5" cols="30">Enter your quotation here.</textarea><br />
42      <input type="submit" name="submit" value="Add This Quote!" />
43  </form>
44
45  </body>
46  </html>
```

3. Check if the form has been submitted:

```
if ($_SERVER['REQUEST_METHOD'] ==
→'POST') {
```

This page both displays and handles the HTML form. The conditional tests if the form has been submitted, in which case the quotation should be written to the text file.

4. Check that a quotation was entered:

```
if ( !empty($_POST['quote']) &&
→($_POST['quote'] != 'Enter your
→quotation here.') ) {
```

This simple conditional validates the user-supplied data. The first part confirms that the **$_POST['quote']** variable isn't empty. The second part confirms that the variable doesn't still have the default value (as shown in Ⓐ).

5. Confirm that the file can be written to

```
if (is_writable($file)) {
```

By placing this function call in a conditional, you make the PHP script attempt to write to the file only if the file is writable.

6. Write the data to the file and then print a message:

```
file_put_contents($file,
→$_POST['quote'] . PHP_EOL,
→FILE_APPEND);
print '<p>Your quotation has been
→stored.</p>';
```

The first line writes the user-submitted data to the file. The **PHP_EOL** constant is concatenated to the written data, so that each submission gets stored on its own line.

If you're not using PHP 5 or later, you'll need to do this instead:

```
$fp = fopen ($file, 'ab')
fwrite($fp, $_POST['quote'] .
→PHP_EOL);
fclose($fp);
```

7. Complete the conditionals:

```
        } else { // Could not open
        →the file.
          print '<p style="color:
          →red;">Your quotation
          →could not be stored due
          →to a system error.</p>';
        }
    } else { // Failed to enter a
    →quotation.
      print '<p style="color:
      →red;">Please enter a
      →quotation!</p>';
    }
} // End of submitted IF.
```

The first **else** completes the conditional that checks if PHP could open the file for writing **B**. If you see this message, there's likely a permissions issue or the file reference is incorrect. The second **else** completes the conditional that checks whether no quotation was entered **C**. The final closing curly bracket marks the end of the main submission conditional.

Because this page handles the form and then displays it again (so that the user may keep entering quotations), the form isn't displayed as part of an **else** statement as it has been in other examples in this book.

8. Complete the PHP section:

   ?>

   Because the rest of this script is standard HTML, exit out of the PHP code by closing the PHP tag.

9. Create the HTML form:

   ```
   <form action="add_quote.php"
   → method="post">
     <textarea name="quote" rows="5"
     → cols="30">Enter your quotation
     → here.</textarea><br />
     <input type="submit" name=
     → "submit" value="Add This
     → Quote!" />
     <input type="hidden" name=
     → "submitted" value="true" />
   </form>
   ```

   This HTML form presents a text box where the user can enter a quotation. The text box has a preset value of *Enter your quotation here.*, created by putting that text between the **textarea** tags.

continues on next page

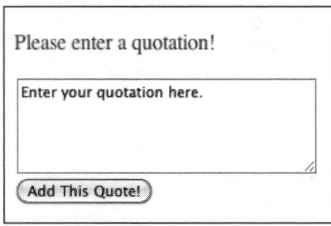

B If the PHP script can't find the **quotes.txt** file, or if it's not writable, the user will see this message.

C The script includes basic form validation.

10. Complete the HTML page:

```
</body>
</html>
```

11. Save the file as **add_quote.php** and place it in the proper directory for your PHP-enabled server.

Again, refer back to in the previous section of the chapter for how the **add_quote.php** and **quotes.txt** should be placed on your server relative to each other. If this arrangement isn't possible for you, or if it's just too confusing, then place both documents within the same directory (the one from which you can execute PHP scripts) and change the **$file** assignment line to

```
$file = 'quotes.txt';
```

12. Run the script several times in your Web browser **D** and **E**.

13. If you want, open the **quotes.txt** file in a text editor to confirm that the data has been written to it.

TIP Note that all of the file- and directory-related functions are usable only on files and directories on the same computer (i.e., server) on which PHP is running. A PHP script on a server has no access to a file on a client's computer (until the file is uploaded to the server).

TIP If you receive a permissions error when you run this script **B**, either the permissions aren't set properly or the PHP script couldn't access the data file. The latter can happen if you misspell the filename or incorrectly reference the file's path on the server.

TIP If your version of PHP is running in safe mode or has the open_basedir directive set, you may be limited in using PHP to access files and directories. Check your phpinfo() script to see these settings for your server.

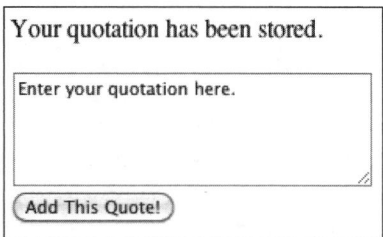

> A book is like a garden carried in the pocket. (Chinese Proverb)
>
> [Add This Quote!]

D Filling out the form...

> ## Your quotation has been stored.
>
> Enter your quotation here.
>
> [Add This Quote!]

E ...and the result if all went well.

TABLE 11.2 flock() Lock Types

Lock	Meaning
LOCK_SH	Shared lock for reading purposes
LOCK_EX	Exclusive lock for writing purposes
LOCK_UN	Release of a lock
LOCK_NB	Nonblocking lock

Locking Files

Although the last example worked fine (hopefully), it could be improved on. If only a single user were submitting the form at one time, there would be no problems. But what if two or more users submitted different quotations simultaneously? In such a case, there could be problems when multiple instances of the PHP script attempt to write to the same text file at once (the file could become corrupted). The solution is to temporarily *lock* the file while PHP is writing to it. If you are running PHP 5.1 or greater, you can add the **LOCK_EX** constant as the third argument to `file_put_contents()`:

```
file_put_contents($file, $data,
→ LOCK_EX);
```

To use both the **LOCK_EX** and **FILE_APPEND** constants, separate them with the binary OR operator (|):

```
file_put_contents($file, $data,
→ FILE_APPEND | LOCK_EX);
```

It doesn't matter in which order you list the two constants. If you're using an earlier version of PHP and have to use **fopen()**, **fwrite()**, and **fclose()**, you can invoke the **flock()** function after opening the file:

```
$fp = fopen($file, 'a+b');
flock($fp, locktype)
```

The different lock types are represented by the constants listed in **Table 11.2**. Note that you should unlock the file once the script is done with it.

As an example, to temporarily lock a file during a write, use this code:

```
$fp = fopen($file, 'a+b');
flock ($fp, LOCK_EX);
fwrite ($fp, $data);
flock ($fp, LOCK_UN);
```

continues on next page

To demonstrate, let's update **add_quote.php** to lock the file during the writing process.

To use file locks:

1. Open **add_quote.php** (Script 11.1) in your text editor or IDE, if it isn't already open.

2. Change the **file_put_contents()** line to the following (**Script 11.2**):

```
file_put_contents($file,
→ $_POST['quote'] . PHP_EOL,
→ FILE_APPEND | LOCK_EX);
```

This command places an exclusive lock on the file so that other scripts can't write to it at the same time.

Again, if you're not able to use **file_put_contents()** and **LOCK_EX**, you'll need to apply **flock()**, as in

```
flock($fp, LOCK_EX);
fwrite($fp, $_POST['quote'] .
→ PHP_EOL);
flock($fp, LOCK_UN);
fclose($fp);
```

Script 11.2 The modified version of the **add_quote.php** script locks the data file for better security and reliability.

```
1    <!DOCTYPE html PUBLIC "-//W3C//DTD XHTML 1.0 Transitional//EN"
2        "http://www.w3.org/TR/xhtml1/DTD/xhtml1-transitional.dtd">
3    <html xmlns="http://www.w3.org/1999/xhtml" xml:lang="en" lang="en">
4    <head>
5        <meta http-equiv="content-type" content="text/html; charset=utf-8" />
6        <title>Add A Quotation</title>
7    </head>
8    <body>
9    <?php // Script 11.1 - add_quote.php
10   /* This script displays and handles an HTML form. This script takes text input and stores it in
      a text file. */
11
12   // Identify the file to use:
13   $file = '../quotes.txt';
14
15   // Check for a form submission:
16   if ($_SERVER['REQUEST_METHOD'] == 'POST') { // Handle the form.
17
18       if ( !empty($_POST['quote']) && ($_POST['quote'] != 'Enter your quotation here.') ) { // Need
         some thing to write.
```

code continues on next page

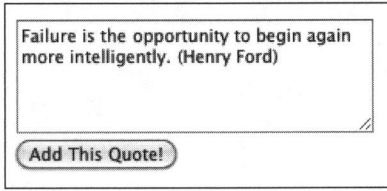

A Using the form once again...

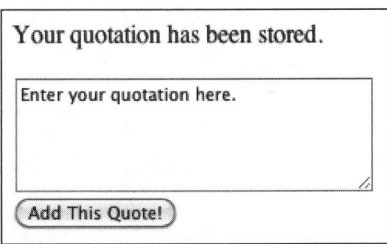

B ...the quotation is still stored without a problem.

3. Save the file, place it in the proper directory for your PHP-enabled server, and test it again in your Web browser **A** and **B**.

TIP When you use `flock()`, the file will automatically be unlocked once `fclose()` is called, but it's good form to specifically unlock it once the file writing is complete.

TIP Technically, if a file is opened in an appending mode, as in this example, not locking it probably won't be a problem even if multiple scripts are writing to the file simultaneously. That said, better safe than sorry!

TIP For file locking to be reliable, every script that writes to a file needs to use locking.

Script 11.2 *continued*

```
19
20        if (is_writable($file)) { // Confirm that the file is writable.
21
22            file_put_contents($file, $_POST['quote'] . PHP_EOL, FILE_APPEND | LOCK_EX); //
              Write the data.
23
24            // Print a message:
25            print '<p>Your quotation has been stored.</p>';
26
27        } else { // Could not open the file.
28            print '<p style="color: red;">Your quotation could not be stored due to a system
              error.</p>';
29        }
30
31    } else { // Failed to enter a quotation.
32        print '<p style="color: red;">Please enter a quotation!</p>';
33    }
34
35  } // End of submitted IF.
36
37  // Leave PHP and display the form:
38  ?>
39
40  <form action="add_quote.php" method="post">
41      <textarea name="quote" rows="5" cols="30">Enter your quotation here.</textarea><br />
42      <input type="submit" name="submit" value="Add This Quote!" />
43  </form>
44
45  </body>
46  </html>
```

Reading from Files

Now that you've created a script that writes data to a file, it's time to create one that can read the information. There are a number of ways to read from a file; which approach you take depends on what your needs are. To read an entire file in as one string, use **file_get_contents()**:

$data = file_get_contents($file);

If the file has some data on each line, as is the case with **quotes.txt**, you're better off using the **file()** function:

$data = file($file);

The **file()** function is a valuable built-in tool in PHP. It reads everything from a file and, unlike **file_get_contents()**, returns that information as an array. Each array element contains one line from the file, where each line is terminated by a newline (**\n** or **\r\n**).

If the document represented by **$file** contains two lines of information, each of which ends with a newline, the corresponding array will contain two elements. The first element will be equal to the first line of **$file**, and the second element will be equal to the second line. Once the data is stored into an array, you can easily manipulate or print it, as you learned in Chapter 7, "Using Arrays."

Next, let's use this knowledge to create a script that randomly displays one of the stored quotations.

Script 11.3 The `view_quote.php` file retrieves all the quotations from the text file and displays one at random.

```
1    <!DOCTYPE html PUBLIC "-//W3C//DTD XHTML
     1.0 Transitional//EN"
2        "http://www.w3.org/TR/xhtml1/DTD/
     xhtml1-transitional.dtd">
3    <html xmlns="http://www.w3.org/1999/
     xhtml" xml:lang="en" lang="en">
4    <head>
5        <meta http-equiv="content-type"
     content="text/html; charset=utf-8" />
6        <title>View A Quotation</title>
7    </head>
8    <body>
9    <h1>Random Quotation</h1>
10   <?php // Script 11.3 - view_quote.php
11   /* This script displays and handles an
     HTML form. This script reads in a file
     and prints a random line from it. */
12
13   // Read the file's contents into an array:
14   $data = file('../quotes.txt');
15
16   // Count the number of items in the array:
17   $n = count($data);
18
19   // Pick a random item:
20   $rand = rand(0, ($n - 1));
21
22   // Print the quotation:
23   print '<p>' . trim($data[$rand]) . '</p>';
24
25   ?>
26   </body>
27   </html>
```

To read from a file:

1. Create a new PHP document in your text editor or IDE, to be named **view_quote.php** (Script 11.3):

```
<!DOCTYPE html PUBLIC "-//W3C//DTD
→ XHTML 1.0 Transitional//EN"
  "http://www.w3.org/TR/xhtml1/
  → DTD/xhtml1-transitional.dtd">
<html xmlns="http://www.w3.org/
→ 1999/xhtml" xml:lang="en"
→ lang="en">
<head>
  <meta http-equiv="content-type"
  → content="text/html;
  → charset=utf-8" />
  <title>View A Quotation</title>
</head>
<body>
<h1>Random Quotation</h1>
```

2. Open a PHP code section:

```
<?php // Script 11.3 -
→ view_quote.php
```

3. Read the file contents and store them in an array:

```
$data = file('../quotes.txt');
```

The function reads the file data into an array called **$data**. Each element of **$data** is a string, which is the submitted quotation.

If the quotes file is not in the parent directory of this script, change the reference here accordingly.

4. Pick a random number based on the number of elements in **$data**:

```
$n = count($data);
$rand = rand(0, ($n - 1));
```

continues on next page

The first line counts how many elements (which is to say, how many quotations) are in the $data array. Then the **rand()** function selects a random number. In order for **rand()** to pick an appropriate number, a little logic is required.

If **$data** has 10 elements, they're indexed between 0 and 9, so that's the range to use for **rand()**. Therefore, to calculate the range for a variable number of lines in the text file, use 0 and 1 less than the number of elements in **$data**.

5. Print out the quotation:

```
print '<p>' . trim($data[$rand]) .
→ '</p>';
```

A simple **print** statement involving concatenation is used to print the random quotation. To retrieve the quotation, you refer to the **$data** array and use the generated **$rand** number as the index. The retrieved quotation is then trimmed to cut off the newline characters from the end of the quotation.

6. Complete the PHP code and the HTML page:

```
?>
</body>
</html>
```

7. Save the file as **view_quote.php**, place it on your Web server (in the same directory as **add_quote.php**), and test it in your Web browser **A**.

8. Reload the page in your Web browser to view another random quote **B**.

> **TIP** If you want to be extra careful, you can use the is_readable() function to test that PHP can read a file before you call the file() function (although it's rare that a file isn't readable).

> **TIP** The readfile() function reads through a file and immediately sends the contents to the Web browser.

> **TIP** Later in the chapter, you'll learn a more complex method of reading a file using fgets() and fgetcsv().

Random Quotation

Nurture your mind with great thoughts, for you will never go any higher than you think. (Benjamin Disraeli)

A A random quotation is displayed each time the page is viewed.

Random Quotation

It is the mark of an educated mind to be able to entertain a thought without accepting it. (Aristotle)

B Subsequent viewings of the **view_quote.php** script display different quotations from the text file.

ⓐ This is how Firefox interprets the file input type.

ⓑ This is how the Safari Web browser interprets the file input type (prior to selecting a file).

Handling File Uploads

As this book has demonstrated, handling HTML forms using PHP is a remarkably easy achievement. Regardless of the data being submitted, PHP can handle it easily and directly. The same is true when the user uploads a file via an HTML form.

To give the user the option of uploading a file, you must make three changes to the standard HTML form. First, the initial **form** tag must include the code **enctype="multipart/form-data"**, which lets the browser know to expect different types of form data:

```
<form action="script.php" enctype=
→ "multipart/form-data" method="post">
```

The form must also always use the POST method.

Second, a special hidden input type should be added to the form:

```
<input type="hidden" name=
→ "MAX_FILE_SIZE" value="30000" />
```

This tells the browser how large a file, in bytes, can be uploaded.

Third, the **file** tag is used to create the necessary form field **ⓐ** and **ⓑ**:

```
<input type="file" name="picture" />
```

The file type of form input allows the user to select a file on their computer, which, upon submission, will be uploaded to the server. Once this has occurred, you can then use PHP to handle the file.

continues on next page

In the PHP script, you refer to the **$_FILES** variable (think of it as the file equivalent of **$_POST**) to reference the uploaded file. The **$_FILES** array contains five elements:

- **name**, the name of the file as it was on the user's computer
- **type**, the MIME type of the file (for example, *image/jpg*)
- **size**, the size of the file in bytes
- **tmp_name**, the temporary name of the file as it's stored on the server
- **error**, an error code if something goes wrong (**Table 11.3**)

Note that, as strange as this may seem, there is no error code 5.

When a file is uploaded, the server first places it in a temporary directory. You can then use the **move_uploaded_file()** function to move the file to its final destination:

```
move_uploaded_file($_FILES['picture']
['tmp_name'], '/path/to/dest/
filename');
```

The first argument is the temporary name of the file on the server. The second argument is the full path and name of the destination.

For PHP to be able to take these steps, you must set several configurations in the **php.ini** file (see the "Configuring PHP for File Uploads" sidebar), and the Web server needs write access to both the temporary and final destination directories. (PHP should have write access to the temporary directory by default.)

TABLE 11.3 $_FILES Error Codes

Code	Meaning
0	No error has occurred.
1	The file exceeds the **upload_max_filesize** setting in **php.ini**.
2	The file exceeds the **MAX_FILE_SIZE** setting in the HTML form.
3	The file was only partially uploaded.
4	No file was uploaded.
6	No temporary directory exists.
7	Failed write to disk.
8	Upload prevented by an extension.

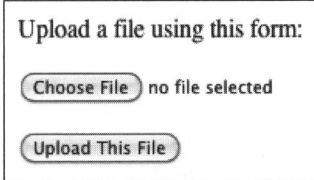

Upload a file using this form:

(Choose File) no file selected

(Upload This File)

C This HTML form lets the user select a file on their computer to upload to the server.

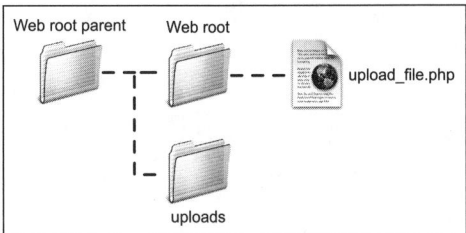

Web root parent   Web root

upload_file.php

uploads

D For this example, a writable **uploads** directory must exist. Here, it's placed in the same directory as the Web root folder. Thus **uploads** is in the directory above the one in which the **upload_file.php** script resides and is not accessible via HTTP.

Next, you'll write a basic script that uploads a file and stores it on the server. Like the **add_quote.php** script, this example also both creates the HTML form **C** and processes it, all in one page. First, though, you'll create a writable directory as the destination point.

To create a writable directory:

1. Create a new folder called **uploads**, located outside of the Web directory root **D**.

2. Using the steps outlined in the first section of this chapter, set the permissions so that everyone can write to, read from, and search (**0777** in Unix terms) the directory.

   Again, if you're running Windows you likely don't need to do anything (try the next script to see for sure). If you're running another operating system, check the list of bullet points in the first section of the chapter for the suggestion that works for your situation.

Configuring PHP for File Uploads

In order for file uploading to work, a number of settings in your **php.ini** configuration file must be set. These may or may not be enabled in your configuration, so you should check them by viewing the **php.ini** file or running a **phpinfo()** script.

For starters, **file_uploads** must be on. Second, the **upload_tmp_dir** value must be set to a directory on the server where PHP can place files (in other words, it must exist and be modifiable by the Web server). If this setting has no value, that's probably fine (meaning that a hidden directory created expressly for purposes such as these will be used).

The **upload_max_filesize** and **post_max_size** settings dictate how large a file can be sent. Whereas the **MAX_FILE_SIZE** hidden form input is a recommendation to the Web browser, these two settings control whether the file is uploaded.

Finally, if really large files will be uploaded (many megabytes or larger), you may need to increase the **memory_limit** and **max_execution_time** settings to give PHP the time and the resources to do what it needs to do.

To use PHP for file uploads:

1. Create a new PHP document in your text editor or IDE, to be named **upload_file.php** (Script 11.4):

```
<!DOCTYPE html PUBLIC "-//W3C//DTD
→ XHTML 1.0 Transitional//EN"
  "http://www.w3.org/TR/xhtml1/
  → DTD/xhtml1-transitional.dtd">
<html xmlns="http://www.w3.org/
→ 1999/xhtml" xml:lang="en"
→ lang="en">
<head>
  <meta http-equiv="content-type"
  → content="text/html;
  → charset=utf-8" />
  <title>Upload a File</title>
</head>
<body>
```

2. Create a section of PHP code:

```
<?php // Script 11.4 -
→ upload_file.php
```

continues on page 312

Script 11.4 This script handles a file upload by first defining the proper HTML form and, second, invoking **move_uploaded_file()** to move the file to the desired location.

```
1    <!DOCTYPE html PUBLIC "-//W3C//DTD XHTML 1.0 Transitional//EN"
2        "http://www.w3.org/TR/xhtml1/DTD/xhtml1-transitional.dtd">
3    <html xmlns="http://www.w3.org/1999/xhtml" xml:lang="en" lang="en">
4    <head>
5        <meta http-equiv="content-type" content="text/html; charset=utf-8" />
6        <title>Upload a File</title>
7    </head>
8    <body>
9    <?php // Script 11.4 - upload_file.php
10   /* This script displays and handles an HTML form. This script takes a file upload and stores it
     on the server. */
11
12   if ($_SERVER['REQUEST_METHOD'] == 'POST') { // Handle the form.
13
```

code continues on next page

```
14       // Try to move the uploaded file:
15       if (move_uploaded_file ($_FILES['the_file']['tmp_name'], "../uploads/{$_FILES['the_file']
         ['name']}")) {
16
17           print '<p>Your file has been uploaded.</p>';
18
19       } else { // Problem!
20
21           print '<p style="color: red;">Your file could not be uploaded because: ';
22
23           // Print a message based upon the error:
24           switch ($_FILES['the_file']['error']) {
25               case 1:
26                   print 'The file exceeds the upload_max_filesize setting in php.ini';
27                   break;
28               case 2:
29                   print 'The file exceeds the MAX_FILE_SIZE setting in the HTML form';
30                   break;
31               case 3:
32                   print 'The file was only partially uploaded';
33                   break;
34               case 4:
35                   print 'No file was uploaded';
36                   break;
37               case 6:
38                   print 'The temporary folder does not exist.';
39                   break;
40               default:
41                   print 'Something unforeseen happened.';
42                   break;
43           }
44
45           print '.</p>'; // Complete the paragraph.
46
47       } // End of move_uploaded_file() IF.
48
49   } // End of submission IF.
50
51   // Leave PHP and display the form:
52   ?>
53
54   <form action="upload_file.php" enctype="multipart/form-data" method="post">
55       <p>Upload a file using this form:</p>
56       <input type="hidden" name="MAX_FILE_SIZE" value="300000" />
57       <p><input type="file" name="the_file" /></p>
58       <p><input type="submit" name="submit" value="Upload This File" /></p>
59   </form>
60
61   </body>
62   </html>
```

3. Check whether the form has been submitted:

```
if ($_SERVER['REQUEST_METHOD'] ==
→'POST') {
```

Once again, this script both displays and handles the HTML form. If it has been submitted, the uploaded file should be addressed.

4. Attempt to move the uploaded file to its final destination:

```
if (move_uploaded_file
→($_FILES['the_file']['tmp_name'],
→"../uploads/{$_FILES['the_file']
→['name']}")) {
```

The **move_uploaded_file()** function attempts to move the uploaded file (identified by **$_FILES['the_file'] ['tmp_name']**) to its new location (**../uploads/{$_FILES['the_file'] ['name']**). The location is the **uploads** directory, which is located in the folder above the one this script is in. The file's name will be the same as it was on the user's computer.

Placing this function as a condition in an **if** statement makes it easy to respond based on whether the move worked.

5. Print messages indicating the success of the operation:

```
print '<p>Your file has been
→uploaded.</p>';
} else { // Problem!
print '<p style="color: red;">
→Your file could not be
→uploaded because: ';
```

The first **print** statement is executed if the move worked 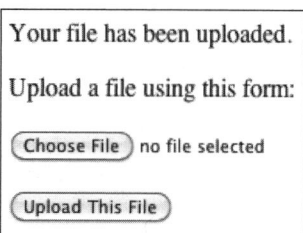. The **else** applies if it didn't work, in which case an error message is begun. This message will be made more explicit in Step 6.

Your file has been uploaded.

Upload a file using this form:

Choose File   no file selected

Upload This File

E If the file was uploaded and moved successfully, a message is printed and the form is displayed again.

6. Print out the error message if the move didn't work:

```
switch ($_FILES['the_file']
['error']) {
  case 1:
    print 'The file exceeds the
    → upload_max_filesize setting
    → in php.ini';
    break;
  case 2:
    print 'The file exceeds the
    → MAX_FILE_SIZE setting in
    → the HTML form';
    break;
  case 3:
    print 'The file was only
    → partially uploaded';
    break;
  case 4:
    print 'No file was uploaded';
    break;
  case 6:
    print 'The temporary folder
    → does not exist.';
    break;
  default:
    print 'Something unforeseen
    → happened.';
    break;
}
```

If a move doesn't work, the **$_FILES['the_file']['error']** variable contains a number indicating the appropriate error message. When you use this in a **switch** conditional, the PHP script can print out the appropriate error message **F**.

You wouldn't normally place code like this in a public site (it's a little too much information), but it's exceptionally good for helping you debug a problem.

7. Complete the error message, and close both conditionals:

```
    print '.</p>'; // Complete the
paragraph.
  } // End of move_uploaded_
file() IF.
} // End of submission IF.
```

8. Exit out of PHP and create the HTML form:

```
?>
<form action="upload_file.php"
→ enctype="multipart/form-data"
→ method="post">
  <p>Upload a file using this
  → form:</p>
  <input type="hidden" name="MAX_
  → FILE_SIZE" value="300000" />
  <p><input type="file"
  → name="the_file" /></p>
  <p><input type="submit"
  → name="submit" value="Upload
  → This File" /></p>
</form>
```

continues on next page

Your file could not be uploaded because: The file exceeds the MAX_FILE_SIZE setting in the HTML form.

Upload a file using this form:

(Choose File) no file selected

(Upload This File)

F If a problem occurred, the script indicates the cause.

The HTML form is simple, containing only two visible elements: a file input type and a submit button. It differs from other HTML forms in this book in that it uses the **enctype** attribute and a **MAX_FILE_SIZE** hidden input type.

Be careful when giving your **file** input a name, because this value must exactly match the index used in the **$_FILES** variable. Here, you use a generic *the_file*.

9. Complete the HTML page:

```
</body>
</html>
```

10. Save the page as **upload_file.php**, place it in the proper directory for your PHP-enabled server relative to the **uploads** directory ⓓ, and test it in your Web browser ⓖ.

Only files smaller than about 300 KB should be allowed, thanks to the **MAX_FILE_SIZE** restriction.

11. Check the **uploads** directory to ensure that the file was placed there.

TIP If the file couldn't be moved and a permissions denied error is shown, check the permissions on the **uploads** directory. Then check that the path to the directory used in the script is correct and that there are no spelling errors.

TIP As you might discover, files uploaded through the Web browser are owned (in terms of permissions) by the Web server application (which put them there).

TIP From a security standpoint, it's better to rename an uploaded file. To do so, you'll need to devise a system that generates a new, unique filename and stores both the original and new filenames in a text file or a database.

TIP A script can handle multiple file uploads as long as they have different names. In such a case, you need only one **MAX_FILE_SIZE** hidden input. In the PHP script, you'd apply the move_uploaded_file() function to $_FILES['filename1'], $_FILES['filename2'], and so on.

TIP You can limit a file upload to a specific size or type by referencing the appropriate index (for example, $_FILES['the_file']['size']) in your PHP script (after the file has been uploaded).

TIP Use unlink() to delete a file without moving or copying it.

TIP You can use the copy() function to make a copy of a file on the server.

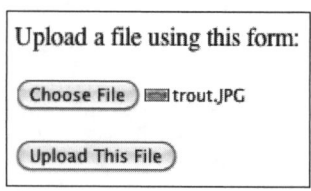

ⓖ Select a file on your computer to upload.

Directories

- ch1
- ch2
- ch3
- templates

Files

Name	Size	Last Modified
add_quote.php	1520 bytes	December 29, 2010
list_dir.php	1562 bytes	December 28, 2010
login.php	1690 bytes	December 28, 2010
register.php	2339 bytes	December 28, 2010
upload_file.php	1844 bytes	December 29, 2010
view_quote.php	773 bytes	December 29, 2010

A The `list_dir.php` script shows the contents of a directory. The top part lists the subfolders, and the bottom table lists the files.

Navigating Directories

The previous PHP scripts work with files, but you can also do many things with directories using PHP. In this example, you'll write a script that lists a directory's contents, but first you'll need to understand the usage and syntax of many of the functions you'll use.

To find all of the contents of a directory, the easiest option is to use the `scandir()` function:

```
$stuff = scandir($dir);
```

This function, added in PHP 5, returns an array of every item—directory or file—found within the given directory. As with the file-related functions, the value of `$dir` can be a relative or an absolute path to the directory in question.

If you're using an earlier version of PHP, you'll need to use `opendir()`, `readdir()`, and `closedir()` instead. See the PHP manual page for `readdir()` for the full syntax and usage.

This next example will make use of `scandir()`, but let's look at a couple more functions first. You'll use the `filesize()` function in this example; it determines how large a file is in bytes. This value can be assigned to a variable or be printed:

```
$size = filesize($file);
```

Similarly, the `filemtime()` function retrieves the modification time of a file. It returns a timestamp, which can be formatted using the `date()` function.

Finally, PHP includes several functions that identify attributes. This chapter has already mentioned `is_writable()` and `is_readable()`, but there are also `is_dir()` and `is_file()`. They return **TRUE** if the item in question is a directory or a file, respectively.

You'll put all of these capabilities together into one page, which will constitute a Web-based control panel for viewing a directory's contents **A**.

To create the directory control panel:

1. Create a new PHP document in your text editor or IDE, to be named **list_dir.php** (Script 11.5):

```
<!DOCTYPE html PUBLIC "-//W3C//DTD
→ XHTML 1.0 Transitional//EN"
  "http://www.w3.org/TR/xhtml1/
  → DTD/xhtml1-transitional.dtd">
<html xmlns="http://www.w3.org/
→ 1999/xhtml" xml:lang="en"
→ lang="en">
<head>
  <meta http-equiv="content-type"
  → content="text/html;
  → charset=utf-8" />
  <title>Directory Contents
  → </title>
</head>
<body>
```

continues on page 318

Script 11.5 This script displays the contents of a directory. First the subdirectories are listed, followed by the files (with their sizes and modification dates) in a table.

```
1    <!DOCTYPE html PUBLIC "-//W3C//DTD XHTML 1.0 Transitional//EN"
2        "http://www.w3.org/TR/xhtml1/DTD/xhtml1-transitional.dtd">
3    <html xmlns="http://www.w3.org/1999/xhtml" xml:lang="en" lang="en">
4    <head>
5        <meta http-equiv="content-type" content="text/html; charset=utf-8" />
6        <title>Directory Contents</title>
7    </head>
8    <body>
9    <?php // Script 11.5 - list_dir.php
10   /* This script lists the directories and files in a directory. */
11
12   // Set the time zone:
13   date_default_timezone_set('America/New_York');
14
15   // Set the directory name and scan it:
16   $search_dir = '.';
17   $contents = scandir($search_dir);
18
```

code continues on next page

```
19   // List the directories first...
20   // Print a caption and start a list:
21   print '<h2>Directories</h2>
22   <ul>';
23   foreach ($contents as $item) {
24       if ( (is_dir($search_dir . '/' . $item)) AND (substr($item, 0, 1) != '.') ) {
25           print "<li>$item</li>\n";
26       }
27   }
28
29   print '</ul>'; // Close the list.
30
31   // Create a table header:
32   print '<hr /><h2>Files</h2>
33   <table cellpadding="2" cellspacing="2" align="left">
34   <tr>
35   <td>Name</td>
36   <td>Size</td>
37   <td>Last Modified</td>
38   </tr>';
39
40   // List the files:
41   foreach ($contents as $item) {
42       if ( (is_file($search_dir . '/' . $item)) AND (substr($item, 0, 1) != '.') ) {
43
44           // Get the file size:
45           $fs = filesize($search_dir . '/' . $item);
46
47           // Get the file's modification date:
48           $lm = date('F j, Y', filemtime($search_dir . '/' . $item));
49
50           // Print the information:
51           print "<tr>
52           <td>$item</td>
53           <td>$fs bytes</td>
54           <td>$lm</td>
55           </tr>\n";
56
57       } // Close the IF.
58
59   } // Close the FOREACH.
60
61   print '</table>'; // Close the HTML table.
62
63   ?>
64   </body>
65   </html>
```

2. Begin the PHP code and set the time zone:

```php
<?php // Script 11.5 - list_dir.php
date_default_timezone_set
→ ('America/New_York');
```

Because this script will make use of the **date()** function, it needs to establish the time zone once. See Chapter 8, "Creating Web Applications," for more and for the reference in the PHP manual where you can find your time zone.

3. Identify the directory to be opened, and scan in its contents:

```php
$search_dir = '.';
$contents = scandir($search_dir);
```

By establishing this value as a variable at the top of the PHP script, it will be easy to find and change as needed. Here you use a single period to refer to the current directory. You could also use an absolute path to another directory (**/Users/larry/Documents** or **C:\\myfiles\\directory**) or a relative path (**../myfiles**), as long as PHP has permission to read the named directory.

The second line scans in the directory's contents and assigns them as an array to the variable **$contents**.

4. List the subdirectories of this directory:

```php
print '<h2>Directories</h2>
<ul>';
foreach ($contents as $item) {
  if ( (is_dir($search_dir . '/' .
  → $item)) AND (substr($item,
  → 0, 1) != '.') ) {
    print "<li>$item</li>\n";
  }
}

print '</ul>';
```

This **foreach** loop accesses every item in the array, assigning each one to the **$item** variable. The script should first

list every directory, so the **is_dir()** function is called to confirm the item's type. That same conditional also checks that the current item isn't the current directory (marked by a single period on Unix systems) or the parent directory (marked by a double period on Unix systems). If this conditional is **TRUE**, then the item's name is printed out, within list item tags, followed by a newline (to make for neater HTML source code).

So that the **is_dir()** function will work when dealing with items found in other directories, the **$search_dir** value, plus a slash, is appended to each item. If the code just referred to **$item** without adding the directory path, the code would only work for the current directory.

5. Create a new heading, and start a table for the files:

```php
print '<hr /><h2>Files</h2>
<table cellpadding="2"
→ cellspacing="2" align="left">
<tr>
<td>Name</td>
<td>Size</td>
<td>Last Modified</td>
</tr>';
```

The script also displays the files' sizes and modification dates. To make this look nicer, the results are placed in an HTML table.

6. Begin looping through the files in this directory:

```php
foreach ($contents as $item) {
  if ( (is_file($search_dir . '/' .
  → $item)) AND (substr($item,
  → 0, 1) != '.') ) {
```

Another **foreach** loop is used to go through the directory contents again. This time, the conditional only wants items that are files (but not hidden files that begin with a single period).

Directories

- ch11
- css
- temp
- templates

Files

Name	Size	Last Modified
add_quote.php	1520 bytes	December 29, 2010
books.php	514 bytes	December 13, 2010
calculator.html	1094 bytes	October 16, 2008
calculator.php	1709 bytes	October 27, 2008
customize.php	1694 bytes	December 20, 2010
event.html	1043 bytes	December 7, 2010

B The directory listing for another folder on the server.

TIP Notice that you need to use double backslashes to create absolute path names on a Windows server. This is necessary because the single backslash, used in Windows path names, is the escape character. So, it must be escaped to be taken literally.

TIP The glob() function lets you search a directory for files whose name matches a pattern (like *something*.jpg or *filename*.doc).

TIP Other file functions you might appreciate include fileperms(), which returns the file's permissions; fileatime(), which returns the last time a file was accessed; and fileowner(), which returns the user who owns the file.

TIP The basename() and dirname() functions are useful for finding subparts of a full directory or file path.

TIP The finfo_file() function is the best way to find a file's MIME type.

Again, the **$search_dir** value and a slash is prepended to each item.

7. Calculate the file's size and modification date, and then print out the information:

```
$fs = filesize($search_dir . '/' .
→ $item);
$lm = date('F j, Y', filemtime
→ ($search_dir . '/' . $item));
print "<tr>
<td>$item</td>
<td>$fs bytes</td>
<td>$lm</td>
</tr>\n";
```

The first line calls the **filesize()** function to retrieve the file's size in bytes. The second line calls the **filemtime()** function, which returns a timestamp of the file's modification time. The timestamp is then fed into the **date()** function, along with the proper formatting, to return a string like *November 24, 2011*. Finally, these two items and the file's name are printed in the appropriate columns of the table.

8. Complete the conditional and the loop:

```
    }
}
```

9. Close the table:

```
print '</table>';
```

10. Complete the PHP code and the HTML page:

```
?>
</body>
</html>
```

11. Save the file as **list_dir.php**, place it in the proper directory for your PHP-enabled server, and test it in your Web browser **A**.

12. If you want, change the value of **$search_dir** and retest the script in your Web browser **B**.

Creating Directories

Understanding how to read from and write to files on the server is only part of the data storage process. It's likely you'll want to use directories for this purpose as well.

The command for creating a directory in PHP is `mkdir()`:

```
mkdir('directory_name', permissions);
```

The directory name is the name of the directory to be created. This value can be relative to the current directory (i.e., the one the script is in) or it can be a full path:

```
mkdir('C:\\inetpub\\users\\george');
```

On Windows servers, the permissions are ignored and therefore not required (as in the preceding example). On non-Windows servers, the permissions are **0777** by default (see the section "File Permissions" earlier in this chapter to learn what those numbers mean).

With this in mind, let's create a script that makes a new directory for a user when the user registers (the theory being that a user could upload files to that directory). This script also records the username and password to a text file, so that the user can be validated when logging in. You'll begin by creating the parent directory (which must be writable so that PHP can create subdirectories in it) and the **users.txt** data file.

To create the directory and the data file:

1. Create a new folder called **users**, located outside of the Web directory root.

   It could be created in the same directory as the **uploads** folder made earlier (see ➍ in "Handling File Uploads").

2. Using the steps outlined in the first section of this chapter, set the permissions so that everyone can write to, read from, and search (**0777** in Unix terms) the directory.

   If you're running Windows, this step will most likely not be necessary.

3. In your text editor, create a new, blank document.

4. Save this file in the **users** directory with the name **users.txt**.

5. Again using the steps outlined earlier in the chapter, set the permissions on **users.txt** so that everyone can write to and read from the file (**0666** in Unix terms).

   Again, this will probably not be necessary if you're running Windows on your PHP server.

TIP Once you create a directory that PHP can write to, PHP should be able to automatically create a `users.txt` file in that directory to which PHP can write. However, it's best not to make assumptions about such things.

To create the registration script:

1. Begin a new PHP document in your text editor or IDE, to be named **register.php** (Script 11.6):

```
<!DOCTYPE html PUBLIC "-//W3C//DTD
→ XHTML 1.0 Transitional//EN"
  "http://www.w3.org/TR/xhtml1/
  → DTD/xhtml1-transitional.dtd">
<html xmlns="http://www.w3.org/
→ 1999/xhtml" xml:lang="en"
→ lang="en">
<head>
  <meta http-equiv="content-type"
  → content="text/html;
  → charset=utf-8" />
  <title>Register</title>
  <style type="text/css"
  → media="screen">
    .error { color: red; }
  </style>
</head>
<body>
<h1>Register</h1>
```

In the page's head, a CSS class is defined that will be used to format errors.

continues on page 323

Script 11.6 The **register.php** script serves two purposes: it records the user's information in a text file and creates a new directory for that user's stuff.

```
1   <!DOCTYPE html PUBLIC "-//W3C//DTD XHTML 1.0 Transitional//EN"
2       "http://www.w3.org/TR/xhtml1/DTD/xhtml1-transitional.dtd">
3   <html xmlns="http://www.w3.org/1999/xhtml" xml:lang="en" lang="en">
4   <head>
5       <meta http-equiv="content-type" content="text/html; charset=utf-8" />
6       <title>Register</title>
7       <style type="text/css" media="screen">
8           .error { color: red; }
9       </style>
10  </head>
11  <body>
12  <h1>Register</h1>
13  <?php // Script 11.6 - register.php
```

code continues on next page

```
14    /* This script registers a user by storing their information in a text file and creating a
      directory for them. */
15
16    // Identify the directory and file to use:
17    $dir = '../users/';
18    $file = $dir . 'users.txt';
19
20    if ($_SERVER['REQUEST_METHOD'] == 'POST') { // Handle the form.
21
22        $problem = FALSE; // No problems so far.
23
24        // Check for each value...
25        if (empty($_POST['username'])) {
26            $problem = TRUE;
27            print '<p class="error">Please enter a username!</p>';
28        }
29
30        if (empty($_POST['password1'])) {
31            $problem = TRUE;
32            print '<p class="error">Please enter a password!</p>';
33        }
34
35        if ($_POST['password1'] != $_POST['password2']) {
36            $problem = TRUE;
37            print '<p class="error">Your password did not match your confirmed password!</p>';
38        }
39
40        if (!$problem) { // If there weren't any problems...
41
42            if (is_writable($file)) { // Open the file.
43
44                // Create the data to be written:
45                $subdir = time() . rand(0, 4596);
46                $data = $_POST['username'] . "\t" . md5(trim($_POST['password1'])) . "\t" .
                   $subdir . PHP_EOL;
47
48                // Write the data:
49                file_put_contents($file, $data, FILE_APPEND | LOCK_EX);
50
51                // Create the directory:
52                mkdir ($dir . $subdir);
53
54                // Print a message:
55                print '<p>You are now registered!</p>';
56
57            } else { // Couldn't write to the file.
58                print '<p class="error">You could not be registered due to a system error.</p>';
59            }
60
```

code continues on next page

2. Begin the PHP code and create two variables:

```php
<?php // Script 11.6 - register.php
$dir = '../users/';
$file = $dir . 'users.txt';
```

These two variables represent the directory and file being used by the example. The file will be in the directory, so its value starts with the directory's value. Change the value of **$dir** so that it's appropriate for your situation.

3. Check whether the form has been submitted:

```php
if ($_SERVER['REQUEST_METHOD'] ==
→ 'POST') {
```

Once again, this page both displays and handles the HTML form. This is accomplished using a conditional that checks how the script is being requested.

continues on next page

Script 11.6 *continued*

```
61      } else { // Forgot a field.
62          print '<p class="error">Please go back and try again!</p>';
63      }
64
65  } else { // Display the form.
66
67  // Leave PHP and display the form:
68  ?>
69
70  <form action="register.php" method="post">
71      <p>Username: <input type="text" name="username" size="20" /></p>
72      <p>Password: <input type="password" name="password1" size="20" /></p>
73      <p>Confirm Password: <input type="password" name="password2" size="20" /></p>
74      <input type="submit" name="submit" value="Register" />
75  </form>
76
77  <?php } // End of submission IF. ?>
78  </body>
79  </html>
```

4. Validate the registration information:

```php
$problem = FALSE;
if (empty($_POST['username'])) {
    $problem = TRUE;
    print '<p class="error">Please
    → enter a username!</p>';
}
if (empty($_POST['password1'])) {
    $problem = TRUE;
    print '<p class="error">Please
    → enter a password!</p>';
}
if ($_POST['password1'] != $_POST
→ ['password2']) {
    $problem = TRUE;
    print '<p class="error">Your
    → password did not match your
    → confirmed password!</p>';
}
```

The registration form is a simpler version of earlier registration forms developed in this book. The same validation process you previously developed is used to check the submitted username and passwords. The **$problem** variable is used as a flag to indicate whether a problem occurred.

5. Check for problems:

```php
if (!$problem) {
```

Again, the **$problem** variable lets you know if it's okay to register the user. If no problems occurred, it's safe to continue.

6. Confirm that the **users.txt** file is writable:

```php
if (is_writable($file)) {
```

Like before, the data file is first confirmed as writable in a conditional, so that the script can respond accordingly. If you're not using PHP 5.1 or greater, use

an **fopen()** line as the condition instead (see earlier in the chapter).

7. Create the data to be written to the file, and then write it:

```php
$subdir = time() . rand(0, 4596);
$data = $_POST['username'] . "\t" .
→ md5(trim($_POST['password1'])) .
→ "\t" . $subdir . PHP_EOL;
file_put_contents($file, $data,
→ FILE_APPEND | LOCK_EX);
```

The name of the directory being created is a number based on the time the user registered and a random value. This system helps to guarantee that the directory created is unique and has a valid name.

Instead of storing a single string as you previously have, this script stores three separate pieces of information: the user's name; an encrypted version of the password (using the **md5()** function; see the first tip); and the directory name, created in the preceding line. The password is trimmed first, to get rid of any extraneous spaces.

To distinguish between the pieces of information, you insert a tab (created using the **\t** code). A newline is used to mark the end of the line, again using the **PHP_EOL** constant.

8. Create the user's directory, and print a message:

```php
mkdir ($dir . $subdir);
print '<p>You are now
→ registered!</p>';
```

The **mkdir()** function creates the directory in the **users** directory. The directory is named whatever random number was generated earlier.

Register

You could not be registered due to a system error.

The result if the **users.txt** file is not writable.

Register

Please enter a username!

Please enter a password!

Please go back and try again!

The script reports any form validation errors.

9. Complete the conditionals:

```
} else { // Couldn't write to
→ the file.
  print '<p class="error">You
  → could not be registered due
  → to a system error.</p>';
}
} else { // Forgot a field.
  print '<p class="error">Please
  → go back and try again!</p>';
}
```

The first **else** completes the conditional if the script couldn't open the **users.txt** file for writing **A**. The second **else** completes the conditional if the user failed to complete the form properly **B**.

10. Add an **else** clause to the main conditional, and exit out of PHP:

```
} else {
?>
```

Unlike the previous examples in this chapter, this PHP script first displays the form and then handles it. Whereas the other scripts would then display the form again, this one does not, as the form creation is part of an **else** statement. Because the rest of the page is just HTML, you exit out of PHP to create the form.

11. Display the HTML form:

```
<form action="register.php"
→ method="post">
  <p>Username: <input type="text"
  → name="username" size="20" /></p>
  <p>Password: <input type=
  → "password" name="password1"
  → size="20" /></p>
  <p>Confirm Password: <input
  → type="password" name=
  → "password2" size="20" /></p>
  <input type="submit" name=
  → "submit" value="Register" />
</form>
```

continues on next page

12. Complete the main conditional:

```php
<?php } // End of submission IF. ?>
```

This final closing curly bracket closes the main submit conditional. For it to work, a new PHP section must first be created.

13. Complete the HTML page:

```html
</body>
</html>
```

14. Save the file as **register.php**, place it in the proper directory for your PHP-enabled server, and test it in your Web browser **C** and **D**.

15. If you want, open the **users.txt** file in your text editor to see its contents (**Script 11.7**).

TIP The md5() function creates a *hash*: a mathematically calculated representation of a string. So this script doesn't actually store the password but a representation of that password (in theory, no two strings would have the same md5() value). You'll soon see how the hashed password is used by a login script.

TIP You can also ensure that the page worked as it should by looking in the **users** directory for the new subdirectories.

TIP The rmdir() function deletes an existing directory, assuming PHP has permission to do so.

Register

Username: larry

Password: ••••

Confirm Password: ••••

(Register)

C The registration form is quite basic but serves its purpose.

Register

You are now registered!

D This is what the user sees if the registration process worked.

Script 11.7 The **users.txt** file lists three tab-delineated fields of information: the username, a scrambled version of the user's password, and their associated directory name.

```
1   larry    1a1dc91c907325c69271ddf0c944bc72    12936537501284
2   john     0cc175b9c0f1b6a831c399e269772661    1293653788455
3   paul     92eb5ffee6ae2fec3ad71c777531578f    12936537931717
4   george   4a8a08f09d37b73795649038408b5f33    1293653799360
5   ringo    8277e0910d750195b448797616e091ad    12936538042144
```

Reading Files Incrementally

In the **view_quote.php** script (Script 11.3), an entire file was read into an array using the **file()** function. But what if you want to read in only a little of the file at a time? Then you need to use the **fgets()** function.

The **fgets()** function reads a string of a certain length. It's most often placed in a **while** loop that uses the **feof()** function to make sure the end of the file hasn't been reached. For example:

```
$fp = fopen($file, 'rb');
while (!feof($fp)) {
        $string = fgets($fp, 1024);
}
fclose ($fp);
```

With that code, 1,023 bytes of data at a time will be read in, as **fgets()** always reads 1 byte less than the length you specify. Or **fgets()** will stop reading once it reaches the end of the line or the end of the file. The second argument is optional, but if present, it should be a number larger than a single line of text in the file. If you want to just read to the end of the line, omit the length argument:

```
$string = fgets($fp);
```

In an example where the data is stored in a *delineated* format (commonly using a comma, hence a CSV—comma-separated values—format), you can use the **fgetcsv()** function instead. It breaks the string into parts, using the marked separator, and returns an array:

```
$array = fgetcsv($fp, length,
  delimiter);
$array = fgetcsv($fp, 1024);
```

Again, the preceding function call returns 1,023 bytes of data, but it breaks the string into an array using the default delimiter—a comma—as an indicator of where to make elements. This function is the equivalent of using the **fgets()** and **explode()** functions together. If you provide a delimiter argument, you can change what character is used to delineate the data.

Finally, because these functions rely on identifying the end of a line, it's a smart extra precaution to enable PHP's **auto_detect_line_endings** setting. You can do so using the **ini_set()** function:

```
ini_set('auto_detect_line_endings', 1);
```

As an example, let's create a login script that uses the **users.txt** file created in the preceding example. It will continue to read a file until a matching username/password combination has been found.

To read a file incrementally:

1. Begin a new PHP document in your text editor or IDE, to be named **login.php** (Script 11.8):

```
<!DOCTYPE html PUBLIC "-//W3C//DTD
→XHTML 1.0 Transitional//EN"
  "http://www.w3.org/TR/xhtml1/
  →DTD/xhtml1-transitional.dtd">
<html xmlns="http://www.w3.org/
  →1999/xhtml" xml:lang="en"
  →lang="en">
<head>
  <meta http-equiv="content-type"
  →content="text/html;
  →charset=utf-8" />
  <title>Login</title>
</head>
<body>
<h1>Login</h1>
```

2. Create the PHP section and identify the file to use:

```
<?php // Script 11.8 - login.php
$file = '../users/users.txt';
```

The value of **$file** should be the same as that in **register.php**.

3. Check whether the form has been submitted:

```
if ($_SERVER['REQUEST_METHOD'] ==
→'POST') {
```

4. Create a dummy variable to use as a flag:

```
$loggedin = FALSE;
```

The **$loggedin** variable is used to indicate whether the user entered the correct username/password combination. When the script first starts, it's assumed that the user has not entered the correct values.

continues on page 380

Script 11.8 The **login.php** script uses the information stored in **users.txt** (created by Script 11.6) to validate a user.

```
1    <!DOCTYPE html PUBLIC "-//W3C//DTD XHTML 1.0 Transitional//EN"
2       "http://www.w3.org/TR/xhtml1/DTD/xhtml1-transitional.dtd">
3    <html xmlns="http://www.w3.org/1999/xhtml" xml:lang="en" lang="en">
4    <head>
5       <meta http-equiv="content-type" content="text/html; charset=utf-8" />
6       <title>Login</title>
7    </head>
8    <body>
9    <h1>Login</h1>
10   <?php // Script 11.8 - login.php
11   /* This script logs a user in by check the stored values in text file. */
12
13   // Identify the file to use:
14   $file = '../users/users.txt';
15
16   if ($_SERVER['REQUEST_METHOD'] == 'POST') { // Handle the form.
17
18       $loggedin = FALSE; // Not currently logged in.
19
20       // Enable auto_detect_line_settings:
21       ini_set('auto_detect_line_endings', 1);
22
```

code continues on next page

Script 11.8 *continued*

```
23      // Open the file:
24      $fp = fopen($file, 'rb');
25
26      // Loop through the file:
27      while ( $line = fgetcsv($fp, 200, "\t") ) {
28
29          // Check the file data against the submitted data:
30          if ( ($line[0] == $_POST['username']) AND ($line[1] == md5(trim($_POST['password']))) 
) {
31
32              $loggedin = TRUE; // Correct username/password combination.
33
34              // Stop looping through the file:
35              break;
36
37          } // End of IF.
38
39      } // End of WHILE.
40
41      fclose($fp); // Close the file.
42
43      // Print a message:
44      if ($loggedin) {
45          print '<p>You are now logged in.</p>';
46      } else {
47          print '<p style="color: red;">The username and password you entered do not match those on
          file.</p>';
48      }
49
50  } else { // Display the form.
51
52  // Leave PHP and display the form:
53  ?>
54
55  <form action="login.php" method="post">
56      <p>Username: <input type="text" name="username" size="20" /></p>
57      <p>Password: <input type="password" name="password" size="20" /></p>
58      <input type="submit" name="submit" value="Login" />
59  </form>
60
61  <?php } // End of submission IF. ?>
62
63  </body>
64  </html>
```

5. Open the file for reading:

```
ini_set('auto_detect_line_
→ endings', 1);
$fp = fopen($file, 'rb');
```

Unlike the **file()** function, the **fgetcsv()** function requires a file pointer. Therefore, the **users.txt** file must be opened with the **fopen()** function, using the appropriate mode. Here, that mode is **rb**, meaning the file should be opened for reading in a binary safe mode.

First, though, just to be safe, PHP's **auto_detect_line_endings** setting is enabled.

6. Loop through each line of the file:

```
while ( $line = fgetcsv($fp,
→ 200, "\t") ) {
```

This **while** loop reads another 200 bytes or one line of the file—whichever comes first—with each iteration. The data being read is broken into an array, using the tab to indicate the separate elements.

Because the **users.txt** file stores its data in the format *username tab password tab directory newline*, the **$line** array contains three elements indexed at 0 (*username*), 1 (*password*), and 2 (*directory*).

7. Check the submitted values against the retrieved values:

```
if ( ($line[0] == $_POST['username'])
→ AND ($line[1] == md5(trim($_POST
→ ['password']))) ) {
```

This two-part conditional checks the submitted username against the stored username (**$line[0]**) and checks

the submitted password against the stored password (**$line[1]**). However, because the stored password was scrambled using **md5()**, apply **md5()** to the submitted value and then make the comparison.

8. If a match was found, set **$loggedin** to **TRUE** and exit the **while** loop:

```
$loggedin = TRUE;
break;
```

If the conditional is **TRUE**, the submitted username and password match those on file. In this case, the **$loggedin** flag is set to **TRUE**, and the **break** statement is used to exit the **while** loop. The benefit of this system is that only as much of the file is read as is required to find a match.

9. Close the conditional, the **while** loop, and the file:

```
    }
  }
fclose ($fp);
```

10. Print a message to the user:

```
if ($loggedin) {
    print '<p>You are now logged
    → in.</p>';
} else {
    print '<p style="color: red;">
    → The username and password you
    → entered do not match those on
    → file.</p>';
}
```

Using the **$loggedin** flag, the script can now say whether the user is "logged in." You could add some functionality to this process by storing the user's directory in a session and then sending them to a file-upload page.

Login

Username: larry

Password: ••••

(Login)

Ⓐ The login form takes a username and password.

Login

You are now logged in.

Ⓑ If the submitted username and password match those previously recorded, the user sees this message.

Login

The username and password you entered do not match those on file.

Ⓒ The result if the user submits a username and password combination that doesn't match the values previously recorded.

11. Continue the main submit conditional, and exit PHP:

```
} else {
?>
```

12. Create the HTML form:

```
<form action="login.php"
→ method="post">
  <p>Username: <input type="text"
  → name="username" size="20" /></p>
  <p>Password: <input type=
  → "password" name="password"
  → size="20" /></p>
  <input type="submit" name=
  → "submit" value="Login" />
</form>
```

13. Return to PHP to complete the main conditional:

```
<?php } // End of submission IF. ?>
```

14. Finish the HTML page:

```
</body>
</html>
```

15. Save the file as **login.php**, place it in the proper directory for your PHP-enabled server, and test it in your Web browser Ⓐ, Ⓑ, and Ⓒ.

TIP As of PHP 4.3, the `fgetcsv()` function takes another optional argument: the string being used to enclose the elements.

TIP As of PHP 5.3, the `fgetcsv()` function takes another optional argument: the character used to escape problematic characters. Naturally, the default escape character is the backslash.

TIP If a line is blank, `fgetcsv()` returns an array containing a single null value.

Review and Pursue

If you have any problems with the review questions or the pursue prompts, turn to the book's supporting forum (www.LarryUllman.com/forum/).

Review

- What version of PHP are you running?

- What steps did you need to take to make a file or directory writable for your server?

- What is the *Web root directory* (as a concept)? What is the Web root directory for your Web site (whether on your own computer or on a live server)?

- What are two ways you can write data to a file?

- How do you append new data to existing files (as opposed to replacing any existing data)?

- How do you ensure that new data is placed on its own line?

- In order for a form to accept file uploads, what attributes must the opening **form** tag have?

- In what variable will a PHP script be able to access an uploaded file? What function is used to move the file to its final destination on the server?

- How does the **fgetcsv()** function differ from **file()** or **file_get_contents()**?

Pursue

Check out some of the other file system related functions in the PHP manual (start at www.php.net/manual/en/ref.filesystem.php).

Modify **add_quote.php** so that it confirms that the **quotes.txt** file exists, prior to checking if it's writable.

Make the text area in **add_quote.php** sticky.

Change **add_quote.php** so that it takes the quotation and the attribution as separate inputs and writes them separately to the text file. Then modify **view_quote.php** so that it retrieves and displays both pieces of data.

Modify **view_quote.php** so that it displays two random quotations.

Update **upload_file.php**, making it confirm that the **uploads** directory is writable.

View the PHP manual page for the **glob()** function to see what it can do and how to use it.

Update **list_dir.php** to display other information about the files in a directory.

- Create a system to guarantee unique usernames in **register.php**. Hint: Before you attempt to create the directory, use PHP to check your list of existing usernames for a match to the just-registered name. If no match is found, the new name is acceptable. If the username is already in use, then PHP can create an error message requesting a new username.

- Use the combination of writing to and reading from text files, plus either sessions or cookies, to create a real registration and login system.

Intro to Databases

The Internet wouldn't be where it is today if not for the existence of databases. In fact, PHP probably wouldn't be as popular or as useful if not for its built-in support for numerous types of databases. This chapter will use MySQL as the example database management system (DBMS). Although MySQL—which is available for most platforms—may not be as powerful as the highest-end commercial database servers, MySQL has enough speed and functionality for most purposes. And its price—free for most uses—makes it the common choice for Web development.

This chapter walks through the development of a simple database for running a basic blog. Although you'll learn enough here to get started working with database, you will want to visit Appendix B, "Resources and Next Steps," once you've finished this chapter to find some references where you can learn more about the topic.

In This Chapter

Introduction to SQL	334
Connecting to MySQL	336
MySQL Error Handling	340
Creating and Selecting a Database	343
Creating a Table	347
Inserting Data into a Database	352
Securing Query Data	358
Retrieving Data from a Database	361
Deleting Data in a Database	366
Updating Data in a Database	372
Review and Pursue	378

Introduction to SQL

A *database* is a collection of tables (made up of columns and rows) that stores information. Most databases are created, updated, and read using SQL (Structured Query Language). There are surprisingly few commands in SQL (**Table 12.1** lists the seven most important), which is both a blessing and a curse.

SQL was designed to be written a lot like the English language, which makes it very user friendly. But SQL is still extremely capable, even if it takes some thought to create more elaborate SQL statements with only the handful of available terms. In this chapter you'll learn how to execute all the fundamental SQL commands.

For people new to PHP, confusion can stem from PHP's relationship to HTML (i.e., PHP can be used to generate HTML but PHP code is never executed in the Web browser). When you incorporate a database, the relationships can become even fuzzier. The process is quite simple: PHP is used to send SQL statements to the database application, where they are executed. The result of the execution—the creation of a table, the insertion of a record, the retrieval of some records, or even an error—is then returned by the database to the PHP script **A**.

With that in mind, PHP's `mysql_query()` function will be the most-used tool in this chapter. It sends an SQL command to MySQL:

```
$result = mysql_query(SQL command,
 database connection);
```

TABLE 12.1 Common SQL Commands

Command	Purpose
ALTER	Modifies an existing table
CREATE	Creates a database or table
DELETE	Deletes records from a table
DROP	Deletes a database or table
INSERT	Adds records to a table
SELECT	Retrieves records from a table
UPDATE	Updates records in a table

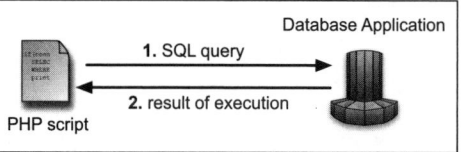

A PHP will be used to send an SQL statement to MySQL. MySQL will execute the statement and return the result to the PHP script.

MySQL Support in PHP

Support for the MySQL database server has to be built into PHP in order for you to use PHP's MySQL-specific functions. For most PHP installations, this should already be the case. You can confirm support for MySQL by calling the `phpinfo()` function, which reveals details of your installation.

When working through this chapter, if you see an error message saying … *undefined function mysql_…*, this means the version of PHP you're using doesn't have support for MySQL (or you misspelled the function name, which you should also check).

Enabling support for MySQL takes a little effort, but it can be done if you have administrative-level control over your server. For more information, see the PHP manual.

I start this chapter with this prologue because the addition of SQL and MySQL to the Web development process will complicate things. When problems occur—and undoubtedly they will—you'll need to know how solve them.

When a PHP script that interacts with a MySQL database does not perform as expected, the first step is to determine if the problem is in the query itself—number 1 in Ⓐ—or in the results of the query—number 2 in Ⓐ. To take this step, you can start by printing out the query being executed, using code such as the following:

```
print $query;
```

Assuming that **$query** represents the complete SQL command, often containing the values of PHP variables, this one, simple line will reveal to you the actual SQL statement being run.

Next, you would take the printed query and execute it using another application. The two most common options are:

- The MySQL client Ⓑ, a command-line tool for interacting with MySQL
- phpMyAdmin Ⓒ, a PHP-based MySQL interface

One or both of these should be provided to you by your hosting company or the software you installed on your own computer. For a demonstration of using each, see Appendix A, "Installation and Configuration."

> **TIP** Technically, a DBMS, or database application, is the software that interfaces with the database proper. However, most people use the terms *database* and *DBMS* synonymously.

> **TIP** Lots of other applications are available for interacting with MySQL aside from the MySQL client and phpMyAdmin. Some are free, and others cost. A quick search using Google for *MySQL*, *admin*, and your operating system should turn up some interesting results.

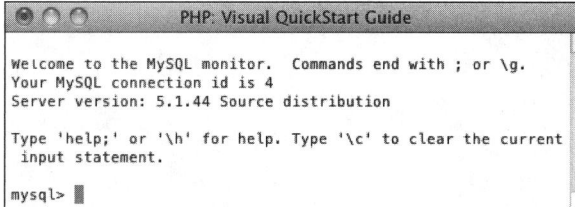

Ⓑ The MySQL client comes with the MySQL database software and can be used to execute queries without the need for a PHP script.

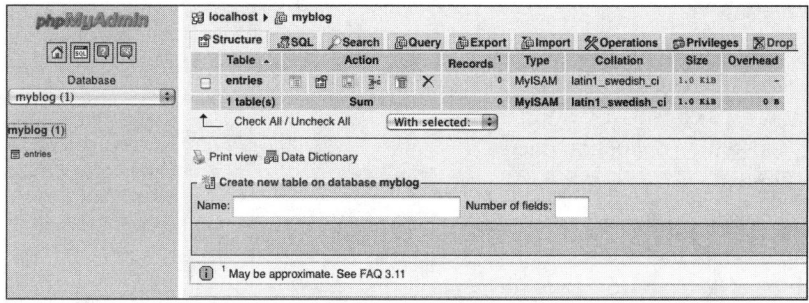

Ⓒ phpMyAdmin is perhaps the most popular software written in PHP. It provides a Web-based interface for a MySQL database.

Connecting to MySQL

When you worked with text files in Chapter 11, "Files and Directories," you saw that some functions, such as **fwrite()** and **fgets()**, require that you first create a file pointer using **fopen()**. This pointer then acts as a reference to that open file. You use a similar process when working with databases. First, you have to establish a connection to the database server (in this case, MySQL). This connection is then used as the access point for any future commands. The syntax for connecting to a database is

$dbc = mysql_connect(*hostname, username, password*);

The database connection (assigned to **$dbc** in the above) is established using at least three arguments: the host, which is almost always *localhost*; the username; and the password for that username.

If you're using a database through a hosting company, the company will most likely provide you with the host name, username, and password to use. If you're running MySQL on your own computer, see Appendix A to learn how you create a user.

Once you're done working with a database, you can close the connection, just as you'd close an open file:

mysql_close($dbc);

The PHP script will automatically close the database connection when the script terminates, but it's considered good form to formally close the connection once it's no longer needed.

For the first example of this chapter, you'll write a simple script that attempts to connect to MySQL. Once you have this connection working, you can proceed through the rest of the chapter.

Script 12.1 Being able to connect to the MySQL server is the most important step. This script tests that process.

```
1    <!DOCTYPE html PUBLIC "-//W3C//DTD XHTML
     1.0 Transitional//EN"
2        "http://www.w3.org/TR/xhtml1/DTD/
         xhtml1-transitional.dtd">
3    <html xmlns="http://www.w3.org/1999/
     xhtml" xml:lang="en" lang="en">
4    <head>
5        <meta http-equiv="content-type"
         content="text/html; charset=utf-8" />
6        <title>Connect to MySQL</title>
7    </head>
8    <body>
9    <?php // Script 12.1 - mysql_connect.php
10   /* This script connects to the MySQL
     server. */
11
12   // Attempt to connect to MySQL and print
     out messages:
13   if ($dbc = mysql_connect('localhost',
     'username', 'password')) {
14
15       print '<p>Successfully connected to
         MySQL!</p>';
16
17       mysql_close($dbc); // Close the
         connection.
18
19   } else {
20
21       print '<p style="color: red;">Could
         not connect to MySQL.</p>';
22
23   }
24
25   ?>
26   </body>
27   </html>
```

To connect to MySQL:

1. Begin a new PHP document in your text editor or IDE, to be named **mysql_connect.php** (Script 12.1):

   ```
   <!DOCTYPE html PUBLIC "-//W3C//DTD
   → XHTML 1.0 Transitional//EN"
     "http://www.w3.org/TR/xhtml1/
       → DTD/xhtml1-transitional.dtd">
   <html xmlns="http://www.w3.org/
   → 1999/xhtml" xml:lang="en"
   → lang="en">
   <head>
     <meta http-equiv="content-type"
     → content="text/html;
     → charset=utf-8" />
     <title>Connect to MySQL</title>
   </head>
   <body>
   ```

2. Start the section of PHP code:

   ```
   <?php // Script 12.1 -
   → mysql_connect.php
   ```

3. Connect to MySQL, and report on the results:

   ```
   if ($dbc = mysql_connect
   → ('localhost', 'username',
   → 'password')) {
     print '<p>Successfully connected
     → to MySQL!</p>';
     mysql_close($dbc);
   } else {
     print '<p style="color:
     → red;">Could not connect to
     → MySQL.</p>';
   }
   ```

   By placing the connection attempt as the condition in an **if-else** statement, you make it easy to report on whether the connection worked.

   This chapter will continue to use *username* and *password* as values.

   continues on next page

For your scripts, you'll need to replace these with the values provided by your Web host or set them when you add a user using the steps outlined in Appendix A.

If a connection was established, a positive message is printed and then the connection is closed. Otherwise, a message stating the opposite is printed, and there is no need to close the database connection (because it wasn't opened).

4. Complete the PHP code and the HTML page:

```
?>
</body>
</html>
```

5. Save the file as **mysql_connect.php**, place it in the proper directory of your PHP-enabled computer, and test it in your Web browser 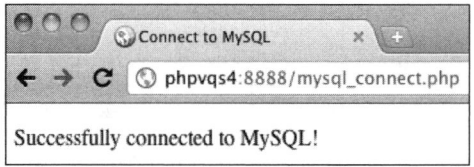.

If you see results like those in **B**, double-check the username and password values. They should match up with those provided to you by your Web host or those you used to create the user. You can always test your connection username and password by using them in the MySQL client (again, see Appendix A).

If you see *call to undefined function mysql_connect...*, your version of PHP doesn't support MySQL (see the "MySQL Support in PHP" sidebar).

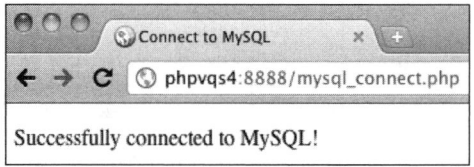

A If PHP has support for MySQL and the username/password/host combination you used was correct, you should see this simple message.

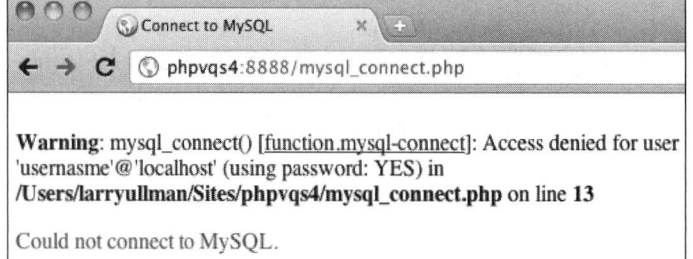

B If PHP couldn't connect to MySQL, you'll probably see something like this. The warning message may or may not appear, depending on your error management settings.

MySQL Extensions

PHP can communicate with MySQL using different extensions. The first, used in this chapter, is the "standard" MySQL extension. It has been around for years and works with all versions of PHP and MySQL. All of the standard MySQL extension functions begin with *mysql_*.

The second extension is called *MySQLi* (Improved MySQL Extension). This extension was added in PHP 5 and can be used with MySQL 4.1 or greater. These functions all begin with *mysqli_* and take advantage of some of the added features in MySQL. If possible, it's preferable to use the MySQLi functions, but as the older extension is more universally enabled, this book uses it exclusively. See the PHP manual or my book *PHP 6 and MySQL 5 for Dynamic Web Sites: Visual QuickPro Guide* (Peachpit Press, 2007) for details on the MySQLi extension.

TIP The database connection (`$dbc` in this case) in most `mysql_something()` functions is optional. Regardless of that, in this book you'll see it always used, as it's not optional in the `mysqli_something()` functions and you should be prepared to provide the database connection when you move to those functions later (see the "MySQL Extensions" sidebar).

TIP The *localhost* value is used as the hostname when both the PHP script and the MySQL database reside on the same computer. You can use PHP to connect to a MySQL database running on a remote server by changing the hostname in the PHP script and creating the proper permissions in MySQL.

TIP PHP has built-in support for most databases, including dBase, FilePro, SQLite, MySQL, Oracle, PostgreSQL, and Sybase. If you're using a type of database that doesn't have direct support—for example, Access or SQL Server—you'll need to use PHP's ODBC (Open Database Connectivity) functions along with that database's ODBC drivers to interface with the database.

TIP The combination of using PHP and MySQL is so common that you may run across terms that identify servers configured with both PHP and MySQL: *LAMP, MAMP*, and *WAMP*. These stand for the operating system—Linux, Mac OS X, or Windows—plus the Apache Web server, the MySQL DBMS, and PHP.

TIP You'll be working with MySQL, so all the functions you use in this chapter are MySQL specific. For example, to connect to a database in MySQL the proper function is `mysql_connect()`, but if you're using PostgreSQL, you'd instead write `pg_connect()`. If you aren't using a MySQL DBMS, use the PHP manual (available through www.PHP.net) to find the appropriate function names.

MySQL Error Handling

Before this chapter gets too deep into working with MySQL, it would be best to discuss some error-handling techniques up front. Common errors you'll encounter are

- Failure to connect to MySQL
- Failure to select a database
- Inability to run a query
- No results returned by a query
- Data not inserted into a table

Experience will teach you why these errors normally occur, but immediately seeing what the problem is when running your scripts can save you much debugging time. To have your scripts give informative reports about errors that occur, use the `mysql_error()` function. This function returns a textual version of the error that the MySQL server returned.

Along with this function, you may want to use some PHP tools for handling errors. Specifically, the error suppression operator (@), when used preceding a function name, suppresses any error messages or warnings the function might invoke:

```
@function_name();
```

Note that this operator doesn't stop the error from happening; it just prevents the message from being immediately displayed. You'd use it in situations where you intend to handle the error yourself, should one occur.

To use error handling:

1. Open **mysql_connect.php** (Script 12.1) in your text editor or IDE.

2. Suppress any PHP errors created by the **mysql_connect()** function by changing the **if** conditional as follows (**Script 12.2**):

   ```
   if ($dbc = @mysql_connect
   → ('localhost', 'username',
   → 'password')) {
   ```

   Rather than have PHP print out an error message when the **mysql_connect()** function backfires (**B** in the previous section), the message will be suppressed here using the **@** symbol. The errors still occur, but they're handled by the change made in the next step.

   continues on next page

Script 12.2 By adding error control to the script (the **@** symbol and the **mysql_error()** function), you can more purposefully address problems that occur.

```
1    <!DOCTYPE html PUBLIC "-//W3C//DTD XHTML 1.0 Transitional//EN"
2        "http://www.w3.org/TR/xhtml1/DTD/xhtml1-transitional.dtd">
3    <html xmlns="http://www.w3.org/1999/xhtml" xml:lang="en" lang="en">
4    <head>
5        <meta http-equiv="content-type" content="text/html; charset=utf-8" />
6        <title>Connect to MySQL</title>
7    </head>
8    <body>
9    <?php // Script 12.2 - mysql_connect.php #2
10   /* This script connects to the MySQL server. */
11
12   // Attempt to connect to MySQL and print out messages:
13   if ($dbc = @mysql_connect('localhost', 'username', 'password')) {
14
15       print '<p>Successfully connected to MySQL!</p>';
16
17       mysql_close($dbc); // Close the connection.
18
19   } else {
20
21       print '<p style="color: red;">Could not connect to MySQL:<br />' . mysql_error() . '.</p>';
22
23   }
24
25   ?>
26   </body>
27   </html>
```

3. Add the `mysql_error()` function to the `print` statement in the `else` section:

```
print '<p style="color: red;">Could
→ not connect to MySQL:<br />' .
→ mysql_error() . '.</p>';
```

Instead of printing a message or relying on whatever error PHP kicks out (see **B** in the previous section), the script now prints the MySQL error within this context. You accomplish this by printing some HTML concatenated with the `mysql_error()` function.

You should note that the `mysql_error()` function, in this case, is not provided with the database connection—**$dbc**—as an argument, since no database connection was made.

4. Save the file and test it again in your Web browser **A**.

If there was a problem, this result now looks better than what would have been shown previously. If the script connected, the result is like that shown in **A** in the previous section, because neither of the error-management tools is involved.

TIP In this chapter, error messages are revealed to assist in the debugging process. Live Web sites should not have this level of explicit error messages shown to the user.

TIP You can use the @ symbol to suppress errors, notices, or warnings stemming from any function, not just a **MySQL**-related one. For example:

```
@include('./filename.php');
```

TIP You may also see code where `die()`, which is an alias for `exit()`, is called when a connection error occurs. The thinking is that since a database connection cannot be made, there's no point in continuing. In my opinion, that's too heavy-handed of an approach.

A Using PHP's error-control functions, you can adjust how errors are handled.

Creating and Selecting a Database

Before a PHP script can interact with a database, the database must first be selected. Of course, in order for you to select a database, it must exist. You can create a database using PHP, the MySQL client, phpMyAdmin, or any number of tools, as long as the MySQL hostname/username/password combination you are using has permission to do so.

Database permissions are a bit more complicated than file permissions, but you need to understand this: Different types of users can be assigned different database capabilities. For example, one DBMS user may be able to create new databases and delete existing ones (you may have dozens of databases in your DBMS), but a lower-level user may only be able to create and modify tables within a single database. The most basic user may just be able to read from, but not modify, tables.

If you're using PHP and MySQL for a live, hosted site, the hosting company will most likely give you the second type of access—control over a single database but not the DBMS itself—and establish the initial database for you. If you're working on your own server or have administrative access, you should have the capability to create new users and databases.

To create a database with PHP, you use the **mysql_query()** function to execute a **CREATE DATABASE** *databasename* SQL command:

```
mysql_query('CREATE DATABASE somedb',
↪ $dbc);
```

Once you've done this, you can select the database using **mysql_select_db()**:

```
mysql_select_db('somedb', $dbc);
```

Note that you have to create a database only once, but it must always be selected before any other queries are run on it. In other words, some readers will need to perform the first step, but every reader must take the second step with every PHP script.

In this example, you'll create a new database and then select it. To repeat, creating a database requires that you have administrator access. If your Web host restricts your access, the hosting company should create the initial database for you upon request; you can just write the second part of this script, which selects the database.

To create and select a database:

1. Open **mysql_connect.php** (Script 12.2) in your text editor or IDE.

2. After the first **print** statement, create the new database, if necessary (**Script 12.3**):

```
if (@mysql_query('CREATE DATABASE
→ myblog', $dbc)) {
  print '<p>The database has been
  → created!</p>';
} else {
  print '<p style="color: red;">
  → Could not create the database
  → because:<br />' .
  → mysql_error($dbc) . '.</p>');
}
```

If you need to create the database, use this construct to handle the task

Script 12.3 Creating a new database consists of three steps: connecting to the database, running a **CREATE DATABASE** query using the **mysql_query()** function, and then closing the connection.

```
1    <!DOCTYPE html PUBLIC "-//W3C//DTD XHTML 1.0 Transitional//EN"
2        "http://www.w3.org/TR/xhtml1/DTD/xhtml1-transitional.dtd">
3    <html xmlns="http://www.w3.org/1999/xhtml" xml:lang="en" lang="en">
4    <head>
5        <meta http-equiv="content-type" content="text/html; charset=utf-8" />
6        <title>Create the Database</title>
7    </head>
8    <body>
9    <?php // Script 12.3 - create_db.php
10   /* This script connects to the MySQL server. It also creates and selects the database. */
11
12   // Attempt to connect to MySQL and print out messages:
13   if ($dbc = @mysql_connect('localhost', 'username', 'password')) {
14
15       print '<p>Successfully connected to MySQL!</p>';
16
17       // Try to create the database:
18       if (@mysql_query('CREATE DATABASE myblog', $dbc)) {
19           print '<p>The database has been created!</p>';
20       } else { // Could not create it.
21           print '<p style="color: red;">Could not create the database because:<br />' .
                 mysql_error($dbc) . '.</p>';
22       }
23
```

code continues on next page

cleanly and effectively. The query—**CREATE DATABASE myblog**—is run using the **mysql_query()** function. The **@** symbol is used to suppress any error messages, which are instead handled by **print** in conjunction with the **mysql_error()** function in the **else** clause.

Note that this invocation of **mysql_error()** can be provided with the specific database connection: **$dbc**.

If the database has already been created for you, skip this step.

3. Attempt to select the database:

```
if (@mysql_select_db('myblog',
→ $dbc)) {
  print '<p>The database has been
  → selected!</p>';
} else {
  print '<p style="color: red;">
  → Could not select the database
  → because:<br />' .
  → mysql_error($dbc) . '.</p>';
}
```

continues on next page

Script 12.3 *continued*

```
24     // Try to select the database:
25     if (@mysql_select_db('myblog', $dbc)) {
26         print '<p>The database has been selected!</p>';
27     } else {
28         print '<p style="color: red;">Could not select the database because:<br />' .
           mysql_error($dbc) . '.</p>';
29     }
30
31     mysql_close($dbc); // Close the connection.
32
33 } else {
34
35     print '<p style="color: red;">Could not connect to MySQL:<br />' . mysql_error() . '.</p>';
36
37 }
38
39 ?>
40 </body>
41 </html>
```

This conditional has the same structure as that in Step 2. If PHP can select the database, a message is printed. If it can't select the database, the specific MySQL error will be displayed instead.

Every PHP script that runs queries on a database must connect to MySQL and select the database in order to work.

4. If you want, change the page title to reflect this script's new purpose:

```
<title>Create the Database</title>
```

5. Save your script as **create_db.php**, place it in the proper directory for your PHP-enabled server, and test it in your Web browser **A** and **B**.

TIP You probably won't create databases with any frequency and may not normally do so using a PHP script. Still, this example demonstrates both how you execute simple queries using PHP as well as the SQL command needed to create a database.

TIP You haven't done so in these examples, but in general it's a good idea to set your database information—hostname, username, password, and database name—as variables or constants. Then you can plug them into the appropriate functions. By doing so, you can separate the database specifics from the functionality of the script, allowing you to easily port that code to other applications.

> Successfully connected to MySQL!
>
> The database has been created!
>
> The database has been selected!

A If the database could be created and selected, you'll see this result in the Web browser.

> Successfully connected to MySQL!
>
> Could not create the database because:
> Access denied for user 'username'@'localhost' to database 'myblog'.
>
> Could not select the database because:
> Unknown database 'myblog'.

B If the MySQL user doesn't have the authority to create a database, you'll see a message like this. A similar result will occur if the user doesn't have permission to select the database.

Creating a Table

Once you've created and selected the initial database, you can begin creating individual tables in it. A database can consist of multiple tables, but in this simple example you'll create one table in which all the chapter's data will be stored.

To create a table in the database, you'll use SQL—the language that databases understand. Because SQL is a lot like spoken English, the proper query to create a new table reads like this:

```
CREATE TABLE tablename (column1
→ definition, column2 definition,
→ etc.)
```

For each column, separated by commas, you first indicate the column name and then the column type. Common types are **TEXT, VARCHAR** (a variable number of characters), **DATETIME**, and **INT** (integer).

Because it's highly recommended that you create a column that acts as the *primary key* (a column used to refer to each row), a simple **CREATE** statement could be

```
CREATE TABLE my_table (
id INT PRIMARY KEY,
information TEXT
)
```

A table's primary key is a special column of unique values that is used to refer to the table's rows. The database makes an index of this column in order to more quickly navigate through the table. A table can have only one primary key, which you normally set up as an automatically incremented column of integers. The first row has a key of 1, the second has a key of 2, and so forth. Referring back to the key always retrieves the values for that row.

You can visit the MySQL Web site for more information on SQL and column definitions. By following the directions in this section, though, you should be able to accomplish some basic database tasks. The table that you'll create in this example is represented by **Table 12.2**.

In this example, you'll create the database table that will be used to store information submitted via an HTML form. In the next section of the chapter, you'll write the script that inserts the submitted data into the table created here.

TABLE 12.2 The entries Table

Column Name	Column Type
entry_id	Positive, non-null, automatically incrementing integer
title	Text up to 100 characters in length
entry	Text of any length
date_entered	A timestamp including both the date and the time the row was added

To create a new table:

1. Begin a new PHP document in your text editor or IDE, to be named **create_table.php** (Script 12.4):

```
<!DOCTYPE html PUBLIC "-//W3C//DTD
→ XHTML 1.0 Transitional//EN"
  "http://www.w3.org/TR/xhtml1/
    → DTD/xhtml1-transitional.dtd">
<html xmlns="http://www.w3.org/
→ 1999/xhtml" xml:lang="en"
→ lang="en">
<head>
  <meta http-equiv="content-type"
  → content="text/html;
  → charset=utf-8" />
  <title>Create a Table</title>
</head>
<body>
```

Script 12.4 To create a database table, define the appropriate SQL statement and then invoke the `mysql_query()` function.

```
1    <!DOCTYPE html PUBLIC "-//W3C//DTD XHTML 1.0 Transitional//EN"
2        "http://www.w3.org/TR/xhtml1/DTD/xhtml1-transitional.dtd">
3    <html xmlns="http://www.w3.org/1999/xhtml" xml:lang="en" lang="en">
4    <head>
5        <meta http-equiv="content-type" content="text/html; charset=utf-8" />
6        <title>Create a Table</title>
7    </head>
8    <body>
9    <?php // Script 12.4 - create_table.php
10   /* This script connects to the MySQL server, selects the database, and creates a table. */
11
12   // Connect and select:
13   if ($dbc = @mysql_connect('localhost', 'username', 'password')) {
14
15       // Handle the error if the database couldn't be selected:
16       if (!@mysql_select_db('myblog', $dbc)) {
17           print '<p style="color: red;">Could not select the database because:<br />' .
             mysql_error($dbc) . '.</p>';
18           mysql_close($dbc);
19           $dbc = FALSE;
20       }
21
22   } else { // Connection failure.
23       print '<p style="color: red;">Could not connect to MySQL:<br />' . mysql_error() . '.</p>';
24   }
```

code continues on next page

```
25
26    if ($dbc) {
27
28        // Define the query:
29        $query = 'CREATE TABLE entries (
30    entry_id INT UNSIGNED NOT NULL
      AUTO_INCREMENT PRIMARY KEY,
31    title VARCHAR(100) NOT NULL,
32    entry TEXT NOT NULL,
33    date_entered DATETIME NOT NULL
34    )';
35
36        // Execute the query:
37        if (@mysql_query($query, $dbc)) {
38            print '<p>The table has been
             created!</p>';
39        } else {
40            print '<p style="color: red;">
             Could not create the table
             because:<br />' .
             mysql_error($dbc) . '.</p>
             <p>The query being run was: ' .
             $query . '</p>';
41        }
42
43        mysql_close($dbc); // Close the
          connection.
44
45    }
46    ?>
47    </body>
48    </html>
```

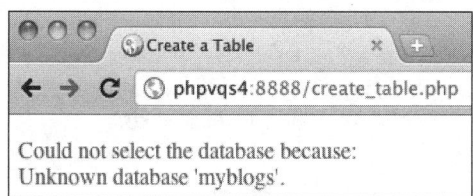

> Could not select the database because:
> Unknown database 'myblogs'.

Ⓐ Between the MySQL error message and printing out the query being executed, you should be able to figure out what the problem is if the script does not work properly.

2. Begin a section of PHP code:

```
<?php // Script 12.4 -
→ create_table.php
```

3. Connect to the MySQL server, and select the database:

```
if ($dbc = @mysql_connect
→ ('localhost', 'username',
→ 'password')) {
  if (!@mysql_select_db('myblog',
  → $dbc)) {
    print '<p style="color:
    → red;">Could not select the
    → database because:<br />' .
    → mysql_error($dbc) . '.</p>';
    mysql_close($dbc);
    $dbc = FALSE;
  }
} else {
  print '<p style="color:
  → red;">Could not connect to
  → MySQL:<br />' . mysql_error()
  → . '.</p>';
}
```

This is an alternative version of the code used in the preceding script. The main difference is that no messages are printed if each step was successful (hopefully you have connection and database selection working by this point).

If for some reason a connection could not be made to the database, or the database could not be selected, then error messages will be displayed Ⓐ. If a connection could be made but the database could not be selected, the connection is then closed, as the connection won't be useful. To indicate that scenario, the **$dbc** variable, which had represented the connection, is set to **FALSE**, which will prevent the **CREATE** query from being executed (see Step 4).

continues on next page

4. Define the query for creating the table:

```
if ($dbc) {
   $query = 'CREATE TABLE entries (
entry_id INT UNSIGNED NOT NULL
→ AUTO_INCREMENT PRIMARY KEY,
title VARCHAR(100) NOT NULL,
entry TEXT NOT NULL,
date_entered DATETIME NOT NULL
)';
```

First, if **$dbc** still has a value, the table can be created. If not—meaning that no connection could be made or the database couldn't be selected—then none of the following code will be executed.

As for the query itself, let's break that into more recognizable parts. First, to create a new table, you write **CREATE TABLE** *tablename* (where *tablename* is replaced by the desired table name). Then, within parentheses, you list every column you want with each column separated by a comma. Your table and column names should be alphanumeric, with no spaces.

The first column in the table is called **entry_id**; it's an unsigned integer (**INT UNSIGNED**—which means that it can only be a positive whole number). By including the words **NOT NULL**, you indicate that this column must have a value for each row. The values automatically increase by 1 for each

row added (**AUTO INCREMENT**) and stand as the primary key.

The next two columns consist of text. One, called **title**, is limited to 100 characters. The second, **entry**, can be vast in size. Each of these fields is also marked as **NOT NULL**, making them required fields.

Finally, the **date_entered** column is a timestamp that marks when each record was added to the table.

5. Execute the query:

```
if (@mysql_query($query, $dbc)) {
   print '<p>The table has been
   → created.</p>';
} else {
   print '<p style="color:
   → red;">Could not create the
   → table because:<br />' .
   → mysql_error($dbc) .
   → '.</p><p>The query being run
   → was: ' . $query . '</p>';
}
```

To create the table, call the **mysql_query()** function using the **$query** variable as the first argument and the database connection as the second. If a problem occurred, the MySQL error is printed, along with the value of the **$query** variable. This last step—printing the actual query being executed—is a particularly useful debugging technique **Ⓑ**.

Could not create the table because:
CREATE command denied to user 'username'@'localhost' for table 'entries'.

The query being run was: CREATE TABLE entries (entry_id INT UNSIGNED NOT NULL AUTO_INCREMENT PRIMARY KEY, title VARCHAR(100) NOT NULL, entry TEXT NOT NULL, date_entered DATETIME NOT NULL)

Ⓑ If the query caused an error, the MySQL error will be reported and the query itself displayed (for debugging purposes).

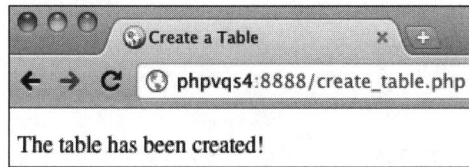

The table has been created!

C If all went well, all you'll see is this message.

6. Close the database connection and complete the **$dbc** conditional:

```
mysql_close($dbc);
}
```

7. Complete the PHP code and the HTML page:

```
?>
</body>
</html>
```

8. Save the script as **create_table.php**, place it in the proper directory for your PHP-enabled server, and test it in your Web browser **C**.

TIP It's not necessary to write your SQL keywords in all capital letters as I do here, but doing so helps to distinguish the SQL terms from the table and column names.

TIP On larger Web applications, I highly recommended that you place the database connection and selection code (lines 13 through 24 here) in a separate file, located outside of the Web directory. Then, each page that requires the database can include this external file. You'll see an example of this in Chapter 13, "Putting It All Together."

TIP The `mysql_query()` function returns TRUE if a query was successfully run on a database. That result doesn't necessarily mean the desired result occurred.

TIP This chapter presents the basics of MySQL- and SQL-related knowledge (including column types). You'll want to check out other resources—listed in Appendix B—once you're comfortable with the fundamentals.

TIP You wouldn't normally use a PHP script to create a table, just as you wouldn't normally create a database using a PHP script, but when you're just starting with MySQL, this is an easy way to achieve the desired results.

Inserting Data into a Database

As mentioned, this database will be used as a simple blog, an online journal. Blog entries—consisting of a title and text—will be added to the database using one page and then displayed on another page.

With the last script, you created the table, which consists of four columns: `entry_id`, `title`, `entry`, and `date_entered`. The process of adding information to a table is similar to creating the table itself in terms of which PHP functions you use, but the SQL query is different. To insert records, use the **INSERT** SQL command with either of the following syntaxes:

```
INSERT INTO tablename VALUES (value1,
→ value2, value3, etc.)
INSERT INTO tablename (column1_name,
→ column2_name) VALUES (value1, value2)
```

The query begins with **INSERT INTO** *tablename*. Then you can either specify which columns you're inserting values for or not. The latter is more specific and is therefore preferred, but it can be tedious if you're populating a slew of columns. In either case, you must be certain to list the right number and type of values for each column.

The values are placed within parentheses, with each value separated by a comma. Non-numeric values—strings and dates—need to be quoted, whereas numbers do not:

```
INSERT INTO example (name, age)
→ VALUES ('Jonah', 1)
```

The query is executed using the `mysql_query()` function. Because **INSERT** queries can be complex, it makes sense to assign each query to a variable and send that variable to the `mysql_query()` function (as previously demonstrated).

To demonstrate, let's create a page that adds blog entries to the database. Like many of the examples in the preceding chapter, this one will both display and handle the HTML form. Before getting into the example, though, I'll say that this script knowingly has a security hole in it; it'll be explained and fixed in the next section of the chapter.

Building on This Example

The focus in this chapter is on explaining and demonstrating the basics of using PHP with MySQL. This also includes the core components of SQL. However, this chapter's examples do a few things that you wouldn't want to do in a real site, such as allow anyone to insert, edit, and delete database records.

In the next chapter, a different example will be developed that is also database driven. That example will use cookies to restrict what users can do with the site.

To enter data into a database from an HTML form:

1. Begin a new PHP document in your text editor or IDE, to be named **add_entry. php** (Script 12.5):

```
<!DOCTYPE html PUBLIC "-//W3C//DTD
→ XHTML 1.0 Transitional//EN"
   "http://www.w3.org/TR/xhtml1/
   → DTD/xhtml1-transitional.dtd">
<html xmlns="http://www.w3.org/
→ 1999/xhtml" xml:lang="en"
→ lang="en">
<head>
  <meta http-equiv="content-type"
  → content="text/html;
  → charset=utf-8" />
  <title>Add a Blog Entry</title>
</head>
<body>
<h1>Add a Blog Entry</h1>
```

continues on next page

Script 12.5 The query statement for adding information to a database is straightforward enough, but be sure to match the number of values in parentheses to the number of columns in the database table.

```
1    <!DOCTYPE html PUBLIC "-//W3C//DTD XHTML 1.0 Transitional//EN"
2        "http://www.w3.org/TR/xhtml1/DTD/xhtml1-transitional.dtd">
3    <html xmlns="http://www.w3.org/1999/xhtml" xml:lang="en" lang="en">
4    <head>
5        <meta http-equiv="content-type" content="text/html; charset=utf-8" />
6        <title>Add a Blog Entry</title>
7    </head>
8    <body>
9    <h1>Add a Blog Entry</h1>
10   <?php // Script 12.5 - add_entry.php
11   /* This script adds a blog entry to the database. */
12
13   if ($_SERVER['REQUEST_METHOD'] == 'POST') { // Handle the form.
14
15       // Connect and select:
16       $dbc = mysql_connect('localhost', 'username', 'password');
17       mysql_select_db('myblog', $dbc);
18
19       // Validate the form data:
20       $problem = FALSE;
21       if (!empty($_POST['title']) && !empty($_POST['entry'])) {
```

code continues on next page

2. Create the initial PHP section and check for the form submission:

```php
<?php // Script 12.5 -
→ add_entry.php
if ($_SERVER['REQUEST_METHOD'] ==
→ 'POST') {
```

3. Connect to and select the database:

```php
$dbc = mysql_connect('localhost',
→ 'username', 'password');
mysql_select_db('myblog', $dbc);
```

At this point, if you're running these examples in order, I'll assume you have a working connection and selection process down, so I'll dispense with all the conditionals and error reporting (mostly to shorten the script). If you have problems connecting to and selecting the database, apply the code already outlined in the chapter.

Script 12.5 *continued*

```
22          $title = trim(strip_tags($_POST['title']));
23          $entry = trim(strip_tags($_POST['entry']));
24      } else {
25          print '<p style="color: red;">Please submit both a title and an entry.</p>';
26          $problem = TRUE;
27      }
28
29      if (!$problem) {
30
31          // Define the query:
32          $query = "INSERT INTO entries (entry_id, title, entry, date_entered) VALUES
            (0, '$title', '$entry', NOW())";
33
34          // Execute the query:
35          if (@mysql_query($query, $dbc)) {
36              print '<p>The blog entry has been added!</p>';
37          } else {
38              print '<p style="color: red;">Could not add the entry because:<br /> .
                mysql_error($dbc) . '.</p><p>The query being run was: ' . $query . '</p>';
39          }
40
41      } // No problem!
42
43      mysql_close($dbc); // Close the connection.
44
45  } // End of form submission IF.
46
47  // Display the form:
48  ?>
49  <form action="add_entry.php" method="post">
50      <p>Entry Title: <input type="text" name="title" size="40" maxsize="100" /></p>
51      <p>Entry Text: <textarea name="entry" cols="40" rows="5"></textarea></p>
52      <input type="submit" name="submit" value="Post This Entry!" />
53  </form>
54  </body>
55  </html>
```

Add a Blog Entry

Please submit both a title and an entry.

Entry Title: [   ]

[   ]

Entry Text: [   ]

[Post This Entry!]

A The PHP script performs some basic form validation so that empty records are not inserted into the database.

4. Validate the form data:

```
$problem = FALSE;
if (!empty($_POST['title']) &&
→ !empty($_POST['entry'])) {
  $title = trim(strip_tags
  → ($_POST['title']));
  $entry = trim(strip_tags
  → ($_POST['entry']));
} else {
  print '<p style="color:
  → red;">Please submit both a
  → title and an entry.</p>';
  $problem = TRUE;
}
```

Before you use the form data in an **INSERT** query, it ought to be validated. Just a minimum of validation is used here, guaranteeing that some values are provided. If so, new variables are assigned those values, after trimming away extraneous spaces and applying **strip_tags()** (to prevent cross-site scripting attacks and other potential problems). If either of the values was empty, an error message is printed **A** and the **$problem** flag variable is set to **TRUE** (because there is a problem).

5. Define the **INSERT** query:

```
if (!$problem) {
  $query = "INSERT INTO entries
  → (entry_id, title, entry,
  → date_entered) VALUES
  → (0, '$title', '$entry', NOW())";
```

The query begins with the necessary **INSERT INTO** *tablename* code. Then it lists the columns for which values will be submitted. After that is **VALUES**, followed by four values (one for each column, in order) separated by commas. When assigning this query to the **$query** variable, use double quotation marks so that the values of the variables will

continues on next page

be automatically inserted by PHP. The `$title` and `$entry` variables are strings, so they must be placed within single quotation marks in the query itself.

Because the `entry_id` column has been set to **AUTO_INCREMENT**, you can use 0 as the value and MySQL will automatically use the next logical value for that column. To set the value of the `date_entered` column, use the MySQL **NOW()** function. It inserts the current time as that value.

6. Run the query on the database:

```
if (@mysql_query($query, $dbc)) {
  print '<p>The blog entry has
  → been added!</p>';
} else {
  print '<p style="color: red;">
  → Could not add the entry
  → because:<br />' . mysql_
  → error($dbc) . '.</p><p>The
  → query being run was: ' .
  → $query . '</p>';
}
```

The query, once defined, is run using the `mysql_query()` function. By calling this function as the condition of an **if-else** statement, you can print simple messages indicating the result of the query execution.

As an essential debugging tool, if the query didn't run properly, the MySQL error and the query being run are both printed to the Web browser **B**.

7. Close the `$problem` conditional, the database connection, and complete the main conditional and the PHP section:

```
} // No problem!
mysql_close($dbc);
} // End of form submission IF.
?>
```

From here on out, the form will be displayed.

8. Create the form:

```
<form action="add_entry.php"
→ method="post">
  <p>Entry Title: <input type=
  → "text" name="title" size="40"
  → maxsize="100" /></p>
  <p>Entry Text: <textarea
  → name="entry" cols="40"
  → rows="5"></textarea></p>
  <input type="submit" name=
  → "submit" value="Post This
  → Entry!" />
</form>
```

Add a Blog Entry

Could not add the entry because:
You have an error in your SQL syntax; check the manual that corresponds to your MySQL server version for the right syntax to use near 's January 1st, 2011, the first day of six weeks of writing the date incorrectly.' at line 1.

The query being run was: INSERT INTO entries (entry_id, title, entry, date_entered) VALUES (0, 'Happy New Year!', 'It's January 1st, 2011, the first day of six weeks of writing the date incorrectly.', NOW())

B If the **INSERT** query didn't work, the MySQL error is printed along with the query that was run.

C This is the form for adding an entry to the database.

D If the **INSERT** query ran properly, a message is printed and the form is displayed again.

The HTML form is very simple, requiring only a title for the blog entry and the entry itself. As a good rule of thumb, use the same name for your form inputs as the corresponding column names in the database. Doing so makes errors less likely.

9. Finish the HTML page:

```
</body>
</html>
```

10. Save the script as **add_entry.php**, place it in the proper directory for your PHP-enabled server, and test it in your Web browser **C** and **D**.

You should probably avoid using apostrophes in your form values or you might see results like those in **B**. Turn the page for the explanation and solution.

TIP MySQL allows you to insert several records at once, using this format:

INSERT INTO *tablename* (*column1_name*, → *column2_name*) VALUES (*value1*, → *value2*), (*value3*, *value4*);

Most other database applications don't support this construct, though.

TIP To retrieve the automatically incremented number created for an AUTO_INCREMENT column, call the `mysql_insert_id()` function.

TIP Because of the way auto-incrementing primary keys work, this query is also fine:

INSERT INTO entries (title, entry, → date_entered) VALUES ('$title', → '$entry', NOW())";

Securing Query Data

As I mentioned in the introduction to the preceding sequence of steps, the code as written has a pretty bad security hole in it. As it stands, if someone submits text that contains an apostrophe, that data will break the SQL query **A** (security concerns aside, it's also a pretty bad bug). The result is obviously undesirable, but why is it insecure?

If a malicious user knows they can break a query by typing an apostrophe, they may try to run their own queries using this hole. If someone submitted *';DROP TABLE entries;* as the blog post title, the resulting query would be

```
INSERT INTO entries (entry_id,
→ title, entry, date_entered) VALUES
→ (0, '';DROP TABLE entries;', '<entry
→ text>', NOW())
```

The initial apostrophe in the provided entry title has the effect of completing the blog title value part of the query. The semicolon then terminates the **INSERT** query itself. This will make the original query syntactically invalid. Then the database will be provided with a second query—**DROP TABLE entries**, with the hope that it will be executed when the original **INSERT** query fails. This is called an *SQL injection attack*, but fortunately it's easy to prevent.

To do so, send potentially insecure data to be used in a query through the `mysql_real_escape_string()` function. This function will escape—preface with a backslash—any potentially harmful characters, making the data safe to use in a query:

```
$var = mysql_real_escape_string
→ ($var, $dbc);
```

Let's apply this function to the preceding script.

Add a Blog Entry

Could not add the entry because:
You have an error in your SQL syntax; check the manual that corresponds to your MySQL server version for the right syntax to use near ';DROP TABLE entries;', '', NOW())' at line 1.

The query being run was: INSERT INTO entries (entry_id, title, entry, date_entered) VALUES (0, '';DROP TABLE entries;', '', NOW())

A The apostrophe in the conjunction *It's* breaks the query because apostrophes (or single quotation marks) are used to delimit strings used in queries.

Showing MySQL Errors

Even if MySQL doesn't execute an injected SQL command (normally MySQL will only run a single SQL query sent through the `mysql_query()` function), hackers will provide bad characters in form data in the hopes that the syntactically broken query generates a database error. By seeing the database error, the hacker seeks to gain knowledge about the database that can be used for malicious purposes. For this reason, it's imperative that a live site never reveal the actual MySQL errors or queries being executed. The scripts in this chapter do so only for your own debugging purposes.

To secure query data:

1. Open **add_entry.php** (Script 12.5) in your text editor or IDE, if it is not already open.

2. Update the assignment of the **$title** and **$entry** variables to read (**Script 12.6**) as follows:

```
$title = mysql_real_escape_string
→ (trim(strip_tags($_POST
→ ['title'])), $dbc);
$entry = mysql_real_escape_string
→ (trim(strip_tags($_POST
→ ['entry'])), $dbc);
```

These two lines will greatly improve the security and functionality of the script. For both posted variables, their values are first trimmed and stripped of tags, then sent through **mysql_real_escape_string()**. The result will be safe to use in the query.

If the application of three functions to one variable is too confusing for you, you can separate the code into discrete steps:

```
$title = $_POST['title'];
$title = trim(strip_tags($title));
$title = mysql_real_escape_
string($title, $dbc);
```

continues on next page

Script 12.6 To better secure the Web application and the database, the **mysql_real_escape_string()** function is applied to the form data used in the query.

```
1    <!DOCTYPE html PUBLIC "-//W3C//DTD XHTML 1.0 Transitional//EN"
2        "http://www.w3.org/TR/xhtml1/DTD/xhtml1-transitional.dtd">
3    <html xmlns="http://www.w3.org/1999/xhtml" xml:lang="en" lang="en">
4    <head>
5        <meta http-equiv="content-type" content="text/html; charset=utf-8" />
6        <title>Add a Blog Entry</title>
7    </head>
8    <body>
9    <h1>Add a Blog Entry</h1>
10   <?php // Script 12.6 - add_entry.php #2
11   /* This script adds a blog entry to the database. It now does so securely! */
12
13   if (isset($_POST['submitted'])) { // Handle the form.
14
15       // Connect and select:
16       $dbc = mysql_connect('localhost', 'username', 'password');
17       mysql_select_db('myblog', $dbc);
18
19       // Validate and secure the form data:
20       $problem = FALSE;
21       if (!empty($_POST['title']) && !empty($_POST['entry'])) {
22           $title = mysql_real_escape_string(trim(strip_tags($_POST['title'])), $dbc);
23           $entry = mysql_real_escape_string(trim(strip_tags($_POST['entry'])), $dbc);
24       } else {
25           print '<p style="color: red;">Please submit both a title and an entry.</p>';
26           $problem = TRUE;
27       }
28
```

code continues on next page

3. Save the script, place it on your PHP-enabled server, and test it in your Web browser **Ⓑ** and **Ⓒ**.

TIP If you see (later in the chapter) that the displayed blog posts have extra backslashes before apostrophes, this is likely because you're using a version of PHP with Magic Quotes enabled. (Magic Quotes automatically escapes problematic characters in form data, although not as well as `mysql_real_escape_string()`). If that's the case, you'll need to apply the `stripslashes()` function to remove the extraneous slashes from the submitted values:

```
$title = mysql_real_escape_string
→ (stripslashes(trim(strip_tags
→ ($_POST['title']))), $dbc);
```

Add a Blog Entry

Entry Title: [It's Another Test!]

Entry Text: ["Will these quotes and apostrophes cause problems?", you ask. I don't think so!]

[Post This Entry!]

Ⓑ Now apostrophes in form data...

Add a Blog Entry

The blog entry has been added!

Ⓒ ...will not cause problems.

Script 12.6 *continued*

```
29      if (!$problem) {
30
31          // Define the query:
32          $query = "INSERT INTO entries (entry_id, title, entry, date_entered) VALUES (0, '$title',
            '$entry', NOW())";
33
34          // Execute the query:
35          if (@mysql_query($query, $dbc)) {
36              print '<p>The blog entry has been added!</p>';
37          } else {
38              print '<p style="color: red;">Could not add the entry because:<br />' .
                mysql_error($dbc) . '.</p><p>The query being run was: ' . $query . '</p>';
39          }
40
41      } // No problem!
42
43      mysql_close($dbc); // Close the connection.
44
45  } // End of form submission IF.
46
47  // Display the form:
48  ?>
49  <form action="add_entry.php" method="post">
50      <p>Entry Title: <input type="text" name="title" size="40" maxsize="100" /></p>
51      <p>Entry Text: <textarea name="entry" cols="40" rows="5"></textarea></p>
52      <input type="submit" name="submit" value="Post This Entry!" />
53      <input type="hidden" name="submitted" value="true" />
54  </form>
55  </body>
56  </html>
```

Retrieving Data from a Database

The next process this chapter demonstrates for working with databases is retrieving data from a populated table. You still use the `mysql_query()` function to run the query, but retrieving data is slightly different than inserting data—you have to assign the query result to a variable and then use another function in order to fetch the data.

The basic syntax for retrieving data is the **SELECT** query:

```
SELECT what columns FROM what table
```

The easiest query for reading data from a table is

```
SELECT * FROM tablename
```

The asterisk is the equivalent of saying *every column*. If you only require certain columns to be returned, you can limit your query, like so:

```
SELECT name, email FROM users
```

This query requests that only the information from two columns (**name** and **email**) be gathered. Keep in mind that this structure doesn't limit what rows (or records) are returned, just what columns for those rows.

Another way to alter your query is to add a conditional restricting which rows are returned, accomplished using a **WHERE** clause:

```
SELECT * FROM users WHERE
→ name='Larry'
```

Here you want the information from every column in the table, but only from the rows where the **name** column is equal to *Larry*.

This is a good example of how SQL uses only a few terms effectively and flexibly.

The main difference in retrieving data from a database as opposed to inserting data into a database is that you need to handle the query differently. You should first assign the results of the query to a variable:

```
$result = mysql_query($query, $dbc);
```

Just as **$dbc** is a reference to an open database connection, **$result** is a reference to a query result set. This variable is then provided to the `mysql_fetch_array()` function, which retrieves the query results:

```
$row = mysql_fetch_array($result);
```

The function fetches one row from the result set at a time, creating an array in the process. The array will use the selected column names as its indexes: **$row['name']**, **$row['email']**, and so on. As with any array, you must refer to the columns exactly as they're defined in the database (the keys are case-sensitive). So, in this example, you must use **$row['email']** instead of **$row['Email']**.

If the query will return multiple rows, execute the `mysql_fetch_array()` function within a loop to access them all:

```
while ($row = mysql_fetch_array
→ ($result)) {
        // Do something with $row.
}
```

With each iteration of the loop, the next row of information from the query (referenced by **$result**) is assigned to an array called **$row**. This process continues until no more rows of information are found. Within the loop, you would do whatever you want with **$row**.

continues on next page

The best way to understand this new code is to try it. You'll write a script that retrieves the posts stored in the **entries** table and displays them **Ⓐ**. You may want to run through **add_entry.php** a couple more times to build up the table first.

To retrieve data from a table:

1. Begin a new PHP document in your text editor or IDE, to be named **view_entries.php** (Script 12.7):

```
<!DOCTYPE html PUBLIC "-//W3C//DTD
→ XHTML 1.0 Transitional//EN"
   "http://www.w3.org/TR/xhtml1/
   → DTD/xhtml1-transitional.dtd">
<html xmlns="http://www.w3.org/
→ 1999/xhtml" xml:lang="en"
→ lang="en">
<head>
   <meta http-equiv="content-type"
   → content="text/html;
   → charset=utf-8" />
   <title>View My Blog</title>
</head>
<body>
   <h1>My Blog</h1>
```

My Blog

It's Another Test!

"Will these quotes and apostrophes cause problems?", you ask. I don't think so!
Edit Delete

___

Happy New Year!

Today is January 1st, 2011, the first day of six weeks of writing the date incorrectly.
Edit Delete

Ⓐ This dynamic Web page uses PHP to pull data from a database.

Script 12.7 The SQL query for retrieving all data from a table is quite simple; but in order for PHP to access every returned record, you must loop through the results one row at a time.

```
1    <!DOCTYPE html PUBLIC "-//W3C//DTD XHTML 1.0 Transitional//EN"
2        "http://www.w3.org/TR/xhtml1/DTD/xhtml1-transitional.dtd">
3    <html xmlns="http://www.w3.org/1999/xhtml" xml:lang="en" lang="en">
4    <head>
5        <meta http-equiv="content-type" content="text/html; charset=utf-8" />
6        <title>View My Blog</title>
7    </head>
8    <body>
9        <h1>My Blog</h1>
10   <?php // Script 12.7 - view_entries.php
11   /* This script retrieves blog entries from the database. */
12
```

code continues on next page

2. Begin a PHP section and connect to the database:

```php
<?php // Script 12.7 -
→ view_entries.php
$dbc = mysql_connect('localhost',
→ 'username', 'password');
mysql_select_db('myblog', $dbc);
```

3. Define the **SELECT** query:

```php
$query = 'SELECT * FROM entries
→ ORDER BY date_entered DESC';
```

This basic query tells the database that you'd like to fetch every column of every row in the **entries** table. The returned records should be sorted, as indicated by the **ORDER BY** clause, by the order in which they were entered (recorded in the **date_entered** column), starting with the most recent first. This last option is set by **DESC**, which is short for *descending*. If the query was **ORDER BY date_entered ASC**, the most recently added record would be retrieved last.

4. Run the query:

```php
if ($r = mysql_query($query,
→ $dbc)) {
```

The **SELECT** query is run like any other. However, the result of the query is assigned to a **$result** (or, more tersely, **$r**) variable, which will be referenced later.

continues on next page

Script 12.7 *continued*

```php
13    // Connect and select:
14    $dbc = mysql_connect('localhost', 'username', 'password');
15    mysql_select_db('myblog', $dbc);
16
17    // Define the query:
18    $query = 'SELECT * FROM entries ORDER BY date_entered DESC';
19
20    if ($r = mysql_query($query, $dbc)) { // Run the query.
21
22        // Retrieve and print every record:
23        while ($row = mysql_fetch_array($r)) {
24            print "<p><h3>{$row['title']}</h3>
25            {$row['entry']}<br />
26            <a href=\"edit_entry.php?id={$row['entry_id']}\">Edit</a>
27            <a href=\"delete_entry.php?id={$row['entry_id']}\">Delete</a>
28            </p><hr />\n";
29        }
30
31    } else { // Query didn't run.
32        print '<p style="color: red;">Could not retrieve the data because:<br />' . mysql_error($dbc)
         . '.</p><p>The query being run was: ' . $query . '</p>';
33    } // End of query IF.
34
35    mysql_close($dbc); // Close the connection.
36
37    ?>
38    </body>
39    </html>
```

5. Print out the returned results:

```
while ($row = mysql_fetch_array
→ ($r)) {
  print "<p><h3>{$row['title']}</h3>
  {$row['entry']}<br />
  <a href=\"edit_entry.php?id=
  → {$row['entry_id']}\">Edit</a>
  <a href=\"delete_entry.php?
  → id={$row['entry_id']}\">
  → Delete</a>
  </p><hr />\n";
}
```

This loop sets the variable **$row** to an array containing the first record returned in **$r**. The loop then executes the following command (the **print** statement). Once the loop gets back to the beginning, it assigns the next row, if it exists. It continues to do this until there are no more rows of information to be obtained.

Within the loop, the array's keys are the names of the columns from the table—hence, **entry_id**, **title**, and **entry** (there's no need to print out the **date_entered**).

At the bottom of each post, two links are created: to **edit_entry.php** and **delete_entry.php**. These scripts will be written in the rest of the chapter. Each link passes the posting's database ID value along in the URL. That information will be necessary for those other two pages to edit and delete the blog posting accordingly.

6. Handle the errors if the query didn't run:

```
} else { // Query didn't run.
  print '<p style="color: red;">
  → Could not retrieve the
  → data because:<br />' .
  → mysql_error($dbc) . '.</p>
  → <p>The query being run
  → was: ' . $query . '</p>';
} // End of query IF.
```

My Blog

This is the newest post!

This is so absolutely amazing that I'm downright speechless!
Edit Delete

It's Another Test!

"Will these quotes and apostrophes cause problems?", you ask. I don't think so!
Edit Delete

Happy New Year!

B Thanks to the **SELECT** query, which orders the returned records by the date they were entered, the most recently added entry is always listed first.

```
            <h1>My Blog</h1>
<p><h3>This is the newest post!</h3>
              This is so absolutely amazing that I'm dow
              <a href="edit_entry.php?id=4">Edit</a>
              <a href="delete_entry.php?id=4">Delete</a>
              </p><hr />
<p><h3>It's Another Test!</h3>
              "Will these quotes and apostrophes cause p
so!<br />
              <a href="edit_entry.php?id=3">Edit</a>
              <a href="delete_entry.php?id=3">Delete</a>
              </p><hr />
<p><h3>Happy New Year!</h3>
              Today is January 1st, 2011, the first day
incorrectly.<br />
              <a href="edit_entry.php?id=2">Edit</a>
              <a href="delete_entry.php?id=2">Delete</a>
              </p><hr />
```

C Part of the HTML source of the page. Note that the two links have *?id=X* appended to each URL.

If the query couldn't run on the database, it should be printed out, along with the MySQL error (for debugging purposes).

7. Close the database connection:

   ```
   mysql_close($dbc);
   ```

8. Complete the PHP section and the HTML page:

   ```
   ?>
   </body>
   </html>
   ```

9. Save the script as **view_entries.php**, place it in the proper directory for your PHP-enabled server, and test it in your Web browser **A**.

10. If you want, add another record to the blog using the **add_entry.php** page (Script 12.6), and run this page again **B**.

11. Check the source code of the page to see the dynamically generated links **C**.

TIP The `mysql_fetch_array()` function takes another argument, which is a constant indicating what kind of array should be returned. `MYSQL_ASSOC` returns an associative array, whereas `MYSQL_NUM` returns a numerically indexed array.

TIP The `mysql_num_rows()` function returns the number of records returned by a SELECT query.

TIP It's possible to paginate returned records so that 10 or 20 appear on each page (like the way Google works). Doing so requires more advanced coding than can be taught in this book, though. See my book *PHP 6 and MySQL 5 for Dynamic Web Sites: Visual QuickPro Guide* (Peachpit Press, 2007), or look online for code examples and tutorials.

Deleting Data in a Database

Sometimes you might also want to run a **DELETE** query on a database. Such a query removes records from the database. The syntax for a delete query is

DELETE FROM *tablename* **WHERE**
→ *column=value*

The **WHERE** clause isn't required, but if it's omitted, you'll remove every record from the table. You should also understand that once you delete a record, there's no way to recover it (unless you have a backup of the database).

As a safeguard, if you want to delete only a single record from a table, add the **LIMIT** clause to the query:

DELETE FROM *tablename* **WHERE**
→ *column=value* **LIMIT 1**

This clause ensures that only one record is deleted at most. Once you've defined your query, it's again executed using the **mysql_query()** function, like any other query.

To see if a **DELETE** query worked, you can use the **mysql_affected_rows()** function. This function returns the number of rows affected by an **INSERT**, **DELETE**, or **UPDATE** query.

As an example, let's write the **delete_entry.php** script, which is linked from the **view_blog.php** page. This page receives the database record ID in the URL. It then displays the entry to confirm that the user wants to delete it **A**. If the user clicks the button, the record will be deleted **B**.

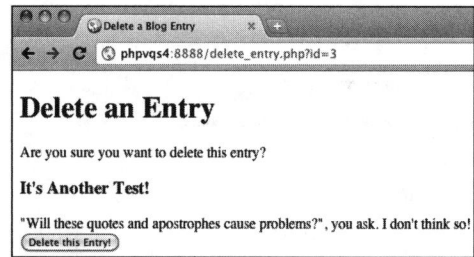

A When the user arrives at this page, the blog entry is shown and the user must confirm that they want to delete it.

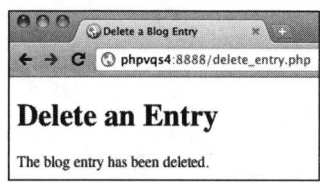

B If the delete query worked properly, the user sees this result.

To delete data from a database:

1. Begin a new PHP document in your text editor or IDE, to be named **delete_entry.php** (Script 12.8):

```
<!DOCTYPE html PUBLIC "-//W3C//DTD
→ XHTML 1.0 Transitional//EN"
  "http://www.w3.org/TR/xhtml1/
  → DTD/xhtml1-transitional.dtd">
<html xmlns="http://www.w3.org/
→ 1999/xhtml" xml:lang="en"
→ lang="en">
<head>
  <meta http-equiv="content-type"
  → content="text/html;
  → charset=utf-8" />
  <title>Delete a Blog Entry
  → </title>
</head>
<body>
<h1>Delete an Entry</h1>
```

2. Start the PHP code and connect to the database:

```
<?php // Script 12.8 -
→ delete_entry.php
$dbc = mysql_connect('localhost',
→ 'username', 'password');
mysql_select_db('myblog', $dbc);
```

continues on page 369

Script 12.8 The **DELETE** SQL command permanently removes a record (or records) from a table.

```
1    <!DOCTYPE html PUBLIC "-//W3C//DTD XHTML 1.0 Transitional//EN"
2       "http://www.w3.org/TR/xhtml1/DTD/xhtml1-transitional.dtd">
3    <html xmlns="http://www.w3.org/1999/xhtml" xml:lang="en" lang="en">
4    <head>
5       <meta http-equiv="content-type" content="text/html; charset=utf-8" />
6       <title>Delete a Blog Entry</title>
7    </head>
8    <body>
9    <h1>Delete an Entry</h1>
10   <?php // Script 12.8 - delete_entry.php
11   /* This script deletes a blog entry. */
12
```

code continues on next page

```
13    // Connect and select:
14    $dbc = mysql_connect('localhost', 'username', 'password');
15    mysql_select_db('myblog', $dbc);
16
17    if (isset($_GET['id']) && is_numeric($_GET['id']) ) { // Display the entry in a form:
18
19        // Define the query:
20        $query = "SELECT title, entry FROM entries WHERE entry_id={$_GET['id']}";
21        if ($r = mysql_query($query, $dbc)) { // Run the query.
22
23            $row = mysql_fetch_array($r); // Retrieve the information.
24
25            // Make the form:
26            print '<form action="delete_entry.php" method="post">
27            <p>Are you sure you want to delete this entry?</p>
28            <p><h3>' . $row['title'] . '</h3>' .
29            $row['entry'] . '<br />
30            <input type="hidden" name="id" value="' . $_GET['id'] . '" />
31            <input type="submit" name="submit" value="Delete this Entry!" /></p>
32            </form>';
33
34        } else { // Couldn't get the information.
35            print '<p style="color: red;">Could not retrieve the blog entry because:<br />' .
                  mysql_error($dbc) . '.</p><p>The query being run was: ' . $query . '</p>';
36        }
37
38    } elseif (isset($_POST['id']) && is_numeric($_POST['id'])) { // Handle the form.
39
40        // Define the query:
41        $query = "DELETE FROM entries WHERE entry_id={$_POST['id']} LIMIT 1";
42        $r = mysql_query($query, $dbc); // Execute the query.
43
44        // Report on the result:
45        if (mysql_affected_rows($dbc) == 1) {
46            print '<p>The blog entry has been deleted.</p>';
47        } else {
48            print '<p style="color: red;">Could not delete the blog entry because:<br />' .
                  mysql_error($dbc) . '.</p><p>The query being run was: ' . $query . '</p>';
49        }
50
51    } else { // No ID received.
52        print '<p style="color: red;">This page has been accessed in error.</p>';
53    } // End of main IF.
54
55    mysql_close($dbc); // Close the connection.
56
57    ?>
58    </body>
59    </html>
```

Delete an Entry

This page has been accessed in error.

C If the script does not receive an *id* value in the URL, an error is reported.

3. If the page received a valid entry ID in the URL, define and execute a **SELECT** query:

```
if (isset($_GET['id']) && is_numeric
→ ($_GET['id']) ) {
  $query = "SELECT title, entry
  → FROM entries WHERE
  → entry_id={$_GET['id']}";
  if ($r = mysql_query($query,
  → $dbc)) {
```

To display the blog entry, the page must confirm that a numeric ID is received by the page. Because that value should first come in the URL (when the user clicks the link in **view_blog.php**, see **C** in the previous section), you reference **$_GET['id']**.

The query is like the **SELECT** query used in the preceding example, except that the **WHERE** clause has been added to retrieve a specific record. Also, because only the two stored values are necessary—the title and the entry itself—only those are being selected.

This query is then executed using the **mysql_query()** function.

4. Retrieve the record, and display the entry in a form:

```
$row = mysql_fetch_array($r);
print '<form action="delete_entry.
→ php" method="post">
<p>Are you sure you want to
→ delete this entry?</p>
<p><h3>' . $row['title'] . '</h3>' .
$row['entry'] . '<br />
<input type="hidden" name="id"
→ value="' . $_GET['id'] . '" />
<input type="submit" name="submit"
→ value="Delete this Entry!" /></p>
</form>';
```

continues on next page

Instead of retrieving all the records using a **while** loop, as you did in the previous example, use one call to the **mysql_fetch_array()** function to assign the returned record to the **$row** variable. Using this array, the record to be deleted can be displayed.

The form first shows the blog entry details, much as it did in the **view_blog. php** script. When the user clicks the button, the form will be submitted back to this page, at which point the record should be deleted. In order to do so, the blog identification number, which is passed to the script as **$_GET['id']**, must be stored in a hidden input so that it exists in the **$_POST** array upon submission (because **$_GET['id']** won't have a value at that point).

5. Report an error if the query failed:

```
} else { // Couldn't get the
→ information.
   print '<p style="color: red;">
   → Could not retrieve the blog
   → entry because:<br />' .
   → mysql_error($dbc) . '.</p>
   → <p>The query being run was:
   →' . $query . '</p>';
}
```

If the **SELECT** query failed to run, the MySQL error and the query itself are printed out.

6. Check for the submission of the form:

```
} elseif (isset($_POST['id']) &&
→ is_numeric($_POST['id']))
→ { // Handle the form.
```

This **elseif** clause is part of the conditional begun in Step 3. It corresponds to the second usage of this same script (the form being submitted). If this conditional is **TRUE**, the record should be deleted.

7. Define and execute the query:

```
$query = "DELETE FROM entries
→ WHERE entry_id={$_POST['id']}
→ LIMIT 1";
$r = mysql_query($query, $dbc);
```

This query deletes the record whose **entry_id** has a value of **$_POST['id']**. The ID value comes from the form, where it's stored as a hidden input. By adding the **LIMIT 1** clause to the query, you can guarantee that only one record, at most, is removed.

8. Check the result of the query:

```
if (mysql_affected_rows($dbc) ==
→ 1) {
   print '<p>The blog entry has
   → been deleted.</p>';
} else {
   print '<p style="color: red;">
   → Could not delete the blog
   → entry because:<br />' .
   → mysql_error($dbc) . '.</p>
   → <p>The query being run
   → was: ' . $query . '</p>';
}
```

The `mysql_affected_rows()` function returns the number of rows altered by the most recent query. If the query ran properly, one row was deleted, so this function should return 1. If so, a message is printed. Otherwise, the MySQL error and query are printed for debugging purposes.

9. Complete the main conditional:

```
} else { // No ID received.
  print '<p style="color: red;">
  →This page has been accessed
  →in error.</p>';
} // End of main IF.
```

If no numeric ID value was passed to this page using either the GET method or the POST method, then this `else` clause takes effect **C**.

10. Close the database connection, and complete the page:

```
mysql_close($dbc);
?>
</body>
</html>
```

11. Save the script as **delete_entry.php**, place it in the proper directory for your PHP-enabled server, and test it in your Web browser **A** and **B**.

To test this script, you must first run **view_blog.php**. Then, click one of the Delete links to access **delete_entry.php**.

TIP You can empty a table of all of its records by running the query TRUNCATE TABLE *tablename*. This approach is preferred over using DELETE FROM *tablename*. TRUNCATE will completely drop and rebuild the table, which is better for the database.

TIP It's a fairly common error to try to run the query DELETE * FROM *tablename*, like a SELECT query. Remember that DELETE doesn't use the same syntax as SELECT, because you aren't deleting specific columns.

Updating Data in a Database

The final type of query this chapter will cover is **UPDATE**. It's used to alter the values of a record's columns. The syntax is

```
UPDATE tablename SET column1_name=
→ value, column2_name=value2 WHERE
→ some_column=value
```

As with any other query, if the values are strings, they should be placed within single quotation marks:

```
UPDATE users SET first_name=
→ 'Eleanor', age=7 WHERE user_id=142
```

As with a **DELETE** query, you should use a **WHERE** clause to limit the rows that are affected. If you don't do this, every record in the database will be updated.

To test that an update worked, you can again use the **mysql_affected_rows()** function to return the number of records altered.

To demonstrate, let's write a page for editing a blog entry. It will let the user alter an entry's title and text, but not the date entered or the blog ID number (as a primary key, the ID number should never be changed). This script will use a structure like that in **delete_entry.php** (Script 12.8), first showing the entry **A**, and then handling the submission of that form **B**.

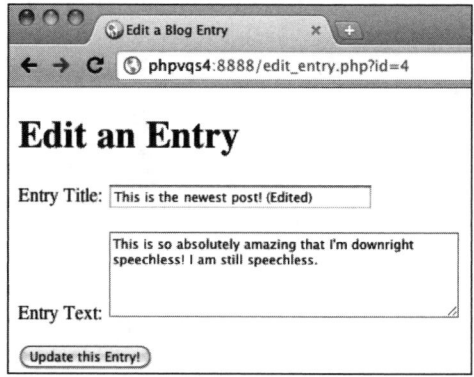

A When the user arrives at the edit page, the form is shown with the existing values.

B Upon submitting the form, the user sees a message like this.

To update data in a database:

1. Begin a new PHP document in your text editor or IDE, to be named **edit_entry.php** (Script 12.9).

```
<!DOCTYPE html PUBLIC "-//W3C//DTD
→ XHTML 1.0 Transitional//EN"
  "http://www.w3.org/TR/xhtml1/
   → DTD/xhtml1-transitional.dtd">
<html xmlns="http://www.w3.org/
→ 1999/xhtml" xml:lang="en"
→ lang="en">
<head>
  <meta http-equiv="content-type"
  → content="text/html;
  → charset=utf-8" />
  <title>Edit a Blog Entry</title>
</head>
<body>
<h1>Edit an Entry</h1>
```

continues on page 375

Script 12.9 You can edit records in a database table by using an **UPDATE** SQL command.

```
1    <!DOCTYPE html PUBLIC "-//W3C//DTD XHTML 1.0 Transitional//EN"
2        "http://www.w3.org/TR/xhtml1/DTD/xhtml1-transitional.dtd">
3    <html xmlns="http://www.w3.org/1999/xhtml" xml:lang="en" lang="en">
4    <head>
5        <meta http-equiv="content-type" content="text/html; charset=utf-8" />
6        <title>Edit a Blog Entry</title>
7    </head>
8    <body>
9    <h1>Edit an Entry</h1>
10   <?php // Script 12.9 - edit_entry.php
11   /* This script edits a blog entry using an UPDATE query. */
12
13   // Connect and select:
14   $dbc = mysql_connect('localhost', 'username', 'password');
15   mysql_select_db('myblog', $dbc);
16
17   if (isset($_GET['id']) && is_numeric($_GET['id']) ) { // Display the entry in a form:
18
19       // Define the query.
20       $query = "SELECT title, entry FROM entries WHERE entry_id={$_GET['id']}";
21       if ($r = mysql_query($query, $dbc)) { // Run the query.
22
23           $row = mysql_fetch_array($r); // Retrieve the information.
24
```

code continues on next page

```
25          // Make the form:
26          print '<form action="edit_entry.php" method="post">
27      <p>Entry Title: <input type="text" name="title" size="40" maxsize="100" value="' .
        htmlentities($row['title']) . '" /></p>
28      <p>Entry Text: <textarea name="entry" cols="40" rows="5">' . htmlentities($row['entry']) . '</
        textarea></p>
29      <input type="hidden" name="id" value="' . $_GET['id'] . '" />
30      <input type="submit" name="submit" value="Update this Entry!" />
31      </form>';
32
33          } else { // Couldn't get the information.
34          print '<p style="color: red;">Could not retrieve the blog entry because:<br />' . mysql_
        error($dbc) . '.</p><p>The query being run was: ' . $query . '</p>';
35          }
36
37      } elseif (isset($_POST['id']) && is_numeric($_POST['id'])) { // Handle the form.
38
39          // Validate and secure the form data:
40          $problem = FALSE;
41          if (!empty($_POST['title']) && !empty($_POST['entry'])) {
42              $title = mysql_real_escape_string(trim(strip_tags($_POST['title'])), $dbc);
43              $entry = mysql_real_escape_string(trim(strip_tags($_POST['entry'])), $dbc);
44          } else {
45              print '<p style="color: red;">Please submit both a title and an entry.</p>';
46              $problem = TRUE;
47          }
48
49          if (!$problem) {
50
51              // Define the query.
52              $query = "UPDATE entries SET title='$title', entry='$entry' WHERE entry_id=
        {$_POST['id']}";
53              $r = mysql_query($query, $dbc); // Execute the query.
54
55              // Report on the result:
56              if (mysql_affected_rows($dbc) == 1) {
57                  print '<p>The blog entry has been updated.</p>';
58              } else {
59                  print '<p style="color: red;">Could not update the entry because:<br />' .
        mysql_error($dbc) . '.</p><p>The query being run was: ' . $query . '</p>';
60              }
61
62          } // No problem!
63
64      } else { // No ID set.
65          print '<p style="color: red;">This page has been accessed in error.</p>';
66      } // End of main IF.
67
68      mysql_close($dbc); // Close the connection.
69
70      ?>
71      </body>
72      </html>
```

2. Start your PHP code and connect to the database:

```php
<?php // Script 12.9 -
→ edit_entry.php
$dbc = mysql_connect('localhost',
→ 'username', 'password');
mysql_select_db('myblog', $dbc);
```

3. If the page received a valid entry ID in the URL, define and execute a **SELECT** query:

```php
if (isset($_GET['id']) &&
→ is_numeric($_GET['id']) ) {
  $query = "SELECT title,
  → entry FROM entries WHERE
  → entry_id={$_GET['id']}";
  if ($r = mysql_query($query,
  → $dbc)) {
```

This code is exactly the same as that in the delete page; it selects the two column values from the database for the provided ID value.

4. Retrieve the record, and display the entry in a form:

```php
$row = mysql_fetch_array($r);
  print '<form action="edit_entry.
  → php" method="post">
<p>Entry Title: <input type=
→ "text" name="title" size="40"
→ maxsize="100" value="' .
→ htmlentities($row['title']) .
→ '" /></p>
<p>Entry Text: <textarea name=
→ "entry" cols="40" rows="5">' .
→ htmlentities($row['entry']) .
→ '</textarea></p>
<input type="hidden" name="id"
→ value="' . $_GET['id'] . '" />
<input type="submit" name="submit"
→ value="Update this Entry!" />
</form>';
```

Again, this is almost exactly the same as in the preceding script, including the most important step of storing the ID value in a hidden form input. Here, though, the stored data isn't just printed but is actually used as the values for form elements. For security and to avoid potential conflicts, each value is run through **htmlentities()** first.

5. Report an error if the query failed:

```php
} else { // Couldn't get the
→ information.
  print '<p style="color:
  → red;">Could not retrieve
  → the blog entry because:
  → <br />' . mysql_error($dbc) .
  → '.</p><p>The query being run
  → was: ' . $query . '</p>';
}
```

6. Check for the submission of the form:

```php
} elseif (isset($_POST['id']) &&
→ is_numeric($_POST['id'])) {
```

This conditional will be **TRUE** when the form is submitted.

7. Validate and secure the form data:

```php
$problem = FALSE;
if (!empty($_POST['title']) &&
→ !empty($_POST['entry'])) {
  $title = mysql_real_escape_
  → string(trim(strip_tags($_POST
  → ['title'])), $dbc);
  $entry = mysql_real_escape_
  → string(trim(strip_tags($_POST
  → ['entry'])), $dbc);
} else {
  print '<p style="color: red;">
  → Please submit both a title
  → and an entry.</p>';
  $problem = TRUE;
}
```

continues on next page

This code comes from the page used to add blog postings. It performs minimal validation on the submitted data and then runs it through the `mysql_real_escape_string()` function to be safe. Because the form data can be edited, the form should be validated as if it were a new record being created.

8. Define and execute the query:

```
if (!$problem) {
    $query = "UPDATE entries SET
    → title='$title', entry='$entry'
    → WHERE entry_id={$_POST['id']}";
    $r = mysql_query($query, $dbc);
```

The **UPDATE** query sets the **title** column equal to the value entered in the form's title input and the **entry** column equal to the value entered in the form's entry text area. Only the record whose **entry_id** is equal to **$_POST['id']**, which comes from a hidden form input, is updated.

9. Report on the success of the query:

```
if (mysql_affected_rows($dbc) == 1) {
    print '<p>The blog entry has
    → been updated.</p>';
} else {
    print '<p style="color: red;">
    → Could not update the entry
    → because:<br />' . mysql_
    → error($dbc) . '.</p><p>The
    → query being run was: ' .
    → $query . '</p>';
}
```

If one row was affected, then a success message is returned. Otherwise, the MySQL error and the query are sent to the Web browser.

10. Complete the conditionals:

```
    } // No problem!
} else { // No ID set.
    print '<p style="color: red;">
    → This page has been accessed
    → in error.</p>';
} // End of main IF.
```

If no numeric ID value was passed to this page using either the GET method or the POST method, then this **else** clause takes effect.

11. Close the database connection, and complete the page:

```
mysql_close($dbc);
?>
</body>
</html>
```

12. Save the file as **edit_entry.php**, place it in the proper directory for your PHP-enabled server, and test it in your Web browser **Ⓐ** and **Ⓑ**.

As in the preceding example, to edit an entry, you must click its *Edit* link in the **view_blog.php** page.

13. Revisit `view_blog.php` to confirm that the changes were made 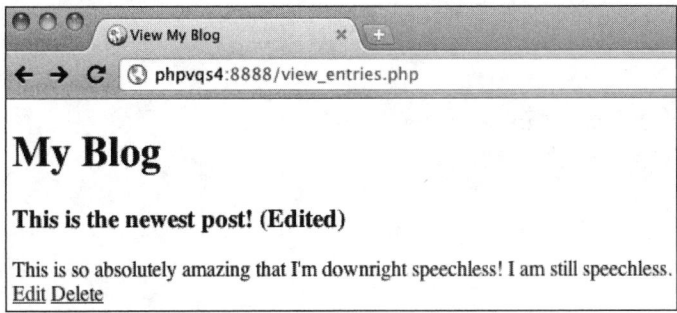.

> **TIP** The id is a primary key, meaning that its value should never change. By using a primary key in your table, you can change every other value in the record but still refer to the row using that column.

> **TIP** The `mysql_real_escape_string()` function does not need to be applied to the ID values used in the queries, as the `is_numeric()` test confirms they don't contain apostrophes or other problematic characters.

> **TIP** More thorough edit and delete pages would use the `mysql_num_rows()` function in a conditional to confirm that the SELECT query returned a row prior to fetching it:

```
if (mysql_num_rows($r) == 1) {…
```

> **TIP** If you run an update on a table but don't change a record's values, `mysql_affected_rows()` will return 0.

> **TIP** It can't hurt to add a `LIMIT 1` clause to an UPDATE query, to ensure that only one row, at most, is affected.

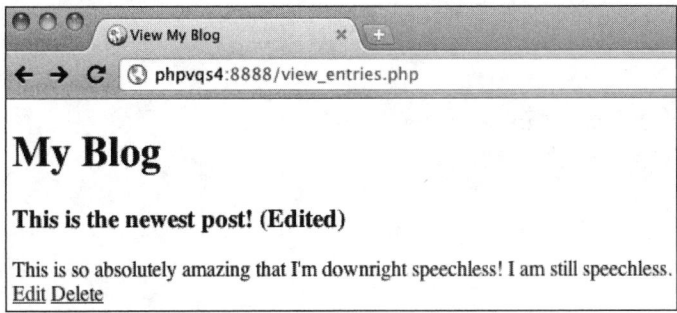

C Reloading the `view_blog.php` script reflects the changes made to the entries.

Review and Pursue

If you have any problems with the review questions or the pursue prompts, turn to the book's supporting forum (www.LarryUllman.com/forum/).

Review

- What version of MySQL are you using? What values do you personally use to connect to MySQL?

- How does a PHP script connect to a MySQL server? How does it disconnect?

- What is the error suppression operator? What does it do?

- What function returns MySQL-reported errors?

- What debugging techniques should you use when having problems with a PHP script that interacts with MySQL?

- How do you select which database to use?

- What SQL command is used to create a table? To add new records? To retrieve records? To modify records? To remove records?

- What function should string values be run through to prevent SQL injection attacks?

Pursue

- Find the version of the MySQL manual that corresponds to your version of MySQL. Start reading!

- Move the code for connecting to and selecting the database to a separate script, then include that script in the PHP pages that interact with the database.

- Make the **add_entry.php** form sticky.

- Change the code in **view_entry.php** so that it converts newline characters in each entry into HTML break tags.

13

Putting It All Together

The 12 chapters to this point have covered all the fundamentals of using PHP for Web development. In this chapter, you'll use your accumulated knowledge to create a complete and functional Web site. And even though the focus of this chapter is on applying your newfound knowledge, you'll still learn a few new tricks. In particular, you'll see how to develop a full-scale Web application from scratch.

In This Chapter

Getting Started	380
Connecting to the Database	382
Writing the User-Defined Function	383
Creating the Template	385
Logging In	388
Logging Out	392
Adding Quotes	393
Listing Quotes	397
Editing Quotes	400
Deleting Quotes	406
Creating the Home Page	410
Review and Pursue	414

Getting Started

The first step when starting any project is identifying the site's goals. The primary goal of this chapter is to apply everything taught in the book thus far (a lofty aim, to be sure). The example I came up with for doing so combines the models from the previous two chapters, creating a site that will store and display quotations. Instead of using a file to do so, as in Chapter 11, "Files and Directories," this site will use a MySQL database as the storage repository. But as with the blog example from Chapter 12, "Intro to Databases," the ability to create, edit, and delete quotations will be implemented. Further, the public user will be able to view the most recent quotation by default **Ⓐ**, or a random one, or a random quotation previously marked as a favorite.

For improved security, the site will have an administrator who can log in and log out. And only the logged-in administrator will be allowed to create, edit, or delete quotations **Ⓑ**.

The site will use a simple template to give every page a consistent look, with CSS handling all the formatting and layout. The site will also make use of one user-defined function, stored in an included file.

As in Chapter 12, you must first create the database and its one table. The database could be named *myquotes* (or something else if you'd rather). You create its one table with this SQL command:

Ⓐ The site's simple home page.

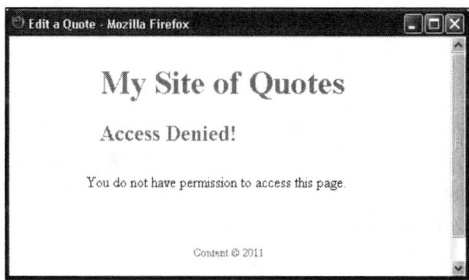

Ⓑ Nonadministrators are denied access to certain pages.

```
CREATE TABLE quotes (
  quote_id INT UNSIGNED NOT NULL
  ↪ AUTO_INCREMENT,
  quote TEXT NOT NULL,
  source VARCHAR(100) NOT NULL,
  favorite TINYINT(1) UNSIGNED NOT
  ↪ NULL,
  date_entered TIMESTAMP NOT NULL
  ↪ DEFAULT CURRENT_TIMESTAMP,
  PRIMARY KEY (quote_id)
)
```

The **quote_id** is the primary key, and it will automatically be incremented to the next logical value with each new submission. The **quote** field stores the quote itself, with the **source** field storing the attribution (unlike in Chapter 11, where the quote and the source were stored together). The **favorite** field stores a 1 or a 0, marking the quote as a favorite or not. Finally, the **date_entered** column is a timestamp, automatically set to the current timestamp when a new record is created.

You can create this table using a PHP script, such as Script 12.4, or a third-party application (like the MySQL client or phpMyAdmin).

Finally, a word about how the site should be organized on the server **C**. Ideally the **mysql_connect.php** script, which establishes a database connection, would be stored outside the Web root directory. If that is not possible in your case, you can place it in the **includes** folder, then change the code in the other scripts accordingly.

Once you've created the database, the database table, and the necessary folders, you can begin coding.

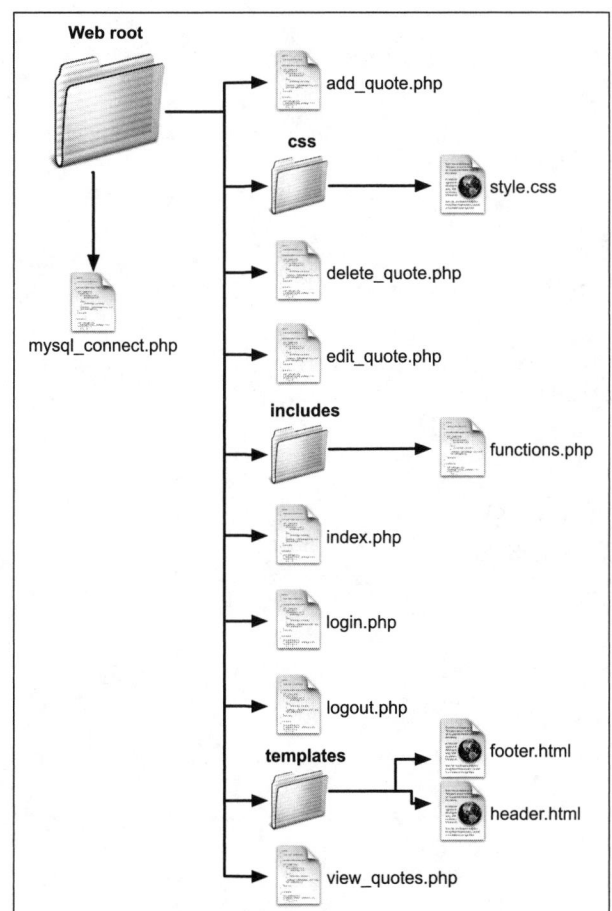

C The structure and organization of the files on the server.

Connecting to the Database

Unlike the scripts in Chapter 12, which connected to the database using code repeated in each script, this site will use the more common practice of placing the repeated code in a stand-alone file. Every script that interacts with the database—which will be most but not all of them—will then include this file. As you can see in Figure **C** in the previous section, this file should be stored outside of the Web root directory or, if that's not possible, within the **includes** folder.

To create mysql_connect.php:

1. Begin a new PHP script in your text editor or IDE, to be named **mysql_connect.php** (Script 13.1):

   ```
   <?php
   ```

2. Connect to the database server:

   ```
   $dbc = mysql_connect('localhost', 'username', 'password');
   ```

   Naturally, you'll need to change the values used here to be appropriate for your server.

3. Select the database:

   ```
   mysql_select_db('myquotes', $dbc);
   ```

   If you named your database something else, change this value accordingly.

4. Complete the script:

   ```
   ?>
   ```

5. Save the file as **mysql_connect.php**.

Script 13.1 This script connects to the database server and selects the database to be used.

```
1   <?php // Script 13.1 - mysql_connect.php
2   /* This script connects to and selects
    the database. */
3
4   // Connect:
5   $dbc = mysql_connect('localhost',
    'username', 'password');
6
7   // Select:
8   mysql_select_db('myquotes', $dbc);
9
10  ?>
```

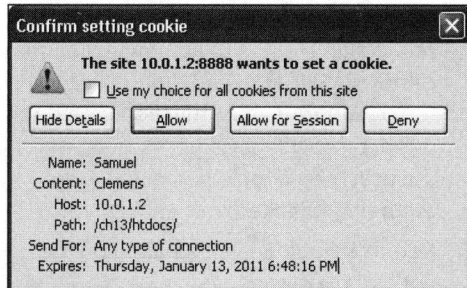

A This cookie will be used to identify the administrator.

Writing the User-Defined Function

The site will have a single user-defined function. As discussed in Chapter 10, "Creating Functions," the best time to create your own functions is when a script or a site might have repeating code. In this site there are a couple such instances, but the most obvious one is this: Many scripts will need to check whether or not the current user is an administrator. In this next script, you'll create your own function that returns a Boolean value indicating if the user is an administrator. But what will be the test of administrative status?

Upon successfully logging in, a cookie will be sent to the administrator's browser, with a name of *Samuel* and a value of *Clemens* **A**. This may seem odd or random, and it is. When using something simple, like a cookie, for authentication, it's best to be obscure about what constitutes verification. If you went with something more obvious, such as a name of *admin* and a value of *true*, that'd be quite easy for anyone to guess and falsify. With this cookie in mind, this next function simply checks if a cookie exists with a name of *Samuel* and a value of *Clemens*.

To create functions.php:

1. Begin a new PHP script in your text editor or IDE, to be named **functions.php** (Script 13.2):

   `<?php // Script 13.2 - functions.php`

   Even though, as written, the script only defines a single function, I'm naming the file using the plural—*functions*—with the understanding that more user-defined functions might be added to the script in time.

2. Begin defining a new function:

   `function is_administrator($name =`
   `→ 'Samuel', $value = 'Clemens') {`

   The function takes two arguments: the cookie's name and its value. Both have default values.

   Since the function checks only a single cookie with a single expected value, it doesn't need to take arguments at all, let alone default ones. But by having the function take arguments, it can be used in different ways should the

site's functionality expand (e.g., if you had multiple types of authentication to perform). Still, by using default values for those arguments, function calls don't need to provide argument values when the assumed cookie name and value are being checked.

3. Return a Boolean value based on the cookie's existence and value:

   `if (isset($_COOKIE[$name]) &&`
   `→ ($_COOKIE[$name] == $value)) {`
   `    return true;`
   `} else {`
   `    return false;`
   `}`

   If the cookie exists and has the appropriate value, the Boolean true is returned. Otherwise the function returns false.

4. Complete the function and the script:

   `} // End of is_administrator()`
   `→ function.`
   `?>`

5. Save the file as **functions.php**, stored in the **includes** directory.

Script 13.2 The **is_administrator()** function, defined in an includable script, will be called on any page that needs to verify administrator status.

```
1    <?php // Script 13.2 - functions.php
2    /* This page defines custom functions. */
3
4    // This function checks if the user is an administrator.
5    // This function takes two optional values.
6    // This function returns a Boolean value.
7    function is_administrator($name = 'Samuel', $value = 'Clemens') {
8
9        // Check for the cookie and check its value:
10       if (isset($_COOKIE[$name]) && ($_COOKIE[$name] == $value)) {
11           return true;
12       } else {
13           return false;
14       }
15
16   } // End of is_administrator() function.
17
18   ?>
```

Ⓐ If the person viewing any page is an administrator, they'll see some additional links.

Script 13.3 The header file includes the `functions.php` script and begins the HTML page.

```
1    <?php // Script 13.3 - header.html
2
3    // Include the functions script:
4    include('includes/functions.php'); ?>
5    <!DOCTYPE html PUBLIC "-//W3C//DTD XHTML
     1.0 Transitional//EN"
6        "http://www.w3.org/TR/xhtml1/DTD/
         xhtml1-transitional.dtd">
7    <html xmlns="http://www.w3.org/1999/
     xhtml" xml:lang="en" lang="en">
8    <head>
9        <meta http-equiv="content-type"
         content="text/html; charset=utf-8" />
10       <link rel="stylesheet" media="all"
         href="css/style.css" />
11       <title><?php // Print the page title.
12       if (defined('TITLE')) { // Is the title
         defined?
13           print TITLE;
14       } else { // The title is not defined.
15           print 'My Site of Quotes';
16       }
17       ?></title>
18   </head>
19   <body>
20       <div id="container">
21           <h1>My Site of Quotes</h1>
22           <br />
23           <!-- BEGIN CHANGEABLE CONTENT. -->
```

Creating the Template

Now that the two helper files have been created, it's time to move on to the template. As illustrated in Chapter 8, "Creating Web Applications," the site's layout will be controlled by two includable files: a header and a footer. Both will be stored in the **templates** directory. The header also references a style sheet, to be stored in the **css** folder. You can find the style sheet by downloading the book's code from www.LarryUllman.com (the file will be in the **ch13** folder of the download).

Besides generating the primary HTML for the site, the header file must include the functions script. The footer file should also display some administration links **Ⓐ**, should the current user be an administrator.

To create header.html:

1. Begin a new HTML document in your text editor or IDE, to be named **header.html** (Script 13.3).

    ```
    <?php // Script 13.3 - header.html
    include('includes/functions.php'); ?>
    ```

    The header will start with a PHP section in order to include the **functions.php** script, which will be required by multiple pages on the site. The reference to the script is relative to the pages that will be including the header: files in the main directory.

continues on next page

2. Begin the HTML document:

```
<!DOCTYPE html PUBLIC "-//W3C//DTD
→ XHTML 1.0 Transitional//EN"
  "http://www.w3.org/TR/xhtml1/
    → DTD/xhtml1-transitional.dtd">
<html xmlns="http://www.w3.org/
→ 1999/xhtml" xml:lang="en"
→ lang="en">
<head>
  <meta http-equiv="content-type"
  → content="text/html;
  → charset=utf-8" />
  <link rel="stylesheet" media=
  → "all" href="css/style.css" />
```

Again, the style sheet needs to be downloaded from the book's corresponding Web site. And the reference to that style sheet is relative to the scripts that include the header, all found within the main directory.

3. Print the page's title:

```
<title><?php
if (defined('TITLE')) {
  print TITLE;
} else {
  print 'My Site of Quotes';
}
?></title>
```

This code also comes from Chapter 8, printing either the default title or a custom one, if set as a constant.

4. Complete the head:

```
</head>
```

5. Begin the page's body:

```
<body>
  <div id="container">
    <h1>My Site of Quotes</h1>
    <br />
    <!-- BEGIN CHANGEABLE
    → CONTENT. -->
```

6. Save the file as **header.html**, stored in the **templates** directory.

To create footer.html:

1. Begin a new HTML document in your text editor or IDE, to be named **footer.html** (Script 13.4):

```
<!-- END CHANGEABLE CONTENT. -->
```

2. Check if it's appropriate to display general administration links:

```
<?php
if ( (is_administrator() &&
→ (basename($_SERVER['PHP_SELF'])
→ != 'logout.php'))
OR (isset($loggedin) &&
→ $loggedin) ) {
```

This conditional is a bit complicated. To start, most pages can confirm that the current user is an administrator by just invoking the **is_administrator()** function. But because of how cookies work, that function will return inappropriate results on two pages: **login.php** and **logout.php**. On the **logout.php**, the script will have received the administrative cookie prior to deleting it. So on that page, it will seem like the user is an administrator (because they just were), but links to the administrative pages should not be shown as the user will be blocked from using them (because when they get to those pages, the cookie will no longer exist). Hence, the first part of the conditional requires that **is_administrator()** return true and that the current page not be **logout.php**. The code **basename($_SERVER['PHP_SELF'])** is a reliable way to get the current script (and because the footer file is included by another script, **$_SERVER['PHP_SELF']** will have the value of the *including* script.

The second part of the conditional, after the **OR**, checks if the **$loggedin** variable is set and has a true value. This will be the case on the **login.php** page, after the user successfully logged in. The

is_administrator() function won't return a true value at that juncture, because the cookie will have been just sent by the script, and therefore won't be available to be read.

3. Create the links:

```
print '<hr /><h3>Site Admin</h3>
➝ <p><a href="add_quote.php">Add
➝ Quote</a> <->
<a href="view_quotes.php">View All
➝ Quotes</a> <->
<a href="logout.php">Logout</a></p>';
```

Three links are created: to a page for adding new quotes, to a page for viewing every quote, and to the logout page.

4. Complete the conditional and the PHP section:

```
}
?>
```

5. Complete the HTML page:

```
</div><!-- container -->
<div id="footer">Content &copy;
➝ 2011</div>
</body>
</html>
```

6. Save the file as **footer.html**, stored in the **templates** directory.

Script 13.4 The footer file displays general administrative links, when appropriate, and completes the HTML page.

```
1    <!-- END CHANGEABLE CONTENT. -->
2    <?php // Script 13.4 - footer.html
3
4    // Display general admin links...
5    // - if the user is an administrator and it's not the logout.php page
6    // - or if the $loggedin variable is true (i.e., the user just logged in)
7    if ( (is_administrator() && (basename($_SERVER['PHP_SELF']) != 'logout.php'))
8    OR (isset($loggedin) && $loggedin) ) {
9
10       // Create the links:
11       print '<hr /><h3>Site Admin</h3><p><a href="add_quote.php">Add Quote</a> <->
12       <a href="view_quotes.php">View All Quotes</a> <->
13       <a href="logout.php">Logout</a></p>';
14
15   }
16
17   ?>
18       </div><!-- container -->
19       <div id="footer">Content &copy; 2011</div>
20   </body>
21   </html>
```

Logging In

Next, it's time to create the script through which the administrator can log in. The end result will be very similar to the scripts in Chapter 9, "Cookies and Sessions," with one structural difference: that chapter used *output buffering*, allowing you to lay out your script however you want. This site does not use output buffering, so the handling of the form must be written in such a way that the cookie can be sent without generating *headers already sent* errors (see Chapter 9 if this isn't ringing a bell for you). In other words, the script must check for a form submission prior to including the header. To still be able to reflect errors and other messages within the context of the page, you must therefore use variables.

To create login.php:

1. Begin a new PHP document in your text editor or IDE, to be named **login.php** (**Script 13.5**):

   ```
   <?php // Script 13.5 - login.php
   ```

2. Define two variables with default values:

   ```
   $loggedin = false;
   $error = false;
   ```

   These two variables will be used later in the script. Here they are given default values, indicating that the person is not logged in and no errors have yet occurred.

3. Check if the form has been submitted:

   ```
   if ($_SERVER['REQUEST_METHOD'] ==
   → 'POST') {
   ```

Script 13.5 The login script both displays and handles a form, sending a cookie upon a successful login attempt.

```
1   <?php // Script 13.5 - login.php
2   /* This page lets people log into the
    site. */
3
4   // Set two variables with default values:
5   $loggedin = false;
6   $error = false;
7
8   // Check if the form has been submitted:
9   if ($_SERVER['REQUEST_METHOD'] == 'POST')
{
10
11      // Handle the form:
12      if (!empty($_POST['email']) &&
        !empty($_POST['password'])) {
13
14          if ( (strtolower($_POST['email'])
            == 'me@example.com') && ($_
            POST['password'] == 'testpass') ) {
            // Correct!
15
16              // Create the cookie:
17              setcookie('Samuel', 'Clemens',
                time()+3600);
18
19              // Indicate they are logged in:
20              $loggedin = true;
21
22          } else { // Incorrect!
23
24              $error = 'The submitted email
                address and password do not
                match those on file!';
25
26          }
27
28      } else { // Forgot a field.
29
30          $error = 'Please make sure you
            enter both an email address and a
            password!';
31
32      }
33
34  }
35
```

code continues on next page

```
36   // Set the page title and include the
     header file:
37   define('TITLE', 'Login');
38   include('templates/header.html');
39
40   // Print an error if one exists:
41   if ($error) {
42       print '<p class="error">' . $error .
'</p>';
43   }
44
45   // Indicate the user is logged in, or
     show the form:
46   if ($loggedin) {
47
48       print '<p>You are now logged in!</p>';
49
50   } else {
51
52       print '<h2>Login Form</h2>
53       <form action="login.php"
         method="post">
54       <p><label>Email Address <input type=
         "text" name="email" /></label></p>
55       <p><label>Password <input
         type="password" name="password" />
         </label></p>
56       <p><input type="submit" name="submit"
         value="Log In!" /></p>
57       </form>';
58
59   }
60
61   include('templates/footer.html');
     // Need the footer.
62   ?>
```

4. **Handle the form:**

   ```
   if (!empty($_POST['email']) &&
   → !empty($_POST['password'])) {
     if ( (strtolower($_POST['email'])
   → == 'me@example.com') && ($_POST
   → ['password'] == 'testpass') ) {
   ```

   Similar to examples in Chapter 9, this script first confirms that both **$_POST['email']** and **$_POST['password']** are not empty. The second conditional compares the submitted values against what they need to be.

5. **Create the cookie:**

   ```
   setcookie('Samuel', 'Clemens',
   → time()+3600);
   ```

   The cookie has a name of *Samuel* and a value of *Clemens*. It's set to expire in an hour.

6. **Indicate that the user is logged in:**

   ```
   $loggedin = true;
   ```

   This variable will be used later in this same script, and in the footer file (see Script 13.4).

7. **Create error messages for the two other conditions:**

   ```
   } else { // Incorrect!
     $error = 'The submitted
   → email address and
   → password do not match
   → those on file!';
   }
   } else { // Forgot a field.
     $error = 'Please make sure
   → you enter both an email
   → address and a password!';
   }
   }
   ```

continues on next page

The first **else** clause applies if an email address and password were provided but were wrong. The second **else** clause applies if no email address or password was submitted. In both cases, the message is assigned to a variable so that it may be used later in the script.

8. Set the page title and include the header file:

```
define('TITLE', 'Login');
include('templates/header.html');
```

9. Print an error if one exists:

```
if ($error) {
  print '<p class="error">' .
  → $error . '</p>';
}
```

The error itself will be determined in Step 7, but it can't be printed at that point because the HTML header will not have been included. The solution is to have this code check for a non-false **$error** value and then print **$error** within some HTML and CSS **A**.

My Site of Quotes

The submitted email address and password do not match those on file!

Login Form

Email Address

A Error messages are displayed after the header is included but before the HTML form.

My Site of Quotes

You are now logged in!

Site Admin

Add Quote <-> View All Quotes <-> Logout

Content © 2011

B The result upon successfully logging in.

My Site of Quotes

Login Form

Email Address [ ]

Password [ ]

[Log In!]

Content © 2011

C The basic login form.

---

10. Indicate that the user is logged in, or display the form:

```
if ($loggedin) {
  print '<p>You are now logged
  ↪ in!</p>';
} else {
  print '<h2>Login Form</h2>
  <form action="login.php"
  ↪ method="post">
  <p><label>Email Address <input
  ↪ type="text" name="email" />
  ↪ </label></p>
  <p><label>Password <input
  ↪ type="password" name=
  ↪ "password" /></label></p>
  <p><input type="submit" name=
  ↪ "submit" value="Log In!" /></p>
  </form>';
}
```

If the **$loggedin** variable has a true value—its value is false by default—then the user just successfully logged into the site and a message saying so is displayed **B**. If the **$loggedin** variable still has its default value, then the form should be shown **C**.

11. Include the footer and complete the page:

```
include('templates/footer.html');
?>
```

12. Save the file as **login.php**.

13. Test the file in your Web browser (Figures **A**, **B**, and **C**).

I purposefully omitted creating a link to the login section (as a security measure), so you'll need to enter the correct URL in your Web browser's address bar.

TIP Note that, as written, the script requires administrators to log back in after an hour, whether or not they continue to be active in the site.

Logging Out

If you write a login process, there must be a logout process, too. In this case, just using cookies, it's a very simple script.

To create logout.php:

1. Begin a new PHP document in your text editor or IDE, to be named **logout.php** (**Script 13.6**):

   ```
   <?php // Script 13.6 - logout.php
   ```

2. Destroy the cookie, but only if it already exists:

   ```
   if (isset($_COOKIE['Samuel'])) {
     setcookie('Samuel', FALSE,
     → time()-300);
   }
   ```

   As an extra security measure, the script only attempts to delete the cookie if it exists. By making this check, the script prevents hackers from discovering the name of the cookie used by the site by accessing the logout script without having first logged in.

   To delete the existing login cookie, another cookie is sent with the same name, a value of FALSE, and an expiration time in the past.

3. Define a page title and include the header:

   ```
   define('TITLE', 'Logout');
   include('templates/header.html');
   ```

4. Print a message:

   ```
   print '<p>You are now logged
   → out.</p>';
   ```

5. Include the footer:

   ```
   include('templates/footer.html');
   ?>
   ```

6. Save the file as **logout.php**.

7. Test the file in your Web browser  and .

Script 13.6 The logout script deletes the administrator-identifying cookie.

```
1    <?php // Script 13.6 - logout.php
2    /* This is the logout page. It destroys
     the cookie. */
3
4    // Destroy the cookie, but only if it
     already exists:
5    if (isset($_COOKIE['Samuel'])) {
6        setcookie('Samuel', FALSE,
         time()-300);
7    }
8
9    // Define a page title and include the
     header:
10   define('TITLE', 'Logout');
11   include('templates/header.html');
12
13   // Print a message:
14   print '<p>You are now logged out.</p>';
15
16   // Include the footer:
17   include('templates/footer.html');
18   ?>
```

Ⓐ This cookie deletes the existing cookie.

Ⓑ The resulting logout page.

A The form for adding quotations to the database.

Script 13.7 The `add_quote.php` script allows only administrators to add new quotations to the database.

```
1    <?php // Script 13.7 - add_quote.php
2    /* This script adds a quote. */
3
4    // Define a page title and include the
     header:
5    define('TITLE', 'Add a Quote');
6    include('templates/header.html');
7
8    print '<h2>Add a Quotation</h2>';
9
10   // Restrict access to administrators only:
11   if (!is_administrator()) {
12       print '<h2>Access Denied!</h2><p
         class="error">You do not have
         permission to access this page.</p>';
13       include('templates/footer.html');
14       exit();
15   }
16
17   // Check for a form submission:
18   if ($_SERVER['REQUEST_METHOD'] == 'POST')
     { // Handle the form.
19
20       if ( !empty($_POST['quote']) &&
         !empty($_POST['source']) ) {
21
```

code continues on next page

Adding Quotes

Now that the administrator has the ability to log in, she or he should be able to start adding quotations. The script for doing so is a lot like the one for adding blog postings (from Chapter 12), but the form will have an additional checkbox for marking the quotation as a favorite **A**.

Because this script creates records in the database, security must be a primary concern. As an initial precaution, the script will make sure that only the administrator can use the page. Second, values to be used in the SQL command will be sanctified to prevent invalid queries.

To create add_quote.php:

1. Begin a new PHP document in your text editor or IDE, to be named **add_quote.php** (Script 13.7):

   ```
   <?php // Script 13.7 -
   → add_quote.php
   define('TITLE', 'Add a Quote');
   include('templates/header.html');
   print '<h2>Add a Quotation</h2>';
   ```

2. Deny access to the page if the user is not an administrator:

   ```
   if (!is_administrator()) {
     print '<h2>Access Denied!</h2>
   → <p class="error">You do not
   → have permission to access
   → this page.</p>';
     include('templates/footer.html');
     exit();
   }
   ```

   continues on next page

By invoking the **is_administrator()** function, the script can quickly test for that condition. If the user is not an administrator, an *Access Denied* error is displayed, the footer is included, and the script is terminated **B**.

3. Check for a form submission:

```
if ($_SERVER['REQUEST_METHOD'] ==
→'POST') {
```

4. Check for values:

```
if ( !empty($_POST['quote']) &&
→!empty($_POST['source']) ) {
```

This script performs a minimum of validation, checking that the two variables aren't empty. With large blocks of text, such as a quotation, there's not much more that can be done in terms of validation.

5. Prepare the values for use in the query:

```
$quote = mysql_real_escape_
→string(trim(strip_tags($_POST
→['quote'])), $dbc);
$source = mysql_real_escape_
→string(trim(strip_tags($_POST
→['source'])), $dbc);
```

To make the two textual values safe to use in the query, they're run through the **mysql_real_escape_string()** function (see Chapter 12). To make the values safe to later display in the Web page, the **strip_tags()** function is applied, too (see Chapter 5, "Using Strings").

6. Create the *favorite* value:

```
if (isset($_POST['favorite'])) {
  $favorite = 1;
} else {
  $favorite = 0;
}
```

My Site of Quotes

Add a Quotation
Access Denied!

You do not have permission to access this page.

Content © 2011

B Any user not logged in as an administrator is denied access to the form.

Script 13.7 *continued*

```
22    // Need the database connection:
23    include('../mysql_connect.php');
24
25    // Prepare the values for storing:
26    $quote = mysql_real_escape_
      string(trim(strip_tags($_
      POST['quote'])), $dbc);
27    $source = mysql_real_escape_
      string(trim(strip_tags($_
      POST['source'])), $dbc);
28
29    // Create the "favorite" value:
30    if (isset($_POST['favorite'])) {
31        $favorite = 1;
32    } else {
33        $favorite = 0;
34    }
35
36    $query = "INSERT INTO quotes
      (quote, source, favorite) VALUES
      ('$quote', '$source', $favorite)";
37    $r = mysql_query($query, $dbc);
38
39    if (mysql_affected_rows($dbc) ==
      1) {
40        // Print a message:
41        print '<p>Your quotation has
          been stored.</p>';
42    } else {
43        print '<p class="error">Could
          not store the quote because:<br
          />' . mysql_error($dbc) . '.</
          p><p>The query being run was: '
          . $query . '</p>';
```

code continues on next page

```
44          }
45
46          // Close the connection:
47          mysql_close($dbc);
48
49     } else { // Failed to enter a quotation.
50          print '<p class="error">Please
            enter a quotation and a source!</p>';
51     }
52
53  } // End of submitted IF.
54
55  // Leave PHP and display the form:
56  ?>
57
58  <form action="add_quote.php"
    method="post">
59      <p><label>Quote <textarea
        name="quote" rows="5" cols="30">
        </textarea></label></p>
60      <p><label>Source <input type="text"
        name="source" /></label></p>
61      <p><label>Is this a favorite? <input
        type="checkbox" name="favorite"
        value="yes" /></label></p>
62      <p><input type="submit" name="submit"
        value="Add This Quote!" /></p>
63  </form>
64
65  <?php include('templates/header.html');
    ?>
```

In the database, a quotation's status as a favorite is indicated by a 1. Nonfavorites are represented by a 0. To determine which number to use, all the PHP script has to do is check for a **$_POST ['favorite']** value. If that variable is set, regardless of what its value is, it means the user checked the favorite checkbox. If the user didn't do that, then the variable won't be set, and the **$favorite** variable will be assigned the value 0.

7. Define and execute the query:

   ```
   $query = "INSERT INTO quotes
   → (quote, source, favorite) VALUES
   → ('$quote', '$source', $favorite)";
   $r = mysql_query($query, $dbc);
   ```

   The query specifies values for three fields and uses the variables already defined. The remaining two table columns—**quote_id** and **date_ entered**—will automatically be assigned values, thanks to the table's definition.

8. Print a message based on the results:

   ```
   if (mysql_affected_rows($dbc) ==
   → 1) {
      print '<p>Your quotation has
      → been stored.</p>';
   } else {
      print '<p class="error">Could
      → not store the quote because:
      → <br />' . mysql_error($dbc) .
      → '.</p><p>The query being run
      → was: ' . $query . '</p>';
   }
   ```

   If the **INSERT** query created one new row in the database, a message indicating such is displayed. Otherwise, debugging information is shown so that you can try to figure out what went wrong.

   continues on next page

9. Complete the validation conditional:

```
} else { // Failed to enter a
→ quotation.
  print '<p class="error">Please
  → enter a quotation and a
  → source!</p>';
}
```

10. Complete the submission conditional and the PHP block:

```
} // End of submitted IF.
?>
```

11. Create the form:

```
<form action="add_quote.php"
→ method="post">
  <p><label>Quote <textarea
  → name="quote" rows="5"
  → cols="30"></textarea>
  → </label></p>
  <p><label>Source <input
  → type="text" name="source" />
  → </label></p>
  <p><label>Is this a favorite?
  → <input type="checkbox"
  → name="favorite" /></label></p>
  <p><input type="submit"
  → name="submit" value="Add This
  → Quote!" /></p>
</form>
```

The form has one text area, one text input, and a checkbox (plus the submit button, of course). It is not designed to be sticky: that's a feature you could add later, if you wanted.

12. Include the footer:

```
<?php include('templates/
→ footer.html'); ?>
```

13. Save the file as **add_quote.php** and test in your Web browser **C**.

TIP The ability to create (i.e., INSERT), retrieve (SELECT), update, and delete database records is collectively referred to as *CRUD*.

My Site of Quotes

Add a Quotation

Your quotation has been stored.

Quote

C The result after adding a quotation.

My Site of Quotes

All Quotes

> *Nothing astonishes men so much as common sense and plain dealing.*

- Ralph Waldo Emerson

Quote Admin: Edit <-> Delete

> *It is the mark of an educated mind to be able to entertain a thought without accepting it.*

- Aristotle [Favorite!]

Quote Admin: Edit <-> Delete

> *In all affairs it's a healthy thing now and then to hang a question mark on the things you have long*

A The full list of stored quotations, with links to edit or delete each.

Script 13.8 This script lists every quotation currently stored, providing links for the administrator to edit or delete them.

```
1    <?php // Script 13.8- view_quotes.php
2    /* This script lists every quote. */
3
4    // Include the header:
5    define('TITLE', 'View All Quotes');
6    include('templates/header.html');
7
8    print '<h2>All Quotes</h2>';
9
10   // Restrict access to administrators only:
11   if (!is_administrator()) {
12       print '<h2>Access Denied!</h2><p
         class="error">You do not have
         permission to access this page.</p>';
13       include('templates/footer.html');
14       exit();
15   }
16
17   // Need the database connection:
18   include('../mysql_connect.php');
19
```

code continues on next page

Listing Quotes

The administrative side of the site will have a page that lists every quote stored in the database **A**. Although the same script could easily be adapted for the public side, its primary purpose is to provide quick links for the administrator to edit or delete any quote (as opposed to searching randomly through the public side for the right quote to manage).

Like the **add_quote.php** script, this page will restrict access to just administrators.

To create view_quotes.php:

1. Begin a new PHP document in your text editor or IDE, to be named **view_quotes.php** (Script 13.8):

   ```
   <?php // Script 13.8-
   → view_quotes.php
   define('TITLE', 'View All Quotes');
   include('templates/header.html');
   print '<h2>All Quotes</h2>';
   ```

2. Terminate the script if the user isn't an administrator:

   ```
   if (!is_administrator()) {
       print '<h2>Access Denied!</h2>
   → <p class="error">You do not
   → have permission to access
   → this page.</p>';
       include('templates/footer.html');
       exit();
   }
   ```

continues on next page

This is the exact same code as that in **add_quote.php**. Except for the browser's title, the result for nonadministrators will be the same as in **B** in the previous section of the chapter.

3. Include the database connection and define the query:

```
include('../mysql_connect.php');
$query = 'SELECT quote_id, quote,
→ source, favorite FROM quotes
→ ORDER BY date_entered DESC';
```

```
<!-- BEGIN CHANGEABLE CONTENT. --><h2>All Quo
<p><b>Quote Admin:</b> <a href="edit_quote.php?id=13">Edit</a
                 <a href="delete_quote.php?id=13">Delete</a></
<div><blockquote>It is the mark of an educated mind to be abl
  <strong>Favorite!</strong><p><b>Quote Admin:</b> <a href="ed
                 <a href="delete_quote.php?id=9">Delete</a></p>
<div><blockquote>In all affairs it's a healthy thing now and
mark on the things you have long taken for granted.</blockquo
<p><b>Quote Admin:</b> <a href="edit_quote.php?id=5">Edit</a>
                 <a href="delete_quote.php?id=5">Delete</a></p
<div><blockquote>Nurture your mind with great thoughts, for y
<p><b>Quote Admin:</b> <a href="edit_quote.php?id=6">Edit</a>
                 <a href="delete_quote.php?id=6">Delete</a></p
```

B The HTML source code for the page shows how the **quote_id** value is passed in the URL to the linked pages.

Script 13.8 *continued*

```
20    // Define the query:
21    $query = 'SELECT quote_id, quote, source, favorite FROM quotes ORDER BY date_entered DESC';
22
23    // Run the query:
24    if ($r = mysql_query($query, $dbc)) {
25
26        // Retrieve the returned records:
27        while ($row = mysql_fetch_array($r)) {
28
29            // Print the record:
30            print "<div><blockquote>{$row['quote']}</blockquote>- {$row['source']}\n";
31
32            // Is this a favorite?
33            if ($row['favorite'] == 1) {
34                print ' <strong>Favorite!</strong>';
35            }
36
37            // Add administrative links:
38            print "<p><b>Quote Admin:</b> <a href=\"edit_quote.php?id={$row['quote_id']}\">Edit</a> <->
39            <a href=\"delete_quote.php?id={$row['quote_id']}\">Delete</a></p></div>\n";
40
41        } // End of while loop.
42
43    } else { // Query didn't run.
44        print '<p class="error">Could not retrieve the data because:<br />' . mysql_error($dbc) . '.</
p><p>The query being run was: ' . $query . '</p>';
45    } // End of query IF.
46
47    mysql_close($dbc); // Close the connection.
48
49    include('templates/footer.html'); // Include the footer.
50    ?>
```

The query returns four columns—all but the date entered—from the database for every record. The results will be returned in order by the date they were entered.

4. Execute the query and begin retrieving the results:

```
if ($r = mysql_query($query,
→ $dbc)) {
  while ($row = mysql_fetch_
  → array($r)) {
```

The **while** loop code was explained in Chapter 12, even though it wasn't used in that chapter. This construct is how you fetch every record returned by a query.

5. Begin printing the record:

```
print "<div><blockquote>
→ {$row['quote']}</blockquote>-
→ {$row['source']}\n";
```

This code starts a DIV, places the quotation itself within **blockquote** tags, and then shows the quote's attribution.

6. Indicate that the quotation is a favorite, if applicable:

```
if ($row['favorite'] == 1) {
  print ' <strong>Favorite!
  → </strong>';
}
```

The value of **$row['favorite']** will be either 1 or 0. If it's 1, the word *Favorite!*, emphasized, is displayed along with the record.

7. Add administrative links for editing and deleting the quote:

```
print "<p><b>Quote Admin:</b>
→ <a href=\"edit_quote.php?id=
→ {$row['quote_id']}\">Edit</a> <->
<a href=\"delete_quote.php?id=
→ {$row['quote_id']}\">Delete</a>
→ </p></div>\n";
```

For each quote, two links must be created. The first is to **edit_quote.php** and the second to **delete_quote.php**. Each link must also pass the **quote_id** value along in the URL, as the code in Chapter 12 does **B**.

The end of the **print** statement closes the DIV for the specific quotation (begun in Step 5).

8. Complete the **while** loop and the **mysql_query()** conditional:

```
  } // End of while loop.
} else { // Query didn't run.
  print '<p class="error">Could
  → not retrieve the data
  → because:<br />' . mysql_
  → error($dbc) . '.</p><p>The
  → query being run was: ' .
  → $query . '</p>';
} // End of query IF.
```

9. Close the database connection:

```
mysql_close($dbc);
```

10. Complete the page:

```
include('templates/footer.html');
?>
```

11. Save the view as **view_quotes.php** and test in your Web browser.

TIP As some of the queries in this chapter demonstrate, you can use a column or value in an ORDER BY clause even if it's not selected by the query.

Editing Quotes

The **view_quotes.php** page (and later, **index.php**) has links to **edit_quote.php**, where the administrator can update a quote. Functionally, this script will be very similar to **edit_entry.php** from Chapter 12:

1. The script needs to receive an ID value in the URL.

2. Using the ID, the record is retrieved and used to populate a form 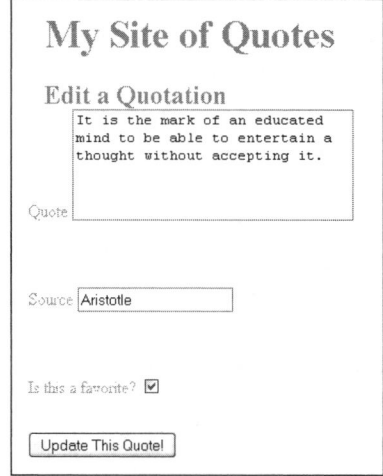.

3. Upon form submission, the form data will be validated (even if only slightly).

4. If the form data passes validation, the record will be updated in the database.

For the most part, this script is just another application of what you've already seen. But one new thing you'll learn here is how to check or not check a form's checkbox element based on a preexisting value.

To create edit_quote.php:

1. Begin a new PHP document in your text editor or IDE, to be named **edit_quote.php** (Script 13.9):

```php
<?php // Script 13.9 -
→ edit_quote.php
define('TITLE', 'Edit a Quote');
include('templates/header.html');
print '<h2>Edit a Quotation</h2>';
```

2. Terminate the script if the user isn't an administrator:

```php
if (!is_administrator()) {
  print '<h2>Access Denied!</h2>
  → <p class="error">You do not
  → have permission to access
  → this page.</p>';
  include('templates/footer.html');
  exit();
}
```

A The form's elements are prepopulated, and pre-checked, using the record's existing values.

Script 13.9 The **edit_quote.php** script gives the administrator a way to update an existing record.

```php
1   <?php // Script 13.9 - edit_quote.php
2   /* This script edits a quote. */
3
4   // Define a page title and include the
    header:
5   define('TITLE', 'Edit a Quote');
6   include('templates/header.html');
7
8   print '<h2>Edit a Quotation</h2>';
9
10  // Restrict access to administrators only:
11  if (!is_administrator()) {
12      print '<h2>Access Denied!</h2>
        <p class="error">You do not have
        permission to access this page.</p>';
13      include('templates/footer.html');
14      exit();
15  }
16
17  // Need the database connection:
18  include('../mysql_connect.php');
19
20  if (isset($_GET['id']) && is_numeric
    ($_GET['id']) && ($_GET['id'] > 0) ) { //
    Display the entry in a form:
21
22      // Define the query.
```

code continues on next page

3. Include the database connection:

```
include('../mysql_connect.php');
```

Both phases of the script—displaying the form and handling the form—require a database connection, so the included file is incorporated at this point.

4. Validate that a numeric ID value was received in the URL:

```
if (isset($_GET['id']) &&
→ is_numeric($_GET['id']) &&
→ ($_GET['id'] > 0) ) {
```

This conditional is like one from Chapter 12, with the addition of checking that the ID value is greater than 0. Adding that clause doesn't do anything for the security of the script—the `is_numeric()` test confirms that the value is safe to use in a query, but prevents the query from being executed if the ID has an unusable value.

5. Define and execute the query:

```
$query = "SELECT quote, source,
→ favorite FROM quotes WHERE
→ quote_id={$_GET['id']}";
if ($r = mysql_query($query,
→ $dbc)) {
  $row = mysql_fetch_array($r);
```

The query returns three columns for a specific record.

continues on next page
continues on next page

Script 13.9 *continued*

```
23    $query = "SELECT quote, source, favorite FROM quotes WHERE quote_id={$_GET['id']}";
24    if ($r = mysql_query($query, $dbc)) { // Run the query.
25
26        $row = mysql_fetch_array($r); // Retrieve the information.
27
28        // Make the form:
29        print '<form action="edit_quote.php" method="post">
30            <p><label>Quote <textarea name="quote" rows="5" cols="30">' . htmlentities($row['quote'])
            . '</textarea></label></p>
31            <p><label>Source <input type="text" name="source"value="' . htmlentities($row['source'])
            . '" /></label></p>
32            <p><label>Is this a favorite? <input type="checkbox" name="favorite" value="yes"';
33
34        // Check the box if it is a favorite:
35        if ($row['favorite'] == 1) {
36            print ' checked="checked"';
37        }
38
39        // Complete the form:
40        print ' /></label></p>
41            <input type="hidden" name="id" value="' . $_GET['id'] . '" />
42            <p><input type="submit" name="submit" value="Update This Quote!" /></p>
43        </form>';
44
45    } else { // Couldn't get the information.
46        print '<p class="error">Could not retrieve the quotation because:<br />' . mysql_
        error($dbc) . '.</p><p>The query being run was: ' . $query . '</p>';
47    }
48
```

code continues on next page

6. Begin creating the form:

```
print '<form action="edit_quote.php"
→ method="post">
<p><label>Quote <textarea name=
→ "quote" rows="5" cols="30">' .
→ htmlentities($row['quote']) .
⋯ '</textarea></label></p>
```

```
<p><label>Source <input type=
→ "text" name="source"value="' .
→ htmlentities($row['source']) .
→ '" /></label></p>
<p><label>Is this a favorite?
→ <input type="checkbox"
→ name="favorite" value="yes"';
```

Script 13.9 *continued*

```
49   } elseif (isset($_POST['id']) && is_numeric($_POST['id']) && ($_POST['id'] > 0)) { // Handle the form.
50
51       // Validate and secure the form data:
52       $problem = FALSE;
53       if ( !empty($_POST['quote']) && !empty($_POST['source']) ) {
54
55           // Prepare the values for storing:
56           $quote = mysql_real_escape_string(trim(strip_tags($_POST['quote']))), $dbc);
57           $source = mysql_real_escape_string(trim(strip_tags($_POST['source']))), $dbc);
58
59           // Create the "favorite" value:
60           if (isset($_POST['favorite'])) {
61               $favorite = 1;
62           } else {
63               $favorite = 0;
64           }
65
66       } else {
67           print '<p class="error">Please submit both a quotation and a source.</p>';
68           $problem = TRUE;
69       }
70
71       if (!$problem) {
72
73           // Define the query.
74           $query = "UPDATE quotes SET quote='$quote', source='$source', favorite=$favorite WHERE
             quote_id={$_POST['id']}";
75           if ($r = mysql_query($query, $dbc)) {
76               print '<p>The quotation has been updated.</p>';
77           } else {
78               print '<p class="error">Could not update the quotation because:<br /> . mysql_
                 error($dbc) . '.</p><p>The query being run was: ' . $query . '</p>';
79           }
80
81       } // No problem!
82
83   } else { // No ID set.
84       print '<p class="error">This page has been accessed in error.</p>';
85   } // End of main IF.
86
87   mysql_close($dbc); // Close the connection.
88
89   include('templates/footer.html'); // Include the footer.
90   ?>
```

The form is posted back to this same page. It starts with a text area, whose value will be prepopulated with the quote value retrieved from the database. That value is run through **htmlentities()** as a safety precaution.

Next, a text input is created, prepopulated with the quotation's source. Finally, the checkbox for the indication of the favorite is begun. Note that this checkbox element is not completed, as the script needs to next determine whether or not to check the box (in Step 7).

7. Check the box if it is a favorite:

```
if ($row['favorite'] == 1) {
  print ' checked="checked"';
}
```

If the record's **favorite** value equals 1, then the administrator previously marked this quotation as a favorite. In that case, additional HTML needs to be added to the checkbox input to pre-check it. After this point in the code, the favorite checkbox's underlying HTML will be either

```
<input type="checkbox"
→ name="favorite" value="yes"
```

or **B**

```
<input type="checkbox"
→ name="favorite" value="yes"
→ checked="checked"
```

continues on next page

```
<textarea name="quote" rows="5" cols="30">It is the mark of an educated mind to be ab.
 <input type="text" name="source"value="Aristotle" /></label></p>
s a favorite? <input type="checkbox" name="favorite" value="yes" checked="checked" />·
.den" name="id" value="9" />
```

B The HTML source code for the page, upon first arriving, shows how the favorite checkbox can be pre-checked.

8. Complete the form:

```
print ' /></label></p>
<input type="hidden" name="id"
→ value="' . $_GET['id'] . '" />
<p><input type="submit" name=
→ "submit" value="Update This
→ Quote!" /></p>
</form>';
```

The **print** statement starts by closing the checkbox. Then the form must also store the ID value in a hidden input, so that it's available to the script upon the form submission.

9. Create an error if the record could not be retrieved:

```
} else { // Couldn't get the
→ information.
  print '<p class="error">Could
→ not retrieve the quotation
→ because:<br />' . mysql_
→ error($dbc) . '.</p><p>The
→ query being run was: ' .
→ $query . '</p>';
}
```

10. Check for a form submission:

```
} elseif (isset($_POST['id']) &&
→ is_numeric($_POST['id']) &&
→ ($_POST['id'] > 0)) {
```

This conditional begins the second phase of the script: handling the submission of the form. The validation is the same as in Step 4, but now **$_POST['id']** is referenced instead of **$_GET['id']**.

11. Validate the form data:

```
$problem = FALSE;
if ( !empty($_POST['quote']) &&
→ !empty($_POST['source']) ) {
```

The form validation for the edit page mirrors that in the **add_quote.php** script (Script 13.7).

12. Prepare the values for use in the query:

```
$quote = mysql_real_escape_string
→ (trim(strip_tags($_POST
→ ['quote'])), $dbc);
$source = mysql_real_escape_
→ string(trim(strip_tags($_POST
→ ['source'])), $dbc);
if (isset($_POST['favorite'])) {
  $favorite = 1;
} else {
  $favorite = 0;
}
```

This code is also taken straight from **add_quote.php**.

13. Indicate a problem if the form wasn't completed:

```
} else {
  print '<p class="error">Please
→ submit both a quotation and
→ a source.</p>';
  $problem = TRUE;
}
```

14. If no problem occurred, update the database:

```
if (!$problem) {
  $query = "UPDATE quotes SET
→ quote='$quote', source=
→ '$source', favorite=$favorite
→ WHERE quote_id={$_POST['id']}";
  if ($r = mysql_query($query,
→ $dbc)) {
  print '<p>The quotation has
→ been updated.</p>';
```

C The result upon successfully editing a record.

The **UPDATE** query updates the values of three of the record's columns. The two string values are enclosed in single quotation marks (within the query); the numeric **$favorite** value is not.

The **WHERE** clause, which dictates the record to be updated, is the critical piece.

Finally, a simple message indicates the success of the operation **C**.

15. Indicate a problem if the query failed:

```
} else {
  print '<p class="error">Could
  → not update the quotation
  → because:<br />' . mysql_
  → error($dbc) . '.</p><p>The
  → query being run was: ' .
  → $query . '</p>';
}
```

16. Complete the conditionals:

```
  } // No problem!
} else { // No ID set.
  print '<p class="error">This
  → page has been accessed in
  → error.</p>';
} // End of main IF.
```

The **else** clause applies if no valid ID value is received by the page via either GET or POST.

17. Close the database connection and complete the page:

```
mysql_close($dbc);
include('templates/footer.html');
?>
```

18. Save the file and test in your Web browser (by clicking a link on **view_quotes.php**).

Deleting Quotes

The script for deleting existing quotations mimics **delete_entry.php** from Chapter 12. Upon first arriving, assuming that a valid record ID was passed along in the URL, the quote to be deleted is displayed **Ⓐ**. If the administrator clicks the submit button, the form will be submitted back to this same page, at which point the record will be removed from the database **Ⓑ**.

To create delete_quote.php:

1. Begin a new PHP document in your text editor or IDE, to be named **delete_quote.php** (Script 13.10):

```
<?php // Script 13.10 -
→ delete_quote.php
define('TITLE', 'Delete a Quote');
include('templates/header.html');
print '<h2>Delete a Quotation</h2>';
```

Ⓐ The first step for deleting a record is confirming the record to be removed.

Ⓑ Upon submission of the form, the quotation is deleted and a message is printed.

Script 13.10 The **delete_quote.php** script provides the administrator with a way to delete an existing record.

```
1    <?php // Script 13.10 - delete_quote.php
2    /* This script deletes a quote. */
3
4    // Define a page title and include the header:
5    define('TITLE', 'Delete a Quote');
6    include('templates/header.html');
7
8    print '<h2>Delete a Quotation</h2>';
9
10   // Restrict access to administrators only:
11   if (!is_administrator()) {
12       print '<h2>Access Denied!</h2>
         <p class="error">You do not have permission to access this page.</p>';
13       include('templates/footer.html');
14       exit();
15   }
16
17   // Need the database connection:
18   include('../mysql_connect.php');
19
20   if (isset($_GET['id']) && is_numeric($_GET['id']) && ($_GET['id'] > 0) ) { // Display the quote
     in a form:
```

code continues on next page

2. Terminate the script if the user isn't an administrator:

```php
if (!is_administrator()) {
    print '<h2>Access Denied!</h2>
    → <p class="error">You do not
    → have permission to access
    → this page.</p>';
    include('templates/footer.html');
    exit();
}
```

3. Include the database connection:

```php
include('../mysql_connect.php');
```

continues on next page

Script 13.10 *continued*

```php
21
22      // Define the query:
23      $query = "SELECT quote, source, favorite FROM quotes WHERE quote_id={$_GET['id']}";
24      if ($r = mysql_query($query, $dbc)) { // Run the query.
25
26          $row = mysql_fetch_array($r); // Retrieve the information.
27
28          // Make the form:
29          print '<form action="delete_quote.php" method="post">
30          <p>Are you sure you want to delete this quote?</p>
31          <div><blockquote>' . $row['quote'] . '</blockquote>- ' . $row['source'];
32
33          // Is this a favorite?
34          if ($row['favorite'] == 1) {
35              print ' <strong>Favorite!</strong>';
36          }
37
38          print '</div><br /><input type="hidden" name="id" value="' . $_GET['id'] . '" />
39          <p><input type="submit" name="submit" value="Delete this Quote!" /></p>
40          </form>';
41
42      } else { // Couldn't get the information.
43          print '<p class="error">Could not retrieve the quote because:<br />' . mysql_error($dbc) .
                '.</p><p>The query being run was: ' . $query . '</p>';
44      }
45
46  } elseif (isset($_POST['id']) && is_numeric($_POST['id']) && ($_POST['id'] > 0) ) { // Handle the
    form.
47
48      // Define the query:
49      $query = "DELETE FROM quotes WHERE quote_id={$_POST['id']} LIMIT 1";
```

code continues on next page

4. Validate that a numeric ID value was received in the URL:

```
if (isset($_GET['id']) &&
→ is_numeric($_GET['id']) &&
→ ($_GET['id'] > 0) ) {
```

This is the same conditional used in **edit_quote.php**.

5. Retrieve the record to be deleted:

```
$query = "SELECT quote, source,
→ favorite FROM quotes WHERE
→ quote_id={$_GET['id']}";
if ($r = mysql_query($query, $dbc))
→ { $row = mysql_fetch_array($r);
```

The standard three fields are retrieved from the database for the record. Because only one record is being addressed in this script, the **mysql_ fetch_array()** function is called once, outside of any loop.

6. Begin creating the form:

```
print '<form action="delete_quote.
→ php" method="post">
<p>Are you sure you want to
→ delete this quote?</p>
<div><blockquote>' . $row['quote'] .
→ '</blockquote>- ' .
$row['source'];
```

The form, for the most part, just displays the quotation.

7. Indicate if the quotation is a favorite:

```
if ($row['favorite'] == 1) {
  print ' <strong>Favorite!
  → </strong>';
}
```

This code is the same as that on the **view_quotes.php** page, indicating that the quote is, in fact, a favorite.

Script 13.10 *continued*

```
50    $r = mysql_query($query, $dbc); // Execute the query.
51
52    // Report on the result:
53    if (mysql_affected_rows($dbc) == 1) {
54        print '<p>The quote entry has been deleted.</p>';
55    } else {
56        print '<p class="error">Could not delete the blog entry because:<br />' . mysql_
          error($dbc) . '.</p><p>The query being run was: ' . $query . '</p>';
57    }
58
59    } else { // No ID received.
60        print '<p class="error">This page has been accessed in error.</p>';
61    } // End of main IF.
62
63    mysql_close($dbc); // Close the connection.
64
65    include('templates/footer.html');
66    ?>
```

8. Complete the form:

```php
print '</div><br />
<input type="hidden" name="id"
→ value="' . $_GET['id'] . '" />
<p><input type="submit" name=
→ "submit" value="Delete this
→ Quote!" /></p>
</form>';
```

The form must contain a hidden input that will pass the quote ID back to the page upon form submission.

9. Complete the `mysql_query()` conditional:

```php
} else { // Couldn't get the
→ information.
  print '<p class="error">Could
→ not retrieve the quote
→ because:<br />' . mysql_
→ error($dbc) . '.</p><p>The
→ query being run was: ' .
→ $query . '</p>';
}
```

If the query failed, the MySQL error, and the query itself, are displayed for debugging purposes.

10. Check for a form submission:

```php
} elseif (isset($_POST['id']) &&
→ is_numeric($_POST['id']) &&
→ ($_POST['id'] > 0) )) {
```

This conditional begins the second phase of the script: handling the submission of the form. The validation is the same as in Step 4, but now **$_POST['id']** is referenced instead of **$_GET['id']**.

11. Delete the record:

```php
$query = "DELETE FROM quotes
→ WHERE quote_id={$_POST['id']}
→ LIMIT 1";
$r = mysql_query($query, $dbc);
```

The **DELETE** query will remove the record. The **WHERE** conditional indicates which specific record is to be removed, and the **LIMIT 1** clause is applied as an extra precaution.

12. Report on the result:

```php
if (mysql_affected_rows($dbc)
→ == 1) {
  print '<p>The quote entry has
→ been deleted.</p>';
} else {
  print '<p class="error">Could
→ not delete the blog entry
→ because:<br />' . mysql_
→ error($dbc) . '.</p><p>The
→ query being run was: ' .
→ $query . '</p>';
}
```

If the query succeeded, then one record will have been affected, and a message is displayed to the user **B**.

13. Complete the conditionals:

```php
} else { // No ID received.
  print '<p class="error">This
→ page has been accessed in
→ error.</p>';
} // End of main IF.
```

The **else** clause applies if no valid ID value is received by the page via either GET or POST.

14. Close the database connection and complete the page:

```php
mysql_close($dbc);
include('templates/footer.html');
?>
```

15. Save the file and test in your Web browser (by clicking a link on **view_quotes.php**).

Creating the Home Page

Last, but certainly not least, there's the home page. For this site, the home page will be the only page used by the public at large. The home page will show a single quotation, but the specific quotation can be one of the following:

- The most recent (the default)
- A random quotation
- A random favorite quotation

To achieve this effect, links will pass different values in the URL back to this same page .

The script should also display administrative links—edit and delete—for the currently displayed quote, if the user is an administrator **B**.

To create index.php:

1. Begin a new PHP document in your text editor or IDE, to be named **index.php** (Script 13.11):

   ```php
   <?php // Script 13.11 - index.php
   ```

2. Include the header:

   ```php
   include('templates/header.html');
   ```

   The home page does not need a custom title, so no constant is defined before including the header.

3. Include the database connection:

   ```php
   include('../mysql_connect.php');
   ```

4. Begin defining the query to be run:

   ```php
   if (isset($_GET['random'])) {
     $query = 'SELECT quote_id,
   → quote, source, favorite FROM
   → quotes ORDER BY RAND() DESC
   → LIMIT 1';
   ```

A Values passed in the URL trigger the execution of different queries.

B When an administrator views the home page, extra links are displayed.

Script 13.11 The home page of the site shows a single quotation at a time, plus administrative links (when appropriate).

```
1   <?php // Script 13.11 - index.php
2   /* This is the home page for this site.
    It displays:
3   - The most recent quote (default)
4   - OR, a random quote
5   - OR, a random favorite quote */
6
7   // Include the header:
8   include('templates/header.html');
9
10  // Need the database connection:
11  include('../mysql_connect.php');
12
13  // Define the query...
```

code continues on next page

If a $_GET['random'] variable is set, the user clicked a link requesting a random quotation. It doesn't matter what value this variable has, so long as it is set.

For all of the queries, four columns—quote_id, the quote, the source, and favorite—from one row will be returned. To only retrieve one row, a LIMIT 1 clause is used.

To select a random row in MySQL, use the ORDER BY RAND() clause. This code uses MySQL's RAND() function, short for *random*, to return the records in a random order. So this query first selects every record in random order, and then returns only the first in that set.

5. Define the query that selects a random favorite record:

```
} elseif (isset($_GET['favorite'])) {
  $query = 'SELECT quote_id,
  ⇥ quote, source, favorite FROM
  ⇥ quotes WHERE favorite=1 ORDER
  ⇥ BY RAND() DESC LIMIT 1';
```

This query is similar to that in Step 4, but it uses a WHERE clause to restrict the pool of possible quotations to just those whose favorite value equals 1.

6. Define the default query:

```
} else {
  $query = 'SELECT quote_id,
  ⇥ quote, source, favorite FROM
  ⇥ quotes ORDER BY date_entered
  ⇥ DESC LIMIT 1';
}
```

If no value was passed in the URL, then the home page should display the most recently added quotation. To do that, the query orders all of the quotes in descending order of date entered, and then limits the results to just a single record.

7. Execute the query and fetch the returned record:

```
if ($r = mysql_query($query, $dbc)) {
  $row = mysql_fetch_array($r);
```

continues on next page

Script 13.11 *continued*

```
14   // Change the particulars depending upon values passed in the URL:
15   if (isset($_GET['random'])) {
16       $query = 'SELECT quote_id, quote, source, favorite FROM quotes ORDER BY RAND() DESC LIMIT 1';
17   } elseif (isset($_GET['favorite'])) {
18       $query = 'SELECT quote_id, quote, source, favorite FROM quotes WHERE favorite=1 ORDER BY
         RAND() DESC LIMIT 1';
19   } else {
20       $query = 'SELECT quote_id, quote, source, favorite FROM quotes ORDER BY date_entered DESC
         LIMIT 1';
21   }
22
23   // Run the query:
24   if ($r = mysql_query($query, $dbc)) {
25
26       // Retrieve the returned record:
27       $row = mysql_fetch_array($r);
28
29       // Print the record:
30       print "<div><blockquote>{$row['quote']}</blockquote>- {$row['source']}";
```

code continues on next page

8. Print the quotation:

```
print "<div><blockquote>{$row
→ ['quote']}</blockquote>-
→ {$row['source']} ";
```

This code is similar to that in **view_quotes.php**, but only needs to be used once.

9. Indicate if the quotation is a favorite and complete the DIV:

```
if ($row['favorite'] == 1) {
  print ' <strong>Favorite!
  → </strong>';
}
print '</div>';
```

The conditional is the same as in **delete_quote.php** and **view_quotes.php**.

10. If the user is an administrator, create links to edit or delete this record:

```
if (is_administrator()) {
  print "<p><b>Quote Admin:</b>
  → <a href=\"edit_quote.php?
  → id={$row['quote_id']}\">Edit
  → </a> - + | + -
  <a href=\"delete_quote.php?
  → id={$row['quote_id']}\">
  → Delete</a>
  </p>\n";
}
```

If the user is an administrator, links to the edit and delete scripts will be added to the page. The links themselves have values just like those in **view_quotes.php**.

Script 13.11 *continued*

```
31
32      // Is this a favorite?
33      if ($row['favorite'] == 1) {
34          print ' <strong>Favorite!</strong>';
35      }
36
37      // Complete the DIV:
38      print '</div>';
39
40      // If the admin is logged in, display admin links for this record:
41      if (is_administrator()) {
42          print "<p><b>Quote Admin:</b> <a href=\"edit_quote.php?id={$row['quote_id']}\">Edit</a> <->
43          <a href=\"delete_quote.php?id={$row['quote_id']}\">Delete</a>
44          </p>\n";
45      }
46
47  } else { // Query didn't run.
48      print '<p class="error">Could not retrieve the data because:<br />' . mysql_error($dbc) .
            '.</p><p>The query being run was: ' . $query . '</p>';
49  } // End of query IF.
50
51  mysql_close($dbc); // Close the connection.
52
53  print '<p><a href="index.php">Latest</a> <-> <a href="index.php?random=true">Random</a> <->
        <a href="index.php?favorite=true">Favorite</a><p>';
54
55  include('templates/footer.html'); // Include the footer.
56  ?>
```

11. If the query didn't run, print an error message:

```
} else { // Query didn't run.
  print '<p class="error">Could
  → not retrieve the data
  → because:<br /> . mysql_error
  → ($dbc) . '.</p><p>The query
  → being run was: ' . $query .
  → '</p>';
} // End of query IF.
```

This code is for your own debugging purposes. You would not display a MySQL error, or the query that caused it, to the general public.

12. Close the database connection:

```
mysql_close($dbc);
```

The database connection will no longer be needed, so it can be closed at this point.

13. Create links to other pages:

```
print '<p><a href="index.php">
  → Latest</a> <-> <a href=
  → "index.php?random=true">
  → Random</a> <-> <a href=
  → "index.php?favorite=true">
  → Favorite</a><p>';
```

Three public links are added to the page, each back to this same script. The first link, which passes no values in the URL, will always show the most recent quotation. The second, which passes a *random* value in the URL, will trigger the query in Step 4, thereby retrieving a random record. The third link, which passes a *favorite* value in the URL, will trigger the query in Step 5, thereby retrieving a random favorite record.

14. Include the footer and complete the page:

```
include('templates/footer.html');
?>
```

15. Save the file and test in your Web browser **C**.

> **TIP** Normally the home page is one of the first scripts written, not the last. But in this case I wanted to build up to this point in the example.

C The latest quotation (note the URL).

Review and Pursue

If you have any problems with the review questions or the pursue prompts, turn to the book's supporting forum (www.LarryUllman.com/forum/).

Review

- How would the `is_administrator()` function be called to check for the same cookie—named *Samuel*—with a different value? A different cookie—not named *Samuel*—with a different value?

- Why is the reference to the style sheet in the header file **css/style.css** instead of **../css/style.css**? How else could the style sheet be referenced?

- Why is the **login.php** script structured the way it is? How could that script be organized more linearly?

- What would be some other good ideas for user-defined functions with this site? Hint: look for repeated code.

Pursue

- Make the login form sticky.

- Define the login credentials—the cookie name and value—as constants in a configuration file. Then include that configuration file on every page and use those constants for creating, deleting, and confirming the value of the cookie.

- Limit the cookie's expiration to only 15 minutes, and then re-send the cookie on each page, if appropriate (i.e., if the cookie exists).

- Use sessions instead of a cookie.

- Make the **add_quote.php** and **edit_quote.php** forms sticky.

- Change **view_quotes.php** so that the administrator can list the quotes in different order. Hint: Create links back to the page like those on **index.php** and change the query accordingly.

- Before putting this site on a live server (should you do that), update all the code so that no MySQL error is ever shown to a nonadministrative user.

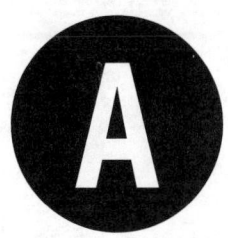

Installation and Configuration

There are three technical requirements for executing all of this book's examples: MySQL (the database application), PHP (the scripting language), and the Web server application (that PHP runs through). This appendix describes the installation of these tools on two different platforms—Windows XP and Mac OS X. If you are using a hosted Web site, all of this will already be provided for you, but these products are all free and easy enough to install, so putting them on your own computer still makes sense.

After the installation section, this appendix demonstrates some basics for working with MySQL and configuring PHP. The PHP and MySQL manuals cover installation and configuration in a reasonable amount of detail. You may want to also peruse them, particularly if you encounter problems.

Installation on Windows

Although you can certainly install a Web server (like Apache, Abyss, or IIS), PHP, and MySQL individually on a Windows computer, I strongly recommend you use an all-in-one installer instead. It's simply easier and more reliable to do so.

There are several all-in-one installers out there for Windows. The two that I see mentioned most frequently are XAMPP (www.apachefriends.org) and WAMP (www.wampserver.com). For this appendix, I'll use XAMPP, which runs on Windows 2000, 2003, XP, and Vista. (The XAMPP site makes no mention of Windows 7, but you should be able to use XAMPP on that version of Windows.)

Along with Apache, PHP, and MySQL, XAMPP also installs:

- PEAR (PHP Extension and Application Repository), a library of PHP code
- phpMyAdmin, the Web-based interface to a MySQL server
- A mail server (for sending email)
- Several useful extensions

As of this writing, XAMPP (Version 1.7.3) installs PHP 5.31, MySQL 5.1.41, Apache 2.2.14, and phpMyAdmin 3.2.4.

I'll run through the installation process in these next steps. Note that if you have any problems, you can use the book's supporting forum (www.LarryUllman.com/forum/), but you'll probably have more luck turning to the XAMPP site (it is their product, after all). Also, the installer works really well and isn't that hard to use, so rather than detail every single step in the process, I'll highlight the most important considerations.

On Firewalls

A firewall prevents communication over *ports* (a port is an access point to a computer). Versions of Windows starting with Service Pack 2 of XP include a built-in firewall. You can also download and install third-party firewalls. Firewalls improve the security of your computer, but they may also interfere with your ability to run Apache, MySQL, and some of the other tools used by XAMPP because they all use ports.

When running XAMPP for the first time, if you see a security prompt indicating that the firewall is blocking Apache, MySQL, or the like, choose Unblock. Otherwise, you can configure your firewall manually (for example, on Windows XP, it's done through Control Panel > Security Center). The ports that need to be open are as follows: 80 (for Apache), 3306 (for MySQL), and 25 (for the Mercury mail server). If you have any problems starting or accessing one of these, disable your firewall and see if it works then. If so, you'll know the firewall is the problem and that it needs to be reconfigured.

Just to be clear, firewalls aren't found just on Windows, but in terms of the instructions in this appendix, the presence of a firewall will more likely trip up a Windows user than any other.

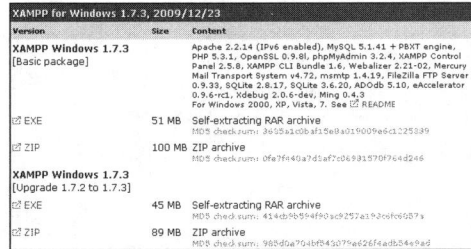

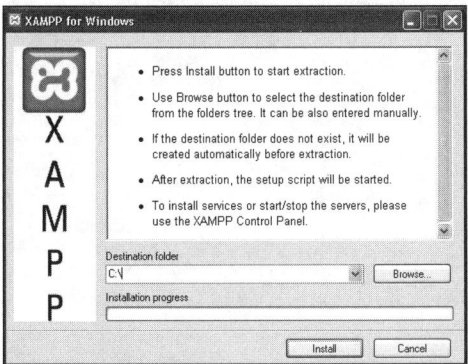

A From the Apache Friends Web site, grab the latest installer for Windows.

B Select where XAMPP should be installed.

C The XAMPP console window.

To install XAMPP on Windows:

1. Download the latest release of XAMPP for Windows from www.apachefriends.org.

   You'll need to click around a bit to find the download section, but eventually you'll come to an area where you can find the download **A**. Then click *EXE*, which is the specific item you want.

2. On your computer, double-click the downloaded file in order to begin the installation process.

3. When prompted **B**, install XAMPP somewhere other than in the Program Files directory.

   You shouldn't install it in the Program Files directory because of a permissions issue in Windows Vista. I recommend installing XAMPP in your root directory (e.g., **C:**).

   Wherever you decide to install the program, make note of that location, as you'll need to know it several other times as you work through this appendix.

4. If you want, create Desktop and Start Menu shortcuts **C**.

   During the installation process, XAMPP will open a console window, where you'll be prompted for additional options.

5. When prompted, have XAMPP locate the paths correctly.

6. When prompted, do not make a portable XAMPP without drive letters.

7. Continue through the remaining prompts, reading them and pressing Enter/Return to continue.

   You'll be notified that the installation is successful, what time zone was set in the PHP configuration, and so forth. Nothing that significant here.

   continues on next page

8. After the installation process has done its thing **D**, enter 1 to start the control panel.

   Upon completion of the installation, you'll be given a few options, still within the console window. One option is to start the control panel, which can also be done using the Desktop or Start Menu shortcuts, assuming you chose to create those in Step 4.

9. To start, stop, and configure XAMPP, use the XAMPP control panel **E**.

10. Using the control panel, start Apache, MySQL, and Mercury.

    Apache has to be running for every chapter in this book. MySQL must be running for Chapter 12, "Intro to Databases." Mercury is the mail server that XAMPP installs. It needs to be running in order to send email using PHP (see Chapter 8, "Creating Web Applications").

11. Immediately set a password for the root MySQL user.

    How you do this is explained later in the chapter.

> **TIP** The XAMPP control panel's various admin links will take you to different Web pages (on your server) and other resources **F**.

> **TIP** See the "PHP Configuration" section to learn how to configure PHP by editing the php.ini file.

> **TIP** Your Web root directory—where your PHP scripts should be placed in order to test them—is the htdocs folder in the directory where XAMPP was installed. Following my installation instructions, this would be C:\xampp\htdocs.

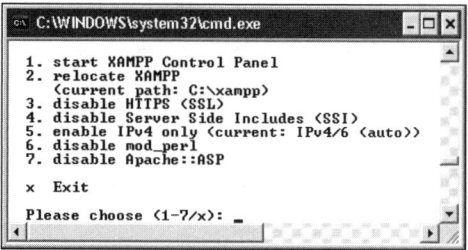

D The installation of XAMPP is complete!

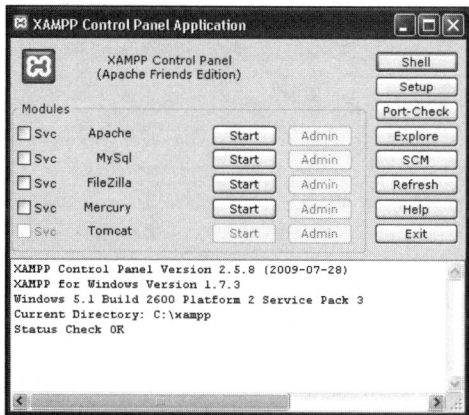

E The XAMPP control panel, used to manage the software.

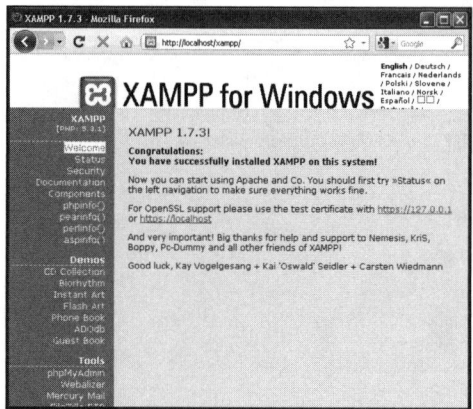

F The Web-based splash page for XAMPP, linked from the control panel.

Installation on Mac OS X

Thanks to some ready-made packages, installing MySQL and PHP on Mac OS X used to be surprisingly easy (and may still be for you). Mac OS X already uses Apache as its Web server and comes with a version of PHP installed but not enabled. Thanks to Marc Liyanage (www.entropy.ch), who does a ton of work supporting the Mac operating system, more current and feature-rich versions of PHP can be easily installed.

I say that installation "used to be" and "may still be" easy because it depends on the hardware and operating system you're using. Starting with Mac OS X 10.5 (Leopard), the version of Apache included is 64-bit (assuming your computer supports it), meaning that PHP must also be 64-bit, as must every library that PHP uses. This is not easily done.

Because of the complications that have arisen from Mac OS X 10.5 using the 64-bit version of Apache (if possible), I've decided to take a more universally foolproof route and recommend that you use the all-in-one MAMP installer (www.mamp.info). It's available in both free and commercial versions, is very easy to use, and won't affect the Apache server built into the operating system.

Along with Apache, PHP, and MySQL, MAMP also installs phpMyAdmin, the Web-based interface to a MySQL server, along with lots of useful PHP extensions. As of this writing, MAMP (Version 1.9.4) installs both PHP 5.2.13 and 5.3.2, in addition to MySQL 5.1.44, Apache 2.0.63, and phpMyAdmin 3.2.5.

continues on next page

I'll run through the installation process in these next steps. If you have any problems, you can use the book's supporting forum (www.LarryUllman.com/forum/), but you'll probably have more luck turning to the MAMP site (it is their product, after all). Also, the installer works really well and isn't that hard to use, so rather than detail every single step in the process, I'll highlight the most important considerations.

To install MAMP on Mac OS X:

1. Download the latest release of MAMP from www.mamp.info.

   On the front page, click *Download*, and then click *MAMP & MAMP PRO 1.9.4* 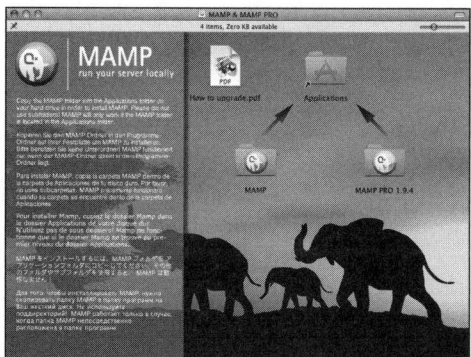. (As new releases of MAMP come out, the link and filename will obviously change accordingly.)

   The same downloaded file is used for both products. In fact, MAMP Pro is just a nicer interface for controlling and customizing the same MAMP software.

2. On your computer, double-click the downloaded file in order to mount the disk image **B**.

3. Copy the MAMP folder from the disk image to your **Applications** folder.

   If you think you might prefer the commercial MAMP PRO, copy that folder as well (again, it's an interface to MAMP, so both folders are required). MAMP PRO comes with a free 14-day trial period.

   Whichever folder you choose, note that you must place it within the **Applications** folder. It cannot go in a subfolder or another directory on your computer.

Download: MAMP & MAMP PRO 1.9.4

Published: 2010-10-26

This download package contains the free MAMP and a free 14-day trial of MAMP PRO. MAMP can be used stand-alone without MAMP PRO.

The trial Version of MAMP PRO can be upgraded to the full version by buying a serial number. You can order a serial number at our shop.

All MAMP PRO updates in the current major version (1.x) are free of charge. If you want to update MAMP PRO from e.g. 1.7.2 to 1.9.4 just use the serial number you already got.

- **Requirements:** min. Mac OS X 10.4
  (This version of MAMP & MAMP PRO is indeed compatible with Mac OS X 10.6 Snow Leopard.)
- **Platform:** Universal Binary
- **File type:** dmg
- **File size:** app. 170 MB
- **Translations MAMP:** English, French, German, Italian, Japanese, Russian, Spanish
- **Translations MAMP PRO:** English, German, Japanese

A Download MAMP from this page at www.mamp.info.

B The contents of the downloaded MAMP disk image.

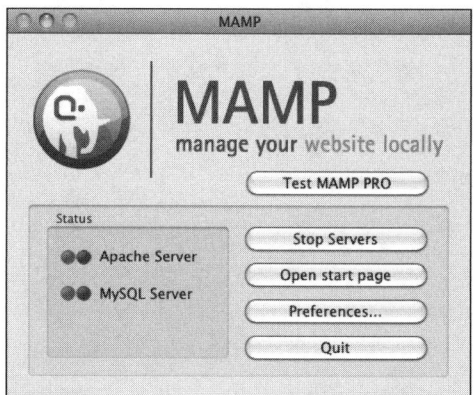

C The simple MAMP application, used to control and configure Apache, PHP, and MySQL.

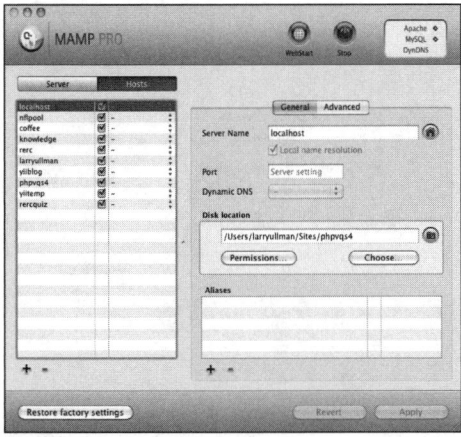

D The MAMP PRO application, used to control and configure Apache, PHP, MySQL, and more.

4. Open the **Applications/MAMP** (or **Applications/MAMP PRO**) folder.

5. Double-click the MAMP (or MAMP PRO) application to start the program **C**.

   It may take just a brief moment to start the servers, but then you'll see a result like that in **C** for MAMP or **D** for MAMP PRO.

   When starting MAMP, a start page should also open in your default Web browser **E**. Through this page you can view the version of PHP that's running, as well as how it's configured, and interface with the MySQL database using phpMyAdmin.

   With MAMP PRO, you can access that same page by clicking the WebStart button **D**.

continues on next page

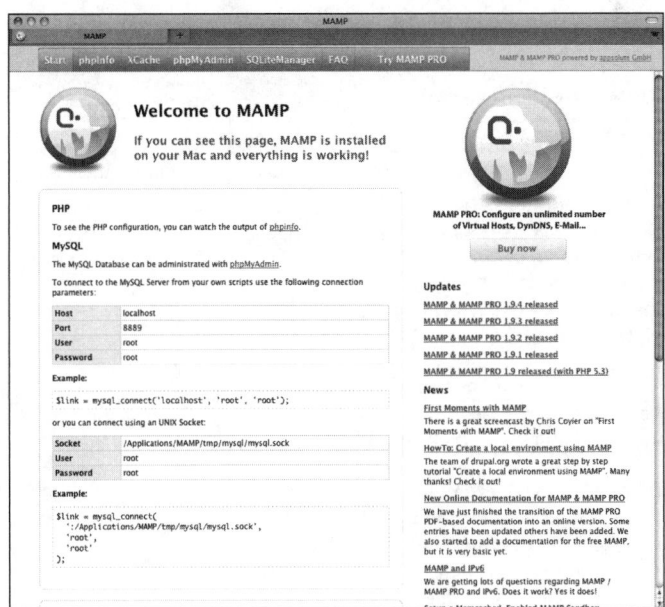

E The MAMP Web start page.

6. To start, stop, and configure MAMP, use the MAMP or MAMP PRO application **C** or **D**.

   There's not much to the MAMP application itself (which is a good thing), but if you click Preferences, you can tweak the application's behavior **F**, set the version of PHP to run, and more.

   MAMP PRO also makes it easy to create different *virtual hosts* (i.e., different sites), adjust how Apache is configured and runs, use dynamic DNS, change how email is sent, and more.

7. Immediately change the password for the root MySQL user.

   How you do this is explained later in the chapter.

TIP Personally, I appreciate how great MAMP alone is, and that it's free. I also don't like spending money. But I've found the purchase of MAMP PRO to be well worth the relatively little money it costs.

TIP See the "PHP Configuration" section to learn how to configure PHP by editing the `php.ini` file.

TIP You may want to change the Apache Document Root **G** to the `Sites` directory in your home folder. By doing so, you assure that your Web documents will backed up along with your other files (and you are performing regular backups, right?).

TIP MAMP also comes with a Dashboard widget you can use to control the Apache and MySQL servers.

TIP Your Web root directory—where your PHP scripts should be placed in order to test them—is the `htdocs` folder in the directory where MAMP was installed. For a standard MAMP installation without alteration, this would be `Applications/MAMP/htdocs`.

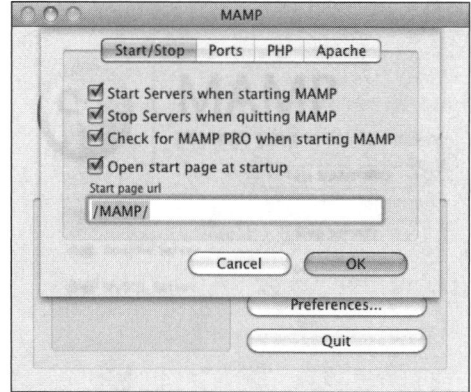

F These options dictate what happens when you start and stop the MAMP application.

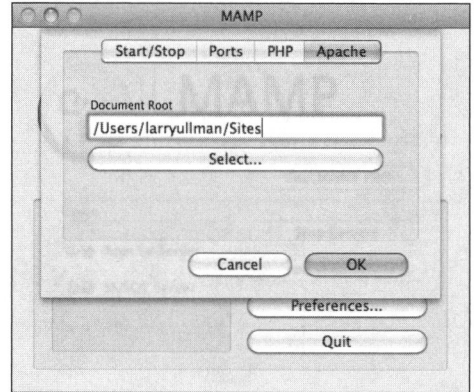

G MAMP allows you to change where the Web documents are placed.

PHP Configuration

One of the benefits of installing PHP on your own computer is that you can configure it however you prefer. How PHP runs is determined by the **php.ini** file, which is normally created when PHP is installed.

Two of the most important settings you may want to consider adjusting are **display_errors** and **error_reporting** (both are discussed in Chapter 3, "HTML Forms and PHP"). To change any setting, open the PHP configuration file, edit it as needed, then save it and restart the Web server.

To alter PHP's configuration:

1. In your Web browser, execute a script that invokes the phpinfo() function **A**.

   The **phpinfo()** function, discussed in Chapter 1, "Getting Started with PHP," reveals oodles of information about the PHP installation.

2. In the browser's output, search for Loaded Configuration File.

   The value next to this text is the location of the active configuration file. This will be something like **C:\xampp\ php\php.ini** or **/Library/Application Support/appsolute/MAMP PRO/conf/ php.ini**.

   If there is no value for the Loaded Configuration File, your server has no active **php.ini** file. In that case, you'll need to download the PHP source code, from www.php.net, to find a sample configuration file.

continues on next page

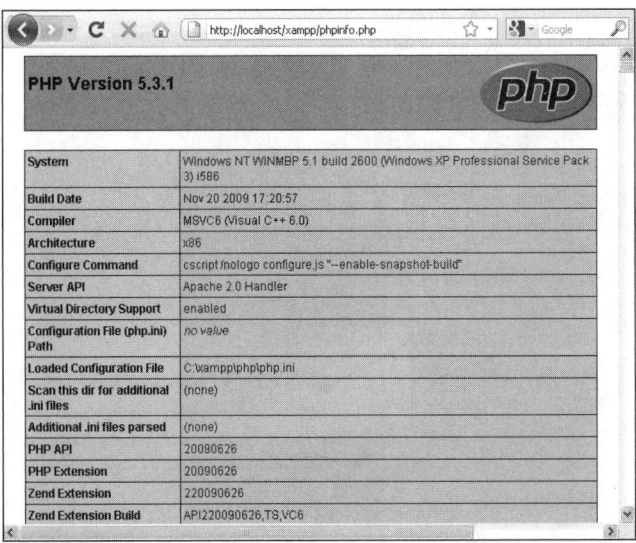

A Some of the output from calling the **phpinfo()** function.

3. Open the `php.ini` file in any text editor.

4. Change the settings as you wish.

   Depending on your operating system, you may need to be an administrator or enter a password to make changes to this file.

   Many instructions are included in the file. Lines are commented out (made inactive) by preceding them with a semicolon.

5. Save the `php.ini` file.

6. Restart your Web server.

   You don't need to restart the entire computer, just the Web server (e.g., Apache).

TIP You can also use the `phpinfo()` function to confirm that your configuration changes have taken effect.

TIP If you edit the `php.ini` file and restart the Web server but your changes don't take effect, make sure you're editing the proper `php.ini` file (you may have more than one on your computer).

TIP MAMP PRO on Mac OS X uses a template for the `php.ini` file that must be edited within MAMP PRO itself. To change the PHP settings when using MAMP PRO, select File > Edit Template > PHP *X.X.X* php.ini.

Enabling Mail

The `mail()` function works only if the computer running PHP has access to sendmail or another mail server. One way to enable the `mail()` function is to set the `smtp` value in the `php.ini` file (for Windows only). This approach works, for example, if your Internet provider has an SMTP address you can use. Unfortunately, you can't use this value if your ISP's SMTP server requires authentication.

For Windows, there are also a number of free SMTP servers, like Mercury. It's installed along with XAMPP, or you can install it yourself if you're not using XAMPP.

Mac OS X comes with a mail server installed—postfix and/or sendmail—that needs to be enabled. Search Google for instructions on manually enabling your mail server on Mac OS X.

Alternatively, you can search some of the PHP code libraries to learn how to use an SMTP server that requires authentication.

MySQL Interfaces

In Chapter 12 and Chapter 13, "Putting It All Together," a PHP script will be used to interact with a MySQL database. As I explain in Chapter 12, being able to interact with MySQL independent of your PHP scripts is the most valuable debugging tool there is. Knowing how to use a separate MySQL interface is therefore critical information. I'll quickly introduce the two most common options.

Using the MySQL Client

The MySQL software comes with an important tool called the MySQL *client*. This application provides a simple interface for communicating with the MySQL server. It's a command-line tool that must be accessed using the Terminal application on Linux and Mac OS X or through the command (DOS) prompt on Windows.

To use the MySQL client:

1. Make sure the MySQL server is running.

2. Find the MySQL **bin** directory.

   To connect to the client, you'll need to know where it's located. The MySQL client is found within the **bin** directory for your installation. I'll run through the common possibilities.

   If you installed MySQL yourself, the client's location depends on where you installed the software, but it's most likely

   C:\mysql\bin\mysql (Windows)

   or

   /usr/local/mysql/bin/mysql
   (Mac OS X and Unix)

   continues on next page

If you used XAMPP on Windows, it's **C:\ xampp\mysql\bin\mysql** (assuming you installed XAMPP in **C:**). If you installed MAMP on Mac OS X, the MySQL directory is **/Applications/MAMP/ Library/bin/mysql**.

3. Access a command prompt.

On Mac OS X and Unix, you can accomplish this by running the Terminal application. On Mac OS X, it's found within the **Applications/Utilities** folder.

On Windows, click the Start menu, select Run, and then type **cmd** and press Enter or click OK at the prompt 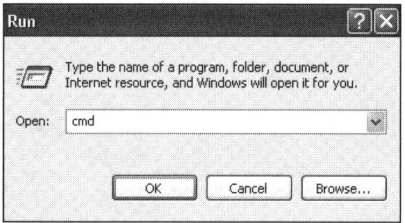.

4. Attempt to connect to the MySQL server.

To connect, enter the pathname identified in Step 2 plus **-u** *username* **-p**. So, the command might be

c:\mysql\bin\mysql -u *username* **-p** (Windows)

or

/usr/local/mysql/bin/mysql -u *username* **-p** (Unix and Mac OS X)

or

C:\xampp\mysql\bin\mysql -u *username* **-p** (Windows)

or

/Applications/MAMP/Library/bin/ mysql -u *username* **-p** (Mac OS X)

Replace *username* with the username you want to use. If you haven't yet created any other users, this will be *root* (root is the supreme MySQL user). If you haven't yet established a root user password (the default behavior for XAMPP), you can omit the **-p** flag.

A Use the Run prompt to access a console window on Windows.

5. Enter the password at the prompt 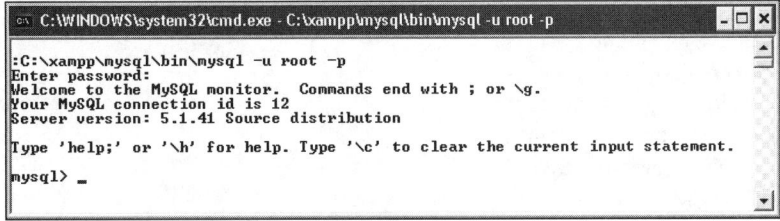.

The password requested is the MySQL password for the user named during the connection. You'll see this prompt only if you used the **-p** option in Step 4.

If you installed MAMP on Mac OS X, the password for the root user will be *root*. If you installed XAMPP on Windows, there is no password initially set.

6. List the available databases **C**:

SHOW DATABASES;

The **SHOW DATABASES** command is an SQL query that lists every database hosted on that MySQL installation that the connected user can see.

7. Exit the MySQL client.

To do so, type **exit** or **quit**.

> **TIP** If you see a *Can't connect to local MySQL server through socket...* error message, it normally means MySQL isn't running.

> **TIP** The MySQL client is one of the best tools for debugging PHP scripts that work with MySQL. You can use the MySQL client to check user permissions and to run queries outside of the PHP script.

B Successfully accessing the MySQL client on Windows.

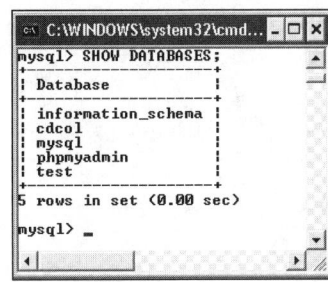

C After a fresh MySQL installation, there will be only a couple of default databases.

Using phpMyAdmin

phpMyAdmin (www.phpmyadmin.net) is a Web-based interface for interacting with a MySQL server, allowing you to create tables, import and export records, and much more, without having to use a command-line interface. It is arguably the most popular Web software written in PHP, as every PHP hosting company provides it. In fact, the all-in-one XAMPP and MAMP installers include it, too. phpMyAdmin is well documented and easy to use, but I'll highlight a couple of quick points.

To use phpMyAdmin:

1. Access phpMyAdmin in your Web browser 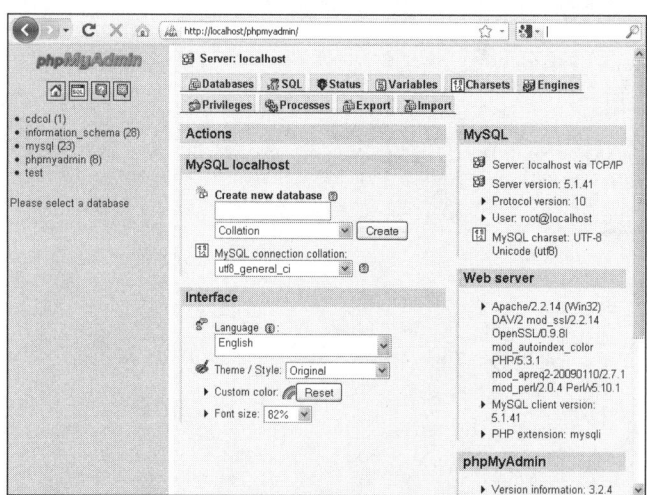.

   When using XAMPP, phpMyAdmin is available at http://localhost/phpmyadmin/, also found by clicking the MySQL admin link in the control panel. On MAMP, phpMyAdmin is available by first going to http://localhost:8888/MAMP/.

2. Click a database name in the left column to select that database.

D The phpMyAdmin front page.

3. Click a table name in the left column to select that table 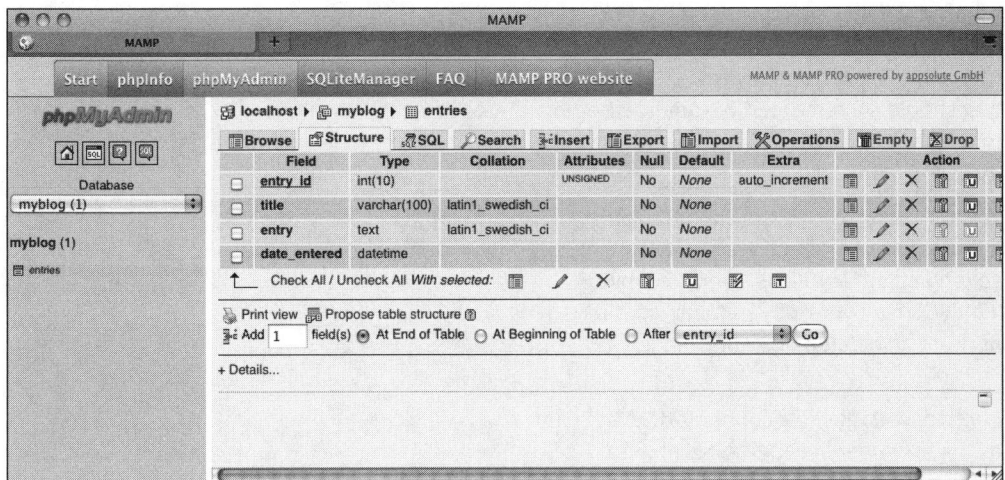.

   You don't always have to select a table, but by doing so you can simplify some tasks.

4. Use the tabs and links (on the right side of the page) to perform common tasks.

   For the most part, the tabs and links are shortcuts to common SQL commands. For example, the Browse tab performs a **SELECT** query and the Insert tab creates a form for adding new records.

5. Use the SQL tab to execute any SQL command.

   You can alternatively use the SQL Query Window, linked just above the list of database or table names. Using either interface, you can test queries that your PHP scripts are using, without the added complication of the script itself.

TIP There are many other clients for interacting with a MySQL database, but the MySQL command-line client and phpMyAdmin are the two most common.

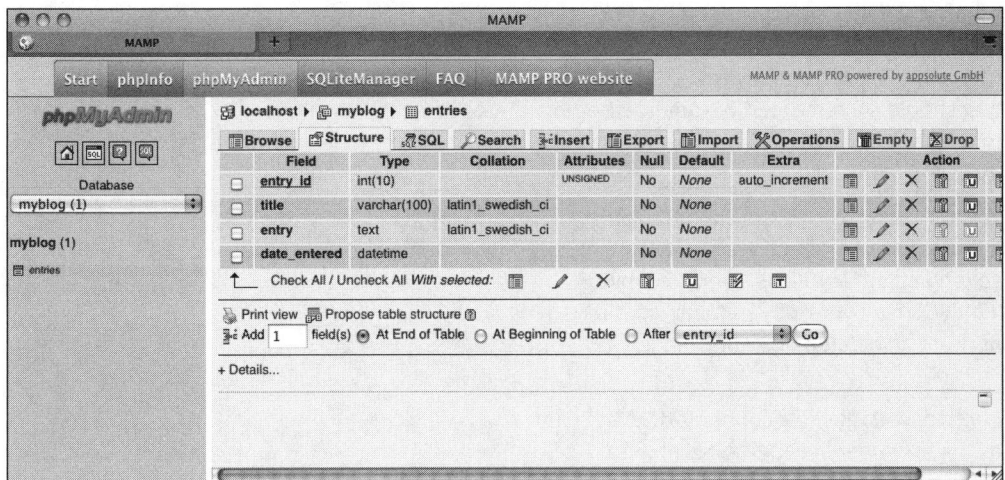

E Selecting a database or a table, from the left column, changes the options on the right side of the page.

Managing MySQL Users

Once you've successfully installed MySQL, you can begin creating MySQL users. A MySQL user is a fundamental security concept, limiting access to, and influence over, stored data. Just to clarify, your databases can have several different users, just as your operating system might. But MySQL users are different from operating system users. While learning PHP and MySQL on your own computer, you don't necessarily need to create new users, but live production sites need to have dedicated MySQL users with appropriate permissions.

The initial MySQL installation comes with one user (named *root*) with no password set (except when using MAMP, which sets a default password of *root*). At the very least, you should create a new, secure password for the root user after installing MySQL.

After that, you can create other users with more limited permissions. As a rule, you shouldn't use the root user for normal, day-to-day operations.

Setting the root user password

When you install MySQL, no value—or no secure password—is established for the root user. This is certainly a security risk that should be remedied before you begin to use the server (as the root user has unlimited powers).

You can set any user's password using either phpMyAdmin or the MySQL client, so long as the MySQL server is running. If MySQL isn't currently running, start it now using the steps outlined earlier in the appendix.

Second, you must be connected to MySQL as the root user in order to be able to change the root user's password.

To assign a password to the root user via the MySQL client:

1. Connect to the MySQL client.

   See the preceding set of steps for detailed instructions.

2. Enter the following command, replacing *thepassword* with the password you want to use :

   ```
   SET PASSWORD FOR
   → 'root'@'localhost' =
   → PASSWORD('thepassword');
   ```

   Keep in mind that passwords in MySQL are case-sensitive, so *Kazan* and *kazan* aren't interchangeable. The term **PASSWORD** that precedes the actual quoted password tells MySQL to encrypt that string. And there cannot be a space between *PASSWORD* and the opening parenthesis.

3. Exit the MySQL client:

   ```
   exit
   ```

4. Test the new password by logging into the MySQL client again.

   Now that a password has been established, you need to add the **-p** flag to the connection command. You'll see an *Enter password:* prompt, where you enter the just-created password.

A Updating the root user's password using SQL within the MySQL client.

To assign a password to the root user via phpMyAdmin:

1. Open phpMyAdmin in your Web browser.

   See the preceding set of steps for detailed instructions.

2. On the home page, click the Privileges tab.

   You can always click the home icon, in the upper-left corner, to get to the home page.

3. In the list of users, click the Edit Privileges icon on the root user's row **B**.

4. Use the Change Password form **C**, found further down the resulting page, to change the password.

5. Change the root user's password in phpMyAdmin's configuration file, if necessary.

The result of changing the root user's password will likely be that phpMyAdmin is denied access to the MySQL server. This is because phpMyAdmin, on a local server, normally connects to MySQL as the root user, with the root user's password hard-coded into a configuration file. After following Steps 1–4, find the **config.inc.php** file in the phpMyAdmin directory—likely **/Applications/MAMP/bin/phpMyAdmin** (Mac OS X with MAMP) or **C:\xampp\phpMyAdmin** (Windows with XAMPP). Open that file in any text editor or IDE and change this next line to use the new password:

```
$cfg['Servers'][$i]['password']
→ = 'the_new_password';
```

Then save the file and reload phpMyAdmin in your Web browser.

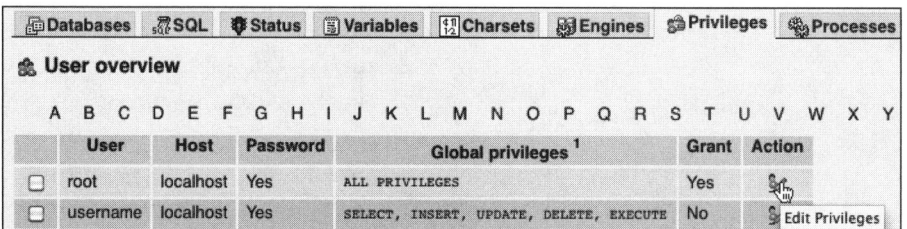

B The list of MySQL users, as shown in phpMyAdmin.

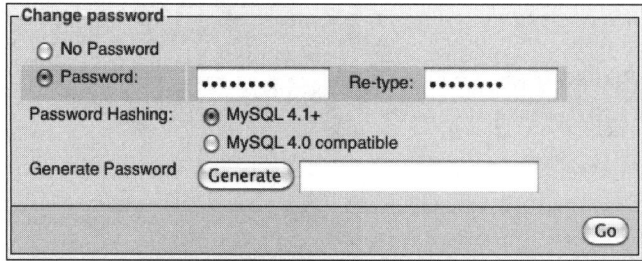

C The form for updating a MySQL user's password within phpMyAdmin.

TABLE A.1 MySQL Privileges

PRIVILEGE	ALLOWS
SELECT	Read rows from tables.
INSERT	Add new rows of data to tables.
UPDATE	Alter existing data in tables.
DELETE	Remove existing data from tables.
INDEX	Create and drop indexes in tables.
ALTER	Modify the structure of a table.
CREATE	Create new tables or databases.
DROP	Delete existing tables or databases.
RELOAD	Reload the grant tables (and therefore enact user changes).
SHUTDOWN	Stop the MySQL server.
PROCESS	View and stop existing MySQL processes.
FILE	Import data into tables from text files.
GRANT	Create new users.
REVOKE	Remove users' permissions.

Creating users and privileges

After you have MySQL successfully up and running, and after you've established a password for the root user, you can add other users. To improve the security of your databases, you should always create new users to access your databases rather than using the root user at all times.

The MySQL privileges system was designed to ensure proper authority for certain commands on specific databases. This technology is how a Web host, for example, can let several users access several databases without concern. Each user in the MySQL system can have specific capabilities on specific databases from specific hosts (computers). The root user—the MySQL root user, not the system's—has the most power and is used to create subusers, although subusers can be given rootlike powers (inadvisably so).

When a user attempts to do something with the MySQL server, MySQL first checks to see if the user has permission to connect to the server at all (based on the username, the user's host, the user's password, and the information in the `mysql` database's `user` table). Second, MySQL checks to see if the user has permission to run the specific SQL statement on the specific databases—for example, to select data, insert data, or create a new table. **Table A.1** lists most of the various privileges you can set on a user-by-user basis.

continues on next page

There are a handful of ways to set users and privileges in MySQL, but I'll start by discussing the **GRANT** command. The syntax goes like this:

```
GRANT privileges ON database.* TO
→'username'@'hostname' IDENTIFIED
→ BY 'password';
```

For the *privileges* aspect of this statement, you can list specific privileges from Table A.1, or you can allow for all of them by using **ALL** (which isn't prudent). The **database.*** part of the statement specifies which database and tables the user can work on. You can name specific tables using the **database.tablename** syntax or allow for every database with ***.*** (again, not prudent). Finally, you can specify the username, hostname, and a password.

The username has a maximum length of 16 characters. When you're creating a username, be sure to avoid spaces (use the underscore instead), and note that usernames are case-sensitive.

The hostname is the computer from which the user is allowed to connect. This could be a domain name, such as www.example.

com, or an IP address. Normally, *localhost* is specified as the hostname, meaning that the MySQL user must be connecting from the same computer that the MySQL database is running on. To allow for any host, use the hostname wildcard character (%):

```
GRANT privileges ON database.*
→TO 'username'@'%' IDENTIFIED
→ BY 'password';
```

But that is also not recommended. When it comes to creating users, it's best to be explicit and confining.

The password has no length limit but is also case-sensitive. The passwords are encrypted in the MySQL database, meaning they can't be recovered in a plain text format. Omitting the **IDENTIFIED BY 'password'** clause results in that user not being required to enter a password (which, once again, should be avoided).

As an example of this process, you'll create two new users with specific privileges on a new database named *temp*. Keep in mind that you can only grant permissions to users on existing databases. This next sequence will also show how to create a database.

Creating Users in phpMyAdmin

To create users in phpMyAdmin, start by clicking the Privileges tab on the phpMyAdmin home page. On the Privileges page, click Add A New User. Complete the Add A New User form to define the user's name, host, password, and privileges. Then click Go. This creates the user with general privileges but no database-specific privileges.

On the resulting page, select the database to apply the user's privileges to and then click Go. On the next page, select the privileges this user should have on that database, and then click Go again. This completes the process of creating rights for that user on that database. Note that this process allows you to easily assign a user different rights on different databases.

Finally, click your way back to the Privileges tab on the home page and then click the reload the privileges link.

To create new users using GRANT:

1. Log in to the MySQL client as a root user.

   Use the steps already explained to do this. You must be logged in as a user capable of creating databases and other users.

2. Create a new database 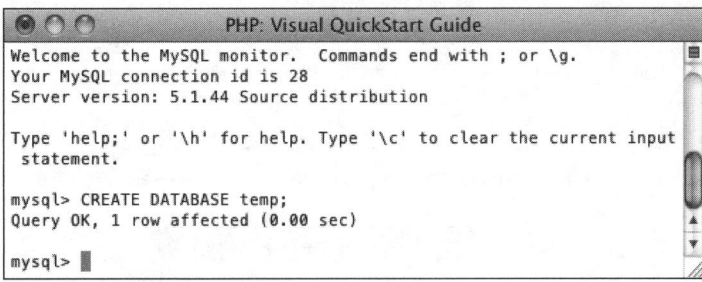:

   ```
   CREATE DATABASE temp;
   ```

   If your MySQL server doesn't yet have a **temp** database, create one using **CREATE DATABASE temp** (followed by a semicolon, as is required by the MySQL client).

3. Create a user with administrative-level privileges on the **temp** database:

   ```
   GRANT SELECT, INSERT, UPDATE,
   → DELETE, CREATE, DROP,
   → ALTER, INDEX ON temp.* TO
   → 'llama'@'localhost' IDENTIFIED
   → BY 'camel';
   ```

   This user, *llama*, can create tables, alter tables, insert data, update data, and so forth, on the **temp** database. This essentially includes every administrative-level capability aside from creating new users. Be certain to use a password—perhaps one more clever than used here—and, preferably, specify a particular host.

continues on next page

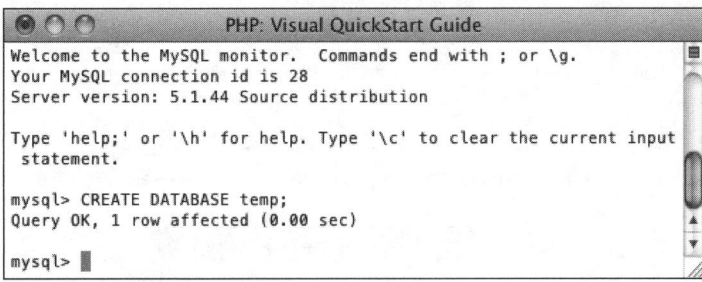

D Creating a new database.

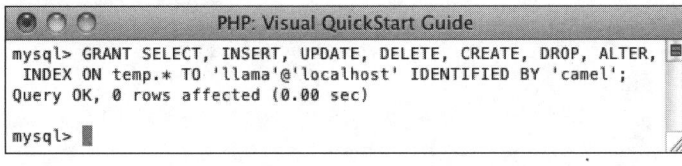

E Creating an administrative-level user for a single database.

4. Create a user with basic access to the databases 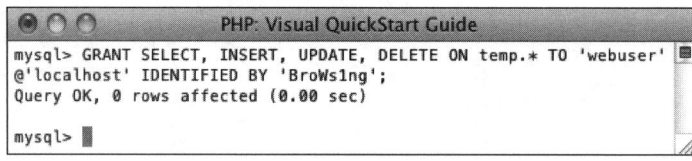:

```
GRANT SELECT, INSERT,
→ UPDATE, DELETE ON temp.* TO
→ 'webuser'@'localhost' IDENTIFIED
→ BY 'BroWs1ng';
```

Now the generic *webuser* can browse through records (**SELECT** from tables) as well as add, edit, and delete them, but this user can't alter the structure of the database. When you're establishing users and privileges, work your way from the bottom up, allowing the bare minimum of access at all times.

5. Apply the changes **G**:

FLUSH PRIVILEGES;

The changes just made won't take effect until you've told MySQL to reset the list of acceptable users and privileges, which is what this command does. Forgetting this step and then being unable to access the database using the newly created users is a common mistake.

TIP Any database whose name begins with *test_* can be modified by any user who has permission to connect to MySQL. Therefore, be careful not to create a database named this way unless it truly is experimental.

TIP The REVOKE command removes users and permissions.

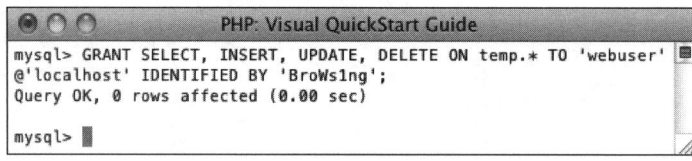

```
PHP: Visual QuickStart Guide
mysql> GRANT SELECT, INSERT, UPDATE, DELETE ON temp.* TO 'webuser'
@'localhost' IDENTIFIED BY 'BroWs1ng';
Query OK, 0 rows affected (0.00 sec)

mysql>
```

F This user has more restricted rights to the same database.

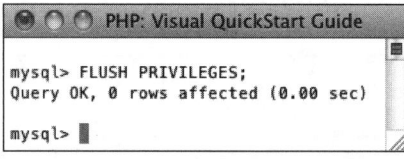

```
PHP: Visual QuickStart Guide
mysql> FLUSH PRIVILEGES;
Query OK, 0 rows affected (0.00 sec)

mysql>
```

G Don't forget this step before you try to access MySQL using the newly created users.

Resources and Next Steps

This book was written to give beginning PHP programmers a good foundation on which to base their learning. A few topics have been either omitted or glossed over, as the book focuses on covering the absolute fundamentals. This appendix lists a number of useful PHP-related Internet resources; briefly discusses where to obtain more information for databases and some uncovered topics; and includes a few tables, both old and new.

Along with those sites included here, you should check out the book's companion Web site, found at www.LarryUllman.com. There you'll find all of the book's code, a support forum, an errata page, and more.

Before getting to it, consider that when the first edition of this book was written, few good PHP sites were available. Now there are literally dozens (and hundreds of not-so-good ones). The best, most obvious ones are included here, but a quick Internet search will always be a great resource for you.

Online PHP Resources

If you have questions specifically about PHP, you should be able to find the answer with ease. This section of the appendix highlights the best Internet-specific tools for you to use.

The PHP manual

All PHP programmers should familiarize themselves with, and possibly acquire, some version of the PHP manual before beginning to work with the language. The manual is available from the official PHP site—www.php.net/docs.php—as well as from a number of other locations.

You can download the manual in nearly a dozen languages in different formats. The official Web site also has an annotated version of the manual available at www.php. net/manual/en/ (in English), where users have added helpful notes and comments. If you're having problems with a particular function, reading the manual's page for that function will likely provide an answer.

A trick pointed out in Chapter 1, "Getting Started with PHP," is that you can quickly access the documentation page for any specific function by going to www.php.net/*functionname*. For example, the page for the `number_format()` function is www.php.net/number_format.

General PHP Web sites

This section mentions a few of the many useful Web sites you can turn to when you're programming, but I'll leave it up to you to discover the ones you like best. Most of these also contain links to other PHP-related sites. The first, and most obvious, site to bookmark is PHP.net (www.php.net), the official site for PHP.

You should familiarize yourself with Zend (www.zend.com), the home page for the creators of PHP's core. The site contains numerous downloads plus a wealth of other resources—straight from the masters, so to speak.

For information on specific topics, PHPBuilder (www.phpbuilder.com) is one of many good places to turn. The site has dozens of articles explaining how to do particular tasks using PHP. On top of that, PHPBuilder provides support forums and a code library where programmers have uploaded sample scripts.

You can also find useful articles at PHP Zone (http://php.dzone.com) and phplarchitect (www.phparch.com), which also puts out a monthly PHP magazine.

W3Schools (www.w3schools.com) is a good general Web development site, but it also focuses a good portion of its energies on PHP. For a cohesive look at developing dynamic Web sites using PHP, HTML, CSS, and JavaScript, this is an excellent place to turn.

When a good resource, PHP or otherwise, comes across my desk, I'll normally reference it on my site. You can find any post related to PHP under the "PHP" category here: www.larryullman.com/category/php/.

Code repositories

There's no shortage of code libraries online these days. Due to the generous (and often showy) nature of PHP programmers, many sites have scores of PHP scripts, organized and available for download. The best online code repositories are as follows:

- HotScripts (www.hotscripts.com/PHP/)
- PHP Resource Index (http://php.resourceindex.com)
- PHP Classes Repository (www.phpclasses.org)
- PX: The PHP Code Exchange (http://px.sklar.com)

You can also find code examples at Zend and PHPBuilder or by searching the Web. There's even a search engine dedicated to finding code: www.koders.com.

Newsgroups and mailing lists

If you have access to newsgroups, you can use them as a great sounding board for ideas as well as a place to get your most difficult questions answered. Of course, you can always give back to the group by offering your own expertise to those in need.

The largest English-language PHP newsgroup is comp.lang.php. You may be able to access it through your ISP or via a pay-for-use Usenet organization. Newsgroups are also available in languages other than English.

The PHP Web site lists the available mailing lists you can sign up for at www.php.net/mailing-lists.php.

Before you post to any newsgroup or mailing list, it will behoove you to read Eric Steven Raymond's "How to Ask Questions the Smart Way" at www.catb.org/~esr/faqs/smart-questions.html. The 10 minutes spent reading that document will save you hours when you go asking for assistance.

Database Resources

Which database resources will be most useful to you depends, obviously, on which database management system (DBMS) you're using. The most common database used with PHP is probably MySQL, but PHP supports all the standard database applications.

To learn more about using MySQL, begin with the official MySQL Web site (www.mysql.com). You can download the MySQL manual to use as a reference while you work. A handful of books are also available specifically on MySQL, including my own *MySQL: Visual QuickStart Guide, 2nd Edition* (Peachpit Press, 2006).

If you're using MySQL, don't forget to download and install phpMyAdmin (www.phpmyadmin.net). Written in PHP, this is an invaluable tool for working with a database. If you're using PostgreSQL or even Oracle, you can find similar tools available for interfacing with them. Every database application also has its own mailing lists and newsgroups.

Another area of database resources you should delve into is SQL. Web sites discussing SQL, the language used by every database application, include the following:

- SQL Course (www.sqlcourse.com)

- A Gentle Introduction to SQL (www.sqlzoo.net)

- W3Schools' SQL Tutorial (www.w3schools.com/sql/)

- SQL.org (www.sql.org)

My *PHP 6 and MySQL 5 for Dynamic Web Sites: Visual QuickPro Guide* (Peachpit Press, 2008) also discusses SQL and MySQL in much greater detail than this book.

Top 10 Frequently Asked Questions (or Problems)

Debugging is a valuable skill that takes time and experience to fully develop. But rather than send you off on that journey ill-equipped, I've included the 10 most frequently seen problems in PHP scripts, along with the most likely causes. First, though, here are 5 of my best pieces of advice when it comes to debugging a problem:

1. Know what version of PHP you're running.

   Some problems are specific to a version of PHP. Use the `phpinfo()` function to test the version in use whenever you go to use a server for the first time. Also make sure you know what version of MySQL you're using, if applicable; the operating system; and the Web server (e.g., Apache 2.2).

2. Run all PHP scripts through a URL.

   If you don't run a PHP script through a URL—and this includes the submission of a form to a PHP script—the Web server will not handle the request, meaning that PHP will never execute the code.

3. Trust the error message!

   Many beginners have more difficulty than they should in solving a problem because they don't pay attention to the error message they see. Although some of PHP's error messages are cryptic and even a few can be misleading, if PHP says there's a problem on line 22, the problem is probably on line 22.

4. Avoid "trying" things to fix a problem!

   If you're not sure what's causing the problem and what the proper fix is, avoid trying random things as a solution. You'll likely create new issues this way and only further confuse the original problem.

5. Take a break!

   The best piece of advice I can offer is to step away from the computer and take a break. I've solved many, many problems this way. Sometimes a clear head is what you need.

Moving on, here are the top 10 likely problems you'll encounter in PHP:

1. Blank Web pages

   If you see a blank screen in your Web browser after submitting a form or loading a PHP script, it's most likely because an error occurred that terminated the execution of the page. First check the HTML source code to see if it's an HTML problem. Then turn on `display_errors` in your `php.ini` configuration file or PHP script to see what PHP problem could be occurring.

2. *Undefined variable* or *undefined index* error Ⓐ

   These errors occur when error reporting is set on its highest level, and they may or may not indicate a problem. Check the spelling of each variable or array index to make sure it's correct. Then, either change the error reporting settings or initialize variables prior to referring to them. Also make sure, of course, that variables that should have a value actually do!

3. Variables that don't have a value

   Perhaps you referred to a variable by the wrong name. Double-check your capitalization and spelling of variable names, and then be certain to use **$_GET**, **$_POST**, **$_COOKIE**, and **$_SESSION** as appropriate. If need be, use the **print_r()** function to see the value of any variable.

4. *Call to undefined function…* error

   Such an error message means you're attempting to use a function that PHP doesn't have. This problem can be caused by a misspelling of a function name, failure to define your own function before calling it, or using a function that's not available in your version of PHP. Check your spelling and the PHP manual for a non-user-defined function to find the problem.

5. *Headers already sent* error Ⓑ

   This error message indicates that you've used an HTTP header-related function—**header()**, **setcookie()**, or **session_start()**—after the Web browser has already received HTML or even a blank space. Double-check what occurs in a script before you call any of these functions. You can also make use of output buffering to prevent these errors from occurring.

6. *Access denied* error Ⓒ

   If you see this message while attempting to work with a database, then the username, password, and host combination you're using doesn't have permission to access the database. This isn't normally a PHP issue. Confirm the values that are being used, and attempt to connect to the database using a different interface (such as the MySQL client).

continues on next page

Notice: Undefined index: Name in /Users/larryullman/Sites/phpvqs4/handle_form.php on line 16

Thank you, Mr. , for your comments.

Ⓐ Errors complaining about undefined variables or indexes often come from spelling or capitalization mistakes.

Warning: Cannot modify header information – headers already sent by (output started at /Users/larryullman/Sites/phpvqs4/templates/header.html:4) in /Users/larryullman/Sites/phpvqs4/login.php on line 22

Ⓑ Some functions create *headers already sent* errors if called at the wrong time.

7. *Supplied argument is not a valid MySQL result resource* error

   This is another database-related error message. The message means that a query result is being used inappropriately. Most frequently, this is because you're trying to fetch rows from a query that didn't return any records. To solve this problem, print out the query being run and test it using another tool (such as the MySQL client or phpMyAdmin). Also check that you've been consistent with your variable names.

8. Preset HTML form values are cut off

   You must put the value attribute of an HTML form input within double quotation marks. If you fail to do so, only the part of the value up to the first space will be set as that input's value.

9. Conditionals or loops behave unpredictably

   These logical errors are quite common. Check that you haven't used the wrong operator (such as = instead of ==) and that you refer to the proper variables. Then use **print** statements to let you know what the script is doing.

10. Parse errors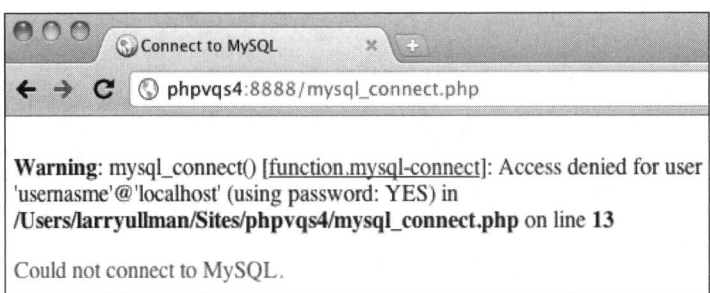

   Parse errors are the most ubiquitous problems you'll deal with. Even the most seasoned PHP programmer sees them occasionally. Check that every statement concludes with a semicolon and that all quotation marks, parentheses, square braces, and curly brackets are evenly paired. If you still can't find the parse error, comment out large sections of the script using the **/*** and ***/** characters. Uncomment a section at a time until you see the parse error again. Then you'll know where in the script the problem is (or most likely is).

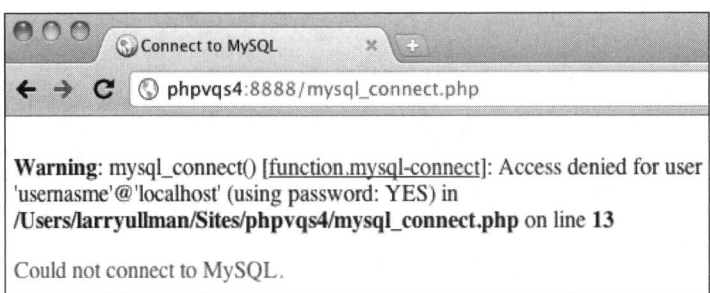

Warning: mysql_connect() [function.mysql-connect]: Access denied for user 'usernasme'@'localhost' (using password: YES) in **/Users/larryullman/Sites/phpvqs4/mysql_connect.php** on line **13**

Could not connect to MySQL.

C If the MySQL access information is incorrect, you'll see a message saying that database access has been denied.

Parse error: syntax error, unexpected T_ENCAPSED_AND_WHITESPACE, expecting T_STRING or T_VARIABLE or T_NUM_STRING in **/Users/larryullman/Sites /phpvqs4/handle_form.php** on line **19**

D Parse errors are all too common and prevent scripts from executing.

Next Steps

This book will get you started using PHP, but there are a few topics that you may want to investigate further.

Security

Web servers, operating systems, databases, and PHP security are all topics that merit their own books. Although this book demonstrates writing secure Web applications, there's always room for you to learn more in this area. Start by checking out these sites:

- A Study in Scarlet (www.securereality. com.au/studyinscarlet.txt)

- W3C Security Resources (www.w3.org/ Security/)

The first is an article about writing secure PHP code. The second is the World Wide Web Consortium's resources page for Web-related security issues.

You should also read the relevant sections of the PHP manual and the manual for the database you're using. Searching the Internet for *PHP* and *security* will turn up many interesting articles as well.

Object-oriented programming

The subject of objects and object-oriented programming (OOP) is not covered in this book for two reasons:

1. It's well beyond the scope of a beginner's guide.

2. You won't be restricted as to what you can do in PHP by not understanding objects.

When you decide you want to learn the subject, you can search the PHP sites for tutorials, check out a framework (see the next section of the appendix), or read my

PHP 5 Advanced: Visual QuickPro Guide (Peachpit Press, 2007). I dedicate around 150 pages of that book just to OOP (and there are still aspects of OOP that I didn't get to)!

Frameworks

A framework is an established library of code that you can use to develop sophisticated Web applications. By reusing someone else's proven code, you can quickly build parts or all of a Web site.

There are many PHP frameworks available, starting with PEAR. The PEAR library is an immense repository of PHP code, written using objects (classes, technically). Even if you don't use objects yourself or you barely understand the concept, you can still get a lot of value out of the PEAR Web site (http://pear.php.net). PEAR and its Web site provide free, wonderful code and demonstrate good PHP coding style. PECL (http://pecl.php.net) is PEAR's more powerful sibling.

Another framework to consider is the Zend Framework (http://framework.zend.com). This framework was created by some of the key people behind PHP and is well documented.

My personal favorite PHP framework, as of this writing, is Yii (www.yiiframework.com). I write about Yii extensively on my site.

Many people love frameworks and what they offer. On the other hand, it does take some time to learn how to use a framework, and customizing the framework's behavior can be daunting.

JavaScript and Ajax

JavaScript is a client-side technology that runs in the Web browser. It can be used to add various dynamic features to a Web site, from simple eye candy like image rollovers to interactive menus and forms. Because it runs within the Web browser, JavaScript provides some functionality that PHP cannot. And, like PHP, JavaScript is relatively easy to learn and use. For more, see:

- JavaScript.com (www.javascript.com)
- W3School's JavaScript pages (www.w3schools.com/js/)

Ajax (which either means Asynchronous JavaScript and XML or doesn't, depending on whom you ask) has been all the rage in the Web development community since around 2005. This technology uses JavaScript to communicate with the server without the user knowing it. The net effect is a Web site that behaves more like a desktop application. For more, see Ajaxian (www.ajaxian.com) or search online.

I highly recommend you consider learning jQuery (www.jquery.com) to help you with your JavaScript, Ajax, and other dynamic Web needs. jQuery is a JavaScript framework that's easy to use, powerful, and pretty well documented.

Other books

It is my hope that after reading this book you'll be interested in learning more about PHP and Web development in general. While I could recommend books by other writers, there's an inherent conflict there and my opinion as a rival writer would not be the same as yours as a reader. So, instead, I'll just quickly highlight a couple of my other books and how they compare to this one.

The *PHP 6 and MySQL 5 for Dynamic Web Sites: Visual QuickPro Guide* (Peachpit Press, 2008) is kind of a sequel to this one (a new edition, tentatively titled *PHP and MySQL for Dynamic Web Sites: Visual QuickPro Guide, Fourth Edition*, should be published in 2011). There is

some overlap in content, particularly in the early chapters, but the examples are different and it goes at a faster pace. MySQL and SQL in particular get a lot more coverage, and there are three different example chapters: a multilingual forum, a user registration and login system, and an e-commerce setup.

My *PHP 5 Advanced: Visual QuickPro Guide* (Peachpit Press, 2007) is kind of a sequel to the PHP and MySQL book just mentioned. This book is much more advanced, spending a lot of time on topics such as OOP and PEAR. It's not intended to be read as linearly as this one, but rather each chapter focuses on a specific topic.

MySQL: Visual QuickStart Guide, Second Edition (Peachpit Press, 2006) looks almost exclusively at just MySQL and SQL. Although there are four chapters covering languages used to interact with MySQL— PHP, Perl, and Java, plus a techniques chapter—this book largely addresses things like installation, administration, and maximizing your MySQL knowledge.

My newest book (written just before the one you're reading now) is *Effortless E-Commerce with PHP and MySQL* (New Riders, 2011). The book covers everything you need to know to create fully functioning e-commerce sites. The book uses two specific examples for doing so, and incorporates two different payment systems. Complete comfort with PHP and MySQL is assumed, however.

Finally, my *Building a Web Site with Ajax: Visual QuickProject Guide* (Peachpit Press, 2008) walks through the process of coding an Ajax-enabled Web site. It also uses PHP and MySQL, but those technologies aren't taught in the same way that JavaScript and Ajax are.

Tables

This book has a handful of tables scattered about, the three most important of which are reprinted here as a convenient reference. You'll also find one new table that lists operator precedence (Table B.1). This partial list goes from highest to lowest (for example, multiplication takes precedence over addition).

Table B.2 lists PHP's main operators and their types. It's most important to remember that a single equals sign (=) assigns a value to a variable, whereas two equals signs (==) are used together to check for equality.

Table B.3 indicates the modes you can use when opening a file. Which you choose determines what PHP can do with that file—write to it, read from it, and so forth.

The various formats for the **date()** function may be one of the hardest things to remember. Keep **Table B.4** nearby when you're using the **date()** function.

TABLE B.1 Operator Precedence

! ++ --
* / %
+ - .
< <= > >=
== != ===
&&
||
= += -= *= /= .= %=
and
xor
or

TABLE B.2 PHP's Operators

Operator	Usage	Type
+	Addition	Arithmetic
-	Subtraction	Arithmetic
*	Multiplication	Arithmetic
/	Division	Arithmetic
%	Modulus (remainder of a division)	Arithmetic
++	Incrementation	Arithmetic
--	Decrementation	Arithmetic
=	Assigns a value to a variable	Assignment
==	Equality	Comparison
!=	Inequality	Comparison
<	Less than	Comparison
>	Greater than	Comparison
<=	Less than or equal to	Comparison
>=	Greater than or equal to	Comparison
!	Negation	Logical
AND	And	Logical
&&	And	Logical
OR	Or	Logical
||	Or	Logical
.	Concatenation	String
XOR	Or not	Logical
.=	Concatenates to the value of a variable	Combined concatenation and assignment
+=	Adds to the value of a variable	Combined arithmetic and assignment
-=	Subtracts from the value of a variable	Combined arithmetic and assignment

TABLE B.3 fopen() Modes

Mode	Meaning
r	Read only; begin reading at the start of the file.
r+	Read or write; begin at the start of the file.
w	Write only; create the file if it doesn't exist, and overwrite any existing contents.
w+	Read or write; create the file if it doesn't exist, and overwrite any existing contents (when writing).
a	Write only; create the file if it doesn't exist, and append the new data to the end of the file (retain any existing data and add to it).
a+	Read or write; create the file if it doesn't exist, and append the new data to the end of the file (when writing).
x	Write only; create the file if it doesn't exist, but do nothing (and issue a warning) if the file does exist.
x+	Read or write; create the file if it doesn't exist, but do nothing (and issue a warning) if the file already exists (when writing).

TABLE B.4 Date() Function Formatting

Character	Meaning	Example
Y	Year as 4 digits	2011
y	Year as 2 digits	11
L	Is it a leap year?	1 (for yes)
n	Month as 1 or 2 digits	2
m	Month as 2 digits	02
F	Month	February
M	Month as 3 letters	Feb
j	Day of the month as 1 or 2 digits	8
d	Day of the month as 2 digits	08
l (lowercase L)	Day of the week	Monday
D	Day of the week as 3 letters	Mon
w	Day of the week as a single digit	0 (Sunday)
z	Day of the year: 0 to 365	189
t	Number of days in the month	31

TABLE B.4 continued

Character	Meaning	Example
S	English ordinal suffix for a day, as 2 characters	rd
g	Hour; 12-hour format as 1 or 2 digits	6
G	Hour; 24-hour format as 1 or 2 digits	18
h	Hour; 12-hour format as 2 digits	06
H	Hour; 24-hour format as 2 digits	18
i	Minutes	45
s	Seconds	18
u	Microseconds	1234
a	am or pm	am
A	AM or PM	PM
U	Seconds since the epoch	1048623008
e	Timezone	UTC
I (capital i)	Is it daylight savings?	1 (for yes)
O	Difference from GMT	+0600

Index

Symbols

.., using with directories, 293
\\, using with absolute paths, 320
' (apostrophe), in MySQL, 358, 360
@ (at symbol), using in MySQL, 342
\ (backslash), using with strings, 39
<!-- --> comment characters, 27
(comments), using with scripts, 25, 27
// (comments), using with scripts , 25, 27
/* */ (comments), using with scripts, 25, 27
{} (curly brackets), using with array values, 163
$ (dollar sign), preceding variables with, 36
$ (dollar sign), printing, 79
( ) (parentheses)
   using in calculations, 84–85
   using in conditionals, 125
" (double quotation marks)
   error caused by, 22
   using with strings, 39
   using with variables, 45–47
\n (newline character), using with HTML, 23
; (semicolon), using in MySQL, 358
' (single quotation marks)
   using with arrays, 160
   using with strings, 39
   using with variables, 45–47
_ (underscore), using with variables, 36
- operator, using, 77–80, 129
-- operator, 129
! operator, 129, 133
!= = operator, 129
!= operator, 130
% operator, 129
&& operator, 129, 133
* operator, 77–80, 129
*= operator, 87
. operator, 129
/ operator, 77–80, 129
/= operator, 87
| operator, 129
|| operator, 133
+ operator, 77–80, 129
++ operator, 86–87, 129
+= operator, 87
< operator, 129
<= operator, 129
== operator, 129
= operator, 129
-= operator, 87
> operator, 129
>= operator, 129

A

abs()math function, 89
absolute paths
   creating on Windows servers, 319
   start of, 293
   using with external files, 194
action attribute, including in form tag, 50, 53
add_entry.php script
   creating, 353
   saving, 357
   securing query data, 359–360
add_quote.php script
   creating, 296
   file locks, 302
   for sample site, 393–396
   saving, 300
addition (+) operator, using, 77–80, 129
Ajax resources, 443–444
ALTER command in SQL, 334
AND operator, 129, 133–134
Apache Web site, 10
apostrophe ('), in MySQL, 358, 360
arguments. See also PHP functions
   error, 266
   using with functions, 265–270
arithmetic
   assignment operators, 87, 129
   performing, 77–80
array() calls, nesting, 167
array elements
   accessing, 161–163, 167
   deleting, 158
   pointing to, 164
   referring to, 157
array() function, 154–155, 157
array indexes, using strings for, 161
array syntax, using, 176–178
array values, accessing, 163

arrays, 40. *See also* superglobals
    adding items to, 158–160
    associative, 40
    for checkbox input names, 177
    versus constants, 200
    contents of, 152
    creating, 154–157
    creating from forms, 176–181
    deleting, 158
    examples of, 153
    grocery list example, 152
    indexed, 40, 157
    indexing, 154, 157
    merging, 160
    multidimensional, 164–167
    overview, 152
    printing values of, 162–163
    sorting, 168–171
    $soups, 155
    superglobals, 153
    syntactical rules, 153
    using single quotation marks with, 160
arrays and strings, transforming between, 172–175
arsort()function, 168, 170
asort()function, 168–170
assignment versus comparison operators, 130
at symbol (@), using in MySQL, 342
attributes, identifying, 315

B

backslash (\), using with strings, 39
banners, creating for Web pages, 186
BBEdit Web site, 4
birth year, creating input for, 117
blank Web pages, debugging, 440–441
blog entry
    adding, 355–358
    editing, 372–377
    retrieving data from, 362
    securing query data, 360
$books array, 164–165
books.php script
    creating, 165, 198
    saving, 199
**
** tag
    using for newlines, 98–99
    using in XHTML pages, 6
break, language construct, 144
breaks, converting newlines to, 98–99, 102
browser
    sending **Hello, world!** greeting to, 16–17
    sending HTML to, 22–24
    sending text to, 15–17
    testing scripts in, 12–14
buffer size, setting maximum for, 224
buttons. *See* radio buttons; submit button

C

calculations, using parentheses in, 84–85
calculator.html script
    creating, 74–76
    saving, 76
calculator.php script
    function returning value, 275–278
    saving, 278
    variable scope, 281–285
Cascading Style Sheets (CSS), adding to Web
    pages, 3
case of strings, adjusting, 111
cell()math function, 89
characters
    counting in strings, 109
    escaping, 59
    indexed positions of, 108
check boxes
    creating for form, 118
    presetting status of, 216
checkdate() validation function, 128
code repositories, 438
comments
    # type of, 25, 27
    // type of, 25, 27
    /* */ type of, 25, 27
    <!-- --> type of, 27
    adding to scripts, 25–27
comparison operators
    versus assignment operators, 130
    using, 129–132
concatenating strings, 95–97
concatenation
    operator, 129
    using with functions, 106
conditionals. *See also* **if** conditional
    debugging, 442
    if-else, 126–127
    nesting, 133
    nesting for login form, 207
    reverse, 132
    using in functions, 125
    using parentheses in, 125
conditions, TRUE versus FALSE, 133
configuration changes, confirming, 424
constants
    versus arrays, 200
    benefits of, 285
    global scope of, 200
    naming, 200
    predefined, 200
    printing, 199–200
    using in Web applications, 197–200
control structures. *See also* loops
    else, 126–128
    elseif, 138–141
    foreach loop, 146, 162–163
    HTML form for, 116–118

if conditional, 119–121, 124
for loop, 146–149, 163
switch conditional, 142–145
while loop, 146, 149
cookies
   adding **expiration** arguments to, 242–244
   adding parameters to, 242–243
   creating, 234–238
   debugging, 233
   deleting, 245–247
   features of, 234
   output buffering, 238
   overview, 232–233
   reading from, 239–241
   in sample site, 383
   secure value, 243
   sending, 235–238
   versus sessions, 248
   testing compatibility, 247
cost, calculating, 79
count() function, 160
CREATE command in SQL, 334
create_table.php script
   beginning, 348
   saving, 351
Crimson Editor Web site, 4
cross-site scripting (XSS) attacks, 100
CRUD, explained, 396
crypt() function, using with strings, 106
CSS (Cascading Style Sheets), adding to
   Web pages, 3
CSS code, adding to layout model, 185
CSS templates, 191. *See also* templates
curly brackets (**{}**), using with array values, 163
customize.php script
   creating for cookies, 235
   expiration date, 243–244
   saving, 238

D

database code, placement of, 351
database information, setting, 346
database management system (DBMS), 335
database records
   CRUD, 396
   editing in databases, 373–374
   inserting via MySQL, 357
   paginating returned, 365
database resources, 439
database tables
   columns in, 347
   creating, 347–351
   creating for sample site, 380–381
   emptying of records, 371
   entries example, 347
   primary keys, 347
   using commas in, 347

databases. *See also* sample site
   connecting to, 382
   creating, 343–346
   defined, 334
   deleting data in, 366–371
   editing records in, 373–374
   id primary key, 377
   INSERT INTO command, 352
   inserting data into, 352–357
   permissions for, 343
   queries, 352
   retrieving data from, 361–365
   securing query data, 358–360
   selecting, 343–346
   updating data in, 372–377
date() function, 201–203, 295, 446
day of month, drop-down menu for, 147–148
day pull-down menu, creating, 262
$dbc reference
   explained, 361
   setting, 364
DBMS (database management system), 335
debugging
   cookies, 233
   FAQs (frequently asked questions), 440–442
   PHP scripts, 28–29, 63
   variables without values, 441
decrementation operator, 129
default case, adding to **switch** conditional, 145
DELETE queries, 334
   error related to, 371
   using in MySQL, 366–371
delete_entry.php script
   creating, 367
   saving, 371
delete_quote.php script
   creating, 406
   saving, 409
deleting
   arrays, 158
   cookies, 245–247
   data in databases, 366–371
   directories, 326
   files, 314
   sessions, 254–255
deprecated functions, listing in PHP manual, 21
die(), calling in MySQL, 342
die, language construct, 144
directories
   deleting, 326
   finding contents of, 315
   finding parts of, 319
   navigating, 315–319
   parent folders, 293
   permissions for, 320
   referring to, 293
   saving, 320–326
   scandir() function, 315
   searching files in, 319

directory control panel, creating, 316–319

display_errors setting. *See also* errors
  enabling for debugging scripts, 63
  turning on, 29, 62
  viewing, 61

division (**/**) operator, using, 77–80, 129

documents, creating for XHTML pages, 4

dollar sign (**$**), preceding variables with, 36

dollar sign ($), printing, 79

double quotation marks (**"**)
  error caused by, 22
  using with strings, 39
  using with variables, 45–47

Dreamweaver Web site, 4

DROP command in SQL, 334

drop-down menu. *See also* menu
  creating for form, 118
  for day of month, 147–148
  selecting options from, 181

E

edit_entry.php script
  creating, 373
  saving, 376

edit_quote.php script
  creating, 400
  saving, 405

EditPlus Web site, 4

else conditional, 126–128

elseif conditional, 138–141

email, sending, 217–221

email address
  adding text input for, 52
  adding to HTML form, 93
  creating inputs for, 117

email body, creating lines in, 221

empty() validation function, 122–123

encoding, selecting, 5

equality operator, 129

error handling
  applying to PHP scripts, 70
  in **handle_calc.php** document, 78

error messages
  for sample site, 390
  trusting, 440

error reporting. *See also* **display_errors** setting
  adjusting level of, 65–66
  constants, 64

error settings, placing in external files, 196

Error type, 64

error types
  Error, 64
  Notice, 64
  Parse error, 64
  Warning, 64

error-handling techniques, 340

errors. *See also* **display_errors** setting
  Access denied, 441
  "Call to undefined function," 264

Call to undefined function..., 441
  database queries, 350
  DELETE queries, 371
  displaying in scripts, 61–63
  file permissions, 300
  $FILES variable, 308
  Headers already sent, 441
  parsing, 442
  related to **foreach** loop, 181
  related to functions, 264
  related to **header()** call, 222
  Supplied argument is not valid MySQL result resource, 442
  Undefined index, 441
  Undefined variable, 44
  Undefined variable, 441

escape sequences, using with files, 293

escaping characters, 59

event.html script
  creating, 177
  saving, 178

event.php script
  creating, 179–181
  saving, 181

exit(), alias for, 342

exit, language construct, 144

explode() function, 172, 174

extensions, explained, 9

external files
  placing error settings in, 196
  using with Web applications, 192–196
  writing to, 296–300

F

FALSE versus TRUE conditionals, 133, 137

FAQs (frequently asked questions), 440–442

fclose() function, 295, 302

feedback.html script
  adding **method** attribute to, 55–56
  creating, 51
  saving, 53
  using with HTML forms, 60

fgetcsv() function, 331

fgets() function, 327

file access, returning time of, 319

file() function, 304

file navigation, 194

file owner, returning, 319

file paths, 293, 319

file permissions
  versus database permissions, 343
  for directories, 320
  error, 300
  overview, 288–289
  quotes.txt file, 289–290
  returning, 319
  setting, 291–292

File Transfer Protocol (FTP), using, 10–11

file uploads
  configuring PHP for, 307
  file tag, 307
  $FILES variable, 308
  form tag, 307
  hidden input type, 307
  using PHP for, 310–314
  writable directory, 309
file_get_contents() function, 304
file_put_contents() function, 293–294
files
  copying on server, 314
  deleting, 314
  locking, 301–303
  modification times of, 315
  opening, 294
  reading from, 303–306
  reading incrementally, 327–331
  writing to, 293–300
$FILES variable
  elements of, 308
  error codes, 308
FileZilla, using to upload scripts, 10–11
Firebug extension for Firefox, 233, 238
firewalls, using, 416
first name, adding to HTML form, 93
flag variable
  creating for sticky form, 213
  using with if conditional, 120–121
floating-point numbers and integers, 38
flock() lock types, 301–303
floor() math function, 89
footer file, creating for Web pages, 190–191
footer.html script
  for sample site, 386–387
  saving, 190
fopen() modes, 294, 446
for loop. *See also* loops
  executing, 146–147
  variables in, 149
  writing, 147–149
foreach loop, 146
  error related to, 181
  using to access array elements, 162–163
form inputs, quoting attributes in, 216
form submission, determining, 204–205. *See also* HTML forms
form tags, 50
  adding to **feedback.html** file, 51–52
  for **calculator.html** document, 75
  creating for **register.html** script, 117
  for **posting.html** script, 92
frameworks resources, 443
frequently asked questions (FAQs), 440–442
FTP (File Transfer Protocol), using, 10–11
function calls, using spaces between, 83
function definitions, looking up, 20–21
function design theory, 285
function_exists() function, 264

functions. *See also* PHP functions; user-defined functions
  calling, 17
  deprecated, 21
  looking up in PHP manual, 18
functions.php script, creating for sample site, 384–385
fwrite() function, 295

G

garbage collection, 255
GET method
  using with HTML forms, 54–56
  using with **welcome.php** page, 229
$_GET predefined variable, 57
getrandmax() math function, 89
glob() function, 319
global statement, using with variable scope, 279–285
$grades array, 169, 171
GRANT command, using in MySQL, 434–435
greater than operator, 129
greater than or equal to operator, 129
greetings, creating in PHP scripts, 70–71
$groceries array, 164

H

handle_calc.php script
  creating, 77
  precedence example, 85–87
  saving, 79, 83
  using to format numbers, 82–83
handle_form.php script
  adjusting error reporting in, 65–66
  creating, 58
  displaying errors in, 62–63
  saving, 59, 62
  slashes displayed in, 60
handle_post.php script
  creating, 96
  functions in, 101–102
  saving, 97, 99
  string variables sent to, 95
  substring example, 109
  urlencode() example, 103–105
handle_reg.php script
  comparison operators examples, 130–132
  creating, 120
  else control structure example, 126–128
  elseif example, 139–141
  form validation example, 123–125
  logical operators example, 134–137
  saving, 121, 124
  switch conditional example, 143–145
hash, creating, 326
header file, creating for Web pages, 188–189
header() function, 222, 225–229

header.html script
   date() function, 202–203
   modifying, 199–200
   output, 222
   printing constants, 199–200
   for sample site, 385
   saving, 199, 203
headers_sent() function, 229
Hello, world! greeting
   enhanced version of, 23
   sending to browser, 16–17
hello2.php script
   adding comments to, 26
   saving, 23
   source code, 24
hello3.php file, saving, 26
hello.html script, creating, 68
hello.php file, saving, 17
hello.php script
   creating, 70
   versus **hello.html**, 71
   running directly, 71
hidden input, using with HTML forms, 60
home page, creating for sample site, 410–413
HTML (HyperText Markup Language)
   outside of PHP tags, 24
   versus PHP documents, 7
   resource, 6
   sending to browser, 22–24
   versus XHTML, 6
HTML code, spacing, 23
HTML comments, location of, 27
html entities() function, 100–102
HTML form data
   accessing, 60
   receiving in PHP, 57–60
   validating, 120–121, 123–125
HTML forms. *See also* form submission
   adding menus to, 52
   adding radio buttons to, 52
   adding submit buttons to, 53
   for control structures, 116–118
   creating, 50–53
   creating arrays from, 176–181
   GET method, 54–56
   handling with PHP, 204–209
   hidden input, 60
   making sticky, 210–216
   method attribute, 54–56
   for numbers, 74–76
   POST method, 54–56
   preset values cut off, 442
   printing out user data from, 60
   redisplaying immediately, 209
   select element, 52
   for strings, 92–94
   for strings and arrays, 173–174
   textarea, 53

using with databases, 353–357
   viewing information in, 56
HTML pages
   creating to receive data, 67–69
   with input types, 51
   sending data to manually, 67–71
HTML syntax, 2–4
HTML tags, using PHP functions with, 100–101.
      See also PHP tags; tags
html_entity_decode function, 102
htmlspecialchars() function, 100, 102
HTTP headers, manipulating, 225–226
HTML (HyperText Markup Language)
   outside of PHP tags, 24
   versus PHP documents, 7
   resource, 6
   sending to browser, 22–24
   versus XHTML, 6

I

id primary key, using in databases, 377
if conditional. *See also* conditionals
   = versus == operators in, 132
   creating, 119–121
   for validating form data, 124
if-else conditional, 126–127, 135
if-else statements, troubleshooting, 137
if-elseif conditionals, simplifying, 142–144
if-elseif-else conditional, 138–141
implode() function, 172, 174
include() function, 192–193, 196
increment (**++**) operator, using, 86–87, 129
incrementing numbers, 86–87
index.php script
   creating, 193
   running in browser, 195
   for sample site, 410–413
   saving, 194, 410–413
inequality operator, 129
ini_set() function, using with scripts, 62
INSERT command in SQL, 334
INSERT INTO command, using with
      queries, 352, 357
INSERT query, using form data in, 355
installation
   on Mac OS X, 419–422
   on Windows, 415–418
integers and floating-point numbers, 38
is_numeric() validation function, 123, 125
is_readable() function, 306
is_writable() function, 295
isset() validation function, 122–123, 125

J

JavaScript resources, 443–444
join() function, 174

K

key-value pairs, using with arrays, 40
krsort()function, 168
ksort()function, 168–171

L

language constructs
  break, 144
  die, 144
  exit, 144
  print, 144
last name, adding to HTML form, 93
layout model, creating for Web pages, 185–187
layout.html script, footer file, 190–191
less than operator, 129
less than or equal to operator, 129
links
  creating to PHP scripts, 68–69
  using to send values to scripts, 71
list() function, 181
list of words, alphabetizing, 172
list_dir.php script
  creating, 316–317
  displaying, 315–319
  saving, 319
list.html script
  creating, 173–174
  saving, 174
list.php script
  creating, 174
  saving, 175
locking files, 301–303
$loggedin flag, 330
logical operators, using, 133–137
login form
  checking for hidden input, 209
  creating for Web page, 205–209
login script, creating, 327–331
login.php script
  creating, 206, 328–329
  header() function, 226
  $loggedin flag, 330
  for sample site, 388–391
  saving, 209, 331, 391
  sessions, 250–251
logout.php script
  creating, 254–255
  for sample site, 392
  saving, 255
loops. *See also* control structures; **for** loop
  debugging, 442
  nesting, 149

M

Mac OS X, installation on, 419–422
Magic Quotes, 59–60. *See also* quotation marks
mail() function, 218–221, 424
mailing lists, 439

make_date_menus() function, 263
make_text_input() function, 269
MAMP, installing on Mac OS X, 420–422
mathematical functions
  abs(), 89
  ceil(), 89
  floor(), 89
  getrandmax(), 89
  mt_rand(), 89
  rand(), 89
  round(), 89
mathematical operators, 84–85, 87.
    See also operators
mathematics, principles of, 77
mcrypt_encrypt() function, using with strings, 106
md5() function, 326
menu, adding to HTML form, 52. *See also*
    drop-down menu; pull-down menu
menu variables, values of, 60
menus.php script
  creating, 260
  saving, 263
message, printing in browser, 16
method attribute, using with HTML forms, 54–56
MIME type, finding, 319
mkdir() command,, 320
modulus operator, 129
money_format() function, 83
month pull-down menu, creating, 260
monthly payment, calculating, 79
move_uploaded_file() script, 310–311
mt_rand()math function, 89
multidimensional arrays
  using, 164–167
  viewing, 167
multilingual page, creating, 5
multiplication (*) operator, using, 77–80, 129
My Blog example. *See* blog entry
My Site of Quotes, setting up, 380
MySQL
  alias for **exit()**, 342
  auto-incrementing primary keys, 357
  calling **die()**, 342
  connecting to, 336–340
  DELETE queries, 366–371
  error handling, 340–342
  extensions, 339
  GRANT command, 434–435
  inserting records, 357
  localhost value, 339
  paginating returned records, 365
  REVOKE command, 436
  SELECT queries, 361
  support for, 334–335
  TRUNCATE TABLE command, 371
  WHERE clauses, 361
MySQL client, using, 425–427
MySQL errors, showing, 358
MySQL privileges, creating, 433–436

MySQL symbols
  ; (semicolon), 358
  @ (at sign), 342
  ' (apostrophe), 358, 360
MySQL users
  creating, 433–436
  setting root user password, 430–432
`mysql_connect.php` script
  creating, 337
  creating databases, 344–346
  error-handling, 341
  sample site, 382
  saving, 338, 342, 382
  selecting databases, 344–346
`mysql_error()` function, 340
`mysql_fetch_array()` function, 365
`mysql_num_rows()` function, 365, 377
`mysql_query()` function
  invoking, 348, 350
  returning **TRUE**, 350
  using, 356
`mysql_real_escape_string()` function, 377

N

name, adding to HTML form, 93
name value, using with greetings, 70–71
$name variable, creating via concatenation, 96
`natcasesort()` function, 171
`natsort()`function, 171
negation operator, 129
nesting
  conditionals, 133
  conditionals for login form, 207
  loops, 149
newline character (**\n**), using with HTML, 23
newlines
  converting to breaks, 98–99, 102
  inserting into strings, 99
newsgroups, 439
`nl2br()` function. *See also* functions
  in PHP manual, 18
  using with HTML in PHP, 101–102
  using with newlines, 99
not equal to operator, 130
Not Found server response, receiving, 13
not operator, 133–134
Notice error type, 64
number class, using with `handle_calc.php`
    document, 77
number variables, 38
`number_format()` function, 81–83
numbers. *See also* random numbers
  creating HTML forms for, 74–76
  decrementing, 86–87
  formatting, 81–83
  incrementing, 86–87
  integers and floating-point, 38
  `round()` function, 81, 83
  valid versus invalid, 38

O

`ob_clean()` function, 224
`ob_end_clean()` function, 222
`ob_end_flush()` function, 222, 224
`ob_flush()` function, 224
`ob_get_contents()` function, 224
`ob_get_length()` function, 224
`ob_start()` function, 222–223
object-oriented programming resources, 443
$okay conditional, using with **else**, 126–127
online resources. *See also* Web sites
  code repositories, 438
  newsgroups, 439
  PHP manual, 437–438
  Web sites, 438
operators. *See also* mathematical operators
  arithmetic, 129
  comparison, 129–132
  logical, 133–137
  precedence of, 84–85, 445
  table of, 129, 445
  using, 77–80
OR operator, 129, 133
ORDER BY clause, contents of, 399
output buffering, 222–224, 238

P

pages. *See* HTML pages; Web pages
parameters, using with functions, 265–270
parentheses (**()**)
  using in calculations, 84–85
  using in conditionals, 125
parse errors, 64
  debugging, 442
  for variable values, 44
password values, validating, 130–133
passwords
  assigning to root user in MySQL, 431–432
  creating inputs for, 117
  validating for sticky forms, 214
permissions. *See* databases; file permissions
PHP. *See also* sample site
  case-insensitivity of, 17
  configuring, 423–424
  as server-side technology, 203
PHP code, placing in files, 224
.php extension, 9
PHP function list, 20
PHP functions. *See also* arguments; functions;
    nl2br() function; sorting functions;
    validation functions
  with arguments, 265–270
  array(), 154–155, 157
  count(), 160
  creating and calling, 260–264
  crypt(), 106
  date(), 201–203, 446
  explode(), 172, 174

fclose(), 295, 302
fgetcsv(), 331
fgets(), 327
file(), 304
file_get_contents(), 304
file_put_contents(), 293–294
flock() lock types, 301–303
fopen() modes, 294, 446
formatting, 259
function_exists(), 264
fwrite(), 295
glob(), 319
header(), 222, 225–229
headers_sent(), 229
html entities() function, 100–102
html_entity_decode, 102
implode(), 172, 174
include(), 192–193, 196
is_readable(), 306
is_writable(), 295
join(), 174
list(), 181
mail(), 218–221, 424
make_date_menus() function, 263
make_text_input(), 269
mcrypt_encrypt(), 106
md5(), 326
move_uploaded_file(), 310
mysql_error(), 340
mysql_fetch_array(), 365
mysql_num_rows(), 365, 377
mysql_query(), 348, 356
mysql_real_escape_string() function, 377
naming, 258
ob_clean(), 224
ob_end_clean(), 222
ob_end_flush(), 222, 224
ob_flush(), 224
ob_get_contents(), 224
ob_get_length(), 224
ob_start(), 222–223
omitting spaces from, 258
readfile(), 306
require(), 192–193, 196
returning values, 274–278
rmdir(), 326
scandir() function, 315
session_start(), 222, 249
setcookie(), 222, 234, 238
sizeof(), 160
srtoupper(), 111
str_ireplace(), 111–113
str_word_count(), 109
strcasecmp(), 107
strcmp(), 107
strip_tags() function, 100–102
stripos(), 107
stristr(), 107

strlen(), 109
strnatcasecmp(), 107
strnatcmp(), 107
strpos(), 107
strstr(), 107
strtok(), 107
strtolower(), 111
substr(), 108
trim(), 111–113, 132
ucfirst(), 111
ucwords(), 111
unlink(), 314
unset(), 158
urldecode(), 105
urlencode(), 103–105
user-defined, 258
using concatenation with, 106
using conditionals in, 125
using with HTML tags, 100–101
var_dump(), 157
wordwrap(), 102
PHP installation
on Mac OS X, 419–422
on Windows, 415–418
PHP manual
accessing, 18
deprecated functions in, 21
looking up function definitions, 20–21
nl2br() function page, 18
print function page, 18
using, 18–19, 437–438
PHP scripts
accessing via URLs, 14
adding comments to, 25–27
blank pages displayed in, 63
creating, 8–9
creating for HTML pages, 70–71
creating links to, 68–69
debugging, 28–29
displaying errors in, 61–63
executing, 9
as open source software, 10
passing data to, 67
passing preset values to, 60
running, 10
running through URLs, 28, 440
sending to server via FTP, 10–11
testing in browsers, 12–14
PHP scripts, running through URLs, 7
PHP syntax, 7–8
PHP tags, 7, 16. See also HTML tags; tags
PHP version, confirming, 28, 440
PHP versus HTML documents, 7
PHP Web sites, 438
PHP-enabled server, obtaining, 10
phpinfo() function
calling, 8
running to display errors, 61

/phpinfo.php, adding to URL, 13
phpinfo.php script
  creating, 8
  saving, 9
  uploading to server, 11
phpMyAdmin, 335
  assigning root user, 432
  creating users in, 432
  using, 428–429
$_POST elements, adding to calculator, 78
POST method, using with HTML forms, 54–56
$_POST predefined variable, 57–59
posting.html script
  creating, 92
  saving, 94
  string variables in, 95
<pre></pre> tags, using with variables, 35
precedence of operators managing, 84–85, 445.
    See also operators
predefined variables, 32–35, 57. *See also*
    variables
predefined.php file, saving, 34
print statement
  language construct, 144
  in PHP manual, 18
  typing, 15
  using on variable types, 41
  using over multiple lines, 17
  using to send HTML to browser, 22
  using with HTML in PHP, 101
  using with sales cost calculator, 79
  using with substrings, 110
  using with **urlencode()** function, 104
print_r() function, calling, 33, 35
printf() function, using to format numbers, 83
printing
  $ (dollar sign), 79
  constants, 199–200
  message in browser, 16
  predefined variables, 33–35
  values of arrays, 162–163
  variable values, 41–42
projects, identifying goals of, 380
pull-down menu. *See also* menu
  creating for form, 260–261
  preselecting, 216

Q

queries, executing, 352
query data, securing, 358–360
query statement, 353–354
quotation marks. *See also* Magic Quotes
  using, 45–47
  using with strings, 39
  using with variables, 45
quotations
  adding to sample site, 393–396
  deleting, 406–409

displaying randomly, 304–306
  editing, 400–405
  storing in text file, 296–300
quotes.php file, saving, 47
quotes.txt file
  creating, 289–290
  referencing, 297

R

radio buttons
  adding to HTML forms, 52
  presetting status of, 216
  values of, 60
rand() function, invoking, 89
random numbers, generating, 88–89. *See also*
    numbers
random.php script, creating, 88
range() function, using to create arrays, 157
readfile() function, 306
reading from files, 304–306
records
  CRUD, 396
  editing in databases, 373–374
  inserting via MySQL, 357
  paginating returned, 365
register.html script
  creating for control structures, 116–118
  for loop example, 147–149
  saving, 118
register.php script
  directories, 321–326
  mail() function, 218
  saving, 216
  sticky form, 212
registration form, creating shell of, 211–216
registration script, creating for directory, 321–326
relative paths
  start of, 293
  using with external files, 193–194
require() function, 192–193, 196
resources
  Ajax, 443–444
  books, 444
  code repositories, 438
  frameworks, 443
  JavaScript, 443–444
  newsgroups, 439
  object-oriented programming, 443
  PHP manual, 437–438
  security, 443
  Web sites, 438
reverse conditionals, 132
REVOKE command, using in MySQL, 436
rmdir() function, 326
round() function, using with numbers, 81, 83, 89
$row reference, explained, 361
rsort() function, 168

S

sales cost calculator, creating, 77–80

sample site. *See also* databases; PHP; Web sites
  adding quotes, 393–396
  connecting to database, 382
  creating database for, 380
  creating home page, 410–413
  creating tables for, 380
  creating template, 385–387
  deleting quotes, 406–409
  editing quotes, 400–405
  listing quotes, 397–399
  logging in, 388–391
  logging out, 392
  organizing, 381
  `quote_id` primary key, 381
  structure of, 381
  writing user-defined function, 383–384

scalar variable, defined, 152. *See also* variables

`scandir()` function, 315

scripts. *See* PHP scripts

security resources, 443

`select` element, using with HTML forms, 52

`SELECT` queries, 334
  defining, 361, 363
  running, 363

semicolon (;), using in MySQL, 358

server
  configuring to send email, 221
  requesting information from, 55
  setting time zone, 203
  uploading **phpinfo.php** script to, 11

`$_SERVER` predefined variable, 57

server-side technology, 7

`$_SESSION` array, 252

session values, deleting, 255

session variables
  accessing, 252–253
  verifying, 253

`session_start()` function, 222, 249

sessions
  versus cookies, 248
  creating, 249–251
  deleting, 254–255
  overview, 248
  using without cookies, 255

`setcookie()` function, 222, 234, 238

short tags, 9

`shuffle()`function, using with arrays, 168

single quotation marks (')
  using with arrays, 160
  using with strings, 39
  using with variables, 45–47

site structure, 194

sites. *See* sample site; Web sites

`sizeof()` function, 160

`sort()` function, 168

sorting functions. *See also* PHP functions
  `arsort()`, 168, 170
  `asort()`, 168–170
  `krsort()`, 168
  `ksort()`, 168–171
  `natcasesort()`, 171
  `natsort()`, 171
  `rsort()`, 168
  `shuffle()`, 168
  `sort()`, 168
  `uasort()`, 171
  `ursort()`, 171
  `usort()`, 171

`sort.php` file
  creating, 169
  saving, 171

`$soups` array, 155, 162

`soups1.php` script
  creating, 159
  opening, 159
  saving, 156

`soups3.php` script
  creating, 162
  saving, 163

spaces, using between function calls, 83

spacing HTML code, 23

`sprintf()` function, using to format numbers, 83

SQL (Structured Query Language), 334–335

SQL injection attack, 358

SQL keywords, writing, 351

sticky forms, making, 210–216

`sticky1.php` script
  creating, 268
  functions with default values, 272
  saving, 270

`sticky2.php` script, saving, 273

`str_ireplace()` function, 111–113

`str_word_count()` function, 109

`strcasecmp()` function, 107

`strcmp()` function, 107

string case, adjusting, 111

string operator, 129

string values, comparing, 132

string variables, 39

strings. *See also* substrings
  comparing, 107
  concatenating, 95–97
  counting words and characters in, 109
  decrypting, 106
  empty, 39
  encoding and decoding, 103–106
  encrypting, 106
  HTML form for, 92–94
  inserting newlines into, 99
  linking via concatenation, 97
  replacing parts of, 111–113
  using for array indexes, 161
  using in **switch** conditionals, 145

strings and arrays, transforming between, 172–175
strip_tags() function, 100–102
stripos() function, 107
stristr() function, 107
strlen() function, 109
strnatcasecmp() function, 107
strnatcmp() function, 107
strpos() function, 107
strstr() function, 107
strtok() function, 107
strtolower() function, 111
Structured Query Language (SQL), 334–335
strupper() function, 111
subdirectories, listing, 318
submit button
    adding to HTML forms, 53
    creating for **register.html script**, 118
substr() function, 108
substrings. *See also* strings
    finding, 107–110
    replacing, 111–113
subtraction (-) operator, using, 77–80, 129
superglobals, 153, 285. *See also* arrays
support forum, 6
switch conditional, using, 142–145

T

tables. *See* database tables
tags, 9. *See also* HTML tags; PHP tags
tax rate
    calculating, 79
    recalculating, 86–87
template system, files in, 196
template.html script
    creating, 185–187
    header file, 188–189
    saving, 187
templates. *See also* CSS templates; Web
       applications; Web pages
    creating, 184
    creating for sample site, 385–387
    footer file, 190–191
    header file, 188–189
    layout model, 185–187
    using with external files, 193–194
text, sending to browser, 15–17
text area, presetting value of, 216
text input, adding to email address, 52
textarea form element
    adding to HTML forms, 53
    using with newlines, 98–99
TextMate Web site, 4
time zone, setting for server, 203
token substring, explained, 107
trim() function, using with strings, 111–113, 132
TRUE versus FALSE conditionals, 133, 137
TRUNCATE TABLE command, 371

U

uasort() function, 171
ucfirst() function, using with strings, 111
ucwords() function, using with strings, 111
Undefined variable error, 44
underscore (_), using with variables, 36
Unicode encoding, 5
unlink() function, 314
unset() function, 158
UPDATE command in SQL, 334
UPDATE queries
    LIMIT 1 clause, 377
    using with databases, 372–377
upload_file.php script
    creating, 310
    saving, 314
uploads folder, creating, 309
urldecode() function, 105
urlencode() function, 103–105
URLs
    accessing scripts from, 13
    adding **/phpinfo.php** to, 13
    running PHP scripts through, 28
ursort() function, 171
user-defined functions. *See also* functions
    creating, 258–259
    memory requirements, 264
    writing for sample site, 383–384
users folder, creating, 320
users.txt file
    displaying, 326
    login script, 327–331
    saving, 320
usort() function, 171
UTF-8 encoding, using, 5

V

validating
    form data, 120–121, 123–125
    password values, 130–133
    variables, 141
    year values, 130–133
validation, repeating for sticky form, 213–214
validation functions. *See also* PHP functions
    checkdate(), 128
    empty(), 122–123
    is_numeric(), 123, 125
    isset(), 122–123, 125
values, assigning to variables, 129
var_dump() function, 157
variable names
    case sensitivity of, 36
    conventions, 37
variable scope
    $arg and **$var** values, 280
    global statement, 279–285
    overview, 279–281

variable syntax, 36–37
variable types
    arrays, 40
    numbers, 38
    strings, 39
    using `print` statement on, 41
variable values
    assigning, 41–44
    incrementing, 86–87
    parse errors, 44
    printing, 35, 41–42
variables. *See also* predefined variables;
    scalar variable
    `$_SERVER`, 34–35
    assigning values to, 129
    documenting purpose of, 37
    minimizing bugs in, 37
    nonexisting, 60
    overview, 32
    predefined, 32–35
    referring to, 37
    valid versus invalid, 37
    validating, 141
    without values, 441
`variables.php` file, saving, 44
`view_blog.php` script, 366, 369–371, 376–377
`view_entries.php` script
    creating, 362
    saving, 365
`view_quote.php` script
    creating, 305–306
    for sample site, 397–399
    saving, 306
`view_settings.php` script
    saving, 241
    using with cookies, 239

W

Warning error type, 64
weakly typed, explained, 97
Web applications. *See also* templates
    constants, 197–200
    date and time, 201–203
    external files, 192–196
    HTTP headers, 225–229
    output buffering, 222–224
    sending email, 217–221
    sticky forms, 210–216
Web document root, 12
Web pages. *See also* templates
    adding CSS to, 3
    banners, 186
    blank, 440–441
    content, 187
    defining titles for, 198
    footer, 187, 190–191
    header area, 186
    header file, 188–189
    layout model, 185–188
    login form, 205–209
    sidebars, 187
Web root directory, 288
Web sites. *See also* online resources; sample site
    Apache, 10
    BBEdit, 4
    Crimson Editor, 4
    Dreamweaver, 4
    EditPlus, 4
    identifying goals of, 380
    support forum, 6
    TextMate, 4
Web-page extensions, 9
`welcome.html` file, saving, 6
`welcome.php` page
    creating, 227–229
    session variables, 252
`WHERE` clauses, using in queries, 361
`while` loop, 146, 149
white space, using, 23
Windows, installation on, 415–418
word list, alphabetizing, 172
`wordwrap()` function, 102

X

XAMPP, installing on Windows, 417–419
XHTML
    attributes, 2
    CSS, 2
    versus HTML, 2
    resource, 6
    rules, 50–51
    tags, 2–3
XHTML code sample document, 4
XHTML page
    body section, 5–6
    body tags, 6
    `<br />` tag, 6
    creating, 4–6
    head section, 5
    header lines, 4–5
    saving, 6
    testing, 6
XOR operator, 133–134
XSS (cross-site scripting) attacks, 100

Y

year pull-down menu, creating, 262
year validation, 137
year values, validating, 130–133, 135
year variable, checking digits in, 135–136

WATCH
READ
CREATE

Unlimited online access to all Peachpit, Adobe Press, Apple Training and New Riders videos and books, as well as content from other leading publishers including: O'Reilly Media, Focal Press, Sams, Que, Total Training, John Wiley & Sons, Course Technology PTR, Class on Demand, VTC and more.

No time commitment or contract required! Sign up for one month or a year. All for $19.99 a month

SIGN UP TODAY
peachpit.com/creativeedge